Citroën BX
Service and Repair Manual

I M Coomber and Christopher Rogers

Models covered

(908 - 336 - 1AA12)

Citroën BX Hatchback & Estate models with petrol engines (inc. GTi, 16 valve & special/limited editions)
1360 cc, 1580 cc & 1905 cc

Does not cover diesel engine variants or 4x4 models

© Haynes Publishing 1997

ABCDE
FGHIJ
KLMNO
PQ
3

A book in the **Haynes Service and Repair Manual Series**

ISBN **1 85960 190 1**

British Library Cataloguing in Publication Data
A catalogue record for this book is available from the British Library

Printed by **J H Haynes & Co Ltd, Sparkford, Nr Yeovil, Somerset BA22 7JJ, England**

Haynes Publishing
Sparkford, Nr Yeovil, Somerset BA22 7JJ, England

Haynes North America, Inc
861 Lawrence Drive, Newbury Park, California 91320, USA

Editions Haynes S.A.
Tour Aurore - La Défense 2, 18 Place des Reflets, 92975 PARIS LA DEFENSE Cedex, France

Haynes Publishing Nordiska AB
Box 1504, 751 45 UPPSALA, Sweden

Contents

LIVING WITH YOUR CITROEN BX

Roadside Repairs

Weekly Checks

Tyre pressures

Lubricants, fluids and capacities

MAINTENANCE

Routine Maintenance and Servicing

Contents

The Citroën BX was introduced in France in October of 1982 and became available in the UK in September 1983. The original models available in the range were the BX, BX 14 E, BX 14 RE, BX 16 RS and BX 16 TRS. The types of engine, transmission and equipment fitted being dependent on the model and the body design being that of a Hatchback.

For the 1985 model year, the BX 19 GT was made available for the driver requiring a higher performance model. Also in 1985, the BX Leader replaced the BX and BX 14 models, the Leader being fitted with the same engine and transmission as the BX 14. In the second half of 1985 the Estate was introduced, two versions being available, the BX 16 RS Estate and the BX 16 TRS Estate.

Changes for the 1987 model year included the introduction of the BX 16 RE Hatchback, the BX 19 GTi (fuel injection and ABS braking), the BX 19 GTi 16v (16 valve engine) and the replacement for the BX 19 GT, the BX 19 TRS. Also, a BX 19 TRS Estate fitted with automatic transmission became available. The facia and instruments were modified on all models, with round instruments being used. Other aesthetic improvements were made to improve the external appearance of certain models.

For the 1988 model year, all BX 14 models were equipped with the K1G engine with 2CA type 4 or 5-speed manual gearbox.

For the 1989 model year, BX 16 and BX 19 models were equipped with the BE3 5-speed manual gearbox to replace the earlier BE1 5-speed type.

In early 1990, BX 19 TZi Hatchback and Estate models became available, these being equipped with catalytic converters.

In late 1992, BX 16 TXi catalytic converter equipped Hatchback and Estate models were added to the range.

On all models, the engine and transmission is mounted transversely and drives the front wheels through two driveshafts. The transmission available (depending on model type) is a 4 or 5-speed manual gearbox or a 4-speed automatic unit.

All models are extremely comfortable to ride in, thanks to the hydropneumatic suspension and luxurious interior trim. The unique design suspension is self-levelling and the ride height is maintained automatically over all road conditions. A ground clearance lever inside the car may be used to adjust the ride height when travelling over rough ground, this also makes changing a roadwheel much simpler.

Citroën BX 16 TRS

Citroën BX 19 GTi

The Citroën BX Team

Haynes manuals are produced by dedicated and enthusiastic people working in close co-operation. The team responsible for the creation of this book included:

Authors	Ian Coomber Christopher Rogers
Sub-editors	Sophie Yar Carole Turk
Editor & Page Make-up	Steve Churchill Bob Jex
Workshop manager	Paul Buckland
Photo Scans	John Martin Paul Tanswell Steve Tanswell
Cover illustration & Line Art	Roger Healing

We hope the book will help you to get the maximum enjoyment from your car. By carrying out routine maintenance as described you will ensure your car's reliability and preserve its resale value.

Your Citroën BX Manual

The aim of this Manual is to help you get the best value from your vehicle. It can do so in several ways. It can help you decide what work must be done (even should you choose to get it done by a garage), provide information on routine maintenance and servicing, and give a logical course of action and diagnosis when random faults occur. However, it is hoped that you will use the Manual by tackling the work yourself. On simpler jobs it may even be quicker than booking the car into a garage and going there twice, to leave and collect it. Perhaps most important, a lot of money can be saved by avoiding the costs a garage must charge to cover its labour and overheads.

The Manual has drawings and descriptions to show the function of the various components so that their layout can be understood. Then the tasks are described and photographed in a clear step-by-step sequence.

Acknowledgements

Thanks are due to Champion Spark Plug who supplied the illustrations showing spark plug conditions, and to Duckhams Oils, who provided lubrication data. Certain other illustrations are the copyright of Citroën (UK) Limited and are used with their permission. Thanks are also due to Sykes-Pickavant Limited, who supplied some of the workshop tools, and to all those people at Sparkford who helped in the production of this Manual.

We take great pride in the accuracy of information given in this manual, but vehicle manufacturers make alterations and design changes during the production run of a particular vehicle of which they do not inform us. No liability can be accepted by the authors or publishers for loss, damage or injury caused by any errors in, or omissions from the information given.

Working on your car can be dangerous. This page shows just some of the potential risks and hazards, with the aim of creating a safety-conscious attitude.

General hazards

Scalding

• Don't remove the radiator or expansion tank cap while the engine is hot.
• Engine oil, automatic transmission fluid or power steering fluid may also be dangerously hot if the engine has recently been running.

Burning

• Beware of burns from the exhaust system and from any part of the engine. Brake discs and drums can also be extremely hot immediately after use.

Crushing

• When working under or near a raised vehicle, always supplement the jack with axle stands, or use drive-on ramps. *Never venture under a car which is only supported by a jack.*
• Take care if loosening or tightening high-torque nuts when the vehicle is on stands. Initial loosening and final tightening should be done with the wheels on the ground.

Fire

• Fuel is highly flammable; fuel vapour is explosive.
• Don't let fuel spill onto a hot engine.
• Do not smoke or allow naked lights (including pilot lights) anywhere near a vehicle being worked on. Also beware of creating sparks (electrically or by use of tools).
• Fuel vapour is heavier than air, so don't work on the fuel system with the vehicle over an inspection pit.
• Another cause of fire is an electrical overload or short-circuit. Take care when repairing or modifying the vehicle wiring.
• Keep a fire extinguisher handy, of a type suitable for use on fuel and electrical fires.

Electric shock

• Ignition HT voltage can be dangerous, especially to people with heart problems or a pacemaker. Don't work on or near the ignition system with the engine running or the ignition switched on.

• Mains voltage is also dangerous. Make sure that any mains-operated equipment is correctly earthed. Mains power points should be protected by a residual current device (RCD) circuit breaker.

Fume or gas intoxication

• Exhaust fumes are poisonous; they often contain carbon monoxide, which is rapidly fatal if inhaled. Never run the engine in a confined space such as a garage with the doors shut.
• Fuel vapour is also poisonous, as are the vapours from some cleaning solvents and paint thinners.

Poisonous or irritant substances

• Avoid skin contact with battery acid and with any fuel, fluid or lubricant, especially antifreeze, brake hydraulic fluid and Diesel fuel. Don't syphon them by mouth. If such a substance is swallowed or gets into the eyes, seek medical advice.
• Prolonged contact with used engine oil can cause skin cancer. Wear gloves or use a barrier cream if necessary. Change out of oil-soaked clothes and do not keep oily rags in your pocket.
• Air conditioning refrigerant forms a poisonous gas if exposed to a naked flame (including a cigarette). It can also cause skin burns on contact.

Asbestos

• Asbestos dust can cause cancer if inhaled or swallowed. Asbestos may be found in gaskets and in brake and clutch linings. When dealing with such components it is safest to assume that they contain asbestos.

Special hazards

Hydrofluoric acid

• This extremely corrosive acid is formed when certain types of synthetic rubber, found in some O-rings, oil seals, fuel hoses etc, are exposed to temperatures above 400°C. The rubber changes into a charred or sticky substance containing the acid. *Once formed, the acid remains dangerous for years. If it gets onto the skin, it may be necessary to amputate the limb concerned.*
• When dealing with a vehicle which has suffered a fire, or with components salvaged from such a vehicle, wear protective gloves and discard them after use.

The battery

• Batteries contain sulphuric acid, which attacks clothing, eyes and skin. Take care when topping-up or carrying the battery.
• The hydrogen gas given off by the battery is highly explosive. Never cause a spark or allow a naked light nearby. Be careful when connecting and disconnecting battery chargers or jump leads.

Air bags

• Air bags can cause injury if they go off accidentally. Take care when removing the steering wheel and/or facia. Special storage instructions may apply.

Diesel injection equipment

• Diesel injection pumps supply fuel at very high pressure. Take care when working on the fuel injectors and fuel pipes.

⚠️ *Warning: Never expose the hands, face or any other part of the body to injector spray; the fuel can penetrate the skin with potentially fatal results.*

Remember...

DO

• Do use eye protection when using power tools, and when working under the vehicle.

• Do wear gloves or use barrier cream to protect your hands when necessary.

• Do get someone to check periodically that all is well when working alone on the vehicle.

• Do keep loose clothing and long hair well out of the way of moving mechanical parts.

• Do remove rings, wristwatch etc, before working on the vehicle – especially the electrical system.

• Do ensure that any lifting or jacking equipment has a safe working load rating adequate for the job.

DON'T

• Don't attempt to lift a heavy component which may be beyond your capability – get assistance.

• Don't rush to finish a job, or take unverified short cuts.

• Don't use ill-fitting tools which may slip and cause injury.

• Don't leave tools or parts lying around where someone can trip over them. Mop up oil and fuel spills at once.

• Don't allow children or pets to play in or near a vehicle being worked on.

The following pages are intended to help in dealing with common roadside emergencies and breakdowns. You will find more detailed fault finding information at the back of the manual, and repair information in the main chapters.

If your car won't start and the starter motor doesn't turn

☐ If it's a model with automatic transmission, make sure the selector is in 'P' or 'N'.
☐ Open the bonnet and make sure that the battery terminals are clean and tight.
☐ Switch on the headlights and try to start the engine. If the headlights go very dim when you're trying to start, the battery is probably flat. Get out of trouble by jump starting (see next page) using a friend's car.

If your car won't start even though the starter motor turns as normal

☐ Is there fuel in the tank?
☐ Is there moisture on electrical components under the bonnet? Switch off the ignition, then wipe off any obvious dampness with a dry cloth. Spray a water-repellent aerosol product (WD-40 or equivalent) on ignition and fuel system electrical connectors like those shown in the photos. Pay special attention to the ignition coil wiring connector and HT leads.

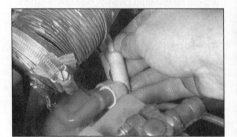

A Check that the HT lead connections at the distributor are clean and secure.

B Check that the HT lead connections at the spark plugs are clean and secure.

C Check that the HT and LT lead connections at the ignition coil are clean and secure.

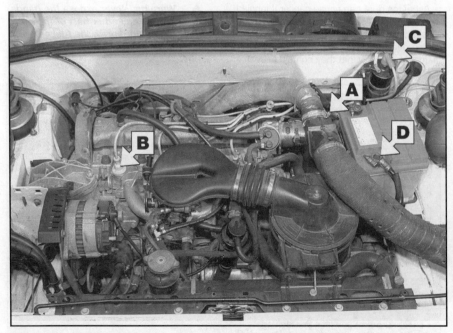

Check that electrical connections are secure (with the ignition switched off) and spray them with a water dispersant spray like WD40 if you suspect a problem due to damp

D Check the security and condition of the battery connections.

E Check all wiring block connectors are clean and secure.

Jump starting

Jump starting will get you out of trouble, but you must correct whatever made the battery go flat in the first place. There are three possibilities:

1 The battery has been drained by repeated attempts to start, or by leaving the lights on.

2 The charging system is not working properly (alternator drivebelt slack or broken, alternator wiring fault or alternator itself faulty).

3 The battery itself is at fault (electrolyte low, or battery worn out).

When jump-starting a car using a booster battery, observe the following precautions:

✔ Before connecting the booster battery, make sure that the ignition is switched off.

✔ Ensure that all electrical equipment (lights, heater, wipers, etc) is switched off.

✔ Make sure that the booster battery is the same voltage as the discharged one in the vehicle.

✔ If the battery is being jump-started from the battery in another vehicle, the two vehcles MUST NOT TOUCH each other.

✔ Make sure that the transmission is in neutral (or PARK, in the case of automatic transmission).

1 Connect one end of the red jump lead to the positive (+) terminal of the flat battery

2 Connect the other end of the red lead to the positive (+) terminal of the booster battery.

3 Connect one end of the black jump lead to the negative (-) terminal of the booster battery

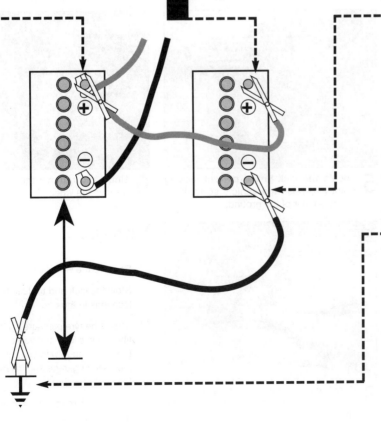

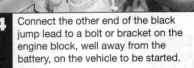

4 Connect the other end of the black jump lead to a bolt or bracket on the engine block, well away from the battery, on the vehicle to be started.

5 Make sure that the jump leads will not come into contact with the fan, drive-belts or other moving parts of the engine.

6 Start the engine using the booster battery, then with the engine running at idle speed, disconnect the jump leads in the reverse order of connection.

Wheel changing

Some of the details shown here will vary according to model. For instance, the location of the spare wheel and jack is not the same on all cars. However, the basic principles apply to all vehicles.

 Warning: Do not change a wheel in a situation where you risk being hit by other traffic. On busy roads, try to stop in a lay-by or a gateway. Be wary of passing traffic while changing the wheel – it is easy to become distracted by the job in hand.

Preparation

☐ When a puncture occurs, stop as soon as it is safe to do so.
☐ Park on firm level ground, if possible, and well out of the way of other traffic.

☐ Use hazard warning lights if necessary.
☐ If you have one, use a warning triangle to alert other drivers of your presence.
☐ Apply the handbrake.

☐ Chock the wheel diagonally opposite the one being removed – a couple of large stones will do for this.
☐ If the ground is soft, use a flat piece of wood to spread the load under the jack.

Changing the wheel

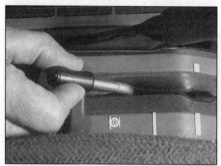

1 With the handbrake applied and engine set to idle, move ground clearance selector lever to maximum height position.

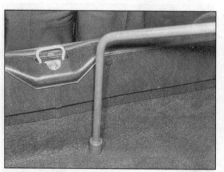

2 Turn the wheelbrace 6 to 8 turns to lower the spare wheel carrier.

3 Remove the spare wheel and jack.

4 Use the wheel brace to slightly loosen the bolts of the wheel to be removed.

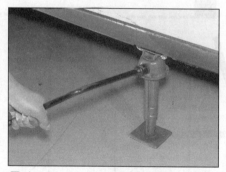

5 Locate the jack in the correct jacking point and raise the vehicle so that the wheel is clear of the ground.

6 Undo and remove the wheel bolts and remove the wheel.

7 Fit the spare wheel, nipping tight the bolts. Lower to the ground and tighten the bolts to correct torque setting.

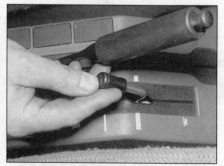

8 Reset the ground clearance lever to normal driving position before using the vehicle.

Finally...

☐ Remove the wheel chocks.

☐ Stow the jack and tools in the correct locations in the car.

☐ Check the tyre pressure on the wheel just fitted. If it is low, or if you don't have a pressure gauge with you, drive slowly to the nearest garage and inflate the tyre to the right pressure.

☐ Have the damaged tyre or wheel repaired as soon as possible.

Identifying leaks

Puddles on the garage floor or drive, or obvious wetness under the bonnet or underneath the car, suggest a leak that needs investigating. It can sometimes be difficult to decide where the leak is coming from, especially if the engine bay is very dirty already. Leaking oil or fluid can also be blown rearwards by the passage of air under the car, giving a false impression of where the problem lies.

 Warning: Most automotive oils and fluids are poisonous. Wash them off skin, and change out of contaminated clothing, without delay.

 The smell of a fluid leaking from the car may provide a clue to what's leaking. Some fluids are distinctively coloured. It may help to clean the car carefully and to park it over some clean paper overnight as an aid to locating the source of the leak.
Remember that some leaks may only occur while the engine is running.

Sump oil

Engine oil may leak from the drain plug...

Oil from filter

...or from the base of the oil filter.

Gearbox oil

Gearbox oil can leak from the seals at the inboard ends of the driveshafts.

Antifreeze

Leaking antifreeze often leaves a crystalline deposit like this.

Brake fluid

A leak occurring at a wheel is almost certainly brake fluid.

Power steering fluid

Power steering fluid may leak from the pipe connectors on the steering rack.

Towing

When all else fails, you may find yourself having to get a tow home – or of course you may be helping somebody else. Long-distance recovery should only be done by a garage or breakdown service. For shorter distances, DIY towing using another car is easy enough, but observe the following points:
☐ Use a proper tow-rope – they are not expensive. The vehicle being towed must display an 'ON TOW' sign in its rear window.
☐ Always turn the ignition key to the 'on' position when the vehicle is being towed, so that the steering lock is released, and that the direction indicator and brake lights will work.
☐ Only attach the tow-rope to the towing eyes provided.

☐ Before being towed, release the handbrake and select neutral on the transmission (Refer to the *Warning* on the right).
☐ The driver of the car being towed must keep the tow-rope taut at all times to avoid snatching.
☐ Make sure that both drivers know the route before setting off.
☐ Only drive at moderate speeds and keep the distance towed to a minimum. Drive smoothly and allow plenty of time for slowing down at junctions.
☐ Remember that if the engine is not running, there will be no hydraulic pressure (Refer to the *Warning* on the right).

 Warning: BX, BX14 and Leader with manual gearbox and all automatic transmission models should be towed with the front wheels clear of the ground. If this is impossible, restrict towing speed to 30 MPH and distance to 30 miles maximum. Disregard of these instructions may cause transmission damage due to lack of lubrication. If in doubt, do not tow, or transmission damage may result.
Once the reserve of hydraulic pressure has been exhausted, the footbrake will not work and the handbrake will have to be used instead. Power steering assistance (when applicable) will also be lost.

Introduction

There are some very simple checks which need only take a few minutes to carry out, but which could save you a lot of inconvenience and expense.

These "Weekly checks" require no great skill or special tools, and the small amount of time they take to perform could prove to be very well spent, for example;

☐ Keeping an eye on tyre condition and pressures, will not only help to stop them wearing out prematurely, but could also save your life.

☐ Many breakdowns are caused by electrical problems. Battery-related faults are particularly common, and a quick check on a regular basis will often prevent the majority of these.

☐ If your car develops a brake fluid leak, the first time you might know about it is when your brakes don't work properly. Checking the level regularly will give advance warning of this kind of problem.

☐ If the oil or coolant levels run low, the cost of repairing any engine damage will be far greater than fixing the leak, for example.

Underbonnet check points

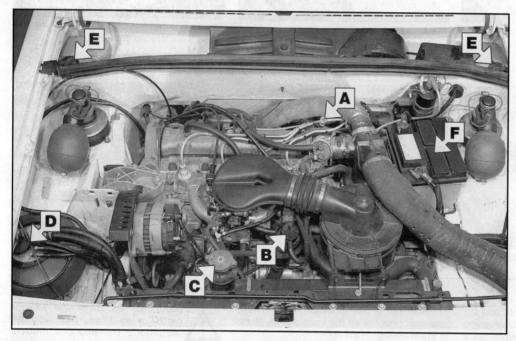

◀ **BX 16 RE**

All other models similar

A *Engine oil level dipstick (may be at front or rear of engine)*

B *Engine oil filler cap*

C *Coolant filler cap*

D *Hydraulic fluid reservoir*

E *Screen washer fluid reservoir*

F *Battery*

Engine oil level

Before you start

✔ Make sure that your car is on level ground.
✔ Check the oil level before the car is driven, or at least 5 minutes after the engine has been switched off.

 If the oil is checked immediately after driving the vehicle, some of the oil will remain in the upper engine components, resulting in an inaccurate reading on the dipstick!

The correct oil

Modern engines place great demands on their oil. It is very important that the correct oil for your car is used (See "Lubricants, fluids and capacities").

Car Care

● If you have to add oil frequently, you should check whether you have any oil leaks. Place some clean paper under the car overnight, and check for stains in the morning. If there are no leaks, the engine may be burning oil *(see "Fault Finding")*.

● Always maintain the level between the upper and lower dipstick marks (see photo 3). If the level is too low severe engine damage may occur. Oil seal failure may result if the engine is overfilled by adding too much oil.

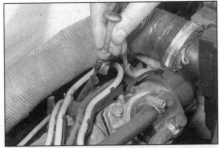

1 Depending on engine type, the dipstick is located either at the back or the front of the engine (see *"Underbonnet Check Points"* on pages 0•10 for exact location). Withdraw the dipstick.

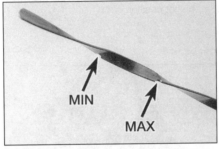

3 Note the oil level on the end of the dipstick, which should be between the upper ("MAX") mark and lower ("MIN") mark. Approximately 1.0 litre of oil will raise the level from the lower mark to the upper mark.

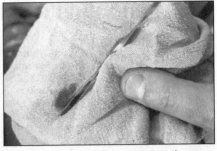

2 Using a clean rag or paper towel remove all oil from the dipstick. Insert the clean dipstick into the tube as far as it will go, then withdraw it again.

4 Oil is added through the filler cap. Unscrew the cap and top-up the level; a funnel may help to reduce spillage. Add the oil slowly, checking the level on the dipstick often. Don't overfill (see *"Car Care"* left).

Coolant level

 Warning: DO NOT attempt to remove the expansion tank pressure cap when the engine is hot, as there is a very great risk of scalding. Do not leave open containers of coolant about, as it is poisonous.

Car Care

● With a sealed-type cooling system, adding coolant should not be necessary on a regular basis. If frequent topping-up is required, it is likely there is a leak. Check the radiator, all hoses and joint faces for signs of staining or wetness, and rectify as necessary.

● It is important that antifreeze is used in the cooling system all year round, not just during the winter months. Don't top-up with water alone, as the antifreeze will become too diluted.

1 The coolant level varies with engine temperature. To check the level, wait until the engine is **cold** then unscrew the filler cap until a hissing sound is heard. When the hissing ceases, indicating that all pressure is released, slowly unscrew and remove the cap. If more hissing is heard, wait until it stops before unscrewing the cap completely. At all times keep well away from the filler opening.

2 On early BX models, the coolant depth, when cold, must be 250 to 300 mm from the top of the filler neck. The engine oil dipstick can be used to check the level but wipe it off before and after use. Later models have a tubular dipstick in the filler neck, the coolant must be between the MIN and MAX marks on the dipstick.

3 If necessary, add the recommended mixture of water and antifreeze through the filler orifice, until the coolant is up to the maximum level. Refit the cap, ensuring it is secure.

Hydraulic fluid level

Warning:
● **Use only LHM mineral hydraulic fluid in the hydraulic system of the Citroën BX. The use of any other fluid will ruin the rubber rings and seals. LHM fluid is green in colour. Keep the fluid, carefully sealed, in its original container.**

● *Make sure that your car is on level ground.*
● *Cleanliness is of great importance when dealing with the hydraulic system, so take care to clean around the reservoir cap before topping-up. Use only clean LHM fluid.*

Safety First!

● If the reservoir requires repeated topping-up, this is an indication of a fluid leak somewhere in the hydraulic system, which should be investigated immediately. The Citroën BX relies on the main hydraulic reservoir to supply the hydropneumatic suspension, the braking system and the power steering (where fitted).

● If a leak is suspected, the car should not be driven until the suspension, braking and steering systems have been checked. Never take any risks where any of these systems are concerned.

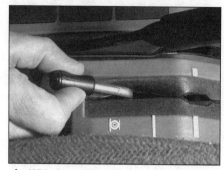

1 With the engine idling, move the ground clearance selector lever to the maximum height position.

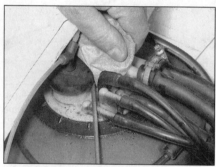

3 If topping-up is necessary, clean the filler cap and the surrounding area then remove the cap.

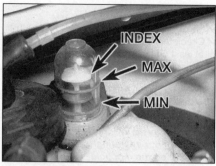

2 The hydraulic fluid reservoir is located on the front of the right-hand side engine bay bulkhead. Locate the hydraulic fluid sight level indicator on the top of the reservoir. The yellow indicator float (index) must be between the two red rings on the sight level glass.

4 Using genuine green LHM fluid, top-up the reservoir until the indicator reaches the upper red mark, then refit the cap and switch off the engine. The difference between the upper and lower red rings is approximately 0.45 litre of fluid.

Screen washer fluid level

Screenwash additives not only keep the winscreen clean during foul weather, they also prevent the washer system freezing in cold weather - which is when you are likely to need it most. Don't top up using plain water as the screenwash will become too diluted, and will freeze during cold weather. *On no account use coolant antifreeze in the washer system - this could discolour or damage paintwork.*

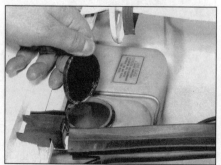

1 The reservoirs for the windscreen and rear window washer systems are located on either side of the engine compartment, at the rear.

2 When topping-up each reservoir, a screenwash additive should be added in the quantities recommended on the bottle.

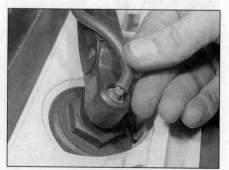

3 Check the operation of the windscreen and rear window washers. Check that the screenwash supply pipe to each wiper blade is correctly connected and free from blockage.

Tyre condition and pressure

It is very important that tyres are in good condition, and at the correct pressure - having a tyre failure at any speed is highly dangerous. Tyre wear is influenced by driving style - harsh braking and acceleration, or fast cornering, will all produce more rapid tyre wear. As a general rule, the front tyres wear out faster than the rears. Interchanging the tyres from front to rear ("rotating" the tyres) may result in more even wear. However, if this is completely effective, you may have the expense of replacing all four tyres at once! Remove any nails or stones embedded in the tread before they penetrate the tyre to cause deflation. If removal of a nail does reveal that the tyre has been punctured, refit the nail so that its point of penetration is marked. Then immediately change the wheel, and have the tyre repaired by a tyre dealer.

Regularly check the tyres for damage in the form of cuts or bulges, especially in the sidewalls. Periodically remove the wheels, and clean any dirt or mud from the inside and outside surfaces. Examine the wheel rims for signs of rusting, corrosion or other damage. Light alloy wheels are easily damaged by "kerbing" whilst parking; steel wheels may also become dented or buckled. A new wheel is very often the only way to overcome severe damage.

New tyres should be balanced when they are fitted, but it may become necessary to re-balance them as they wear, or if the balance weights fitted to the wheel rim should fall off. Unbalanced tyres will wear more quickly, as will the steering and suspension components. Wheel imbalance is normally signified by vibration, particularly at a certain speed (typically around 50 mph). If this vibration is felt only through the steering, then it is likely that just the front wheels need balancing. If, however, the vibration is felt through the whole car, the rear wheels could be out of balance. Wheel balancing should be carried out by a tyre dealer or garage.

1 *Tread Depth - visual check*
The original tyres have tread wear safety bands (B), which will appear when the tread depth reaches approximately 1.6 mm. The band positions are indicated by a triangular mark on the tyre sidewall (A).

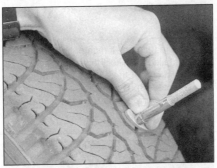

2 *Tread Depth - manual check*
Alternatively, tread wear can be monitored with a simple, inexpensive device known as a tread depth indicator gauge.

3 *Tyre Pressure Check*
Check the tyre pressures regularly with the tyres cold. Do not adjust the tyre pressures immediately after the vehicle has been used, or an inaccurate setting will result. The tyre pressures are shown on page 0•15.

Tyre tread wear patterns

Shoulder Wear

Underinflation (wear on both sides)
Under-inflation will cause overheating of the tyre, because the tyre will flex too much, and the tread will not sit correctly on the road surface. This will cause a loss of grip and excessive wear, not to mention the danger of sudden tyre failure due to heat build-up.
Check and adjust pressures
Incorrect wheel camber (wear on one side)
Repair or renew suspension parts
Hard cornering
Reduce speed!

Centre Wear

Overinflation
Over-inflation will cause rapid wear of the centre part of the tyre tread, coupled with reduced grip, harsher ride, and the danger of shock damage occurring in the tyre casing.
Check and adjust pressures

If you sometimes have to inflate your car's tyres to the higher pressures specified for maximum load or sustained high speed, don't forget to reduce the pressures to normal afterwards.

Uneven Wear

Front tyres may wear unevenly as a result of wheel misalignment. Most tyre dealers and garages can check and adjust the wheel alignment (or "tracking") for a modest charge.
Incorrect camber or castor
Repair or renew suspension parts
Malfunctioning suspension
Repair or renew suspension parts
Unbalanced wheel
Balance tyres
Incorrect toe setting
Adjust front wheel alignment
Note: *The feathered edge of the tread which typifies toe wear is best checked by feel.*

Electrical systems

✔ Check all external lights and the horn. Refer to the appropriate Sections of Chapter 13 for details if any of the circuits are found to be inoperative.

✔ Visually check all accessible wiring connectors, harnesses and retaining clips for security, and for signs of chafing or damage.

 HAYNES HINT *If you need to check your brake lights and indicators unaided, back up to a wall or garage door and operate the lights. The reflected light should show if they are working properly.*

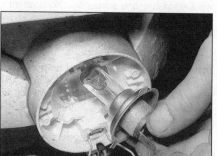

1 If a single indicator light, stop-light or headlight has failed, it is likely that a bulb has blown and will need to be replaced. Refer to Chapter 13 for details. If both stop-lights have failed, it is possible that the switch has failed (see Chapter 10).

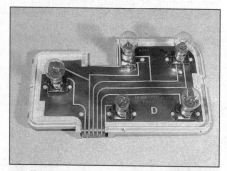

2 If more than one indicator light or tail light has failed it is likely that either a fuse has blown or that there is a fault in the circuit (see Chapter 13). The fuses are located in the passenger compartment, beneath the lower trim panel.

3 To remove a blown fuse, pull it from position. Fit a new fuse of the same rating, available from car accessory shops. It is important that you find the reason for the fuse blowing (see Chapter 13).

Battery

Caution: Before carrying out any work on the vehicle battery, read the precautions given in "Safety first" at the start of this manual.

✔ Make sure that the battery tray is in good condition, and that the clamp is tight. Corrosion on the tray, retaining clamp and the battery itself can be removed with a solution of water and baking soda. Thoroughly rinse all cleaned areas with water. Any metal parts damaged by corrosion should be covered with a zinc-based primer, then painted.

✔ Periodically (approximately every three months), check the charge condition of the battery as described in Chapter 5A.

✔ If the battery is flat, and you need to jump start your vehicle, see *Roadside Repairs*.

HAYNES HINT

Battery corrosion can be kept to a minimum by applying a layer of petroleum jelly to the clamps and terminals after they are reconnected.

1 The battery is located on the left-hand side of the engine compartment. The exterior of the battery should be inspected periodically for damage such as a cracked case or cover. If necessary, top-up using distilled water, so that the plates are covered by 6 mm of electrolyte.

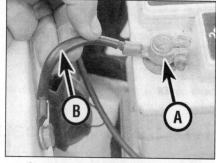

2 Check the tightness of battery clamps (A) to ensure good electrical connections. You should not be able to move them. Also check each cable (B) for cracks and frayed conductors.

3 If corrosion (white, fluffy deposits) is evident, remove the cables from the battery terminals, clean them with a small wire brush, then refit them. Automotive stores sell a tool for cleaning the battery post . . .

4 . . . as well as the battery cable clamps

Wiper blades

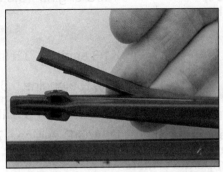 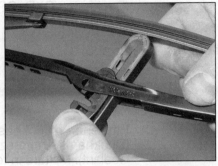

1 Check the condition of the wiper blades; if they are cracked or show any signs of deterioration, or if the glass swept area is smeared, renew them. Wiper blades should be renewed annually.

2 To remove a windscreen wiper blade, pull the arm fully away from the screen until it locks. Swivel the blade through 90°, press the locking tab with your fingers and slide the blade out of the arm's hooked end.

Tyre pressures (cold)

	Front (bar)	Rear (bar)
BX	1.9	2.0
BX 14	1.9	2.0
BX 14 Estate	2.2	2.5
BX 16	1.9	2.1
BX 16 - automatic transmission (from 1987)	2.2	2.2
BX 16 Estate	2.3	2.5
BX 19	2.0	2.2
BX 19 RE	2.0	2.0
BX 19 Estate	2.3	2.5
BX 19 GTi:		
No ABS	2.2	2.2
ABS	2.0	2.2
BX 19 GTi 16v:		
Pre March 1989	2.2	2.1
From March 1989	2.1	2.0

Recommendations may vary. Consult owners handbook or a tyre specialist if in doubt

Component or system	Lubricant or fluid	Capacity
Engine:		
BX and BX14 (with gearbox) pre-August 1988	Multigrade engine oil, viscosity SAE 15W/40 or 20W/50, (Duckhams QXR, QS, Hypergrade Plus or Hypergrade)	150A engine - 4.5 litres (oil change) 150C engine - 5.0 litres (oil change)
BX (from August 88)	As above	K1G engine - 3.5 litres (with filter)
BX16 and BX19	As above	171/159 engine 5.0 litres (oil change)
BX19 GTi 16v	As above	D6C engine - 5.3 litres (with filter)
Cooling system	Ethylene - glycol based antifreeze (Duckhams Antifreeze and Summer Coolant). Mixture in temperate climate - 25% antifreeze to 75% water	D6A/C/D engine - 7.1 litres Others - 6.5 litres
Manual gearbox:		
BX and BX14 pre-Aug. 88	N/A	With engine
Later BX 14 (MA type)	Gear oil, viscosity 75W/80W (Duckhams PT75W/80 Gear Oil)	2 litres
BX16 and BX19 (Type BE1)	As above	2 litres
BX16 and BX19 (Type BE3/5)	As above	Up to serial No. 2445106 - 2.2 litres From serial No. 2445106 - 1.8 litres
Automatic transmission	Dexron IID type ATF (Duckhams Uni-Matic)	From dry - 6.5 litres Drain and refill - 2.5 litres
Hydraulic system	Green LHM fluid (Duckhams LHM fluid)	-
Fuel system	97 to 99 RON leaded or 95 RON unleaded *	BX/BX14 - 44 or 52 litres BX16/BX19 - 52 or 66 litres

* Note: *Models fitted with catalytic converters* **MUST** *use unleaded fuel at all times*

Choosing your engine oil

Oils perform vital tasks in all engines. The higher the engine's performance, the greater the demand on lubricants to minimise wear as well as optimise power and economy. Duckhams tailors lubricants to the highest technical standards, meeting and exceeding the demands of all modern engines.

HOW ENGINE OIL WORKS

• *Beating friction*

Without oil, the surfaces inside your engine which rub together will heat, fuse and quickly cause engine seizure. Oil, and its special additives, forms a molecular barrier between moving parts, to stop wear and minimise heat build-up.

• *Cooling hot spots*

Oil cools parts that the engine's water-based coolant cannot reach, bathing the combustion chamber and pistons, where temperatures may exceed 1000°C. The oil assists in transferring the heat to the engine cooling system. Heat in the oil is also lost by air flow over the sump, and via any auxiliary oil cooler.

• *Cleaning the inner engine*

Oil washes away combustion by-products (mainly carbon) on pistons and cylinders, transporting them to the oil filter, and holding the smallest particles in suspension until they are flushed out by an oil change. Duckhams oils undergo extensive tests in the laboratory, and on the road.

Note: It is antisocial and illegal to dump oil down the drain. To find the location of your local oil recycling bank, call this number free.

Chapter 1
Routine maintenance and servicing

Contents

Degrees of difficulty

Easy, suitable for novice with little experience **Fairly easy,** suitable for beginner with some experience **Fairly difficult,** suitable for competent DIY mechanic **Difficult,** suitable for experienced DIY mechanic 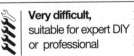 **Very difficult,** suitable for expert DIY or professional

Lubricants, fluids and capacities

Refer to the end of "Weekly checks"

Engine

For engine to model applications refer to Chapter 2, Part A, B, C or D

Oil filter type

150 engine (up to July 1988)	Champion C204
All other engines	Champion F104

Valve clearances (cold)

150 engine:	
Inlet	0.10 to 0.15 mm
Exhaust	0.20 to 0.30 mm
171 and 159 engines:	
Inlet	0.15 to 0.25 mm
Exhaust	0.35 to 0.45 mm
B1A/A engine:	
Inlet	0.15 to 0.20 mm
Exhaust	0.35 to 0.40 mm
D6A engine:	
Inlet	0.10 to 0.15 mm
Exhaust	0.20 to 0.30 mm
K1G engine:	
Inlet	0.20 mm
Exhaust	0.40 mm

Fuel system

Air cleaner element

Carburettor engines:	
BX 14	Champion V402
BX 14 (Aug 1988 to Sept 1991)	Champion V401
BX 14 (Sept 1991 on)	Champion V438
BX 16 (pre June 1987)	Champion W117
BX 16 (Sept 1988 to 1991)	Champion U543
BX 19 (pre June 1987)	Champion W117
BX 19 (from July 1987) and all Fuel-injected engines	Champion U543

Fuel filter type

Carburettor engines	Champion L101
Fuel-injected engines	Champion L201

Idle speed

Carburettor engines:	
BX	700 to 800 rpm
BX 14 (pre August 1988)	800 to 850 rpm
BX 14 (from August 1988)	700 to 800 rpm
BX 16 (pre June 1983 - Weber carburettor)	700 rpm
BX 16 (pre June 1983 - Solex carburettor)	650 to 700 rpm
BX 16 (from July 1983 - Weber carburettor)	650 to 700 rpm
BX 16 (from July 1983 - Solex carburettor)	650 to 700 rpm
BX 16 (automatic transmission and air conditioning)	750 to 800 rpm
BX 16 RE	650 to 750 rpm
BX 16 (from Sept 1988 to 1991):	
Manual gearbox	700 to 900 rpm
Automatic transmission	700 to 800 rpm
BX 19	650 to 750 rpm
BX 19 TRS/TZS (from July 1986 to 1991 - Weber carburettor)	750 to 850 rpm
BX 19 TRS/TZS (from July 1986 to 1991 - Solex carburettor)	650 to 750 rpm
BX 19 TZS (from 1991)	700 to 800 rpm
Fuel-injected engines:	
BX 16	Controlled by ECU
BX 19 GTi (pre July 1990):	
Manual gearbox	800 to 850 rpm
Automatic transmission	850 to 950 rpm
With air conditioning on	950 to 1000 rpm
BX 19 GTi (from July 1990)	850 to 900 rpm
BX 19 GTi 16v (pre 1991)	850 rpm (not adjustable)
BX 19 GTi 16v (from 1991)	850 rpm (not adjustable)
BX 19 TZi with catalytic converter	850 to 950 rpm

Ignition system

	Spark plug type	Electrode gap
Carburettor engines:		
BX	Champion S9YCC / S281YC	0.8 mm / 0.6 mm
BX 14:		
Pre Aug 1988	Champion S9YCC / S281YC	0.8 mm / 0.6 mm
From Aug 1988	Champion RC9YCC / C9YCX	0.8 mm / 0.9 mm
BX16:		
Pre Sept 1988	Champion S7YCC / S279YC	0.8 mm / 0.6 mm
From Sept 1988	Champion RC7YCC / C7YCX	0.8 mm
BX 19:		
Pre July 1987	Champion S7YCC / S279YC	0.8 mm / 0.6 mm
From July 1987	Champion RC7YCC / C7YCX	0.8 mm
Fuel-injected engines:		
BX 16	Champion C9YCX	0.9 mm
BX 19 GTi and GTi 16v	Champion RC7YCC	0.8 mm (1.6 mm - GTi 16v)

Clutch

Pedal free play	Nil
Pedal travel	130 to 150 mm

Braking system

Brake pads

Lining minimum thickness:	
Front	Indicated by warning lamp
Rear	2.0 mm - suggested

Standard discs

Wear limit:	
Front	7.0 mm
Rear	4.0 mm
Maximum run-out	0.2 mm

Steering

Front wheel alignment toe-out	0 to 3.0 mm

Tyre pressures

Refer to the end of "Weekly checks"

Torque wrench settings

	Nm	lbf ft
150 engine		
Rocker cover	10	7
Valve adjuster screw locknuts	17	12
Sump drain plug	28	20
171 and 159 engines		
Cam cover	10	7
Sump drain plug	30	22
K1G engine		
Valve cover	5	4
Oil filter	15	11
Ignition system		
Spark plugs:		
Taper seat type	12	9
Flat seat type (with washer)	25	18
Manual gearbox		
BX and BX 14 - Type BH3:		
Drain plug	25	18
BX and BX 14 - Type MA (2 CA):		
Drain and filler plugs	26	19
BX 16 and BX 19:		
Drain plug:		
Final drive	30	22
Gearbox	10	7

1

The maintenance intervals in this Manual are provided with the assumption that you will be carrying out the work yourself. These are the minimum maintenance intervals recommended by the manufacturer for vehicles driven daily. If you wish to keep your vehicle in peak condition at all times, you may wish to perform some of these procedures more often. We encourage frequent maintenance, because it enhances the efficiency, performance and resale value of your vehicle.

If the vehicle is driven in dusty areas, used to tow a trailer, or driven frequently at slow speeds (idling in traffic) or on short journeys, more frequent maintenance intervals are recommended.

When the vehicle is new, it should be serviced by a factory-authorised dealer service department, in order to preserve the factory warranty.

Every 250 miles (400 km) or weekly
☐ Refer to "Weekly Checks"

Every 1000 miles (1500 km) or monthly - whichever comes first
☐ Check seat belts (Section 3)
☐ Check operation of brakes (Section 4)
☐ Check for signs of fluid leakage (Section 5)

Every 6000 miles (10 000 km) or 6 months
☐ Check exhaust system (Section 6)
☐ Check and lubricate all lock, hinge and latch mechanisms (Section 7)
☐ Check hydraulic lines for condition and security (Section 8)
☐ Renew engine oil and filter (Section 9)
☐ Check automatic transmission fluid level (Section 10)
☐ Check clutch operation (Section 11)
☐ Check brake pads for wear (Section 12)
☐ Check brake discs for wear and condition (Section 13)
☐ Check handbrake adjustment (Section 14)
☐ Check front wheel alignment (Section 15)
☐ Check condition of steering gear, track rod balljoints and gaiters (Section 16)
☐ Check driveshaft bellows (Section 17)

Every 12 000 miles (20 000 km) or 12 months
☐ Check seat belt anchorages (Section 18)
☐ Check drivebelt tensions (Section 19)
☐ Clean and inspect crankcase ventilation hoses (Section 20)
☐ Check valve clearances - BX and BX 14 (Section 21)
☐ Check valve clearances - BX 16 and BX 19 (Section 22)
☐ Check engine idle speed (Section 23)
☐ Renew fuel filter - BX 16 RE (Section 24)
☐ Renew spark plugs (Section 25)
☐ Lubricate clutch pedal and cable (Section 26)
☐ Check front suspension lower balljoints (Section 27)

Every 18 000 miles (30 000 km) or 18 months
☐ Renew air cleaner element (Section 28)
☐ Clean hydraulic system filters (Section 29)

Every 30 000 miles (50 000 km)
☐ Renew engine valve springs - 150 engine (Section 30)

Every 36 000 miles (60 000 km)
☐ Renew camshaft drivebelt - except 150 engine (Section 31)
☐ Renew cooling system antifreeze (Section 32)
☐ Renew automatic transmission fluid (Section 33)
☐ Renew hydraulic system fluid (Section 34)

Every 48 000 miles (80 000 km)
☐ Renew fuel filter - BX 16 fuel-injected (Section 35)

Every 60 000 miles (100 000 km)
☐ Renew fuel filter - BX 19 fuel-injected (Section 36)
☐ Renew manual gearbox oil - except BX and BX 14 pre August 1988 (Section 37)

Underbonnet view of a BX or BX 14 with 150 engine

1 Dipstick
2 Radiator filler cap
3 Hydraulic fluid reservoir
4 Front suspension unit (right-hand side)
5 Rear window washer reservoir
6 Carburettor
7 Oil filler
8 Ignition coil
9 Windscreen washer reservoir
10 Battery
11 Air filter

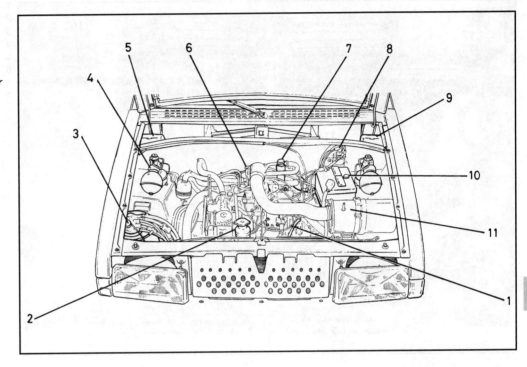

1

Underbonnet view of a BX 14 with K1G engine

1 Front suspension sphere
2 Heater hose bleed screw
3 Air cleaner
4 Battery
5 Right-hand engine mounting
6 Carburettor
7 Fuel pump
8 Hydraulic system fluid reservoir
9 Alternator
10 Engine oil filler cap
11 Ignition coil
12 Hot air intake hose
13 Air intake tube
14 Radiator filler cap
15 Radiator bleed screw
16 Air cleaner Winter/Summer lever
17 Bonnet lock

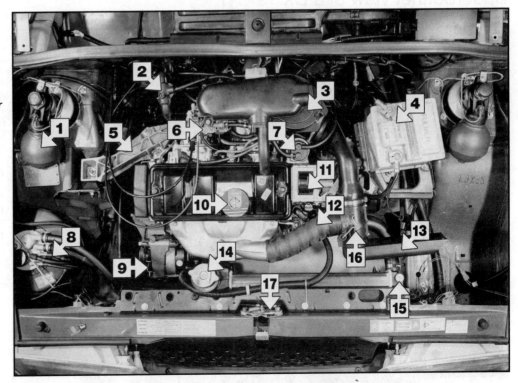

Underbonnet view of a BX 16 with air filter removed for clarity

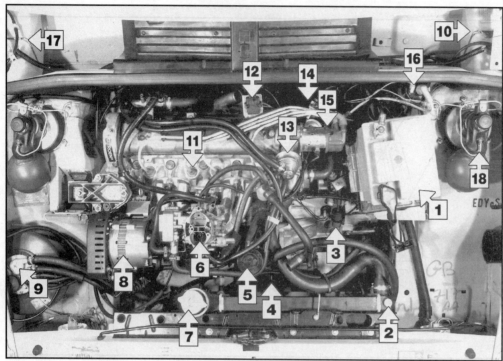

1 Battery
2 Bleed screws - radiator
3 Clutch cable
4 Dipstick
5 Oil filler cap
6 Carburettor
7 Radiator filler cap
8 Alternator
9 Hydraulic system reservoir
10 Rear window washer reservoir
11 Spark plug
12 Diagnostic socket
13 Fuel pump
14 Dipstick - alternative position
15 Distributor
16 Ignition coil
17 Windscreen washer reservoir
18 Front suspension unit - left side

Underbonnet view of a BX 19 GTi

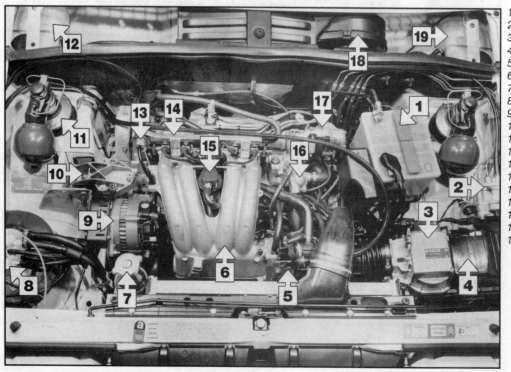

1 Battery
2 ABS hydraulic control unit
3 Airflow meter
4 Air cleaner
5 Throttle butterfly housing
6 Inlet manifold
7 Radiator filler cap
8 Hydraulic system fluid reservoir
9 Alternator
10 Right-hand engine mounting
11 Front suspension unit
12 Rear window washer reservoir
13 Fuel pressure regulator
14 Fuel rail
15 Engine oil filler cap
16 Thermostat housing
17 Distributor
18 Heater blower motor
19 Windscreen washer reservoir

Underbonnet view of a BX 19 GTi 16 valve

1 Rear window washer reservoir
2 Heater blower motor
3 Windscreen washer reservoir
4 Front suspension sphere
5 Timing belt cover
6 Coolant distribution pipe
7 Battery
8 Right-hand engine mounting
9 Camshaft cover
10 Distributor
11 Coolant expansion tank
12 Hydraulic system fluid reservoir
13 Inlet manifold
14 Idle actuator
15 Engine oil filler cap
16 Air intake hose
17 Airflow meter
18 Air cleaner
19 Radiator
20 Throttle butterfly housing

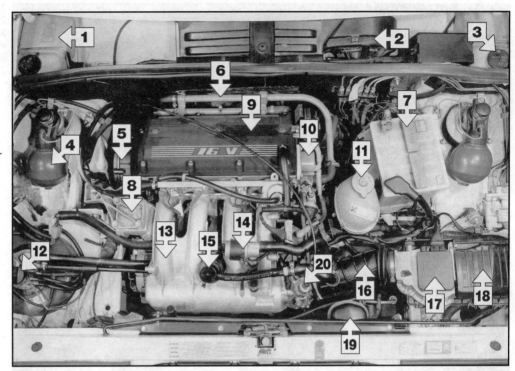

Front underbody view (typical)

1 Exhaust front section
2 Hydraulic system pipes and union
3 Steering track-rod
4 Front suspension arm
5 Driveshaft inboard joint
6 Driveshaft inboard joint
7 Driveshaft intermediate bearing
8 Transmission
9 Exhaust downpipe
10 Oil filter
11 Radiator
12 Hydraulic system fluid pressure regulator
13 Hydraulic system fluid pump
14 Sump
15 Brake disc air deflector

1

Rear underbody view (typical)

1 Fuel filler pipe
2 Rear suspension arm
3 Fuel tank
4 Exhaust system and heat shield
5 Rear suspension unit
6 Spare wheel

Maintenance procedures

1 Introduction

This Chapter is designed to help the home mechanic maintain his/her vehicle for safety, economy, long life and peak performance.

The Chapter contains a master maintenance schedule, followed by Sections dealing specifically with each task in the schedule. Visual checks, adjustments, component renewal and other helpful items are included. Refer to the accompanying illustrations of the engine compartment and the underside of the vehicle for the locations of the various components.

Servicing your vehicle in accordance with the mileage/time maintenance schedule and the following Sections will provide a planned maintenance programme, which should result in a long and reliable service life. This is a comprehensive plan, so maintaining some items but not others at the specified service intervals, will not produce the same results.

As you service your vehicle, you will discover that many of the procedures can - and should - be grouped together, because of the particular procedure being performed, or because of the close proximity of two otherwise-unrelated components to one another. For example, if the vehicle is raised for any reason, the exhaust can be inspected at the same time as the suspension and steering components.

The first step in this maintenance programme is to prepare yourself before the actual work begins. Read through all the Sections relevant to the work to be carried out, then make a list and gather together all the parts and tools required. If a problem is encountered, seek advice from a parts specialist, or a dealer service department.

2 Intensive maintenance

If, from the time the vehicle is new, the Routine Maintenance schedule is followed closely and frequent checks are made of fluid levels and high-wear items, as suggested throughout this Manual, the engine will be kept in relatively good running condition and the need for additional work will be minimised.

It is possible that there will be times when the engine is running poorly due to the lack of regular maintenance. This is even more likely if a used vehicle which has not received regular and frequent maintenance checks is purchased. In such cases, additional work may need to be carried out outside of the regular maintenance intervals.

If engine wear is suspected, a compression test will provide valuable information regarding the overall performance of the main internal components. Such a test can be used as a basis to decide on the extent of the work to be carried out. If, for example, a compression test indicates serious internal engine wear, conventional maintenance as described in this Chapter will not greatly improve the performance of the engine, and may prove a waste of time and money, unless extensive overhaul work is carried out first.

The following series of operations are those most often required to improve the performance of a generally poor-running engine:

Primary operations

a) Clean, inspect and test the battery
b) Check all the engine-related fluids
c) Check the condition and tension of the auxiliary drivebelt(s)
d) Renew the spark plugs
e) Inspect the distributor cap and HT leads - as applicable
f) Check the condition of the air cleaner filter element, and renew if necessary
g) Renew the fuel filter (if fitted)
h) Check the condition of all hoses and check for fluid leaks
i) Check the idle speed and mixture settings - as applicable

5 If the above operations do not prove fully effective, carry out the following secondary operations:

Secondary operations

a) Check the charging system
b) Check the ignition system
c) Check the fuel system
d) Renew the distributor cap and rotor arm - as applicable
e) Renew the ignition HT leads - as applicable

Every 1000 miles or Monthly

3 Seat belt check

1 Check the webbing of each seat belt for signs of fraying, cuts or other damage, pulling the belt out to its full extent to check its entire length.
2 Check the operation of the belt buckles by fitting the belt tongue plate and pulling hard to ensure that it remains locked, then check the retractor mechanism (inertia reel only) by pulling out the belt to the halfway point and jerking hard. The mechanism must lock immediately to prevent any further unreeling but must allow free movement during normal driving.
3 If there is any sign of damage, or any doubt about the condition of a belt, then it must be renewed. If the vehicle has been involved in a collision, any belts in use at the time must be renewed as a matter of course and all other belts should be checked carefully.
4 Use only warm water and non-detergent soap to clean seat belts. Never use chemical cleaners, strong detergents, dyes or bleaches. Keep the belts fully extended until they have dried naturally. Do not apply heat to dry a belt.

4 Brake operation check

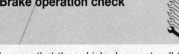

1 Make sure that the vehicle does not pull to one side when braking and that the wheels do not lock prematurely when braking hard.
2 Check that there is no vibration through the steering when braking.
3 Check that the handbrake operates correctly without excessive movement of the lever and that it holds the vehicle stationary on a slope.

5 Fluid leakage check

1 Visually inspect the engine joint faces, gaskets and seals for any signs of coolant or oil leaks. Pay particular attention to the areas around the rocker cover, cylinder head, oil filter and sump joint faces. Bear in mind that over a period of time some very slight seepage from these areas is to be expected but what you are really looking for is any indication of a serious leak (see Haynes Hint). Should a leak be found, renew the offending gasket or oil seal by referring to the appropriate Chapter(s) of this Manual.
2 Similarly, check the transmission for oil leaks and investigate and rectify and problems found.
3 Check the security and condition of all the engine related pipes and hoses. Ensure that all cable-ties or securing clips are in place and in good condition. Clips which are broken or missing can lead to chafing of the hoses, pipes or wiring which could cause more serious problems in the future.
4 From within the engine compartment, check the security of all fuel hose attachments and pipe unions, and inspect the fuel hoses and vacuum hoses for kinks, chafing and deterioration.
5 Carefully check the condition of all coolant, fuel, power steering and brake hoses. Renew any hose which is cracked, swollen or deteriorated. Cracks will show up better if the hose is squeezed. Pay close attention to the hose clips that secure the hoses to the system components. Hose clips can pinch and puncture hoses, resulting in leaks. If wire type hose clips are used, it may be a good idea to replace them with screw-type clips.

6 With the vehicle raised, inspect the fuel tank and filler neck for punctures, cracks and other damage. The connection between the filler neck and tank is especially critical. Sometimes a rubber filler neck or connecting hose will leak due to loose retaining clamps or deteriorated rubber.
7 Carefully check all rubber hoses and metal fuel lines leading away from the fuel tank. Check for loose connections, deteriorated hoses, crimped lines and other damage. Pay particular attention to the vent pipes and hoses which often loop up around the filler neck and can become blocked or crimped. Follow the lines to the front of the vehicle carefully inspecting them all the way. Renew damaged sections as necessary.
8 Inspect all hydraulic system pipes. If any damage or deterioration is discovered, do not drive the vehicle until the necessary repair work has been carried out. Renew any damaged sections of pipe immediately.
9 Check the condition of all exposed wiring harnesses.

HAYNES
HINT

A leak in the cooling system will usually show up as white or rust coloured deposits on the area adjoining the leak

1

Every 6000 miles or 6 Months

6 Exhaust system check

1 With the exhaust system cold, check the complete system from the engine to the end of the tailpipe. Ideally the inspection should be carried out with the vehicle raised and supported on axle stands (see "*Jacking and vehicle support*") to permit unrestricted access.
2 Check the exhaust pipes and connections for evidence of leaks, severe corrosion and damage. Make sure that all brackets and mountings are in good condition and tight. Leakage at any of the joints or in other parts of the system will usually show up as a black sooty stain in the vicinity of the leak.
3 Rattles and other noises can often be traced to the exhaust system, especially the brackets and mountings. Try to move the pipes and silencers. If the components can come into contact with the body or suspension parts, secure the system with new mountings or if possible, separate the joints and twist the pipes as necessary to provide additional clearance.

8.3 Carefully inspect each hydraulic pipe

7 Lock, hinge and latch mechanism check and lubrication

1 Lubricate the hinges of the bonnet, doors and tailgate with a light machine oil.
2 Lightly grease the bonnet release mechanism.
3 The door and tailgate latches, strikers and locks should also be lubricated, wiping off any surplus grease or oil.
4 Do not lubricate the steering lock mechanism with oil or any other lubricant which might foul the ignition switch contacts. If the lock is stiff, try to introduce a graphite-based powder into the mechanism.

8 Hydraulic line condition and security check

1 The hydropneumatic suspension and the braking system are both pressurised by a common hydraulic system. The pipes and hoses of this system must be checked for security and condition and any damaged or corroded components renewed immediately.
2 Start examination of the system from the fluid reservoir and work around the suspension and braking systems in a logical sequence, including the pressure regulator, pump, security valve, compensator control valve, front and rear suspension height corrector units and suspension unit cylinders.
3 Carefully work along the length of each pipe looking for dents, kinks, damage of any sort or corrosion. Corrosion should be polished off. If the depth of pitting is significant then the pipe must be renewed **(see illustration)**.
4 Look for signs of leakage at pipe and hose unions, then examine all flexible hoses for signs of cracking, chafing or deterioration of the rubber. Bend them sharply between the fingers (but do not actually bend them double or the casing may be damaged) and check

that this does not reveal previously hidden cracks, cuts or splits **(see illustrations)**. Check that all pipes and hoses are securely fastened in their clips.

9 Engine oil and filter renewal

Note: *There may be a delay of a few seconds before the oil pressure warning light goes out when the engine is first started after oil renewal*
1 Before starting, gather together all the necessary tools and materials. Make sure that you have plenty of clean rags and newspapers handy to mop up any oil spillage. Ideally, the engine oil should be warm as it will drain better and more built-up sludge will be removed with it. Take care however, not to touch the exhaust or any other hot parts of the engine when working under the vehicle. To avoid any possibility of scalding and to protect yourself from possible skin irritants and other harmful contaminants in used engine oils, it is advisable to wear gloves when carrying out this work.
2 Raise the vehicle to its full height setting to allow improved clearance and support it on axle stands (see "*Jacking and vehicle support*")
3 The engine oil drain plug is located at the lowest point of the sump **(see illustration)**. Remove the oil filler cap and slacken the drain plug about half a turn. Position a suitable container under the drain plug, then remove the plug completely **(see Haynes Hint)**.
4 Allow some time for the old oil to drain, noting that it may be necessary to reposition the container as the flow of oil slows to a trickle. Work can be speeded-up by removing the oil filter while the oil is draining.
5 After all the oil has drained, wipe off the drain plug with a clean rag and (where fitted) renew its sealing washer. Clean the area around the drain plug opening and refit the plug. Tighten the plug securely, to the specified torque.
6 Move the container into position under the oil filter.

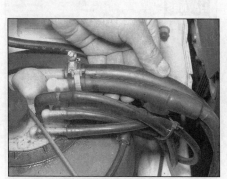

8.4a Examine all hydraulic hoses for signs of leakage, cracking, chafing or deterioration

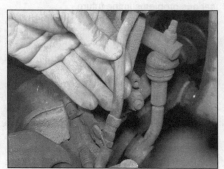

8.4b Examining a brake system hose

9.3 The engine oil drain plug is located at the lowest point of the sump

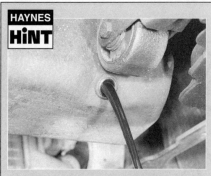

Keep the drain plug pressed into the sump while unscrewing it by hand for the last couple of turns. As the plug releases, move it away sharply so the stream of oil issuing from the sump runs into the container, not up your sleeve!

7 Using a filter removal tool, slacken the filter initially then unscrew it by hand the rest of the way **(see illustration)**. If a tool is not available, pierce the side of the filter with a long pointed tool and use this as a lever to unscrew it from its mounting. Empty the oil in the old filter into the container and allow any residual oil to drain out of the engine.

8 Use a clean rag to remove all oil, dirt and sludge from the filter sealing area on the engine. Check the old filter to make sure that the rubber sealing ring has not stuck to the engine. If it has, carefully remove it.

9 Apply a light coating of clean engine oil to the sealing ring of the new filter and screw the filter into position until it seats. Tighten the filter by hand only, do not use any tools.

10 Remove the old oil and all tools from under the vehicle.

11 Refill the engine with fresh oil, using the correct grade and type of oil. Pour in half the specified quantity of oil first, then wait a few minutes for the oil to fall to the sump. Continue adding oil a small quantity at a time until the level is up to the lower mark on the dipstick *(see Weekly Checks)*. Adding a further 1.0 litre will bring the level up to the upper mark on the dipstick.

12 Start the engine and run it for a few minutes while checking for leaks around the oil filter seal and the sump drain plug.

13 Switch off the engine and wait a few minutes for the oil to settle in the sump once more. With the new oil circulated and the filter now completely full, recheck the level on the dipstick and add more oil as necessary.

14 Dispose of the used engine oil safely.

Note: It is antisocial and illegal to dump oil down the drain. To find the location of your local oil recycling bank, call this number free.

OIL BANK LINE
0800 66 33 66

9.7 Removing the engine oil filter

10 Automatic transmission fluid level check

1 This check should be made directly after the vehicle has been used so that the transmission oil is at its normal operating temperature. Note that the transmission fluid may be very hot, so take precautions to avoid being burnt by it.

2 With the vehicle parked on level ground and the engine running, move the selector lever through all positions a number of times then finally leave it in P. The handbrake must be fully applied throughout the check procedure.

3 With the engine still running, remove the transmission fluid level dipstick, wipe it clean, reinsert it fully then withdraw it again and check the fluid level. The fluid level must be between the MIN and MAX levels on the dipstick **(see illustration)**.

4 If required, top-up the fluid level (but do not overfill) through the dipstick guide tube.

5 Stop the engine and refit the dipstick on completion.

6 If topping-up becomes frequently necessary, inspect the transmission for leaks.

11 Clutch operation check

1 Check that the clutch pedal moves smoothly and easily through its full travel and that the clutch itself functions correctly, with no trace of slip or drag.

2 If excessive effort is required to operate the clutch, check first that the cable is correctly routed and undamaged, then remove the pedal to ensure that its pivot is properly greased before suspecting a fault in the cable itself. If the cable is worn or damaged, or if its adjusting mechanism is no longer effective, then it must be renewed.

3 Check clutch pedal travel by measuring the total distance from the highest to the lowest point of its travel. The recommended travel distance must be within the limits specified.

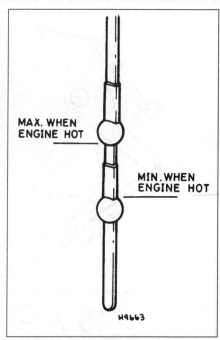

MAX. WHEN ENGINE HOT

MIN. WHEN ENGINE HOT

H9663

10.3 The automatic transmission fluid level dipstick

4 The clutch thrust bearing is of the self-centring ball type and it should be in permanent contact with the release mechanism. Check this by ensuring that there is no clutch pedal free play. Check the clearance between the pedal pin and the pedal unit support aperture lower limit **(see illustrations)**.

5 The clearance measured should be a minimum of 8 mm. If adjustment is necessary, loosen the clutch pushrod locknut and take up any excessive play by turning the adjustment screw. When the adjustment is correct retighten the locknut **(see illustration)**.

12 Brake pad wear check

Warning: When checking brake components, take care not to disperse brake dust into the air or to inhale it, since it may contain asbestos which is injurious to health

Front

1 The brake pad wear warning lamp will indicate that the front brake pads have worn down to the specified limit.

2 To carry out a visual check, chock the rear roadwheels, jack up the front of the vehicle and support it on axle stands (see *"Jacking and vehicle support"*).

3 Remove the front roadwheels, release the handbrake and turn the steering so that one of the brake calipers is facing outboard.

1

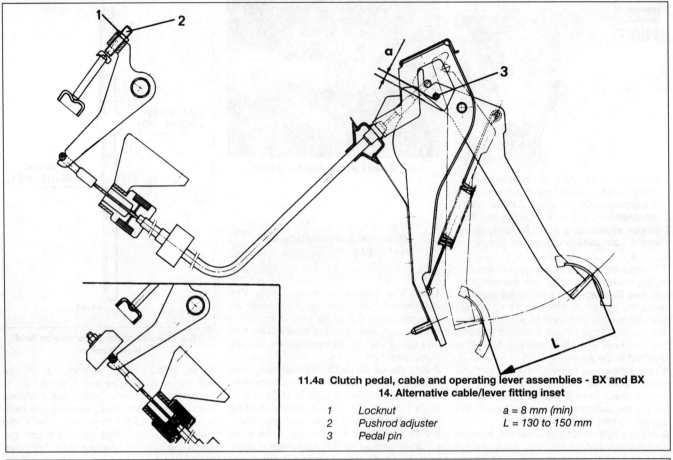

11.4a Clutch pedal, cable and operating lever assemblies - BX and BX 14. Alternative cable/lever fitting inset

1	Locknut	a = 8 mm (min)
2	Pushrod adjuster	L = 130 to 150 mm
3	Pedal pin	

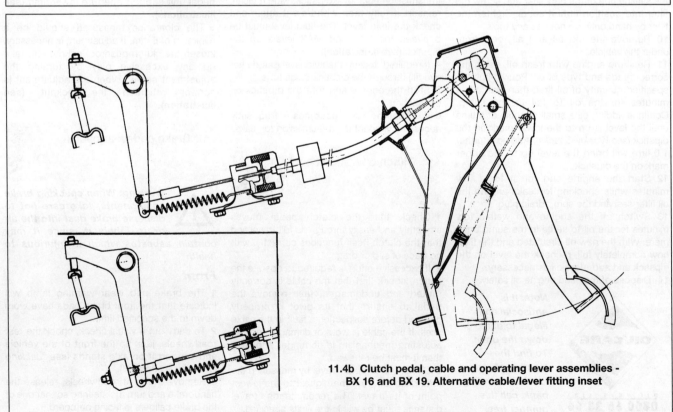

11.4b Clutch pedal, cable and operating lever assemblies - BX 16 and BX 19. Alternative cable/lever fitting inset

11.5 Clutch pushrod and release lever - BX 16

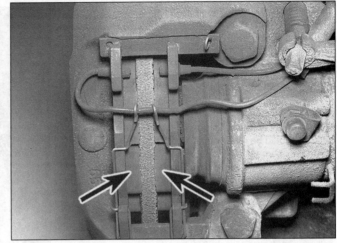

12.4 The thickness of the friction material on each brake pad can be measured through the aperature in the caliper body

4 Check the thickness of the brake pad linings. If worn down to or beyond the minimum allowable thickness they must be renewed without delay **(see illustration)**.

5 Repeat the process on the opposite caliper.

6 When renewing the brake pads, always fit new pads to both calipers.

Rear

7 Apply the handbrake, jack-up the rear of the vehicle and support it on axle stands. Remove both roadwheels.

8 Unscrew and remove the retaining bolt and withdraw the pad cover from each caliper.

9 Check the thickness of the brake pad linings of both calipers. If worn down to or beyond the minimum allowable thickness they must be renewed.

10 When renewing the brake pads, always fit new pads to both calipers.

13 Brake disc wear and condition check

Clean and examine each brake disc for deep scoring or grooving. Light scoring is normal but if it is severe, the disc must be refaced by a competent engineering works or, if worn to the specified wear limit, renewed.

Check each disc for run-out to determine whether it is distorted or buckled. To do this accurately, a dial gauge will be necessary. If a gauge is not available, feeler blades can be used against a fixed block as the disc is rotated slowly. Do not confuse wear in the hub bearings with disc run-out. The mating surfaces of the hub and disc must be perfectly clean or a false reading could be given. If run-out is greater than that specified, renew the disc.

14 Handbrake adjustment check

The handbrake should be capable of holding the parked car stationary, even on steep slopes, when applied with moderate force. The mechanism should be firm and positive in feel with no trace of stiffness or sponginess from the cables and should release immediately the handbrake lever is released. If the mechanism is faulty in any of these respects it must be checked immediately.

To check the setting, apply the handbrake firmly several times to establish correct pad-to-disc clearance, then release the lever fully. Applying normal moderate pressure, pull the handbrake lever to the fully-applied position and count the number of notches required to do so. If the number of notches is more or less than that specified in Chapter 10 (handbrake adjustment), then adjustment is required.

15 Front wheel alignment check

1 Accurate wheel alignment is essential for good steering and slow tyre wear. Before checking, make sure that the suspension heights are correct and that the tyres are correctly inflated.

2 Place the vehicle on level ground with the wheels in the straight-ahead position.

3 With the ground clearance lever in the "normal" position and the engine idling, measure the toe of the front wheels using a wheel alignment gauge. The amount of toe must be as specified.

4 If adjustment is necessary, refer to Chapter 11.

16 Steering gear, track rod balljoint and gaiter check

1 Raise the front of the vehicle and securely support it on axle stands (see *"Jacking and vehicle support"*).

2 Visually inspect the balljoint dust covers and the steering gear rubber gaiters for splits, chafing or deterioration. Any wear of these components will cause loss of lubricant together with dirt and water entry, resulting in rapid deterioration of the balljoints or steering gear.

3 Grasp the roadwheel at the 9 o'clock and 3 o'clock positions and try to rock it. Any movement felt may be caused by wear in the hub bearings or in the track rod balljoints. If a balljoint is worn the visual movement will be obvious. If the inner joint is suspect, it can be felt by placing a hand over the steering gear rubber gaiter and gripping the track rod. If the wheel is now rocked, movement will be felt at the inner joint if wear has taken place.

4 With the vehicle standing on its wheels, have an assistant turn the steering wheel back and forth about an eighth of a turn each way. There should be very little, if any, lost movement between the steering wheel and the roadwheels. If this is not the case, closely observe the joints and mountings previously described, but in addition check for wear of the steering column universal joint and the steering gear itself.

17 Driveshaft bellow check

With the vehicle raised and securely supported on axle stands (see *"Jacking and vehicle support"*), turn the steering onto full lock then slowly rotate the roadwheel. Inspect

1

the condition of the outer constant velocity (CV) joint rubber bellows while squeezing them to open out the folds (see illustration). Check for signs of cracking, splits or deterioration of the rubber which may allow grease to escape and lead to the entry of water and grit into the joint. Also check the security and condition of the retaining clips. Repeat these checks on the inner CV joints. If any damage or deterioration is found, the bellows should be renewed.

At the same time, check the general condition of the CV joints themselves by first holding the driveshaft and attempting to rotate the roadwheel. Repeat this check by holding the inner joint and attempting to rotate the driveshaft. Any appreciable movement indicates wear in the joints, in the driveshaft splines, or a loose driveshaft nut.

17.1 Inspect the CV joint rubber bellows for signs of cracking, splits or deterioration

Every 12 000 miles or 12 Months

18 Seat belt anchorage check

1 Ensure that all belt mounting bolts are securely tightened. Note that some bolts are shouldered so that the belt anchor points are free to rotate.
2 If there is any sign of damage or heavy corrosion around an anchorage point causing a reduction in strength, then it must be repaired immediately
3 If the vehicle has been involved in a collision, then all belt anchorage points must be checked as a matter of course.

19 Drivebelt tension check

Alternator

1 If the alternator drivebelt is too loose, alternator performance will be affected. If the belt is too tight it will cause unnecessary alternator bearing wear. In either case the belt itself will suffer and its life will be shortened.
2 The belt should be tight enough to take up any play in the belt at its mid point on the longest run between the pulleys (see illustration). Whilst tautness is required, the belt must not be overtightened.

HP pump

3 Belt tension must be felt to be taut under a reasonable thumb pressure at the midway point between the pulleys on its longest run. Note that the belt must not be tightened excessively or its will be shortened and

damage to the pulleys and their drive bearings could result.

20 Crankcase ventilation hose check and clean

1 Check the security and condition of all crankcase breather hoses. They must be free of perishing, splits and chafing.
2 If hose blockage is suspected, remove and clean the relevant hose.
3 Ensure that all cable-ties or securing clips attached to the hoses are in place and in good condition. Clips which are broken or missing can lead to chafing of the hose which could cause more serious problems in the future.

21 Valve clearance check - BX and BX 14

Note: *For engine to model applications refer to Chapter 2*

19.2 Checking alternator drivebelt tension

150 engine

Checking

1 This operation must only be done when the engine is cold.
2 Remove the rocker cover.
3 The engine will need to be progressively turned over when checking the valve clearances. To do this, raise the front of the vehicle so that a roadwheel is clear of the ground, then turn the roadwheel with 4th gear engaged and turn the engine over as required. Removal of the spark plugs will allow the engine to be turned over more easily.
4 It is important that each clearance is checked only when the rocker of the valve being adjusted rests on the heel of the cam, that is directly opposite the peak of the cam. This can be ensured by working in the following sequence, which also avoids turning the engine more than necessary:

Valve fully open	Check and adjust valves
1 exhaust	3 inlet and 4 exhaust
3 exhaust	4 inlet and 2 exhaust
4 exhaust	2 inlet and 1 exhaust
2 exhaust	1 inlet and 3 exhaust

5 Each clearance must be as shown in *Specifications*.

Adjustment

6 To adjust a clearance, position the valve fully open and inserting a feeler blade in the gap between the rocker arm and valve stem. Loosen the locknut with a spanner and turn the adjuster screw with a screwdriver (see illustration). Adjust the screw so that the feeler blade slides in the gap with a slight drag. Tighten the locknut, recheck the clearance and readjust if necessary.
7 Check that the rocker cover seal is in good condition and refit the cover. Fit new sealing washers under the retaining bolts and tighten the bolts.

21.6 Adjusting a valve clearance - 150 engine

21.15 Adjusting a valve clearance - K1G engine

K1G engine

Checking

8 Disconnect the crankcase ventilation hose from the rocker cover.

9 Unscrew the nuts and remove the rocker cover.

10 Remove the two spacers and baffle plate from the studs.

11 Prepare to rotate the crankshaft, either by jacking up one front wheel and turning the wheel with 4th gear engaged, or by using a spanner on the crankshaft sprocket bolt. Rotation will be easier if the spark plugs are first removed.

12 Rotate the crankshaft until No 1 exhaust valve (flywheel end) is fully open. No 3 inlet valve and No 4 exhaust valve clearances may now be checked.

13 Insert a feeler blade of the specified thickness between the rocker arm and valve stem. It should be a firm, sliding fit if the clearance is correct.

14 Work in the following sequence:

Valve fully open	Check and adjust valves
1 Exhaust	3 Inlet and 4 Exhaust
3 Exhaust	4 Inlet and 2 Exhaust
4 Exhaust	2 Inlet and 1 Exhaust
2 Exhaust	1 Inlet and 3 Exhaust

Adjustment

15 Where adjustment is necessary, loosen the adjuster nut with a ring spanner, turn the adjuster as required with a screwdriver, then retighten the nut **(see illustration)**.

16 When all valve clearances have been checked and adjusted, refit the baffle plate with its edges pointing downwards, followed by the two spacers.

17 Check that the rubber gasket is re-usable (renew if necessary), then refit the rocker cover and tighten the nuts.

18 Reconnect the crankcase ventilation hose.

---

22 Valve clearance check - BX 16 and BX 19

Note: *For engine to model applications refer to Chapter 2*

171 and 159 engines

Checking

1 Valve clearances must be checked with the engine cold.

2 Remove the camshaft cover, trying not to damage the gasket.

3 Prepare to rotate the crankshaft, either by jacking up one front wheel and turning the wheel with 5th gear engaged, or with a spanner on the crankshaft pulley bolt. The crankshaft will be easier to rotate if the spark plugs are first removed.

4 Have ready a pencil and paper to record the measured clearances.

5 Turn the crankshaft until the cam lobe nearest the pulley end of the engine is pointing vertically upwards **(see illustration)**. Use feeler blades to measure the clearance between the base of the cam and the tappet **(see illustration)**. Record the clearance.

6 Repeat the measurement for the other seven valves, turning the crankshaft as necessary so that the cam lobe in question is always vertically upwards.

7 Calculate the difference between each measured clearance and the specified value. Note that the value for inlet valves is different from that for exhaust. Counting from either end of the engine, the valve sequence is:

Exhaust- Inlet - Inlet- Exhaust- Exhaust - Inlet - Inlet - Exhaust

8 If any clearance is outside the specified tolerance, then it must be adjusted.

9 If all clearances are within tolerance, refit the camshaft cover, using a new gasket if necessary. Note the copper washer under the bolt at the timing belt end **(see illustration)**.

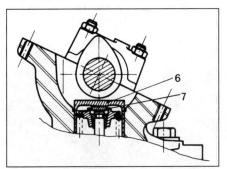

22.5a Valve clearance is measured with the cam lobe pointing vertically upwards - 171 and 159 engines

6 Tappet　　　*7 Shim*

22.5b Measuring a valve clearance - 171 and 159 engines

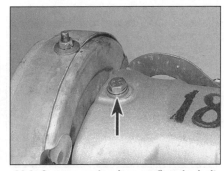

22.9 Copper washer (arrowed) under bolt head

1

Adjustment

10 Remove the camshaft.

11 Lift off a tappet and its shim. Be careful that the shim does not fall out of the tappet. Clean the shim and measure its thickness with a micrometer **(see illustrations)**.

12 Refer to the clearance recorded for the valve concerned. If the clearance was larger than specified, a thicker shim must be fitted. If the clearance was too small, a thinner shim must be fitted.

Sample calculation - clearance too large:
Desired clearance (A) 0.20 mm
Measured clearance (B) 0.28 mm
Difference (B - A) = + 0.08 mm
Original shim thickness 2.62 mm
Reqd. shim thickness 2.62 + 0.08 = 2.70 mm

Sample calculation - clearance too small:
Desired clearance (A) 0.40 mm
Measured clearance (B) 0.23 mm
Difference (B - A) = - 0.17 mm
Original shim thickness 2.86 mm
Reqd. shim thickness 2.86 - 0.17 = 2.69 mm

13 Shims are available in the following thicknesses:
From 2.225 to 3.025 mm in steps of 0.025 mm
From 3.100 to 3.550 mm in steps of 0.075 mm
14 Clean new shims before measuring or fitting them.

23.6a Idle speed adjustment screw (arrowed) - Weber carburettor

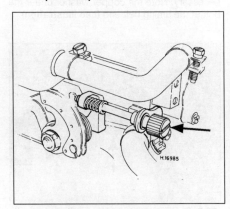

23.6b Idle speed adjustment screw (arrowed) - Weber 36TLP carburettor

22.11a Lifting a tappet

15 Repeat the operations on the other tappets and shims, keeping each tappet identified so that it can be refitted in the same position.

16 When reassembling, oil the shim and fit it on the valve stem, then oil the tappet and lower it smoothly into position. If the tappet is raised at any stage the shim may be dislodged.

17 When all the tappets are in position with their shims, refit the camshaft. Check the valve clearances before refitting the camshaft drivebelt in case a mistake has been made and the camshaft has to be removed again.

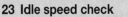

23 Idle speed check

Carburettor models

1 Correct idle speed adjustment can only be achieved if the engine is in generally good condition. Valve clearances must be correct and the ignition system must be in good condition and adjusted correctly.

2 An independent tachometer is necessary to make accurate adjustment and it should be connected to the engine in accordance with the manufacturer's instructions.

3 On automatic transmission models, engage "P".

4 With the air filter fitted, run the engine until warm, as indicated by engagement of the cooling fan.

5 Check the idle speed is that specified.

23.6c Idle speed adjustment screw (arrowed) - Solex 32-34 carburettor

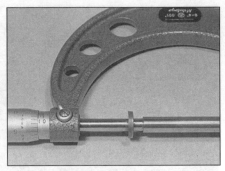

22.11b Measuring shim thickness with a micrometer

6 To adjust the idle speed, turn the adjustment screw **(see illustrations)**.

7 On automatic transmission models, after adjustment to the idle speed has been made, check that the handbrake is fully applied and then place chocks against the roadwheels. Engage a gear and check that the idle speed drops to between 650 to 700 rpm. If required, further adjust the idle speed with the vehicle in gear to obtain this in-gear idle speed.

Fuel injection models

Bosch LE3 Jetronic

8 Before checking the idle speed, the following conditions must be met:
a) *The ignition system must be in good condition and correctly adjusted*
b) *The air cleaner element must be clean*
c) *The throttle initial position must be correctly set, as must the throttle butterfly spindle switch*
d) *The engine must be at its normal operating temperature, the cooling fan having cut in and then out*

9 Connect a tachometer and an exhaust gas analyser to the engine. If the idle speed is incorrect, turn the adjustment screw in the required direction to set the speed to that specified **(see illustration)**.

Motronic ML4.1

10 The idle speed is controlled by the ECU and no adjustment is possible.

Motronic M1.3 without catalyst

11 The idle speed is controlled by the ECU and no adjustment is possible.

23.9 Idle speed adjustment screw (arrowed) - Bosch LE3 Jetronic

23.15 Idle speed adjustment screw (arrowed) - Motronic M1.3 with catalyst

23.19 Idle speed adjustment screw (arrowed) - Motronic MP3.1

24.1 Note direction of arrow on in-line fuel filter - BX 16 RE

Motronic M1.3 with catalyst

12 To adjust the idle speed, run the engine until it reaches normal operating temperature (the cooling fan should have cut in and out), then stop the engine and connect a tachometer in accordance with the manufacturer's instructions.

13 Clamp the fuel vapour recycling hose which connects to the inlet manifold.

14 Where applicable, remove the tamperproof cap from the idle speed adjustment screw on the throttle butterfly housing.

15 With the engine idling, turn the adjustment screw to obtain the specified idle speed **(see illustration)**.

16 On completion, stop the engine. Disconnect the tachometer and where necessary, fit a new tamperproof cap to the idle speed adjustment screw.

Motronic MP3.1

17 Run the engine until it reaches normal operating temperature (the cooling fan should have cut in and out), then stop the engine and connect a tachometer and an exhaust gas analyser in accordance with the manufacturer's instructions.

18 Remove the tamperproof cap from the idle speed adjustment screw on the throttle butterfly housing.

19 With the engine idling, turn the adjustment screw as necessary to obtain the specified idle speed **(see illustration)**.

20 On completion, stop the engine. Disconnect the tachometer and exhaust gas analyser and fit a new tamperproof cap to the adjustment screw.

Magneti Marelli

21 The idle speed is controlled by the ECU and does not normally require adjustment. While experienced home mechanics with a considerable amount of skill and equipment (including a good-quality tachometer and carefully-calibrated exhaust gas analyser) may be able to check the exhaust CO level and idle speed, if these are found to be in need of adjustment then the vehicle must be taken to a suitably-equipped Citroën dealer.

22 Adjustments can be made only by re-programming the ECU, using special diagnostic equipment connected to the system via the diagnostic connector.

24 Fuel filter renewal - BX 16 RE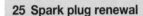

From November 1987, BX 16 RE models have an in-line fuel filter fitted between the fuel pump and the carburettor **(see illustration)**.

When renewing this filter, ensure that the directional arrow on the filter points towards the carburettor and check for leaks at its hose connections after starting the engine.

25 Spark plug renewal

Note: *From July 1987, the engines of BX 19 models are fitted with conventional flat-seat spark plugs with washers, instead of the taper-seat plugs without washer used previously. Flat-seat spark plugs with washers are also fitted to BX 19 GTi and BX GTi 16v engines. BX 14 and BX 16 models followed suit in August and September of 1988 respectively.*

Removal

1 Pull the HT lead from each plug. Grip the rubber end fitting not the lead, otherwise the lead connection may be fractured **(see illustration)**.

> **HAYNES HiNT**
> *Number each HT lead using sticky tape or paint before removal so as to avoid confusion when refitting*

2 The plugs are deeply recessed in the cylinder head. It is recommended that dirt is removed from the recesses using a vacuum cleaner or compressed air before removing the plugs, to prevent dirt dropping into the cylinders.

3 Unscrew each plug.

Fitting

4 Screw each new plug in by hand. This will make sure that there is no chance of cross-threading.

5 Tighten each plug to the specified torque. If a torque wrench is not available, just nip up the plug. It is better to slightly undertighten rather than overdo it and risk stripping the threads from the light alloy cylinder head.

6 Overtightening plugs of the tapered seat type can make them extremely difficult to remove.

7 When reconnecting the plug leads, make sure that they are refitted in their correct order (1 - 3 - 4 - 2) No 1 cylinder being at the flywheel end of the engine.

26 Clutch pedal and cable lubrication

1 Refer to Chapter 6 and remove the clutch cable from the vehicle. Check the cable outer along its length for signs of damage and ensure that the cable inner moves freely in its outer.

2 If the cable inner moves freely, lubricate it thoroughly with light machine oil and refit the cable.

3 If the cable inner is very stiff to move, the best option is to renew the cable.

4 Lubricate all cable linkages with light machine oil.

5 Remove the clutch pedal and grease its pivot.

25.1 Pulling an HT lead from a spark plug

1

27 Front suspension lower balljoint check

1 Raise the front of the vehicle and securely support it on axle stands with both roadwheels clear of the ground (see "Jacking and vehicle support").

2 Using a large screwdriver or flat bar, check for wear in the front suspension lower balljoints by levering between the relevant suspension component and its attachment point. Balljoint wear should be obvious, necessitating renewal.

3 Check the condition of any visible rubber bushes, looking for splits, cracks or contamination of the rubber (see illustration).

4 Check the tightness of all nuts and bolts on the suspension.

27.3 Check each rubber bush for splits, cracks or contamination of the rubber

Every 18 000 miles or 18 Months

28 Air cleaner element renewal

Carburettor models

BX and BX 14

150 engine

1 Release the clip on the large hose at the air cleaner cover. Pull off the hose and twist it aside.

28.5a Prise down the toggle clips . . .

28.5b . . . and withdraw the lid/element assembly - BX 14 with K1G engine

2 Unscrew the cover retaining knob.

3 Withdraw the cover/filter element.

4 Clean out the casing and fit the new filter cartridge, reversing the removal procedure.

K1G engine

5 Prise down the toggle clips and withdraw the lid/element assembly (see illustrations).

6 Wipe out the casing and fit the new element.

BX 16 and BX 19

7 Unscrew the wing nut securing the air cleaner top cover and lift off the cover, complete with the inlet duct, lifting the duct from the carburettor (see illustration).

8 Lift the old element out of the air cleaner case and discard it. Clean out the casing.

9 Insert the new element and check that it is correctly seated.

10 Relocate the top cover and inlet duct. Fasten the cover with the wing nut.

Fuel injection models

Note: For injection system to model applications refer to Chapter 4

28.7 Lift off the cover, complete with inlet duct to expose the air filter element - BX 16 and BX 19

Motronic and Bosch LE3 Jetronic systems

11 Raise and support the bonnet.

12 Undo the air cleaner/airflow meter unit inlet hose clip and detach the hose.

13 Release the retaining clips and lift the air cleaner/airflow meter unit away from the lower cleaner housing.

14 Lift out the old air cleaner element from the housing and discard it (see illustration).

15 Wipe clean the air cleaner housing, then fit the new air cleaner element into position.

16 Refit the air cleaner/airflow meter unit and inlet hose, reversing the removal procedures.

Magneti Marelli system

17 The air cleaner housing is situated in the left-hand front corner of the engine compartment.

18 To remove the filter element, release the five housing lid retaining clips, then lift the lid until there is sufficient clearance to withdraw the element from the air cleaner housing (see illustrations).

28.14 Lifting the air filter element from its housing - Motronic and Bosch systems

28.18a Release the five retaining clips . . .

28.18a . . . remove the lid and withdraw the air filter element - Magneti Marelli system

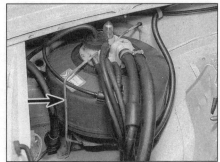

29.3 Spring back the hydraulic reservoir cover retaining clip (arrowed) to release the cover and central block

19 On refitting, ensure that the new element is correctly seated in the housing, then refit the lid and secure it in position with the retaining clips.

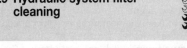
29 Hydraulic system filter cleaning

 Warning: Observe all precautions against fire when cleaning the hydraulic system filters with fuel

Fluid renewal and filter cleaning

1 Move the ground clearance control lever inside the vehicle to the minimum height position.

2 Loosen the pressure regulator bleed screw 1 to 1.5 turns.
3 Spring back the reservoir cover retaining clip and release the cover and central block from the reservoir **(see illustration)**.
4 Remove the overflow and return filter and the supply filter from the central block **(see illustration)**.
5 Clean the filters with fuel and blow them dry with compressed air, observing all precautions against fire.
6 Reassemble the filters and clip the cover assembly back onto the reservoir.
7 Refer to Section 34 of this Chapter and replenish the LHM hydraulic fluid.

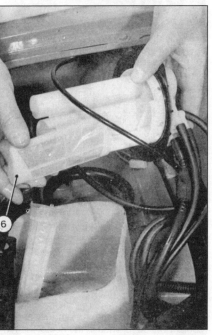

29.4 Remove the hydraulic filter assembly from the central block

Every 30 000 miles

30 Engine valve spring renewal - 150 engine

Citroen recommend that all valve springs fitted to 150 engines must be renewed at this maintenance interval. Valve stem oil seals should be renewed at the same time. Refer to Chapter 2A for details.

Every 36 000 miles

31 Camshaft drivebelt renewal - except 150 engine

The camshaft drivebelt fitted to all engines except the 150 type must be renewed at this maintenance interval. Follow the procedure given in the appropriate Part of Chapter 2. If the belt is not renewed, it may break whilst the engine is running, resulting in serious and expensive engine damage.

32 Cooling system antifreeze renewal

 Warning: Wait until the engine is cold before draining the cooling system

Draining

1 With the system cool, remove the filler cap from the radiator by turning it anti-clockwise.

Note that on BX 19 GTi 16 valve models, no radiator cap is fitted, only the expansion bottle cap.
2 Position a container of sufficient capacity under the bottom hose connection of the radiator. Undo the hose retaining clip and pull the hose from the radiator **(see illustration)**. Once the coolant starts to flow , loosen the system bleed screws **(see illustrations)**. Note that BX 14 models equipped with the K1G engine have only a single screw at the T-piece in the heater hose **(see illustration)**.

1

32.2a The radiator bottom hose
connection - BX 16 and BX 19

32.2b The radiator bleed screw -
all models

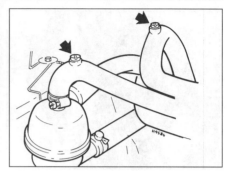

32.2c Bleed screw locations -
BX and BX 14

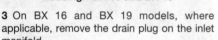

32.2d Bleed screw adjacent to thermostat
housing - BX 16 and BX 19

32.2e Bleed screw at heater hose
connection - BX 16 and BX 19

3 On BX 16 and BX 19 models, where
applicable, remove the drain plug on the inlet
manifold.
4 To fully drain the system, move the heater
control on the facia to the "hot" position.
Where fitted, remove the cylinder block drain
plug **(see illustration)**.
5 When draining is complete, mop up any
spillage.
6 Remember that, without dismantling, it is
impossible to drain the system fully as some
coolant will be retained in the heater matrix.

7 Where appropriate, refit the inlet manifold
drain plug.
8 Unless the system is to be flushed,
reconnect the bottom hose.

Flushing

9 With the system drained, leave the bottom
hose disconnected.
10 Cover the engine (in particular the ignition
system) with plastic sheet.
11 To flush the radiator, direct a flow of water
through its filler neck and allow the water to

run through until it is seen to be clean when
running out of the bottom hose connector. If
the radiator is badly contaminated then
remove it, invert it and reverse flush, directing
the water flow through the bottom hose
connector. If, after a reasonable period, the
water still does not run clear, the radiator
should be flushed with a good proprietary
cleaning agent.
12 To flush the heater matrix, disconnect one
of the heater hoses at the engine
compartment bulkhead and direct a flow of
water through the matrix. On completion,
reconnect the hose.
13 To flush the engine, leave the bottom
hose disconnected. Remove the thermostat
and refit the thermostat housing/hose.
Disconnect the radiator top hose and direct a
flow of water into it. Flush through until clean
water is seen to run from the bottom hose.
Reverse the flow if badly contaminated.

32.2g Heater hose bleed screw

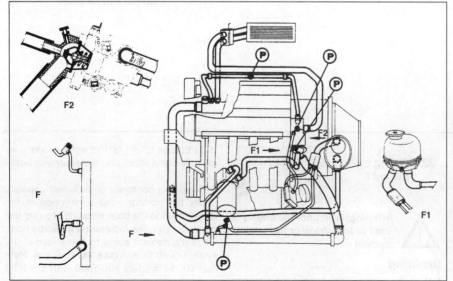

32.2f Bleed screw locations (P) - BX 19 GTi 16v

32.4 Cylinder block coolant drain plug -
K1G engine

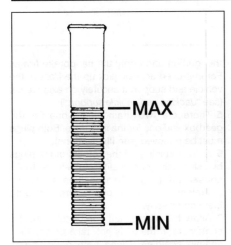

32.19 The integral coolant level dipstick fitted to later models

14 On completion, refit the thermostat and reconnect the hoses. Refill the cooling system as follows.

Filling

15 Before filling the system, check the condition and security of all hoses and connections. Ensure that the drain plug is firmly closed (where appropriate) and that the heater temperature control is in the "hot" position.

16 Fully undo the system bleed screw(s).

17 Fill the system slowly with the correct coolant mixture until the level rises and overflows from the radiator filler neck (or expansion bottle neck on BX 19 GTi 16 valve models). As the level rises, the coolant will emerge from the bleed screws at which point the screws should be tightened.

18 Start the engine and run it at a fast idle speed so that the coolant is warmed up and the electric cooling fan cuts in and then out, at which point stop the engine.

19 With the system cool, carefully remove the filler cap and check the coolant level. If necessary top it up to the required level. On early models, the coolant height in the radiator

header tank should be 250 to 300 mm with the engine cold. This measurement can be checked with a dipstick. Later models have an integral black plastic tube type dipstick. The level must be between the MIN and MAX marks **(see illustration)**.

20 Finally, run the engine again and check the system for any leaks.

33 Automatic transmission fluid renewal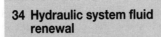

Note: *If fluid is to be drained directly after the vehicle has been driven, the transmission fluid may be very hot, so take precautions to avoid being burnt by it*

1 Position a suitable container with a minimum capacity of 3 litres under the transmission. There are two drain plugs to be removed **(see illustration)**. Remove the plugs, drain the fluid then refit the plugs.

2 Refill, using 2.5 litres of the recommended fluid, through the dipstick guide tube.

3 Recheck the fluid level after a nominal mileage has been covered and, if necessary, top-up the fluid, as described in Section 10 of this Chapter.

34 Hydraulic system fluid renewal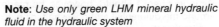

Note: *Use only green LHM mineral hydraulic fluid in the hydraulic system*
Note: *The hydraulic system filters must be cleaned at the same time as the system fluid is renewed*

1 Move the ground clearance control lever inside the vehicle to the minimum height position.

2 Loosen the pressure regulator bleed screw 1 to 1.5 turns.

3 Spring back the reservoir cover retaining clip and release the cover and central block from the reservoir (see illustrations in Section 29).

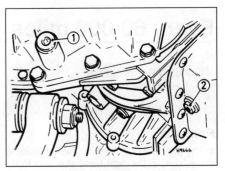

33.1 Automatic transmission drain plug locations

4 Remove the overflow and return filter and the supply filter from the central block.

5 Carefully lift the reservoir from the bulkhead and discard the fluid. Drain the high pressure pump supply pipe.

6 Remove the deflector plate from the bottom of the reservoir.

7 Clean the filters and reservoir with petrol and blow them dry with compressed air, observing all precautions against fire.

8 Refit the reservoir and deflector plate and fill it with 2.5 litres of LHM hydraulic fluid. Reassemble the filters and clip the cover assembly onto the reservoir.

9 Disconnect the high pressure pump supply pipe from the reservoir cover central block and using a small funnel, prime the pump with LHM hydraulic fluid.

10 Loosen the pressure regulator bleed screw 1 to 1.5 turns (if it was retightened). Get an assistant to start the engine then as it is started, quickly reconnect the high pressure pump supply pipe.

11 Grip the return pipe from the pressure regulator unit by hand and as soon as it is felt to throb, retighten the bleed screw at the regulator.

12 When the vehicle height has stabilised, top-up the fluid level in the reservoir so that the indicator is level with the upper (maximum) level mark.

1

Every 48 000 miles

35 Fuel filter renewal - BX 16 fuel-injected

Removal

1 The fuel filter is located on the underside of the vehicle, at the right-hand side, just to the

rear of the fuel tank. The filter is located in a rubber holder, in tandem with the fuel pump unit which is directly beneath it.

2 To remove the fuel filter, proceed as described for fuel pump removal in Chapter 4D. Note that it may not be necessary to completely detach and remove the pump unit in order to remove the filter but this will improve access.

3 As it is removed, note which way round the filter is fitted so as to ensure correct orientation when refitting.

Refitting

4 Refit in the reverse order of removal. On completion, check for satisfactory operation and for any sign of fuel leaks from the pump and filter connections.

Every 60 000 miles

36 Fuel filter renewal - BX 19 fuel-injected

Removal

1 The fuel filter is located on the underside of the vehicle, at the right-hand side, just to the rear of the fuel tank. The filter is located in a rubber holder, in tandem with the fuel pump unit which is directly beneath it.

2 To remove the fuel filter, proceed as described for fuel pump removal in Chapter 4B. Note that it may not be necessary to completely detach and remove the pump unit

37.5a Rear view of manual gearbox showing differential housing drain plug (arrowed)

37.5b Front view of manual gearbox

5 Reversing light switch
6 Oil filler plug
7 Drain plug - gearbox (early models)
8 Reverse gear shaft clamp bolt - Do not remove

in order to remove the filter but this will improve access.

3 As it is removed, note which way round the filter is fitted so as to ensure correct orientation when refitting.

Refitting

4 Refit in the reverse order of removal. On completion, check for satisfactory operation and for any sign of fuel leaks from the pump and filter connections.

37 Manual gearbox oil renewal - except BX and BX 14 pre August 1988

Note: For gearbox to model applications refer to Chapter 7

> **HAYNES HiNT** *Draining the gearbox is quicker and more efficient if the gearbox is warmed up to normal operating temperature*

BX and BX 14 - pre August 1988

1 On these models the engine and transmission share the same lubrication system and therefore there is no separate transmission oil level check requirement. Periodic checks should, however, be made around the differential and driveshaft joints to ensure that there are no serious oil leaks.

BX 14 - from August 1988

2 Routine oil changes for the Type MA (2CA) gearbox are no longer specified.

BX 16 and BX 19 - pre 1986

Draining

3 This operation is much quicker and more efficient if the vehicle is first taken on a journey of sufficient length to warm the gearbox up to normal operating temperature.

4 Park the vehicle on level ground, switch off

the ignition and apply the handbrake firmly. For improved access, jack up the front of the vehicle and support it securely on axle stands (see "*Jacking and vehicle support*").

5 There are two drain plugs, one for the gearbox and one for the final drive. Both plugs must be removed **(see illustrations)**.

6 Avoid rounding-off the corners of the plugs by using only good quality, close-fitting tools. Loosen the plugs, then position a suitable container under each one before removing them completely.

7 Allow the oil to drain completely into the containers. If the oil is hot, take precautions against scalding. Clean both plugs, being especially careful to wipe any metallic particles off their magnetic inserts. Where fitted, discard the original sealing washers which should be renewed whenever they are disturbed **(see illustration)**.

8 When the oil has finished draining, clean the plug threads and those of the gearbox casing, fit new sealing washers and refit the plugs, tightening each one to the specified torque wrench setting. It the vehicle was raised for the draining operation, now lower it to the ground.

Filling

9 When filling, do so through the filler plug orifice. Remember to measure out the specified quantity of oil required beforehand. Do not overfill the gearbox.

10 Dispose of the old oil safely. Do not pour it down a drain.

BX 16 and BX 19 - from 1986

11 From early 1986, the gearbox drain plug was deleted, although the differential drain plug remained.

12 From October 1986, a filler/level plug is fitted in the gearbox end cover. The oil level should be up to the lower edge of the plug hole.

13 From 1990, routine oil changes are no longer specified.

37.7 Gearbox magnetic oil drain plug with sealing washer (arrowed)

Chapter 2 Part A:
150 engine

Contents

Degrees of difficulty

| Easy, suitable for novice with little experience 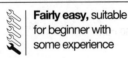 | Fairly easy, suitable for beginner with some experience | Fairly difficult, suitable for competent DIY mechanic 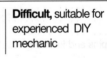 | Difficult, suitable for experienced DIY mechanic | Very difficult, suitable for expert DIY or professional |

Specifications

General

Type	Four-cylinder, in-line, OHC, liquid cooled, transverse mounting
Model application:	
BX	150 A (XY6C)
BX 14 before August 1988	150 C (XY6D)
Bore	75.0 mm
Stroke	77.0 mm
Capacity	1360 cc
Compression ratio	9.3:1
Firing order	1 - 3 - 4 - 2
Location of No 1 cylinder	At clutch end of block
Direction of crankshaft rotation	Clockwise viewed from pulley end
Maximum power DIN (BHP):	
150A engine	62 at 5500 rpm
150C engine	72 at 5750 rpm
Maximum torque DIN (lbf ft):	
150A engine	79.4 at 2500 rpm
150C engine	79.4 at 3000 rpm

Cylinder head

Type	Aluminium alloy, bi-spherical combustion chambers, offset valves and five bearing camshaft
Maximum allowable distortion	0.05 mm
Valve seat maximum contact surface width:	
Inlet	1.45 mm
Exhaust	1.80 mm
Valve seat angle:	
Inlet	120°
Exhaust	90°

Valves

Stem diameter	8.0 mm
Head diameter:	
Inlet	36.8 mm
Exhaust	29.3 mm
Length:	
Inlet	113.19 to 113.63 mm
Exhaust	113.11 to 114.01 mm
Springs:	
Wire diameter	4.3 mm
Length under load:	
Inlet	41/26 mm/kg
Exhaust	30/77 mm/kg
Rocker clearance (cold):	
Inlet	0.10 to 0.15 mm
Exhaust	0.20 to 0.30 mm

Valve timing

	150 A engine	150 C engine
Valve lift	7.25 mm	8.25 mm
Camshaft identification mark	A	S
Inlet opens*	4° ATDC	0° ATDC
Inlet closes*	29° ABDC	42° ABDC
Exhaust opens*	30° BBDC	43° BBDC
Exhaust closes*	5° BTDC	1° BTDC

With valve clearance of 0.7 mm

Camshaft

Endfloat	0.07 to 0.17 mm

Crankshaft and main bearings

Number of bearings	Five
Crankshaft endfloat	0.07 to 0.27 mm
Thrustwasher thicknesses	2.40, 2.50, 2.55, 2.60 mm
Minimum allowable ovality of crankpins and journals	0.007 mm
Crankpin standard diameter	45.0 mm
Main bearing journals:	
Standard diameter	49.981 to 49.965 mm
Regrind diameter	49.681 to 49.665 mm

Connecting rods

Small-end bush diameter	19.463 to 19.476 mm
Big-end diameter	48.655 to 48.671 mm

Cylinder liners

Type	Cast iron, wet type
Liner base seal	O-ring
Liner protrusion - clamped or without seal	0.10 to 0.17 mm
Maximum allowable projection difference between two liners	0.05 mm
Piston offset	1.0 mm
Grades:	
Piston:	
A	One file mark
B	Two file marks
C	Three file marks

Pistons

Type	Aluminium alloy, two compression and one oil control ring. Gudgeon pin free in piston, interference fit in connecting rod
Piston fitting direction	Arrow mark on crown points to the timing gear (DT)
Gudgeon pin classes	Three, colour-coded to marks on piston crown
Running clearance	0.07 to 0.09 mm

Lubrication system

Pump maximum lobe-to-body clearance	0.064 mm
Minimum oil pressure	3 bar at 4000 rpm
Low pressure warning	0.6 bar
Oil filter (up to July 1988)	Champion C204

	150 A	150 C
Oil capacity:		
New or reconditioned engine	5.0 litres (8.8 pints)	5.5 litres (9.7 pints)
After draining	4.5 litres (7.9 pints)	5.0 litres (8.8 pints)
Dipstick minimum to maximum	1 litre (1.76 pints)	1 litre (1.76 pints)

Torque wrench settings

	Nm	lbf ft
Rocker cover	10	7
Rocker adjuster screw locknuts	17	12
Camshaft retaining plate bolt	18	13
Cylinder head bolts:		
Stage 1	50	36
Stage 2	78	56
Crankshaft pulley nut	140	101
Timing cover bolts	12	9
Timing chain guide plate bolts	6	4
Timing chain tensioner (both types)	6	4
Camshaft sprocket bolt	75	54
Oil pressure switch	20	15
Coolant temperature sender unit	45	33
Sump	10	7
Sump drain plug	28	20
Oil suction strainer bolts	10	7
Clutch casing bolts	10	7
Flywheel bolts	68	50
Connecting rod big-end cap bolts	38	27
Gearbox to engine	15	11
Engine mountings:		
A	50	36
B	22	16
C	35	25
Main bearing/casing bolts:		
Stage 1	38	27
Stage 2	53	38
Crankcase flange housing bolts	10	7

2A

1 General information and precautions

General information

The 150 series engine fitted to the Citroën BX and BX 14 models is of 4-cylinder, in-line, overhead camshaft design and mounted transversely.

A manual gearbox is bolted to the bottom of the engine. The final drive to the front roadwheels is via a differential unit on the front of the gearbox. Drive to the gearbox is via a conventional clutch on the left-hand side of the engine, through an input pinion free-running on the crankshaft and located between the clutch and the engine block.

All the major casings and housings are manufactured from pressure die-cast aluminium alloy. The cylinder block has removable wet cylinder liners which are centrifugally cast from special iron alloy and the main bearing caps are made of cast iron. The cylinder head has bi-spherical squish effect combustion chambers, each having one exhaust valve, one inlet valve, and a taper seated spark plug location. Single springs are fitted to the valves which are operated by rockers, each incorporating an adjustable screw and locknut for valve clearance setting.

The aluminium alloy pistons are fitted with three rings, two compression and one "perfect circle" scraper. The pistons are assembled to the forged steel connecting rods by a gudgeon pin which is a force fit in the connecting rod small-end.

The crankshaft is carried in five main bearings and the flywheel and clutch are bolted to its rear end in conventional manner. The other end is keyed to drive the camshaft chain sprocket and also a shaft by which the oil pump, fuel pump and distributor are driven.

A forced feed lubrication system common to both engine and gearbox is employed. The oil pump is attached to the crankcase in the lower section of the timing chest and it incorporates the pressure relief valve. The pump is driven by gears from the crankshaft. Apart from the standard replaceable canister filter located on the outside of the crankcase there is a gauze filter incorporated in the oil pump suction inlet.

Precautions

Because of the unusual layout of the engine and transmission systems, extra care and attention are necessary during maintenance and overhaul procedures which, in many instances, differ from more conventional systems.

Read through the various Sections concerned before tackling any job, and analyse the instructions, so that any snags or possible difficulties can be noted in advance. Because the sub-assembly castings are made from aluminium alloy it is of utmost importance that, where specified, all fastenings are tightened to the correct torque and, in some instances, in the correct sequence.

2 Oil filter - removal and refitting

Refer to Chapter 1, Section 9.

3 Major operations possible with engine in vehicle

Note: *Some of these tasks can only be achieved with the aid of special Citroën tools.*

The following operations are possible with the engine in the vehicle:

a) *Removal and refitting of the cylinder head*
b) *Removal and refitting of the clutch unit*
c) *Removal and refitting of the engine mountings*
d) *Removal and refitting of the timing case*

6.7 Exhaust downpipe ball socket connection

4 Major operations requiring engine removal

The engine must be removed for the following operations:

a) *Removal and refitting of the transmission*
b) *Removal and refitting of the crankshaft and main bearings*
c) *Removal and refitting of the piston and connecting rod assemblies*
d) *Renewal of the big-end bearings*

5 Valve rocker clearances - checking and adjustment

Refer to Chapter 1, Section 21.

6 Cylinder head - removal and refitting

Note: *Citroën tool no 701 2-T will be needed to hold the camshaft sprocket and prevent the timing chain from falling down into the timing case.*

Note: *The following operation was carried out with the engine in the vehicle.*

Removal

1 The cylinder head can be removed and refitted with the engine in position in the vehicle, but a Citroën special tool will be required to hold the camshaft sprocket and prevent the timing chain from falling down into the timing case. This tool (part no 701 2-T) comprises three items, referred to as N1, N2 and N3.

2 When the cylinder head is being removed, there is a risk of disturbing the wet liners in their locations. Because of this, certain checks are necessary to confirm that the liners are correctly located. If it is found that they are not within permissible limits, new O-rings will have to be fitted between the liners and the cylinder block. This job will entail removal of the engine/transmission from the car and the virtual complete dismantling of the unit on the bench. It can be seen that removing the cylinder head on this engine, when installed, should only be undertaken if full facilities are available to remove and dismantle the engine even though they may

not be required. Alternatively, be prepared to have the car towed to your Citroën agent if the liner O-rings have to be removed.

3 Disconnect the battery earth lead.
4 Drain the cooling system.
5 Drain the engine/gearbox oil.
6 Raise and support the vehicle on safety stands.
7 From underneath the vehicle, undo the two retaining nuts and disconnect the exhaust downpipe at the ball socket connection **(see illustration)**. Disconnect the warm air feed pipe.
8 Disconnect the following hoses **(see illustration)** and position them out of the way:
a) *Heater hoses at the bulkhead*
b) *Coolant pump hoses, or unbolt the pump*
c) *Cylinder head hose*
d) *Thermostat hose*
e) *Heater hoses to the carburettor*
f) *Carburettor fuel feed and return hoses. Plug or clamp these hoses*
9 Disconnect the ignition HT and LT wiring from the plugs and distributor. Position the wiring harness out of the way.
10 Remove the spark plugs.
11 Disconnect the accelerator cable from the carburettor and position it out of the way.
12 Remove the cooling system de-aerator unit.
13 Remove the hose carrier from the timing cover.
14 Unbolt and remove the fuel pump and withdraw the operating rod.
15 Remove the distributor.
16 Unbolt and remove the rocker cover.
17 Disconnect the following items, noting their connections:
a) *Idle cut-off lead from the carburettor*
b) *Coolant temperature sensor lead*
c) *Earth cables to the cylinder head*
d) *The Econoscope vacuum hose on the inlet manifold*
18 Unscrew and remove the first extended head bolt and then the end plate which is secured by two bolts **(see illustration)**. Loosen but do not remove the second extended head bolt.
19 Unscrew and remove the bolt retaining the timing gear to the end of the camshaft. Do not disturb the gear as the bolt is withdrawn.

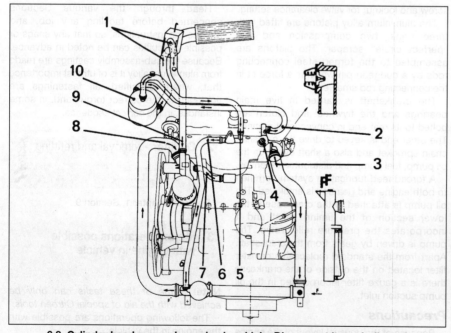

6.8 Cylinder head removal - engine in vehicle. Disconnect items indicated

1 *Heater hoses*	4 *Water temperature*	7 *Water pump hose*
2 *Cylinder head hose*	*sensor*	8 *Water pump hose*
3 *Thermostat hose*	5 *Carburettor hose*	9 *Water pump hose*
	6 *Carburettor hose*	10 *De-aerator unit*

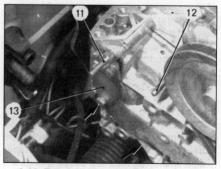

6.18 Extended head bolts (11 and 12) and end plate (13)

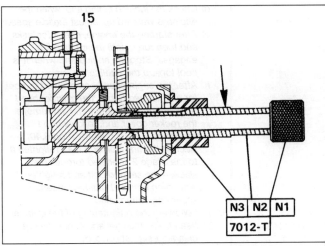

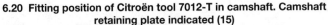

6.20 Fitting position of Citroën tool 7012-T in camshaft. Camshaft retaining plate indicated (15)

6.30 Dowel stop rod (4) guide pins (5) and timing cover extended screw (a)

20 Lubricate the special tool (701 2-T) with oil and fit it into position. Fit the clamp onto the timing case, but do not fully tighten the bolts. The mandrel groove must engage with the fuel pump control cam pin. Tighten the mandrel onto the camshaft. The camshaft and mandrel grooves must be in alignment **(see illustration)**. Mark the relative positions.

21 Turn the engine over slowly so that the mandrel groove mark can be seen to be positioned within the upper quarter of the timing cover face. In this position fully tighten the clamp bolts.

22 Loosen the camshaft retaining plate bolt and withdraw the plate from its groove, then retighten the bolt.

23 Position a piece of modelling clay or similar compound under the front left-hand cylinder head nut to keep it in position when the bolt is removed. Following the tightening sequence in reverse, progressively loosen the 10 cylinder head bolts. As the bolts are loosened, the rocker shaft assembly will lift under the influence of the valve springs. Remove the bolts and the rocker shaft assembly.

24 Loosen the special tool (N1) from the camshaft and slide the camshaft away from the gear by hand. When the camshaft is clear of the gear the cylinder head can be removed. If it appears to be stuck, insert two bars into cylinder head bolt holes, taking care not to damage the head, and rock it free of the block. Do not, on any account, hammer on the cylinder head as it can be damaged very easily. Fit temporary restraining straps made of strip material to the block to keep the cylinder liners in position; secure them with bolts and nuts in the cylinder head bolt holes.

25 Carefully cut and remove the upper, exposed portion of the timing case gasket level with the face of the cylinder block. Clean the mating faces of the block, cylinder head, and timing case free of all jointing materials. Do not use emery cloth or sharp-edged tools as the surfaces must be free of all traces of scores, burns, or impact damage.

26 Note that on engines manufactured after December 1985, the cylinder head location dowels are of a reduced diameter, that is, from 16 mm to 14 mm. The cylinder head gasket is modified to suit. In certain instances (e.g. fitting a new-type head to an old-type block) the use of stepped dowels will be necessary - these are available from Citroën dealers. Ensure that the combination of dowels and gasket is correct.

27 If there is likely to be an appreciable time lapse before reassembly, cover the exposed parts of the engine internals with clean, fluff-free rag.

Refitting

28 Before refitting the cylinder head, check the cylinder liner protrusions.

29 Check that the location dowels are in position in the cylinder block top face. To prevent the rear dowel from being pushed down when fitting the cylinder head, insert a suitable rod into the hole in the crankcase side wall directly beneath the dowel.

30 Locate two guide pins in the cylinder block **(see illustration)**. The pins should be 11 mm in diameter and no more than 95 mm long.

31 Lubricate the cylinder walls with clean engine oil. Remove the cylinder liner retaining straps.

32 Locate the new cylinder head gasket. It must be fitted dry and the arrow mark must point towards the front of the engine. Smear the timing cover mating faces with a suitable sealant.

33 Loosen the rocker adjustment screws.

34 Carefully lower the cylinder head into position on the block and then fit the rocker assembly into position on the cylinder head **(see illustrations)**.

35 Note that on engines manufactured after December 1985, the rocker assembly has a location dowel on each pedestal, instead of one at each end as on earlier models **(see illustration)**. The cylinder head also has corresponding dowel holes. At the same time, the rocker cover retaining screw holes are increased in diameter, and are now 8.5 mm (previously 7.5 mm). The location holes in the rocker assembly are correspondingly increased, and larger bolts used. Ensure any new components are of the correct type. From February 1987, the rocker arms, shaft and rocker cover were further modified. These components can be fitted to earlier engines, provided all the arms, shaft and cover are fitted at the same time.

36 Fit the cylinder head bolts and nuts but leave them untightened for the moment. Remove the guide pins and the dowel support rod.

2A

6.34a Lower cylinder head into position . . .

6.34b . . . then fit rocker assembly onto cylinder head

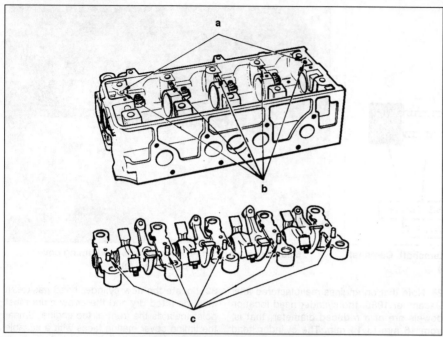

6.35 Rocker assembly positioning dowels

a Early models   b Later models   c Dowel locations on later rocker assembly

37 Locate the timing cover extended head bolt into position (see illustration 6.30) but do not fully tighten it.

38 Align the grooves of the camshaft and the mandrel and tighten it into position. Push the timing gear and the camshaft together ensuring correct engagement. If necessary tap the rear end of the camshaft with a soft-faced mallet.

39 Fit the camshaft retaining plate into its groove and tighten the bolt to the specified torque.

40 Tighten the cylinder head bolts in the sequence shown. The bolts must be tightened in two stages to the specified torque settings (see illustration).

41 Remove the special tool (7012-T) then refit the gear/camshaft retaining bolt and tighten it to the specified torque.

42 Refit the timing cover bolts and tighten them to the specified torque. Before refitting the timing case closing plate smear the mating edges with sealant.

43 Adjust the rocker/valve clearances.

44 Refitting of the remaining components is a reversal of the removal procedure, but note the following special points:

a) *Tighten fasteners to the specified torque settings*

b) *Refill the cooling system and top-up the engine/gearbox oil*

c) *Before restarting the engine, check that all tools and equipment are removed from the engine compartment*

d) *Check the ignition timing and, when the engine is warmed up, adjust the idle speed*

e) *After starting the engine, check for leaks and then run it until the cooling fan engages. Stop the engine and when it is cool top-up the cooling system*

f) *After the engine has been allowed to cool for at least two hours, the cylinder head bolts must be retightened. First remove the rocker cover and, following the sequence shown in* **illustration 6.40**, *slacken the first bolt and then retighten it to the Stage 2 specified torque. Then slacken the second bolt and retighten it, and so on until all bolts have been separately retightened*

g) *Following the retightening of the cylinder head bolts, the inlet and exhaust valve clearances must be reset*

7 Engine/transmission - removal and refitting

Removal

1 The engine/transmission must be removed as a complete assembly and cannot be separated until removed. Certain operations are awkward and care must be taken not to damage adjacent components in the engine compartment, especially during removal. It is necessary to have an assistant readily to hand. Start by removing the bonnet.

2 Chock the rear wheels then raise the vehicle at the front so that the front roadwheels are clear of the ground. With the vehicle supported on safety stands, remove the front roadwheels.

3 Disconnect the positive and negative leads from the battery.

4 Disconnect the earth wires from the cylinder head.

5 Remove the battery and its plastic tray from the engine compartment.

6 Detach and remove the air cleaner unit.

7 Disconnect the following (see illustration):

a) *The HT lead at the coil*

b) *The diagnostic plug negative and positive wires at the coil*

c) *The wiring connector at the distributor*

d) *The Econoscope wiring harness*

e) *The Econoscope vacuum inlet tube*

8 Disconnect the clutch inner cable from the operating lever clevis (see illustration).

9 Undo and detach the speedometer drive cable at its transmission connection. Fold the cable back out of the way.

10 Disconnect and remove the air inlet duct from the wing panel.

11 Disconnect the choke cable and the accelerator cable at the carburettor.

12 Detach the fuel feed hose from the fuel pump and the fuel return hose from the carburettor. Plug the hoses and connections to prevent excessive leakage and the ingress of dirt.

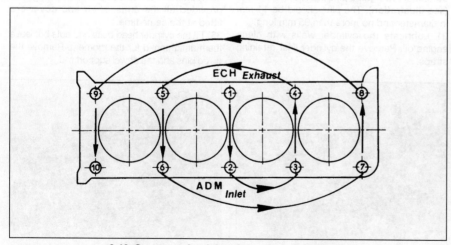

6.40 Sequence for tightening cylinder head bolts

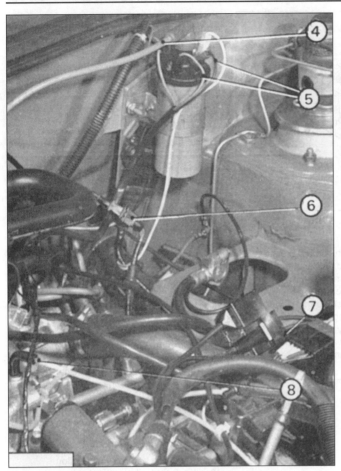

7.7 View showing items to be disconnected

4 Coil HT lead   7 Econoscope connector
5 Coil leads   8 Econoscope tube
6 Distributor connector

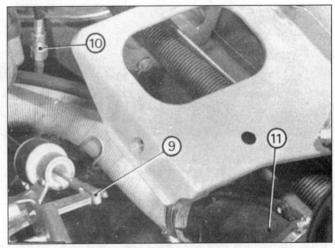

7.8 Disconnect clutch cable (9) speedometer cable (10) and air inlet duct (11)

7.19 View showing reversing lamp switch (7) wiring harness clip (8) and sump drain plug (9)

2A

13 Drain the cooling system.

14 Disconnect and detach the heater flow and return hoses at the coolant pump, the inlet manifold heater hose and the cylinder head-to-radiator coolant hose.

15 Disconnect the wiring connectors from the cooling fan temperature sensor and the coolant level sensor at the radiator.

16 Undo the five radiator top panel retaining bolts. Remove the panel and the radiator, taking care not to damage its core as it is lifted out.

17 Detach and remove the de-aeration chamber from its support on the right-hand side of the engine compartment.

18 Position a suitable container under the sump then remove the drain plug and drain the engine oil.

19 Detach the reversing lamp switch leads and detach the wiring harness from the retaining clip (see illustration).

20 Release the pressure from the hydraulic system.

21 Disconnect the oil suction pipe from the

high pressure (HP) pump. Clean the connections and plug the ports to prevent the ingress of dirt (see illustration).

22 Disconnect the oil return pipe and outlet pipe from the pressure regulator unit (see illustration). Clean the connectors and plug the ports to prevent the ingress of dirt.

23 Disconnect the hydraulic outlet pipe from its location lug and the two pipes from the lugs on the engine front face.

24 Disconnect the link rods from the gearbox.

25 Disconnect the exhaust downpipe at the balljoint.

7.21 Disconnect oil suction pipe (1) from HP pump

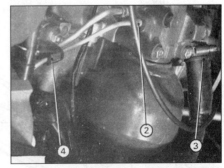

7.22 Disconnect oil return pipe (3) outlet pipe (2) and securing lug at pressure regulator unit (4)

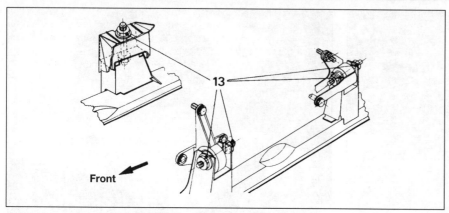

7.29 Undo engine mounting nuts (13)

26 The steering link rods and lower wheel arm balljoints must now be separated. Loosen the retaining nuts and use a suitable separator to disconnect the joints.

27 Pull the driveshafts outwards and release them from the transmission. Support the shafts so that they are out of the way without damaging their rubber gaiters or straining their joints.

28 Connect a sling to the lift brackets at each end of the cylinder head. Lift and just take the weight of the engine/transmission.

29 Unscrew and remove the engine mounting nuts **(see illustration)**.

30 Check that the engine and associated components are fully disconnected and positioned so that they will not be damaged or interfere with engine/transmission removal.

31 Lift the engine/transmission clear of the mountings then guide the unit upwards out of the engine compartment. An assistant will be necessary to steady the unit as it is removed.

32 Once removed from the vehicle, the engine/transmission can be cleaned externally then moved to the work area for dismantling and overhaul.

Refitting

33 Refitting of the engine/transmission is, in general, the reverse of the removal procedure but note the following points.

34 Check that the lift sling is securely located before lifting the unit into position.

35 Check that all loose hoses, wires, hydraulic pipes and components in the engine bay are moved out of the way as the unit is lowered into position.

36 When reconnecting the driveshafts, take care not to damage the oil seals and ensure that the shafts are fully located.

37 Renew the engine mounting self-locking nuts, also those of the lower wheel arm and steering link rod balljoints.

38 Tighten all mounting and connecting bolts and nuts to the specified torque settings **(see illustration)**.

39 Refer to the appropriate Chapter when reconnecting the choke and accelerator cables.

40 Refer to the appropriate Chapter when connecting and adjusting the clutch cable.

41 Check that the cooling system, fuel system and hydraulic system hoses are in good condition before reconnection.

42 Check that all electrical connections are correctly and securely made.

43 Top-up the cooling system.

44 Top-up the engine/transmission oil level.

45 Retighten the hydraulic system pressure regulator bleed screw and top-up the hydraulic fluid level as necessary. The system will need to be repressurised as soon as the engine is started.

46 Go carefully round the engine to make sure that all reconnections have been made. Especially check that the electrical earth connections are made, the drivebelts are correctly tensioned, the carburettor controls are connected and that there are no apparent oil or coolant leaks. Remove all loose tools, rags, etc.

47 Refit the battery and secure with its clamp plate. Reconnect the battery leads and check the operation of the electrical circuits.

48 The engine is now ready for its initial start-up.

8 Engine dismantling - general information

1 A clean and good sized work area will be required, preferably on a bench. Before moving the engine/transmission to the work area it should be cleaned to remove road dirt, oil and grease.

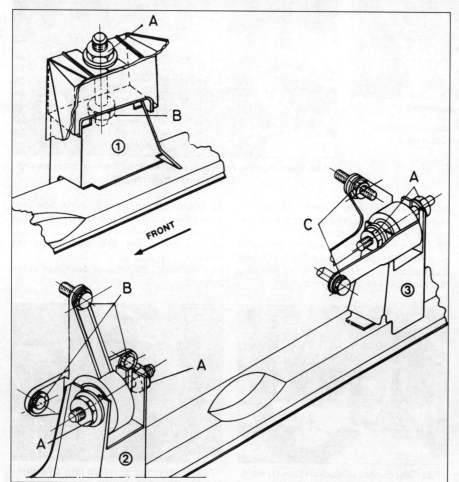

7.38 Engine mountings and securing bolts (refer to the Specifications for torque settings)

2 During the dismantling process, care should be taken to avoid contaminating exposed internal parts of the engine with dirt. Although everything will be cleaned separately before reassembly, road dirt or grit can cause damage to parts during dismantling and could also affect inspection and checks.

3 A good proprietary grease solvent will make the job of cleaning much easier but if this is not available then use paraffin. With a solvent the usual procedure is to apply it to the contaminated surfaces and, after a suitable soaking period has elapsed, to wash it off with a jet of water. Where the grease or oil and dirt mixture is encrusted, the solvent should be worked in using a stiff brush.

4 After rinsing off the solvent and dirt, wipe down the exterior of the unit and then, only when the unit is clean and dry, start the dismantling process.

5 As the unit is stripped, individual parts should be examined before being washed in a bath of paraffin and wiped dry. The examination need only be cursory at this stage but it is sometimes helpful as the cleaning procedure might wash away useful evidence of running conditions. Avoid immersing parts with internal oil passages, such as the crankshaft and the timing case. To clean such parts, use a paraffin-damped rag and clean out the oilways with wire. If an air supply is available, then the oilways can be blown through to clear them.

6 The re-use of old gaskets or oil seals is a false economy and can lead to fuel, oil or coolant leaks, if nothing worse. To avoid the possibility of such problems, always use new gaskets throughout.

7 A suggested procedure for dismantling is to remove the clutch assembly and then the timing mechanism (this order could be reversed if required) followed by the transmission, cylinder head, crankshaft and piston assemblies. A supply of wooden blocks of varying sizes will be useful in supporting the engine as it is being worked on.

8 Wherever possible, refit nuts, bolts and washers finger-tight from wherever they were removed as this helps avoid later loss or muddle. If they cannot be refitted, lay them out in such a fashion that it is clear where they came from. Make sketches or notes if you think you may forget the position of washers, etc.

9 Engine dismantling - ancillary items

1 Irrespective of whether you are going to dismantle the engine completely and rebuild it, or are simply going to exchange it for a new or reconditioned unit, the ancillary components will have to be removed.

2 The only possible method of determining the exact condition of the engine and assessing the extent of reconditioning required is to dismantle it completely. If, having done this, it is decided that a reconditioned short block is needed then the unit can be loosely reassembled, but check that a replacement is available first.

3 Refer to the appropriate Chapters and remove the following components or assemblies:

a) Distributor
b) Fuel pump and operating plunger
c) Carburettor
d) Inlet and exhaust manifolds
e) Coolant pump and drivebelt
f) Alternator and starter motor
g) Diagnostic socket and wiring harness
h) Coolant temperature sender
i) Oil pressure sender
j) Thermostat and housing
k) Oil filter and dipstick tube
l) Clutch assembly
m) Hydraulic system HP pump unit
n) Pressure regulator unit
o) The support mounting

4 If the engine is to be exchanged, check what ancillary items are included in the exchange unit.

10 Engine - separation from transmission

1 If the engine is to be dismantled for overhaul, refer to the previous Section and remove the items listed, then in addition remove the flywheel, as described below.

2 If the two units are to be separated but the engine is not being dismantled, remove the items indicated **(see illustration)** whilst referring to the appropriate Chapters for details where necessary.

3 When the clutch unit is removed, unbolt and remove the flywheel. The retaining bolt positions are not symmetrical so there is no need to mark the fitted position of the flywheel.

4 Unscrew and remove the two bolts and the single nut securing the engine and transmission joint faces at the flywheel end **(see illustration)**.

5 If still in position, unbolt and remove the rocker cover.

10.2 Items to be disconnected to separate engine from gearbox if engine is not being dismantled

1 Engine support mounting	4 Alternator and HP pump drivebelts	6 Pressure regulator unit
2 Starter motor	5 HP pump unit	7 Fuel pump
3 Dipstick tube		

10.4 Engine-to-transmission securing bolts (1) and nut (2) at flywheel end

10.9a Engine-to-transmission securing bolts (arrowed) - inlet side

10.9b Engine-to-transmission securing bolts (arrowed) - exhaust side at timing cover end

10.9c Engine-to-transmission securing bolts (arrowed) - exhaust side at flywheel end

6 Unbolt and detach the HP pump drive pulley from the crankshaft inner pulley. Undo the central retaining bolt and remove the crankshaft pulley. To prevent the crankshaft from turning when undoing the bolts, fit two flywheel bolts into the crankshaft rear end and jam a bar diagonally between the bolts.

7 Unscrew and remove the timing cover retaining bolts. As they are withdrawn note the respective bolt sizes and fitted positions to ensure correct refitting.

11.3a Loosening first type chain tensioner

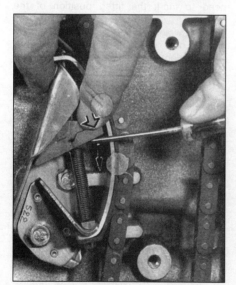

11.3b Releasing second type chain tensioner

8 Carefully remove the timing cover. If it is stuck, gently break the joint by tapping it free with a soft-faced hammer, but do not use excessive force as the light alloy casing can easily be damaged. Remove the timing cover gasket (this must be renewed when reassembling). Retrieve the fuel pump pushrod.

9 Unscrew and remove the engine-to-transmission retaining bolts on each side (**see illustrations**).

10 Support the engine then prise the transmission away from the engine using a suitable length of wood. Take care not to damage the casings. If the two assemblies are reluctant to part, check that there are no retaining bolts or nuts left in position.

11 Engine - complete dismantling

1 Support the engine securely on strong, clean worksurface.

2 Remove any remaining engine ancillary items.

3 Loosen the timing chain tensioner. One of two types will be fitted. With the first type, retract the tensioner by turning the lock in an anti-clockwise direction (**see illustration**). With the second type, use a screwdriver as shown and press down the tensioner to release it (**see illustration**).

4 Unbolt and remove the chain tensioner.

11.9 Oil pump and backplate removal

5 Unbolt and remove the chain guide plate.

6 Unscrew the camshaft sprocket bolt. The crankshaft must be held against rotation for this operation. Do this by screwing two bolts into the flange and passing a long lever between them.

7 Remove the fuel pump eccentric cam.

8 Remove the oil pump socket-headed screws. Some of these are accessible through the holes in the oil pump driven gear.

9 Remove the oil pump and backplate (**see illustration**).

10 Withdraw the camshaft sprocket, timing chain and crankshaft sprocket with Woodruff key (**see illustration**).

11 Unscrew and remove the spark plugs.

12 Remove the cylinder head bolts by unscrewing them in the reverse order to the tightening sequence.

13 Lift off the rocker assembly.

14 Drive down a cylinder head positioning dowel so that the cylinder head can be swivelled rather than lifted from the block. This is to prevent disturbing the cylinder liner base seals. If the liners are to be removed then obviously this precaution is not necessary, neither is the need to fit cylinder liner clamps to hold the liners down once the cylinder head has been removed.

15 Unscrew and remove the bolts which hold the crankcase half sections together (**see illustration**).

16 Split the crankcase and keep the main bearing shells with their crankcase web recesses if the shells are to be used again.

17 Remove the crankshaft oil seal.

18 Mark the rim of the cylinder liners in respect of position in the block and orientation (**see illustration**).

19 Mark the big-end caps and the connecting rods so that they can be refitted in their original sequence and the correct way round. A centre punch or hacksaw blade is useful for this purpose.

20 Unscrew the big-end nuts and remove the caps. If the bearing shells are to be used again, keep them taped to their respective cap or connecting rod.

21 Lift the crankshaft from its crankcase half section, keep the shell bearings in their

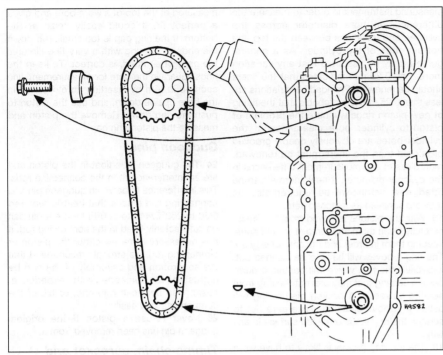

11.10 Timing chain and sprockets removal

original web recesses if they are to be used again and retrieve the semi-circular thrustwashers from either side of Number 2 web.

22 Remove each liner/piston/connecting rod as an assembly from the crankcase. Use a plastic-faced or wooden mallet to tap the liners out if necessary. Make sure that the liners and their respective piston rod assemblies are marked as to position in the block and orientation. A spirit marker is useful for this purpose.

23 Discard the liner base seals which must be renewed.

12 Engine - examination and renovation

General information

1 With the engine dismantled, all components must be thoroughly cleaned and examined for wear, as described in the following Sections.

2 If a high mileage has been covered and general wear is evident, consideration should be given to replacing the engine with a reconditioned unit.

3 If a single component has malfunctioned and the rest of the engine is in good condition, endeavour to find out the cause of its failure if not readily apparent. For example, if a bearing has failed, check that the adjoining oilways are clear. A new bearing will not last long if it is not being lubricated.

4 If uncertain about the condition of any components then seek a second opinion, preferably from a Citroën dealer who will have an expert knowledge of your model and be able to advise on the best course of action.

5 Check on the availability of replacement parts before discarding old ones. Check the new part against the old to ensure that you have the correct replacement.

6 Some of the measurements required will need the use of feeler blades or a micrometer, but in many instances wear will be visually evident or the old component can be compared with a new one.

7 Take care not to damage mating surfaces when cleaning old sealant and/or gaskets from them.

Crankshaft and main bearings

8 Carefully examine the crankpin and main journal surfaces for signs of scoring or scratches and check the ovality and taper of each journal in turn. Use a dial gauge and V-blocks and check the main bearing journals for ovality. If any journals are found to be more than the specified amount out of round then they will have to be reground. If the crankpins are scored or scratched, do not bother measuring them as they will have to be reground.

9 If a bearing has failed after a short period of operation, look for the cause and rectify before reassembly.

10 If the crankshaft is to be reground this will have to be done by your Citroën dealer or a competent automotive engineer. They will also be able to supply the new shell bearings to suit the undersize requirement. New thrustwashers to control endfloat will also be supplied.

11 Main bearing shells themselves are normally a matt grey in colour all over and should show no signs of pitting, ridging or

2A

11.15 Crankshaft half casing retaining bolt locations (arrowed)

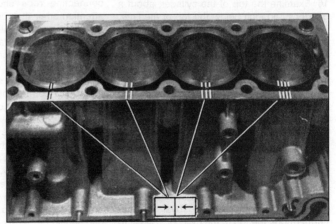

11.18 Cylinder liners and block match marks

discolouration as this usually indicates that the surface bearing metal has worn away and the backing material is showing through.

The shells must be renewed if there is any sign of damage or if the crankshaft has been reground. It is worthwhile renewing the bearing shells anyway if you have gone to the trouble of removing the crankshaft.

12 If the crankshaft is not being reground yet bearing shells are being renewed, make sure that you check whether or not the crankshaft has been reground before. This will be indicated by looking at the back of the bearing shells and will show whether it is undersize or not. The same type of shell bearing must be used when they are renewed.

Big-end bearings

13 Big-end bearings are subject to wear at a greater rate than the crankshaft journals. A sign that one or more big-end bearings are getting badly worn is a pronounced knocking noise from the engine, accompanied by a significant drop in oil pressure due to the increased clearance between the bearing and the journal permitting oil to flow more freely through the resulting larger space.

14 If this happens in an engine which has been neglected, and oil changes and oil filter changes have not been carried out as they should have been, it is most likely that the rest of the engine is in a pretty terrible state anyway. If it occurs in an engine which has been recently overhauled, then it is almost certainly due to a piece of grit or swarf which has got into the oil circulation system and finally come to rest in the bearing shell and scored it. In these instances renewal of the shell alone accompanied by a thorough flushing of the lubrication system may be all that is required.

Cylinder liners, pistons and connecting rods

15 The liner bores may be examined for wear either in or out of the engine block. The cylinder head must, of course, be removed in each case.

16 Examine the top of the cylinder, about a quarter of an inch below the top of the liner. Feel if there is any ridge running round the circumference of the bore. In a worn cylinder bore, a ridge will develop at the point where the top ring on the piston comes to the uppermost limit of its stroke. An excessive ridge indicates that the bore below the ridge is worn. If there is no ridge, it is reasonable to assume that the cylinder is not badly worn.

17 Measure the diameter of the cylinder bore, both in line with the piston gudgeon pin and at right angles to it, at the top and bottom of the cylinder. A cylinder is expected to wear at the sides where the thrust of the piston presses against it. In time this causes the cylinder to assume an oval shape. Furthermore, the top of the cylinder is likely to wear more than the bottom of the cylinder. It will be necessary to use a proper bore

measuring instrument in order to measure the differences in bore diameter across the cylinder, and variations between the top and bottom ends of the cylinder. As a general guide it may be assumed that any variation more than 0.25 mm indicates that the liners should be renewed. Provided all variations are less than 0.25 mm it is probable that the fitting of new piston rings will cure the problem of piston-to-cylinder bore clearances. If the cylinder bores are obviously deeply grooved or scored then the liners must be renewed, regardless of any measurement differences in the cylinder diameter. If new liners are to be fitted, new pistons will be required also, as they are supplied as matched sets.

18 With the pistons removed from the liners, carefully clean them and remove the old rings, keeping them in order and the correct way up. The ring grooves will have to be cleaned out, especially the top, which will contain a burnt carbon coating that may prevent the ring from seating correctly. A broken piston ring will assist in groove cleaning. Take care not to scratch the ring lands or piston surface in any way.

19 The top ring groove is likely to have worn the most. After the groove has been cleaned out, refit the top ring and any excessive wear will be obvious by a sloppy fit. The degree of wear may be checked by using a feeler blade.

20 Examine the piston surface and look for signs of any hairline cracks especially round the gudgeon pin area. Check that the oil drain holes below the oil control ring groove are clear, if not, carefully clean them out using a suitable size drill taking care not to mark the piston.

21 If any of the pistons are obviously badly worn or defective they must be renewed. A badly worn top ring land may be machined to accept a wider, stepped ring, the stop on the outer face of this type of ring being necessary to avoid fouling the unworn ridge at the top of the cylinder bore.

22 Providing the engine has not seized up or suffered any other severe damage, the connecting rods should not require any attention other than cleaning. If damage has occurred or the piston(s) shows signs of irregular wear it is advisable to have the connecting rod alignment checked. This requires the use of specialised tools and should therefore be entrusted to a Citroën agent or a competent automotive engineer, who will be able to check and realign any defective rods.

23 New Citroën rings are supplied with their gaps already preset, but if you intend to use other makes the gaps should be checked and adjusted if necessary. Before fitting the new rings on the pistons, each should be inserted approximately 75 mm down the cylinder bore and the gap measured with a feeler blade. The gap should be between 0.38 and 0.97 mm. It is essential that the gap should be measured at the bottom of the ring travel, as if it is

measured at the top of a worn bore and gives a perfect fit, it could easily seize at the bottom. If the ring gap is too small, rub down the ends of the ring with a very fine file until the gap, when fitted, is correct. To keep the rings square in the bore for measurement, line each up in turn by inserting an old piston in the bore upside down, and use the piston to push the ring down. Remove the piston and measure the piston ring gap.

Gudgeon pins

24 The gudgeon pins float in the piston and are an interference fit in the connecting rods. This interference fit between gudgeon pin and connecting rod means that heat is required (230 to 260°C/446 to 500°F) before a pin can be satisfactorily fitted in the connecting rod. If it is necessary to renew either the piston or connecting rod, we strongly recommend that the separation and assembly of the two be entrusted to someone with experience. Misapplied heat can ruin one, or all, of the components very easily.

25 Never re-use a piston if the original gudgeon pin has been removed from it.

Timing chain, sprocket and tensioner

26 Examine the teeth of both sprockets for wear. Each tooth on a sprocket is an inverted V-shape and wear is apparent when one side of the tooth becomes more concave in shape than the other. When badly worn, the teeth become hook-shaped and the sprockets must be renewed.

27 If the sprockets need to be renewed then the chain will have worn also and should also be renewed. If the sprockets are satisfactory, examine the chain and look for play between the links. When the chain is held out horizontally, it should not bend appreciably. Remember, a chain is only as strong as its weakest link and, being a relatively cheap item, it is worthwhile fitting a replacement anyway.

28 Check the condition of the tensioner slipper. If it is worn, renew it.

29 Inspect the oil pump drive gears for wear or damage and renew if necessary. Always fit a new timing cover oil seal **(see illustration)**.

12.29 Renewing timing cover oil seal

Camshaft and rocker gear

30 The camshaft lobes should be examined for signs of flats or scoring or any other form of wear or damage. At the same time the rocker arms should also be examined, particularly on the faces where they bear against the camshaft, for signs of wear. Very slight wear may be removed by rubbing with an oilstone but maintain the original contour.

31 The camshaft bearing journals should be in good condition and show no signs of pitting or scoring as they are relatively free from stress.

32 If the bearing surfaces are scored or discoloured it is possible that the shaft is not running true. In this case it will have to be renewed. For an accurate check get your Citroën agent to inspect both the camshaft and cylinder head.

33 Worn camshaft bearings in the cylinder head can only be rectified by renewal of the head, an expensive business as the bearings are machined directly in the head.

34 The rocker arms can be removed from the shaft after extracting the circlip (distributor end) and the Allen screw from the opposite end **(see illustrations)**.

12.34a Rocker shaft retaining circlip (arrowed)

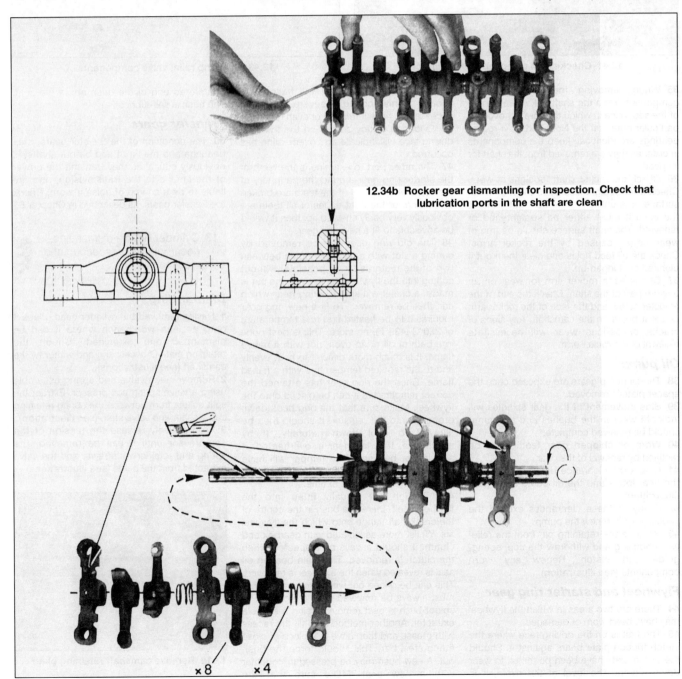

12.34b Rocker gear dismantling for inspection. Check that lubrication ports in the shaft are clean

×8   ×4

2A

12.41 Checking oil pump lobe tip clearance

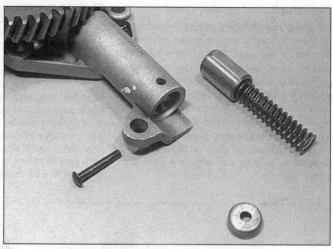

12.43 Oil pump relief valve components

35 When removing the various rocker components from the shaft, take careful note of the sequence in which they are removed. In particular note that the No 2 and No 4 rocker bearings are identical, keep the components in order as they are removed from the shaft for inspection.

36 Check the rocker shaft for signs of wear. Check it for straightness by rolling it on a flat surface. It is unlikely to be bent but if this is the case it must either be straightened or renewed. The shaft surface should be free of wear ridges caused by the rocker arms. Check the oil feed holes and clear them out if blocked or sludged-up.

37 Check each rocker arm for wear on an unworn part of the shaft. Check the end of the adjuster screw and the face of the rocker arm where it bears on the camshaft. Any signs of cracks or serious wear will necessitate renewal of the rocker arm.

Oil pump

38 The oil pump gears are exposed once the spacer plate is removed.

39 Side movement of the gear spindles will indicate wear in the bushes and the pump should be renewed complete.

40 Worn or chipped gear teeth must be rectified by renewal of the gear.

41 Check the clearance between the tip of the gear lobes and the oil pump body **(see illustration)**.

42 If any of these clearances exceed the specified limit, renew the pump.

43 Remove the retaining pin from the relief valve housing and withdraw the cup, spring, guide and piston. Renew any worn components **(see illustration)**.

Flywheel and starter ring gear

44 There are two areas in which the flywheel may have been worn or damaged.

45 The first is on the driving face where the clutch friction plate bears against it. Should the clutch plate have been permitted to wear down beyond the level of the rivets, it is

possible that the flywheel will have been scored. If this scoring is severe it may be necessary to have it refaced or even renewed.

46 Evidence of tiny cracks on the flywheel driving face will indicate that overheating has occurred.

47 The other part to examine is the teeth of the starter ring gear around the periphery of the flywheel. If several of the teeth are broken or missing, or the front edges of all teeth are obviously very badly chewed up, then it would be advisable to fit a new ring gear.

48 The old ring gear can be removed by cutting a slot with a hacksaw down between two of the teeth as far as possible, without cutting into the flywheel itself. Once the cut is made, a chisel will split the ring gear which can then be removed. To fit a new ring gear requires it to be heated first to a temperature of 220°C (435°F), no more. This is best done in a bath of oil or an oven, not with a naked flame. It is much more difficult to heat evenly and to the required temperature with a naked flame. Once the ring gear has attained the correct temperature it can be placed onto the flywheel. Make sure that the ring beds down properly onto the register. It should then be allowed to cool down naturally. If by mischance, the ring gear is overheated, it should not be used. The temper will have been lost, thereby softening it, and it will wear out in a very short space of time.

49 Although not actually fitted into the flywheel itself, there is a bush in the centre of the crankshaft flange onto which the flywheel fits. Whilst more associated with gearbox and clutch, it should always be inspected when the clutch is removed. The main bearing oil seal is revealed when the flywheel is removed. This can be prised out with a screwdriver but must always be renewed once removed. The spigot bush is best removed using a suitable extractor. Another method is to fill the recess with grease and then drive in a piece of close fitting steel bar. This should force the bush out. A new bush may be pressed in, together with a new seal. Make sure that the

chamfered end of the bush abuts the seal. The bush is self-lubricating.

Transfer gears

50 The condition of the transfer gears, their bearings and the input and output shafts, is obviously critical as they transmit the power of the engine to the transmission, and are liable to be a source of noise if worn. Check the transfer gears, as described in Chapter 6.

---

13 Cylinder head - dismantling, decarbonising, inspection and reassembly

Dismantling

1 Having removed the cylinder head, place it onto a clean workbench where it can be dismantled and examined. Unbolt the retaining plate (if necessary) and withdraw the camshaft **(see illustrations)**.

2 Remove each valve and spring assembly using a valve spring compressor. Extract the split collets from between the spring retaining cup washer and valve stem **(see illustration)**.

3 Progressively release the tension of the compressor until it can be removed, the spring and retainer withdrawn, and the valve extracted from the guide **(see illustrations)**.

13.1a Remove camshaft retaining plate ...

13.1b ... to allow camshaft withdrawal

13.2 Compress valve spring ...

13.3a ... and remove spring cup retainer, spring ...

13.3b ... and valve

4 As the valves are removed, keep them in order by inserting them in a card having suitable holes punched in it, numbered from 1 to 8. Discard the valve stem oil seals.

Decarbonising

5 Wash the cylinder head clean and carefully scrape away the carbon build-up in the combustion chambers and exhaust ports, using a scraper which will not damage the surfaces to be cleaned. If a rotary wire brush and drill is available this may be used for removing the carbon.
6 The valves may also be scraped and wire-brushed clean in a similar manner.

Inspection

7 With the cylinder head cleaned and dry, examine it for cracks or damage. In particular inspect the valve seat areas for signs of hairline cracks, pitting or burning. Check the head mating surfaces for distortion, the maximum permissible amount being 0.05 mm.
8 Minor surface wear and pitting of the valve seats can probably be removed when the valves are reground. More serious wear or damage should be shown to your Citroën dealer or a competent automotive engineer who will advise you on the action necessary.
9 Carefully inspect the valves, in particular the exhaust valves. Check the stems for distortion and signs of wear. The valve seat faces must be in reasonable condition and if they have covered a high mileage they will probably need to be refaced on a valve grinding machine. Again, this is a job for your Citroën dealer or local automotive machine shop.

10 Insert each valve into its respective guide and check for excessive side play. Worn valve guides allow oil to be drained past the inlet valve stem causing a smoky exhaust, while exhaust leakage through the exhaust valve guide can overheat the valve guide and cause sticking valves.
11 If the valve guides are to be renewed, this is a job best left to your Citroën agent who will have the required specialist equipment.
12 Assuming the valves and seats are in reasonable condition they should be reseated by grinding them using valve grinding carborundum paste. The grinding process must also be carried out when new valves are fitted.
13 The carborundum paste used for this job is normally supplied in a double-ended tin with coarse paste at one end and fine at the other. In addition, a suction tool for holding the valve head so that it may be rotated is also required. To grind in the valve, first smear a trace of the coarse paste onto the seat face and fit the suction grinder to the valve head. Then with a semi-rotary motion grind the valve head into its seat, lifting the valve occasionally to redistribute the grinding paste. When a dull matt continuous line is produced on both the valve seat and the valve then the paste can be wiped off. Apply a little fine paste and finish off the grinding process, then remove all traces of the paste.
14 The width of the line which is produced after grinding indicates the seat width. This width should not exceed 2 mm. If, after a moderate amount of grinding, it is apparent that the seating line is too wide, it probably means that the seat has already been cut back one or more times previously, or else the

valve has been ground several times. Here again, specialist advice is best sought.
15 Examine all the valve springs to make sure that they are in good condition and not distorted. If the engine has covered 30 000 miles (48 000 km) then fit new springs at reassembly. Renew the valve stem oil seals **(see illustration)**.
16 At the same time, renew the valve spring seating washers which sit directly on the cylinder head **(see illustration)**. These wear fairly quickly.

Reassembly

17 Before reassembling the valves and springs to the cylinder head make a final check that everything is thoroughly clean and free from grit **(see illustration)**, then lightly smear all the valve stems with engine oil prior to reassembly. The camshaft can now be refitted in the cylinder head and located with the retaining plate. This is then secured with its bolt and a new shakeproof washer.

2A

13.15 Valve stem oil seal

13.16 Valve spring seating washer

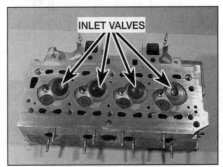

INLET VALVES

13.17 Cylinder head cleaned and reassembled

14 Engine reassembly - general information

It is during the process of engine reassembly that the job is either made a success or a failure. From the start there are certain basic rules to follow, these are as follows:

a) *Absolute cleanliness. The working area, the components of the engine and the hands of the person working on the engine must be completely free of grime and grit. One small piece of carborundum dust or swarf can ruin a bearing surface in no time.*

b) *Always use new gaskets, locking tabs, seals, lock nuts and any other parts mentioned in the Sections in this Chapter. It is pointless to dismantle an engine, spend considerable money and time on it and then waste all this for the sake of something as small as a failed oil seal.*

c) *Do not rush work. The most skilled and experienced mechanic can easily make a mistake if he is rushed.*

d) *Check that all nuts and bolts are clean and in good condition and ideally renew all spring washers, lockwashers and tab washers as a matter of course.*

e) *Obtain a supply of clean engine oil and clean cloths for reassembly.*

f) *A torque wrench is an essential requirement when reassembling the engine. This is because the various housings are manufactured from aluminium alloy. Whilst this gives the advantage of less weight, it also means that the various*

fastenings must be accurately tightened as specified to avoid distortion and/or damage to the components.

15 Engine - preparation for reassembly

1 Assuming that the engine has been completely stripped for reconditioning and that the block is now bare, before any reassembly takes place it must be thoroughly cleaned both inside and out.

2 Clean out the oilways using a bottle brush, wire or other suitable implement, and blow through with compressed air. Squirt some clean engine oil through to check that the oilways are clear.

3 If the core plugs are defective and show signs of weeping, they must be renewed at this stage. To remove, carefully drive a punch through the centre of the plug and use the punch to lever the plug out. Clean the aperture thoroughly and prior to fitting the new plug, smear the orifice with sealant. Use a small-headed hammer and carefully drive the new core plug into position with the convex side outwards. Check that it is correctly seated on completion.

4 As components are assembled, lubricate them with clean engine oil and use a suitable sealant where applicable.

5 Make sure that all blind tapped holes are clean, with any oil mopped out of them. This is because it is possible for a casting to fracture when a bolt is screwed in owing to hydraulic pressure.

16.4 One method of clamping cylinder liners

16 Cylinder liners - checking protrusion

1 Protrusion of the cylinder liners when assembled to the block must be within the prescribed limits so that a gastight seal can be achieved when the head is bolted on. One liner protruding too much or not enough will, despite the cylinder head gasket, make it impossible to secure a gas or watertight joint.

2 An O-ring seal is fitted between each liner mating flange and the cylinder block. These seals compress when the cylinder head is tightened down to effect a watertight seal.

3 Although the actual liner protrusion check method is the same, the procedure differs if the engine is assembled or dismantled.

4 If the cylinder head has been removed with the engine *in situ* the liners must be held under compression with the use of liner clamps **(see illustration)**. Remove the dowels from the cylinder block top face to allow the clamps to be fitted, if necessary.

5 If the engine is dismantled, check that the seal mating surfaces of the liners and the cylinder block are clean then insert each liner into its respective position in the cylinder block without its seal.

6 Check each liner protrusion in turn, measuring the distance between the top face of the liner and the top face of the cylinder block. Use a dial test indicator if available but, failing this, use a metal rule and feeler blades to assess the protrusion **(see illustrations)**.

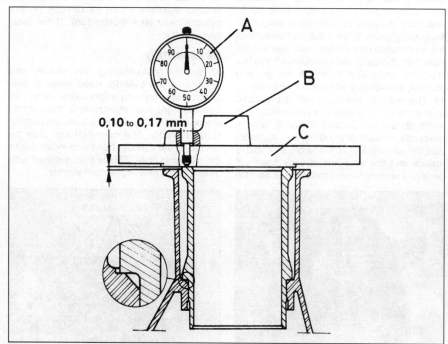

16.6a Cylinder liner protrusion check using a dial gauge

Gauge and mounting (A and B) and flat plate (C)

16.6b Measuring cylinder liner projection with a rule and feeler blades

7 As the protrusion of each liner in turn is checked, ensure that it is squarely located in the cylinder block. The protrusion of each liner should be within the limits specified.

8 Finally check the difference in height between adjacent liners. Use the dial test indicators or rule and feeler blades to measure the difference in height, if any, between adjacent liners at a point on each lying along the centre axis parallel with the crankshaft on the top face. Each difference in level must not exceed the maximum specified.

9 If the checks reveal a discrepancy on an installed engine then it will be necessary to renew the liner O-rings or even one or more liners. In either case the engine/transmission will have to be removed for dismantling.

10 Once the checks have shown the liners to be within limits of protrusion and squareness, reassembly can continue or, if appropriate, temporary retainer clamps/straps should be fitted to hold them in position. Do not turn the crankshaft if the liners are not restrained from movement. Cover the exposed engine internal parts if there is likely to be a delay before completing reassembly.

11 With new liners, once correctly located, mark their sequence in the block and withdraw them so that their piston/rods can be fitted - **(see illustration 11.18)**.

17 Engine - complete reassembly

Pistons and liners

1 Fit the piston rings to the pistons. Always fit the rings from the piston crown end. Use three old feeler blades equally spaced behind the ring so that it will slide down to the lower grooves without dropping into the higher ones **(see illustration)**.

2 Make sure that the rings are correctly located and the right way up **(see illustration)**.

3 Twist the piston rings so that the gap in the oil control ring expander aligns with the gudgeon pin and the gaps in the rails are offset from the gudgeon pin by between 20.0 and 50.0 mm. The caps in the top two compression rings should be equally spaced

17.1 Method of fitting piston rings

(120º) from the gap in the oil control expander around the piston.

4 If new piston/liner assemblies have been supplied, the identification marks on the piston and liner **(see illustration)** should be as follows:

Piston	Liner
A	One file mark on rim
B	Two file marks on rim
C	Three file marks on rim

5 All four pistons should be of the same grading.

6 Fit the liners to the piston/connecting rod assemblies so that when installed in the cylinder block, the rim mark on the liner will be towards the oil gallery side and the arrow on the piston crown facing towards the timing chain cover end of the engine **(see illustration)**. Piston-to-rod relationship is not important.

7 Oil the piston rings liberally and fit a compressor to the piston and compress the rings fully. When fitted, the top edge of the ring compressor should be 4 to 5 mm below the crown of the piston.

8 Lubricate the bore of the liner and insert the piston. As this is done, the compressor will be pushed off **(see illustration)**.

9 Push the liner down so that the piston crown is level with or just below the top edge of the liner.

10 With the pistons and liners reassembled, fit a new O-ring seal over the bottom end of each liner in turn, ensuring that the seals are not twisted as they are fitted **(see illustration)**.

2A

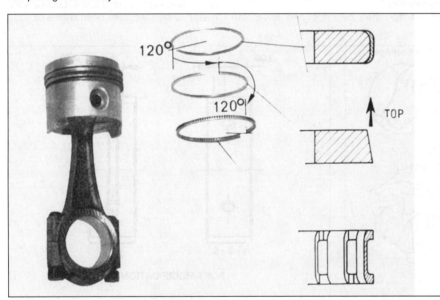

17.2 Piston rings showing correct orientation

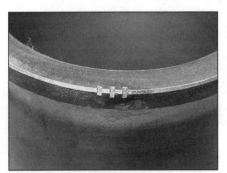

17.4 Piston/liner grading mark

17.6 Piston crown showing directional arrow

17.8 Fitting the piston/rod assembly to its cylinder liner

17.10 Cylinder liner O-ring seal

17.12 Installing piston/liner assembly

11 Remove the big-end caps, wipe the recesses in rod and cap absolutely clean and fit the bearing shells. If the original shells are being used again, make sure that they are being returned to their original locations.
12 Push the liner/rod assemblies into the block, without disturbing the seals and aligning the location marks **(see illustration)**.
13 Fit clamps to hold the liners in the block.

Crankshaft

14 Place the block so that it rests on its top face, wipe out the recesses and fit the main bearing shells. Note that on engines manufactured after December 1985, the main bearing shell location tags and their slots in the crankcase upper and lower half-sections have been modified. If renewing the bearing shells, ensure that the correct type is fitted **(see illustrations)**.
15 Fit the semi-circular thrustwashers which control crankshaft endfloat. The oil grooves of the thrustwashers must be against the machined face of the crankshaft **(see illustration)**.
16 Oil the shell bearings and lower the crankshaft into position **(see illustration)**.
17 Now check the crankshaft endfloat. Do this by first pushing the crankshaft fully in one direction and then in the other. A dial gauge or feeler blades should be used to measure the endfloat **(see illustration)**. If the endfloat is not within the specified limits, change the thrustwashers and fit alternatives of suitable thickness. Thrustwashers are available in a choice of four thicknesses.
18 Lubricate and fit the big-end caps, complete with bearing shells. Make sure that the cap/rod matching marks are in alignment. This will ensure that both tongues of the shells are on the same side **(see illustration)**.
19 Tighten the big-end nuts to the specified torque.

Crankcase housing

20 Check that the three location dowels are in position in the cylinder block flange face and fit a new O-ring seal to each **(see illustration)**.
21 Clean the recesses in the remaining crankcase housing section and fit the main bearing shells. Note that the grooved shells are located in positions 2 and 4. Lubricate the main bearing shells with clean engine oil.

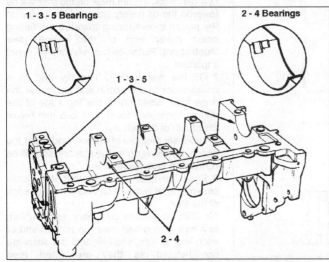

17.14a Main bearing shell location tags - crankcase lower half shown (post December 1985)

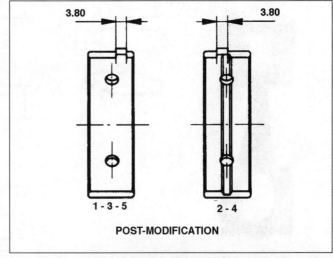

17.14b Main bearing shell identification - post December 1985

17.15 Crankshaft thrustwashers

17.16 Lowering crankshaft into position

17.17 Checking crankshaft endfloat

17.18 Fitting a big-end cap

17.20 Crankcase flange O-ring seal in position on dowel

17.23 Fitting crankcase housing

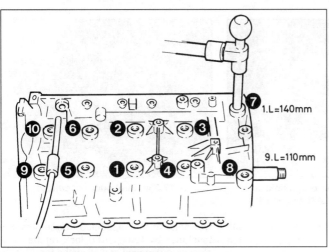
17.25 Main bearing/casing bolt tightening sequence

17.26 Crankcase housing flange bolts

2A

22 Apply an even layer of jointing compound to the mating flange of the crankcase.
23 Locate the crankcase housing, taking care not to displace the bearing shells (see illustration).
24 Lubricate the bolt threads then screw in the ten main bearing/casing bolts with flat washers. Note that the two longer bolts are at the flywheel housing end and the very long one at the crankshaft pulley end on the oil pump side.
25 Tighten the bolts in the sequence given in two stages to the specified torque (see illustration).
26 Now screw in and tighten the seven

housing flange bolts with their spring washers (see illustration).
27 Grease the lips of a new crankshaft oil seal and drive it squarely into position (see illustration).

Cylinder head
28 Refit the cylinder head, referring to the appropriate Section of this Chapter.

Timing chain and sprockets
29 Fit the timing chain tensioner oil filter and the crankshaft sprocket Woodruff key. Bolt the chain tensioner into position (see illustrations).

30 Rotate the crankshaft by temporarily screwing in two flywheel bolts and placing a bar between them until the key is in alignment with the crankcase joint.
31 Temporarily fit the camshaft sprocket and rotate the camshaft until the keyway is positioned as shown (see illustration).
32 Fit the crankshaft sprocket (see illustration).
33 Loop the chain around the crankshaft sprocket so that the bright link on the chain is centred on the timing mark on the sprocket (see illustration).
34 Now loop the chain around the camshaft sprocket so that the two bright links are

17.27 Fitting new crankshaft oil seal

17.29a Locate chain tensioner filter ...

17.29b ... then fit tensioner

17.32 Locate crankshaft sprocket

17.33 Timing chain bright link at crankshaft sprocket

17.34 Timing chain bright links at camshaft sprocket timing mark

17.35a Fuel pump eccentric

17.31 Align camshaft and crankshaft sprocket Woodruff key slots as shown

17.35b Tightening sprocket retaining bolt

17.36 Releasing timing chain tensioner - first type

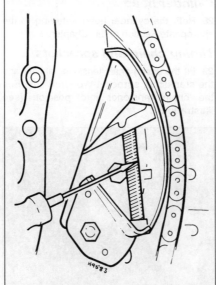

17.37 Arming timing chain tensioner - second type

17.39 Fitting oil pump with spacer plate

positioned one on each side of the sprocket timing mark. Push the sprocket with chain onto the camshaft, if necessary move the camshaft a fraction to align the keyway **(see illustration)**.

35 Screw in the camshaft sprocket bolt with fuel pump eccentric and tighten to the specified torque **(see illustrations)**.

36 Where the first type chain tensioner is fitted, check that the tensioner shoe is locked in the retracted position and assemble the two retaining bolts and locking washers, the joint gasket and the spacer plate to the tensioner. Fit the tensioner to the block and tighten the

two bolts to their specified torque. Arm the tensioner by turning the lock ratchet in a clockwise direction and allow the tensioner to automatically take up the chain tension. Do not assist the action of the tensioner **(see illustration)**.

37 Where the second type of chain tensioner is fitted, fit the tensioner into position on the block and tighten the retaining bolts. Arm the tensioner by engaging the spring and prising it upwards **(see illustration)**.

38 Refit the timing chain guide plate and tighten the two retaining bolts to the specified torque.

Oil pump

39 Check that the locating dowel is in position and fit the oil pump with spacer plate (no gasket is used). If the pump driven sprocket is hard to turn, release the pump

mounting bolts and turn the pump slightly on its locating dowel. Re-tighten the bolts **(see illustration)**.
40 Fit the oil pump drive sprocket and Woodruff key to the crankshaft **(see illustration)**.

General

41 The engine is now ready for reconnection to the transmission. If required, certain engine ancillary items such as the oil filter, oil pressure sender and coolant pump can be fitted into position before reconnecting the engine to the transmission **(see illustration)**.

---

18 Engine - reconnection to transmission

1 Check that the oil pick-up strainer is in position within the transmission casing.
2 Fit the sump cover using a new gasket.
3 Tighten the fixing bolts and drain plug to the specified torque.
4 Fit the cover plate.
5 Apply jointing compound to the mating surfaces of the engine and transmission. Ensure that an even layer of sealant is applied around the oil duct.
6 On the transmission, locate a new O-ring seal and check that the locating dowels and the studs are in position **(see illustration)**.
7 Offer the transmission to the engine, screw in the connecting bolts and nuts and tighten to the specified torque **(see illustration)**.

17.40 Oil pump drive sprocket

8 The timing cover can now be fitted **(see illustration)**. The new timing cover gasket must be fitted dry and, prior to fitting the cover, check that the centring pin is in position and put the bolt nearest the coolant pump pulley into its cover hole, otherwise the pulley will prevent it from being fitted later **(see illustration)**. Do not tighten the cover bolts yet.
9 Fit the coolant hose retainer under its cover bolts.
10 Use the crankshaft pulley to centralise the timing chain cover and then tighten the cover bolts to the specified torque.
11 Cut off the upper ends of the cover gasket flush. Lubricate the lips of the crankshaft pulley oil seal and locate it onto the crankshaft and into the timing cover. Drive the seal carefully into position using a suitable tube drift or mandrel.

17.41 Oil pressure sender switch

12 Locate the Woodruff key into its groove in the crankshaft, refit the pulley and tighten the retaining nut to the specified torque. When tightening the pulley retaining nut, fit two bolts into the flywheel flange end of the crankshaft and jam a lever between them to prevent the crankshaft from turning. The nut threads should be treated with a suitable locking sealant prior to fitting.
13 Fit the alternator drivebelt pulley into position on the front end of the coolant pump drivebelt pulley and secure with the three bolts.
14 Fit the flywheel. Apply thread locking fluid to clean threads and screw in the flywheel bolts to the specified torque. The flywheel holes are offset so it will only go onto the crankshaft flange in one position **(see illustration)**.
15 Fit the clutch and centralise the friction plate.
16 Fit a new gasket and the flywheel housing complete with transfer gears. Make sure that the engine lifting lug and earth strap are correctly located under their respective bolts.
17 If they were removed, bolt the engine mountings to the flywheel housing.
18 Fit the starter motor. Tighten the bolts and nuts in the following order:
a) *Starter drive end flange to flywheel housing*
b) *Brush end bracket to engine crankcase*
c) *Brush end bracket to starter motor*
19 Adjust the valve clearances and using a new gasket, fit the rocker cover.

2A

18.6 O-ring seal on transmission casing

18.7 Offering transmission to engine

18.8a Refitting timing cover with new gasket

18.8b Timing cover bolt nearest coolant pump pulley

18.14 Tightening flywheel bolts to specified torque

20 Refit the alternator and the remaining engine ancillary items still to be fitted, reversing the removal sequence for the various items and referring to the relevant Chapter for full fitting details.

19 Engine - initial start-up after overhaul

1 Make sure that the battery is fully charged and properly reconnected.
2 Replenish the coolant and all lubricants.
3 Top-up the hydraulic system and prime the high pressure (HP) pump.
4 It will require several revolutions of the engine on the starter motor to pump fuel to the carburettor. As soon as the engine fires and runs, keep it going at a fast tickover and bring it up to the normal working temperature.
5 With the engine running, repressurise the hydraulic system.
6 As the engine warms up there will be odd smells and some smoke from parts getting hot and burning off oil deposits. The signs to look for are leaks of coolant or oil which will be obvious if serious.
7 Check the exhaust pipe and manifold connections. These do not always find their exact gas-tight position until the warmth and vibration have acted on them and it is almost certain that they will need tightening further. This should be done with the engine stopped.
8 When normal running temperature has been reached, adjust the engine idling speed. Run the engine until the cooling fan cuts in and then switch off.
9 Allow at least two hours for the engine to cool down and then retighten the cylinder head bolts after removing the rocker cover. Follow the bolt tightening sequence and, starting with the first, slacken the bolt and retighten it to the specified final tightening torque before loosening the second bolt. Repeat until all bolts have been retightened.
10 Check and adjust the valve clearances.
11 Check the ignition timing.
12 Road test the car to check that the timing is correct and that the engine is giving the necessary smoothness and power. Do not race the engine. If new bearings and/or pistons have been fitted, it should be treated as a new engine and run in at a reduced speed.
13 Change the engine oil at 1000 miles (1600 km) if many of the engine internal components have been renewed. At the same mileage, check the tension of the drivebelt.

Chapter 2 Part B:
171 and 159 engines

Including engine variants B1A/A, B2C, BDY, D2A, D2E, D2F, D6A, D6D and DKZ.
For model applications refer to Specifications

Contents

Degrees of difficulty

Easy, suitable for novice with little experience	**Fairly easy,** suitable for beginner with some experience	**Fairly difficult,** suitable for competent DIY mechanic	**Difficult,** suitable for experienced DIY mechanic	**Very difficult,** suitable for expert DIY or professional

Specifications

Model application

BX 16	171 B or C (XU5S)
BX 19	159 A (XU9S)
BX 16 RE	B1A/A
BX 16 (except TXi model - from September 1988)	B2C (XU52C)
BX 16 - fuel-injected	BDY (XU5M 3Z)
BX 19 TRS (from July 1986)	D2A (XU92C)
BX 19 TRS/TZS (for 1990)	D2E (XU92C+)
BX 19 TZS (from 1991)	D2F (XU92C+)
BX 19 GTi (up to 1991)	D6A (XU9J2)
BX 19 GTi (from 1991)	D6D (XU9J2)
BX 19 TZi with catalytic converter	DKZ (XU9JAZ)

171 engine

General

Type	Four-cylinder, in-line, OHC, liquid cooled, transverse mounting
Bore	83.0 mm
Stroke	73.0 mm
Capacity	1580 cc
Compression ratio	9.5:1
Firing order	1 - 3 - 4 - 2
Location of No 1 cylinder	At clutch end of block
Direction of crankshaft rotation	Clockwise viewed from pulley end
Maximum power DIN (BHP)	92 (94*) at 6000 rpm
Maximum torque DIN (lbf ft)	96.9 at 3500 rpm

171 C engine from October 1984

Cylinder head

Type .... Aluminium alloy, in-line valves and five bearing camshaft
Maximum allowable distortion .... 0.05 mm
Valve seat angle .... 90°
Valve guide bore diameter .... 8.0 to 8.022 mm

Valves

Stem diameter:
  Inlet .... 7.98 to 7.83 mm
  Exhaust .... 7.96 to 7.81 mm
Head diameter:
  Inlet .... 40.0 mm
  Exhaust .... 32.0 mm
Length:
  Inlet .... 107.49 ± 0.1mm
  Exhaust .... 106.92 ± 0.1mm
Springs:
  Wire diameter: .... 4.4 mm
  Length under load:
    Inlet .... 40.5/41 mm/kg
    Exhaust .... 30.0/80 mm/kg
Valve clearance (cold):
  Inlet .... 0.15 to 0.25 mm
  Exhaust .... 0.35 to 0.45 mm
Adjustment shim thickness .... 2.225 mm to 3.025 mm (in steps of 0.025 mm) 3.100 mm to 3.550 mm
                                                   (in steps of 0.075 mm)

Valve timing

Valve lift .... 10.4 mm or 9.7 mm (from December 1983)
Inlet opens* .... 0° 48' BTDC
Inlet closes* .... 37° ABDC
Exhaust opens* .... 35° 36' BBDC
Exhaust closes* .... 2° 12' ATDC
*With valve clearance of 1.0 mm

Camshaft

Endfloat .... 0.07 to 0.16 mm

Crankshaft and main bearings

Number of bearings .... Five
Crankshaft endfloat .... 0.07 to 0.27 mm
Thrustwasher thicknesses .... 2.30, 2.35, 2.40, 2.45, 2.50 mm
Maximum allowable ovality of crankpins and journals ..... 0.007 mm
Crank journal dimensions:
  Standard diameter .... 60.0 to 59.981 mm
  Regrind diameter .... 59.7 to 59.681 mm
Standard main bearing thickness .... 1.842 mm
Replacement main bearing thickness after regrind .... 1.992 mm
Crankpin dimensions:
  Standard diameter .... 45.0 mm
  Regrind diameter .... 44.7 mm
  Standard bearing thickness .... 1.817 mm
  Replacement bearing thickness after regrind .... 1.967 mm

Connecting rods

Small-end bore diameter .... 22.0 mm
Small-end to gudgeon pin .... 0.020 to 0.041 mm
Big-end bore diameter .... 48.655 mm

Cylinder liners

Type .... Cast iron, wet type
Liner base seal .... O-ring
Liner protrusion - clamped or without seal .... 0.08 to 0.15 mm
Maximum allowable projection difference between two liners .... 0.05 mm
Piston offset .... 1.5 mm
Grades:
  Piston:
    A .... One file mark
    B .... Two file marks
    C .... Three file marks

Pistons

Type . . . . Aluminium alloy, two compression and one oil control ring. Gudgeon pin free in piston, interference fit in connecting rod
Piston fitting direction . . . . Arrow mark on crown points to the timing gear (DT)
Gudgeon pin classes . . . . Three, colour-coded to marks on piston crown
Running clearance . . . . 0.07 to 0.09 mm

Lubrication system

Oil pressure at 4000 rpm . . . . 3.5 bar
Oil pressure switch calibration:
    Operates between . . . . 0.44 and 0.58 bar
    Stops operating at . . . . 0.8 bar (maximum)
Oil filter . . . . Champion F104
Oil capacity:
    New or reconditioned engine . . . . 5.2 litres (9.1 pints)
    After draining . . . . 5.0 litres (8.8 pints)
    Dipstick minimum to maximum . . . . 1.5 litres (2.6 pints)

Torque wrench settings

	Nm	lbf ft
Cam cover	10	7
Camshaft bearing cap bolts	15	11
Camshaft sprocket	80	58
Camshaft stop (thrust plate)	15	11
Camshaft inner cover	7	5
Exhaust manifold	22	16
Inlet manifold	22	16
Timing covers	8	6
Mounting bracket	20	15
Cylinder head bolts:		
Stage 1	60	43
Stage 2 (after slackening)	20	15
Stage 3:		
Hexagon headed bolts	Tighten a further 120°	
Torx headed bolts	Tighten a further 300°	
Timing belt tensioner	16	12
Timing belt tensioner lock cam (interlock plunger)	15	11
Crankshaft pulley	110	80
Crankshaft main bearing cap bolts	53	38
Connecting rod big-end cap bolts	49	35
Sump bolts	19	14
Sump drain plug	30	33
Suction drain pipe nuts	5	4
Oil pump bolts	19	14
Crankshaft front cover	16	12
Flywheel bolts	49	35
Coolant temperature sender units	18	13
Engine mountings - See illustration 21.6:		
A	35	25
B	28	20
C	23	17
D	45	33
E	18	13
F	50	36
G	20	15

159 engine

Specification as for the type 171 engine except for the following:

General

Stroke . . . . 88.0 mm
Capacity . . . . 1905 cc
Compression ratio 9.3:1
Maximum power DIN (BHP) . . . . 105 at 5600 rpm
Maximum torque DIN (lbf ft) . . . . 88.1 at 2000 rpm

Valves

Head diameter:
    Inlet . . . . 39.5 mm
    Exhaust . . . . 33.0 mm

2B

Valve timing

Valve lift . . . . 10.3 mm
Inlet opens* . . . . -3° BTDC
Inlet closes* . . . . 46° ABDC
Exhaust opens* . . . . 40° BBDC
Exhaust closes* . . . . 2° ATDC
*With valve clearance of 1.0 mm

B1A/A engine
Specification as for the type 171 engine except for the following:

General
Compression ratio . . . . 9.35 to 1
Maximum power DIN (BHP) . . . . 80 at 5600 rpm
Maximum torque DIN (lbf ft) . . . . 97.6 at 2800 rpm

Valves
Valve clearances (cold):
   Inlet . . . . 0.15 to 0.20 mm
   Exhaust . . . . 0.35 to 0.40 mm

Valve timing
Inlet opens . . . . 5° 6' BTDC
Inlet closes . . . . 23° 7' ABDC
Exhaust opens . . . . 35° 8' BBDC
Exhaust closes . . . . 0° 8' BTDC

B2C engine
Specification as for the type 171C engine except for the following:

General
Compression ratio 8.95:1
Maximum power DIN (BHP) . . . . 94 at 6000 rpm
Maximum torque DIN (lbf ft) . . . . 97 at 3200 rpm

Valves
Length . . . . 108.0 mm
Head diameter:
   Inlet . . . . 41.5 mm
   Exhaust . . . . 34.5 mm

BDY engine
Specification as for the type 171C engine except for the following:

General
Compression ratio 8.95:1
Maximum power DIN (BHP) . . . . 89 at 6400 rpm
Maximum torque DIN (lbf ft) . . . . 97 at 3000 rpm

D2A engine
Specification as for the type 159A engine except for the following:

General
Maximum power DIN (BHP) . . . . 105 at 5600 rpm
Maximum torque DIN (lbf ft) . . . . 119 at 3000 rpm

D2E engine
Specification as for the type 159A engine except for the following:

General
Maximum power DIN (BHP) . . . . 105 at 6000 rpm
Maximum torque DIN (lbf ft) . . . . 118 at 3000 rpm

D2F engine
Specification as for the type 159A engine except for the following:

General
Maximum power DIN (BHP) . . . . 107 at 6000 rpm
Maximum torque DIN (lbf ft) . . . . 122.5 at 3000 rpm

D6A engine

Specification as for the type 159A engine except for the following:

General

Compression ratio	9.3:1
Maximum power DIN (BHP)	125 at 5500 rpm
Maximum torque DIN (lbf ft)	129 at 4500 rpm

Valves

Head diameter:	
Inlet	40.6 mm
Exhaust	33.0 mm
Length	105 mm
Valve clearance (cold):	
Inlet	0.10 to 0.15 mm
Exhaust	0.20 to 0.30 mm

Valve timing

Valve lift	11.5 mm
Inlet opens*	5° 9' BTDC
Inlet closes*	48° ABDC
Exhaust opens*	43° 4' BBDC
Exhaust closes*	1° 10' ABDC

With valve clearance of 0.7 mm

D6D engine

Specification as for the type D6A engine except for the following:

General

Maximum power DIN (BHP)	123 at 5500 rpm
Maximum torque DIN (lbf ft)	127 at 2750 rpm

DKZ engine

Specification as for the type D6A engine except for the following:

General

Compression ratio	9.18:1
Maximum power DIN (BHP)	122 at 6000 rpm
Maximum torque DIN (lbf ft)	115 at 3000 rpm

Valves

Head diameter:	
Inlet	34.5 mm
Exhaust	41.5 mm
Length	108.0 mm

2B

1 General information and precautions

General information

171 and 159 engines

These engines, which are fitted to the Citroën BX 16 and BX 19 models respectively, have four wet liner cylinders, a five bearing crankshaft and an overhead camshaft. The engine is mounted transversely in the engine compartment

Camshaft drive is by toothed belt. The belt is tensioned by a spring-loaded wheel and also drives the coolant pump. The camshaft operates directly on bucket tappets (cam followers). Valve clearance adjustment is by shims inserted between the tappet and the valve stem. The distributor is driven directly from the tail of the camshaft.

A pressure feed lubrication system is fitted, oil being circulated round the engine by a high output rotary pump drawing oil from the sump. This pump is located in the bottom of the timing case and it is driven by a chain connected to a sprocket on the front of the crankshaft. Oil is drawn through a strainer in the sump and delivered to a filter cartridge mounted on the front of the crankcase. A relief valve operates to prevent excessive oil pressure.

A pressure switch located directly above the oil filter will light the oil pressure warning light in the instrument panel if the pressure falls below a certain pressure. In the event of the cartridge filter becoming clogged, a safety bypass valve located in the filter mounting will open to prevent oil starvation. Unfiltered oil is then supplied to the bearing surfaces.

B1A/A and B2C engines

These engines are used in later BX 16 models and are a development of the 171 engine. All modifications are of a minor nature, mainly concerning the fuel and exhaust systems.

All procedures for these engines are as described for the 171 engine. Refer to the relevant text for applicable modifications.

BDY engine

This engine is used in the fuel-injected BX 16 models first introduced in late 1992. The engine is fed by a Magneti Marelli single-point injection engine management system incorporating a closed-loop catalytic converter.

This engine is a development of the 171 engine and all procedures are as described for that engine. Refer to the relevant text for applicable modifications.

D2A, D2E and D2F engines

The D2A engine supersedes the 159A engine used in BX 19 models for the 1987 model year. The D2A engine was itself superseded by the D2E for the 1990 model year. As part of a process of continual development, the D2E engine was replaced by the D2F engine for the 1991 model year. All modifications to these engines are of a minor nature, mainly concerning the fuel and ignition systems.

All procedures for these engines are as described for the 159A engine. Refer to the relevant text for applicable modifications.

D6A and D6D engines

The D6A engine powers the BX 19 GTi model and is a development of the 159A engine. All modifications are of a minor nature, mainly concerned with the cylinder head and the fuel injection system components which replace the carburettor fitted to other BX 19 models.

6.3 Camshaft timing sprocket cover removal

6.4a Set crankshaft pulley and camshaft sprocket dowel holes to positions "a" and "b"

The D6D engine supersedes the D6A engine for the 1991 model year and uses a Motronic engine management system.

All procedures for these engines are as described for the 159A engine. Refer to the relevant text for applicable modifications.

DKZ engine

This engine is used in the BX 19 TZi models from March 1990, and operates in conjunction with a catalytic converter.

The engine is a development of the 159A engine and all procedures are as described for the same. Refer to the relevant text for applicable modifications.

Precautions

Because of the unusual layout of the engine and transmission systems, extra care and attention are necessary during maintenance and overhaul procedures which, in many instances, differ from more conventional systems.

Read through the various Sections concerned before tackling any job, and analyse the instructions, so that any snags or possible difficulties can be noted in advance. Because the sub-assembly castings are made from aluminium alloy it is of utmost importance that, where specified, all fastenings are tightened to the correct torque and, in some instances, in the correct sequence.

2   Oil filter - removal and refitting

Refer to Chapter 1, Section 9.

3   Major operations possible with engine in vehicle

The following items can be removed and refitted with the engine in the vehicle:
a) Cylinder head
b) Camshaft and camshaft drivebelt
c) Clutch and flywheel (after removal of transmission)

6.4b Timing dowels (drills) in position

d) Sump (after removal of the support member between the crossmember and the front cross panel. Disconnect the hydraulic line from the clip attached to the support member)

4   Major operations requiring engine removal

The engine must be removed for the following operation:
a) Removal of the crankshaft and main bearings

5   Valve clearances - checking and adjustment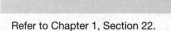

Refer to Chapter 1, Section 22.

6   Camshaft drivebelt - removal and refitting

Note: *The following operation was carried out with the engine in the vehicle.*

171, 159, B1A/A, D2A, D2E and D6A engines. Also B2C, BDY, D2F, D6D and DKZ engines prior to January 1992

Removal

1 Disconnect the battery earth lead.
2 Remove the alternator drivebelt and HP pump drivebelt.
3 Unbolt and remove the camshaft timing sprocket cover **(see illustration)**.
4 Turn the crankshaft until the dowel hole in the pulley is at approximately 12 o'clock and the hole in the camshaft sprocket is at approximately 7 o'clock. In this position a 10 mm dowel should pass through each hole and into the timing recess behind **(see illustration)**. Verify this and then remove the dowels **(see illustration)**.
5 Remove the clutch/torque converter bottom shield. Have an assistant jam the starter ring gear while the crankshaft pulley bolt is undone. This bolt is very tight. Do not jam the pulley by means of the timing dowel as damage will result. Remove the bolts and washer.
6 Check that the 10 mm dowels will still enter the timing holes. Adjust the crankshaft position if necessary by means of the starter ring gear. Remove the crankshaft pulley, retrieving the Woodruff key if it is loose.
7 Remove the timing covers from the front of the camshaft drivebelt **(see illustration)**. Note that from May 1987, a simplified three-piece timing belt cover has been fitted. This simplified cover can be fitted to earlier vehicles but will require the purchase of an additional nut and screw.

8 Slacken the two nuts on the front of the drivebelt tensioner and the single nut at the rear. Use a spanner on the square end of the tensioner cam spindle to turn the cam to the horizontal position and so compress the tensioner spring. Tighten the cam locknut **(see illustration)**.

9 Remove the camshaft drivebelt, taking care not to kink it or contaminate it with oil if it is to be re-used.

Refitting

10 Commence refitting by positioning the belt on the crankshaft sprocket, then refitting the pulley and verifying the correct position of the crankshaft by means of the dowel. Observe the arrows on the belt showing the direction of rotation, and the timing lines which align with marks on the crankshaft and camshaft sprockets **(see illustrations)**. The drivebelt used with the type of tensioner mechanism fitted to these engines should have 113 teeth and white markings.

11 Fit the belt to the camshaft sprocket, around the tensioner and to the coolant pump sprocket.

12 Release the tensioner cam locknut and turn the cam downwards to release the spring. Tighten the locknut and the tensioner front nuts **(see illustrations)**.

13 Remove the timing dowels and turn the crankshaft through two full turns in the normal direction of rotation. Turn the crankshaft further to bring No 1 piston to TDC on the firing stroke (flywheel index mark aligned with the O-mark).

14 Slacken the tensioner front nuts and the cam locknut, then retighten them to the specified torque.

15 Turn the crankshaft further and make sure that the timing dowels can still be inserted. If not, remove the drivebelt and start again.

16 If a new belt has been fitted, it must be run in and retensioned as follows.

17 Tighten the crankshaft pulley bolt to the specified torque, then refit and tension the alternator drivebelt and the HP drivebelt. Temporarily refit the camshaft sprocket cover.

18 Run the engine up to operating temperature (indicated by the cooling fan operating) then stop it and allow it to cool for at least two hours.

6.7 Central timing cover removed for access to tensioner

6.8 Tensioner cam spindle (square end) and locknut

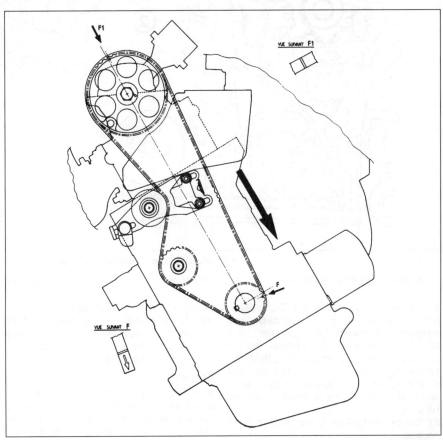

6.10a Timing belt-to-sprockets alignment. Arrow indicates normal direction of belt rotation

6.10b Line on belt aligns with mark on camshaft sprocket

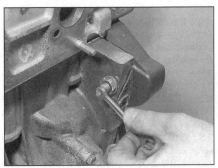

6.12a Turn tensioner cam downwards . . .

6.12b . . . and tighten drivebelt tensioner front nuts

2B

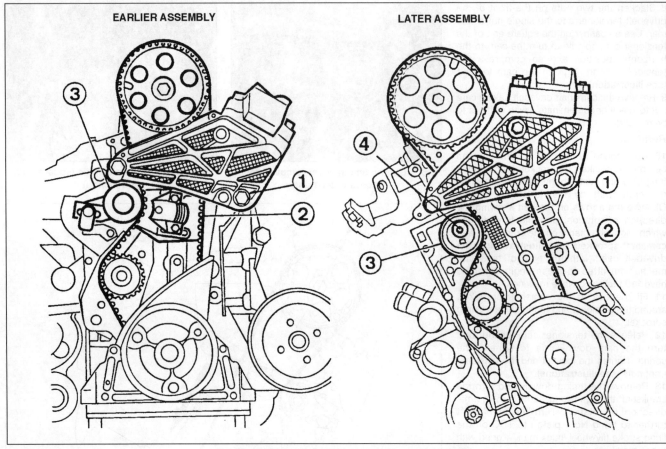

EARLIER ASSEMBLY

LATER ASSEMBLY

6.23 Modified timing belt and tensioner arrangement

1 Right-hand engine mounting   *2 Timing belt*   *3 Tensioner assembly*   *4 Tensioner roller bolt*

19 Rotate the crankshaft to the TDC position, No 1 cylinder firing, then slacken and retighten the tensioner nuts once more.

20 Remove the alternator drivebelt, the HP drivebelt and the crankshaft pulley. Refit and secure the covers, then refit the pulley and tighten its bolt to the specified torque. Refit and tension the alternator drivebelt and the HP drivebelt.

21 Check the ignition timing and adjust if necessary.

B2C, BDY, D2F, D6D and DKZ engines from January 1992

22 On these engines, the tensioner mechanism is of an eccentric roller type.

23 To accommodate this revised mechanism, a number of the surrounding engine components have been changed from those fitted to engines manufactured before January 1992 **(see illustration)**. They are as follows:
a) *Tensioner assembly*
b) *Camshaft drivebelt*
c) *Front crankshaft oil seal carrier plate*
d) *Coolant pump*
e) *Right-hand engine mounting*
f) *Cylinder block (has an extra threaded hole for tensioner centre bolt)*
g) *Camshaft drivebelt covers*

24 Note that the type of camshaft drivebelt fitted to these engines should have 114 teeth and yellow/orange markings. If the drivebelt is to be renewed, ensure that the correct type of replacement drivebelt is obtained.

Removal

Note: *Citroën specify the use of a special tool (SEEM belt tension measuring equipment) to correctly set the belt tension. If this equipment cannot be obtained, an approximate setting can be achieved using the method described below. If the method described here is used, the tension must be checked using the special equipment at the earliest opportunity. Do not drive the vehicle over large distances, or use high engine speeds, until the belt tension is known to be correct. Refer to a Citroën dealer for advice.*

25 Proceed as described in paragraphs 1 to 7, noting that the crankshaft pulley timing dowel must be of 10 mm diameter, stepped down to 8 mm at one end to engage with the smaller hole in the timing recess.

26 With the camshaft timing belt covers removed, slacken the tensioner roller bolt to relieve the belt tension, then withdraw the belt, noting the direction of fitting and the markings.

Refitting

27 Commence refitting by slipping the belt over the camshaft sprocket, followed by the crankshaft sprocket, the coolant pump sprocket, and finally over the tensioner roller. Observe the arrows on the belt indicating the direction of rotation and the timing lines which align with corresponding marks on the crankshaft and camshaft sprockets.

28 With the camshaft timing dowel fitted, rotate the tensioner roller anti-clockwise by hand as far as possible to take up any slack in the belt, then tighten the tensioner roller bolt sufficiently to hold the roller in position. If the special belt tension measuring equipment is available then it should be fitted to the front run of the belt and the tensioner roller should be moved to give a reading of 30 SEEM units. Tighten the roller bolt to the specified torque, taking care not to move the roller as the bolt is tightened.

29 Check that the crankshaft and camshaft are still positioned correctly by temporarily refitting the crankshaft pulley and reinserting the timing dowel.

30 Remove the timing dowels, temporarily refit the crankshaft pulley and turn the crankshaft through two full turns in the normal direction of rotation. Check that both timing

7.7a Undo retaining screw . . .

7.7b . . . and remove camshaft thrust plate

7.16 Locating cover plate with 10 mm dowel

dowels can still be inserted. If not, remove the drivebelt and start again. Never turn the crankshaft backwards during this procedure.

31 If all is well, remove the dowels and turn the crankshaft through two further turns in the normal direction of rotation.

32 Refit the camshaft timing dowel and check that the belt can just be twisted through 90° (using moderate pressure from the forefinger and thumb) at the midpoint of the longest belt run between the camshaft and crankshaft sprockets. If in doubt about this setting, it is better to err on the tight side until the tension can be checked by a Citroën dealer. If the belt is too slack, it may jump on the sprockets resulting in serious engine damage. If the special belt tension measuring equipment is available, it should be refitted to the front run of the belt. The reading should now be between 42 and 46 units.

33 If the tension is not as specified, repeat the tensioning operation.

34 On completion, refit all disturbed components, tightening the crankshaft pulley bolt to the specified torque. Tension the alternator drivebelt and HP pump drivebelt.

7 Camshaft - removal and refitting

Note: *The following operation was carried out with the engine in the vehicle.*

Removal

1 Remove the camshaft drivebelt.

2 Remove the camshaft cover. For ease of access, remove the distributor cap and HT leads also.

3 Remove the distributor and the fuel pump from the thermostat housing.

4 Remove the camshaft lubrication manifold.

5 Lock the camshaft sprocket (eg. with a timing dowel) and remove the sprocket retaining bolt. Remove the sprocket.

6 Unbolt and remove the camshaft sprocket inner cover plate from the cylinder head.

7 Unbolt and remove the camshaft thrust plate **(see illustrations)**.

8 The camshaft bearing caps can now be removed, starting with bearing No 4 at the

distributor end. Make identifying marks if necessary then progressively loosen the bearing cap securing nuts. As the No 4 bearing is removed take care not to damage the seal between the distributor support and the bearing. Be prepared for the camshaft to spring upwards. Remove the camshaft.

Refitting

9 Commence refitting by making sure that the crankshaft is in the correct (doweled) position. If not, move it to this position to avoid possible piston/valve contact.

10 Lubricate the camshaft bearings and lower the camshaft into position so that the fourth and sixth cams are resting on the tappets. Fit the centre bearing cap so that the oil hole is towards the front.

11 Refit the remaining bearing caps and tighten them to the specified torque in a progressive sequence. The seal bearing surface should have sealant applied. If the seal was damaged during dismantling, renew it and coat with a sealing compound.

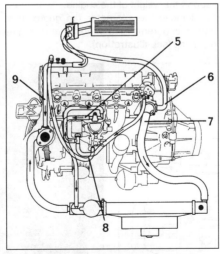

8.5a Disconnect hoses indicated for cylinder head removal

5 *Carburettor heating return hose*
6 *Water outlet duct hose*
7 *Water outlet duct hose*
8 *Inlet manifold hose*
9 *Heater coolant return pipe hose*

12 When renewing the oil seal at the camshaft sprocket end, lubricate it with engine oil and drive it into position.

13 Refit and secure the camshaft stop thrust plate.

14 Check that the camshaft endfloat is as specified and if necessary renew the thrust plate.

15 Check that the valve clearances are as specified.

16 Refit the sprocket rear cover plate, locate it correctly with a 10 mm dowel and tighten its fastenings **(see illustration)**. Fit the camshaft sprocket, dowel it and tighten its securing bolt to the specified torque.

17 Refit the fuel pump, the distributor and the lubrication manifold.

18 Refit the camshaft cover, the HT leads and the distributor cap.

19 Refit the camshaft drivebelt.

8 Cylinder head - removal and refitting

Note: *The following operation was carried out with the engine in the vehicle.*

Removal

1 Disconnect the battery earth lead.

2 Drain the cooling system.

3 Remove the air filter.

4 Disconnect and plug the feed and return hoses at the fuel pump.

5 Disconnect the coolant hoses from the thermostat housing, the inlet manifold and carburettor (heating return) **(see illustrations)**.

8.5b Coolant hose connections to carburettor auto-choke

2B

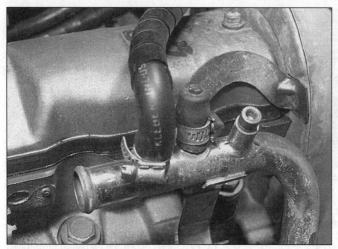

8.6a Heater coolant hose and support clamp

8.6b Dipstick guide tube support bracket

6 Detach the heater coolant return hose from its securing clamp and support lug. Unbolt the dipstick tube support bracket **(see illustrations)**.

7 On engines manufactured before March 1986, remove the engine breather support screw. Engines manufactured after March 1986 are equipped with a modified crankcase breather circuit **(see illustration)**. The oil separator unit fitted to earlier engines is no longer fitted and the rocker cover now has a breather pipe connection.

8 Disconnect the accelerator cable at the carburettor.

9 Disconnect the coolant temperature leads and the lead from the carburettor idle cut-off solenoid.

10 Unclip and remove the distributor cap, detach the HT leads from the spark plugs and place them out of the way. Also disconnect the distributor LT leads. Remove the spark plugs.

11 Detach and remove the lining from the front right-hand wheel arch. This is best achieved with the vehicle raised at the front end and supported on safety stands. The roadwheel can then be removed to improve access under the wing for guard removal and subsequent operations.

12 Locate a spanner onto the crankshaft pulley bolt and turn the engine over to align the dowel hole in the pulley with the timing recess behind it. Insert a 10 mm dowel rod to lock the crankshaft in this position. The pistons must be at the half stroke position in their cylinders.

13 Unbolt and detach the exhaust downpipe.

14 Position a jack under the sump. Place a piece of wood between the jack and sump to protect the sump, then raise the jack to support the weight of the engine.

15 Remove the alternator fan guard, then unbolt and remove the right-hand engine mounting **(see illustration)**.

16 Unbolt and remove the upper and central timing covers.

17 Loosen the camshaft drivebelt tension then disengage the belt from the camshaft sprocket.

18 Remove the camshaft cover. The cylinder head bolts can now be loosened half a turn at a time in the reverse order to that shown for tightening and then removed. Discard the bolts and obtain a new set for refitting. Note that from February 1987, Torx type cylinder head bolts are fitted, replacing the original hex-head bolts. It is not necessary to retighten these bolts once the engine has been warmed up to normal operating temperature. However, they must be renewed whenever they are disturbed.

19 Remove the cylinder head, using a couple of bars through two of the bolt holes and rocking it towards the front of the vehicle **(see illustration)**. Remove the gasket and recover any loose dowels.

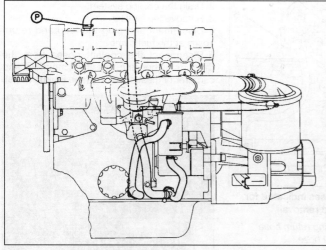

8.7 Modified crankcase breather circuit

P Rocker cover connection

8.15 Right-hand engine mounting

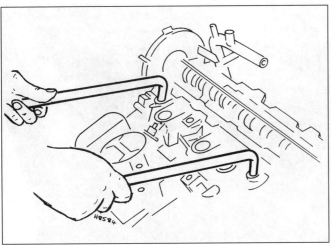

8.19 Cylinder head removal using two bars

8.20 Cylinder liners clamped with washers and bolts

20 Fit cylinder liner clamps, or large washers secured with nuts and bolts, to keep the liners in position **(see illustration)**. If the liners are disturbed, the engine will have to be removed for new seals to be fitted.

21 Before refitting the cylinder head, check that its mating faces are clean. Before removing the liner clamps, the liner protrusions must be checked.

22 The oil filter in the cylinder head should be removed and renewed before refitting the cylinder head **(see illustration)**.

Refitting

23 Commence refitting by fitting the dowels to the cylinder block. Keep the flywheel end dowel raised by inserting a 5 mm punch or large nail through the hole in the front of the block **(see illustration)**. Remove the liner clamps.

24 Fit the new gasket, dry and with the tab at the flywheel end. Lower the cylinder head into position, making sure that it mates with the dowels. Remove the punch or nail.

25 Fit the new cylinder head bolts with their threads cleaned and lightly oiled. Remember to fit the spacer to the bolt above the coolant pump.

26 Progressively tighten the bolts in the order shown to the Stage 1 specified torque **(see illustration)**.

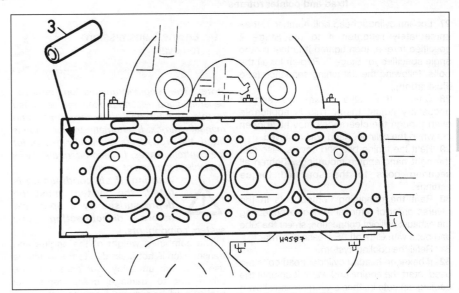

8.22 Oil filter location in cylinder head (3)

8.23 Dowel is kept raised by inserting a rod or nail beneath it

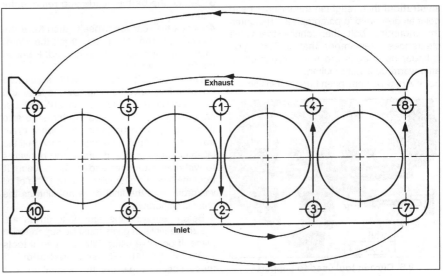

8.26 Cylinder head bolt tightening sequence

2B

8.27 Home-made disc for measuring tightening angle. Disc is fixed and pointer rotates

8.32 Loosen engine mounting bolt indicated (1)

27 Loosen cylinder head bolt number 1, then immediately retighten it to the Stage 2 specified torque, then tighten it further by the angle specified for Stage 3. Repeat for all the bolts, following the tightening sequence (see illustration).

28 Check the valve clearances and if necessary adjust them. This is applicable even though the clearances may have been set when the cylinder head was removed.

29 Refit the timing belt and covers. Also refit the right-hand engine mountings. Tighten all securing bolts to the specified torque settings.

30 Refit the remaining components in the reverse order of removal. When reconnecting the exhaust balljoint connection, smear the tube and bolts with Gripcott AF grease or similar.

31 Refill the cooling system.

32 If hexagon headed cylinder head bolts are used, start the engine and warm it up until the cooling fan cuts in, then switch off and allow it to cool for at least two hours. Loosen the engine mounting bolt indicated (see illustration) then retighten the cylinder head bolts as described in paragraph 27. Retighten the mounting bolt then check the valve clearances. Remember that if Torx type cylinder head bolts are fitted, retightening after warm-up is not required.

33 If a new belt has been fitted, retension it.

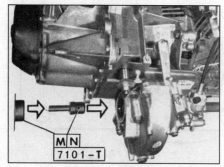

9.6 Citroën tool used to support differential sun gears

9 Engine/transmission - removal

Note: The engine/transmission removal, separation and refitting procedures described in this Chapter deal with the engine and manual gearbox. If automatic transmission is fitted, the procedures are similar except for the control linkages. Limited information was available at the time of writing.

⚠️ Warning: If air conditioning is fitted, the system must be depressurised by a Specialist before disconnecting any system components.

1 The combined weight of the engine and transmission is not great due to the extensive use of aluminium alloy, but care must be taken not to damage components. An assistant will be required for some tasks.

2 Unbolt and remove the bonnet.

3 Detach the battery leads and remove the battery.

4 Chock the rear roadwheels, then raise the vehicle at the front so that the front roadwheels are clear of the ground. Remove the front roadwheels.

5 The driveshafts must now be separated from the final drive housing. On the left-hand side, unbolt and release the anti-roll bar connecting link, then separate the stub axle from the steering balljoint. Position a drain tray under the final drive housing then pull the left-hand driveshaft and wheel hub outwards to withdraw the inner end of the driveshaft from the final drive housing. About 1 litre of oil will drain from the final drive housing as the shaft is withdrawn.

6 Before removing the right-hand driveshaft, the differential sun gears must be supported in place, if possible using Citroën special tools 7101-TM and 7101-TN (see illustration). If these special tools are not available, it is possible to improvise using a suitable length of

wooden dowel or tube approximately 24 mm in diameter, chamfered at the leading end to allow entry into the side gear splines.

7 The right-hand driveshaft is disconnected from the differential housing by removing it completely.

8 The hydraulic circuit must now be depressurised.

9 Remove the air cleaner unit. Also unbolt and remove the air cleaner support bracket (see illustration).

10 Drain the cooling system and remove the radiator.

11 Disconnect the throttle cable from the carburettor by releasing the inner cable nipple from the throttle quadrant then pulling the inner/outer cable from its support bracket. Place the cable out of the way.

12 Disconnect the vent hose from the carburettor (this hose runs down to the radiator left-hand lower side).

13 Disconnect the fuel supply hose to the fuel pump and plug the hose.

14 Note the positions of the spark plug HT leads in the location clips on the top face of the cam cover and release them. Detach the HT leads from the spark plugs and release the distributor cap. Disconnect the LT leads from the distributor, then place the cap and leads out of the way.

9.9 Air cleaner support bracket

9.16 Reversing light switch and lead connections

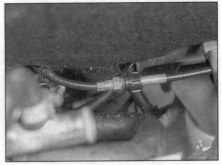

9.21 Speedometer drive cable connection between engine and bulkhead

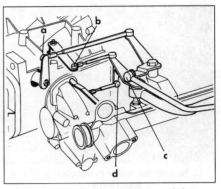

9.26 Disconnect gear linkages at joints a, b, c and d

15 Disconnect the wiring harness connection blocks under the battery support frame, also the wiring terminal block in line with the battery positive lead.
16 Disconnect the reversing light switch leads from the gearbox (see illustration).
17 Undo the retaining nut and detach the battery earth lead from the battery support tray. Remove the tray.
18 Disconnect the clutch cable from the lever by prising the lever rearwards.
19 Disconnect the battery earth lead and the braided earth strap from the gearbox.
20 Detach the diagnostic socket lead connector at the left-hand side under the ignition coil.
21 Disconnect the speedometer drive cable (see illustration).
22 Disconnect the heater coolant hoses at the bulkhead.

23 Disconnect the hydraulic suction pipe from the HP pump and the hydraulic pump from the pressure regulator outlet. Plug the pipes to prevent fluid loss and the ingress of dirt.
24 Detach the hydraulic pipe support clip from the alternator support strap.
25 Disconnect the rigid pipe from the pressure regulator unit and detach the pipe support clip. Position the pipe out of the way, but do not over-distort the pipe. Plug the end of the pipe.
26 Disconnect the gearchange linkages at the points indicated (see illustration). The linkage rods have balljoints which are simply prised apart.
27 Working from underneath the vehicle, unbolt the exhaust downpipe and disconnect it from the manifold.
28 Unclip and detach the coolant bottom hose at connection on the right-hand rear lower corner of the engine. As the hose is pulled free from the connection allow for additional coolant spillage.
29 Fit the lifting sling and hoist into position. Take the weight of the engine and transmission. Arrange the lifting sling so that when connected to the lifting eyes it will allow the gearbox to be tilted downwards at an angle of about 45° when the units are being lifted out (see illustration).
30 Working underneath the vehicle, detach the torque link by unscrewing and removing its through-bolt. If necessary position a jack under the engine to allow it to be raised and allow the bolt to be removed (see illustration).

31 Unbolt and detach the left-hand side transmission mounting (see illustration).
32 Unbolt and remove the right-hand upper engine mounting.
33 Check around the engine/transmission to ensure that all attachments are disconnected. Before lifting out the unit, it is advisable to position a protector plate of some description between the height corrector unit and the engine to prevent damage to the rubber dust cover during removal.
34 Carefully lift the engine/transmission upwards, tilting the transmission downwards as the unit is manoeuvred from the engine compartment. Assistance is necessary to guide the unit clear of its surrounding fittings (see illustration).
35 Once clear of the vehicle, the engine/transmission can be removed for cleaning and repairs as necessary.

10 Engine dismantling - general information

Refer to Section 8 in Part A of this Chapter .

11 Engine dismantling - ancillary items

The extent of engine ancillary items to be removed is dependent on the extent to which the engine is to be dismantled and repaired.

9.29 Engine lift support bracket - front right-hand side

9.30 Torque link and through-bolt (arrowed)

9.31 Left-hand side transmission mounting

9.34 Engine and transmission removal

2B

12.1a Starter motor is secured by three Allen bolts . . .

12.1b . . . and a mounting bracket

13.12 Lock camshaft sprocket with a 10 mm rod

Refer to Section 9 in Part A of this Chapter and remove those items listed which are applicable, ignoring references to the coolant pump and, if the cylinder head is to be removed, the exhaust manifold. These two items are best removed later during the engine dismantling procedures.

Note that the clutch unit is removed after the engine and gearbox are separated.

12 Engine - separation from transmission

1 If still in position, unbolt and remove the starter motor (see illustrations).
2 Unbolt and remove the remaining engine-to-transmission bolts.
3 Support the engine and pull the transmission away from it. Do not allow the weight of the transmission to hang on the primary shaft. Recover any loose dowels.

13 Engine - complete dismantling

1 Support the engine on a clean bench or strong table.
2 Remove any remaining ancillary components still attached to the engine.
3 The exhaust manifold may be removed now, or it can be left in place to serve as a handle until the head is removed.

4 Unbolt and remove the crankshaft pulley. Jam the flywheel teeth when undoing the pulley bolt to stop the crankshaft rotating.
5 Remove the camshaft drivebelt covers, noting the location of the various sizes of bolt.
6 Unbolt and remove the camshaft cover.
7 Rotate the crankshaft by means of the flywheel until a 10 mm diameter rod can be passed through the hole in the camshaft sprocket and into the timing recess. The pistons are now at mid-stroke so piston/valve contact cannot occur.
8 Release the camshaft drivebelt tensioner by slackening its nuts (two at the front and one behind the front plate) and using the square end of the cam spindle to bring the cam into a horizontal position.
9 Remove the camshaft drivebelt, taking care not to kink it and noting its direction of travel if it is to be re-used.
10 Unbolt and remove the camshaft drivebelt tensioner.
11 Remove the belt side covers and crankshaft sprocket. Recover the Woodruff key.
12 Unbolt and remove the camshaft sprocket. Restrain the sprocket from turning if necessary using the 10 mm diameter rod inserted through the timing hole in the sprocket (see illustration).

13.22 Oil pump removal

13 Unbolt and remove the engine mounting bracket, the camshaft sprocket backplate and the coolant pump.
14 Slacken the ten cylinder head bolts, working in the reverse sequence of that used for tightening. Remove the bolts and washers.
15 Remove the cylinder head. If it seems to be stuck, use a couple of metal rods in two of the bolt holes to rock it free. Do not attempt to hammer or lever it off. Retrieve the two locating dowels if they are loose.
16 Fit liner clamps if it is not proposed to remove the pistons and liners then invert the engine.
17 Unbolt and remove the flywheel. It is doweled so it can only be refitted one way.
18 Remove the suction drain pipe from the side of the sump.
19 Unbolt and remove the sump. Note the location of the three Allen-headed bolts (see illustration).
20 Remove the bolts which secure the oil pump, noting the special centring bolt at the rear.
21 Unbolt and remove the oil seal carrier plate.
22 Lower the oil pump into the engine so that its chain can be removed. Withdraw the pump and recover the spacer, the dowel and the chain (see illustration).
23 Pull the oil pump sprocket off the crankshaft and recover the Woodruff key.
24 Unscrew the connecting rod cap bolts. Before removing the caps, check that they are marked in numerical order, also the connecting rods, liners and pistons. Mark them if they are not (see illustration).

13.19 Location of three Allen head bolts

13.24 Relative positions of cylinder liners and block must be marked before removal

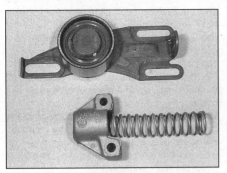

14.9 Camshaft (timing) drivebelt tensioner components

25 If the cylinder liners are being removed, then the pistons, rods and liners can be lifted out of the block as individual units, but mark their relative positions.
26 Remove the bolts from main bearing caps 1, 2, 4 and 5. Also remove the two nuts and the two side bolts from the centre cap. Make alignment marks on the bearing caps and remove them. Keep the bearing shells with their caps if they are to be re-used. Recover the thrustwasher segments from either side of No 2 bearing cap.
27 Remove the oil seal from the flywheel end of the crankshaft.
28 Lift the crankshaft out of the crankcase. Recover the upper half main bearing shells and the other two thrustwasher segments.
29 If the cylinder liners have been left clamped in position in the cylinder block, their protrusions above the cylinder block face must be checked before reassembling the engine.

14 Engine - examination and renovation

General information

1 Refer to Section 12 in Part A of this Chapter.

Crankshaft and main bearings

2 Refer to Section 12 in Part A of this Chapter.
3 Later 171 engines (from 1984 on), in common with 159 engines, have no spigot bush in the crankshaft tail. The diameter of the

14.10 Separating two halves of oil pump

gearbox input shaft is correspondingly increased.
4 Therefore, on 171 engines, if the later type crankshaft is being fitted and being mated to an earlier type input shaft, it will be necessary to obtain and insert a spigot bush.
5 If the reverse situation applies (new input shaft and old crankshaft), extract the spigot bush.

Big-end bearings

6 Refer to Section 12 in Part A of this Chapter.

Cylinder liners, pistons, gudgeon pins and connecting rods

7 Refer to Section 12 in Part A of this Chapter.

Timing drivebelt, sprockets and tensioner

8 Renew the drivebelt as a matter of course unless it is in perfect condition and is known to have covered only a nominal mileage. Renew the sprockets if they are damaged.
9 The drivebelt tensioner should be examined for roughness of the wheel bearing and wear or distortion of the spring (where applicable). Renew as necessary (see illustration). The wheel, bearing and backplate must be renewed as an assembly.

Oil pump

10 Remove the six bolts which hold the two halves of the oil pump together. Separate the halves, being prepared for the release of the relief valve spring and plunger (see illustration).

11 Inspect the rotors and their housing for wear and damage. No wear limits are published for this pump. Any visible wear on the moving parts suggests that renewal is necessary. With the exception of the relief valve spring and plunger, individual components are not available (see illustrations).
12 Lubricate the pump components well before reassembly. Bolt the two halves together, being careful not to trap the spring.
13 If the pump is to be renewed, it is wise to renew the chain and the crankshaft sprocket also.

Camshaft and tappets

14 Inspect the camshaft lobes and bearing journals for wear and damage. If wear and damage is evident, renewal is probably necessary. Also inspect the bearing surfaces in the cylinder head and bearing caps.
15 Clean the camshaft lubrication manifold with solvent and then blow through it with compressed air. All the holes must be clear (see illustration).
16 Inspect the tappets for wear and scuffing and renew as necessary. New tappets must be fitted if the camshaft is renewed, it is also advisable to renew the valve springs.

Flywheel and starter ring gear

17 Refer to Section 12 in Part A of this Chapter but ignore paragraph 49 as this is already dealt with in this Section.

2B

15 Cylinder head - dismantling, decarbonising, inspection and reassembly

Dismantling

1 Unbolt and remove the inlet manifold (with carburettor) and the exhaust manifold. Renew their respective gaskets.
2 Remove the camshaft from the cylinder head.
3 Remove the tappets and shims, identifying their locations if they are to be re-used (see illustration).
4 Extract the oil filter gauze from the oilway.
5 Proceed as described in Section 13 in Part A of this Chapter to remove the valves.

14.11a Inspect pump gears for excessive wear

14.11b Oil pump relief valve spring and plunger

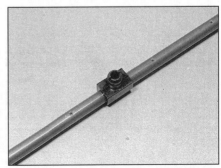

14.15 Pinholes of lubrication manifold must be clear

15.3 Remove tappets and shims and keep in order

Decarbonising and inspection

6 Proceed as described in Section 13 in Part A of this Chapter and clean and inspect the various engine components. Note, however, that the makers state that no machining of the cylinder head surface is permitted. A warped head must therefore be renewed. Factory exchange cylinder heads may have had 0.2 mm machined off the mating face. These heads are identified by the letter R stamped on a boss at the distributor end of the head. A gasket 0.2 mm thicker than normal must be used with such a head. The thicker gasket is identified by a cut-out in the tab at the clutch end.

Reassembly

7 Commence reassembly of the cylinder head by fining new valve stem oil seals into position, then locate the valves, the spring seat washers (lubricated with clean engine oil), the springs and collets. Oil the valve stems liberally. A smear of grease will hold the collets in position while the spring is compressed. The valve springs can be fitted either way up.

8 Lubricate the tappet bores. Secure each shim to its valve stem with a dab of grease and carefully fit the tappets. If new components have been fitted so that the valve clearances are unknown, fit the thinnest possible shims to all valves.

9 Fit the camshaft to the head and oil its lobes and journals (see illustration). Fit the bearing caps, making sure that the middle ones are the right way round. Progressively tighten the bearing cap nuts to the specified torque.

10 Fit the camshaft thrust plate and tighten its securing bolt.

11 Press the lubrication manifold into position (see illustration).

12 Fit a new filter gauze in the oilway (see illustration).

13 Fit the coolant outlet housing, using a new gasket. Fit the thermostat and its elbow to the housing, again with a new gasket.

14 Fit the inlet and exhaust manifolds, using new gaskets, and tighten their fastenings to the specified torque.

15 Fit and secure the fuel pump (new gasket)

and the distributor. If alignment marks were not made when dismantling, set the distributor in mid-slot. The drive is offset so it can only be fitted one way.

16 Fit the carburettor and its heat insulator.

17 Fit a new oil seal to the sprocket end of the camshaft, using a piece of tube to drive it home.

18 If valve clearance adjustment is to be carried out now, temporarily fit the camshaft sprocket and stand the cylinder head on wooden blocks so that open valves do not strike the work surface.

16 Engine reassembly - general information

Refer to Section 14 in Part A of this Chapter.

17 Engine - preparation for reassembly

Refer to Section 15 in Part A of this Chapter.

18 Cylinder liners - checking protrusion

Refer to Section 16 in Part A of this Chapter.

19 Engine - complete reassembly

Pistons and liners

1 Reassemble the piston rings to the pistons and the pistons to the liners. Orientate the piston rings as shown (see illustration) and arrange the oil control rings so that the rail gaps are offset to each other and from the gudgeon pin hole by 20 to 30 mm.

2 The piston and liner assemblies can be fitted to the crankcase at this stage or, if preferred, after the crankshaft has been fitted.

15.9 Fit camshaft into position

15.11 Refit camshaft lubrication manifold

15.12 Insert oil filter gauze in cylinder head oilway

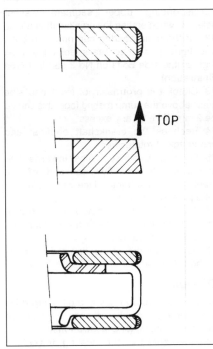

19.1 Fitting direction for standard piston rings

Crankshaft

3 Position the cylinder block for access to the bottom end and fit the main bearing upper shells. Also fit the thrustwasher segments to No 2 bearing, grooved sides outwards (see illustration), retaining them with a smear of

19.3 Fitting thrustwasher upper segments

grease. It will be noted that the main bearing shells supplied comprise plain and grooved type half shells which differ according to engine type as follows:

Early engines

4 On these engines there are two grooved half shells supplied, these being fitted to the No 2 and No 4 bearings on the top (crankcase) side.

Engines manufactured prior to July 1986

5 On these engines, the bearing set contains seven grooved and three plain bearing shells, one plain bearing shell being located at the top (crankcase) side of No 3 bearing and the other two fitted to the No 2 and No 4 bearing caps (see illustrations).

Engines manufactured after July 1986

6 On these engines, there is a further arrangement for the location and fitting of the

bearing shells. The plain bearing shells are fitted to the bearing caps of Nos 2 to 5 bearings inclusive. The No 1 bearing cap and upper half-shells are all grooved (see illustration). The bearing shell location lug recesses in the crankcase are changed to suit the new bearings. Earlier and later-type shell bearings are thus not compatible. When ordering replacement bearing shells, it is therefore important to be specific on which type is required.

Engines manufactured after July 1987

7 As from this date, grooved shells are used in the crankcase seats, and plain shells in the bearing caps.

All engine types

8 Oil the bearing shells and lower the crankshaft into position, taking care not to dislodge the thrustwasher segments (see illustration). Inject some clean engine oil into the crankshaft oilways.

9 Check the crankshaft endfloat by pushing it in one direction then the other along its length. A dial gauge or feeler blades should be used to measure the endfloat. If the endfloat measured is not within the specified limits change the thrustwasher segments and fit alternatives of suitable thickness. Thrustwashers are available in a choice of five thicknesses.

10 Fit new side seals to No 1 main bearing cap. Carefully fit the cap with its bearing shell. Using clean engine oil, lubricate the shell, the sides of the cap and the locating surfaces in the block. There is a risk of displacing or

2B

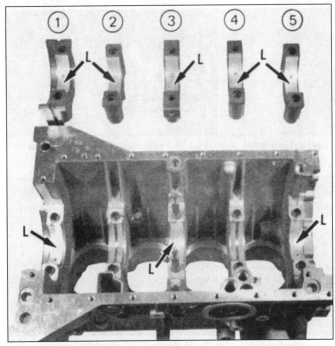

19.5a Main bearing cap fitting positions - early type

L Plain bearing half shell positions

19.5b Main bearing cap fitting positions - later type

L Plain bearing half shell positions

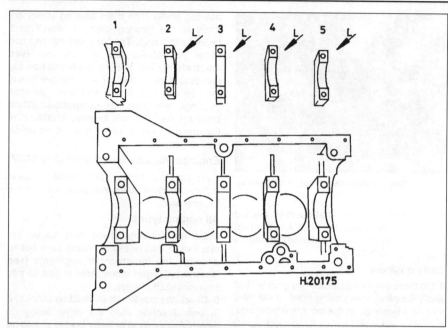
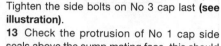

19.6 Main bearing shell locations - BX 16 and BX 19 from July 1986

L Plain shells in caps

distorting the side seals as the cap is fitted, so protect them with a couple of feeler blades or thin strips of tin which can be withdrawn rearwards after fitting the cap **(see illustrations)**.

11 Fit the shells to the other main bearing caps, lubricate them and fit the caps. Fit the thrustwasher segments (grooved side outwards) to No 2 cap. Observe the mating marks made when dismantling. The lug on each bearing cap points towards the timing sprockets. Ensure that the thrustwasher segment on each side of the No 2 main bearing cap is of equal thickness to the

corresponding upper segment washer selected when setting the crankshaft endfloat.

12 Fit the main bearing cap nuts and bolts and tighten them to the specified torque. Tighten the side bolts on No 3 cap last **(see illustration)**.

13 Check the protrusion of No 1 cap side seals above the sump mating face, this should be 2 mm. Trim off any excess.

14 Recheck the crankshaft endfloat and ensure that it rotates freely.

15 Fit a new oil seal (lips inwards and lubricated) to the flywheel end of the crankshaft. Drive it into place with a piece of tube **(see illustration)**.

16 If not already fitted, fit new O-ring seals to the cylinder liners, then fit the pistons and liners **(see illustration)**.

17 Reconnect the connecting rod big-ends to the crankshaft.

Oil pump

18 Fit the Woodruff key and oil pump drive sprocket to the crankshaft nose. Fit the chain over the sprocket **(see illustrations)**.

19 Make sure that the locating dowel is in position, then engage the oil pump sprocket in the chain and offer the pump to the block. Engage the pump on the dowel, then lift it up far enough to slide the L-shaped spacer in underneath it **(see illustrations)**.

20 Fit the oil pump securing bolts, remembering that the special centring bolt is nearest the flywheel, and tighten them to the

19.8 Fitting the crankshaft

19.10a Fitting a side seal to No 1 main bearing

19.10b Protecting side seals with feeler blades

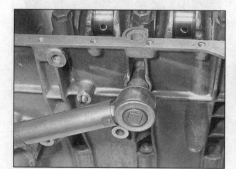

19.12 Tightening No. 3 main bearing side bolt

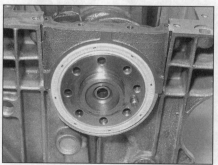

19.15 Crankshaft oil seal - flywheel end

19.16 Arrow mark on piston crowns must point to camshaft sprocket end (letter and number indicate liner and gudgeon pin grade)

19.18a Fitting oil pump drive sprocket

19.18b Oil pump drive chain

19.19a Fitting oil pump - chain must be engaged first

specified torque. Generously lubricate the pump and the chain with clean engine oil (see illustration).

21 Refit the pulley oil seal carrier plate, using silicone jointing compound on the block mating faces. Fit a new oil seal, lubricated lips inwards, and drive it home with a piece of tube.

22 Fit the sump, using a new gasket, and tighten its securing bolts progressively to the specified torque. Remember the correct location of the three Allen-headed bolts.

23 Refit the suction drain pipe, using a new O-ring. Do not overtighten the securing nuts, refer to the *Specifications* for the correct torque setting.

Flywheel and clutch

24 Fit the flywheel to the crankshaft flange and secure with new bolts, using thread locking compound. Tighten the bolts progressively to the specified torque.

25 Fit the clutch friction plate and pressure plate.

Cylinder head

26 Position the engine for access to the cylinder head face. Rotate the crankshaft to bring the pistons to mid-stroke (none at TDC), then remove the liner clamps.

27 Check that the head mating surface is clean and that the two locating dowels are present. Place a 5 mm diameter rod in the hole beneath the dowel at the flywheel end to stop the dowel being displaced downwards.

28 Fit a new cylinder head gasket, dry and with the protruding tab at the flywheel end (see illustration).

29 Lower the assembled cylinder head into position, making sure that it engages with the dowels.

30 Fit the cylinder head bolts, with their threads clean and lightly oiled. Remember to fit the spacer to the bolt above the coolant pump.

31 Tighten the cylinder head bolts progressively in the order shown in illustration 8.26 to the Stage 1 specified torque.

32 Slacken cylinder head bolt number 1, then immediately retighten it to the Stage 2 specified torque, then tighten it further through the angle specified for Stage 3. Repeat this operation on the other bolts in sequence.

Camshaft drivebelt

33 Fit the camshaft sprocket backplate, using a 10 mm rod through the timing hole to locate it precisely before tightening its securing bolts.

19.19b Locating oil pump spacer

34 Fit the camshaft sprocket, washer and bolt. Use the 10 mm rod to lock the sprocket in the correct position and tighten the bolt to the specified torque. Remove the rod.

35 Fit and secure the coolant pump, using a new gasket. Tighten the bolts to the specified torque.

36 Fit the covers around the coolant pump, noting the locations of the various special bolts (see illustration). Smear the large bolt threads with sealant.

37 Fit the Woodruff key and the crankshaft sprocket.

38 Fit the camshaft drivebelt tensioner but leave the nuts slack. Compress the spring by locking the cam in the horizontal position.

19.20 Special bolt location

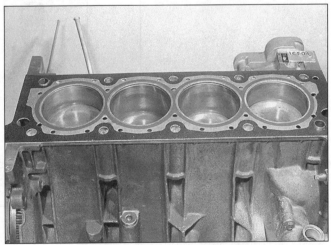

19.28 Head gasket correctly fitted

39 Temporarily fit the crankshaft pulley, its washer and bolt. Lightly tighten the bolt. Carefully turn the crankshaft until a 10 mm rod will pass through the timing hole in the pulley and into the timing recess. If piston/valve contact occurs, back off and try again with the camshaft in a slightly different position. Do not try to force the crankshaft if a piston contacts a valve.

40 Use the 10 mm rod to position the camshaft sprocket, then remove the crankshaft pulley and fit the camshaft drivebelt. Be careful not to kink the belt as it is fitted and observe the arrows showing the correct direction of rotation. The stripes on the belt should align with the timing marks on the sprockets.

41 Withdraw the timing rod. Tension the belt by turning the tensioner cam so that it points downwards and secure it with its locknut. Tighten the two nuts at the front of the tensioner.

42 Turn the crankshaft through two full turns in the normal direction of rotation. Rotate it further to bring Nos 1 and 4 pistons to TDC with the valves on No 1 cylinder open.

43 Slacken the two nuts and the cam locknut on the drivebelt tensioner, then retighten them.

44 Temporarily refit the crankshaft pulley, rotate the crankshaft and check that the timing rods can be inserted simultaneously in the crankshaft pulley and camshaft sprocket holes. If not, remove the belt and try again. Remove the pulley.

45 Fit the engine mounting bracket and tighten its bolts.

46 Refit the drivebelt covers, but note that they will have to be removed later to retension the drivebelt if a new one has been fitted.

47 Fit the crankshaft pulley, washer and bolt, making sure that the Woodruff key is still in position. Jam the starter ring gear teeth and tighten the bolt to the specified torque.

48 Refit the camshaft cover, noting the copper washer at the sprocket end bolt and using a new gasket.

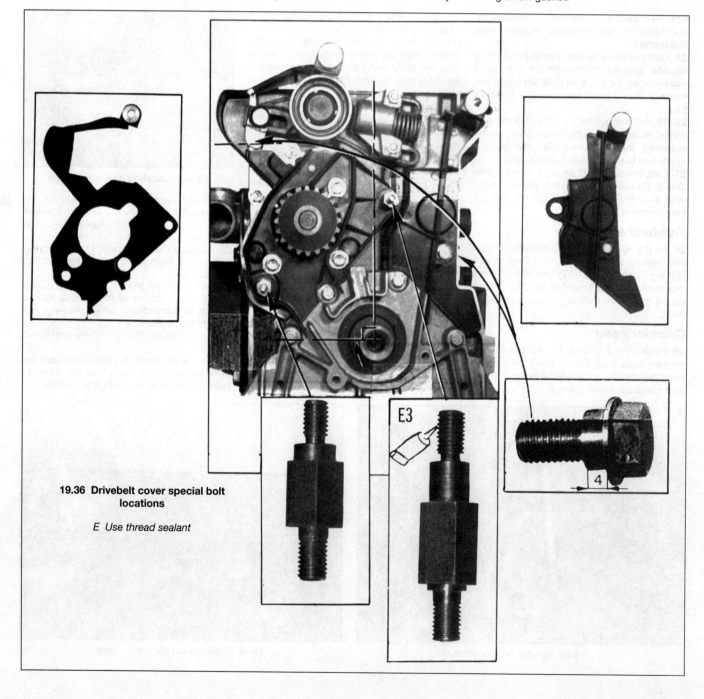

19.36 Drivebelt cover special bolt locations

E Use thread sealant

Ancillary components

49 Refit the ancillary components listed below. It may be preferable to leave delicate items such as the alternator and distributor until after the engine is refitted:
a) *Oil filler/breather pipe*
b) *Oil pressure switch*
c) *Coolant inlet housing and pipe **(see illustration)***
d) *Spark plugs, distributor and HT leads*
e) *HP pump and drivebelt **(see illustration)***
f) *Alternator and drivebelt*

50 Fit a new oil filter with its sealing ring well lubricated. Tighten by hand only.

20 Engine - reconnection to transmission

1 Check that the clutch release components are correctly fitted in the gearbox and that the pressure plate and friction disc are fitted to the flywheel. On automatic transmission models, check that the torque converter is properly located.
2 Smear a little anti-seize compound on the nose and splines of the transmission primary (input) shaft, then offer the transmission to the engine. Do not allow the weight of the transmission to hang on the input shaft. If the input shaft does not wish to pass the clutch, it is possible that the clutch disc is not centred. Check also that the transmission input shaft is compatible with the spigot recess in the crankshaft.
3 Engage the engine-to-transmission dowels and loosely fit the bolts. Also fit the starter

19.49a Securing coolant pipe to inlet housing

motor, which is secured by three Allen bolts and a bracket.
4 On manual gearbox models, fit the clutch cable guide and pivot brackets.

21 Engine/transmission - refitting

1 Arrange the lift sling so that the gearbox tilts down at an angle of 45° when the engine/transmission is raised.
2 An assistant should be at hand to guide the unit into position as it is lowered. Take care not to damage any associated components within the engine compartment, the hydraulic lines in particular. The suspension height corrector control unit can be protected from possible damage by shielding it with a suitable piece of sheet metal. Also, before lowering the combined units into position,

19.49b Refitting HP pump and drivebelt

check that the gearchange return levers are set parallel to the steering gear unit.
3 Carefully lower the engine/transmission into the engine compartment, guiding the gearbox down forwards of the battery tray support. When clear of the support, swivel the gearbox rearwards then raise it so that the mounting stud enters the mounting slot. Locate the mounting rubber (cone face upwards), then fit the flat washer and nut. Do not fully tighten it at this stage.
4 Further lower the lifting hoist to guide the engine down so that it engages with the right-hand mounting and its torque link (underneath towards the rear).
5 Locate a plain nut and washer to secure the right-hand mounting and insert the through-bolt and fit the self-locking nut to secure the torque link.
6 Tighten the mounting nuts and the torque link nut and bolt to their specified torque settings **(see illustration)**.

2B

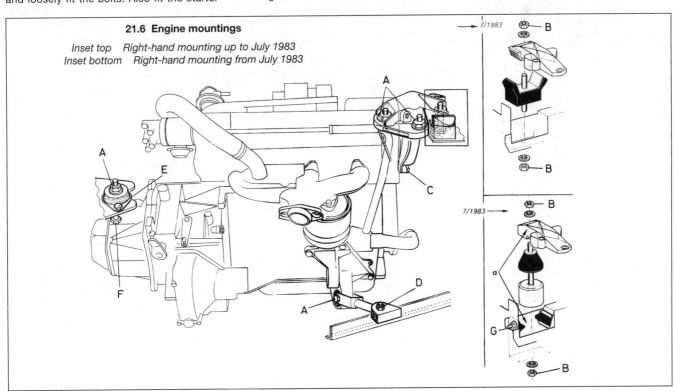
21.6 Engine mountings

Inset top   Right-hand mounting up to July 1983
Inset bottom   Right-hand mounting from July 1983

7 Reconnect the following items, referring where necessary to the relevant Section or Chapter for further details:
  a) *The gearchange link rods*
  b) *The speedometer cable*
  c) *The coolant hoses to the coolant manifold located between the cylinder head and the bulkhead*
  d) *Fuel feed and return hoses*
  e) *The HP pump unit hoses. Retighten the regulator bleed screw*
  f) *Accelerator cable to the carburettor*
  g) *Wiring harnesses*
  h) *Clutch cable to release arm. Lubricate the pushrod with grease at each end before assembling*
  i) *Exhaust downpipe*
  j) *Radiator and coolant hoses*
  k) *Braided earth straps to the gearbox, battery support tray and battery*

8 When refitting the alternator guard, press the retaining grommet into the right-hand engine mounting bracket as shown using a rod and pliers **(see illustration)**. Take care not to pierce the bottom end of the grommet and smear it with a little soapy solution to ease fitting.

21.8 Method devised for securing alternator guard retaining grommet

9 The driveshafts and associated steering/suspension components should be refitted in accordance with the instructions given in the appropriate Chapter. Refit the right-hand drive shaft first.
10 Before refitting the air filter and air ducts, check around the engine/transmission to ensure that all fittings are securely and correctly made.
11 Top-up and bleed the cooling system.
12 Top-up the engine oil level, having checked that the sump plug is securely fitted.
13 Top-up the gearbox oil level with the specified quantity of oil. Note that the gearbox filler plug is not a level plug.

22 Engine - initial start-up after overhaul

1 Follow the check procedures described in paragraphs 1 to 7 inclusive in Section 19 in Part A of this Chapter.
2 If hexagon headed cylinder head bolts are fitted, allow the engine to cool for at least two hours. Loosen the bolt which secures the engine right-hand mounting bracket to the block, then retighten the cylinder head bolts as described in Section 8. Tighten the mounting bracket bolt on completion. No subsequent retightening is necessary. Note that where Torx type cylinder head bolts are fitted, retightening after warm-up is not required.
3 Recheck the valve clearances.
4 If a new camshaft drivebelt was fitted then retension it.

Chapter 2 Part C:
K1G engine

Contents

Degrees of difficulty

Easy, suitable for novice with little experience 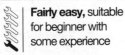	Fairly easy, suitable for beginner with some experience	Fairly difficult, suitable for competent DIY mechanic	Difficult, suitable for experienced DIY mechanic	Very difficult, suitable for expert DIY or professional

Specifications

Specifications are as for the type 150 engine (see Chapter 2A) except for the following:

General
Model application:
BX 14 after August 1988 .... K1G
Maximum power DIN (BHP) .... 72 at 5600 rpm
Maximum torque DIN (lbf ft) .... 78 at 3400 rpm

Valves
Valve clearance (cold):
  Inlet .... 0.20 mm
  Exhaust .... 0.40 mm

Valve timing
Inlet opens* .... 7°14' BTDC
Inlet closes* .... 39° 45' ABDC
Exhaust opens* .... 54° 30' BBDC
Exhaust closes* .... 0° 45' BTDC
*With valve clearance of 0.7 mm

Crankshaft
Endfloat .... 0.052 to 0.452 mm

Cylinder liners
Protrusion from block - without seal .... 0.03 to 0.10 mm
Protrusion difference between liners .... 0.05 mm

Lubrication system
Oil pressure at 90°C (194°F):
  650 rpm .... 1.5 bar
  4000 rpm .... 4.0 bar
Oil filter .... Champion F104
Oil capacity - with filter change .... 3.5 litres (6.2 pints)
Dipstick minimum to maximum .... 1.4 litres (2.5 pints)

Torque wrench settings

	Nm	lbf ft
Crankshaft pulley	102	74
Camshaft sprocket	82	59
Big-end bearing cap	39	28
Flywheel	66	48
Clutch pressure plate bolts	15	11
Distributor/fuel pump housing	8	6
Camshaft thrust fork	17	13
Thermostat housing	8	6
Main bearing cap casting main bearing bolts:		
Stage 1	21	15
Stage 2	Angle-tighten a further 45°	
Oil pump	8	6
Sump	8	6
Main bearing cap casting to block	8	6
Coolant pump housing:		
8 mm bolt	31	22
6 mm bolts	51	37
Cylinder head bolts:		
Stage 1	21	15
Stage 2	Angle-tighten a further 240°	
Timing belt tensioner	21	15
Timing cover	6	4
Valve cover	5	4
Dipstick tube	15	11
Oil pressure switch	29	21
Oil filter	15	11

1 General information and precautions

General information

The K1G engine is fitted to all Citroën BX 14 models after August 1988. It is an all-alloy unit and although the dimensions, clearances and tolerances are similar to those of the type 150C engine dealt with in Chapter 2A, there are several major differences. These differences include the camshaft drive, which is of toothed belt type, and the oil pump, which is chain-driven from the crankshaft.

Precautions

Because of the unusual layout of the engine and transmission systems, extra care and attention are necessary during maintenance and overhaul procedures which, in many instances, differ from more conventional systems.

Read through the various Sections concerned before tackling any job, and analyse the instructions, so that any snags or possible difficulties can be noted in advance. Because the sub-assembly castings are made from aluminium alloy it is of utmost importance that, where specified, all fastenings are tightened to the correct torque and, in some instances, in the correct sequence.

2 Oil filter - removal and refitting

Refer to Chapter 1, Section 9.

3 Major operations possible with engine in vehicle

Note: *Since the sump and cylinder head can be removed in situ, it is possible to renew the pistons, liners and big-end bearings without removing the engine. However, this is not recommended, since the tasks can be performed more easily with the engine removed*

The following components can be removed and refitted with the engine in the vehicle:
a) Timing belt and camshaft
b) Cylinder head
c) Sump and oil pump
d) Clutch and flywheel (after removal of gearbox)

4 Major operations requiring engine removal

The engine must be removed for the following operations:
a) Removal and refitting of the transmission
b) Removal and refitting of the crankshaft and main bearings
c) Removal and refitting of the piston and connecting rod assemblies - see Note, Section 3
d) Renewal of the big-end bearings - see Note, Section 3

5 Valve rocker clearances - checking and adjustment

Refer to Chapter 1, Section 21.

6 Camshaft drivebelt - removal and refitting

Note: *If there is the slightest doubt about the condition of the timing belt then it must be renewed.*
Note: *The following operation can be carried out with the engine in the vehicle.*

Removal

1 Disconnect the battery earth lead.
2 Remove the hydraulic pump (outer) and the alternator (inner) drivebelts.
3 Remove the rocker cover and remove the rubber gasket from the cover (see illustrations).
4 Remove the two spacers and baffle plate from the studs (see illustrations).
5 Unbolt the upper timing cover, followed by the intermediate cover and lower cover (see illustrations).
6 Turn the engine clockwise, using a socket on the crankshaft sprocket bolt, until the small hole in the camshaft sprocket is aligned with the corresponding hole in the cylinder head. Insert the shank of a close-fitting twist drill into the holes (see illustration).
7 Align the TDC holes in the flywheel and cylinder block rear flange, then insert a further twist drill or long bolt (see illustration).

6.3a Removing a rocker cover nut

6.3b Removing rocker cover gasket

6.4a Remove rocker cover spacers (arrowed) . . .

6.4b . . . and baffle plate

6.5a Unbolting upper timing cover

6.5b Removing upper timing cover

2C

6.5c Removing intermediate timing cover

6.5d Removing lower timing cover

contaminate the timing belt with oil

10 Engage the timing belt with the crankshaft sprocket then, keeping it taut, feed it onto the camshaft sprocket, around the tensioner pulley, and onto the coolant pump sprocket.

11 Loosen the nut and turn the tensioner roller anti-clockwise by hand. Tighten the nut.

12 Citroën dealers use the special tool shown **(see illustration)** to tension the timing belt. A similar tool may be fabricated using an 8.0 cm long arm and a 1.5 kg (3.3 lb) weight. The torque applied to the roller will approximate 12 Kgf (10.5 lbf in). Pre-tension the timing belt with the tool and tighten the nut, then remove the timing pins and rotate the crankshaft through two complete turns. Loosen the nut and allow the roller to re-position itself. Tighten the nut.

13 If the special tool is not available, an approximate setting may be achieved by turning the roller hub anti-clockwise, until it is

8 Loosen the timing belt tensioner roller nut **(see illustration)**, turn the tensioner clockwise using a screwdriver or square drive in the special hole, then re-tighten the nut.

9 Mark the normal direction of rotation on the

timing belt, then remove it from the camshaft, coolant pump, and crankshaft sprockets.

Refitting

Caution: Take care not to kink or

6.6 Camshaft sprocket held at TDC

6.7 Using long bolt (arrowed) to align TDC holes in flywheel and cylinder block

6.8 Loosening timing belt tensioner roller nut

just possible to turn the timing belt through 90° by finger and thumb midway between the crankshaft and camshaft sprockets. The square in the roller hub should then be directly below the adjustment nut, and the deflection of the belt in the midway position should be approximately 6.0 mm. If using this method, the tension should be re-checked by a Citroën dealer at the earliest opportunity.

14 Refit the lower, intermediate, and upper timing covers, then tighten the bolts (see illustration).

15 Adjust the valve clearances.

16 Refit the baffle plate with its edges pointing downwards, followed by the two spacers.

17 Fit the rubber gasket to the rocker cover, locate the cover in position and tighten the nuts.

18 Refit and tension the hydraulic pump and the alternator drivebelts.

19 Reconnect the battery earth lead.

---

7 Cylinder head - removal and refitting

Note: *The following operation can be carried out with the engine in the vehicle*

Note: *Illustrations for paragraphs 21 to 26 inclusive can be found in Section 6*

Removal

1 Disconnect the battery.
2 Drain the cooling system.

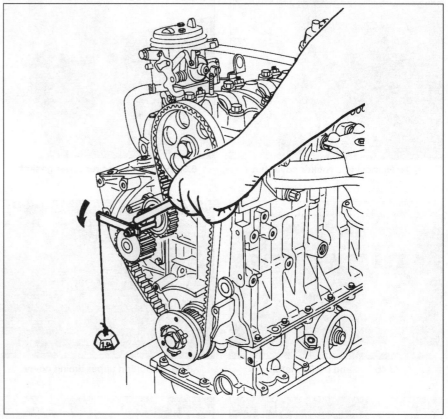

6.12 Using special tool (0132X) to tension timing belt

6.14 Timing cover correctly refitted

3 Remove the air cleaner.
4 Disconnect the choke and throttle cables from the carburettor.
5 Unbolt the exhaust downpipe.
6 Disconnect the HT leads from the spark plugs, unbolt the lead support (see illustration), disconnect the HT lead from the coil, and remove the distributor cap. Remove the spark plugs.
7 Disconnect the vacuum hose between the distributor and carburettor.
8 Disconnect the hoses between the fuel pump and carburettor (beware of fuel spillage and take adequate fire precautions) and between the coolant pump and thermostat housing (see illustration).

9 Unscrew the nuts and remove the inlet manifold complete with carburettor from the studs on the cylinder head (see illustration). Note that there is no gasket.
10 Unbolt and remove the fuel pump and remove the gasket.
11 Loosen the alternator pivot and adjustment bolts, then unscrew the tension bolt and slip the drivebelt from the pulleys. Remove the pivot and adjustment bolts then remove the alternator (see illustration).
12 Unbolt the pulley from the front of the crankshaft (see illustration).
13 Unbolt and remove the coil (see illustration) after unclipping the TDC sensor connector.

7.6 Unbolting HT lead support

7.8 Water pump hose (arrowed) at thermostat housing

7.9 Removing inlet manifold complete with carburettor

7.11 Alternator pivot (A) adjuster (B) and tensioner (C) bolts

7.12 Unbolting crankshaft pulley

7.13 Ignition coil (arrowed) located above distributor

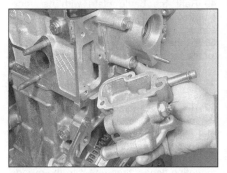

7.17 Removing thermostat housing

7.18 Distributor mounting flange retaining bolts (arrowed)

7.19 TDC sensor mounting bolt (arrowed)

2C

14 Unbolt the exhaust manifold hot air shroud.

15 Unscrew the brass nuts, remove the washers and remove the exhaust manifold from the studs on the cylinder head. Remove the gaskets.

16 Remove the distributor.

17 Remove the thermostat, then unbolt the thermostat housing from the cylinder head (see illustration).

18 Unbolt the distributor mounting flange from the cylinder head (see illustration).

19 Unbolt the TDC sensor from the flywheel end of the cylinder block and unclip the lead from the timing plate (see illustration).

20 Unbolt and remove the timing plate (see illustration).

21 Unscrew the nuts and remove the rocker cover. Remove the rubber gasket from the cover.

22 Remove the two spacers and baffle plate from the studs.

23 Unbolt the upper timing cover, followed by the intermediate cover and lower cover.

24 Turn the engine clockwise, using a socket on the crankshaft sprocket bolt, until the small hole in the camshaft sprocket is aligned with the corresponding hole in the cylinder head. Insert the shank of a close-fitting twist drill into the holes.

25 Align the TDC holes in the flywheel and cylinder block rear flange, then insert a further twist drill or long bolt.

26 Loosen the timing belt tensioner roller nut, turn the tensioner clockwise using a screwdriver or square drive in the special hole, then re-tighten the nut.

27 Mark the normal direction of rotation on the timing belt, then remove it from the

camshaft, coolant pump, and crankshaft sprockets.

28 Unscrew the tensioner nut and remove the tensioner roller.

29 Progressively loosen the cylinder head bolts using the reverse sequence to that shown for tightening, then remove all the bolts.

30 Lift off the rocker arm assembly (see illustration).

31 Rock the cylinder head to free it from the block, then lift it from the location dowels. The two angled metal rods shown may be used for this purpose (see illustrations).

32 Remove the cylinder head gasket from the block.

33 Fit liner clamps (see Section 16 in Part A of this Chapter) if it is not proposed to remove the pistons and liners.

7.20 Timing plate (arrowed)

7.30 Removing rocker arm assembly

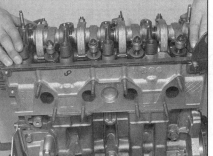

7.31a Using two metal rods to free cylinder head from cylinder block

7.31b Lifting cylinder head from cylinder block

7.35 Cylinder head gasket correctly located

7.37 Camshaft sprocket held at TDC using twist drill

Refitting

34 Clean the cylinder head and block joint faces thoroughly. Also clean the cylinder head bolt holes.

35 Locate the new cylinder head gasket on the block dowels, with the manufacturer's name uppermost **(see illustration)**.

36 Align the TDC holes in the flywheel and block rear flange and insert a twist drill or long bolt.

37 Align the small hole in the camshaft sprocket with the hole in the cylinder head and insert a twist drill or bolt **(see illustration)**.

38 Lower the cylinder head onto the block so that it engages the two dowels.

39 Refit the rocker arm assembly.

40 Lubricate the cylinder head bolt threads and heads with molybdenum disulphide grease. Insert them and tighten to the initial torque using the sequence shown **(see illustration)**.

41 Using the same sequence, angle-tighten the bolts through the specified angle **(see illustration)**.

42 Refit the timing belt tensioner roller, turn it clockwise and tighten the nut.

43 Engage the timing belt with the crankshaft sprocket then, keeping it taut, feed it onto the camshaft sprocket, around the tensioner

pulley, and onto the coolant pump sprocket.

44 Loosen the nut and turn the tensioner roller anti-clockwise by hand. Tighten the nut.

45 Citroën dealers use the special tool shown in **illustration 6.12** to tension the timing belt. A similar tool may be fabricated using an 8.0 cm long arm and a 1.5 kg (3.3 lb) weight. The torque applied to the roller will approximate 12 Kgf (10.5 lbf in). Pre-tension the timing belt with the tool and tighten the nut, then remove the timing pins and rotate the crankshaft through two complete turns. Loosen the nut and allow the roller to re-position itself. Tighten the nut.

46 If the special tool is not available, an approximate setting may be achieved by turning the roller hub anti-clockwise, until it is just possible to turn the timing belt through 90° by finger and thumb midway between the crankshaft and camshaft sprockets. The square in the roller hub should then be directly below the adjustment nut, and the deflection of the belt in the midway position should be approximately 6.0 mm. If using this method, the tension should be re-checked by a Citroën dealer at the earliest opportunity.

47 Refit the lower, intermediate, and upper timing covers, then tighten the bolts - see Section 6.

48 Adjust the valve clearances.

49 Refit the baffle plate with its edges pointing downwards, followed by the two spacers.

50 Fit the rubber gasket to the rocker cover, locate the cover in position and tighten the nuts.

51 Refit the timing plate and tighten the bolts.

52 Refit the TDC sensor and tighten the bolt. Fix the lead in the plastic clip on the timing plate. Note that the main body of the TDC sensor should be 1.0 mm from the flywheel.

53 Apply jointing compound to the distributor mounting flange, then refit it to the cylinder head and tighten the bolts.

54 Apply jointing compound to the thermostat housing, then refit it to the cylinder head and tighten the bolts to the specified torque.

55 Refit the thermostat.

56 Refit the distributor.

57 Refit the exhaust manifold together with new gaskets. Refit the nuts and washers, and tighten securely.

58 Refit the exhaust manifold hot air shroud and tighten the bolts.

59 Locate the coil and bracket over the distributor and tighten the bolts.

60 Position the pulley on the front of the crankshaft. Insert and tighten the bolts.

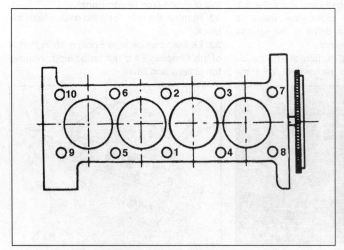

7.40 Cylinder head bolt tightening sequence

7.41 Angle-tightening cylinder head bolts

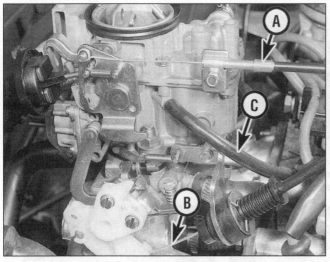

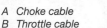

8.8 Carburettor connections

A Choke cable
B Throttle cable

C Distributor vacuum
   hose

8.14 Speedometer cable rubber cotter pin (arrowed)

61 Refit the alternator and insert the pivot and adjustment bolts. Slip the drivebelt onto the pulleys and tighten the tension bolt until the deflection of the belt midway between the pulleys is approximately 6.0 mm under firm thumb pressure. Tighten the pivot and adjustment bolts.

62 Refit the fuel pump with a new gasket and tighten the bolts.

63 Thoroughly clean the mating faces of the inlet manifold and cylinder head and apply jointing compound.

64 Refit the inlet manifold complete with carburettor and tighten the nuts.

65 Reconnect the hose between the fuel pump and carburettor and tighten the clips.

66 Reconnect the vacuum hose between the distributor and carburettor.

67 Refit and tighten the spark plugs.

68 Refit the HT leads and distributor cap.

69 Reconnect the exhaust downpipe.

70 Reconnect the choke and throttle cables to the carburettor.

71 Refit the air cleaner.

72 Replenish the cooling system.

73 Reconnect the battery.

8 Engine/transmission - removal and refitting

Removal

1 The engine/transmission is removed by lifting it upwards out of engine compartment.

2 Remove the bonnet.

3 Remove the battery.

4 Raise the front of the car, and support it securely on axle stands placed under the body sill jacking points.

5 Drain the cooling system.

6 Drain the engine oil.

7 Drain the transmission oil.

8 Disconnect the choke and throttle cables from the carburettor **(see illustration)**.

9 Remove the air cleaner.

10 Disconnect the fuel supply hose from the fuel pump, and the return hose from the T-union.

11 Remove the radiator.

12 Remove both driveshafts.

13 Unbolt and remove the front downpipe from the exhaust manifold, and also the front section of the exhaust system, noting the support bracket on the transmission.

14 Pull out the rubber cotter pin and disconnect the speedometer cable from the transmission **(see illustration)**.

15 Disconnect the gearchange control rods by prising the sockets off the balljoints with an open-ended spanner **(see illustration)**.

16 Remove the bolt from the engine rear mounting **(see illustration)**.

17 Unbolt the rear mounting yoke and the driveshaft support bearing bracket, then remove them.

18 Release the clips which hold the suspension levelling pipeline to the underside of the engine and transmission.

19 Loosen the mounting and belt adjuster link bolts on the hydraulic pump and remove the drivebelt.

20 Set the suspension height control lever in the "low" position and then gently release the screw on the hydraulic pressure regulator through one turn **(see illustration)**.

21 Disconnect the small pipe union on the hydraulic pressure regulator and the one on

2C

8.15 Using an open-ended spanner (arrowed) to disconnect a gearchange rod balljoint

8.16 Engine rear mounting and yoke

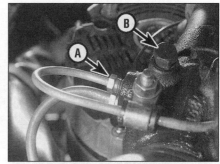

8.20 Hydraulic pressure regulator

A Pipe union   B Pressure relief screw

8.22 Unbolting hydraulic pump/regulator assembly

8.24 Clutch cable connection at release lever

8.26 Heater hose connection at carburettor (arrowed)

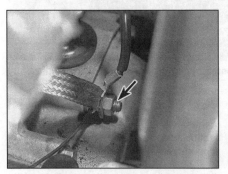

8.27 Earth cables at transmission (arrowed)

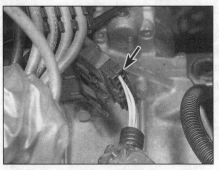

8.28 Temperature switch/oil pressure switch/reversing light switch wiring connector (arrowed)

8.30a Left-hand engine mounting through-bolt (arrowed)

the security valve. Release the fixing clips and withdraw the disconnected section of pipeline from below the car, noting carefully its routing.

22 Unbolt the hydraulic pump/regulator assembly from the cylinder block bracket **(see illustration)**.

23 Raise the assembly and rest it on the crossmember with the hydraulic flexible hose still connected.

24 Disconnect the clutch cable from the release lever on the transmission **(see illustration)**.

25 Disconnect the heater hoses from the engine.

26 Disconnect the heater hose from the carburettor **(see illustration)**.

27 Disconnect the earth cables from the transmission casing **(see illustration)**.

28 Disconnect the wiring from the alternator and the plug which serves the temperature switch, oil pressure switch and reversing light switch **(see illustration)**.

29 Connect a suitable hoist to the engine lifting eyes and take the weight of the engine/transmission.

30 Unscrew the through-bolt of the left-hand mounting, then unbolt and remove the mounting bracket **(see illustrations)**.

31 Unscrew the through-bolt from the right-hand engine mounting **(see illustration)**.

32 Swivel the engine/transmission so that the transmission faces towards the left-hand front corner of the engine compartment.

33 Raise the hoist slowly and lift the engine/transmission out of the engine compartment **(see illustration)**.

34 The transmission can be separated from

the engine after removing the following components:

a) Starter motor
b) TDC sensor
c) Flywheel cover plate
d) Reversing light switch lead connections

35 Undo and remove the clutch bellhousing-to-engine bolts.

Refitting

36 Refitting is a reversal of removal, but observe the following points:

a) Use a plastic protective sleeve to prevent damage to the oil seal lips when fitting the right-hand driveshaft
b) Adjust the clutch cable
c) Refill the engine and transmission with oil
d) Refill the cooling system
e) Tension the drivebelts

8.30b Removing left-hand engine mounting bracket

8.31 Right-hand engine mounting through-bolt (arrowed)

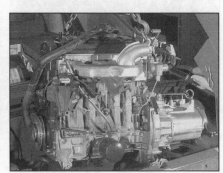

8.33 Lifting engine/transmission unit from vehicle

f) *Top-up the hydraulic system*
g) *The use of self-locking pliers will facilitate reconnection of the gearchange rod balljoints* **(see illustration)**

9 Engine dismantling - general information

Refer to Section 8 in Part A of this Chapter.

10 Engine dismantling - ancillary items

Refer to Section 9 in Part A of this Chapter.

11 Engine - separation from transmission

Refer to Section 10 in Part A of this Chapter.

12 Engine - complete dismantling

1 Disconnect the HT leads from the spark plugs, unbolt the lead support, disconnect the HT lead from the coil, and remove the distributor cap. Remove the spark plugs.
2 Disconnect the vacuum hose between the distributor and carburettor.
3 Disconnect the hoses between the fuel pump and carburettor (beware of fuel spillage and take adequate fire precautions) and between the coolant pump and thermostat housing.
4 Unscrew the nuts and remove the inlet manifold complete with carburettor from the studs on the cylinder head. Note that there is no gasket.

8.36 Reconnecting a gearchange rod balljoint

5 Unbolt and remove the fuel pump, then remove the gasket.
6 Loosen the alternator pivot and adjustment bolts, then unscrew the tension bolt and slip the drivebelt from the pulleys. Remove the pivot and adjustment bolts, then remove the alternator.
7 Unbolt the pulley from the front of the crankshaft.
8 Unbolt and remove the coil after unclipping the TDC sensor connector.
9 Unbolt the exhaust manifold hot air shroud.
10 Unscrew the brass nuts, remove the washers and remove the exhaust manifold from the studs on the cylinder head. Remove the gaskets.
11 Remove the distributor.
12 Remove the thermostat, then unbolt the thermostat housing from the cylinder head.
13 Unbolt the distributor mounting flange from the cylinder head.
14 Unbolt the TDC sensor from the flywheel end of the cylinder block and unclip the lead from the timing plate.
15 Unbolt and remove the timing plate.
16 Unscrew and remove the oil filter, using a strap wrench if necessary.
17 Unscrew and remove the oil pressure switch.
18 Unscrew the mounting bolt and pull the

engine oil dipstick holder from the main bearing cap casting. Remove the dipstick from the holder **(see illustration)**.
19 Unscrew the nuts and remove the rocker cover. Remove the rubber gasket from the cover.
20 Remove the two spacers and baffle plate from the studs.
21 Unbolt the upper timing cover, followed by the intermediate cover and lower cover.
22 Turn the engine clockwise, using a socket on the crankshaft sprocket bolt, until the small hole in the camshaft sprocket is aligned with the corresponding hole in the cylinder head. Insert the shank of a close-fitting twist drill into the holes.
23 Align the TDC holes in the flywheel and cylinder block rear flange, then insert a further twist drill or long bolt.
24 Loosen the timing belt tensioner roller nut, turn the tensioner clockwise using a screwdriver or square drive in the special hole, then re-tighten the nut.
25 Mark the normal direction of rotation on the timing belt, then remove it from the camshaft, coolant pump, and crankshaft sprockets.
26 Unscrew the tensioner nut and remove the tensioner roller.
27 Progressively loosen the cylinder head bolts using the reverse sequence to that shown, then remove all the bolts.
28 Lift off the rocker arm assembly.
29 Rock the cylinder head to free it from the block, then lift it from the location dowels. Two angled metal rods may be used for this purpose.
30 Remove the cylinder head gasket from the block.
31 Fit liner clamps (see Section 16 in Part A of this Chapter) if it is not proposed to remove the pistons and liners.
32 Progressively loosen the clutch pressure plate bolts and remove the pressure plate and friction disc from the flywheel **(see illustration)**.

12.18 Unbolting dipstick holder upper mounting

12.32 Removing clutch pressure plate and friction disc

2C

12.34a Removing crankshaft sprocket bolt . . .

12.34b . . . the hub/sprocket . . .

12.34c . . . and timing belt guide plate

33 Unbolt the coolant pump housing from the side of the block and prise out the O-ring.

34 Have an assistant hold the flywheel stationary with a wide-bladed screwdriver inserted between the starter ring gear teeth,

12.35 Prising out crankshaft front oil seal

then unscrew the crankshaft sprocket bolt and remove the hub/sprocket and timing belt guide plate (see illustrations).

35 Using a screwdriver, prise the front oil seal from the block and main bearing casting (see illustration).

36 Hold the flywheel stationary and unscrew the flywheel bolts. Lift the flywheel from the dowel on the crankshaft rear flange.

37 Prise out the crankshaft rear oil seal using a screwdriver.

38 Invert the engine and support it on blocks of wood.

39 Unscrew the nuts and bolts securing the sump to the main bearing casting, then remove it by carefully prising it free of the jointing compound (see illustration).

40 Unbolt the oil pump and tilt it to release the drive sprocket from the chain (see illustrations).

41 Support the block on its flywheel end.

42 Mark the liners for position, starting with No 1 (at the flywheel end). Similarly mark the big-end bearing caps.

43 Temporarily refit the crankshaft sprocket bolt and turn the crankshaft so that Nos 1 and 4 pistons are at bottom dead centre (BDC).

44 Unscrew the nuts and remove the big-end bearing caps (see illustration). Remove the lower big-end shells, keeping them identified for position.

45 Remove the clamps and withdraw the liners, complete with pistons, from the block (see illustration).

46 Remove the liner bottom O-rings.

47 Repeat the procedure for Nos 2 and 3 pistons and liners.

48 Invert the engine again and unscrew the bolts securing the main bearing cap casting to the block (see illustrations).

12.39 Removing the sump

12.40a Unscrew oil pump retaining bolts . . .

12.40b . . . and remove oil pump

12.44 Removing a big-end bearing cap

12.45 Removing a liner/piston assembly

12.48a Unscrew main bearing cap casting front bolts . . .

12.48b . . . and side bolts (arrowed)

12.50 Removing oil pump chain from crankshaft

51 Lift the crankshaft from the block and remove the main bearing shells, keeping them identified for location. Also remove the endfloat thrustwashers from No 2 main bearing location (see illustrations).

13 Engine - examination and renovation

General information

1 Refer to Section 12 in Part A of this Chapter.

Camshaft drivebelt

2 The drivebelt should be renewed when the engine is overhauled, or if it has become contaminated with oil. There is no specified renewal mileage. When handling the timing belt, do not bend it sharply as this may damage the internal fibres.

Camshaft

3 Refer to Section 12 in Part A of this Chapter but note that there is no camshaft lubrication manifold, as the camshaft runs in an oil bath.

All other components

4 Refer to Section 12 in Part A of this Chapter.

12.51a Removing a main bearing shell . . .

12.51b . . . and endfloat thrustwasher

49 Progressively unscrew the main bearing bolts and lift the main bearing cap casting from the block. Gently tap it with a wooden or soft-headed mallet to release it. Prise out the main bearing shells, keeping them identified for location.
50 Remove the oil pump sprocket and chain from the crankshaft (see illustration).

2C

14 Cylinder head - dismantling, decarbonising, inspection and reassembly

Dismantling

1 Remove the twist drill from the camshaft sprocket, then hold the sprocket stationary using an oil filter strap wrench or tool as shown. Unscrew the bolt and remove the sprocket (see illustrations).
2 Unbolt and remove the camshaft thrust fork (see illustration).
3 Prise out the oil seal, and carefully withdraw the camshaft from the cylinder head (see illustrations).

14.1a Using home-made tool to hold camshaft sprocket stationary

14.1b Unscrew camshaft sprocket bolt . . .

14.1c . . . and remove bolt, washer and sprocket - note location peg and cut-out (arrowed)

14.2 Camshaft thrust fork (arrowed)

14.3a Prise out camshaft oil seal . . .

14.3b . . . and withdraw camshaft

14.4a Compress valve spring and remove split collets . . .

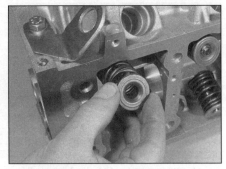

14.4b . . . the retainer . . .

14.4c . . . the spring . . .

14.4d . . . the spring seat . . .

14.4e . . . and the valve

4 Remove the valves and springs, keeping them in order by inserting them in a card having suitable holes punched in it, numbered from 1 to 8. Discard the valve stem oil seals **(see illustrations)**.

Decarbonising

5 Refer to Section 13 in Part A of this Chapter.

Inspection

6 Refer to Section 13 in Part A of this Chapter.

Reassembly

7 Refit the valves and springs with reference to Section 13 in Part A of this Chapter.
8 Oil the camshaft bearings and insert the camshaft into the cylinder head.
9 Refit the camshaft thrust fork, and tighten the bolt.
10 Dip the new oil seal in oil then press it into the cylinder head until flush, using a metal tube or large socket and hammer.
11 Refit the camshaft sprocket so that the location peg enters the cut-out. Insert and tighten the bolt while holding the sprocket stationary, using the method described in paragraph 1.

15 Engine reassembly - general information

Refer to Section 14 in Part A of this Chapter.

16 Engine - preparation for reassembly

Refer to Section 15 in Part A of this Chapter.

17 Cylinder liners - checking protrusion

Refer to Section 16 in Part A of this Chapter.

18 Engine - complete reassembly

Note: *Maintain conditions of absolute cleanliness when reassembling the engine*

Crankshaft

1 With the cylinder block upside-down on the bench, press the main bearing upper shells into position. Note that the grooved bearings are fitted to positions No 2 and 4.
2 Smear a little grease on the thrustwashers and locate them each side of No 2 bearing with their grooves facing outwards.
3 Oil the bearings and lower the crankshaft into position **(see illustration)**.
4 Check that the crankshaft endfloat is as given in the *Specifications*, using a feeler blade between a thrustwasher and the crankshaft web. The thrustwashers are

available in four thicknesses.
5 Fit the oil pump sprocket and chain to the front of the crankshaft, locating the sprocket on the Woodruff key.
6 Press the main bearing lower shells into position in the main bearing cap casting, noting that the grooved bearings are fitted to positions No 2 and 4.
7 Apply jointing compound to the mating face, then lower the main bearing cap casting into position over the crankshaft **(see illustrations)**. At the same time, feed the oil pump chain through the aperture.
8 Insert the main bearing bolts dry, then tighten them evenly to the initial torque wrench setting. Angle-tighten the bolts by a further 45° **(see illustration)**
9 Refit the bolts securing the main bearing cap casting to the block, and tighten them to the specified torque.

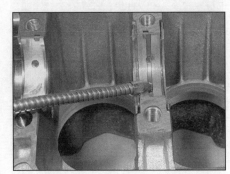

18.3 Oiling main bearing shells

18.7a Apply jointing compound to crankcase mating face . . .

18.7b . . . then lower main bearing cap casting into position

Pistons and liners

10 Support the cylinder block on its flywheel end.

11 Check that the lower big-end bearing shells are fitted to the big-end caps and the upper shells to the connecting rods.

12 Oil the liner bores and piston rings.

13 Position the piston ring end gaps at 120° from each other, so that none is in line with another.

14 Fit a piston ring compressor to each piston in turn and push the pistons in their respective liners using a hammer handle **(see illustrations)**. Make sure that the arrows on the piston crowns face the front (timing belt end) of the liners.

15 Fit the bottom O-rings to the liners, taking care not to twist them.

16 Check that the crankshaft rotates freely, then position Nos 1 and 4 crankpins at bottom dead centre (BDC). Oil the crankpins.

17 Insert No 1 liner/piston into the block and guide the connecting rod big-end onto the crankpin. Refit the big-end bearing cap and tighten the nuts evenly to the specified torque **(see illustration)**.

18 Check that the crankshaft rotates freely while holding the liner in position with a clamp. Temporarily refit the crankshaft sprocket bolt to turn the crankshaft.

19 Repeat the procedure to fit the remaining pistons and liners.

Oil pump

20 Support the block upside-down on the bench.

21 Check that the oil pump location pin is fitted to the main bearing casting, then refit the oil pump, tilting it to engage the drive sprocket with the chain. Insert and tighten the bolts.

Sump

22 Apply jointing compound to the mating faces of the sump and main bearing casting. Refit the sump, insert the bolts and tighten them to the specified torque.

Crankshaft rear oil seal

23 Dip the new crankshaft rear oil seal in clean engine oil and locate it over the rear of the crankshaft **(see illustration)**.

24 Citroën dealers use a special tool (0132U) to fit the seal but it can be fitted by using the flywheel. Temporarily locate the flywheel on the crankshaft using four bolts, then tighten the bolts evenly until the flywheel contacts the rear flange. Remove the flywheel and use a metal tube or block of wood to drive the oil seal fully into position.

2C

18.8 Angle-tightening main bearing cap bolts

18.14a Fitting a piston ring compressor

18.14b Using a hammer handle to push a piston into its liner

18.17 Tightening a big-end bearing cap nut

18.23 Crankshaft rear oil seal located over rear of crankshaft

18.25 Applying locking fluid to a flywheel bolt

18.27 Crankshaft front oil seal located over front of crankshaft

18.28 Tightening crankshaft sprocket bolt

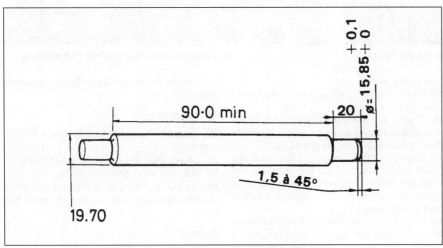

18.31a Clutch centralising tool dimensions

Dimensions in mm

Flywheel

25 Apply locking fluid to the threads of the flywheel bolts. Locate the flywheel on the crankshaft dowel then insert the bolts and tighten them to the specified torque while holding the flywheel stationary with a wide-bladed screwdriver inserted between the starter ring gear teeth **(see illustration)**.

Crankshaft front oil seal

26 Support the engine upright.
27 Dip the crankshaft front oil seal in clean engine oil, locate it over the front of the crankshaft and drive it in flush with the front of the block using a metal tube or socket **(see illustration)**. There is no seating, so take care not to drive it in too far.
28 Fit the oil seal flange, followed by the hub/sprocket. Insert the sprocket bolt and spacer, and tighten the bolt to the specified torque while holding the flywheel stationary **(see illustration)**.

Coolant pump housing

29 Refit the coolant pump housing, together with a new O-ring, and tighten the bolts to the specified torque.

Clutch friction disc and pressure plate

30 Locate the clutch friction disc and pressure plate on the flywheel with the dowels engaged. Insert the bolts finger-tight.
31 Centralise the friction disc using a universal tool, or by making a wooden adapter to the dimensions shown **(see illustrations)**.
32 Tighten the pressure plate bolts evenly to the specified torque **(see illustration)**.

Cylinder head

33 Clean the cylinder head and block joint faces thoroughly. Also clean the cylinder head bolt holes.

18.31b Centralising clutch friction disc using a universal tool

18.32 Tightening a clutch pressure plate bolt

34 Locate the new cylinder head gasket on the block dowels, with the manufacturer's name uppermost.

35 Align the TDC holes in the flywheel and block rear flange, then insert a twist drill or long bolt.

36 Align the small hole in the camshaft sprocket with the hole in the cylinder head, then insert a twist drill or bolt.

37 Lower the cylinder head onto the block so that it engages the two dowels.

38 Refit the rocker arm assembly.

39 Lubricate the cylinder head bolt threads and heads with molybdenum disulphide grease. Insert them and tighten to the initial torque using the sequence shown **(see illustration 7.40)**.

40 Using the same sequence, angle-tighten the bolts through the specified angle.

Timing belt and covers

41 Refit the timing belt tensioner roller, turn it clockwise and tighten the nut.

42 Engage the timing belt with the crankshaft sprocket then, keeping it taut, feed it onto the camshaft sprocket, around the tensioner pulley, and onto the coolant pump sprocket.

43 Loosen the nut and turn the tensioner roller anti-clockwise by hand. Tighten the nut.

44 Citroën dealers use the special tool shown **(see illustration 6.12)** to tension the timing belt. A similar tool may be fabricated using an 8.0 cm long arm and a 1.5 kg (3.3 lb) weight. The torque applied to the roller will approximate 12 kgf cm (10.5 lbf in). Pre-tension the timing belt with the tool and tighten the nut, then remove the timing pins and rotate the crankshaft through two complete turns. Loosen the nut and allow the roller to re-position itself. Tighten the nut.

45 If the special tool is not available, an approximate setting may be achieved by turning the roller hub anti-clockwise, until it is just possible to turn the timing belt through 90° by finger and thumb midway between the crankshaft and camshaft sprockets. The square in the roller hub should then be directly below the adjustment nut, and the deflection of the belt in the midway position should be approximately 6.0 mm. If using this method, the tension should be re-checked by a Citroën dealer at the earliest opportunity.

46 Refit the lower, intermediate and upper timing covers, then tighten the bolts.

Remaining components

47 Adjust the valve clearances.

48 Refit the baffle plate with its edges pointing downwards, followed by the two spacers.

49 Fit the rubber gasket to the rocker cover, locate the cover in position and tighten the nuts.

50 Apply a little sealant to the end of the engine oil dipstick holder and insert it in the main bearing cap casting. Insert and tighten the mounting bolt.

51 Insert and tighten the oil pressure switch.

52 Smear a little oil on the sealing ring and tighten the oil filter into position by hand only.

53 Refit the timing plate and tighten the bolts.

54 Refit the TDC sensor and tighten the bolt. Fix the lead in the plastic clip on the timing plate. Note that the main body of the TDC sensor should be 1.0 mm from the flywheel.

55 Apply jointing compound to the distributor mounting flange, then refit it to the cylinder head and tighten the bolts.

56 Apply jointing compound to the thermostat housing, then refit it to the cylinder head and tighten the bolts to the specified torque.

57 Refit the thermostat.

58 Refit the distributor.

59 Refit the exhaust manifold together with new gaskets. Refit the nuts and washers and tighten securely.

60 Refit the exhaust manifold hot air shroud and tighten the bolts.

61 Locate the coil and bracket over the distributor and tighten the bolts.

62 Position the pulley on the front of the crankshaft. Insert and tighten the bolts.

63 Refit the alternator and insert the pivot and adjustment bolts. Slip the drivebelt onto the pulleys and tighten the tension bolt until the deflection of the belt midway between the pulleys is approximately 6.0 mm under firm thumb pressure. Tighten the pivot and adjustment bolts.

64 Refit the fuel pump with a new gasket and tighten the bolts.

65 Thoroughly clean the mating faces of the inlet manifold and cylinder head and apply jointing compound.

66 Refit the inlet manifold complete with carburettor and tighten the nuts.

67 Reconnect the hose between the fuel pump and carburettor and tighten the clips.

68 Reconnect the vacuum hose between the distributor and carburettor.

69 Refit and tighten the spark plugs.

70 Refit the HT leads and distributor cap.

---

19 Engine - reconnection to transmission

Refer to Section 18 in Part A of this Chapter.

2C

---

20 Engine - initial start-up after overhaul

---

1 Refer to Section 19 in Part A of this Chapter.

2 Note that the cylinder head bolts of this engine do not require re-tightening and the timing belt does not require re-tensioning.

3 If new bearings and/or pistons have been fitted, treat the engine as new, and run it in at reduced speeds. Also change the engine oil at 1000 miles (1500 km).

Notes

Chapter 2 Part D:
D6C engine

Contents

Degrees of difficulty

Easy, suitable for novice with little experience	Fairly easy, suitable for beginner with some experience	Fairly difficult, suitable for competent DIY mechanic	Difficult, suitable for experienced DIY mechanic	Very difficult, suitable for expert DIY or professional

Specifications

Specifications are as for the type 159 engine (see Chapter 2B) except for the following:

General
Model application:
BX 19 GTi 16 valve D6C (XU9J4)
Compression ratio 10.4:1
Maximum power DIN (BHP) . . . . 160 at 6500 rpm
Maximum torque DIN (lbf ft) . . . . 133 at 5000 rpm

Valves
Head diameter:
Inlet . . . . 34.7 mm
Exhaust . . . . 29.7 mm
Cam followers . . . . Hydraulic (valve clearance adjustment not required)

Valve timing
Valve lift 9.2 mm
Inlet opens* . . . . 1° 35' BTDC
Inlet closes* . . . . 45° 50' ABDC
Exhaust opens* . . . . 47° 0' BBDC
Exhaust closes* . . . . 0° 30' ATDC
*With valve clearance of 1.0 mm

Crankshaft
Endfloat thrustwasher thicknesses . . . . 2.33 to 2.53 mm (in increments of 0.05 mm)
Crank journal diameter . . . . 59.7 to 60.0 mm
Crankpin diameter . . . . 49.7 to 50.0 mm

Lubrication system
Oil pressure:
At 850 rpm . . . . 2.0 bar
At 3000 rpm . . . . 4.8 bar
Oil filter . . . . Champion F104
Oil capacity (with filter change) . . . . 5.3 litres (9.3 pints)
Dipstick minimum to maximum . . . . 1.5 litres (2.6 pints)

Torque wrench settings

	Nm	lbf ft
Camshaft bearing cap Allen screws	10	7
Main bearing cap bolts and nuts	50	37
Centre main bearing cap side bolts	25	18
Sump pan bolts	20	15
Big-end bearing cap nuts:		
Stage 1	40	30
Stage 2: slacken, then tighten to	20	15
Stage 3: then immediately	Tighten a further 70°	
Oil pump bolts	20	15
Flywheel bolts	50	37
Clutch cover bolts	25	18
Crankshaft sprocket bolt	110	82
Coolant pump bolts	15	11
Camshaft sprocket bolts	45	33
Timing belt tensioner locking screw	20	15
Engine mounting bracket at timing cover end:		
Larger bolts	72	53
Smaller bolts	45	33
Crankshaft damper bolts	25	18
Camshaft rear pulley bolt	45	33
Inlet manifold bolts	20	15
Exhaust manifold bolts	25	18
Cylinder head bolts:		
Stage 1	60	43
Stage 2: slacken, and then tighten each bolt in turn to	20	15
Stage 3: then immediately	Tighten a further 300°	

1 General information and precautions

General information

The D6C engine is fitted to all BX 19 GTi 16 valve models and is a development of the D6A engine, which itself is based upon the 159A engine dealt with in Chapter 2B.

Introduced in July 1987, the essential difference is the 16 valve double overhead camshaft cylinder head, the camshafts being driven by a toothed belt tensioned by two idler rollers.

The need for valve clearance adjustment is eliminated by the incorporation of Hydraulic tappets (cam followers).

The pistons have been re-designed, with valve head recesses machined in the piston crown and the gudgeon pins are now of the "floating" type, secured by circlips in the piston. The undersides of the pistons are cooled by oil jets located in lubrication pipes within the crankcase.

The crankshaft has lighter balancing counterweights with a damper fitted to the sprocket end.

Pressurised oil is supplied by an oil pump located within the sump pan, the pump being driven by chain from the crankshaft.

Due to an oil cooler being fitted, oil capacity has increased. The oil filter is of disposable screw-on canister type, mounted on the oil cooler housing. The oil filler pipe is an independent assembly, remote from the engine, in order to provide a reasonable position for pouring oil into the steeply-canted engine.

Precautions

Because of the unusual layout of the engine and transmission systems, extra care and attention are necessary during maintenance and overhaul procedures which, in many instances, differ from more conventional systems.

Read through the various Sections concerned before tackling any job, and analyse the instructions, so that any snags or possible difficulties can be noted in advance. Because the sub-assembly castings are made from aluminium alloy it is of utmost importance that, where specified, all fastenings are tightened to the correct torque and, in some instances, in the correct sequence.

2 Oil filter - removal and refitting

Refer to Chapter 1, Section 9.

3 Major operations possible with engine in vehicle

The following items can be removed and refitted with the engine in the vehicle:
a) Timing belt and camshafts.
b) Cylinder head.
c) Sump pan
d) Oil pump.
e) Engine mountings.

4 Major operations requiring engine removal

The engine must be removed for the following operation:
a) Removal of the crankshaft and main bearings

5 Timing belt - removal and refitting

Note: *If there is the slightest doubt about the condition of the timing belt then it must be renewed.*

Note: *The following operation was carried out with the engine in the vehicle.*

Note: *Accurate adjustment of the timing belt entails the use of Citroën special tools. An approximate setting can be achieved using the method described in this Section but is essential that the tension is checked by a dealer on completion.*

Removal

1 Disconnect the battery.

2 Remove the front right-hand roadwheel, then unclip and remove the wheel arch blanking panel to provide access to the timing cover, the crankshaft sprocket and damper **(see illustration)**.

3 Loosen the alternator mounting bolts and the belt adjuster link, then remove the alternator drivebelt.

5.2 Removing front right-hand wheel arch blanking panel

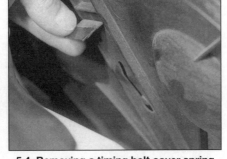

5.4 Removing a timing belt cover spring clip

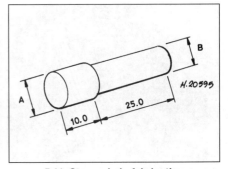

5.11 Stepped pin fabrication

a 8.43 mm   *b 6.38 mm*

4 Pull out the keyhole slot-type spring clips from the front face of the timing belt cover **(see illustration)**.

5 Extract the screws and remove the timing belt cover.

6 Using the centre bolt in the crankshaft damper, turn the crankshaft until the slot in the crankshaft sprocket is aligned with the one on the oil pump cover, and the pin holes in the camshaft sprockets are aligned with the holes in the cylinder head.

7 Unscrew the bolts and take off the damper from the front end of the crankshaft.

8 Remove the timing belt lower cover.

9 Using an Allen key, release the belt tensioner locking screws.

10 Remove the timing belt.

Refitting

Caution: Take care not to kink or contaminate the timing belt with oil

11 Setting tools will be required when fitting the new belt. In the absence of Citroën special tools (01 53M and 01 53G), make up two stepped pins as shown **(see illustration)**. Obtain a short length of rod which will be a snug fit in the cut-outs of the crankshaft sprocket and the oil pump cover.

12 Insert the camshaft sprocket stepped pins and the crankshaft rod **(see illustrations)**.

13 Fit the new timing belt in a clockwise direction, following the numerical sequence shown **(see illustration)**. Adjust the tensioning pulleys on both sides to make the belt taut. Check that the longest run of the belt can be twisted through 45° when gripped

5.12a Camshaft sprocket locking pins in position

between the finger and thumb. Tighten the tensioner screws to the specified torque. Note that in this application, the tensioners serve two purposes, both to tension the belt and to provide fine adjustment of the valve timing.

14 Remove the two stepped pins and the rod.

15 Turn the crankshaft through two complete revolutions. Fit the crankshaft sprocket locking rod.

16 The two stepped pins should now slide smoothly through the holes of the camshaft sprockets into the holes in the cylinder head. Even the slightest misalignment will require re-adjustment of the tensioner pulleys to provide perfect alignment.

17 Remove the pins and rod, and recheck after turning the crankshaft through two more complete revolutions. It is strongly recommended that the belt tension should be

5.12b Crankshaft sprocket locking rod in position

checked by your Citroën dealer using the special tensioner device (Seemtronic 87).

18 Fit the timing belt lower cover, the crankshaft damper and the belt main cover **(see illustrations)**.

19 Refit and reconnect all the other components in reverse order of removal, referring to the *Specifications* for the appropriate torque wrench settings.

6 Cylinder head - removal, overhaul and refitting

Note: The following operation was carried out with the engine in the vehicle.

Removal

1 Drain the engine cooling system and disconnect the battery.

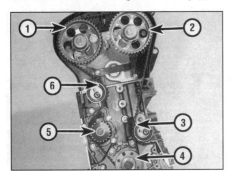

5.13 Fit timing belt in clockwise direction, starting at No 1

5.18a Timing belt lower cover refitted

5.18b Fitting a crankshaft damper bolt

6.2 Removing camshaft centre cover plate

6.8a Extracting a camshaft cover screw

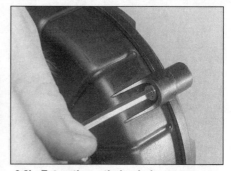

6.8b Extracting a timing belt cover screw

2 Release the screws and remove the cover plate from the centre of the camshaft cover **(see illustration)**.

3 Disconnect the spark plug leads from the spark plugs and disconnect the coolant temperature sender lead.

4 Extract the screws and remove the distributor cap, complete with leads.

5 Disconnect the fuel hose from the fuel rail.

6 Disconnect the fuel injector wiring plugs and then unbolt the fuel rail and remove complete with injectors.

7 Disconnect the coolant hoses from their cylinder head connections.

8 Extract the screws and take off the camshaft cover and the timing belt cover **(see illustrations)**.

9 Using the centre bolt in the crankshaft damper, turn the crankshaft until the slot in the crankshaft is aligned with the one on the oil pump cover and the pin holes in the camshaft sprockets are aligned with the holes in the cylinder head. Use two stepped pins to lock the sprockets in this position as shown in **illustration 5.12a**.

10 Release the tension of the timing belt by slackening the Allen screws in the two tensioner rollers. Mark the direction of rotation on the belt then slip the belt from the camshaft sprockets.

11 Pull the lubrication pipes from the camshaft bearing caps. The camshafts can be removed independently of the cylinder head if required, or the complete cylinder head can be removed and then dismantled.

12 Assuming that the cylinder head is to be removed complete, release and remove the high pressure pump drivebelt from the end of the exhaust valve camshaft.

13 Note that the camshaft bearing caps are numbered 1 to 5 from the flywheel end of the engine and are doweled so that they can only be fitted one way.

14 Progressively unscrew the Allen screws in the reverse order to that shown for tightening. Remove the camshaft bearing caps in the following order - No 4 first, then Nos 2, 3, 1 and 5.

15 Lift out the camshafts, labelling them "Exhaust" and "Inlet".

16 Disconnect the air inlet duct from the air cleaner and the hoses, control cables and leads from the inlet manifold and throttle housing.

17 Unscrew the inlet manifold nuts and lift the manifold from the cylinder head.

18 Unscrew the exhaust manifold nuts and pull it away from the cylinder head. The lower nuts are more accessible from underneath.

19 Using a TX55 Torx bit, unscrew and remove the cylinder head bolts in the reverse order to that shown for tightening.

20 Remove the cylinder head. If it is stuck, rock it using pieces of wood inserted in the inlet ports. Discard the cylinder head gasket.

21 As soon as the head is removed, fit liner clamps to prevent the liner base seals being disturbed.

Overhaul

22 Remove the hydraulic tappets (cam followers), keeping them in order of installation.

23 Removal of the valves and decarbonising are as described in Section 13 in Part A of this Chapter but the valves must be identified as to original location **(see illustrations)**.

24 When refitting a valve, some difficulty may be experienced in inserting the split collets. Use of a pencil magnet or a dab of thick grease will help.

25 The valve stem oil seals can be removed with a pair of long-nosed pliers. Fit the new ones using a piece of tubing of suitable bore.

Refitting

26 Ensure that all components are clean and new gaskets are to hand. Remember that as refitting proceeds, all nuts and bolts must be tightened to the torque wrench settings given in *Specifications*. Remove the liner clamps.

27 Smear the hydraulic tappets (cam followers) with grease, then refit them in their original locations.

28 Place a new cylinder head gasket on the top of the cylinder block **(see illustration)**.

29 Lower the cylinder head onto the positioning dowels.

30 Lightly oil the cylinder head bolts, then insert and tighten them in the order shown to the torque wrench settings given in *Specifications* **(see illustrations)**.

31 Locate the camshafts with new oil seals. Assuming that the crankshaft has not been moved from its position aligned with the oil pump housing, the camshafts should be set with the keyways at the 3 o'clock position. This is so that when the camshaft sprockets are fitted, the pin holes will be in alignment with the corresponding holes in the cylinder head.

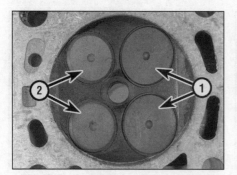

6.23a View of combustion chamber showing inlet valves (1) and exhaust valves (2)

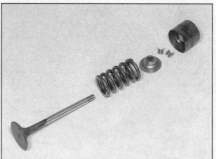

6.23b Valve components

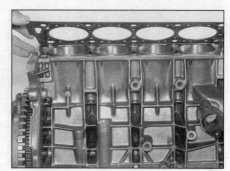

6.28 Fitting a new cylinder head gasket

6.30a Angle-tightening a cylinder head bolt

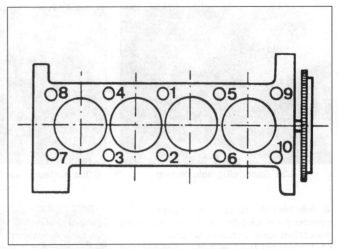

6.30b Cylinder head bolt tightening sequence

32 Fit the camshaft bearing caps and tighten the bolts to the specified torque in the sequence shown **(see illustrations)**.
33 Fit the camshaft lubrication pipes **(see illustration)**.
34 Fit the timing belt rear cover and the camshaft sprockets, ensuring that the alignment is correct by using the stepped pins

described earlier. Use an open-ended spanner on the flats of the camshaft to hold it whilst tightening the sprocket bolt to the specified torque **(see illustrations)**.
35 Refit the timing belt.
36 Fit the timing belt cover. Check that the spark plug hole oil seals are in position **(see illustration)** and then fit the cam cover.

37 Fit the distributor cap and connect the spark plug leads.
38 Using new gaskets, reconnect the inlet and exhaust manifolds to the cylinder head **(see illustrations)**.
39 Reconnect and tension the drivebelts, then connect the air cleaner inlet.

2D

6.32a Fitting a camshaft bearing cap

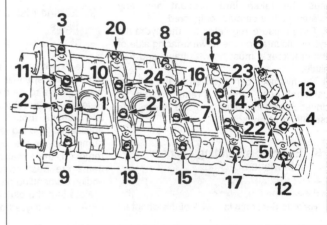

6.32b Camshaft bearing cap bolt tightening sequence

6.33 Camshaft lubrication pipe - note seal on spigot

6.34a Timing belt rear cover correctly refitted

6.34b Fitting a camshaft sprocket bolt

6.36 Spark plug hole oil seal

6.38a Exhaust manifold gasket correctly located

6.38b Exhaust manifold fitted

40 Reconnect the electrical leads to the cylinder head switches and then reconnect the coolant hoses and control cables.
41 Reconnect the fuel hoses, fuel rail and injectors **(see illustration)**.
42 Reconnect the battery.
43 Refill the cooling system.

7 Engine/transmission - removal

1 This operation is essentially as described in Part B of this Chapter. The connections for the Motronic engine management system must be taken into account and any references to a carburettor ignored.
2 The pressure regulator for the hydraulic system (located on the forward-facing side of the crankcase) must be withdrawn and tied aside.
3 The hydraulic pump (driven by the exhaust camshaft pulley) must be removed from its drivebelt and mounting and tied to one side **(see illustrations)**.

8 Engine dismantling - general information

Refer to Section 8 in Part A of this Chapter.

6.38c Inlet manifold fitted

9 Engine dismantling - ancillary items

The extent of engine ancillary items to be removed is dependent on the extent to which the engine is to be dismantled and repaired. Refer to Section 9 in Part A of this Chapter and remove those items listed which are applicable, ignoring references to the coolant pump and, if the cylinder head is to be removed, the exhaust manifold. These two items are best removed later during the engine dismantling procedures.

Note that the clutch unit is removed after the engine and gearbox are separated.

6.41 Fitting fuel rail and injectors

10 Engine - separation from transmission

Refer to Section 12 in Part B of this Chapter.

11 Engine - complete dismantling

Note: *As dismantling of the engine requires the timing belt to be removed, it is advisable to read the procedure for timing belt removal and refitting before starting work.*
1 Support the engine on a clean bench or strong table.
2 Clean away all external dirt using water-soluble solvent or paraffin and a stiff brush.
3 Unbolt the ignition coil from the inlet manifold.
4 Withdraw the engine oil dipstick.
5 Remove the oil filler pipe assembly.
6 Unplug the fuel injectors, release the fuel rail (two screws) and withdraw the rail/injector assembly.
7 Remove the cover plate from the centre of the cam cover then remove the cam cover itself. Disconnect and withdraw the spark plug HT leads.
8 Unscrew and remove the spark plugs.
9 Disconnect the hoses and remove the coolant distribution pipe.

7.3a Hydraulic pump drive pulley (arrowed)

7.3b Hydraulic pump (arrowed)

11.23a Removing crankshaft sprocket bolt and spacer

11.23b Removing crankshaft sprocket

11.32a Extract Allen screws (arrowed) . . .

10 Unbolt and remove the inlet manifold complete with throttle housing. Discard the gasket.

11 Unbolt and remove the thermostat housing.

12 Unbolt the exhaust manifold and discard its gasket.

13 Unbolt and remove the coolant multi-union from the exhaust side of the crankcase.

14 Unbolt and remove the mounting bracket from the front of the cylinder block.

15 Remove the distributor and drive flange.

16 Remove the pulley and plastic guard from the rear end of the exhaust camshaft. The camshaft may be held against rotation using the spanner flats on the camshaft.

17 Unscrew and remove the oil pressure, temperature and level switches.

18 Remove the oil filter.

19 If necessary, remove the oil cooler by disconnecting the hoses and then unscrewing the large fixing nut.

20 Extract the Allen screws, slide the timing belt cover upwards and remove it.

21 Remove the timing belt.

22 Hold the flats on the camshafts with an open-ended spanner, unscrew the bolts which secure the camshaft sprockets, then remove the sprockets.

23 Unbolt and remove the crankshaft sprocket. Take out the Woodruff key **(see illustrations)**.

24 Remove the timing belt guide plate from the crankshaft.

11.32b . . . and remove sump spacer plate

25 Remove the timing belt upper cover backplate.

26 Remove the coolant pump.

27 Pull off the camshaft lubrication pipes.

28 Remove the cylinder head.

29 Unbolt and remove the clutch assembly.

30 Unbolt and remove the flywheel.

31 Remove the sump pan securing bolts and remove the sump pan.

32 Extract the Allen screws and remove the sump spacer plate **(see illustrations)**.

33 Extract the bolts and remove the front oil seal carrier plate.

34 Extract the bolts and withdaw the oil pump, at the same time sliding the drivechain and sprocket off the crankshaft. Note the adjustment shim used to tension the drivechain during production **(see illustrations)**.

35 Mark the adjacent surfaces of the connecting rods and their caps by

11.34a Oil pump in position

centre-punching 1 to 4 from the flywheel end on the inlet manifold side.

36 Unbolt the big-end cap nuts and remove the caps, keeping the shell bearings with their respective rods or caps if they are to be used again.

37 Mark the upper rims of the cylinder liners 1 to 4 from the flywheel end, using paint marks as shown **(see illustration)**. Make the marks on the inlet side if the original liners are to be used again.

38 Discard the liner base seals after the piston, connecting rod and liner assemblies have been withdrawn.

39 If the piston rings are to be removed, push the piston and connecting rod out of the liner and insert three old feeler blades at equidistant points behind the top ring. Remove the ring off the top of the piston using a twisting motion.

11.34b Removing oil pump with drivechain and sprocket

11.34c Removing oil pump drivechain tension adjustment shim

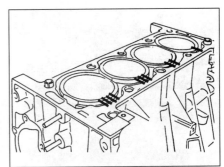

11.37 Method of marking cylinder liner numbering from flywheel end

2D

40 Extract the circlips and push the gudgeon pin out of the piston and connecting rod. If the pin is tight, immerse the piston in very hot water.

41 Note the marking of the main bearing caps - N at the flywheel end and then 2, 3, 4 and 5, read from the flywheel end.

42 Unscrew the main bearing cap bolts or the nuts on the centre cap. The centre cap is also secured by bolts entered from each side of the crankcase.

43 Remove the main bearing caps, keeping the bearing shells with their respective caps if the shells are to be used again.

44 Semi-circular thrustwashers are located at No 2 main bearing cap.

45 Lift out the crankshaft. Retrieve the thrustwashers from their crankcase seats at No 2 main bearing.

46 If necessary, remove the lubrication pipes.

12 Engine - examination and renovation

General information

1 Refer to Section 12 in Part A of this Chapter.

Component examination and renovation

2 Refer to Section 12 in Part A of this Chapter, ignoring references to rocker gear and timing chain.

12.4 Removing a hydraulic tappet

3 The rubber toothed timing belt and the oil pump drive chain should be renewed at the time of major overhaul.

4 The hydraulic tappets (cam followers) cannot be dismantled. Noisy operation will indicate the need for renewal **(see illustration)**.

13 Engine reassembly - general information

Refer to Section 14 in Part A of this Chapter.

14 Engine - preparation for reassembly

Refer to Section 15 in Part A of this Chapter.

15 Cylinder liners - checking protrusion

Refer to Section 16 in Part A of this Chapter.

16 Engine - complete reassembly

Note: *Maintain conditions of absolute cleanliness when reassembling the engine*

Crankshaft

1 With the crankcase clean and oil galleries probed clean, commence reassembly by fitting the lubrication pipes. Note that the pipes are offset towards the crankcase webs **(see illustration)**.

2 Wipe out the main bearing shell seats in the crankcase and fit the grooved shells **(see illustration)**.

3 Using thick grease, place the thrustwashers (oil grooves visible) on each side of No 2 web **(see illustration)**.

4 Lubricate the shells with clean engine oil and lower the crankshaft into the crankcase **(see illustration)**.

5 Fit the plain shells in the main bearing caps and fit the caps in numbered sequence, making sure that the thrustwashers are located in No 2 cap **(see illustrations)**.

16.1 Fitting a crankcase lubrication pipe

16.2 Fitting a grooved bearing shell to the crankcase

16.3 Fitting a crankshaft thrustwasher

16.4 Lowering crankshaft into crankcase

16.5a Main bearing cap with plain shell fitted

16.5b Fitting a main bearing cap

16.6 Flywheel end main bearing cap showing side sealing strip

16.8 Centre main bearing cap side bolt

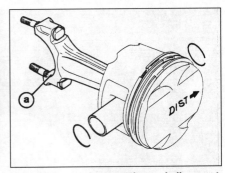

16.9a Piston-to-connecting rod alignment

a Bearing shell notch

6 Fit the crankshaft rear oil seal before tightening down the main bearing cap at the flywheel end. Make sure that the new cap side sealing strips are correctly located **(see illustration)**.

7 Tighten the main bearing cap bolts and nuts to the specified torque. Using a dial gauge or feeler blades, check the crankshaft endfloat as described in Part A of this Chapter. If necessary, change the thrustwashers to bring the endfloat within tolerance.

8 Fit and tighten the centre main bearing cap side bolts to the specified torque **(see illustration)**.

Pistons and liners

9 Assemble the pistons to the connecting rods. The gudgeon pin should be a sliding fit in the piston and connecting rod small end. If necessary, immerse the piston in hot water to ease gudgeon pin installation. The gudgeon pin is retained by circlips which have the gaps facing the rings when fitted. Make sure that the piston-to-rod alignment is correct, as shown **(see illustrations)**.

10 Fit the piston rings as shown **(see illustration)** and space the ring gaps at 120° either side of the scraper (bottom) ring gap.

16.9b Inserting a gudgeon pin circlip

11 Using a piston ring compressor and plenty of clean engine oil, slide the piston assemblies into their liners.

12 Fit a new O-ring seal to the base of each cylinder liner and install each piston/connecting rod/liner assembly into the block. If old assemblies are being fitted, ensure that they are located in their original positions. Check that the pistons are correctly aligned with the arrow on the piston crown towards the timing belt. Fit cylinder liner retaining clamps **(see illustrations)**.

13 Push the pistons down their bores and connect the connecting rod big-end (complete

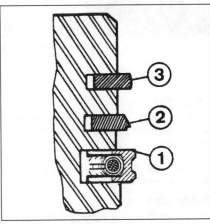

16.10 Piston ring fitting

1 Oil control ring (scraper)
2 Second compression ring
3 Top compression ring

with shell bearing) to the crankshaft.

14 Fit the big-end caps (complete with shell bearings) to their respective connecting rods.

15 Screw on the nuts and tighten to the specified torque. The crankshaft may have to be turned to facilitate fitting the bearing caps and to tighten the nuts **(see illustration)**.

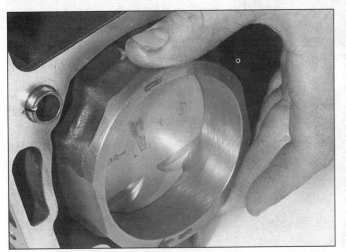

16.12a Fitting a piston/connecting rod/liner assembly

16.12b Typical cylinder liner clamps fitted

2D

16.15 Angle-tightening a big-end cap nut

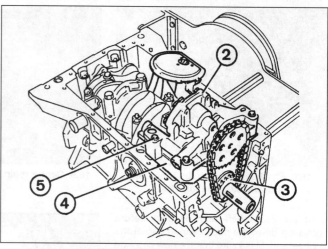

16.17 Fitting the oil pump

| 2 Pump body | 4 L-shaped shim |
| 3 Chain and sprocket | 5 Centralising bolt |

Oil pump

16 Before refitting the oil pump, fit a new oil seal. A new pump must be primed with clean engine oil.

17 Use a new pump gasket and note that bolt "5" (see illustration) centralises the pump and should be fitted first.

Sump pan

18 Use silicone-type instant gasket (applied to clean surfaces) to seal the sump spacer plate to the crankcase (see illustration).

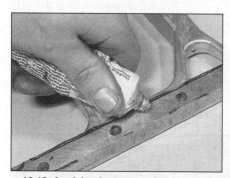

16.18 Applying instant gasket to sump spacer plate

16.20 Tightening a flywheel bolt

19 With the mating surfaces clean and using a new gasket, refit the sump pan, ensuring that the gasket does not move (see illustration). Tighten the retaining bolts to the specified torque wrench settings.

Flywheel and clutch

20 Bolt the flywheel to the end of the crankshaft (the flywheel has a positioning dowel). Apply thread-locking fluid to the cleaned bolt threads and tighten to the specified torque (see illustration).

21 Fit the clutch driven plate with the longer

16.19 Refitting sump pan and gasket

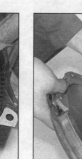

16.21 Fitting clutch components

projecting hub facing the clutch cover (see illustration). Remember to align the driven plate.

Cylinder head and camshafts

22 Fit the cylinder head and camshafts as described earlier in Section 6.

23 Fit the camshaft lubrication pipes.

Coolant pump

24 Fit the coolant pump as described in Chapter 3.

Timing belt and sprockets

25 Fit the timing belt upper cover backplate.

26 Fit the Woodruff key to the crankshaft, then push on the timing belt guide and the sprocket. Apply thread-locking fluid to the bolt threads, then fit the bolt and spacer. Tighten the bolt to the specified torque.

27 Fit the two camshaft sprockets, tightening the securing bolts to the specified torque.

28 Fit and tension the timing belt as described in Section 5.

Remaining components

29 Fit the timing belt lower cover, then bolt on the crankshaft damper, tightening the bolts to the specified torque.

16.32 Fitting oil cooler retaining tube and nut

16.34 Oil temperature switch in sump pan

16.35a Refitting oil pressure switch

2D

30 Locate the spark plug hole seals and fit the camshaft cover, tightening the bolts to the specified torque.
31 Fit the main timing belt cover.
32 Fit the oil cooler using a new gasket, then tighten the fixing nut **(see illustration)**.
33 Apply a smear of clean engine oil to the rubber seal of a new oil filter, then screw it on, using hand pressure only.
34 Screw the oil temperature switch into the sump pan **(see illustration)**.
35 Screw the oil pressure switch into the crankcase. Refit the oil level sensor **(see illustrations)**.
36 Fit the plastic guard and the pulley to the rear end of the exhaust camshaft **(see illustration)**.
37 Fit the distributor components to the end of the inlet camshaft.
38 Bolt the engine mounting bracket to the front of the cylinder block.
39 Bolt the coolant multi-hose union to the exhaust side of the crankcase **(see illustration)**.

16.35b Refitting oil level sensor

40 Fit the exhaust manifold with new gaskets.
41 Bolt on the thermostat housing.
42 Bolt on the inlet manifold using new gaskets. Note the support strut at the front of the manifold.
43 Connect and secure the coolant distribution pipe **(see illustration)**.
44 Fit the fuel rail and injectors.

16.36 Camshaft plastic guard and pulley correctly refitted

45 Fit the oil filler pipe assembly.
46 Insert the oil dipstick.
47 Bolt the ignition coil to its bracket.
48 Screw in the spark plugs using a suitable plug spanner.
49 Connect and route the HT leads and then fit the cover plate to the centre of the cam cover. Do not overtighten the two fixing screws.

16.39 Coolant multi-hose union correctly refitted

16.43 Coolant distribution pipe (arrowed)

17 Engine - reconnection to transmission

Refer to Section 20 in Part B of this Chapter.

18 Engine/transmission - refitting

This operation is essentially as described in Part B of this Chapter with the addition of the following, mentioned in Section 7 of this Chapter:

a) Connections for the Motronic engine management system
b) References to carburettor (to be ignored)
c) Pressure regulator for the hydraulic system
d) Hydraulic pump connections

19 Engine - initial start-up after overhaul

1 Ensure that the battery is fully charged.
2 Ensure that lubricants, coolant and fuel are replenished.
3 Top-up the hydraulic system and prime the high pressure (HP) pump.
4 As soon as the engine fires and runs, keep it going at a fast tickover only and bring it up to the normal working temperature.
5 With the engine running, repressurise the hydraulic system.
6 As the engine warms up, there will be odd smells and some smoke from parts getting hot and burning off oil deposits. Look for oil and coolant leaks, which will be obvious if serious.
7 Check the exhaust pipe and manifold connections, as these do not always find their exact gas-tight position until warmth and vibration have acted on them. It is almost certain that they will need tightening further. This should be done with the engine stopped.
8 Check all fuel system connections for any sign of leakage.
9 Road test the car to check that the ignition timing is correct and that the engine is giving the necessary smoothness and power. Do not race the engine. If new bearings and/or pistons have been fitted, the engine should be treated as new and run-in at a reduced speed.
10 If many of the engine internal components have been renewed, then change the engine oil at 1000 miles (1600 km).

Chapter 3
Cooling, heating and air conditioning systems

Contents

Degrees of difficulty

		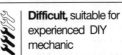	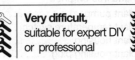

Easy, suitable for novice with little experience

Fairly easy, suitable for beginner with some experience

Fairly difficult, suitable for competent DIY mechanic

Difficult, suitable for experienced DIY mechanic

Very difficult, suitable for expert DIY or professional

Specifications

For engine to model applications refer to Chapter 2

System

Type .... Pressurised, front mounted radiator (with integral header tank), coolant pump and thermostat. Electric cooling fan

Capacity (including heater):
- 150 engine .... 6.5 litres (11.4 Imp pints)
- 171 and 159 engines .... 6.5 to 7.0 litres (11.4 to 12.3 Imp pints)
- K1G engine .... 6.5 litres (11.4 Imp pints)
- D6A, D6C and D6D engines .... 7.1 litres (12.5 Imp pints)

Thermostat

Travel (minimum) .... 7.5 mm
Opening temperature:
- 150 and 171 engines:
  - Starts to open .... 82°C (180°F)
  - Fully open .... 93°C (200°F)
- 159 engine:
  - Starts to open .... 79°C (174°F)
  - Fully open .... 82°C (180°F)
- K1G engine:
  - Starts to open .... 88°C (190°F)
  - Fully open .... 102°C (216°F)
- D6A, D6C and D6D engines:
  - Starts to open .... 79°C (174°F)
  - Fully open .... 82°C (180°F)

Cooling fan

Cut-in temperature:
- 150 engine .... 91° to 96°C (196° to 205°F)
- 171 engine:
  - 1st speed .... 84° to 90°C (183° to 194°F)
  - 2nd speed .... 90° to 96°C (194° to 205°F)
- 159 engine:
  - 1st speed .... 86° to 90°C (186° to 194°F)
  - 2nd speed .... 90° to 94°C (194° to 201°F)
- K1G engine .... 90°C (194°F)
- D6A, D6C and D6D engines:
  - 1st speed .... 86° to 90°C (186° to 194°F)
  - 2nd speed .... 90° to 94°C (194° to 201°F)

3

Coolant temperature switch

Operational temperatures:

150 engine	110° to 113°C (230° to 235°F)
159 engine	105° to 112°C (221° to 233°F)
171 engine:	
Yellow connection	110° to 114°C (230° to 237°F)
Blue connection	103° to 107°C (217° to 224°F)
K1G engine	110°C (230°F)
D6A, D6C and D6D engines	105 to 112°C (221 to 233°F)

Radiator

Cap pressure	1 bar

Torque wrench settings

	Nm	lbf ft
150 engine		
Coolant pump	18	14
Coolant temperature switch	45	33
Thermostat housing cover	17	13
171 and 159 engines		
Coolant pump	15	11
Coolant temperature switch	18	14
Coolant housing	16	12
Coolant housing plug	20	15
Thermostat housing cover	17	13
K1G engine		
Coolant pump upper stud	16	12
Coolant pump lower bolt	8	6
Housing inlet elbow	8	6
Housing to block:		
8 mm bolts	31	22
10 mm bolts	51	37

1 General information and precautions

General information

Cooling system

The cooling system is of the pump-assisted thermal syphon type and is pressurised by means of a pressure valve filler cap. The main components of the system are the radiator, the coolant pump, the thermostat, the cooling fan, the heater and the connecting hoses.

Cold coolant from the bottom of the radiator is pumped into the passages of the cylinder block and head. Heat from the combustion chambers and moving parts of the engine is absorbed by the coolant which is then directed to the upper section of the radiator. The passage of air through the radiator cools the coolant as it passes down through the matrix and the cycle is then repeated.

To accelerate the warming-up process when starting the engine, and thereafter to maintain the correct operating temperature, a thermostat is fitted in the coolant outlet from the engine to the radiator top hose. When the coolant is cold, the thermostat is closed and circulation is limited to the engine coolant passages by means of a bypass route. As coolant temperature rises, the thermostat opens to allow coolant to flow through the radiator.

The system is pressurised to raise the boiling point of the coolant. This allows the engine to achieve its most efficient operating temperature as well as reducing the amount of coolant needed.

Hot coolant is tapped from the system to supply the vehicle heater matrix and also to supply heat to the carburettor and inlet manifold to improve fuel vaporisation.

The cooling fan is driven by an electric motor and this only cuts in above a certain temperature when activated by a coolant temperature sensor switch.

On BX and BX 14 models equipped with the 150 engine, the coolant pump is driven in tandem with the alternator by a drivebelt driven from the crankshaft pulley.

On BX 14 models equipped with the K1G engine, the coolant pump is located at the timing case end of the cylinder block and is driven by the timing belt.

On BX 16 and BX 19 models, the coolant pump is located in the front of the cylinder block at the timing case end and is driven by the timing belt.

On BX 16 and BX 19 models manufactured after July 1985, the cooling system circuit is modified, the main differences being a revised carburettor heating circuit and coolant inlet casing. The opening temperatures for the thermostat, and the temperature switch operating temperatures, are also revised.

Heating and ventilation system

The heater is located centrally under the facia and supplies warm air for interior heating or windscreen demisting. Hot coolant is piped from the engine through a heater matrix and back to the engine when a manually operated valve is opened.

Fresh air inlets are located at the ends of the facia and any stale air from the car interior is exhausted through slots in the tailgate closure recess.

Air conditioning system

Air conditioning is available as an optional extra on some models. To allow for fitting of the system, the engine crankcase is modified to suit and the Weber carburettor fitted with a butterfly opener controlled by an "Elbi" electrovalve which is located underneath the battery tray. A battery of increased capacity is also fitted. The heater system continues to work on the normal principle in conjunction with the cooling system and incorporates its own booster motor.

Precautions

Cooling system maintenance

Do not remove the expansion tank filler cap or disturb any part of the cooling system whilst it is hot, as there is a very great risk of scalding. If the filler cap must be removed before the system is cool, then the pressure in the system must first be released. Cover the cap with a thick layer of cloth, to avoid scalding, and slowly unscrew the cap until a hissing sound can be heard. When the hissing has stopped, then system pressure is released. Slowly unscrew the cap until it can be removed. If more hissing sounds are heard, wait until they have stopped before unscrewing the cap completely. At all times keep well away from the filler opening.

If the engine is hot, the electric cooling fan may start rotating even if the engine is not running. Be careful to keep hands, hair and loose clothing well clear of the fan when working in the engine compartment.

Antifreeze mixture

Antifreeze mixture is poisonous. Keep it out of reach of children and pets. Never leave antifreeze lying around, it is fatal if ingested.

Do not allow antifreeze to come in contact with your skin or the painted surfaces of the vehicle. Rinse off spills immediately with plenty of water.

Air conditioning refrigerant

Although the refrigerant is not itself toxic, in the presence of a naked flame (or a lighted cigarette) it forms a highly toxic gas. Liquid refrigerant spilled on the skin will cause frostbite. If refrigerant enters the eyes, rinse them with a dilute solution of boric acid and seek medical advice immediately.

In view of the above points, and of the need for specialised equipment for evacuating and recharging the system, any work which requires the disconnection of a refrigerant line must be left to a specialist.

Do not allow refrigerant lines to be exposed to temperatures above 230°F (110°C) - eg. during welding or paint drying operations. Do not operate the air conditioning system if it is known to be short of refrigerant, or further damage may result.

2 Cooling system - draining, flushing and filling

Refer to Chapter 1, Section 32.

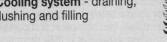

3.4b Air inlet duct attached to crosspanel - GTi

3.3 Temperature sensor unit location in radiator

3 Radiator - removal, inspection, cleaning and refitting

⚠ *Warning: Never work on the cooling system when it is hot. Take care to avoid any possibility of scalding*

Removal

1 Drain the cooling system.
2 Unclip and disconnect the top hose and the smaller expansion return hose from the radiator.
3 Disconnect the wiring connections from the radiator temperature sensor unit **(see illustration)** and, where applicable, the coolant level indicator unit
4 Pivot the bonnet stay out of the way, then unscrew and remove the five radiator front crosspanel securing bolts. Remove the crosspanel **(see illustration)**. Note that on GTi models, the crosspanel has the fuel system air inlet duct attached. The inlet duct hose will need to be detached from the panel and moved out of the way **(see illustration)**.
5 Carefully lift the radiator out of the engine compartment **(see illustration)**.

Inspection

6 Extensive damage should be repaired by a specialist or the unit exchanged for a new or reconditioned radiator. The radiator matrix, header and bottom tanks should be thoroughly examined for signs of damage, deterioration and leakage. Very often, a white

3.5 Lifting radiator out of vehicle

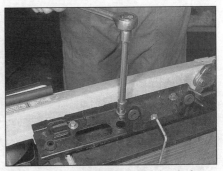
3.4a Undoing radiator retaining bolts

or rusty sediment will have been deposited where a leak has occurred.

Cleaning

7 After inspection, the radiator should be flushed and the matrix and exterior cleaned of dirt and dead flies with a strong jet of water.

Refitting

8 Refitting the radiator is a reversal of the removal procedure, but the following additional points should be noted:
a) *Examine and renew any clips, hoses and rubber mounting washers which have deteriorated*
b) *Refill the cooling system*

4 Cooling fan - removal and refitting

Removal

1 Raise and support the bonnet.
2 Disconnect the battery earth lead.
3 Undo the retaining screws and detach the front grille panel.
4 Undo the fan unit retaining bolt **(see illustration)** at the top and lift out the fan unit sufficiently to detach the wiring connector, then fully remove the fan unit.

Refitting

5 Refit in the reverse order of removal and check for correct operation of the fan on completion.

3

4.4 Cooling fan retaining bolt

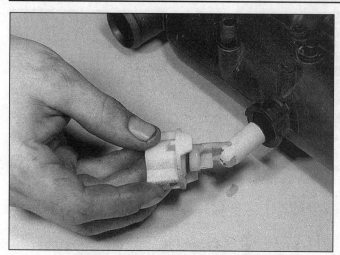

6.3 Coolant low level warning switch removal

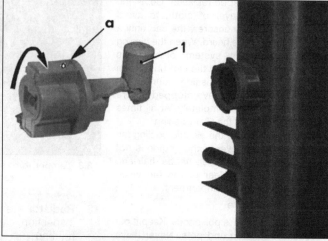

6.4 Coolant low level warning switch showing correct orientation when fitted - mark "a" at top

5 Cooling fan thermal switch - removal and refitting

Removal

1 This switch is fitted into the rear face of the radiator bottom section and its purpose is to switch the cooling fan on and off in accordance with the coolant temperature.
2 To remove the switch, first drain the coolant from the radiator.
3 Disconnect the switch wiring connector then unscrew and remove the switch.

Refitting

4 Refit the switch in the reverse order to removal. If the original switch is being refitted, check that the sealing washer is in good condition and renew if necessary.
5 Top-up the coolant level on completion then run the engine and check that the cooling fan operates when the engine is warmed up.

6 Coolant low level warning switch - removal and refitting

Removal

1 If fitted, this switch is located in the radiator.
2 To remove the switch, first partially drain the cooling system.
3 Disconnect the switch wiring connector then twist the switch anti-clockwise and withdraw it (see illustration).

Refitting

4 Refit the switch in the reverse order to removal but ensure that its orientation is correct with the counterweight to the top (see illustration).

5 On completion, top-up and bleed the cooling system.

7 Coolant temperature switch - removal and refitting

Removal

1 Where a single switch is fitted, it will be screwed into the cylinder head, adjacent to the thermostat housing.
2 Alternatively, where there are two switches fitted, both are screwed into the thermostat housing itself. The switch with the blue lead connector makes the warning lamp blink when the coolant temperature reaches 105°C (221°F) and the switch with the yellow lead connector actuates the warning lamp when the coolant temperature reaches 112°C (233°F) (see illustration).
3 It is difficult to test a temperature switch without special equipment and the best method to use if a fault develops is to substitute a new switch, but only after the wiring to the gauge has been thoroughly checked.
4 To remove a switch, drain the coolant, disconnect the wiring from the switch and unscrew the switch.

Refitting

5 When refitting a switch, make sure that its seal is in good condition. Do not overtighten the switch.
6 Refill the cooling system.
7 If a switch is changed and the gauge still does not register, then the gauge should be checked by a competent auto-electrician. Access to the gauge is obtained after removing the instrument panel.

8 Thermostat - removal, testing and refitting

Removal

1 The thermostat is located at the engine end of the radiator top hose, under a cover secured to the cylinder head/adapter. The one exception being on BX 19 GTi 16 valve models, where it is located at the flywheel end of the cylinder block and where its housing incorporates the coolant temperature switch, a sensor for the Motronic engine management system and a bleed screw (see illustrations).
2 To remove the thermostat, first partially drain the cooling system and then disconnect the top hose from the thermostat housing outlet.

7.2 Coolant temperature switches - BX 16 and BX 19

8.1a Thermostat housing in position - BX 19 GTi 16v

8.1b Thermostat housing dismantled - BX 19 GTi 16v

8.1c Thermostat housing bleed screw (arrowed) - BX 19 GTi 16v

8.3 Thermostat housing cover - BX and BX 14

8.4 The thermostat

3 Unscrew and remove the two retaining bolts and carefully lift the coolant outlet away from the cylinder head/adapter **(see illustration)**.
4 Extract the thermostat from its recess and remove the old gasket **(see illustration)**.
5 Clean the faces of the cylinder head/adapter and the mating thermostat cover so that they are free of all traces of gasket and sealant.

Testing

6 To test whether the thermostat is serviceable, suspend it by a piece of string in a pan of water. Heat the water whilst ensuring that the thermostat does not touch the pan. Use a similarly suspended thermometer to check the operating temperatures of the thermostat with reference to the information given in *Specifications*. If the thermostat is faulty it must be renewed.

Refitting

7 Refitting the thermostat is a reversal of the removal procedure, noting the following:
 a) *Use a new thermostat gasket*
 b) *Ensure that the mating surfaces of the water outlet and head or manifold are clean and free of excessive corrosion*
 c) *Ensure that the thermostat vent pin is positioned upwards to allow air to escape from the system*
 d) *Refill the cooling system*

9 Coolant pump (BX and BX 14) - removal and refitting

150 engine

1 Drain the engine coolant.
2 Loosen the drivebelt tension and disengage the belt from the pump pulley.
3 Undo the retaining clips and detach the coolant hoses from the pump **(see illustration)**. Unbolt the pump and remove it.
4 Any wear in the pump or leakage of coolant at the shaft gland will mean renewal of the pump, as repair is not possible.
5 Always renew the O-ring seal before fitting the pump to the cylinder block **(see illustrations)**.
6 Tighten the pump bolts to the specified torque.
7 Refit and adjust the drivebelt, referring to the information given for the alternator drivebelt.

8 Refill the cooling system.

K1G engine

9 Drain the cooling system.
10 Unbolt and remove the upper and intermediate timing covers, leaving the lower cover in position.
11 Turn the engine clockwise, using a socket on the crankshaft pulley bolt until the small hole in the camshaft sprocket is aligned with the corresponding hole in the cylinder head. Insert a close-fitting twist drill or bolt into the holes.
12 Align the TDC holes in the flywheel and cylinder block rear flange, then insert a further twist drill or long bolt.
13 Loosen the timing belt tensioner roller nut, turn the tensioner clockwise using a screwdriver or square drive in the special hole, then re-tighten the nut.
14 Release the timing belt from the pump sprocket.
15 Unscrew the nut from the right-hand engine mounting.
16 Using a trolley jack and block of wood, lift the right-hand side of the engine as far as possible.
17 Unscrew the nuts and remove the mounting bracket from the pump housing.
18 Disconnect the hoses from the housing, then unbolt the housing from the block. Remove the housing O-ring seal **(see illustrations)**.
19 Unbolt the pump from the housing and remove the pump O-ring **(see illustrations)**. If necessary, similarly remove the inlet elbow.

9.3 Coolant pump hoses

9.5a Coolant pump O-ring seal

9.5b Fitting coolant pump

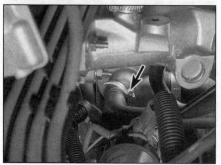

9.18a Bypass hose connection to coolant pump housing (arrowed)

9.18b Coolant pump housing securing bolts (arrowed)

9.18c Coolant pump housing O-ring seal (arrowed)

20 Refitting is a reversal of removal, noting the following points.
  a) *Renew the pump and housing O-rings.*
  b) *Make sure that the housing-to-block location dowels are in position.*
  c) *Tighten all nuts and bolts to the specified torque.*
  d) *Refit and tension the timing belt*
  e) *Refill the cooling system.*

10 Coolant pump (BX 16 and BX 19) - removal and refitting

D6C engine

Note: *As removal of the pump fitted to this engine requires the timing belt to be removed, it is advisable to read the procedure for timing belt removal and refitting before commencing work*

1 Drain the cooling system.
2 Remove the alternator drivebelt.
3 Release the tension on the timing belt and slip the belt from the two camshaft pulleys.
4 Remove the camshaft cover, then holding each camshaft using an open-ended spanner on the camshaft flats, undo and remove the bolts and the camshaft sprockets.
5 Remove the timing cover upper backplate.
6 Unscrew the pump fixing bolts and withdraw the pump **(see illustration)**.
7 Refitting is a reversal of removal, noting the following:
  a) *Use a new gasket.*

9.19a Removing coolant pump from housing

  b) *Tension the timing belt and drivebelts*
  c) *Top-up the cooling system*

All other engines

8 Drain the cooling system.
9 Remove the camshaft drivebelt.
10 Remove the camshaft drivebelt tensioner.
11 Remove the plastic shield, noting the locations of the different types of bolt.
12 Remove the five bolts which secure the coolant pump. Remove the pump and recover the gasket **(see illustration)**.
13 The pump cannot be repaired and if defective, it must be renewed.
14 Refit in the reverse order of removal, noting the following:
  a) *Use a new gasket*
  b) *Tighten the securing bolts to the specified torque*
  c) *Refit and tension the camshaft timing belt*
  d) *Top-up the cooling system*

9.19b Coolant pump O-ring (arrowed)

11 Heater unit (non air conditioned models) - removal and refitting

Early models

1 Disconnect the battery earth lead.
2 Drain the engine coolant.
3 Detach the lower facia panel on the passenger side. It is secured by two screws on the outer end face and a single screw at the other end. Now undo the four screws securing the glovebox lid **(see illustration)** and remove the lid and lower facia panel.
4 Undo and remove the single screw retaining the heater unit from within the glovebox.
5 Remove the retaining screws and lower the speaker unit. Detach the wiring connector and remove the unit.

10.6 Withdrawing coolant pump

10.12 Coolant pump removal

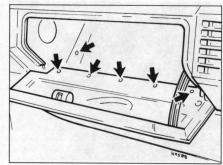

11.3 Remove screws indicated in glovebox

11.6 Heater/ventilation control knob removal

11.8 Heater/ventilation control plate removal

11.10 Remove screws indicated (9 and 10)

6 Withdraw the ashtray and pull free the heater/ventilation control knobs **(see illustration)**.
7 Unscrew the two retaining screws and remove the ashtray support.
8 Remove the heater/ventilation control plate **(see illustration)**.
9 Remove the radio and where applicable, its housing unit.
10 Unscrew and remove the screws from the positions shown **(see illustration)**.
11 Remove the upper and lower retaining screws from the opposite side of the heater/ventilation facia unit and withdraw the unit. As it is withdrawn, detach the ashtray and heater control light lamps.
12 Remove the cigar lighter and its lamp.
13 If applicable, remove the door lock electronic unit.
14 Unscrew and remove the driver's side lower finishing panel retaining screw.

11.21 Heater flow and return hose connections at bulkhead/heater

11.17 Rear passenger compartment heater nozzle

15 Prise free the blanking plugs (at the front and rear of the gear lever) from the console, then undo the retaining nut (front) and bolt (rear).
16 Remove the two plastic dowels retaining the console to the heater unit. Prise free the gear lever rubber gaiter, pull on the handbrake lever and withdraw the front section of the console.
17 Detach the heater nozzle to the rear passenger compartment **(see illustration)**.
18 Undo the two screws from the top end of the underside of the steering column and release the upper column shroud.
19 Undo and remove the three screws from the positions shown **(see illustration)**, then withdraw the lower driver's side facia, leaving the choke control attached (manual choke models).
20 Detach the heater unit wiring harness connector and plug.

11.19 Remove screws from positions 7, 8 and "a". Steering column lower shroud upper retaining screw positions also shown (6) - Left-hand drive

21 Loosen the feed and return coolant hose retaining clips and detach the hoses from the heater unit **(see illustration)**.
22 Carefully detach the bonnet seal rubber, then remove the plastic cover from over the windscreen wiper motor.
23 Undo the two retaining screws and remove the heater air inlet grille.
24 Unscrew and remove the nuts from the positions shown **(see illustration)**.
25 Remove the central directional vent grilles. Insert a screwdriver between the grille and housing to release each grille and withdraw them **(see illustration)**.
26 Using a screwdriver, prise out the vent grille housing by releasing the retaining clips. Remove the vent surround and grille **(see illustration)**.

11.24 Remove heater retaining nuts (1)

11.25 Withdraw vent grille . . .

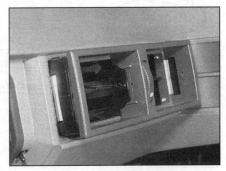

11.26 . . . and grille housing

11.27 Heater coolant drain hose

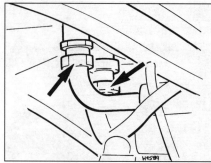

12.4 Air conditioning Freon pipe connections to heater (arrowed)

27 Detach the heater coolant drain pipe from its housing (see illustration).
28 Prise free and detach the heater coolant pipe (feed and return) scuttle seal, then withdraw the heater unit from the passenger side. As it is withdrawn disengage it from the side vent ducts.
29 Refitting is a direct reversal of the removal

procedure, noting the following:
a) Ensure that the heater feed and return hoses are securely connected
b) Ensure that all wiring connections are correctly and securely made
c) Check the operation of all items disconnected during removal
d) Top-up the cooling system

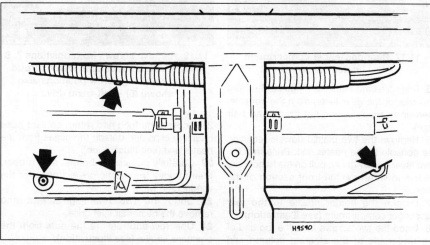

12.5 Additional heater retaining screw locations (arrowed)

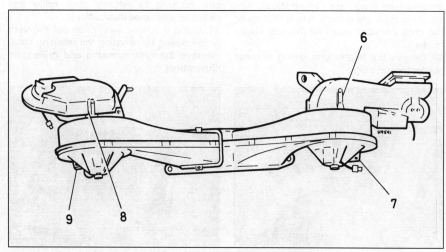

12.6 Remove screws (7 and 9) and clips (6 and 8)

Later models

30 Although the heater unit is much the same as that fitted to earlier models, the controls and the blower motor differ.
31 The blower motor will need to be removed to gain access to the heater unit retaining bolts. Access to the heater motor unit differs, in that the later-type facia panel and assemblies will have to be removed for access.
32 The heater unit retaining bolt positions are as shown in illustration 11.24.
33 Disconnect the fresh air/heater ducts from the heater unit, then remove the main facia unit.
34 The heater unit can now be removed in a similar manner to that described for earlier models.
35 Refitting of the heater unit and the associated fittings is a reversal of the removal procedure, noting the points listed in paragraph 29.

12 Heater unit (air conditioned models) - removal and refitting

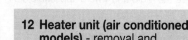

Warning: Where fitted, the air conditioning system must be depressurised and drained by a Citroën dealer or refrigeration specialist. Do not attempt this yourself

Removal

1 The following procedures closely follow those given for the heater unit fitted to non air conditioned models but the following differences apply.
2 Before starting the removal procedure, have the air conditioning system depressurised and drained by your Citroën dealer or refrigeration specialist. Do not attempt this yourself.
3 Prise free and detach the wiring from the air recirculation switch mounted in the control console.
4 Loosen the retaining nuts and detach the two Freon pipes from the heater unit (engine compartment side) (see illustration). Recover the O-ring seals.
5 Undo the retaining screws shown (see illustration) in addition to those shown in illustration 11.24.
6 Remove the screws at positions 7 and 9, and the clips 6 and 8 (see illustration). Lift the two air inlet pipes for access to the unit retaining screws.
7 Release both the coolant pipe and Freon pipe seals at the bulkhead panel when removing the unit.

Refitting

8 Refit in the reverse order of removal. Ensure that the Freon pipe O-ring seals are located when attaching the pipes.

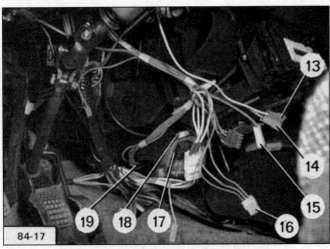

12.9 Heater unit wiring harness connections

13 *Red plug - air blower control*
14 *Blue plug - compressor control*
15 *Yellow plug - air blower control*
16 *3-way orange connector*
17 *4-way brown connector*
18 *Green plug - heater unit control lighting*
19 *Relay (behind the heater unit)*

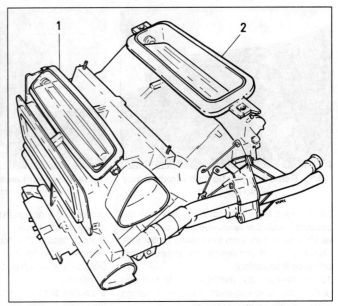

13.2 Heater unit foam gasket location (1 and 2)

9 When reconnecting the heater unit wiring harness, note the connections shown (see illustration).

13 Heater blower motor - removal and refitting

Early models

1 Remove the heater unit.
2 Carefully prise free and remove the foam gaskets (see illustration).
3 Undo the five screws retaining the control bracket, drill out the rivet and retrieve its washer then release the eleven securing clips (see illustration). Separate the housing.

4 Remove the five flaps.
5 Detach the wiring connectors from the blower motor and then pull the motor out of the housing.
6 To remove the grille from the blower motor, undo the two retaining nuts.
7 Undo the two screws and withdraw the blower motor from the support.
8 Refitting is a reversal of the removal procedure. When refitting the flaps, you will need three "end pieces" manufactured in 5 mm diameter steel wire, 50 mm in length. When the flaps are fitted to their pivot points, operate them to ensure correct fitting then fit the end pieces to the free end of flap numbers 6, 7 and 9 (see illustration).
9 When the half housings are reassembled and the clips are in position, the end pieces can be removed.

10 When fitting the 4 mm rivet, insert the plain washer.

Later models

11 Disconnect the battery earth lead.
12 Remove the windscreen wiper arm and spindle nut.
13 The heater blower motor is located in the bulkhead cavity just forward of the windscreen, beneath a plastic cover. Remove the plastic cover by prising free the rubber seal along its front edge and releasing the retaining clips at the rear edge (see illustration).
14 Removal of the air inlet grille at the base of the windscreen is advisable, this is secured by plastic clips. Carefully prise free the clips and remove the grille (see illustration).

3

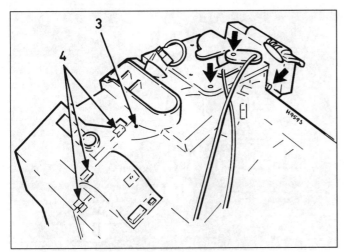

13.3 Remove rivets (3), clips (4) and screws (arrowed)

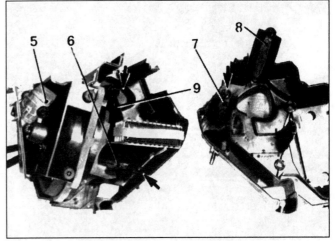

13.8 Heater unit showing flaps (5, 6, 7, 8 and 9). End piece locations arrowed

13.13 Removing plastic cover from heater blower motor

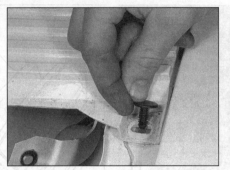

13.14 Removing an air inlet grille securing clip

13.15 Blower motor unit support bracket screws (arrowed)

15 Remove the single retaining bolt and the support bracket screws, then disconnect the wiring connectors from the blower motor unit. Carefully lift out and remove the blower motor unit **(see illustration)**.

16 To remove the motor from its housing unit, unclip and separate the half-housings and undo the retaining screws.

17 Refit in the reverse order of removal and check for satisfactory operation.

14 Heater matrix - removal and refitting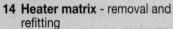

Early models

1 Drain the cooling system.

2 Undo the retaining screws and remove the lower facia finishing panel on the driver's side.

3 Undo the four screws retaining the heater tap to the heater matrix **(see illustration)**.

4 Undo the two screws retaining the matrix to the heater unit and the tap-to-heater unit screw. Reach up with a socket and extension from underneath for the tap-to-heater screw. As the tap is separated from the heater, allow for a certain amount of coolant spillage by

positioning a rag and/or container underneath it **(see illustration)**.

5 Prise apart the four locating clips and withdraw the matrix from the heater unit. Detach the control links as the matrix is withdrawn.

6 Loosen the hose retaining clips and detach the coolant pipes. Remove the gasket and the tap.

7 Loosen the cable clamp screw, disengage the location clip and then remove the control cable.

8 Refit in the reverse order to removal. During assembly, check that the heater control lever fully opens and closes the tap. Move the location clip position to adjust if necessary.

9 Prior to refitting the lower facia finishing panel, top-up the cooling system then check the heater hoses for any sign of leaks.

Later models

10 Drain the cooling system.

11 Remove the upper and lower steering column shrouds. These are secured by screws recessed into the lower shroud.

12 Unbolt the upper and lower steering column mountings.

13 Unbolt and separate the upper-to-lower column universal joint, then withdraw the

upper steering column unit so that it clears the matrix unit. Complete removal of the upper steering column will necessitate detaching the column switch wiring at the harness connectors.

14 The heater matrix is now accessible for withdrawal and can be removed in the same manner described for the earlier variants.

15 Refit in the reverse order of removal.

15 Heater control panel (later models) - removal and refitting

Removal

1 Disconnect the battery earth lead.

2 Pull free the heater/ventilation control knobs.

3 Undo the two retaining screws **(see illustration)**.

4 Remove the two ventilation grilles from their apertures above the heater control panel. Pull to release the retaining clips each side and withdraw the outer control panel.

5 Disconnect the wiring from the rear face of the cigar lighter.

6 The inner control unit is secured by four screws, but it cannot be removed on its own.

14.3 Heater tap (control) unit retaining screws (arrowed)

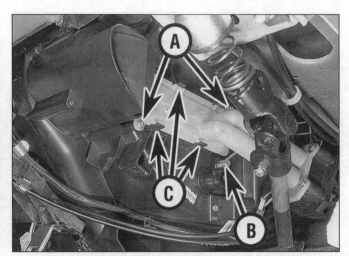

14.4 Heater matrix retaining screws (A) and control link connection (B). Location clips (C) also shown

15.3 Removing a heater/ventilation control panel retaining screw

Either remove it together with the heater unit, or detach the controls at the heater and withdraw the control unit **(see illustration)**.

Refitting

7 Refit in the reverse order of removal, and check for satisfactory operation.

16 Air conditioning system - maintenance

1 The air conditioning system layout and main components are as shown **(see illustration)**.

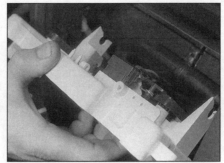

15.6 Withdrawing the heater control unit

2 To allow for fitting of the system the engine crankcase is modified to suit and the Weber carburettor fitted with a butterfly opener controlled by an "Elbi" electrovalve which is located underneath the battery tray. A battery of increased capacity is also fitted.

3 The heater system works on the normal principle in conjunction with the engine cooling system and incorporates its own booster (blower) motor.

4 If it is necessary to disconnect any part of the refrigeration system in order to undertake work on other components, then refer to "*Precautions*" at the beginning of this Chapter.

5 Due to the nature of the refrigerant used in the system, no servicing other than a few basic inspection tasks can be undertaken by the home mechanic.

6 Check the condition and tension of the alternator/compressor drivebelt. Renew the belt if it shows signs of excessive wear.

7 Check the system components for security and condition. Any components which are suspect must be renewed by a specialist. If the system has developed a leak, take care not to allow body contact with the fluid.

8 If the system is not used regularly, then it must be run for a period of about ten minutes once a month to keep it in good condition.

9 No maintenance is required for the electrical wiring part of the system, apart from the occasional check to ensure that the wiring and connections are in good condition and securely located. A line fuse is incorporated into the circuit and in the event of this blowing, the cause should be located and rectified before fitting a new fuse.

10 The fan control module for air conditioning on models manufactured after January 1987 is located on the fan motor casing within the scuttle plenum chamber, instead of being mounted on the steering column support bracket as on earlier models.

3

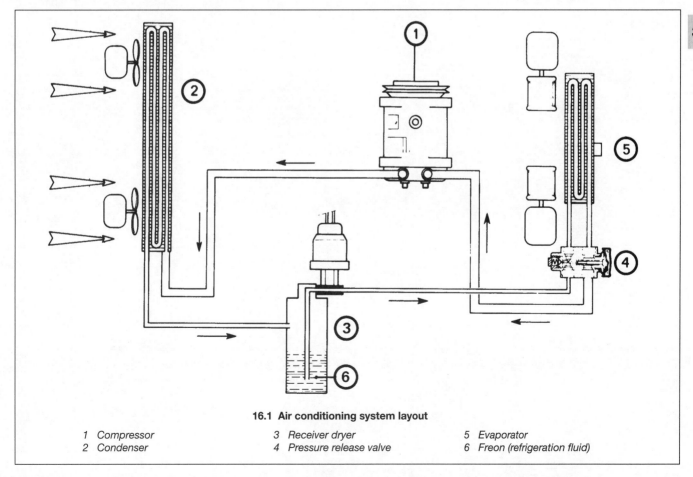

16.1 Air conditioning system layout

1 Compressor	3 Receiver dryer	5 Evaporator
2 Condenser	4 Pressure release valve	6 Freon (refrigeration fluid)

Chapter 4 Part A:
Fuel and exhaust systems - carburettor models

Contents

4A

Degrees of difficulty

Easy, suitable for novice with little experience	**Fairly easy,** suitable for beginner with some experience	**Fairly difficult,** suitable for competent DIY mechanic 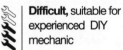

Difficult, suitable for experienced DIY mechanic	**Very difficult,** suitable for expert DIY or professional

Specifications

For engine to model applications refer to Chapter 2

Air cleaner

Type . . . . Dry type with replaceable cartridge. Manual or automatic air temperature controlled inlet system

Element:
BX 14 . . . . Champion V402
BX 14 (Aug 1988 to Sept 1991) . . . . Champion V401
BX 14 (Sept 1991 on) . . . . Champion V438
BX 16 (pre June 1987) . . . . Champion W117
BX 16 (Sept 1988 to 1991) . . . . Champion U543
BX 19 (pre June 1987) . . . . Champion W117
BX 19 (from July 1987) . . . . Champion U543
BX 19 (1991 on) . . . . Champion U543

Fuel filter

Type . . . . Champion L101

Fuel pump

Type . . . . Mechanical diaphragm, driven by eccentric on camshaft

Carburettor - BX

Engine application .... 150 A
Carburettor type .... Solex 30-30 z2 CIT 329

	Primary	Secondary
Venturi	24	25
Main jet	112.5	125
Air corrector jet and emulsion tube	165 ZD	180 ZC
Idle jet	40	-
Bypass jet	-	50
Pneumatic enrichment device	50	-
Pump injector	35	-
Econostat	-	80
Needle valve	1.6 mm	
Float level setting	33 ± 1 mm	
Primary choke valve opening (strangler valve fully shut)	0.9 mm	
Strangler flap opening (by anti-flood capsule) under vacuum of 350 mbar	3.2 ± 0.5 mm	
Idle speed	700 to 800 rpm	
CO percentage in exhaust gas	0.8 to 1.15	

Carburettor - BX 14 (pre August 1988)

Engine application .... 150 C
Carburettor type .... Solex 32-34 Z2 CIT 348

	Primary	Secondary
Venturi	24	25
Main jet	115	120
Air corrector jet and emulsion tube	155 ZE	160 ZC
Idle jet	40	-
Bypass jet	-	50
Pneumatic enrichment device	45	-
Pump injector	35	35
Econostat	-	80
Needle valve	1.6 mm	
Float level setting	33 ± 1 mm	
Primary choke valve opening (strangler valve fully shut)	0.75 mm	
Strangler flap opening (by anti-flood capsule) under vacuum of 350 mbar	3.7 ± 0.5 mm	
Idle speed	800 to 850 rpm	
CO percentage in exhaust gas	0.8 to 1.5	

Carburettor - BX 14 (from August 1988)

Engine application K1G
Carburettor type .... Solex 34 PBISA 17
Venturi 26
Main jet 132
Air correction jet 155
Emulsion tube .... EC
Idle jet .... 42 to 46
Enrichment jet 55
Accelerator pump jet 40
Float chamber needle valve .... 1.6 mm
Idle speed .... 750 ± 50 rpm
CO percentage in exhaust gas .... 0.8 to 1.2

Carburettor - BX 16 (pre June 1983)

Engine application 171
Carburettor type .... Weber 32-34 DRTC 100 W 121-50

	Primary	Secondary
Venturi	24	26
Main jet	107	115
Air corrector jet	165	160
Emulsion tube	F27	F27
Idle jet	45	-
Bypass jet	-	70
Pump injector	55	-
Econostat	-	60
Needle valve	175	
Primary choke valve opening at 20°C	0.50 mm	
Strangler flap opening (by anti-flood capsule)	4.5 mm	
Float level setting	7.25 ± 0.25 mm	
Idle speed	700 rpm	
C0 percentage in exhaust gas	0.8 to 1.5	

Carburettor - BX 16 (pre June 1983)

	Primary	Secondary
Engine application	171	
Carburettor type	Solex 32-34 Z1 CIT 319	
Venturi	24	26
Main jet	140	120
Air corrector jet	200	155
Emulsion tube	23	18
Idle jet	42	70
Accelerator pump injector	40	35
Needle valve diameter	1.8 mm	
Float setting	33.0 mm	
Primary choke valve opening (strangler flap fully shut)	0.45 mm	
Strangler flap opening (by anti-flood capsule)	6.0 mm	
Idle speed	650 to 700 rpm	
CO percentage in exhaust gas	1 to 2	

Carburettor - BX 16 (from July 1983)

	Primary	Secondary
Engine application	171	
Carburettor type	Weber 32-34 DRTC 2/100 W 128-50	
Venturi	24	26
Main jet	107	112
Air corrector jet	170	160
Emulsion tube	F27	F27
Idle jet	45	-
Bypass jet	-	50
Pump injector	50	-
Econostat	-	60
Needle valve	1.75	
Float setting	6.75 ± 0.25 mm	
Maximum difference between floats	1.0 mm	
Primary choke valve opening (strangler flap fully shut) at 20ºC	0.45 mm	
Strangler flap opening (by anti-flood capsule)	4.5 mm	
Idle speed	650 to 700 rpm	
CO percentage in exhaust gas	0.8 to 1.5	

Carburettor - BX 16 (from July 1983)

	Primary	Secondary
Engine application	171	
Carburettor type	Solex 32-34 Z1 W 319	
Venturi	24	26
Main jet	140	120
Air corrector jet	200	155
Emulsion tube	23	18
Idle jet	42	
Bypass jet	-	70
Pump injector	40	35
Enrichment device jet	55	-
Econostat	-	80
Needle valve diameter	1.8 mm	
Primary choke valve opening (1st choke at 20ºC)	0.45 mm	
Strangler flap opening (by anti-flood capsule) under vacuum	6.0 mm	
Idle speed	650 to 700 rpm	
CO percentage in exhaust gas	0.8 to 1.5	

Carburettor - BX 16 (from March 1984)

	Primary	Secondary
Engine application	171	
Carburettor type	Solex 32-34 Z1 CIT 319-1	

This carburettor differs from the Solex 32-34 Z1 CIT 319 carburettor in the following ways:

	Primary	Secondary
Idling air correction jet	180	150
Enrichment device jet	55	-

Carburettor - BX 16 (automatic transmission)

Engine application	171
Carburettor type	Weber 32-34 DRTC 4 100 W 130-50

This carburettor is the same as the Weber 32-34 DRTC 2/100 W 128-50 with the following exception:

CO percentage in exhaust gas	1 to 2

Carburettor - BX 16 (automatic transmission and air conditioning)

Engine application 171
Carburettor type .... Weber 32-34 DRTC 8/100 W 136-50
This carburettor is the same as the Weber 32-34 DRTC 4 100 W 130-50 with the following exception:
Idle speed .... 750 to 800 rpm

Carburettor - BX 16 RE

Engine application B1A/A
Carburettor type .... Weber 36 TLP 1/100
Venturi 28
Main jet 142
Air correction jet 150
Emulsion tube F80
Idle jet .... 47 to 51
Enrichment jet 50
Accelerator pump injector 50
Float chamber needle valve .... 1.5 mm
Idle speed .... 700 ± 50 rpm
CO percentage in exhaust gas .... 1 to 2

Carburettor - BX 16 (from Sept 1988 to 1991)

Engine application B2C
Carburettor type .... Solex 32-34 Z1 PSA

	Primary	Secondary
Venturi	24	26
Main jet	112.5	125
Air correction jet	145	140
Emulsion tube	ZD	ZC
Idling jet	44	50
Air correction jet	180	150
Enrichment jet	55	-
Econostat jet	-	80
Accelerator pump jet	40	40
Fuel inlet needle valve	1.8	

Idle speed:
   Manual gearbox .... 800 ± 100 rpm
   Automatic transmission .... 750 ± 50 rpm
CO percentage in exhaust gas .... 0.8 to 1.5

Carburettor - BX 19

Engine application 159
Carburettor type .... Solex CISAC 34-34 Z1 381

	Primary	Secondary
Venturi	25	17
Main jet	115	125
Air corrector jet	150	160
Emulsion tube	18	20
Idle jet	43	90
Idle air correction jet	145	145
Enrichment device jet	50	-
Econostat	-	80
Pump injector	40	35
Needle valve	1.8 mm	
Float adjustment	33 mm	
Primary choke valve opening (strangler flap fully shut) at 20°C	0.45 mm	
Strangler flap opening (by anti-flood capsule)	5 to 7 mm	
Manual de-flooding	7 to 9 mm	
Idle speed	650 to 750 rpm	
CO percentage in exhaust gas	1.5 ± 0.5	

Carburettor - BX 19 TRS/TZS (from July 1986 to 1991)

Engine applications .... D2A and D2E
Carburettor types:
   Manual gearbox .... Solex 34-34 Z1 CIT 391
   Manual gearbox with air conditioning .... Solex 34-34 Z1 CIT 291-1
   Automatic transmission .... Weber 34-34 DRTC 14/100
   Automatic transmission with air conditioning .... Weber 34-34 DRTC 15/100

Carburettor - BX 19 TRS/TZS (from July 1986 to 1991) (continued)

Solex carburettors	Primary	Secondary
Venturi	25	27
Main jet	115	115
Air correction jet	150	160
Emulsion tube	ZD	ZC
Idling jet	43	90
Idling air correction jet	145	145
Enrichment device jet	50	-
Econostat calibration	-	70
Pump injector	40	56
Needle valve diameter	1.8 mm	
Float adjustment	33 mm	
Positive opening of primary valve (at 20ºC)	0.45 mm	
Strangler flap opening by anti-flood capsule	5 to 7 mm	
Manual anti-flooding	7 to 9 mm	
Idle speed	700 ± 50 rpm	
Fast idling (air conditioning)	900 ± 50 rpm	
CO percentage in exhaust gas	1.0 to 2.0	

Weber carburettors	Primary	Secondary
Venturi	25	27
Main jet	110	125
Air correction jet	160	150
Emulsion tube	F45	F27
Idling jet	52	50
Idling air correction jet	150	70
Enrichment device jet	55	-
Econostat calibration	-	85
Pump injector	50	
Float adjustment	7 mm	
Positive opening of primary valve (at 20ºC)	0 ± 1 mm	
Strangler flap opening by anti-flood capsule	4.5 ± 1 mm	
Manual anti-flooding	8.5 mm	
Idle speed	800 ± 50 rpm	
Fast idling (air conditioning)	900 ± 50 rpm	
CO percentage in exhaust gas	1.0 to 2.0	

Carburettor - BX 19 TZS (from 1991)

Engine application	D2F	
Carburettor type	Solex 34-34 Z1	

	Primary	Secondary
Venturi	26	27
Main jet	115 ± 5	122 ± 5
Air correction jet	140 ± 20	160 ± 20
Emulsion tube	3Z	ZC
Idling jet:		
Manual	45 ± 5	110 ± 10
Automatic	44 ± 3	110 ± 10
Idling air correction jet:		
Manual	145 ± 20	145 ± 20
Automatic	145 ± 20	140 ± 20
Enrichment jet	50 ± 20	-
Econostat jet	-	50 ± 20
Accelerator pump jet	45	40
Fuel inlet needle valve	1.8 mm	
Idle speed	750 ± 50 rpm	
CO percentage in exhaust gas	0.8 to 1.2	

Torque wrench settings

	Nm	lbf ft
Carburettor to inlet manifold	15	11
Inlet manifold to cylinder head	22	16
Exhaust manifold to cylinder head	22	16

4A

1 General information and precautions

General information

The fuel system is conventional in layout and operation. The fuel tank is mounted on the underside of the vehicle directly beneath the rear passenger seats. Fuel is drawn from the tank by a mechanical diaphragm pump operated by an eccentric on the camshaft and fed via a fuel filter (some models) to a carburettor of Solex or Weber manufacture. Depending on model type, a manually operated or automatic choke is fitted.

The air cleaner is of the renewable element type. On BX and BX14 models, the temperature of the air entering the air cleaner unit has a manual control for seasonal setting. Other models in the range have an automatic temperature control fitted to the air cleaner.

All models are fitted with a basic emission control system which relies mainly on the correct setting of the carburettor and the ignition system to keep exhaust emission levels to a minimum.

The admission of warm air to the air cleaner on all models keeps the intake air at the carburettor at a constant temperature and this too makes for clean combustion.

The engine crankcase ventilation system transfers oil fumes and blow-by gases which get past the piston rings into the air cleaner where they are consumed during the normal combustion process.

Precautions

Fuel warning

Many of the procedures in this Chapter require the removal of fuel lines and connections which may result in some fuel spillage. Before carrying out any operation on the fuel system refer to the precautions given in Safety first! at the beginning of this Manual and follow them implicitly. Petrol is a highly dangerous and volatile liquid and the precautions necessary when handling it cannot be overstressed.

3.2a Air intake disconnected from air cleaner casing

Tamperproof adjustment screws

Certain adjustment points in the fuel system are protected by "tamperproof" caps, plugs or seals. The purpose of such tamperproofing is to discourage, and to detect, adjustment by unqualified operators.

In some EEC countries (though not yet in the UK), it is an offence to drive a vehicle with missing or broken tamperproof seals. Before disturbing a seal, satisfy yourself that you will not be breaking local or national anti-pollution regulations by doing so. Fit a new seal when adjustment is complete, when this is required by law.

Do not break tamperproof seals on a vehicle which is still under warranty.

Unleaded petrol - usage

As a general rule, all pre-1988 carburettor models are not suitable for running on unleaded petrol, and must be run on 97 RON leaded fuel only. Models manufactured between 1988 and 1991 should also only be run on 97 RON leaded fuel, but most models produced between these dates are suitable for running on 95 RON unleaded fuel if the suitable adjustments are first carried out. For full information on the use of unleaded petrol, consult your Citroën dealer who will be able to inform you if your vehicle is capable of running on unleaded fuel and, where possible, of the necessary adjustments required. The use of unleaded fuel in a vehicle not designed, or suitably adjusted, to run on unleaded fuel will lead to serious damage of the valve seats.

3.2b Removing insulated hose from exhaust manifold hot air collector plate

2 Air cleaner element - renewal

Refer to Chapter 1, Section 28.

3 Air cleaner - removal and refitting

BX 14 - K1G engine

1 Remove the air cleaner element.
2 Release the large clip, then separate and remove the air intake from the air cleaner casing. Note the insulated hose connecting with the exhaust manifold hot air collector plate (see illustrations).
3 Disconnect the air intake duct from the carburettor and the crankcase vent hoses, then withdraw the air cleaner casing upwards. Note the locating spigot at the base of the casing (see illustrations).
4 Refitting is a reversal of removal. On completion, set the Winter/Summer lever to the appropriate position (see illustration).

All other models

5 Detach the hoses/air ducts to the cleaner unit.
6 On BX and BX 14 models, unclip the retaining strap.

3.3a Disconnecting crankcase vent hose from air cleaner

3.3b Removing air intake duct from carburettor and air cleaner

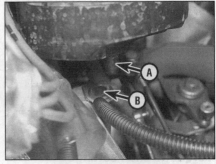

3.3c Air cleaner casing

A Base locating spigot
B Spigot grommet

3.4 Air cleaner Winter/Summer lever

7 Undo the retaining bolt(s) and remove the unit.
8 Refit in the reverse order to removal.

4 Air intake heating system - operation and maintenance

Operation

1 To maintain engine performance in cold conditions, warm air is admitted to the air intake before entering the air cleaner. Air is preheated by a muff on the exhaust manifold and its intake is controlled manually by means of a lever on the top face of the intake ducting (BX and BX 14 models) or automatically by an integral thermostat (BX 16 and 19 models).
2 The manual adjustment lever has three adjustment positions **(see illustration)**.
3 On automatic control models, the integral thermostat operates a valve which directs warm air from the exhaust manifold ducting or cool air through the normal air intake duct on the air cleaner unit **(see illustration)**.

Maintenance

4 This system calls for no special maintenance but, on manual control models, the adjustment lever must be set to the appropriate position as the season demands. Failure to make the seasonal adjustment will reduce efficiency, may cause the carburettor to ice up, and will certainly create emulsion in the engine breather pipes and rocker cover in very cold weather.

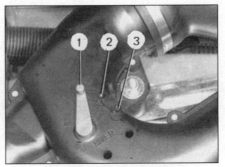

4.2 Manual air intake control

1 ETE (summer) setting
2 Mixte (Mixture) setting
3 Hiver (Winter) setting

5 Fuel pump - testing

1 If the performance of the fuel pump is in doubt, first examine for fuel leaks and check that the fuel line connections are all sound.
2 Disconnect the fuel hose at the carburettor inlet connection and disconnect the high tension lead from the coil. Ensure that the tank contains fuel.
3 Direct the fuel feed hose into a suitable container and have an assistant operate the starter to crank the engine. A good spurt of fuel should be delivered on every second revolution of the engine. If not, check that the hose is not blocked. If the hose is clear, then the pump will have to be removed for examination or renewal.

6 Fuel pump - cleaning

1 The fuel pump may be one of several types and inspection will determine which type of pump is fitted. On one type, the filter cover is simply unbolted and removed. On the other type, the pump cover is retained by two screws. With some pumps, the fuel outlet hose must be removed in order to be able to withdraw the pump cover **(see illustrations)**.

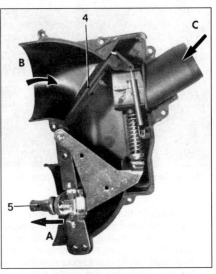

4.3 Automatic air intake control

4 Air control flap
5 Temperature sensor
A Air supply to filter
B Ambient air intake
C Heater air intake

2 With the cover removed, take out the filter screen and wash it in fuel until it is free from fluff and dirt **(see illustration)**.
3 Mop out the fuel from the pump body and wipe out any sediment.
4 Refit the filter screen and cover, making sure that the gasket is in good condition.

7 Fuel pump - removal, overhaul and refitting

4A

Note: *Have a repair kit available before dismantling the fuel pump*

Removal

1 Disconnect the fuel lines from the pump and plug them to prevent ingress of contamination **(see illustration)**.
2 Note that on BX 16 and BX 19 models manufactured after November 1985, the fuel lines have reduced inside diameter connections and are now 6 mm in diameter instead of 8 mm as on earlier models. All

6.1a Fuel pump cover removal - non-removable filter type

6.1b Fuel pump cover removal - removable filter type

6.2 Fuel pump filter removal

7.1 Fuel supply hose removal from fuel pump

7.3a Fuel pump showing retaining nuts and black insulator block - BX 16

7.3b Fuel pump removal - BX 14

connections to the pump, carburettor, fuel filter and fuel flow meter are now of the same diameter. Early and later-type connections are not directly interchangeable. Note also that the later-type fuel lines are secured with clips.

3 Unscrew the pump mounting bolts/nuts and lift the pump away **(see illustrations)**.

4 An insulator block with a gasket each side is fitted between the pump flange and the mounting flange on the engine. The gaskets must be renewed when refitting the pump.

5 Where applicable, withdraw the pump operating pushrod **(see illustration)**.

Overhaul

6 Further dismantling may not be possible on some types of pump. Even if it is, it should only be attempted if you have a repair kit. First, mark the top and bottom halves of the pump for reassembly and then progressively loosen and remove the screws holding the two halves together. The diaphragm is connected to the operating mechanism beneath, and details will vary with different pumps. Note the sequence of assembly so that reassembly can be achieved in the same order.

7 Renew all defective parts. The repair kit will contain a variety of seals or gaskets which should automatically be fitted in place of the originals, regardless of the fact that they may appear fit for further use.

8 Reassembly is the reverse of the dismantling sequence. Make sure that the upper and lower halves of the pump body are aligned and tighten the joint screws progressively and diagonally. Do not overtighten the top cover screws.

9.3 Fuel level transmitter

Refitting

9 Before refitting the pump, check that the operating pushrod is in position (where applicable). Locate a new gasket each side of the insulator and refit the pump.

10 Tighten the securing bolts and make sure that the fuel hoses are reconnected to their correct pump connections.

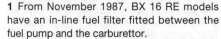

8 In-line fuel filter (BX 16 RE) - renewal

1 From November 1987, BX 16 RE models have an in-line fuel filter fitted between the fuel pump and the carburettor.

2 When renewing this filter, ensure that the directional arrow on the filter points towards the carburettor and check for leaks at its hose connections after starting the engine (see Chapter 1).

3 Note that on BX 16 and BX 19 models manufactured after November 1985, the fuel lines have reduced inside diameter connections and are now 6 mm in diameter instead of 8 mm as on earlier models. All connections to the filter, carburettor, fuel pump and fuel flow meter are now of the same diameter. Early and later-type connections are not directly interchangeable. Note also that the later-type fuel lines are secured with clips.

9 Fuel level transmitter - removal and refitting

Removal

1 Disconnect the battery earth lead.

2 Fold the rear seat forwards and remove the insulator mat.

3 Prise free the circular plastic cover to expose the fuel level transmitter and disconnect the wiring from it **(see illustration)**.

4 Using a suitable tool, unscrew the transmitter mounting plate to release it from the securing tabs. Withdraw the transmitter unit.

7.5 Fuel pump pushrod - BX 14

Refitting

5 Refitting is a reversal of removal. Use a new sealing ring if there is any doubt about the condition of the original one.

10 Fuel tank - removal, inspection and refitting

Removal

1 The fuel tank will normally only need to be removed if it is severely contaminated or damaged, or for any repair work to the adjacent body structure or mechanical components.

2 As there is no drain plug incorporated in the tank, the best time to remove it is when it is nearly empty. If this is not possible, syphon as much as fuel as possible from the tank into a container which can be sealed. Before doing so, observe the following precautions:
 a) *Disconnect the battery*
 b) *Do not smoke or allow any naked lights near the working area*
 c) *Avoid placing the vehicle over an inspection pit as fuel vapour is heavier than air*

3 Raise the rear of the vehicle and support it on axle stands (see *"Jacking and vehicle support"*).

4 From within the vehicle, disconnect the wiring from the fuel level transmitter.

5 Disconnect the fuel supply and return pipes from the fuel tank top face. Note that the fuel

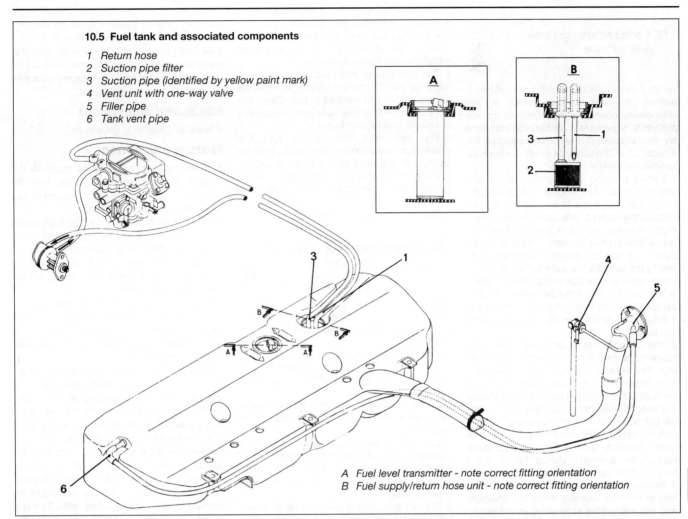

10.5 Fuel tank and associated components

1 Return hose
2 Suction pipe filter
3 Suction pipe (identified by yellow paint mark)
4 Vent unit with one-way valve
5 Filler pipe
6 Tank vent pipe

A Fuel level transmitter - note correct fitting orientation
B Fuel supply/return hose unit - note correct fitting orientation

4A

supply pipe is marked with yellow paint for identification. Plug the pipes to prevent fuel leakage and the ingress of dirt **(see illustration)**.

6 Remove the exhaust system.

7 Detach the height control linkage, complete with its intermediate bearing **(see illustration)**.

8 Detach the fuel filler pipe from the tank inlet nozzle.

9 Unfasten and peel back the carpet edging from the floor panel above the leading edge of the tank, then unscrew the two front tank retaining screws. Support the weight of the tank from underneath.

10 Unscrew and remove the three retaining bolts along the rear edge of the tank unit (from above), then lower the tank. As it is lowered, disconnect the ventilation pipe from the side of the tank. On BX and BX 14 models, this pipe is connected to the right-hand side, whilst on BX 16 and 19 models, the pipe connection is on the left-hand side.

Inspection

11 If the tank is damaged, remove the fuel level transmitter unit and renew the tank. It cannot be repaired.

12 If the tank contains sediment, remove the fuel level transmitter and wash out the tank using paraffin, then rinse it out with clean fuel whilst observing all precautions against fire.

Refitting

13 Refit in the reverse order of removal.

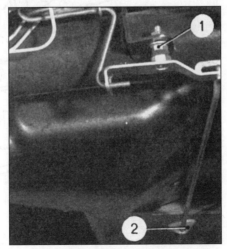

10.7 Height control linkage (1) and intermediate bearing (2)

Ensure that all hose connections are securely made.

11 Carburettors - general information

1 The carburettor fitted is a single Solex or Weber of twin or single choke downdraught design.

2 The type of carburettor fitted is dependent on engine type. Refer to the *Specifications* for application details. Depending on vehicle type, a manually operated or automatic choke is fitted.

3 All carburettors are conventional in operation and have a primary and main jet system and a mechanically operated acceleration pump. All carburettors incorporate exhaust emission control anti-pollution.

4 The type identification number is stamped on a plate attached to the carburettor.

5 The Weber carburettor fitted to BX 16 models with automatic transmission is identical in design to other Weber carburettor types fitted to manual gearbox models, except that it also has a kickdown cam fitted.

12 Carburettors - general maintenance

Note: *A complete carburettor strip-down is unlikely to cure a fault which is not immediately obvious without introducing new problems. If persistent carburation problems are encountered, it is recommended that the advice of a Citroen dealer or carburettor specialist is sought.*

1 Before blaming the carburettor for any shortcomings in engine performance, remember that there is no reason why the carburettor should lose tune. What usually happens is that, as the engine gets older and less efficient, more or less fruitless attempts may be made to restore performance by interfering with the carburettor. In countries where exhaust emission is regulated by law, it is inadvisable and may be illegal, to alter carburettor settings without monitoring exhaust emission levels using special equipment.

2 The ultimate cause of most carburettor problems is wear in moving parts or dirt in the jets. The Solex and the Weber carburettors have no continuously moving parts (except for the float and the throttle spindle) which makes it a very reliable device so long as dirt does not get in. A drop of oil on the various linkages and flap spindle will ensure that they last for years without trouble. In consequence, carburettor overhaul should be no more frequent than major engine overhaul.

3 Routine carburettor maintenance consists only of periodic cleaning of the float chamber and jets and (where applicable) an occasional look at the small gauze filters fitted in the fuel inlet connection and on the accelerator pump inlet valve. These tasks can be undertaken with the carburettor fitted to the engine.

4 Before separating the top of the carburettor from the bottom, give the outside a good clean using paraffin or a proprietary cleaner and a stiff brush, afterwards drying with clean rag. It is well worth taking this extra trouble to reduce the risk of dirt getting into the carburettor.

5 After removing the jets, clean them by first washing in clean fuel and then blowing air through them. Never use a piece of wire as jet calibration can be easily altered.

6 The float can be removed after taking out the hinge pin. The float needle valve can then be unscrewed and washed in fuel. Clean any dirt out of the float chamber using clean fuel but do not use rag for drying.

7 The fuel inlet filter gauze and the accelerator pump valve gauze should both be washed in clean fuel and dried in air. Do not use rag to dry them. On refitting the float, check and if necessary adjust, the level setting.

8 On completion check the idle speed.

13 Carburettors - idle speed and mixture adjustment

Note: *Before carrying out any carburettor adjustments, ensure that the ignition timing, valve clearances and spark plug gaps are correctly set*

Note: *After resetting the mixture, have an exhaust CO reading taken by your Citroën dealer to ensure that it is within the specified limits*

Note: *Information for adjustment of the Solex carburettor 34 PBISA 17 is contained in Section 16*

1 Generally speaking, unless the carburettor is obviously out of tune or is malfunctioning, it is not advisable to tamper with it. In any case, the only running adjustment that can be made is to the idling.

2 Correct adjustment can only be achieved provided that the engine is in generally good condition. Valve clearances must be correct and the ignition system must be in good condition and adjusted correctly.

3 An independent tachometer is necessary to make accurate adjustment and it should be connected to the engine in accordance with the manufacturer's instructions.

Idle speed adjustment

4 Refer to Chapter 1, Section 23.

Mixture adjustment

5 Where adjustment is to be made to the mixture control screw, it may first be necessary to prise free the tamperproof cap for access **(see illustrations)**.

6 With the air filter fitted, run the engine until warm, as indicated by the engagement of the cooling fan. When the cooling fan cuts out, adjustments can be made. During prolonged adjustments take care as the cooling fan will cut-in again periodically.

7 Turn the mixture screw to the position which provides the highest engine speed. Now reduce the engine speed to approximately 50 rpm above the specified idle speed for your model.

8 Repeat the procedure outlined in paragraph 10, then screw in the mixture control screw to reduce the engine speed by 30 to 50 rpm. Further minor adjustment to the idle speed may be necessary to bring the engine speed to within the idle speed range specified.

9 Whenever the mixture control screw setting has been reset, it is advisable to have an exhaust CO reading taken by your Citroën dealer to ensure that the CO reading at the exhaust is within the specified limits. This is of particular importance in territories where strict emission controls are enforced.

13.5a Solex 32-34 - mixture adjustment screw location (6)

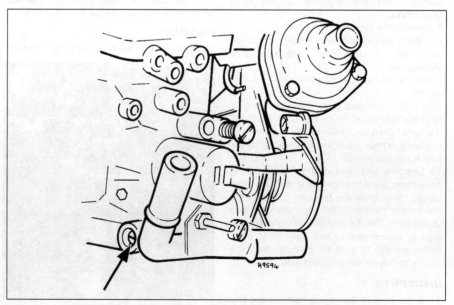

13.5b Weber carburettor - mixture adjustment screw (arrowed)

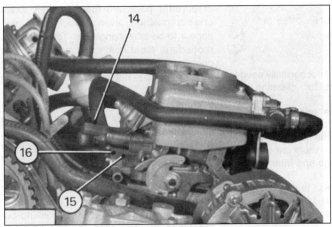

14.3 Weber carburettor - idle cut-off (14), spacer flange (15) and screws (16)

14.4a Weber carburettor removal - items to be disconnected

a and b Coolant hoses to   *11 Fuel return pipe*
     automatic choke   *12 and 13 Coolant hose*
9 Air filter duct   *retaining clips*
10 Fuel inlet pipe

14 Carburettors - removal and refitting

Removal

1 Disconnect the battery earth lead.
2 Unclip and detach the air ducting between the carburettor and the air cleaner unit. Where a Solex 34 PBISA 17 carburettor is fitted, the air cleaner must be removed.

14.4b Solex 32-34 - fuel supply and return hoses

3 Disconnect the wire from the idle cut-off solenoid **(see illustration)**.
4 Disconnect the fuel supply and return lines from the carburettor **(see illustrations)**. Plug the hoses to prevent the ingress of contamination.
5 Note that on BX 16 and BX 19 models manufactured after November 1985, the fuel lines have reduced inside diameter connections and are now 6 mm in diameter instead of 8 mm as on earlier models. All connections to the carburettor, fuel pump, fuel filter and fuel flow meter are now of the same diameter. Early and later-type connections are not directly interchangeable. The only exception to this is if a later-type Solex carburettor is fitted. In this instance, it will be necessary to renew the fuel feed connection to suit. Note also that the later-type fuel lines are secured with clips.
6 Detach the accelerator inner cable from the quadrant and the outer cable from its support at the carburettor and fold it back out of the way.
7 On manual choke models, detach the choke cable by loosening the inner cable clamp screw. Unscrew the outer cable location clamp bolt and move the cable out of the way.

8 On automatic choke models, clamp the coolant hoses each side of the choke unit, then loosen the securing clips and detach the hoses from the choke unit **(see illustration)**. If the hoses are not clamped, the cooling system will have to be partially drained to prevent coolant loss when the hoses are detached.
9 On BX 16 models fitted with the Solex 32-34 Z1 CIT 319-1 carburettor, disconnect the ventilation hoses from the float chamber. Note that the upper hose is connected to the air filter at the other end **(see illustration)**.
10 Where applicable, disconnect the vacuum hose from the carburettor **(see illustration)**.
11 Unscrew and remove the space flange retaining screw and pull the flange away from the carburettor body.
12 Unscrew and remove the four nuts securing the carburettor to the inlet manifold, then lift the carburettor away from it for removal. Retrieve the old joint gasket and place a piece of clean cloth over the aperture in the manifold to prevent the ingress of contamination while the carburettor is removed.

4A

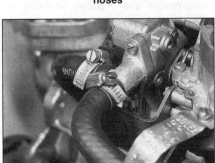

14.8 Solex 32-34 - coolant hose connections

14.9 Solex 32-34 - ventilation hose connections

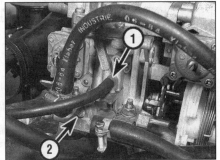

14.10 Solex 32-34 - vacuum hose connection (1) and spacer flange connection (2)

Refitting

13 Refitting the carburettor is the reverse of the removal procedure. Remove all traces of the old gasket and use a new one on installation.

14 After fitting the carburettor, reconnect the accelerator cable and (where applicable) the choke cable. When the choke control cable is fitted and the choke knob is pushed fully in, the flap should be fully open and there should be a small amount of possible additional movement on the control knob. Check that the flap closes when the control is pulled.

15 After reconnecting the two coolant hoses, remove any clamps used.

16 Top up the cooling system.

17 Adjust the idle speed on completion.

15 Solex carburettors - overhaul

1 The carburettor should not normally need to be dismantled except for cleaning and checking the float level.

2 The carburettor is a relatively delicate instrument and requires careful handling. Use the correct tools for the job and do not interchange jets or clean them out with wire which will cause damage and interfere with calibration.

3 Before dismantling, clean the outside of the carburettor and prepare a clean work area.

4 It is sound policy to ensure that individual carburettor parts are fitted in their exact original position, even though they may appear to be interchangeable. To help in this procedure, label items, put small parts in containers so that they do not become mixed up, and lay parts out in order of assembly on clean paper.

5 Identify the relevant illustration for the carburettor being dismantled **(see illustrations)**.

6 Undo the retaining screws and the choke link connecting screw, seen behind the arm of the spring **(see illustration)** and lift the carburettor top cover away from the main body **(see illustration)**

7 The float can be removed by pushing out the hinge pin and then the needle valve assembly can be unscrewed from the cover. Unscrew the fuel inlet connection and remove the gauze filter. Examine the filter for contamination.

8 Remove the accelerator pump operating rod and then remove the cover by progressively undoing the four retaining screws whilst restraining it against the action of the spring under the diaphragm. Examine the diaphragm for splits or damage.

9 Remove the accelerator pump inlet valve cover located in the bottom of the float chamber, taking care not to lose the ball valve. Examine the filter for contamination.

10 Unscrew and remove the jets, checking them for dirt or blockage.

11 It should not be necessary to interfere with any adjusting screws but, if this is necessary, count the number of turns required to remove the screw so that it can be refitted in approximately the same position.

12 Do not disturb the choke flap and throttle butterfly valve or spindles. Their actuating mechanisms are external and normally require no attention unless excessively worn. If the spindles are worn in the carburettor body then serious consideration should be given to renewing the complete carburettor. Air leaks around a worn spindle makes it impossible to tune the carburettor correctly and poor performance and impaired economy will inevitably result.

13 The respective chambers, passages and jet seats can be brush cleaned using clean fuel and then blown dry. Do not use cloth. Clean and blow through the jets in a similar manner.

14 Reassembly is the reverse of the dismantling procedure. Use new washers, gaskets, or seals, wherever fitted. During reassembly, check and adjust the float level.

15 On refitting the carburettor, check the idle speed setting and adjust as necessary. Further "on vehicle" carburettor adjustments may be necessary, check with the appropriate carburettor Section.

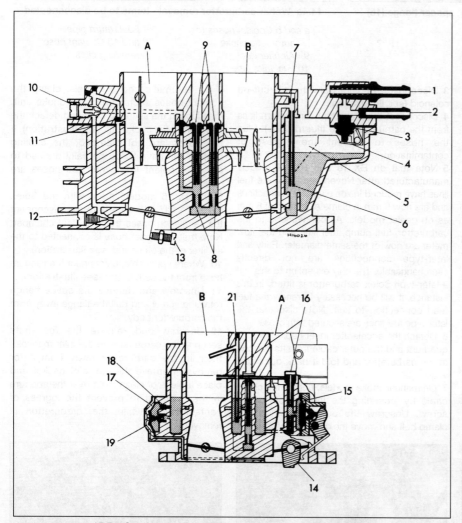

15.5a Sectional view of Solex carburettor - BX and BX 14

1 Fuel inlet	9 Air correction jets	15 Accelerator pump
2 Fuel return	10 Idle jet	16 Accelerator pump injectors
3 Needle valve	11 Idle air calibration	17 Power enrichener
4 Float level adjusting tab	12 Idle mixture adjustment	18 Enrichener calibration
5 Float	screw	19 Enrichener valve
6 Progression fuel jet	13 Idle speed adjustment	21 Econostat
7 Progression air jet	screw	A Primary barrel
8 Main jet	14 Accelerator pump cam	B Secondary barrel

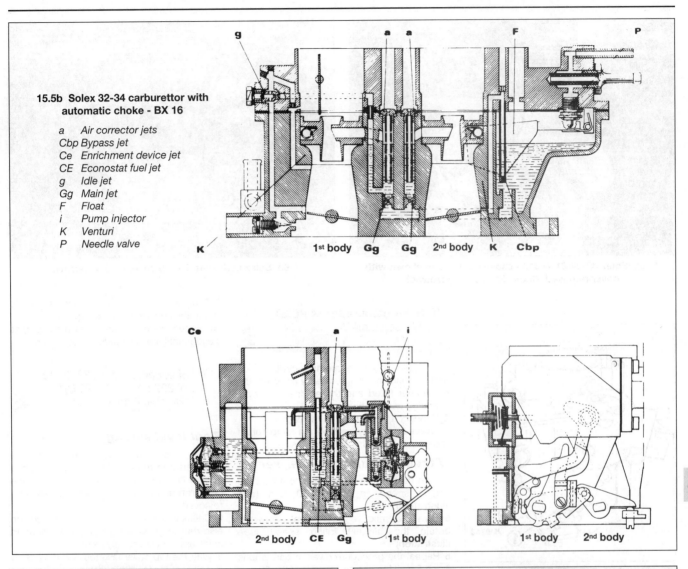

15.5b Solex 32-34 carburettor with automatic choke - BX 16

a   Air corrector jets
Cbp Bypass jet
Ce   Enrichment device jet
CE   Econostat fuel jet
g   Idle jet
Gg   Main jet
F   Float
i   Pump injector
K   Venturi
P   Needle valve

4A

15.5c Solex 30-30 and 32-34 Z 2 - top view with cover removed

1 Main jet (primary)
2 Secondary venturi
3 Main jet/air corrector
   jet/emulsion tube (secondary)
4 Primary venturi
5 Pump injector

15.5d Solex 32-34 and 34-34 Z 2 - top view with cover removed

1 Main jet
2 Primary venturi
3 Pump injector
4 Main jet/air corrector
   jet/emulsion tube (primary)
5 Secondary venturi

15.6a Solex 32-34 Z1 W 319 - choke control unit shown with cover removed. Choke link screw (arrowed)

15.6b Solex carburettor - top cover screws (arrowed)

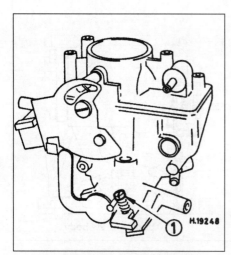

16.4 Solex 34 PBISA - throttle stop screw (1)

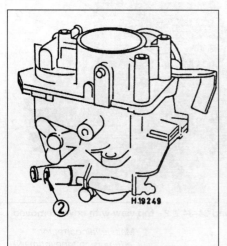

16.5 Solex 34 PBISA - mixture adjustment screw (2)

16 Solex carburettor 34 PBISA 17 - adjustment

1 The following adjustments must be made with the ignition timing correctly adjusted, the air cleaner fitted and the engine at normal operating temperature.
2 Connect a tachometer to the engine.
3 Where necessary, remove the tamperproof cap from the mixture adjustment screw.

Without exhaust gas analyser

4 Turn the throttle stop screw to adjust the engine speed to 750 ± 50 rpm **(see illustration)**.
5 Turn the mixture adjustment screw to obtain the highest idling speed **(see illustration)**.
6 Repeat the procedure given in paragraphs 4 and 5 until the engine speed is 750 ± 50 rpm (i.e. after adjusting the mixture screw).
7 Screw in the mixture adjustment screw slightly until the engine speed starts to decrease.

With exhaust gas analyser

8 Turn the throttle stop screw to adjust the engine speed to 750 ± 50 rpm.

17.3 Solex 30-30 and 32-34 Z 2 - float level setting (A)

9 Turn the mixture adjustment screw to obtain the specified CO reading.
10 Repeat the procedure given in paragraphs 8 and 9 until the idle speed is 750 ± 50 rpm.

17 Solex carburettors 30-30 Z2 CIT 329 and 32-34 Z2 CIT 348 - adjustment

Float level setting

1 This check can be made with the carburettor in the vehicle but the air cleaner duct will need to be detached and the carburettor top cover disconnected and removed.
2 Check that the floats are not punctured and also that the float arm pivot pin and support holes are not excessively worn.
3 With the top cover inverted and the gasket in position, measure the distance (A) from the gasket to the tip of the float **(see illustration)**. This distance should be in accordance with the float level specified for the carburettor type.
4 If adjustment is necessary, carefully bend the float tongue (which bears on the needle) in the required direction and recheck the level setting. Further adjustment may be necessary to achieve the correct adjustment **(see illustration)**.
5 If the difference in height of each float exceeds 1 mm, bend the float link arms so that they are level then recheck the float setting.
6 When refitting the top cover to the carburettor main body, use a new gasket.

Strangler (choke) flap setting

7 This check can be made with the carburettor in the vehicle but the air duct must be detached. Run the engine to provide the necessary manifold vacuum.
8 Pull the choke lever to its full extent and retain it in position. This will subject the

17.4 Solex carburettor - float level setting adjustment

1 Float arm link   *2 Float tongue*

17.8 Solex carburettor - strangler (choke) flap clearance (B)

anti-flooding capsule to a vacuum of 350 mbar and should open the strangler flap the specified amount. To check the flap opening, insert a gauge or twist drill down between the flap and the inner wall of the venturi (B) **(see illustration)**.

9 If necessary, adjustment can be made to open or close the flap to the specified clearance by turning the adjustment screw **(see illustration)** in the required direction.

Primary choke valve (throttle) setting

10 The carburettor must be removed and inverted for this check.

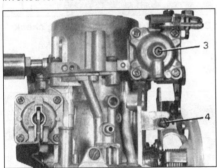

17.9 Solex 30-30 and 32-34 Z 2 - choke flap adjuster (3) and idle screw (4)

17.11 Primary choke (throttle) valve-to-venturi clearance (C)

11 Hold the strangler flap in the closed position and check the clearance between the outer edge of the butterfly valve and the venturi wall **(see illustration)**. To check the clearance, insert a gauge or twist drill of the same diameter as the specified clearance between the two.

12 If adjustment is necessary, prise free the tamperproof cap from the adjustment screw and turn the screw in the required direction to set the clearance **(see illustration)**. On completion, a new tamperproof cap should be fitted but this must be entrusted to your Citroën dealer as a special tool is required.

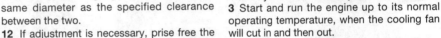

18 Solex carburettors 32-34 Z1 CIT 319, W 319 and 34-34 Z1 381 - adjustment

Note: *The following adjustments were made with the carburettor in the vehicle*

Float level setting

1 The float level setting check and adjustment procedure is similar to that described in the previous Section for other Solex carburettors.

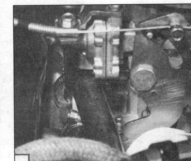

17.12 Solex 30-30 and 32-34 Z 2 - primary choke valve adjuster screw location (5)

Strangler (choke) flap setting

2 A special Citroën gauge (OUT 180143-T) is required to make this check. If this gauge is not available, then the check will have to be made by a Citroën dealer **(see illustration)**.

3 Start and run the engine up to its normal operating temperature, when the cooling fan will cut in and then out.

4 Remove the air intake duct from the carburettor.

5 Remove the cover from the automatic choke housing **(see illustration 15.6a)**.

6 Locate the gauge into position and check that the mobile roller is correctly positioned between the two gauge slots. If not, turn the adjustment screw of the heat-extensible capsule to meet this requirement **(see illustration)**. Prevent the nut from turning by using a 3 mm diameter drill **(see illustration)**.

7 Now reposition the gauge so that it is as shown **(see illustration)** and, with the engine running at idle speed, check that the strangler flap is open to give a gap of 6 ± 1 mm between its outer edge and the wall of the carburettor. Use a gauge or twist drill of suitable diameter to assess the clearance. If adjustment is necessary, turn the adjustment screw (A).

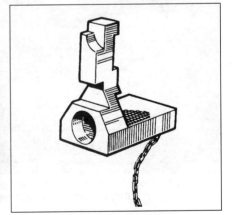

18.2 Special automatic choke gauge (OUT 180 143-T) for Solex carburettors

4A

18.6a Solex 32-34 Z1 W 319 - access aperture for screwdriver to adjust heat extensible capsule screw (arrowed)

8 Turn off the engine and leave the gauge in the previously set position. Open up the accelerator to its full extent, hold it in this position and check the strangler flap to-carburettor wall clearance which should be 8 mm. If this clearance is incorrect, prise open the actuating fork jaws (to increase the clearance) or pinch them together (to reduce the clearance) as necessary.

Primary choke valve (throttle) setting

9 Leave the gauge in the previously set position, connect up a tachometer to the manufacturer's instructions and restart the engine.

10 The engine speed should increase to between 2350 to 2450 rpm for models fitted with a shim on the choke cam or between 1700 and 1800 rpm for models without this shim. If the engine speed is not within these limits, adjust screw D.

11 Note that the above mentioned shim was fitted during manufacture to increase the engine speed during the choke phase when used during the first 600 miles. If still in position after this mileage has been covered, it can be removed by prising it free with a thin screwdriver **(see illustration)**.

12 On completion, remove the gauge and tachometer, refit the choke cover and reconnect the air filter duct.

18.6b Solex 32-34 and 34-34 Z 1 - mobile roller adjustment for automatic choke control

4 Screwdriver	6 3 mm drill
5 Special gauge (OUT 180 143-T)	7 Nut
	8 Movable roller

18.7 Solex 32-34 and 34-34 Z 1 - strangler flap opening check

A Adjuster screw	D Primary choke valve
B Gauge/twist drill	adjuster screw
C Actuator fork jaws	

18.11 Solex 32-34 Z1 CIT 319-1 - temporary shim (1). Remove after initial 600 miles

19.2a Solex 32-34 Z1 and 34-34 Z1 - strangler (choke) flap setting

1 Refer to illustration 19.2b	4 Primary choke flap
3 Roller	adjustment screw

Temperature in C degrees	Dimension "a" in mm
5	29.5
10	28.8
15	28.4
20	27.6
25	27
30	26.3

19.2b Table relating temperature to distance "a" in illustration 19.2a

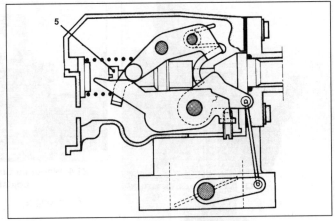

19.3 Solex 32-34 Z1 and 34-34 Z1 - strangler (choke) flap adjustment screw (5)

19 Solex carburettors 32-34 Z1 and 34-34 Z1 - adjustment

Note: *The carburettor must be removed from the vehicle for these adjustments*

Strangler (choke) flap setting

1 Remove the cover from the automatic choke housing.
2 Measure the distance from the top of the choke housing to the roller (see illustration) and compare it with the value in the accompanying table (see illustration).
3 Adjust if necessary, using a screwdriver inserted through the hole just above the deflooding capsule - **see illustration 18.6a. (see illustration).**

Primary choke valve (throttle) setting

4 With the ambient temperature at a steady 20°C (68°F), insert a gauge or drill shank to establish the opening of the primary choke throttle valve (see illustration 17.12).
5 This opening should be as specified. If not, adjust the appropriate screw (see illustration 19.2a).

Anti-flood capsule setting

6 Using pliers, push the anti-flood capsule link rod back into the capsule as far as it will go. Measure the strangler (choke) flap opening with the link rod in this position. If the opening does not correspond to that specified, adjust by means of the locknut and screw on the outside of the anti-flood capsule. Release the link rod (see illustration).

Mechanical (forced) deflooding

7 Fully open the primary throttle valve and measure the strangler flap opening in this position. It should be 8 mm. Adjust if nec-essary by bending the actuator fork jaws (see illustration 18.7).
8 Refit the choke housing cover when adjustments are complete.

20 Weber carburettors - overhaul

1 The overhaul procedure for Weber carburettors is similar to that described for Solex carburettors but note the information given for the Weber 36 TLP carburettor in Section 22.
2 Refer to the accompanying illustration for guidance on component location (see illustration).
3 Before refitting the top cover, check the float level setting. Also make other checks and adjustments as necessary.

4A

19.6 Solex 32-34 Z1 and 34-34 Z1 - anti-flood capsule adjustment

1 Link rod (arrow indicates rest position)
2 Locknut
3 Adjustment screw

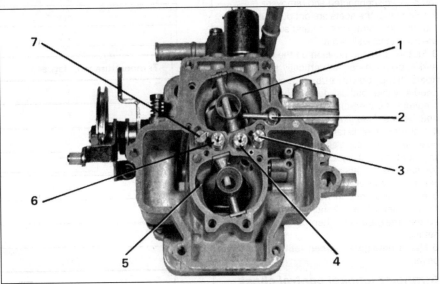

20.2 Weber 32-34 DRTC - top view with cover removed

1 Primary venturi
2 Pump injector
3 Idle jet
4 Main jet/air corrector jet/emulsion tube
5 Secondary venturi
6 Main jet (secondary)/air corrector jet/emulsion tube
7 Bypass jet

21.3 Weber carburettor - float level check

a = float-to-gasket face clearance

21 Weber carburettors - adjustment

Float level setting

1 This check can be made with the carburettor in position in the vehicle. The air cleaner duct will need to be detached and the top cover disconnected and removed.

2 Check that the floats are not punctured and that the float arm pivot pin and support holes are not excessively worn.

3 Fit the gasket in position on the cover face and support the cover vertically so that the floats hang downwards. Check that the needle valve ball is not pushed in, then measure the clearance between the gasket and the float **(see illustration)**.

4 Compare the distance measured with the specified float setting and, if necessary, adjust the float setting by bending the float arm tongue (which bears against the needle valve). Recheck the level setting **(see illustration)**.

5 If the difference in height between each float exceeds 1 mm, bend the float link arms so that they are level then recheck the float setting.

6 Use a new gasket when refitting the top cover.

Strangler (choke) control check

7 Before making this check, the engine must have been switched off for a minimum period of 30 minutes to allow the ambient temperature around the choke thermostatic capsule to have stabilised. You will need a

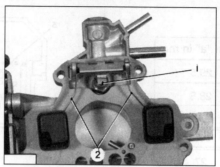

21.4 Weber carburettor - float level adjustment

1 Float tongue   2 Float link arm

thermometer to measure the air temperature when making the check.

8 Measure the distance between the lever end face and the roll **(see illustration)**. Measure the air temperature around the thermostatic capsule then refer to the temperature/distance tables and compare the

21.8a Weber carburettor - strangler (choke) control check

Measure distance (b) between lever endface (3) and roll (4)

readings taken **(see illustration)**. Where the temperature measured is not shown on the table, an estimate can be made.

9 If adjustment is necessary, turn the adjuster screw in the required direction to the point where the correct distance is given **(see illustration)**.

Temperature in C degrees	Dimension « b » in mm
5	22.7
10	23.7
15	24.7
20	25.6
25	26.4
30	27.2
35	28
40	29.1
45	30.2

A

Temperature in C degrees	Dimension ''b'' in mm
5	19
10	20.1
15	21.5
20	22.7
25	24.3
30	25.7
35	27.5
40	28.9
45	30.1

B

21.8b Dimension "b" in illustration 21.8a must be in accordance with temperature at thermostatic capsule

A 32-34 DTRC 100 W 121-50   *B 32-34 DTRC 2/100 W 128-50*

21.9 Weber carburettor - automatic choke adjuster screw (5)

Primary choke valve (throttle) setting

10 This check can only be made with the carburettor removed. When making this check, the ambient temperature and the carburettor temperature should be 20ºC.
11 Insert a gauge of the specified diameter between the venturi wall and the primary choke valve.

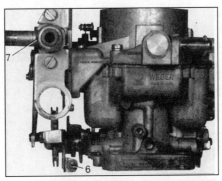

21.12 Weber carburettor - turn screw (6) to alter primary choke valve opening. Thermostatic capsule (7) also indicated

12 If the clearance is not as specified, adjust it by turning the adjustment screw (clockwise to decrease the opening or anti-clockwise to increase the opening) (see illustration).
13 As with the strangler control check, the opening should be checked after the thermostatic capsule temperature has been allowed to stabilise for a minimum period of 30

minutes. If the ambient temperature around the capsule differs from that specified then the primary choke valve opening will differ also, and reference should then be made to the table shown (see illustration). The valve opening should be in accordance with the ambient temperature shown.
14 Where the ambient temperature differs from those given, an estimate can be made.

Strangler (choke) flap setting

15 Before checking the strangler flap opening, certain preliminary checks must be made. First remove the control spring by detaching the retaining circlip at each end (see illustration). With the control spring removed, check that the length measured between the end rings is between 40.3 and 40.7 mm (see illustration). If this measurement is not correct, renew the control spring.
16 Remove the two anti-flooding capsule retaining screws and unclip the capsule control rod retaining circlip. Remove the capsule unit and check that the port is clear (see illustration), also the gallery opening in the base of the carburettor.
17 Refit the anti-flood capsule and the control spring.

	Temperature in C degrees	Dimension « c » in mm
A	5	0.65
	10	0.60
	15	0.55
	20	0.50
	25	0.45
	30	0.40
	35	0.37
	40	0.35
	45	0.33

	Temperature in C degrees	Dimension ''c'' in mm
B	5	0.60
	10	0.55
	15	0.50
	20	0.45
	25	0.40
	30	0.37
	35	0.30
	40	0.25
	45	0.20

21.13 Weber carburettor - primary choke valve opening to be in accordance with temperature at thermostatic capsule

A 32-34 DTRC 100 W 121-50   *B 32-34 DTRC 2/100 W 128-50*

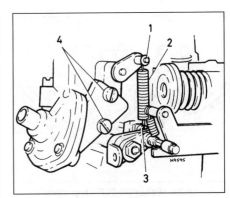

21.15a Weber carburettor - strangler flap opening check

1 Circlip   3 Circlip
2 Control spring   4 Screws

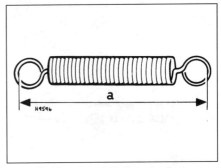

21.15b Measure control spring between end rings

a = 40.5 ±0.2 mm

4A

21.16 Weber carburettor - check that port (6) is clear

21.18 Weber carburettor - strangler flap opening adjustment

6 *Anti-flood capsule*
7 *Clamp (dimension b to equal 103 mm)*
8 *Shaft/heater pipe of thermal capsule*
9 *Lever*

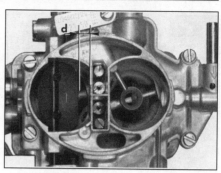

21.19 Weber carburettor - strangler flap opening (d)

18 The strangler flap opening can now be checked. A clamp will need to be fabricated to hold the strangler in the low temperature position. Note the clamp dimension and fitting position **(see illustration)**. The clamp is fitted to ensure that the strangler flap is fully opened for the check. Position the clamp over the shaft and the thermostatic capsule heating pipe.
19 Push against the anti-flood capsule control rod and check the strangler flap opening using a gauge rod or twist drill of the same diameter as the specified clearance **(see illustration)**.

20 If the strangler flap opening is not as specified, adjust it by turning the screw within the anti-flood capsule in the appropriate direction. On completion remove the bracket.

22 Weber carburettor 36 TLP - overhaul and adjustment

1 This carburettor is a single choke downdraught type with a manual choke.

Overhaul

2 For overhaul refer to Section 15 for general principles and to the accompanying illustrations for jet location **(see illustrations)**.

Idle speed and mixture adjustment

3 These adjustments are essentially as described in Section 13 **(see illustration)**.

Float level setting

4 For float level setting, make up a gauge as shown **(see illustration)**. Remove the float chamber cover and hold it vertically. With the gasket in position, the gauge should just contact the floats **(see illustration)**. Bend the float tongue and connecting bars if necessary.

Cold start (choke) adjustments

5 These are not routine adjustments but should be performed if difficult cold starting is experienced.

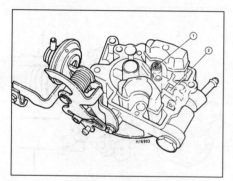

22.2a Weber 36 TLP - top cover

1 *Main jet*
2 *Fuel inlet needle valve*

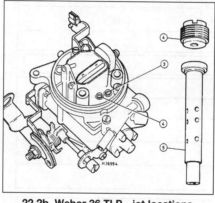

22.2b Weber 36 TLP - jet locations

3 *Idle jet*   5 *Emulsion tube*
4 *Air correction jet*

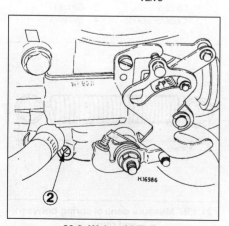

22.3 Weber 36 TLP - mixture adjustment screw (2)

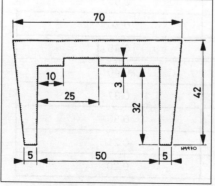

22.4a Weber 36 TLP - float level setting gauge

Dimensions in mm

22.4b Weber 36 TLP - checking float level

1 *Gasket*

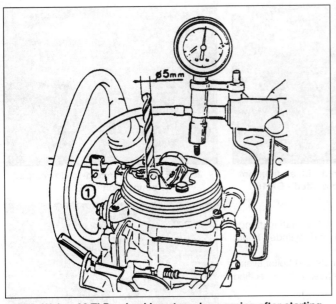

22.8 Weber 36 TLP - checking strangler opening after starting

1 Anti-flood capsule adjustment screw

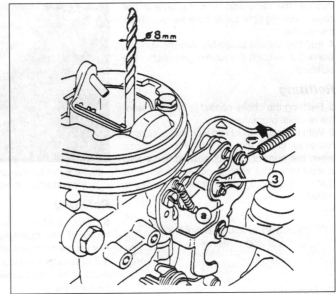

22.11 Weber 36 TLP - checking strangler mechanical opening

a Cam   *3 Roller*

Strangler opening after starting

6 Remove the air inlet from the top of the carburettor. Pull the choke control knob out fully to close the strangler flap.

7 Disconnect the vacuum pipe from the anti-flood capsule. Connect a hand vacuum pump to the capsule.

8 Apply vacuum (400 mm Hg approx.) to the capsule. The strangler flap should open far enough to admit a gauge of 5 mm diameter **(see illustration)**.

9 Adjust if necessary by means of the screw on the anti-flood capsule.

10 Disconnect the vacuum pump, remake the original vacuum connection and close the strangler flap.

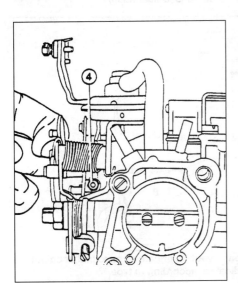

22.13 Weber 36 TLP - strangler mechanical opening adjustment nut (4)

Mechanical opening

11 Having adjusted the anti-flood capsule as just described, move the strangler opening roller into the recess of the cam as shown **(see illustration)**.

12 Check that the strangler flap opening just admits a gauge of 8 mm diameter.

13 Adjustment is carried out by turning the nut shown after removing the carburettor **(see illustration)**.

14 When adjustment is complete, refit the carburettor and air inlet.

23 Accelerator cable - removal and refitting

Removal

1 Pivot the carburettor throttle control quadrant and hold it in the open throttle position. Release the accelerator inner cable from the quadrant groove.

2 Release the outer cable from the location bracket on the carburettor **(see illustration)**.

3 Working inside the vehicle, detach the cable end fitting from the end of the accelerator foot pedal. Withdraw the cable from the vehicle by pulling it into the passenger compartment, at the same time feeding it through the bulkhead grommet.

Refitting

4 Before fitting a new cable, lubricate the inner cable with engine oil.

5 Refitting an accelerator cable is the reverse of the removal procedure. On completion check cable operation is satisfactory through its range of travel and allows full throttle

opening and closing on its return. If necessary, adjust the outer cable at the location bracket as required and fit the securing clip.

6 On automatic transmission models, the accelerator cable and kickdown cable adjustment checks are described in Chapter 7B.

24 Choke cable - removal and refitting

4A

Removal

1 Loosen the clamp bolt securing the inner cable to the choke flap operating link.

2 Loosen the bolt securing the clamp plate which holds the outer sheath on the carburettor bracket. Detach the inner cable and outer sheath from the carburettor.

3 Working inside the vehicle, remove the knob from the choke control cable and undo the control retaining nut. Push the control

23.2 Solex carburettor - accelerator cable location bracket. Adjustment/securing clip of outer cable is indicated

through the facia and then disconnect the choke warning light cable from the switch on the control.

4 Pull the control assembly into the vehicle, working it through the rubber grommet in the bulkhead.

Refitting

5 Refitting the choke control is the reverse of the removal procedure.

6 With the cable fitted and with the air cleaner removed, check that the choke is fully open when the control knob is pushed home and closed when the knob is pulled. Check also that the warning light is on when the choke is pulled.

25 Inlet and exhaust manifolds - removal and refitting

Removal

1 The inlet and exhaust manifolds are located on opposite sides of the cylinder head. They can be removed individually or together with the cylinder head. Removal of the exhaust manifold with the cylinder head in situ is more difficult due to its close proximity to the bulkhead.

2 The inlet manifold can be removed with or without the carburettor attached. Whichever method is employed, the carburettor connections and associated coolant hoses must first be detached.

3 When removing the exhaust manifold, first raise and support the vehicle at the front end to allow access to the manifold and exhaust downpipe flange connection nuts/bolts (see illustrations).

4 If on removal, the manifolds are found to be damaged in any way, then they must be renewed.

25.3a Exhaust manifold with air filter hot air collector cowling fitted - BX 16

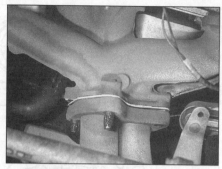
25.3b Exhaust manifold-to-downpipe connection - BX 16

Refitting

5 Before refitting, clean the mating flange faces of the manifold and cylinder head. Always use new gaskets.

6 Tighten the retaining nuts and bolts, evenly and in a diagonal sequence, to the specified torque setting.

26 Exhaust system - maintenance, removal and refitting

Maintenance

1 Refer to Chapter 1, Section 6.

Removal

2 When removing an old system, do not waste time trying to undo rusted and seized nuts, bolts or clamps. Cut them off. New ones will be required in any case if they are that bad.

Refitting

3 When fitting a system, use an exhaust joint sealant when assembling pipe sections to ensure that the joints are free from leaks. Get the system into position, but do not tighten

26.3 Exhaust system flexible hanger (arrowed)

connections until everything is properly located. If the flexible hangers have deteriorated then they must be renewed (see illustration).

4 When reassembling the spring-loaded joint coupling, the joint and retaining screw heads must be lubricated with a special high temperature grease which can be obtained from a Citroën dealer. On BX and BX 14 models, tighten the joint bolts evenly to the point where the compressed spring length is 22 mm. On BX 16 and BX 19 models tighten the bolts evenly until the cup contacts the screw shoulder (see illustration).

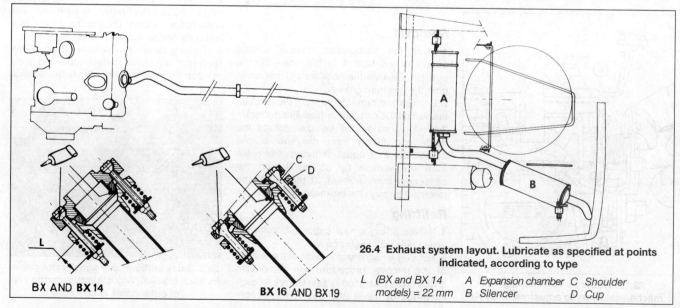
26.4 Exhaust system layout. Lubricate as specified at points indicated, according to type

BX AND BX 14   BX 16 AND BX 19

L (BX and BX 14 models) = 22 mm
A Expansion chamber C Shoulder
B Silencer D Cup

Chapter 4 Part B:
Fuel and exhaust systems - Bosch LE3 Jetronic injection

Contents

4B

Degrees of difficulty

Easy, suitable for novice with little experience	**Fairly easy,** suitable for beginner with some experience	**Fairly difficult,** suitable for competent DIY mechanic	**Difficult,** suitable for experienced DIY mechanic	**Very difficult,** suitable for expert DIY or professional 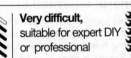

Specifications

For engine to model applications refer to Chapter 2

Air cleaner
Element .... Champion U543

Fuel filter
Type .... Champion L201

System
Type .... Bosch LE3 Jetronic electronic injection, with integral electronic control unit
Model application .... BX 19 GTi (pre July 1990)
Fuel pressure (at idle speed) .... 2 bar
Idle speed:
   Manual gearbox .... 825 ± 25 rpm
   Automatic transmission .... 900 ± 50 rpm
   With air conditioning on (where applicable) .... 975 ± 25 rpm
CO percentage in exhaust gas (maximum) 2.0

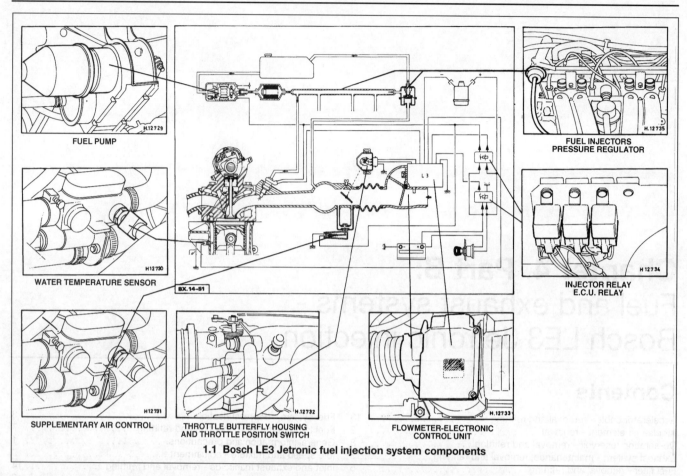

1.1 Bosch LE3 Jetronic fuel injection system components

FUEL PUMP

WATER TEMPERATURE SENSOR

SUPPLEMENTARY AIR CONTROL

THROTTLE BUTTERFLY HOUSING AND THROTTLE POSITION SWITCH

FLOWMETER-ELECTRONIC CONTROL UNIT

FUEL INJECTORS PRESSURE REGULATOR

INJECTOR RELAY E.C.U. RELAY

1 General information and precautions

General information

Operation of the Bosch LE3 Jetronic fuel injection system is as follows. A roller-type electric fuel pump draws fuel from the tank and pumps it through a filter to the injectors via a distribution pipe. The electronic control unit, which is triggered by the ignition circuit, sends impulses to the injectors, which operate simultaneously and inject fuel in the vicinity of the inlet valves. The electronic control unit is provided with sensors to determine engine temperature, speed and load, and the quantity of air entering the engine. This information is computed to determine the period of injection **(see illustration)**.

For cold starting, additional air is provided by a supplementary air device. This excess air "tricks" the system into providing more fuel.

A fuel vapour recirculation system is integrated into the fuel system **(see illustration)**. The fuel tank is vented via the charcoal filter canister. When the engine is started, any fuel vapour in the de-aerating reservoir and charcoal canister is drawn through the airflow meter and into the throttle

housing by the normal induction method, it is then burnt in the engine.

Precautions

Fuel warning

Many of the procedures in this Chapter require the removal of fuel lines and connections which may result in some fuel spillage. Before carrying out any operation on the fuel system refer to the precautions given in Safety first! at the beginning of this Manual and follow them implicitly. Petrol is a highly dangerous and volatile liquid and the precautions necessary when handling it cannot be overstressed.

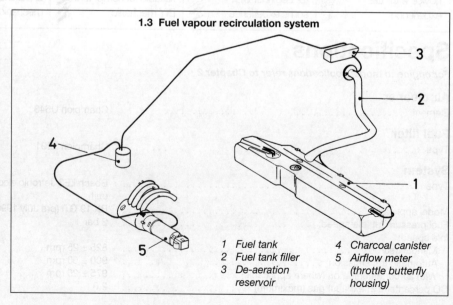

1.3 Fuel vapour recirculation system

1 Fuel tank
2 Fuel tank filler
3 De-aeration reservoir
4 Charcoal canister
5 Airflow meter (throttle butterfly housing)

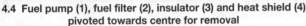

4.4 Fuel pump (1), fuel filter (2), insulator (3) and heat shield (4) pivoted towards centre for removal

4.5 Fuel pump wiring connections

System maintenance

Residual fuel pressure will remain in the system lines long after the vehicle is used. Before disconnecting any fuel line, depressurise the fuel system.

In order to prevent damage to the electrical components of the system, observe the following precautions:

a) *Never disconnect the battery with the engine running*
b) *Never disconnect the electronic control unit with the ignition on*
c) *Never use a test light for checking system circuits*

Tamperproof adjustment screws

Certain adjustment points in the fuel system are protected by "tamperproof" caps, plugs or seals. The purpose of such tamperproofing is to discourage, and to detect, adjustment by unqualified operators.

In some EEC countries (though not yet in the UK), it is an offence to drive a vehicle with missing or broken tamperproof seals. Before disturbing a seal, satisfy yourself that you will not be breaking local or national anti-pollution regulations by doing so. Fit a new seal when adjustment is complete, when this is required by law.

Do not break tamperproof seals on a vehicle which is still under warranty.

Unleaded petrol - usage

Models equipped with the Bosch LE3 Jetronic injection system should be run on 97 RON leaded petrol only. However, it is possible to run on 95 RON unleaded fuel if suitable adjustments are first carried out. Consult your Citroën dealer for further information. Note that the use of unleaded fuel in a vehicle not suitably adjusted will lead to serious damage of the valve seats.

2 Air cleaner element - renewal

Refer to Chapter 1, Section 28.

3 Fuel system - depressurisation

Note: *Depressurise the fuel system before carrying out any work on its component parts*

⚠️ **Warning: The following procedure will merely relieve the pressure in the fuel system. Remember that fuel will still be present in system components, so take precautions accordingly before disconnecting them**

1 The fuel system is defined as the fuel pump, filter, injectors and pressure regulator, also the metal pipes and flexible hoses of the lines between these components. All these components contain fuel which will be under pressure while the engine is running and/or while the ignition is switched on. Pressure will remain for some time after the ignition has been switched off and must be released before any of these components are disturbed for servicing work. Proceed as follows:

2 Disconnect the battery earth lead.

3 Place a suitable container beneath the relevant union to be disconnected and have a large rag ready to soak up any escaping fuel not being caught by the container.

4 Slowly loosen the union to avoid a sudden release of pressure and position the rag around the connection to catch any fuel spray which may be expelled.

5 Once pressure is released, disconnect the union and insert plugs into its open ends to minimise fuel loss and to prevent the entry of contamination into the system.

4 Fuel pump - removal and refitting

Removal

1 The fuel pump is located on the underside of the vehicle, at the rear on the right-hand side, just to the rear of the fuel tank. The pump unit is housed in a rubber insulator, together with the fuel filter unit which is located directly above it.

2 For access to the pump (and/or filter), raise and support the vehicle at the rear.

3 Disconnect the battery earth lead.

4 Unclip and swing the heat shield, insulator, pump and filter units towards the centre **(see illustration)**.

5 Pull back the rubber protective gaiter from the end of the fuel pump and then detach the wiring connectors. Note that, whilst both wires are yellow, one has a white connector sleeve for identification. Note which has the sleeve and its connection **(see illustration)**.

6 Bearing in mind the information given on depressurising the fuel system, loosen the clips and remove the fuel lines from the front and rear of the pump unit.

7 Carefully pull and withdraw the pump unit from the insulator.

Refitting

8 Refitting is a reversal of the removal procedure. Ensure that all connections are correctly and securely made. On completion, check for satisfactory operation, and for any signs of fuel leaks from the pump connections.

5 Fuel filter - removal and refitting

Refer to Chapter 1, Section 36.

4B

6 Fuel level transmitter - removal and refitting

Refer to Section 9 in Part A of this Chapter.

7 Fuel tank - removal, inspection and refitting

The fuel tank is of similar design to that fitted to carburettor models.

Note the information given for depressurising the fuel system when disconnecting the tank fuel lines **(see illustration)** before following the procedure given in Section 10 in Part A of this Chapter.

8 De-aeration reservoir - removal and refitting

Removal

1 The de-aeration reservoir is located at the rear of the car, under the right-hand rear wheel arch **(see illustration)**. It is connected to the fuel filler pipe and the charcoal filter canister, their function being to vent the fuel tank. Any fuel vapour stored in them is drawn into the throttle housing when the engine is started.

8.1 De-aeration reservoir location - GTi

7.2 Fuel tank supply and return hoses - GTi

2 If removing the de-aeration reservoir, take the same precautions as those mentioned for fuel tank removal. Detach the hoses from the reservoir, undo the retaining strap and mounting bolts, then lower and remove it **(see illustration)**.

3 A vent valve is also fitted and is located near the de-aeration reservoir. This can be removed by detaching the hoses and unclipping the valve **(see illustration)**.

Refitting

4 Refitting is a reversal of the removal procedure. Renew any hoses or clips as necessary and check for leakage and security on completion.

9 Idle speed and mixture - adjustment

1 Before making any adjustments to the fuel system, the following conditions must be met:
a) The ignition system must be in good condition and correctly adjusted
b) The air cleaner element must be clean
c) The throttle initial position must be correctly set, as must the throttle butterfly spindle switch
d) The engine must be at its normal operating temperature, the cooling fan having cut in and then out

Idle speed adjustment

2 Refer to Chapter 1, Section 23.

Mixture adjustment

3 To adjust the mixture setting, you will need to punch a hole in the tamperproof plug over the mixture screw and prise out the plug. Turn the mixture adjustment screw to give a maximum CO reading of 2.0%. If required, readjust the idle speed as described previously **(see illustration)**.

4 Recheck the CO reading and readjust the mixture setting and idle speed settings as necessary.

5 On completion, a new tamperproof plug should be fitted over the mixture screw. Disconnect the tachometer and the exhaust gas analyser to complete.

10 Throttle initial position - setting

Note: *This is not a routine adjustment. It should only be necessary if new components have been fitted, or if the setting has been accidentally disturbed.*

1 Remove the tamperproof plug from the throttle butterfly stop screw (located on the other side of the throttle housing from the idle speed adjuster screw).

2 Unscrew the throttle butterfly stop screw until it is no longer in contact with its stop and the butterfly is fully closed. Screw it in again until it just contacts the stop. From this position, screw it in exactly one quarter of a turn.

3 Fit a new tamperproof plug, when required.

4 Check the throttle butterfly switch setting.

11 Throttle position switch - setting

1 Disconnect the multi-plug from the throttle position switch. Connect an ohmmeter or continuity tester between switch terminals 2 and 18.

2 Insert a 0.30 mm feeler blade between the butterfly stop screw and its stop.

3 Slacken the switch mounting screws. Turn the switch in either direction until the contacts

8.2 De-aeration reservoir retaining strap and mounting bolt (arrowed)

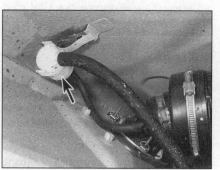

8.3 Vent valve location (arrowed) - GTi

9.3 Mixture adjustment screw (arrowed)

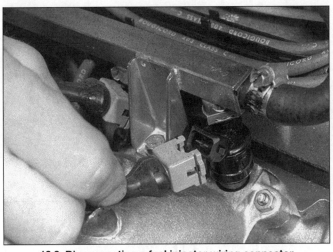

12.2 Disconnecting a fuel injector wiring connector

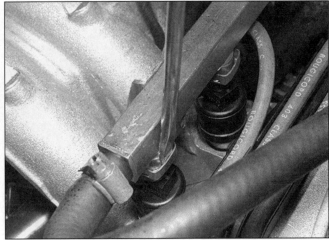

12.3a Prising fuel rail free from injectors

are just closed (continuity or zero resistance). Tighten the screws in this position.

4 Remove the feeler blade and insert another of 0.70 mm thickness. With this blade inserted, the contacts must be open (no continuity, or infinite resistance). If not, repeat the adjustment. Remove the feeler blade.

5 Transfer the ohmmeter to terminals 3 and 18. Have an assistant depress the throttle pedal to the floor. At full-throttle, the contacts must be closed.

6 Disconnect the test equipment and reconnect the multi-plug.

12.3b Fuel rail/injector clip

12 Fuel injectors - removal and refitting

Removal

1 Disconnect the battery earth lead.

2 Detach the wiring connections from the injectors by prising open the wire retaining clip in the connector (see illustration).

3 Prise free the injector-to-fuel supply rail (tube) retaining clip, using a screwdriver as a lever (see illustrations).

4 Bearing in mind the information given on depressurising the fuel system, undo the retaining bolts and remove the fuel supply rail. The hoses and pressure regulator can be left attached (see illustrations).

5 Withdraw the injectors. Ensure that no contamination is allowed to enter the fuel system whilst disconnected.

Refitting

6 Refitting is a reversal of the removal procedure. Use new injector seals. To ease fitting of the injectors to their cylinder head ports, lubricate the seals with a small amount of soapy solution. Check for signs of fuel leakage on completion.

13 Accelerator cable - removal and refitting

This procedure is similar to that described in Section 23 in Part A of this Chapter. However, the cable connection to the throttle housing differs (see illustration).

Cable adjustment is the same as for the carburettor type. Whenever the cable has been disturbed, check the idle speed.

14 Inlet and exhaust manifolds - removal and refitting

1 The basic procedures are much the same as those given in Part A of this Chapter.

2 When removing the inlet manifold, items such as the injectors and ignition coil will need to be detached. The manifold can either be removed together with, or separate from, the throttle housing. Disconnect as appropriate but note the hose connections.

3 Always use new gaskets when refitting.

4B

12.4a Fuel supply rail retaining bolt (arrowed)

12.4b Pressure regulator attached to fuel rail

13.1 Accelerator cable adjustment ferrule (arrowed)

15 Exhaust system -
maintenance, removal and
refitting

Note the information given in Part A of this
Chapter. The exhaust system fitted to fuel
injection models differs from that fitted to
carburettor models, the main difference being
that the front pipe section incorporates an
expansion chamber. All other components in
the system are also specific to model type
and this must be considered when ordering
replacement parts **(see illustration)**.

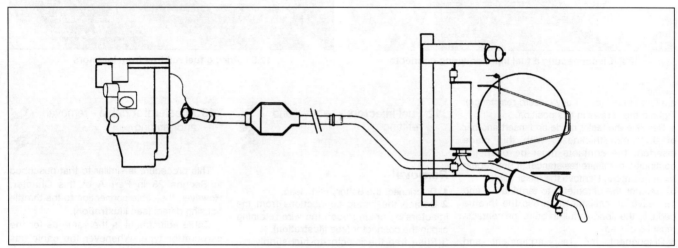

15.1 Exhaust system - BX 19 GTi

Chapter 4 Part C:
Fuel and exhaust systems - Motronic injection

Contents

Degrees of difficulty

Easy, suitable for novice with little experience 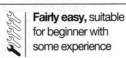	Fairly easy, suitable for beginner with some experience	Fairly difficult, suitable for competent DIY mechanic 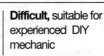	Difficult, suitable for experienced DIY mechanic	Very difficult, suitable for expert DIY or professional

4C

Specifications

For engine to model applications refer to Chapter 2

Air cleaner
Element .... Champion U543

Fuel filter
Type .... Champion L201

System
Model application/Type:
  BX 19 GTi 16v (pre 1991) .... Motronic ML4.1
  BX 19 GTi (from July 1990) .... Motronic MP3.1
  BX 19 GTi 16v (from 1991) .... Motronic M1.3
  BX 19 TZi with catalytic converter .... Motronic M1.3
Idle speed:
  Motronic ML4.1 .... 850 rpm (not adjustable)
  Motronic MP3.1 .... 850 to 900 rpm
  Motronic M1.3:
    BX 19 GTi 16v .... 850 rpm (not adjustable)
    BX 19 TZi .... 850 to 950 rpm
CO percentage in exhaust gas:
  Motronic ML4.1 .... 0.8 to 1.5
  Motronic MP3.1 .... 1.0 to 2.0
  Motronic M1.3:
    BX 19 GTi 16v .... 0.8 to 1.5
    BX 19 TZi .... Controlled by ECU

1.6a Idle actuator (arrowed)

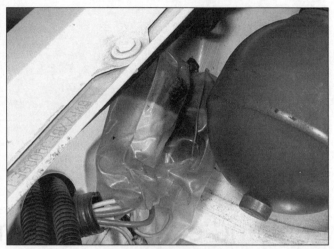

1.6b Injector and fuel pump relays protected by plastic cover -
GTi 16v with Motronic ML4.1

1 General information and precautions

General information

Three types of Motronic engine management systems have been fitted to the Citroën BX range, their model applications being listed in *Specifications*.

To provide fine control of the engine to suit prevailing operating conditions, the system controls the functions of both the fuel injection and ignition systems.

The Electronic Control Unit (ECU) receives signals from various sensors and computes the optimum volume of fuel to be injected and the optimum ignition advance setting to suit the prevailing conditions.

In the event of the failure of a system component, the ECU has the capability to permit the engine to operate, albeit at reduced power and efficiency, until the fault can be investigated by a Citroën dealer who will have access to the necessary specialist test equipment.

The following sensors supply the ECU with information:

a) Airflow meter - measures the volume of air entering the engine
b) Air temperature sensor - measures the temperature of the air entering the engine (integral with the airflow meter)
c) Throttle position switch - senses the position of the throttle valve
d) Coolant temperature sensor
e) TDC sensor - measures engine speed and crankshaft position
f) Knock sensor (only fitted to BX 19 GTi 16v with Motronic M1.3) - senses the engine vibrations associated with pre-ignition, which may cause engine damage unless the ignition timing is retarded as a preventative measure
g) Lambda (oxygen) sensor (only fitted to

models equipped with Motronic M1.3 and catalytic converter) - measures the oxygen content of the exhaust gases

Additionally, the Motronic systems comprise the following components:

a) Air cleaner - located on the left-hand front wing valance, the casing incorporates the airflow meter
b) Fuel pump and filter
c) Fuel pulsation damper - located in the fuel line close to the filter, reduces fuel pump noise
d) Fuel pressure regulator - located on the end of the fuel rail within the engine compartment, maintains a constant fuel pressure
e) Fuel injectors
f) Idle actuator - (BX 19 GTi 16v with Motronic M1.3 or ML4.1) - controls the volume of air bypassing the throttle valve at idle, thus maintaining a suitable idle speed during warm-up and a constant speed when the engine is warm **(see illustration)**
g) Supplementary air device (models with Motronic M1.3 and catalytic converter, and Motronic MP3.1 system) - provides supplementary air to the idling circuit as an aid to starting and warm-up
h) Throttle butterfly housing - two throttle valves open simultaneously and the housing is coolant-heated to improve fuel atomization
i) Electronic control unit (ECU) - located under the driver's seat, the ECU controls the system components
j) HT distributor (all except Motronic MP3.1) - the distributor simply distributes HT current to the spark plugs and consists of a rotor arm on the end of the camshaft (inlet camshaft on 16v models) and a conventional distributor cap.
k) Ignition coil - for the Motronic ML4.1 and M1.3 systems, a conventional ignition coil is used, being triggered by signals from

the ECU. The Motronic MP3.1 system uses a distributorless ignition system with a double coil which operates on the "wasted-spark" principle, supplying current directly to the spark plugs when triggered by signals from the ECU
l) Relays - injector and fuel pump relays are fitted, both being controlled by the ECU **(see illustration)**
m) Idle mixture (CO) adjustment potentiometer - for the Motronic ML4.1 and M1.3 (non-catalyst) systems, the idle mixture adjustment potentiometer is incorporated in the airflow meter casing. The Motronic MP3.1 system uses a remotely-mounted potentiometer located in the engine compartment on the inner right-hand wing panel. Note that on models equipped with the M1.3 system and catalytic converter, no adjustment of idle mixture is possible

All Motronic systems function in a similar manner, the differences between systems being of a minor nature, mainly associated with system sensors and the programming of the ECU.

Precautions

Fuel warning

Many of the procedures in this Chapter require the removal of fuel lines and connections which may result in some fuel spillage. Before carrying out any operation on the fuel system refer to the precautions given in Safety first! at the beginning of this Manual and follow them implicitly. Petrol is a highly dangerous and volatile liquid and the precautions necessary when handling it cannot be overstressed.

System maintenance

Residual fuel pressure will remain in the system lines long after the vehicle is used. Before disconnecting any fuel line, depressurise the fuel system.

In order to prevent damage to the electrical components of the system, observe the following precautions:

a) *Never disconnect the battery with the engine running*
b) *Never disconnect the electronic control unit with the ignition on*
c) *Never use a test light for checking system circuits*

Tamperproof adjustment screws

Certain adjustment points in the fuel system are protected by "tamperproof" caps, plugs or seals. The purpose of such tamperproofing is to discourage, and to detect, adjustment by unqualified operators.

In some EEC countries (though not yet in the UK), it is an offence to drive a vehicle with missing or broken tamperproof seals. Before disturbing a seal, satisfy yourself that you will not be breaking local or national anti-pollution regulations by doing so. Fit a new seal when adjustment is complete, when this is required by law.

Do not break tamperproof seals on a vehicle which is still under warranty.

Unleaded petrol - usage

Pre-1991 GTi 16 valve models are suitable for running on 97 RON leaded petrol only and cannot be run on unleaded petrol. All other models not equipped with a catalytic converter can be run on either 97 RON leaded fuel or 95 RON unleaded fuel without adjustment.

Models equipped with a catalytic converter must be run on 95 RON unleaded fuel only. The use of leaded fuel will seriously damage the converter.

Catalytic converters

The catalytic converter is a reliable and simple device which needs no maintenance in itself but there are some facts of which an owner should be aware if the converter is to function properly for its full service life.

a) *DO NOT use leaded petrol in a vehicle equipped with a catalytic converter - the lead will coat the precious metals, reducing their converting efficiency, and will eventually destroy the converter.*
b) *Always keep the ignition and fuel systems well-maintained, in accordance with the manufacturer's schedule. Ensure that the air cleaner element, the fuel filter (where fitted) and the spark plugs are renewed at the correct intervals. If the inlet air/fuel mixture is allowed to become too rich due to neglect, the unburned surplus will enter and burn in the catalytic converter, overheating the element and eventually destroying the converter.*
c) *If the engine develops a misfire, do not drive the vehicle until the fault is cured. The misfire will allow unburned fuel to enter the converter, which will result in its overheating.*
d) *DO NOT push-start the car. This will soak the catalytic converter in unburned fuel,*

causing it to overheat when the engine does start.
e) *DO NOT switch off the ignition at high engine speeds or "blip" the throttle before switching off. If the ignition is switched off at anything above idle speed, unburned fuel will enter the very hot catalytic converter, with the possible risk of its igniting on the element and damaging the converter.*
f) *DO NOT use fuel or engine oil additives as these may contain substances harmful to the catalytic converter.*
g) *DO NOT continue to use the vehicle if the engine burns oil to the extent of leaving a visible trail of blue smoke. Unburned carbon deposits will clog the converter passages and reduce its efficiency. In severe cases, the element will overheat.*
h) *The converter operates at very high temperatures, causing the heat shields on the vehicle underbody and the casing to become hot enough to ignite combustible materials which brush against it. DO NOT park the vehicle in dry undergrowth, or over long grass or piles of dead leaves.*
i) *The converter is FRAGILE. Do not strike it during servicing work and take great care when working on the exhaust system. Ensure that the converter is well clear of any jacks or other lifting gear used to raise the vehicle and do not drive the vehicle over rough ground, road humps etc. in such a way as to "ground" the exhaust system.*
j) *In some cases, particularly when the vehicle is new or is used for stop/start driving, a sulphurous smell may issue from the exhaust. This is common to many converter-equipped cars and seems to be due to the small amount of sulphur found in some petrols reacting with hydrogen in the exhaust to produce hydrogen sulphide (H_2S) gas. Although this gas is toxic, it is not produced in sufficient amounts to be a problem. Once the vehicle has covered a few thousand miles, the problem should disappear. In the meanwhile, a change of driving style or petrol brand may effect a solution.*
k) *A converter used on a well-maintained and well driven car, should last for*

5.1 Fuel pump location - GTi 16v with Motronic ML4.1

between 50 000 and 100 000 miles. From this point on, careful checks should be made at all specified service intervals of the CO level, to ensure that the converter is still operating efficiently. If the converter is no longer effective, it must be renewed.

2 Air cleaner element - renewal

Refer to Chapter 1, Section 28.

3 Airflow meter - removal and refitting

1 The airflow meter is integral with the air cleaner casing.
2 To remove the assembly, disconnect the battery negative lead and the sensor wiring plug, then release the retaining clips and lift the assembly away from the air cleaner body.
3 Refitting is a reversal of removal.

4 Fuel system - depressurisation

Refer to Section 3 in Part B of this Chapter.

5 Fuel pump - removal and refitting

Refer to Section 4 in Part B of this Chapter **(see illustration)**.

6 Fuel filter - removal and refitting

Refer to Chapter 1, Section 36.

7 Fuel level transmitter - removal and refitting

Refer to Section 9 in Part A of this Chapter.

8 Fuel tank - removal, inspection and refitting

Refer to Section 7 in Part B of this Chapter.

4C

10.3 Idle mixture adjustment screw tamperproof cap (arrowed)

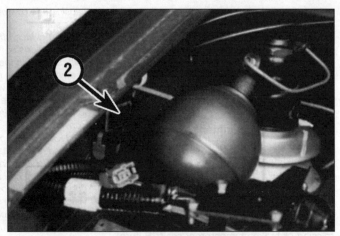

10.13 Idle mixture adjustment potentiometer location (2)

9 De-aeration reservoir - removal and refitting

Refer to Section 8 in Part B of this Chapter.

10 Idle speed and mixture - adjustment

Motronic ML4.1

Idle speed adjustment

1 The idle speed and ignition timing are controlled by the ECU and no adjustment is possible.

Mixture adjustment

2 To adjust the idle mixture, run the engine until it reaches normal operating temperature (the cooling fan should have cut in and out), then stop the engine and connect an exhaust gas analyser in accordance with the manufacturer's instructions.
3 Where applicable, remove the tamperproof cap from the mixture (CO) adjustment screw on the airflow meter **(see illustration)**.
4 With the engine idling, turn the adjustment screw as necessary to obtain the specified CO content.
5 On completion, stop the engine. Disconnect the exhaust gas analyser and where necessary, fit a new tamperproof cap to the mixture adjustment screw.

Motronic M1.3 without catalyst

Idle speed adjustment

6 On non-catalyst equipped models with Motronic M1.3, the idle speed and ignition timing are controlled by the ECU and no adjustment is possible.

Mixture adjustment

7 The idle mixture can be adjusted as described for the Motronic ML4.1 system.

Motronic M1.3 with catalyst

Idle speed adjustment

8 Refer to Chapter 1, Section 23.

Mixture adjustment

9 The idle mixture and ignition timing are controlled by the ECU and no adjustment is possible.

Motronic MP3.1

10 Both idle speed and mixture can be adjusted on this system but the ignition timing is controlled by the ECU.

Idle speed adjustment

11 Refer to Chapter 1, Section 23.

Mixture adjustment

12 Run the engine until it reaches normal operating temperature (the cooling fan should have cut in and out), then stop the engine and connect a tachometer and an exhaust gas analyser in accordance with the manufacturer's instructions.
13 Remove the tamperproof plug from the idle mixture adjustment potentiometer (located on the right-hand inner wing panel) **(see illustration)**.
14 Turn the adjustment screw as necessary to obtain the specified CO reading.
15 If necessary, readjust the idle speed, then recheck the CO reading.

11.1 Removing a fuel injector from the rail

16 If necessary, repeat the procedure given in paragraph 22 until the idle speed and CO values are as specified.
17 On completion, stop the engine. Disconnect the tachometer and exhaust gas analyser and fit a new tamperproof cap to the idle mixture adjustment potentiometer.

11 Fuel injectors - removal and refitting

Refer to Section 12 in Part B of this Chapter **(see illustration)**.

12 Accelerator cable - removal and refitting

Refer to Section 13 in Part B of this Chapter but note that there is no need to check the idle speed after refitting. Instead, check that the throttle butterfly is fully closed with the accelerator pedal in the rest position.

13 Inlet and exhaust manifolds - removal and refitting

Refer to Section 14 in Part B of this Chapter

14 Exhaust system - maintenance, removal and refitting

Refer to Section 15 in Part B of this Chapter but note that on models fitted with a catalytic converter, it will be necessary to disconnect the wiring from the lambda sensor before removing the exhaust front section. It may also be necessary to remove the heat shield from the underbody area around the catalytic converter to allow sufficient clearance to remove the exhaust system.

Chapter 4 Part D:
Fuel and exhaust systems - Magneti Marelli injection

Contents

4D

Degrees of difficulty

Easy, suitable for novice with little experience	**Fairly easy,** suitable for beginner with some experience	**Fairly difficult,** suitable for competent DIY mechanic 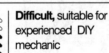	**Difficult,** suitable for experienced DIY mechanic	**Very difficult,** suitable for expert DIY or professional

Specifications

For engine to model applications refer to Chapter 2

Air cleaner
Element . . . . Champion U543

Fuel filter
Type . . . . Champion L201

System
Model application/type:
  BX 16 fuel injection . . . . Magneti Marelli G6.10
Regulated operating pressure . . . . 0.8 bar
Idle speed . . . . Controlled by ECU
CO percentage in exhaust gas . . . . Controlled by ECU

1 General information and precautions

General information

On fuel-injected BX 16 models, a fully-integrated Magneti Marelli G6.10 engine management system is used to control both the single-point fuel injection and ignition systems. This system also incorporates a closed-loop catalytic converter and an evaporative emission control system, complying to the very latest emission control standards. The system operates as follows.

The fuel pump (mounted on the rear of the subframe) pumps fuel from the tank to injector via a filter. Fuel supply pressure is controlled by the pressure regulator in the throttle body

assembly, which lifts to allow excess fuel to return to the tank when the optimum operating pressure of the system is exceeded.

The electrical control system consists of the ECU, along with the following sensors **(see illustration)**:

a) *Manifold absolute pressure (MAP) sensor - informs the ECU of engine load*
b) *Crankshaft sensor - informs the ECU of crankshaft position and engine speed*
c) *Throttle potentiometer - informs the ECU of throttle valve position and rate of throttle opening/closing*
d) *Coolant temperature sensor - informs the ECU of engine temperature*
e) *Fuel/air mixture temperature sensor - informs the ECU of temperature of fuel/air mixture charge entering cylinders*
f) *Lambda (oxygen) sensor - informs the ECU of oxygen content of exhaust gases*

The ECU senses battery voltage, adjusting the injector pulse width to suit and using the stepper motor to increase the idle speed and therefore, the alternator output if the voltage is too low. Short-circuit protection and diagnostic capabilities are incorporated. The ECU can both receive and transmit information via the engine management circuit diagnostic connector, thus permitting engine diagnosis and tuning by special diagnostic equipment.

All the above signals are compared by the ECU which then selects the appropriate response and controls the ignition HT coil (varying the ignition timing as required), and the fuel injector (varying its pulse width the length of time the injector is held open - to provide a richer or weaker mixture, as appropriate). The mixture, idle speed and ignition timing are constantly varied by the ECU to provide the best settings for cranking, starting and engine warm-up, idle, cruising and acceleration.

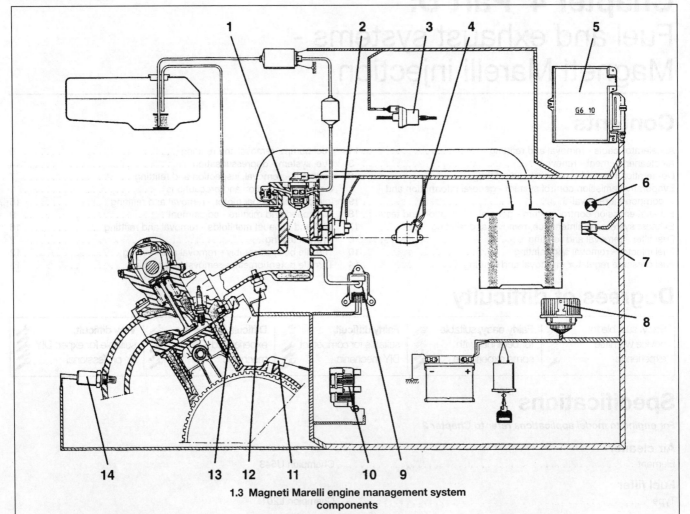

1.3 Magneti Marelli engine management system components

1 *Throttle body injector housing*
2 *Idle speed stepper motor*
3 *Charcoal canister purge valve*
4 *Throttle potentiometer*
5 *ECU*

6 *Instrument panel warning light*
7 *Diagnostic wiring connector*
8 *Relay unit*
9 *Manifold absolute pressure (MAP) sensor*

10 *Ignition HT coil*
11 *Crankshaft sensor*
12 *Fuel/air mixture temperature sensor*
13 *Coolant temperature sensor*
14 *Lambda (oxygen) sensor*

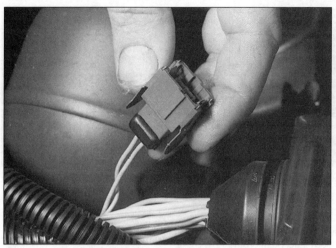

2.3 System diagnostic connector

5.1 Fuel pump and filter (plastic cover unclipped for clarity)

The ECU also regulates the engine idle speed via a stepper motor which is fitted to the throttle body. The motor has a pushrod which controls the opening of an air passage which bypasses the throttle valve. When the throttle valve is closed, the ECU controls the movement of the pushrod, which in turn regulates the amount of air which flows through the throttle body, so controlling the idle speed. The bypass passage is also used as an additional air supply during cold starting. There is no provision for adjustment of the idle speed, except by reprogramming of the ECU using special diagnostic equipment. The idle speed will vary constantly under ECU control.

The ECU controls the ignition side of the engine management system (see Chapter 5) and the exhaust and evaporative emission control systems described later in this Chapter.

If there is an abnormality in any of the readings obtained from any of engine management circuit sensors, the ECU has a back-up facility. It ignores any abnormal sensor signals and assumes a pre-programmed value which will allow the engine to continue running at reduced efficiency. On entering the back-up facility, the ECU will illuminate the engine management warning light in the instrument panel, thereby informing the driver of the fault. It then stores the relevant fault code in the ECU memory. If the warning light is illuminated, the vehicle should be taken to a Citroën dealer for system testing at the earliest opportunity.

Precautions

Refer to the precautions listed in Part C of this Chapter, noting the following:

Unleaded petrol - usage

As with all models equipped with a catalytic converter, these models must be run on 95 RON unleaded fuel only. The use of leaded fuel will seriously damage the catalytic converter.

2 System testing

Note: *Ensure that all wiring connectors are secure and free of corrosion before checking for faults in the engine management system.*

1 If a fault appears in the engine management (ignition/fuel injection) system, first ensure that all the system wiring connectors are securely connected and free of corrosion.

2 Ensure that any fault is not due to poor maintenance. That is, check that the air cleaner element is clean, the spark plugs are in good condition and correctly gapped, that the valve clearances are correctly adjusted and that the engine breather hoses are clear and undamaged.

3 If these checks fail to reveal the cause of the problem, the vehicle should be taken to a Citroën dealer for testing. A wiring block connector is incorporated in the engine management circuit, into which a special electronic diagnostic tester can be plugged **(see illustration)**. The tester will locate the fault quickly and simply, alleviating the need to test all the system components individually, which is a time-consuming operation that carries a high risk of damaging the ECU.

3 Air cleaner element - renewal

Refer to Chapter 1, Section 28.

4 Fuel system - depressurisation

Refer to Section 3 in Part B of this Chapter.

5 Fuel pump - removal and refitting

Refer to Section 4 in Part B of this Chapter **(see illustration)**.

6 Fuel filter - removal and refitting

Refer to Chapter 1, Section 35.

7 Fuel tank - removal, inspection and refitting

Refer to Section 7 in Part B of this Chapter

8 De-aeration reservoir - removal and refitting

Refer to Section 8 in Part B of this Chapter.

9 Idle speed and mixture - adjustment

The idle speed, mixture adjustment and ignition timing are all monitored and controlled by the ECU, and do not normally require adjustment. While experienced home mechanics with a considerable amount of skill and equipment (including a good-quality tachometer and carefully-calibrated exhaust gas analyser) may be able to check the exhaust CO level and the idle speed, if these are found to be in need of adjustment then the vehicle must be taken to a suitably-equipped Citroën dealer.

4D

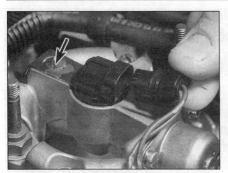

10.2 Disconnecting injector wiring connector - injector retaining screw arrowed

Adjustments can be made only by re-programming the ECU, using special diagnostic equipment connected to the system via the diagnostic connector.

10 Fuel injector - removal and refitting

Note: *If a faulty injector is suspected, before condemning the injector, it is worth trying the effect of one of the proprietary injector-cleaning treatment. If this fails, the vehicle should be taken to a Citroën dealer for testing. At the time of writing, it appears that the fuel Injector is not available separately and, if faulty, the complete upper throttle body assembly must be renewed.*

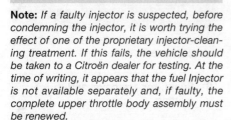

12.2a Disconnect wiring connectors from throttle potentiometer . . .

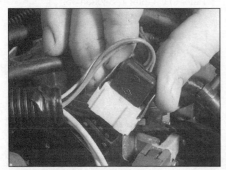

12.2c . . . and the injector wiring loom

12.1a Undo the two nuts . . .

Removal

1 Undo the two nuts securing the **inlet** trunking to the throttle body and position the trunking clear of the body along with its rubber sealing ring.
2 Release the retaining tangs and disconnect the injector wiring connector **(see illustration)**.
3 Undo the retaining screw, then remove the retaining clip and lift the injector out of the housing, noting its sealing ring. As the screw is slackened, place a rag over the injector to catch any fuel spray which may be released.

Refitting

4 Refitting is a reverse of the removal procedure, ensuring that the injector sealing ring is in good condition.

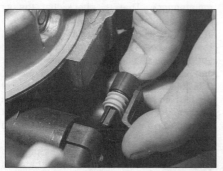

12.2b . . . the idle control stepper motor . . .

12.3 Slacken throttle body fuel feed hose retaining clip

12.1b . . . then disconnect inlet trunking and remove rubber sealing ring

11 Accelerator cable - removal and refitting

Refer to Section 13 in Part B of this Chapter but note that there is no need to check the idle speed after refitting. Adjust the cable until there is only a small amount of freeplay present at the throttle body end of the cable.

12 Throttle body assembly - removal and refitting

Removal

1 Undo the two nuts securing the inlet trunking to the throttle body and position the trunking clear of the body along with its rubber sealing ring **(see illustrations)**.
2 Depress the retaining tabs and disconnect the wiring connectors from the throttle potentiometer, the stepper motor and the injector wiring loom connector which is situated on the front of the throttle body **(see illustrations)**.
3 Bearing in mind the information given on depressurising the fuel system, release the retaining clips and disconnect the fuel feed and return hoses from the throttle body assembly **(see illustration)**.
4 Disconnect the accelerator inner cable from the throttle cam, then free the outer cable from its retaining bracket and position it clear of the throttle body **(see illustration)**.

12.4 Disconnecting accelerator inner cable from throttle cam

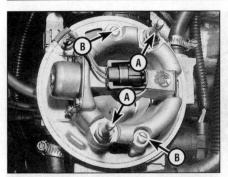

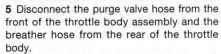

12.7 Throttle body retaining bolts (A) and housing retaining screws (B)

13.2 Throttle potentiometer retaining screws (arrowed)

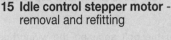

14.2 Fuel pressure regulator retaining screws (arrowed)

5 Disconnect the purge valve hose from the front of the throttle body assembly and the breather hose from the rear of the throttle body.

6 Working quickly to minimise coolant loss, disconnect the two coolant hoses from the rear of the throttle body assembly. Plug each hose end with a suitable bolt or screw.

7 Undo the two retaining bolts and remove the throttle body assembly from the manifold along with its sealing gasket **(see illustration)**.

8 If necessary, with the throttle body removed, undo the two retaining screws and separate the upper and lower sections. Note the gasket which is fitted between the two.

Refitting

9 Refitting is a reverse of the removal procedure, bearing in mind the following points.

a) Where necessary, ensure that the mating surfaces of the upper and lower throttle body sections are clean and dry, then fit a new gasket and reassemble the two, tightening the retaining screws securely.

b) Ensure that the mating surfaces of the manifold and throttle body are clean and dry, then fit a new gasket. Securely tighten the throttle body retaining bolts.

c) Ensure that all hoses are correctly reconnected and, where necessary, that their retaining clips are securely tightened.

d) Adjust the accelerator cable so that only a small amount of freeplay is present at the throttle body end of the cable.

e) If necessary, top-up the cooling system.

13 Throttle potentiometer - removal and refitting

Removal

1 Disconnect the battery negative terminal, then depress the retaining tabs and disconnect the wiring connector from the throttle potentiometer.

2 Undo the two retaining screws and remove the throttle potentiometer from the right-hand side of the throttle body assembly **(see illustration)**.

Refitting

3 Refitting is a reversal of the removal procedure. Ensure that the throttle potentiometer tang is correctly engaged with the throttle spindle.

14 Fuel pressure regulator - removal and refitting

Note: *At the time of writing, it appears that the fuel pressure regulator is not available separately. If the regulator is faulty, then the complete upper throttle body assembly must be renewed. Refer to a Citroën dealer for further information. Although the unit can be dismantled for cleaning, it should not be disturbed unless absolutely necessary.*

Removal

1 Undo the two nuts securing the **inlet** trunking to the throttle body and position the trunking clear of the body along with its rubber sealing ring.

2 Using a suitable marker pen, make alignment marks between the regulator cover and throttle body, then undo the four retaining screws **(see illustration)**. As the screws are slackened, place a rag over the cover to catch any fuel spray which may be released.

3 Lift off the cover, then remove the spring and withdraw the diaphragm, noting its correct fitted orientation.

4 Remove all traces of dirt and examine the diaphragm for signs of splitting. If damage is found, it will be necessary to renew the complete upper throttle body assembly.

Refitting

5 Refitting is a reverse of the removal procedure. Ensure that the diaphragm and cover are fitted the correct way around and the retaining screws are securely tightened.

15 Idle control stepper motor - removal and refitting

Note: *If a faulty stepper motor is suspected, then the vehicle should be taken to a Citroën dealer for testing. At the time of writing, it appears that the stepper motor is not available separately. If faulty, the complete lower throttle body assembly must be renewed.*

To remove the stepper motor, depress the retaining tabs and disconnect the wiring connector. Undo the two retaining screws and withdraw the motor from the rear of the throttle body assembly **(see illustration)**.

Refitting is a reverse of removal.

16 Inlet and exhaust manifolds - removal and refitting

4D

Inlet manifold

1 Remove the throttle body assembly.

2 Drain the cooling system.

3 Disconnect the wiring connector from the fuel/air mixture temperature sensor, located on the right-hand side of the manifold.

4 Undo the nut securing the oil filler cap/breather to the side of the manifold, then release the assembly from its retaining stud and position it clear of the manifold **(see illustration)**.

15.1 Idle control stepper motor location

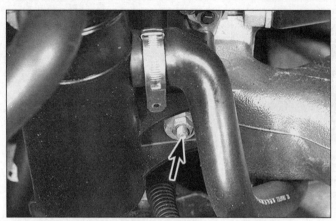

16.4 Oil filler/breather cap retaining nut (arrowed)

16.6 Slackening coolant hose retaining clip from front of inlet manifold - MAP sensor hose arrowed

5 Undo the bolt securing the wiring/hose support bracket to the top of the manifold and position the bracket clear of the manifold.
6 Disconnect the coolant hose and the MAP sensor vacuum hose from the front of the manifold **(see illustration)**.
7 Undo the six manifold retaining nuts and remove the manifold from the **engine**. Remove the gasket and renew it.
8 Refitting is a reverse of the removal procedure, noting the following points.
 a) *Ensure that the manifold and cylinder head mating surfaces are clean and dry before fitting the new gasket.*
 b) *Ensure that all relevant hoses are reconnected to their original positions, and are securely held (where necessary) by the retaining clips.*
 c) *On completion, refill the cooling system.*

Exhaust manifold

9 Refer to Section 14 in Part B of this Chapter

17 Exhaust system - maintenance, removal and refitting

Refer to Section 14 in Part C of this Chapter.

18 Exhaust emission control system - general information and testing

General information

1 To minimise the amount of pollutants which escape into the atmosphere, a catalytic converter is incorporated into the exhaust system. The system is a "closed-loop" type, a lambda sensor in the exhaust system providing the engine management system ECU with constant feedback, thus enabling it to adjust the mixture and provide the best possible conditions for the converter to operate.
2 The lambda sensor has a built-in heating element, controlled by the ECU through the

relay assembly to quickly bring the sensor's tip to an efficient operating temperature. The sensor's tip is sensitive to oxygen and sends the ECU a varying voltage depending on the amount of oxygen in the exhaust gases. If the inlet air/fuel mixture is too rich, the exhaust gases are low in oxygen, so the sensor sends a low-voltage signal. This voltage rises as the mixture weakens and the amount of oxygen in the exhaust gases rises. Peak conversion efficiency of all major pollutants occurs if the inlet air/fuel mixture is maintained at the chemically-correct ratio for the complete combustion of petrol of 14.7 parts (by weight) of air to 1 part of fuel. The sensor output voltage alters in a large step at this point, the ECU using the signal change as a reference point and correcting the **inlet** air/fuel mixture accordingly by altering the fuel injector pulse width.

Testing

3 Regular checks of the lambda sensor's operation should be performed. This can be done only by attaching Citroën diagnostic equipment to the sensor wiring and checking that the voltage varies from low to high values when the engine is running. Do not attempt to "test" any part of the system with anything other than the correct test equipment.

19 Evaporative emission control system - general information and component renewal

General information

1 To minimise the escape of unburned hydrocarbons into the atmosphere, an evaporative emissions control system is incorporated in the Magneti Marelli engine management system. The fuel tank filler cap is sealed and a charcoal canister is mounted underneath the right-hand wing to collect the petrol vapour generated in the tank when the vehicle is parked. This vapour is stored until it can be cleared from the canister (under the control of the engine management system

ECU, via the purge control valve) into the inlet tract, to be burned by the engine during normal combustion.
2 To ensure that the engine runs correctly when it is cold and/or idling, and to protect the catalytic converter from the effects of an over-rich mixture, the purge control valve is not opened by the ECU until the engine has warmed up. The valve solenoid is then modulated on and off to allow the stored vapour to pass into the inlet tract.
3 If the system is thought to be faulty, disconnect the hoses from the charcoal canister and purge control valve and check that they are clear by blowing through them. If the purge control valve or charcoal canister are thought to be faulty, they must be renewed.

Charcoal canister - removal and refitting

4 Disconnect the battery negative terminal.
5 Chock the rear wheels, then jack up the front of the vehicle and support it on axle stands (see "*Jacking and vehicle support*"). Remove the right-hand front roadwheel.
6 Release the retaining clip(s) and disconnect the hoses from the canister.
7 Undo the retaining screw(s) and/or release the retaining clips (as applicable), then free the canister assembly from its retaining bracket and remove it from underneath the wheel arch.
8 Refitting is a reverse of the removal procedure. Ensure that the hoses are correctly routed and securely reconnected.

Purge valve - removal and refitting

9 Disconnect the battery negative terminal.
10 Disconnect the wiring connector from the purge valve, situated just behind the alternator.
11 Disconnect the inlet and outlet hoses, then remove the valve from the engine compartment.
12 Refitting is a reverse of the removal procedure. Ensure that the inlet and outlet hoses are securely reconnected.

Chapter 5 Part A:
Ignition system - carburettor models

Contents

Degrees of difficulty

Easy, suitable for novice with little experience	Fairly easy, suitable for beginner with some experience	Fairly difficult, suitable for competent DIY mechanic 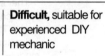	Difficult, suitable for experienced DIY mechanic 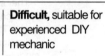	Very difficult, suitable for expert DIY or professional 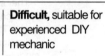

Specifications

For engine to model applications refer to Chapter 2

System
Type .... Electronic (breakerless)

Distributor
Make .... Ducellier or Bosch
Type:
    150 A engine .... Ducellier 525 354
    150 C engine .... Ducellier 525 388
    171 engine .... Ducellier 525 327 or Bosch 0237 009 013
    159 engine .... Ducellier 525 327 or Bosch 0237 009 013

HT leads
Type:
    BX .... Champion LS-04
    BX 14 (pre Aug 1988) .... Champion LS-04
    BX 16 .... Champion LS-14
    BX 19 (pre 1988) .... Champion LS-14

Ignition coil
Type .... Bosch 0221 122 317 or Ducellier 520 015
Primary resistance:
    Bosch .... 0.82 ohm ± 10%
    Ducellier .... 0.8 ohm ± 5%
Secondary resistance:
    Bosch .... 8250 ohms ± 10%
    Ducellier .... 6000 ohms ± 5%

Ignition timing
Dynamic:
    BX .... 8° BTDC at 850 rpm
    BX 14:
        Pre Aug 1988 .... 10° BTDC at 850 rpm
        From Aug 1988 .... 6 to 10° BTDC at 750 rpm
    BX 16:
        Manual gearbox .... 10° BTDC at 900 rpm
        Automatic transmission .... 10° BTDC at 850 rpm
        RE .... 10° BTDC at 700 rpm
        From Sept 1988 .... 10° BTDC at 850 rpm
    BX 19 .... 10° BTDC at 850 rpm

5A

Spark plugs

	Type	Electrode gap
BX	Champion S9YCC / S281YC	0.8 mm / 0.6 mm
BX 14:		
Pre Aug 1988	Champion S9YCC / S281YC	0.8 mm / 0.6 mm
From Aug 1988	Champion RC9YCC / C9YCX	0.8 mm / 0.8 mm
BX16:		
Pre Sept 1988	Champion S7YCC / S279YC	0.8 mm / 0.6 mm
From Sept 1988	Champion RC7YCC / C7YCX	0.8 mm / 0.8 mm
BX 19:		
Pre July 1987	Champion S7YCC / S279YC	0.8 mm / 0.6 mm
From July 1987	Champion RC7YCC / C7YCX	0.8 mm / 0.8 mm

Torque wrench settings

	Nm	lbf ft
Spark plugs:		
Taper seat type	12	9
Flat seat type (with washer)	25	18

1 General information and precautions

General information

The ignition system fitted to all carburettor equipped models is of the electronic type and comprises a 12 volt battery, a high output coil, a transistorised module, a distributor with a magnetic impulser generator and spark plugs (see illustration).

The system relies on the distributor to produce an electrical pulse at each firing point. This pulse is produced by magnetic induction and is amplified by the ignition module which supplies LT current to the coil. HT voltage is generated and distributed in the traditional fashion.

Electronic ignition systems are normally very reliable. Because the effects of contact breaker wear have been eliminated, the system will not go 'off tune'.

Precautions

It is necessary to take extra care when working on the electrical system to avoid damage to semi-conductor devices (diodes and transistors), and to avoid the risk of personal injury. Take note of the following points:

a) Before disconnecting any wiring, or

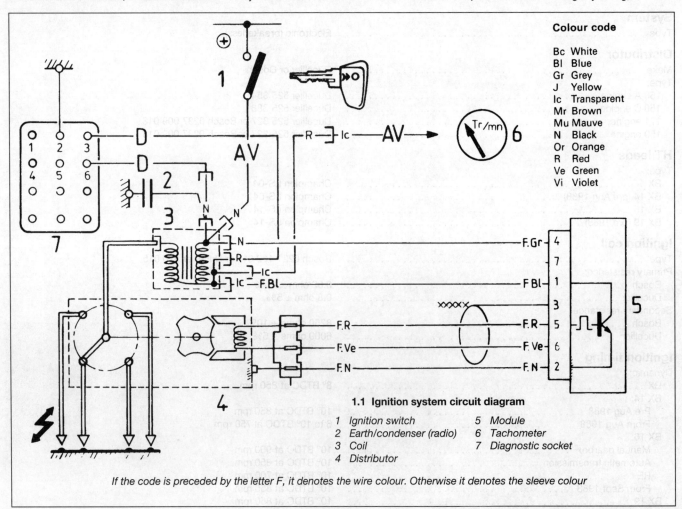

Colour code

Bc White
Bl Blue
Gr Grey
J Yellow
Ic Transparent
Mr Brown
Mu Mauve
N Black
Or Orange
R Red
Ve Green
Vi Violet

1.1 Ignition system circuit diagram

1 Ignition switch
2 Earth/condenser (radio)
3 Coil
4 Distributor
5 Module
6 Tachometer
7 Diagnostic socket

If the code is preceded by the letter F, it denotes the wire colour. Otherwise it denotes the sleeve colour

removing components, always ensure that the ignition is switched off.

b) Always remove rings, watches, etc. before working on the ignition system. Even with the battery disconnected, capacitive discharge could occur if a component live terminal is earthed through a metal object. This could cause a shock or nasty burn.

c) Do not reverse the battery connections. Components such as the alternator or any other having semi-conductor circuitry could be irreparably damaged.

d) If the engine is being started using jump leads and a slave battery, connect the batteries positive to positive and negative to negative. This also applies when connecting a battery charger.

e) Never disconnect the battery terminals, or alternator multi-plug connector, when the engine is running.

f) The battery leads and alternator multi-plug must be disconnected before carrying out any electric welding on the vehicle.

g) Never use an ohmmeter of the type incorporating a hand cranked generator for circuit or continuity testing.

h) The HT voltage generated by an electronic ignition system is extremely high, and in certain circumstances could prove fatal. Persons with surgically-implanted cardiac pacemaker devices should keep well clear of the ignition circuits, components and test equipment.

i) Do not handle HT leads, or touch the distributor or coil when the engine is running. If tracing faults in the HT circuit, use well insulated tools to manipulate live leads.

j) When carrying out welding operations on the vehicle using electric welding equipment, disconnect the battery and alternator.

2 Spark plugs - removal, inspection and fitting

Note: From July 1987, the engines of BX 19 models are fitted with conventional flat-seat spark plugs with washers, instead of the taper-seat plugs without washer used previously. BX 14 and BX 16 models followed suit in August and September of 1988 respectively.

1 The correct functioning of the spark plugs is vital for the correct running and efficiency of the engine. It is essential that the plugs fitted are appropriate for the engine. If the correct type is used and the engine is in good condition, the plugs should not need attention between scheduled replacement intervals. Cleaning is rarely necessary and should not be attempted unless specialised equipment is available as damage can easily be caused to the firing ends.

Removal

2 Pull the HT lead from each plug. Grip the rubber end fitting not the lead, otherwise the lead connection may be fractured **(see illustration)**.
3 The plugs are deeply recessed in the cylinder head. It is recommended that dirt is removed from the recesses using a vacuum cleaner or compressed air before removing the plugs, to prevent dirt dropping into the cylinders.
4 Unscrew each plug.

Inspection

5 Examination of the spark plugs will give a good indication of the condition of the engine.
6 If the insulator nose of the spark plug is clean and white with no deposits, this is indicative of a weak mixture, or too hot a plug.
7 If the top and insulator nose are covered with hard black-looking deposits, this is indicative that the mixture is too rich. Should the plug be black and oily then it is likely that the engine is fairly worn, as well as the mixture being too rich,
8 If the insulator nose is covered with light tan to greyish brown deposits, then the mixture is correct and it is likely that the engine is in good condition.

Gap setting

9 The spark plug gap is of considerable importance as if it is too large or too small, the size of the spark and its efficiency will be seriously impaired.
10 To set the gap, measure it with a feeler blade. Bend open, or close, the outer plug electrode until the correct gap is achieved, see Specifications. The centre electrode should never be bent as this may crack the insulation and cause plug failure if nothing worse.
11 Special gap adjusting tools are available from most motor accessory stores.

Fitting

12 Screw each plug in by hand. This will make sure that there is no chance of cross-threading.
13 Tighten to the specified torque. If a torque wrench is not available, just nip up each plug. It is better to slightly undertighten rather than overdo it and strip the threads from the light alloy cylinder head.

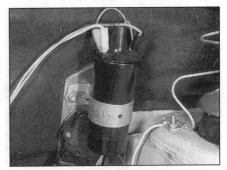

2.2 HT lead removal from spark plug - do not pull on lead

14 Overtightening plugs of the tapered seat type can make them extremely difficult to remove.
15 When reconnecting the plug leads, make sure that they are refitted in their correct order, 1 - 3 - 4 - 2. No 1 cylinder being at the flywheel end of the engine.

3 HT leads - maintenance and fitting

1 Ensure that the HT leads are numbered before removal, to avoid confusion when refitting.
2 Pull each lead from its plug by gripping its end fitting, not the lead, otherwise the lead connection may become fractured.
3 Check inside the end fitting for signs of corrosion, which will look like a white crusty powder. Remove any corrosion found.
4 Push the end fitting back onto the spark plug, ensuring that it is a tight fit. If not, remove the lead again and use pliers to carefully crimp the metal connector inside the end fitting until it fits securely to the plug.
5 Using a clean rag, wipe the entire length of the lead to remove any built-up dirt and grease. Once the lead is clean, check for burns, cracks and other damage. Do not bend the lead excessively or pull the lead lengthways - the conductor inside might break.

4 Ignition coil - maintenance and testing

Maintenance

1 Maintenance of the coil is minimal and is limited to periodically wiping its surfaces clean and dry and ensuring that the lead connectors are secure and free from corrosion **(see illustration)**.
2 High voltages generated by the coil can easily leak to earth over its surface and prevent the spark plugs from receiving the electrical pulses. Water repellent sprays are now available to prevent dampness causing this type of malfunction.

5A

4.1 The ignition coil

Testing

3 Special equipment is required to test a coil and is best left to an auto-electrician. Substitution of another coil is an alternative method of fault tracing.

5 Distributor cap - removal, inspection and refitting

Removal

1 Ensure that the HT leads connected to the distributor cap are numbered before removal, to avoid confusion when refitting.
2 Pull each lead from the cap by gripping its end fitting, not the lead, otherwise the lead connection may become fractured.
3 Unclip the distributor cap. Alternatively, remove the two screws securing the cap in position **(see illustration)**.

Inspection

4 Check inside the HT lead end fittings of the cap for signs of corrosion, which will look like a white crusty powder. Remove any corrosion found.
5 Wipe the cap clean and carefully inspect it inside and out for signs of cracks, carbon tracks (tracking) and worn, burned or loose contacts.
6 Check that the central carbon brush is unworn, free to move against spring pressure and making good contact with the rotor arm.
7 Clean and inspect the rotor arm.
8 If defects are found, then renew the cap or arm.

Refitting

9 Refitting is a reversal of removal. Push the end fitting of each HT lead firmly into the distributor cap, ensuring that it is a tight fit.

6 Distributor - removal and refitting

Removal

1 Disconnect the HT leads from the spark

5.3 Removing the distributor cap - BX 16

plugs by pulling on their end connectors (not the leads).
2 Unclip the distributor cap. Alternatively, remove the two screws securing the cap in position.
3 Release the HT leads from their location clips and position the leads and cap out of the way.
4 Disconnect the LT wiring at the plug connector by releasing the spring retaining clip.
5 Clean the area around the distributor mounting flange and look for a timing alignment mark.
6 On BX and BX 14 models, this alignment mark is normally between the distributor and the cylinder head. On BX 16 and BX 19 models, the mark is between the distributor and fuel pump/thermostat/distributor combined housing **(see illustration)**.
7 If no timing alignment mark is visible, scribe a mark across the two faces.
8 Undo the retaining nuts and withdraw the distributor.

Refitting

9 Refit in the reverse order of removal. The distributor drive is offset so there is no possibility of incorrect assembly **(see illustration)**.
10 Use the alignment marks noted during removal if refitting the old distributor. If fitting a new unit, set it to the middle of the travel allowed by the slotted holes.
11 Check the ignition timing and adjust if necessary.

6.6 Distributor timing alignment mark - BX 16

6.9 Distributor drive engagement dog is offset - BX 16

7 Distributor - dismantling and reassembly

Note: *Before commencing dismantling, check that spares are available. If the mechanical components of the distributor are worn it will be necessary to renew the complete distributor.*

Ducellier

1 Remove the screws which hold together the upper and lower halves of the distributor body. The lugs are offset to guarantee correct reassembly. Separate the body sections **(see illustration)**.
2 The pick-up coil and vacuum unit can now be removed from the upper body section. Note into which hole the vacuum unit link engages.
3 The rotor and centrifugal advance weights can be removed after extracting the circlip from the shaft. The drive dog is secured to the shaft by a pin.
4 Reassemble in the reverse order to dismantling.

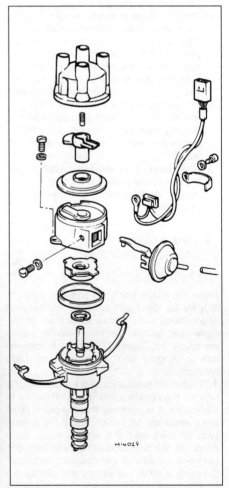

7.1 Exploded view of Ducellier breakerless distributor

7.5 Remove top plate for access to rotor - Bosch distributor

7.6 Bosch distributor drive dogs and O-ring seal (arrowed)

Bosch

5 This procedure is similar to that given for the Ducellier distributor but the distributor body is in one piece (see illustration).
6 Before refitting the distributor, fit a new O-ring seal into the groove in its base (see illustration).

8 Ignition timing

Note: *The ignition timing can only be checked dynamically. A stroboscopic timing light and HT type tachometer will be needed.*
1 Start the engine and run it up to its normal operating temperature (cooling fan cuts in). Switch off the engine.
2 Turn the engine over slowly by hand so that the timing mark on the flywheel periphery can be seen through the aperture in the clutch housing. Highlight the timing mark with white chalk or paint (see illustration).
3 Disconnect the distributor vacuum advance hose.
4 Connect up the timing light and tachometer in accordance with the manufacturer's instructions.
5 Restart the engine and run it at the recommended idle speed. Point the timing light at the timing marks. They should appear stationary and in alignment. If they are not in alignment, loosen the distributor retaining nuts just enough to allow the distributor to be rotated by hand. Turn the distributor body in the required direction to bring the timing marks in alignment, then retighten the distributor retaining nuts.
6 Switch off the engine and remove the timing light and tachometer. Reconnect the ignition vacuum advance hose.
7 Once the timing has been reset, make a timing alignment mark across the faces of the distributor flange and the cylinder head or distributor housing. This will then act as a timing position guide when the distributor is next removed.

9 Diagnostic test socket

The Citroën BX range of models is fitted with a diagnostic test socket for electronic monitoring of engine performance and ignition system condition. Although this facility is of no use to the home mechanic, it does enable a suitably equipped garage to make a quick assessment and with greater accuracy than the usual procedures (see illustration).
With the appropriate equipment the following checks or adjustments can be made:
a) *Primary (LT) circuit condition*
b) *Setting of initial advance*
c) *Centrifugal and vacuum advance curves*
d) *Engine speed*

5A

8.2 Flywheel timing mark aligned with advance timing mark on timing plate - BX 16

9.1 Diagnostic test socket - BX 16

10 Ignition switch and steering lock

Removal and separation of the switch and lock is described in Chapter 11 **(see illustration)**.

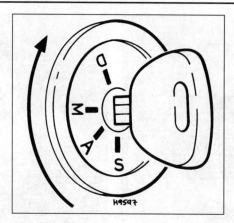

10.1 Ignition switch positions

S Off. Steering locked when key removed
A Ignition off, accessories on
M Ignition on
D Starter motor energised

Chapter 5 Part B:
Ignition system - fuel injection models

Contents

Degrees of difficulty

Easy, suitable for novice with little experience		**Fairly easy,** suitable for beginner with some experience		**Fairly difficult,** suitable for competent DIY mechanic		**Difficult,** suitable for experienced DIY mechanic		**Very difficult,** suitable for expert DIY or professional	

5B

Specifications

For engine to model applications refer to Chapter 2

System

Model application/Type:

BX 19 GTi (pre July 1990)	Bosch LE3 Jetronic
BX 19 GTi 16v (pre 1991)	Motronic ML4.1
BX 19 GTi (from July 1990)	Motronic MP3.1
BX 19 GTi 16v (from 1991)	Motronic M1.3
BX 19 TZi with catalytic converter	Motronic M1.3
BX 16 fuel injection	Magneti Marelli G6.10

HT leads

Type:

BX 19 GTi	Champion LS-10

Spark plugs

	Type	**Electrode gap**
BX 16	Champion C9YCX	0.9 mm
BX 19 GTi	Champion RC7YCC	0.8 mm
BX 19 GTi 16v	Champion RC7YCC	1.6 mm

Torque wrench settings

	Nm	**lbf ft**
Spark plugs:		
Taper seat type	12	9
Flat seat type (with washer)	25	18

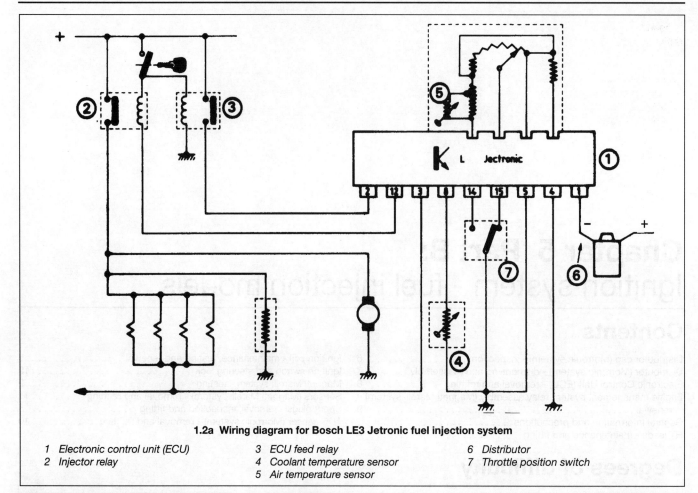

1.2a Wiring diagram for Bosch LE3 Jetronic fuel injection system

1 *Electronic control unit (ECU)*	3 *ECU feed relay*	6 *Distributor*
2 *Injector relay*	4 *Coolant temperature sensor*	7 *Throttle position switch*
	5 *Air temperature sensor*	

1 General information and precautions

General information

Bosch LE3 Jetronic system

Fitted to BX 19 GTi models manufactured before July 1990, operation of this system is fully explained in Chapter 4B.

The electronic control unit (ECU) incorporated in the system is triggered by the ignition circuit and sends impulses to the injectors, which operate simultaneously and inject fuel in the vicinity of the inlet valves. The ECU is provided with sensors to determine engine temperature, speed and load, and the quantity of air entering the engine **(see illustrations)**.

Motronic system

Three types of Motronic engine management systems have been fitted to the Citroën BX range, their model applications being as follows:

BX 19 GTi 16v (pre 1991) *Motronic ML4.1*
BX 19 GTi (from July 1990) *Motronic MP3.1*
BX 19 GTi 16v (from 1991) *Motronic M1.3*
BX 19 TZi with catalytic
converter   *Motronic M1.3*

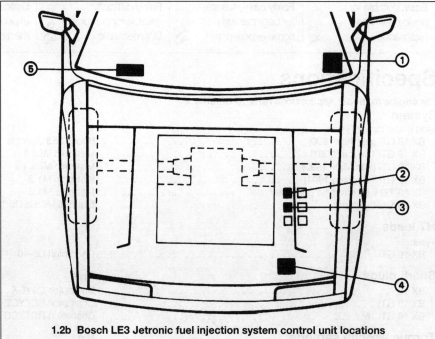

1.2b Bosch LE3 Jetronic fuel injection system control unit locations

1 *Junction/fusebox*	3 *ECU feed relay*	5 *Interface unit (fuel*
2 *Injector relay*	4 *Airflow meter/ECU*	*consumption data for*
		computer, if fitted)

Operation of these system types is fully explained in Chapter 4C, the main components of the ignition function of each system type being as follows:

a) *Electronic control unit (ECU) - located under the driver's seat, the ECU controls the system components and receives signals from various sensors.*

b) *Ignition coil - for the Motronic ML4.1 and M1.3 systems, a conventional ignition coil is used, being triggered by signals from the ECU. The Motronic MP3.1 system uses a distributorless ignition system with a double coil which operates on the "wasted-spark" principle, supplying current directly to the spark plugs when triggered by signals from the ECU*

c) *HT distributor (all except Motronic MP3.1) - the distributor simply distributes HT current to the spark plugs and consists of a rotor arm on the end of the camshaft (inlet camshaft on 16v models) and a conventional distributor cap.*

The following sensors supply the ECU with information:

a) *Air temperature sensor - measures the temperature of the air entering the engine (integral with the airflow meter)*

b) *Throttle position switch - senses the position of the throttle valve*

c) *Coolant temperature sensor*

d) *Knock sensor (only fitted to BX 19 GTi 16v with Motronic M1.3) - senses the engine vibrations associated with pre-ignition, which may cause engine damage unless the ignition timing is retarded as a preventative measure*

e) *Lambda (oxygen) sensor (only fitted to models equipped with Motronic M1.3 and catalytic converter) - measures the oxygen content of the exhaust gases*

f) *TDC sensor - measures engine speed and crankshaft position*

Magneti Marelli system

Fitted to fuel-injected BX 16 models, operation of this system is fully explained in Chapter 4D.

On the ignition side of this system, the ECU has full control. The ignition system is of the static, distributorless type and consists solely of an ignition HT coil with four outputs. The ignition coil comprises two separate HT coils which supply two cylinders each (one coil supplies cylinders 1 and 4 - the other coil cylinders 2 and 3). Under control of the ECU, the ignition coil operates on the "wasted-spark" principle, ie. each spark plug sparks twice for every cycle of the engine, once on the compression stroke and once on the exhaust stroke.

The ECU uses its inputs from the various sensors to calculate the required ignition advance setting and coil charging time. These sensors are as follows:

a) *Manifold absolute pressure (MAP) sensor - informs the ECU of engine load*

b) *Crankshaft sensor - informs the ECU of crankshaft position and engine speed*

c) *Throttle potentiometer - informs the ECU of throttle valve position and rate of throttle opening/closing*

d) *Coolant temperature sensor - informs the ECU of engine temperature*

e) *Fuel/air mixture temperature sensor - informs the ECU of temperature of fuel/air mixture charge entering cylinders*

f) *Lambda (oxygen) sensor - informs the ECU of oxygen content of exhaust gases*

Precautions

General

Refer to the precautions listed in Part A of this Chapter.

Engine management systems

Engine management modules are very sensitive components and certain precautions must be taken to avoid damaging them. These are as follows:

a) *Although underbonnet-mounted modules will tolerate normal underbonnet conditions, they can be adversely affected by excess heat or moisture. If using pressure washing equipment in the vicinity of the module, take care not to direct jets of water or steam at the module. If this cannot be avoided, remove the module from the vehicle and protect its wiring plug with a plastic bag.*

b) *On models with underbonnet-mounted modules, do not run the engine with the module detached from the body panel, as the body acts as an effective heat sink and the module may be damaged due to internal overheating.*

c) *Do not attempt to improvise fault diagnosis procedures using a test lamp or multimeter, as irreparable damage could be caused to the module.*

d) *After working on engine management system components, ensure that all wiring is correctly reconnected before reconnecting the battery or switching on the ignition.*

2.3 Magneti Marelli system diagnostic connector

2 Magneti Marelli system - testing

1 If a fault appears in the system, first ensure that all system wiring connectors are securely connected and free of corrosion.

2 Ensure that any fault is not due to poor maintenance. That is, check that the air cleaner element is clean, the spark plugs are in good condition and correctly gapped, that the valve clearances are correctly adjusted and that the engine breather hoses are clear and undamaged.

3 If these checks fail to reveal the cause of the problem, the vehicle should be taken to a Citroën dealer for testing. A wiring block connector is incorporated in the engine management circuit, into which a special electronic diagnostic tester can be plugged **(see illustration)**. The tester will locate the fault quickly and simply, alleviating the need to test all the system components individually, which is a time-consuming operation that carries a high risk of damaging the ECU.

3 Spark plugs - removal, inspection and fitting

Refer to the information given in Section 2 in Part A of this Chapter, noting that the flat-seated spark plugs with washers are also fitted to BX 19 GTi and BX GTi 16 valve engines.

4 HT leads - maintenance and fitting

Where applicable, refer to Section 3 in Part A of this Chapter.

5 Ignition coil - maintenance, testing and renewal

Maintenance and testing

1 Refer to Section 4 in Part A of this Chapter.

Renewal

Bosch LE3 Jetronic system

2 Ignition coil type and location on the BX 19 GTi manufactured before July 1990 differs to that on other models in the range.

3 The coil is mounted on the underside of the air inlet manifold **(see illustration)**.

4 To remove the coil, detach the wiring connectors and unbolt the unit, complete with its retaining bracket.

5 Refitting is a reversal of the removal procedure.

5B

5.3 Ignition coil location - GTi with Bosch LE3 system

5.8 Disconnect ignition coil wiring connector

5.9 Disconnect HT leads, noting cylinder number markings on leads and coil (arrowed)

Magneti Marelli system

6 The ignition coil of this system is mounted on the left-hand end of the cylinder head, and can be removed as follows.

7 Disconnect the battery negative terminal.

8 Disconnect the wiring connector from the base of the coil **(see illustration)**.

9 Make a note of the correct fitted positions of the HT leads, then disconnect them from the coil terminals. Note that on genuine Citroën leads, each lead is marked with its cylinder number, indicated by red blocks printed near the end of the lead. The coil terminals are also numbered for identification **(see illustration)**.

10 Undo the four Torx retaining screws and remove the coil from the end of the cylinder head.

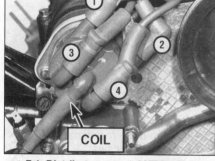

7.1 Distributor cap and HT leads - GTi 16v with Motronic ML4.1

11 Refitting is a reverse of the removal procedure, ensuring that the HT leads are correctly reconnected.

6 Distributor cap (Motronic system) - inspection

1 Check inside the HT lead end fittings of the cap for signs of corrosion, which will look like a white crusty powder. Remove any corrosion found.

2 Wipe the cap clean and carefully inspect it inside and out for signs of cracks, carbon tracks (tracking) and worn, burned or loose contacts.

3 Check that the central carbon brush is unworn, free to move against spring pressure and making good contact with the rotor arm.

4 Clean and inspect the rotor arm.

5 If defects are found, then renew the cap or arm.

7 Distributor (Motronic system) - dismantling and reassembly

1 Disconnect the battery negative lead, then disconnect the HT leads from the spark plugs **(see illustration)**.

2 Loosen the securing screws and withdraw the distributor cap complete with HT leads.

3 Where applicable, remove the three securing screws, then pull the rotor arm from the end of the camshaft **(see illustration)**.

4 On BX 19 GTi 16 valve models, the rotor drive flange can be removed after removing the single Torx retaining screw. The plastic baseplate can then be removed **(see illustration)**.

5 Refitting is a reversal of removal. On BX 19 GTi 16 valve models, clean the threads of the rotor drive flange retaining screw and apply locking fluid before refitting. Note that the components will only fit in one position.

8 Electronic Control Unit (ECU) - removal and refitting

Motronic system

1 The ECU is located under the driver's seat **(see illustration)**.

2 To remove the unit, first disconnect the battery negative lead.

3 To gain access to the unit, unclip the front seat cushion from the seat frame, then release it from the upholstery retaining hooks and remove the seat cushion.

4 Unscrew the bolt securing the unit to its mounting bracket, then disconnect the ECU wiring plug and withdraw the unit.

5 Refitting is a reversal of removal.

7.3 Removing a rotor arm securing screw - GTi 16v with Motronic ML4.1

7.4 Rotor drive flange - GTi 16v with Motronic ML4.1

8.1 ECU location - GTi 16v with Motronic ML4.1

8.6 ECU is located under the driver's seat - Magneti Marelli system

9.1 Engine management relay assembly location - Magneti Marelli system

11.2 Crankshaft sensor wiring connector situated behind ignition coil

Magneti Marelli system

6 Refer to the information given for the Motronic system **(see illustration)**.

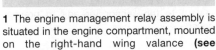

9 Engine management system relay assembly (Magneti Marelli system) - renewal

1 The engine management relay assembly is situated in the engine compartment, mounted on the right-hand wing valance **(see illustration)**.
2 To remove the assembly, first disconnect the battery negative terminal.
3 Disconnect the wiring connector, then undo the retaining screw and remove the relay assembly from the engine compartment.
4 Refitting is a reverse of removal.

10 TDC sensor (Motronic system) - removal and refitting

Removal

1 The TDC sensor is mounted in the gearbox bellhousing.
2 Disconnect the wiring plug, then disconnect the wiring from the sensor.
3 Remove the sensor securing screw and withdraw the sensor from the bellhousing. Where applicable, recover the shim which may be fitted between the sensor and the bellhousing.

Refitting

4 Refitting is a reversal of removal. Note the following.
5 On BX 19 GTi 16 valve models, use a depth gauge to measure the distance between the sensor mounting face and the top of one of the teeth on the flywheel.
6 If the reading obtained is 25 mm, refit the sensor without a shim. If the reading is 24.1 mm, a suitable shim (available from Citroën dealers) must be fitted between the sensor and the bellhousing.

11 Sensors (Magneti Marelli system) - removal and refitting

Crankshaft sensor

1 The crankshaft sensor is fitted to the top of the transmission housing, beside the left-hand end of the cylinder block. To remove it, first disconnect the battery negative terminal.
2 Trace the wiring back from the sensor to its wiring connector, then depress the retaining tabs and disconnect it from the main wiring harness **(see illustration)**.
3 Undo the bolt securing the sensor to the transmission housing and remove the sensor from the vehicle **(see illustration)**.
4 Refitting is a reverse of removal.

Lambda sensor

Note: *This sensor is delicate and will not work*

if dropped or knocked, if its power supply is disrupted, or if any cleaning materials are used on it.
5 Open the bonnet and locate the sensor wiring connectors which are clipped to the right-hand end of the engine compartment bulkhead **(see illustration)**. Disconnect the battery negative terminal, then disconnect both the wiring connectors and free the wiring harness from any relevant retaining clips.
6 Chock the rear wheels, then jack up the front of the car and support it on axle stands (see "*Jacking and vehicle support*").
7 Free the lower end of the sensor wiring from any relevant retaining clips, then unscrew the sensor from the front pipe and remove it along with its sealing washer **(see illustration)**.
8 Prior to refitting, examine the sealing washer for signs of damage and renew as necessary.
9 Ensure that the sensor and manifold threads are clean, then apply a smear of high-temperature anti-seize compound to the sensor's threads.
10 Fit the sealing washer to the sensor, then refit the sensor to the front pipe and tighten it securely.
11 Ensure that the sensor wiring is correctly routed up the bulkhead and secure the wiring in position with any relevant clips or ties.
12 Return to the engine compartment, then reconnect the sensor wiring connectors and secure the wiring to the bulkhead with any remaining clips or ties. Reconnect the battery, and lower the vehicle to the ground.

5B

11.3 Crankshaft sensor location (retaining screw arrowed)

11.5 Lambda sensor wiring connectors (arrowed) situated in right-hand corner of engine compartment

11.7 Lambda sensor location

11.13 Fuel/air mixture temperature sensor location

11.18a Slacken and remove the three retaining nuts and bolts . . .

11.18b . . . then free MAP sensor from bracket and disconnect vacuum hose and wiring connector

Fuel/air mixture temperature sensor

13 This sensor is screwed into the right-hand side of the inlet manifold and is removed as follows (see illustration).

14 Disconnect the battery negative terminal.

15 Disconnect the wiring connector, then unscrew the sensor from the inlet manifold.

16 Refitting is a reverse of the removal procedure, ensuring that the switch is securely tightened.

Manifold absolute pressure (MAP) sensor

17 This sensor is mounted onto a bracket which is situated just behind the alternator. To remove the sensor, first disconnect the battery negative terminal.

18 Slacken and remove the three retaining nuts and bolts, then free the sensor from the bracket. Disconnect the wiring connector and vacuum hose and remove the sensor from the engine compartment (see illustrations).

19 Refitting is a reverse of the removal procedure.

Coolant temperature sensor

20 This sensor is located on the left-hand end of the rear face of the cylinder head, access to it being strictly limited. Either drain the cooling system, or be prepared for some coolant loss as the sensor is removed.

21 To improve access to the sensor, remove the HT coil.

22 Disconnect the wiring connector from the sensor.

23 Unscrew the sensor, then remove it from the cylinder head and plug its aperture to prevent the entry of dirt. If the cooling system has not been drained, work quickly to minimise coolant loss.

24 Refitting is a reverse of removal, noting that any sealing washer must be renewed. If no sealing washer is fitted, apply a smear of sealant to the sensor threads to prevent leakage.

12 Ignition switch and steering lock

Removal and separation of the switch and lock is described in Chapter 11.

Chapter 5 Part C:
Starting and charging systems

Contents

Degrees of difficulty

Easy, suitable for novice with little experience	Fairly easy, suitable for beginner with some experience	Fairly difficult, suitable for competent DIY mechanic	Difficult, suitable for experienced DIY mechanic	Very difficult, suitable for expert DIY or professional

Specifications

For engine to model applications refer to Chapter 2

System
Type . . . . 12 volt, negative earth

Battery
Rating:
  BX and BX 14 . . . . 29 or 35 Ah
  BX 16 and BX 19 . . . . 33, 45 or 50 Ah
  BX 16 and BX 19 with air conditioning . . . . 50 or 60 Ah

Alternator
Make . . . . Bosch, Ducellier, Paris-Rhone or Melco
Application:
  BX and BX 14 (pre Feb 1984) . . . . Bosch 0120 489 163 164
                                                  Ducellier 516 039
                                                  Paris-Rhone A 13 N 43
    Regulator . . . . Bosch 1 197 311 100
                                                  Ducellier 511 020
                                                  Paris-Rhone YH 1639
  BX and BX 14 (from Feb 1984) . . . . Bosch B 120 427 315
                                                  Paris-Rhone A 13 N 38
    Regulator . . . . Bosch 1 1973 11008
                                                  Paris-Rhone YH 1925
  BX 16 and BX 19 (pre Feb 1984) . . . . Melco A 002 T 26 391
                                                  Bosch A 120 427 141
    Regulator . . . . Melco A 866 T 03 870
                                                  Bosch 1 1973 311 100
  BX 16 and BX 19 (from Feb 1984) . . . . Bosch 0 120 489 258 259
                                                  Paris-Rhone A 13 N 95
    Regulator . . . . Bosch 1 197 311 008
                                                  Paris-Rhone YH 1925
  BX 16 - air conditioned models (80A/1120W) . . . . Melco A 3 T 45 191 G
                                                  Melco A 003 T 45 291
    Regulator . . . . Melco 03870 RS 3809
Minimum output at 13.5 volts:
  BX, BX 14, BX 16 and BX 19:
    900 rpm engine speed . . . . 32 amps
    1800 rpm engine speed . . . . 47 amps
  BX 16 - air conditioned models:
    900 rpm engine speed . . . . 54 amps
    1800 rpm engine speed . . . . 75 amps

Starter motor

Make	Ducellier, Paris-Rhone or Bosch
Type	Pre-engaged, 12 volt
Application:	
BX and BX 14	Ducellier 532 014
	Paris-Rhone D 8 E 151
	Bosch 9 000 1 42 002
BX 16 and BX 19	Ducellier 534 039
	Paris-Rhone D 9 E 48
	Bosch A 001 208 316 F
	Bosch 0 001 208 516 E

1 General information and precautions

General information

The system is of the 12 volt negative earth type. Major components comprise a 12 volt battery, a starter motor, and an alternator which is belt-driven from a crankshaft pulley.

The battery supplies a steady amount of current for the ignition and other electrical circuits and provides a reserve of electricity when the current consumed by the electrical equipment exceeds that being produced by the alternator.

The alternator is controlled by a regulator. This ensures a high output if the battery is in a low state of charge or the demand from the electrical equipment is high. Alternatively, it ensures a low output if the battery is fully charged and there is little demand from the electrical equipment.

The starter motor is of the pre-engaged type, its drive pinion being brought into mesh with the starter ring gear on the flywheel before the main current is applied.

When the starter switch is operated, current flows from the battery to the solenoid mounted on top of the starter motor body. The solenoid plunger moves inwards, so causing a centrally pivoted lever to push the drive pinion into mesh with the starter ring gear. When the plunger reaches the end of its travel, it closes an internal contact and full starting current flows to the starter field coils. The armature is then able to rotate the crankshaft, so starting the engine.

Precautions

It is necessary to take extra care when working on the electrical system to avoid damage to semi-conductor devices (diodes and transistors) and to avoid the risk of personal injury. In addition to the precautions given in the "Safety first!" Section at the beginning of this manual, take note of the following points when working on the system.

a) *Before disconnecting any wiring or removing components, always ensure that the ignition is switched off.*
b) *Disconnect the battery leads before using a mains charger.*
c) *Do not reverse the battery connections. Components such as the alternator or any*

other having semi-conductor circuitry could be irreparably damaged.
d) *If the engine is being started using jump leads and a slave battery, connect the batteries positive to positive and negative to negative. This also applies when connecting a battery charger.*
e) *Never disconnect the battery terminals or alternator multi-plug connector when the engine is running.*
f) *The battery leads and alternator multi-plug must be disconnected before carrying out any electric welding on the vehicle.*
g) *Never use an ohmmeter of the type incorporating a hand cranked generator for circuit or continuity testing.*
h) *When carrying out welding operations on the vehicle using electric welding equipment, disconnect the battery and alternator.*

2 Battery - maintenance

Refer to "Weekly Checks".

3 Battery - charging

⚠️ **Warning:** *During battery electrolyte replenishment, never add water to sulphuric acid otherwise it will explode. Always pour the acid slowly onto the water.*

⚠️ **Warning:** *The battery will be emitting significant quantities of (highly-inflammable) hydrogen gas during charging and for approximately 15 minutes afterwards. Do not allow sparks or naked flames near the battery or it may explode.*
Caution: *Specially rapid "boost" charges which are claimed to restore the power of a battery in 1 to 2 hours are not recommended as they can cause serious damage to the battery plates through overheating*
Caution: *If the battery is being charged from an external power source whilst the battery is fitted in the vehicle, both battery leads must be disconnected to prevent damage to the electrical circuits.*

1 In winter when heavy demand is placed on the battery (starting from cold and using more electrical equipment), it is a good idea occasionally to have the battery fully charged from an external source. The charge rate will depend on battery type. For most owners however, the best method will be to use a trickle-charger overnight, charging at a rate of 1.5 amps.
2 Rapid `boost' charges which are claimed to restore the power of the battery in 1 to 2 hours are not recommended, as they can cause serious damage to the battery plates through overheating and may cause a sealed battery to explode.
3 Ideally, the battery should be removed from the vehicle before charging and moved to a well-ventilated area.
4 Continue to charge the battery until all cells are gassing vigorously and no further rise in specific gravity or increase in no-load voltage is noted over a four-hour period. When charging is complete, turn the charger off before disconnecting its leads from the battery.

4 Battery - removal and refitting

Caution: When reconnecting the battery, always connect the positive lead first and the negative lead last.

Removal

1 The battery is on a carrier fitted to the wing valance of the engine compartment.
2 Disconnect the negative and then the positive leads from the battery terminals by releasing the terminal nuts and bolts.
3 Release the battery clamp and carefully lift the battery from its carrier. Hold it vertically to ensure that none of the electrolyte is spilled. Note the earth strap attached to the clamp stud.

Refitting

4 Refitting is a direct reversal of this procedure. Reconnect the positive lead before the negative lead and smear the terminals with petroleum jelly to prevent corrosion. Never use ordinary grease

5 Alternator drivebelt - removal, refitting and adjustment

Removal

1 On BX and BX 14 engines, remove the HP pump drivebelt.
2 Loosen the alternator adjustment and pivot bolts, swivel the alternator towards the engine and remove the drivebelt from the pulley (see illustration).

Refitting

3 Refitting is a reversal of removal but drivebelt adjustment must be made before fully tightening the mounting/adjustment bolts.

Adjustment

4 Correct tensioning of the alternator drivebelt will ensure that it has a long and useful life. If the belt is loose, alternator performance will be affected. If the belt is too tight it will cause unnecessary alternator bearing wear. In either case the belt itself will suffer and its life will be shortened.
5 The drivebelt is tensioned by pivoting the alternator out and securing it when the belt is correctly tensioned.
6 To adjust drivebelt tension, first check that it is correctly located in both pulleys then, with the mounting and adjustment strap bolts loosened, pivot the alternator outwards to tighten the drivebelt. You can use a lever to help achieve this but it must be a wooden one and it must be used only at the pulley end of the alternator. Levering on the case or at the end opposite to the drive pulley can easily cause expensive damage.
7 Tighten the belt as much as possible (but without over stretching it) to take up any play in the belt at its mid point on the longest run between the pulleys. Whilst a taut tension is required the belt must not be overtightened. Tighten the alternator mounting and adjuster strap bolts to set the tension.
8 If a new belt has been fitted, recheck its tension after a nominal mileage has been covered.

5.2 Alternator drivebelt and adjustment strap - BX 16

6 Alternator - removal and refitting

Removal

1 Open the bonnet and disconnect the negative battery terminal followed by the positive battery terminal.
2 Note the location of the alternator supply wires, then disconnect them from the rear cover.
3 On BX and BX 14 engines, remove the HP pump drivebelt.
4 Loosen the alternator adjustment and pivot bolts, swivel the alternator towards the engine and remove the drivebelt from its pulley.
5 Support the alternator and unscrew and remove its adjustment and pivot bolts. The alternator can now be carefully lifted from the vehicle.

Refitting

6 Refitting the alternator is a reversal of the removal procedure. Reconnect the alternator wiring before the battery.
7 Adjust the alternator drivebelt tension and on BX and BX 14 models, refit and adjust the HP pump drivebelt.

7 Alternator - brush renewal

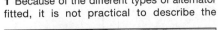

1 Because of the different types of alternator fitted, it is not practical to describe the

procedure for each one in detail. The following procedure applies to the Paris-Rhone 750W alternator. Detail differences will be found with other makes.
2 Remove the alternator from the vehicle.
3 Remove the rear shield. Some force may be needed to prise it off (see illustration).
4 Remove the two screws which secure the regulator/brush holder assembly. Disconnect the regulator lead from the spade terminal and slide the assembly out (see illustrations).
5 In most cases the brushes will have wear limit marks in the form of a groove etched along one face of each brush. When the brushes are worn down to these marks, they are worn out and must be renewed. No dimension is given by Citroen. If in doubt about the condition of the brushes, compare them with ones and if necessary, renew the brushes as a set.
6 The old brushes must be unsoldered and the new ones soldered in their place.

8 Starter motor - testing

Note: *This procedure was carried out with the starter motor in the vehicle*

1 If the starter motor fails to operate, first check the condition of the battery by switching on the headlamps. If they glow brightly, then gradually dim after a few seconds, the battery is in an uncharged condition.
2 If the battery is in good condition, check the terminal connections for security. Also check that the earth lead is making good contact with the body frame.
3 Check the security of the main cable and solenoid cable connections on the starter motor.
4 If the starter motor still fails to turn, check that the solenoid is being energised. To do this, connect a 12 volt test lamp and leads between the large solenoid terminal and earth. When the ignition key is turned to the starting position, the lamp should glow. If not, either the supply circuit is open due to a broken wire or a faulty ignition switch, or the solenoid is defective. If the solenoid is supplying current to the starter motor, the fault must be in the starter motor.

5C

7.3 Removing the rear shield - Paris-Rhone alternator

7.4a Disconnect the regulator lead ...

7.4b ... and remove the regulator and brush holder unit

9.4 Remove the starter motor retaining bolts 1 and 2

9.5 Remove the engine mounting nuts 3 and 4

9.6 Starter motor retaining bolt (5) beyond the mounting

9 Starter motor - removal and refitting

BX and BX 14 models

1 Disconnect the earth lead from the battery terminal.

2 Disconnect the leads from the starter motor and the red identification plug from the solenoid unit.

3 Support the engine/transmission, using a jack underneath or a hoist and sling from above.

4 Unscrew and remove the two starter motor retaining bolts **(see illustration)**.

5 Unscrew and remove the engine mounting nuts **(see illustration)**.

6 Raise the engine/transmission just enough to provide access to the starter motor retaining bolt beyond the mounting **(see illustration)**.

7 Unscrew and remove the two bolts securing the starter motor rear bearing then withdraw the starter motor.

8 Refitting is a reversal of the removal procedure.

BX 16 and BX 19 models

9 Disconnect the battery earth lead from the battery terminal.

10 To improve access to the starter motor, disconnect and remove the air filter duct.

11 Disconnect the wiring from the starter motor, taking note of the connecting positions.

12 Undo the two bolts securing the starter motor mounting bracket to the engine. Note that the lower bolt secures the hydraulic line location clip.

13 Unscrew and remove the three socket-head bolts on the transmission side then withdraw the starter motor, complete with its mounting bracket.

14 Refitting is a reversal of the removal procedure.

BX 19 GTi models

15 Access to the starter motor on this model is poor and the vehicle is best raised and supported at the front end to give a suitable working area underneath. On 16 valve versions, it is possible to remove the starter motor after first taking out the radiator and working through the front grille opening (cover flap removed).

16 Working from underneath, unclip and detach the three crankcase breather hoses from the engine (near the oil filter). Unscrew and remove the oil filter, taking care if the engine is still warm as any oil spillage will be hot.

17 Detach the battery earth lead.

18 Undo the starter motor bracket bolts at the filter end. Unscrew and remove the starter motor-to-clutch housing securing bolts, then withdraw the starter motor. Detach the wiring connections and remove the starter motor from the vehicle.

19 Refitting is a reversal of the removal procedure. In view of its relatively low cost, the oil filter is best renewed.

10 Starter motor - brush renewal

1 Because of the different types of starter motor fitted, it is not practical to describe the procedure for each one in detail. The following procedure applies to the Ducellier starter motor. Other makes are similar **(see illustrations)**.

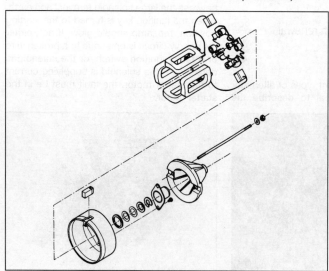

10.1a Brush and cover components - Bosch starter motor fitted to BX 14

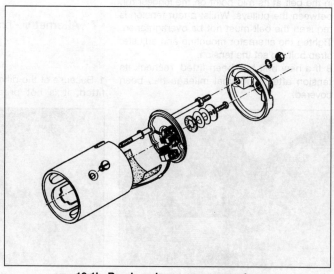

10.1b Brush and cover components - Paris-Rhone starter motor fitted to BX 14

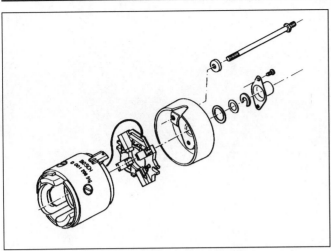

10.1c Brush and cover components -
Bosch starter motor fitted to BX 16

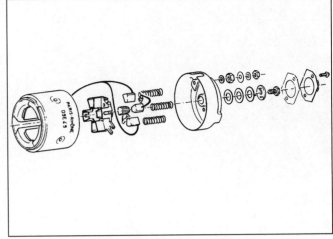

10.1d Brush and cover components -
Paris-Rhone starter motor fitted to BX 16

2 With the motor removed from the vehicle, unscrew the two nuts securing the engine mounting bracket to the motor and remove the bracket. Remove the locknuts and retaining nuts and take off the motor endplate.

3 Prevent the shaft from turning by jamming the drive pinion, and undo the end bearing seal retaining bolt. Remove the seal assembly with its spring (see illustration).

4 To gain access to the brushes, lever the bearing plate from the body. The brushes are mounted on the underside of the plate (see illustration).

10.3 Removing seal assembly and spring

5 In most cases the brushes will have wear limit marks in the form of a groove etched along one face of each brush. When the brushes are worn down to these marks, they are worn out and must be renewed. No dimension is given by Citroen. If in doubt about the condition of the brushes and springs, compare them with new components and if necessary, renew the brushes as a set.

6 To remove each brush, proceed as follows. Lift the positive brush spring and remove the brush from its housing to enable the bearing plate to be removed (see illustration). Note the arrangement of washers on the armature shaft.

7 The brushes can be removed by unsoldering the connecting wires to the holder and to the field coil unit. Take care not to damage the latter during removal and assembly of the brushes (see illustration).

8 If the brushes are serviceable, clean them with a solvent-moistened cloth. Check that the brush spring pressure is equal for all brushes and holds each brush securely against the commutator.

9 Clean the commutator with a solvent-moistened cloth, then check for signs of scoring, burning, excessive wear or severe pitting. If damaged, the commutator should be attended to by an auto-electrician.

10 Undercut the separators of the commutator using an old hacksaw blade to a depth of about 0.5 to 0.8 mm. The commutator may be further cleaned by using a strip of very fine glass paper. Do not use emery cloth for this purpose, as the carborundum particles will become embedded in the copper surfaces.

11 Fitting of the brushes is a reversal of the removal procedure. Make sure that the brushes slide freely in their holders.

5C

10.4 Removing bearing plate

10.6 Bearing plate and brushes

10.7 Brush connections to field coil

Notes

10.16 Brush and cover components –
Paris-Rhone starter motor fitted to BX 19

10.10 Brush and cover components –
Bosch starter motor fitted to BX 19

10.3 Removing seal assembly and spring

10.7 Brush connections to field coil

10.6 Bearing plate and brushes

10.4 Removing bearing plate

Chapter 6
Clutch

Contents

Degrees of difficulty

Easy, suitable for novice with little experience 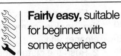	Fairly easy, suitable for beginner with some experience 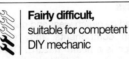	Fairly difficult, suitable for competent DIY mechanic	Difficult, suitable for experienced DIY mechanic	Very difficult, suitable for expert DIY or professional

Specifications

For engine to model applications refer to Chapter 2

Clutch
Type .... Single dry plate with diaphragm spring. Cable operation

Friction plate
Diameter:
  BX and BX 14 .... 180.3 mm
  BX 16 and BX 19 .... 200.6 mm
  BX 19 GTi 16v .... 215.0 mm
Lining thickness (under load) .... 7.7 mm

Release bearing
Type .... Sealed ball

Pedal
Free play .... Nil
Travel (minimum/maximum) .... 130 mm/150 mm

Torque wrench settings

	Nm	lbf ft
Clutch cover bolts	10	7
Transfer gear cover plate bolts	11	8
Lever pivot bolt	25	18
Clutch housing-to-engine mounting bolts	35	25

3.2 Clutch cable connection to release lever - early BX 16

3.3 Clutch and brake pedal assemblies. Brake light switch and wires (arrowed)

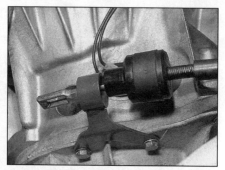

3.5 Withdraw cable from location eye bracket - BX 16

1 General information and precautions

General information

The clutch is of diaphragm spring, single dry plate with cable actuation.

The clutch pedal pivots in a bracket mounted under the facia and operates a cable to the clutch release arm. The release arm operates a thrust bearing (clutch release bearing) which bears on the diaphragm spring of the pressure plate. The diaphragm then releases or engages the clutch driven plate which floats on a splined shaft. On BX and BX 14 models, this shaft (the engine output shaft) is part of the transfer gear assembly which is mounted on the clutch housing. The drive passes via an intermediate pinion to the gearbox primary (input) shaft.

The clutch release mechanism comprises a fork and bearing which are in permanent contact with release fingers on the pressure plate assembly. The fork pushes the release bearing forwards to bear against the release fingers, so moving the centre of the diaphragm spring inwards. The spring is sandwiched between the two rings which act as fulcrum points. As the centre of the spring is pushed in, the outside of the spring is

pushed out, so moving the press plate backwards and disengaging it from the clutch disc.

When the clutch pedal is released, the diaphragm spring forces the pressure plate into contact with the friction linings on the clutch friction plate and at the same time pushes the plate a fraction of an inch forwards on its splines, so engaging the plate with the flywheel. The plate is now firmly sandwiched between the pressure plate and the flywheel, so the drive is taken up.

A self-centring ball thrust bearing is employed and this is in permanent contact with the release mechanism. By using this type of thrust bearing, no clutch pedal free play is required and wear in the linings of the friction plate is automatically compensated for.

Precautions

Dust, created by clutch wear and deposited on the clutch components, may contain asbestos which is a health hazard. Observe the following:
a) *Do not inhale any asbestos dust from the clutch components.*
b) *Do not blow dust off the clutch components with compressed air.*
c) *Do not use petrol or petroleum-based solvents to clean off the dust.*
d) *Use brake system cleaner or methylated*

spirit to flush dust into a suitable receptacle.
e) *Wipe clean all clutch components and dispose of contaminated rags and cleaner in a sealed, marked container.*

2 Clutch - adjustment

Refer to Chapter 1, Section 11.

3 Clutch cable - removal and refitting

Removal

1 For improved access to the clutch cable in the engine compartment, remove the air cleaner unit.

2 Push the clutch operating lever towards the cable and disconnect the spring and inner cable from the lever, then remove the pushrod **(see illustration)**.

3 Working from inside the vehicle, disconnect the brake stop-light switch wire connectors from the switch **(see illustration)**.

4 Undo the two socket-head bolts and the two nuts securing the brake and clutch pedal bracket. Withdraw the bracket from the bulkhead sufficiently to enable the clutch cable to be disconnected from the pedal.

5 Pull the cable through the bulkhead grommet into the engine compartment then withdraw the outer cable and location bush from the locating eye bracket on the transmission and remove the cable **(see illustration)**.

6 The clutch cable fitted to later models has a steel weight fitted at the operating lever end. This is fitted to eliminate cable rattle. It does not affect cable adjustment or fitting and is fully interchangeable with the earlier type **(see illustration)**.

Refitting

7 Refit the clutch cable in the reverse order to removal. When refitting the pedal bracket, align the brake pedal with the pushrod. On completion, check clutch adjustment.

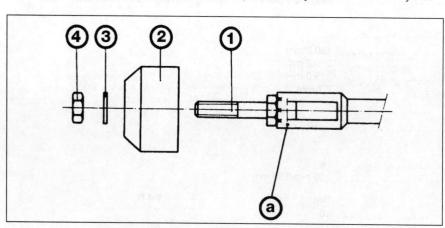

3.6 Clutch cable end components on later models

1 Bolt welded to yoke (a)   2 Steel weight   3 Washer   4 Nut

4 Clutch - removal and refitting

Warning: Do not inhale asbestos dust when working on clutch components

BX and BX 14 models

Removal

1 The clutch unit can be removed with the engine/transmission in position in the vehicle. If the engine/transmission has been removed, proceed from paragraph 17.
2 Drain the engine and gearbox oil.
3 Disconnect and remove the battery. With the battery removed, unbolt and remove the battery fixing clamp and support tray.
4 Unclip and detach the air inlet duct between the carburettor and the air filter unit.
5 Disconnect the air inlet pipe at the air filter heater pipe.
6 Disconnect the clutch cable at the operating lever and retrieve the pushrod.
7 Disconnect the wiring harness connectors where they join above the transfer casing.
8 Detach and remove the heater pipe and the air filter bracket.
9 Raise and support the vehicle at the front so that the roadwheel on the left-hand side can be unbolted and removed.
10 Prise free the retaining clips and remove the mud shield from the left-hand wheel arch.
11 Unbolt and remove the clutch cable bracket.
12 Unbolt the diagnostic socket with its support from the top of the clutch housing.
13 Position a jack underneath the engine and raise it to support the weight of the engine. To prevent possible damage to the engine, locate a suitable flat piece of wood between the engine and the jack saddle.
14 Unscrew the engine mounting nuts and washers **(see illustration)**.
15 Raise the jack to lift the engine and free the mountings from the slotted holes.
16 Undo and remove the bolts from the points indicated **(see illustration 4.14)**. Remove the engine mountings.
17 Undo and remove the clutch casing retaining bolts, noting that one bolt is hidden under the rib **(see illustration)**. Also unbolt and remove the lift sling bracket.
18 Check that all of the retaining bolts and fastenings have been disconnected then carefully withdraw the clutch/transfer gear case housing unit from the engine. The housing may need to be tapped free with a plastic-faced hammer applied to the casting bosses.
19 Unscrew the clutch fixing bolts. Jam the teeth of the flywheel ring gear to prevent rotation as the bolts are unscrewed.
20 Lift away the cover and friction plate.

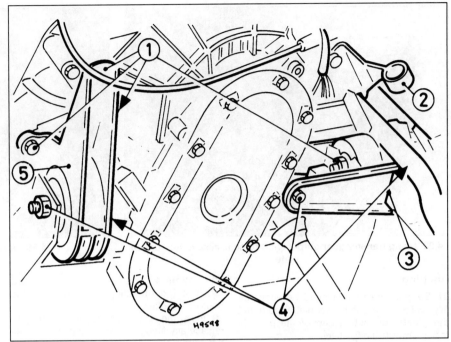

4.14 Clutch removal disconnection points

1 Bolts	3 Engine mounting	5 Engine mounting
2 Cable bracket	4 Mounting nuts and washers	

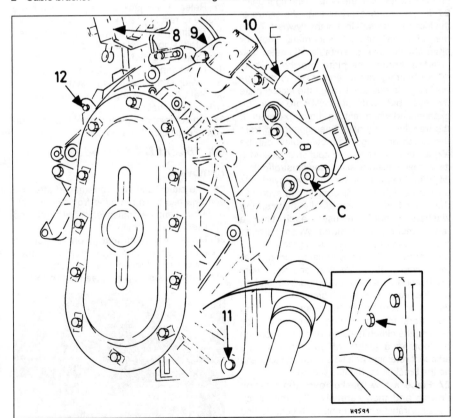

4.17 Clutch removal disconnection points

8 Diagnostic socket and support	9 Lift sling bracket	12 Extended head bolt
	10 Clutch bracket	c Dowel
	11 Retaining bolt	Inset shows hidden bolt

6

4.23 Using transfer gear output shaft to centralise clutch driven plate

4.36 Undo the clutch unit retaining bolts

Refitting

21 Support the friction plate between the flywheel and the clutch lever unit. Ensure that the greater projecting hub of the plate is facing towards the flywheel.

22 Locate the clutch cover unit into position on the flywheel, engaging with the three projecting dowels. Retain the cover in position on the flywheel with the bolts (hand tight only).

23 It is now necessary to align the centre of the friction plate with that of the flywheel. To do this, use a special alignment tool or alternatively use a suitable diameter bar inserted through the plate into the flywheel spigot bearing, but take care not to damage the seal. It is possible to align the friction plate by eye but difficulty will probably be experienced when refitting the output shaft. If the transfer gears have been separated from the clutch housing, the friction plate can be aligned using the engine output shaft located in its normal running position **(see illustration)**.

24 With the plate centralised, the cover bolts should be tightened diagonally and evenly to the specified torque. Ideally new spring washers should be used each time a replacement clutch is fitted. When the bolts are tight, remove the centralising tool.

25 Before refitting the housing, check that the mating surfaces are clean and dry. Smear the bearing surface of the withdrawal pad on the diaphragm spring with grease.

26 To prevent the clutch release operating lever (fork) from becoming disengaged when refitting the clutch housing, retain it in position by looping a length of cord through the adjacent retaining bolt hole in the housing and tie the bracket so that it is secure.

27 Place a new gasket over the location dowels and then carefully offer the clutch housing/transfer pinion unit to the engine and insert the output and input shafts.

28 To assist the respective shaft splines to engage, rotate the flywheel and gearbox input shaft alternately until they slide home into position. Loosely locate bolts 11 and 12 (see

illustration 4.17) then remove the cord retaining the operating lever to allow the housing to fit flush.

29 Insert the retaining bolts, remembering to replace any fittings retained by them. Tighten the bolts progressively to the specified torque.

30 Refit the engine mountings and tighten their retaining bolts to the specified torque settings.

31 Release the jack and slowly lower the engine to rest in position on the bearers. Refit the retaining nuts with washers and tighten them to the specified torque setting.

32 Grease the clutch pushrod at each end then reconnect the clutch cable and check/adjust the pedal height setting.

33 Refit the remaining items in the reverse order of removal.

34 On completion, lower the vehicle and top-up the engine and gearbox oil.

BX 16 and BX 19 models

Removal

35 The clutch unit can be removed after the gearbox has been removed from the vehicle or with the engine/ transmission removed and then separated.

36 Make alignment marks on the clutch pressure plate and the flywheel, then progressively slacken the six bolts which secure the pressure plate **(see illustration)**.

4.38 Centring the clutch friction plate using a proprietary tool

37 Remove the bolts, the pressure plate and the clutch friction plate.

Refitting

38 Commence refitting by offering the clutch friction plate to the flywheel, making sure it is the right way round. It will only fit one way. Retain the disc in position by inserting a centring mandrel. Various proprietary centring tools are available, or alternatively, one can be made from a piece of dowel or bar built up with tape **(see illustration)**.

39 Fit the pressure plate, observing the alignment marks made when dismantling if the old plate is being refitted. Insert the six bolts and just nip them up so that the friction plate is lightly gripped.

40 Make sure that the friction plate is accurately centred, either by visual inspection or by inserting an old gearbox input (friction plate) shaft. If the disc is not centred, it will be impossible to refit the gearbox.

41 With the centring mandrel in position, tighten the pressure plate securing bolts progressively to the specified torque. Remove the centring mandrel.

42 Refit the gearbox on completion.

---

5 Clutch - inspection and repair

 Warning: Do not use petrol or petroleum-based solvents to clean dust off clutch components

1 The clutch friction plate should be inspected for wear and oil contamination. Wear is gauged by the depth of the rivet heads below the surface of the friction material. If this is less than 0.6 mm, the linings are worn enough to justify renewal.

2 Examine the friction faces of the flywheel and clutch pressure plate. These should be bright and smooth. If the linings have worn too much, it is possible that the metal surfaces may

6.10a Release arm and bearing

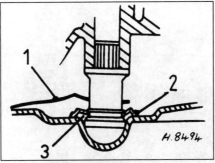

6.10b Clutch release lever spring retaining clip (1) and rubber cover (2). Lubricate with grease (3)

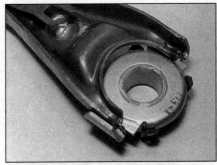

6.11a Release bearing retaining clips

have been scored by the rivet heads. Dust and grit have the same effect. If the scoring is very severe it could mean that, even with a new clutch plate, slip and juddering and other malfunctions will recur. Deep scoring on the flywheel face is serious because the flywheel will have to be removed and machined by a specialist, or renewed and this can be costly. The same applies to the pressure plate in the cover, although this is a less costly affair.

3 If the friction linings seem unworn yet are blackened and shiny, then the cause is almost certainly due to oil. Such a condition also requires renewal of the plate. The source of the oil must be traced. It could be due to a leaking seal on the gearbox primary shaft or from a leaking crankshaft oil seal.

4 If the reason for removal of the clutch has been because of slip and the slip has been allowed to go on for any length of time, it is possible that the heat generated will have adversely affected the diaphragm spring in the cover with the result that the pressure is now uneven and/or insufficient to prevent slip, even with a new friction plate. It is recommended that under such circumstances a new assembly is fitted.

5 Do not attempt to reline the plate or dismantle the pressure plate cover. Obtain new or factory reconditioned units which are sometimes supplied on an exchange basis.

6 Clean away all old gasket from the housing mating flanges without scratching or scoring the surfaces of the metal. Obtain a new gasket.

7 Before refitting the clutch unit, check the clutch release mechanism components for wear and renew any parts as necessary.

6 Clutch release mechanism - removal, overhaul and refitting

BX and BX 14 models

1 The clutch actuating rod can be removed by slackening the operating adjustment and unhooking the return spring.

2 To remove or overhaul the withdrawal bearing and fork, the clutch flywheel housing must be removed.

3 With the housing removed, the withdrawal fork and bearing can be withdrawn from the output shaft for inspection.

4 Wipe clean and inspect the release bearing. If excessive wear is obvious, renew the bearing.

5 Inspect the fork retaining ball-stud and if obviously distorted or worn, renew it. Drift the ball-stud from the housing using a suitable diameter drift. Fit the new one, together with a new rubber cup, by driving it carefully into position using a soft-faced hammer. Support the housing during this operation to prevent it from being damaged.

6 Before reassembly, check the clutch primary shaft oil seal. If it is leaking, then the complete guide bush/seal assembly must be renewed as the seal is not supplied separately.

7 Press the guide bush out of the flywheel housing.

8 Press the new bush/seal assembly fully into its recess so that it seats firmly.

9 Any wear in the spigot bush (located in the centre of the crankshaft rear flange and supporting the output shaft) can be rectified by renewal of the bush.

10 To refit the fork, fit the spring blade so that it is located under the rubber cover as shown (see illustrations).

11 Position the release bearing over the engine output shaft and engage the retainers behind the fork fingers. The release bearing can be slid along the sleeve whilst holding the fork (see illustrations).

12 Check the fork and bearing for correct operation and then refit the housing. Readjust the clutch operating clearance on completion.

BX 16 and BX 19 models

13 Access to the clutch release mechanism is gained after removing the gearbox or engine/transmission from the vehicle. If the latter method is used, separate the unit.

14 The clutch release bearing may be removed by freeing its spring clips from the release fork (see illustration).

15 The clutch release fork can be pulled or levered off its balljoint.

16 Renew the pivot bush if it is worn.

17 To remove the release fork balljoint, use a slide hammer fitted with a suitable claw.

18 To refit the balljoint, apply thread locking compound to the splines and carefully drive it into position.

19 When refitting the clutch release fork to the balljoint, lubricate the joint with grease (see illustration).

20 Refit the release bearing and connect the release fork to it, reversing the removal procedure.

6

6.11b Release arm lever and bearing engaged on ball stud

6.14 Detach clutch release bearing from release fork

6.19 Refitting clutch release fork assembly to balljoint

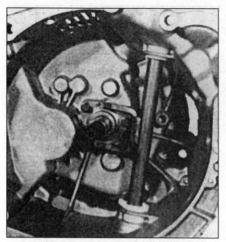

6.21 Clutch release mechanism

BX 19 GTi 16v and all models with BE3/5 gearbox

21 The release mechanism comprises a release fork supported on a pivot shaft (see illustration).
22 To gain access to the mechanism components, the gearbox or engine/transmission must be removed from the vehicle. If the latter method is used, separate the unit.
23 Pull the clutch release bearing from the guide sleeve, and (where applicable) release the spring clips from the fork ends.
24 Using a suitable punch, drive out the roll pin securing the release lever to the pivot shaft. Withdraw the release lever, noting its orientation.
25 Prise the upper pivot shaft bush from the bellhousing.

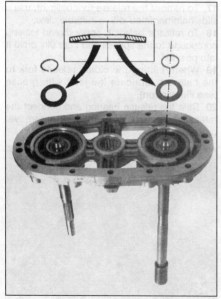

7.14 Input and output shaft reassembly. Note orientation of Belleville washers (concave towards bearing)

7.5 Transfer gears and intermediate plate removal

26 Lift the lower end of the release lever pivot shaft from the lower bush in the bellhousing, then lower the pivot shaft into the bellhousing and manipulate it as necessary to enable removal.
27 If desired, the lower pivot bush can be prised from the bell housing.
28 Reassembly is a reversal of dismantling. Ensure that the pivot bushes are correctly located in the bellhousing and that the release lever is correctly orientated, as noted before removal.
29 Note that there have been some reported cases of the release lever breaking away from its pivot shaft. To resolve this problem, new release lever assemblies are reinforced by fitting a 5 mm thick washer onto the top of the release lever and welding it to the lever and pivot shaft. Refer to your Citroën dealer for further information.

7 Transfer gears (BX and BX 14 models) - removal, overhaul and refitting

Removal

1 The transfer gears are located under a cover plate at the end of the clutch/flywheel housing. Their purpose is to transmit power from the engine crankshaft and clutch to the transmission primary (input) shaft which lies below the engine.
2 The gears are housed in the intermediate plate attached to the clutch/flywheel housing. Removal of the intermediate plate, complete with transfer gears, necessitates removal of the clutch/flywheel housing.
3 Unbolt and remove the cover plate and its gasket.
4 Remove the clutch release bearing and operating lever.
5 Remove the transfer gear intermediate plate (see illustration). The plate will probably require tapping off with a plastic-faced hammer. Take care that the intermediate gear does not drop out as the plate is removed. Only tap the plate on the exposed lugs.
6 Remove the intermediate gear (see illustration).
7 Clean away all old gasket material and obtain a new gasket.

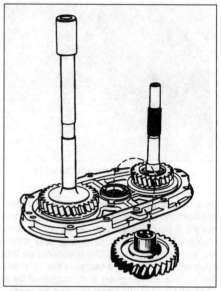

7.6 Intermediate plate and gear removed

Overhaul

8 To remove the input and output shaft units from the intermediate plate, expand the retaining clips and drive or press the shaft units from the plate.
9 Clean the input and output shaft ball-bearings and check them for excessive play and/or signs of damage. Inspect the intermediate shaft needle roller bearings. Renew any suspect or worn bearings. If a bearing has collapsed due to general wear and fatigue, then the chances are that the other bearings are close to failure and it is therefore advisable to renew all the bearings.
10 Carefully inspect the transfer gears. If excessive transmission noise has been experienced, it may be reduced by changing the transfer gears. If the teeth are worn or damaged, then the gears should be renewed. Renew the gear set rather than a single gear. It is not good practice to mesh new gears with old as the wear rate of both is increased and they will be noisy in operation.
11 Check the input and output shafts and inspect their splines for wear or damage. Renew them if necessary.
12 To remove the bearings, use circlip pliers and fully expand the circlip before pressing the shaft out of the bearing or the shaft/bearing out of the intermediate plate.
13 When reassembling, remember that the shorter shaft is located at the narrower end of the intermediate plate. Always use new circlips and support the plate adequately during the pressing operation.
14 Always use a new Belleville washer under the circlip so that its concave face is towards the bearing (see illustration).
15 With the gears reassembled, check that the circlips are fully engaged by measuring their outside diameter which must not exceed 22.6 mm (see illustration).

7.15 Check outside diameter of circlips does not exceed that specified

7.16 Fitting a new intermediate gear roller bearing into its housing using gear and suitable draw bolt

16 If the intermediate gear needle race is to be renewed in the intermediate plate, press the old one out and use the intermediate gear as an installation tool. Make sure that the gear teeth do not lock with those of the other gears during the pressing operation **(see illustration)**.

Refitting

17 Lubricate the bearings and fit the intermediate gear. It must be flush with the input and output gears when fitted.
18 Wind some plastic insulation tape around the output shaft splines to protect the seal during reassembly **(see illustration)**.
19 Check that the dowels are in position in the clutch housing, apply sealant to the joint

faces and locate the transfer gear housing over the dowels **(see illustrations)**.
20 Refit the cover plate using a new gasket and tighten the retaining bolts to the specified torque **(see illustrations)**.
21 Remove the protective tape from the output shaft splines.
22 On completion, refit the clutch release bearing and operating lever.

6

7.18 Bind output shaft splines with tape to protect clutch housing seal

7.19a Apply sealant to mating surface . . .

7.19b . . . and assemble clutch housing to intermediate gear unit

7.20a Locate new gasket . . .

7.20b . . . and refit cover plate

Chapter 7 Part A:
Manual gearbox

Contents

Degrees of difficulty

Easy, suitable for novice with little experience	**Fairly easy,** suitable for beginner with some experience	**Fairly difficult,** suitable for competent DIY mechanic 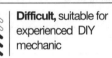	**Difficult,** suitable for experienced DIY mechanic 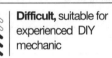	**Very difficult,** suitable for expert DIY or professional 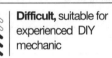

Specifications

For engine to model applications refer to Chapter 2

Gearbox

Type	4 or 5 forward speeds and reverse, synchromesh on all forward gears

Designations:

Type BH3:

BX	2 BT 52, BT 69, BT 78 (4-speed)
BX 14	2 BT 28, BT 73, BT 84 (5-speed)

Type MA:

BX 14 (pre Oct 1989)	2 CA 16 (4-speed) or 2 CA 14 (5-speed)
BX 14 (Oct 1989 to Sept 1990)	2 CA 51 (4-speed) or 2 CA 49 (5-speed)
BX 14 (Sept 1990 to Sept 1991)	2 CA 77 (4-speed) or 2 CA 91 (5-speed)
BX 14 (from Sept 1991)	2 CB 35 (4-speed) or 2 CB 48 (5-speed)

Type BE1:

BX 16	2 BL 03, BL 64, BN 45 (5-speed)
BX 19	BL 61, BL 68, BN 46, BL 62, BL 66, BN 44 (5-speed)
BX 19 GTi	BN10, BN47
BX 19 GTi 16 valve	BN48

Type BE3:

BX 16 (from April 1989)	BE3 (5-speed)
BX 19 (from April 1989)	BE3 (5-speed)

Torque wrench settings

	Nm	lbf ft

BX and BX 14 - Type BH3

	Nm	lbf ft
Drain plug	25	18
Sump cover	10	7
Oil pick-up screen	10	7
Detent plugs	12	9
Secondary shaft nut:		
4-speed	25	18
5-speed	95	69
Primary shaft nut	45	33
Speedometer drivegear	30	22
Reverse light switch	25	18
Reverse fork lock plate bolt	10	7
Crownwheel retaining bolts	60	44

BX and BX 14 - Type MA (2 CA)

Gearbox housing to clutch/final drive housing	18	13
Intermediate plate to clutch/final drive housing	51	37
Pressed-steel housing	18	13
Bearing half-rings	18	13
Output shaft nut (2CA 14)	143	103
Drain and filler plugs	26	19
Gearbox to engine	46	33

BX 16 and BX 19

Engine-to-gearbox bolts	40	29
Starter motor bolts	40	29
Gearbox support shaft	35	25
Gearbox support nut	35	25
Gearbox support bolt	18	13
Clutch release bearing guide tube bolts	12	9
Fifth gear end cover bolts*	12	9
Primary and secondary shaft nuts	50	36
Selector rod lock plate bolt	15	11
Secondary shaft bearing retainer bolts	15	11
Reverse idler gear spindle bolt	20	15
Reversing light switch	25	18
Gearbox main casing-to-clutch housing bolts	12	9
Selector shaft spring bracket nut	15	11
Final drive extension bolts	10	7
Final drive half housing bolts:		
10 mm	40	29
7 mm	12	9
Crownwheel securing bolts	60	44
Drain plug:		
Final drive	30	22
Gearbox	10	7

Apply locking compound to the threads

1 General information and precautions

General information

Type BH3 (2 BT 52 and 2 BT 28)

This gearbox is mounted transversely below and to the rear of the engine. The gearbox and engine share a common lubrication system.

The gearbox casing is constructed in light alloy and incorporates the final drive and differential.

Power from the crankshaft is transmitted through the gearbox output shaft and transfer gears to the primary shaft. Drive to the front roadwheels is transmitted through driveshafts from the differential side gears.

The gearbox is of 4 or 5-speed type, depending upon the vehicle. Both types are similar except for the 5th gear located on the ends of the primary and secondary shafts.

The gearbox is of conventional two shaft, constant-mesh layout. There are four pairs of gears, one for each forward speed. The gears on the primary shaft are fixed to the shaft. The gears on the secondary or pinion shaft float, each being locked to the shaft when engaged by the synchromesh unit. The reverse idler gear is on a third shaft.

On 5-speed units, the 5th speed gears are of fixed type with an extra synchromesh assembly.

The gear selector forks engage in the synchromesh unit. These slide axially along the shaft to engage the appropriate gear. The forks are mounted on selector shafts which are located in the base of the gearbox.

The helical gear on the end of the pinion shaft drives directly onto the crownwheel mounted on the differential unit. The latter differs from normal practice in that it runs in shell bearings and the end thrust is taken up by thrustwashers in a similar manner to the engine crankshaft.

Type MA (2CA)

This gearbox is mounted on the left-hand side of the engine.

The gearbox has either four or five forward gears depending on the model (all with synchromesh) and one reverse gear. All the synchromesh units are located on the output shaft and the differential unit is located in the main gearbox casing.

Type BE1 (2 BL 03, BL 61 and BL 62)

This gearbox is mounted transversely in-line with the engine, the drive being taken direct from the crankshaft and not through transfer gears as on smaller engine variants.

The gearbox has five forward gears, all with synchromesh and one reverse. The 5th gear

components are on the far side of an intermediate plate which carries one pair of shaft bearings.

The differential (final drive) unit is contained in its own housing which is bolted to the gearbox casing. The gearbox and differential share the same lubricant.

The gearbox is conventional in operation (as described for the 2 BT 52 and 2 BT 28 types) and has lubrication separate to the engine.

Type BE3

This gearbox is a development of the BE1 5-speed gearbox, being introduced in 1989 to progressively replace its predecessor. It can be identified by the revised gearchange pattern, with reverse positioned opposite (behind) 5th gear.

Most of the procedures described for the BE1 gearbox are applicable to this type, although many of the internal components have been modified.

Precautions

Type BH3 (2 BT 52 and 2 BT 28)

If it is necessary to have the vehicle towed for anything other than short distances, lift the front wheels clear of the ground or the gearbox could seize due to lack of lubrication.

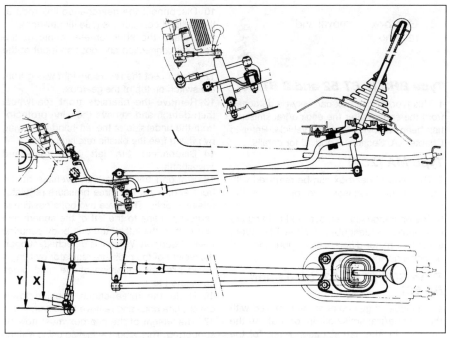

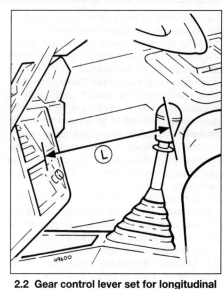

2.2 Gear control lever set for longitudinal adjustment

L = 235 mm (2 BT 52 and 2 BT 28)
L = 215 mm (2 BL 03 and BL 61)

2.1 Gearchange linkage - Type BH3 (2 BT 52 and 2 BT 28) gearboxes

Y = 162 to 172 mm   *X = 90 to 100 mm*

2 Gearchange linkage - adjustment

Type BH3 (2 BT 52 and 2 BT 28)

1 The gearchange linkage does not normally require adjustment. If new parts have been fitted, set the balljointed link rods so that the distance between the centres of the balljoints is as shown **(see illustration)**.

2 When making a longitudinal adjustment of the control lever, position the gear lever in neutral so that the distance from the centre of the knob to the centre of the heater/fresh air control and radio facia panel is approximately 235 mm **(see illustration)**.

3 Measure the distance between the centre of the gearchange link rod balljoints **(Y in illustration 2.1)**. The distance should be between 162 and 172 mm. If adjustment is necessary, loosen the link rod balljoint locknut, separate the joint and turn it in the required direction to set it at the required distance. Decreasing the distance will move the gear lever forward and vice versa. With the distance correctly set, reconnect the balljoint and tighten the locknut.

4 Check the lateral adjustment of the control lever by first checking to see if, when in neutral, it is vertical when viewed in line with the vehicle. Now check the distance between the link rod balljoints **(X in illustration 2.1)**. The correct distance requirement is between 90 and 100 mm.

5 If adjustment is necessary, proceed to adjust the link rod X in the same manner as

that described for Y. Note that decreasing the link rod length moves the gear control lever to the left and vice versa (when viewed from the front of the vehicle).

6 When making adjustment to the link rods, the balljoints must be centralised when tightening the locknut.

Type BE1 (2 BL 03, BL 61 and BL 62)

7 The gearchange linkage does not normally require adjustment. If new parts have been

fitted, set the gearchange control lever to the neutral position.

8 First check the adjustment of the selector control. Check that the selector control lever is in the upright position **(see illustration)**. The reaction link rod length between the balljoint centres should be between 70 and 80 mm.

9 If necessary, adjust the length of the reaction link rod by detaching at the balljoints, loosening the locknut and turning the balljoint in the required direction to the specified length. Retighten the locknut and reconnect

7A

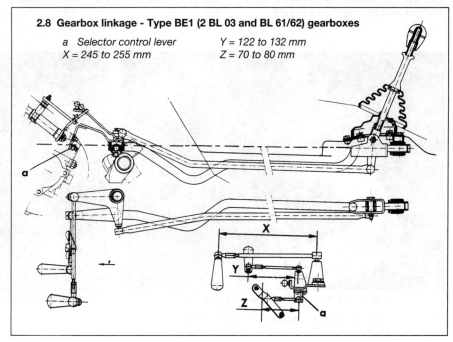

2.8 Gearbox linkage - Type BE1 (2 BL 03 and BL 61/62) gearboxes

a Selector control lever   *Y = 122 to 132 mm*
X = 245 to 255 mm   *Z = 70 to 80 mm*

the balljoint. Check that each joint is centralised over its ball when connected.

10 With the gear lever still in neutral, check the distance between the centre of the knob and the centre of the heater/fresh air control and radio facia panel **(see illustration 2.2)**. This should be 215 mm. If adjustment is necessary, adjust the length of the gearchange link rod **(X in illustration 2.1)** to between 245 to 255 mm in the same manner as that described in paragraph 9. When decreasing the length of the link rod, the gearchange control lever moves forwards and vice versa.

11 Engage 2nd or 4th gear, prise free the rubber gaiter of the gear lever from the centre console and then check that the lever to the rear part of the box clearance (b) is between 4 and 5 mm (minimum) **(see illustration)**.

12 To check the lateral adjustment of the gearchange control lever, first check that, when in neutral, the lever is upright when viewed in line with the vehicle. If it is not, change the length of link rod Y (as described in paragraph 9) so that the length between the centre of the balljoints is between 122 and 132 mm. Decreasing the link rod length moves the control lever towards the left and vice versa.

13 Adjustment to 1st and 2nd gear selection is possible by loosening the gearchange control box retaining bolts then setting the gear lever into the 2nd gear position. Move the box to give a free play movement of 2 to 3 mm between the box and the lever guide block (J). Retighten the box retaining bolts.

14 Move the gear selector through all forward gears and the reverse gear position to check for satisfactory engagement. Also check the gears for satisfactory selection on a road test. Further minor adjustment of 1st and 2nd gear selection may be necessary.

3 Gearbox - removal and refitting

Type BH3 (2 BT 52 and 2 BT 28)

1 This type of gearbox can only be detached from the engine after the engine/transmission has been removed from the vehicle. Refer to Chapter 2A, Sections 7 and 10 for details.

Type MA (2CA)

2 This type of gearbox can be removed with the engine/transmission in or out of the vehicle.

3 The operations for removal and refitting are essentially as described for the BH3 type, except for minor differences in mounting, and gearchange linkage design.

Type BE1 (2 BL 03, BL 61 and BL 62)

4 This type of gearbox can be removed with the engine/transmission in or out of the vehicle. In the latter case, refer to the appropriate part of Chapter 2 for details. With the engine/transmission in the vehicle, proceed as follows.

5 Raise and support the vehicle so that the front and rear roadwheels are clear of the ground. When raised, the vehicle must be level and securely supported (see *"Jacking and vehicle support"*).

6 Disconnect and remove the battery.

7 Disconnect and remove the air filter unit and its support.

8 Unbolt and disconnect the battery earth lead from the top of the gearbox.

9 Disconnect the clutch cable from the operating lever and retrieve the connecting rod.

10 Disconnect the gearchange link rods at the balljoint connections **(see illustration)**.

11 Detach the speedometer cable at the gearbox connection and position it out of the way.

12 Disconnect the reversing light wiring from the switch on top of the gearbox.

13 Remove the nearside front roadwheel then detach and remove the wing protector from the underside of the left-hand front wing by prising free the plastic retaining clips.

14 Disconnect the left and right-hand driveshafts.

15 Working underneath the vehicle at the front end, undo the three pressure regulator retaining bolts. There are two bolts positioned vertically in line to the left of the sphere and one bolt to the left of the unit body securing the rear support. When it is detached, support the weight of the pressure regulator by tying it up to prevent distortion of the rigid pipes connected to it.

16 Undo the three clutch housing lower cover plate bolts and remove the cover.

17 The weight of the gearbox must now be supported. This is best achieved using a lifting sling and hoist and supporting it from above. Failing this, it may be possible to support it from underneath using a suitable trolley jack, but ensure that it is securely located.

18 Unbolt and remove the gearbox support and the support spindle.

19 Position a jack or blocks under the engine to support it.

20 Unbolt and remove the engine-to-gearbox coupling bolts and the starter motor bolts.

21 Check that gearbox associated fittings are detached and positioned out of the way, then withdraw the gearbox sideways from the engine. When the gearbox input shaft is clear of the clutch unit, carefully lower the gearbox and remove it from underneath the vehicle.

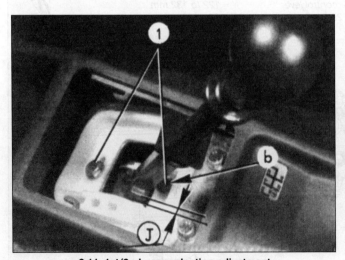

2.11 1st/2nd gear selection adjustment

1 Gear control box retaining bolts
b = at least 4 to 5 mm
J = 2 to 3 mm

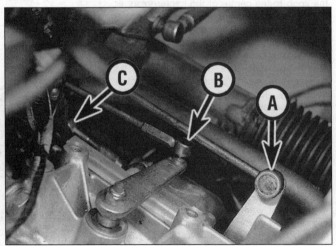

3.10 Disconnect gearchange link rods at joints indicated (A, B and C)

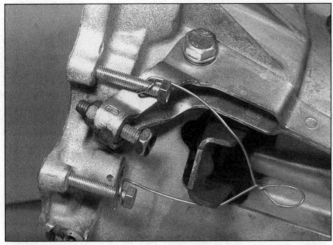

3.23 Retain clutch release lever with two bolts and length of wire

5.3 Driveshaft oil seal at transmission

22 Refitting the gearbox is a reversal of the removal procedure. Note the following.

23 Prior to lifting the gearbox into position make a temporary provision to hold the clutch thrust bearing in position against the guide. This can be achieved by fitting two bolts into the clutch housing/engine bolt holes adjacent to the clutch release lever. Wind wire around the bolt heads and then twist the wire round the release lever to keep the thrust bearing against the guide **(see illustration)**.

24 Apply a small amount of grease to the thrust bearing guide and the control shaft.

25 When fitting the gearbox to the engine, check that the two alignment dowels are in position on the engine flange face (one each side). Centring rods of suitable diameter fitted inside the dowels will assist in aligning the two assemblies as they are joined. Turn the flywheel to align the splines of the clutch friction plate with the gearbox input shaft.

26 When the gearbox is fitted flush to the engine, insert the retaining bolts and tighten them evenly to the specified torque setting. If used, remove the alignment centring rods and remove the wire holding the clutch release lever in position.

27 When refitting the gearbox support shaft, apply a locking sealant to the threads. Tighten the shaft, and the support nut and bolt to the specified torque settings.

28 When refitting the right-hand drive-shaft to the final drive unit, an oil seal protector must be used to protect the oil seal as the shaft splines pass through it.

29 When reconnecting the steering and suspension connections, use new nuts on the balljoints.

30 On completion, check that all connections are securely made and top-up the gearbox oil level.

31 Check that gear selection is satisfactory and if necessary, adjust the linkage.

4 Gearbox - overhaul

Note: *If a gearbox develops a fault or becomes noisy, the best course of action is to have the unit overhauled by a specialist or to obtain an exchange reconditioned unit*

1 Overhauling a gearbox is a difficult and involved job for the DIY home mechanic. In addition to dismantling and reassembling many small parts, clearances must be precisely measured and, if necessary, changed by selecting shims and spacers. Gearbox internal components are also often difficult to obtain and in many instances extremely expensive. Because of this, if the gearbox develops a fault or becomes noisy, the best course of action is to have the unit overhauled by a specialist or to obtain an exchange reconditioned unit.

2 Nevertheless, it is not impossible for the more experienced mechanic to overhaul a gearbox provided that the special tools are available and the job is done in a deliberate step-by-step manner so that nothing is overlooked.

3 The tools necessary for a typical overhaul include internal and external circlip pliers, bearing pullers, a slide- hammer, a set of pin punches, a dial test indicator and possibly an

hydraulic press. In addition, a large sturdy workbench and a vice will be required.

4 All work should be done in conditions of extreme cleanliness. When dismantling, make careful notes of how each component is fitted. This will facilitate accurate and straightforward reassembly.

5 Before dismantling the gearbox, it will help to have some idea of which component is malfunctioning. Certain problems can be related to specific areas in the gearbox which can in turn make component examination and replacement more straightforward. Refer to *Fault diagnosis* in the *Reference* section of this Manual for more information.

5 Differential/driveshaft oil seals - renewal

1 The differential oil seals can be removed and refitted with the engine/transmission in the vehicle, but the driveshafts will obviously have to be removed.

2 With the driveshafts withdrawn, the old oil seals can be extracted from the differential housing using a suitable screwdriver.

3 Clean out the seating before fitting a new seal. Lubricate the seal to assist assembly and drift it carefully into position with its lip facing inwards. Fill the seal lips with grease **(see illustration)**.

4 Always take care not to damage the oil seals when removing or refitting the driveshafts.

7A

Chapter 7 Part B:
Automatic transmission

Contents

Degrees of difficulty

| Easy, suitable for novice with little experience | | Fairly easy, suitable for beginner with some experience | | Fairly difficult, suitable for competent DIY mechanic | | Difficult, suitable for experienced DIY mechanic | | Very difficult, suitable for expert DIY or professional | |

Specifications

For engine to model applications refer to Chapter 2

Transmission

Type .... ZF with 4 forward speeds and one reverse
Designations:
BX 16 (from July 1984)	7 HP 14
BX 16 (from Sept 1988)	4 HP 14
BX 19 (from Sept 1988)	7 HP 14
BX 19 GTi (from Sept 1988)	4 HP 14
BX 19 TRi (from Sept 1988)	4 HP 14

Torque wrench settings

	Nm	lbf ft
Transmission-to-engine bolts	39	29
Starter motor bolts	39	29
Flexible mounting centre bolt	34	25
Flexible mounting plate screws	18	13
Driveplate-to-torque converter bolts	34	25
Torque converter housing screws	24	18
Fluid sump pan screws	10	7
Dipstick guide tube union nut	43	32
Fluid cooler centre fixing screw	49	36

1 General information and precautions

General information

The automatic transmission has four forward speeds and one reverse. In the interests of fuel economy the torque converter is completely bypassed in 4th gear and partially bypassed in 3rd. This reduces losses due to torque converter slip.

Gearchanging is automatic in use, the transmission responding to changes in speed and load. The usual kickdown facility is provided for enhanced acceleration when the throttle is depressed fully.

Cooling is by means of a coolant/oil heat exchanger mounted on the side of the transmission.

Precautions

Observe the following precautions to avoid damage to the automatic transmission:
 a) *Do not attempt to start the engine by*

pushing or towing the vehicle.
 b) *If the vehicle has to be towed for recovery, only tow it with the front wheels clear of the ground.*
 c) *Restrict towing speed to 30 mph and the distance to 30 miles.*
 d) *Only engage 'P' when the vehicle is stationary.*
 e) *Ensure that the handbrake is fully applied and the selector lever is in P whenever the vehicle is parked or being serviced.*

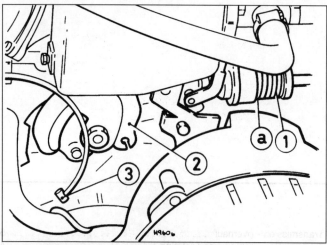

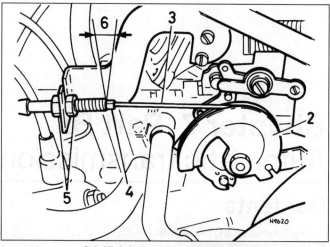

2.3 Accelerator cable sheath stop pin (1) and clearance point (a) with kickdown cable (3) detached from cam (2)

2.4 Kickdown cable attachments

2 Cam
3 Inner cable
4 Crimped stop

5 Sleeve end fitting nuts
6 Crimped stop-to-sleeve clearance (0.5 mm)

2 Kickdown cable - adjustment

BX 16 and BX 19 pre Sept 1988

1 This adjustment must be made with the engine at its normal operating temperature, the electric cooling fan having cut in then off.
2 Check and if necessary adjust the engine idle speed.
3 With the engine switched off, first check the accelerator cable for correct adjustment. Detach the kickdown cable from the cam on the carburettor. Pull the accelerator cable sheath stop pin out and reposition it to allow a small clearance at (a) **(see illustration)**. Depress the accelerator pedal fully and simultaneously check that the throttle valves of the carburettor are fully opened. Reset the cable sheath stop pin on completion.
4 Reconnect the kickdown cable to the cam, then loosen the kickdown outer cable adjustment nuts at the bracket and check that the inner cable is free but not slack **(see illustration)**.
5 Pivot the kickdown cam and check that the crimped stop moves as soon as the cam is rotated.
6 Get an assistant to fully depress the accelerator pedal and check the crimped stop movement, which should be 50 mm **(see illustration)**.

7 If necessary, adjust the outer cable at the bracket. Note that a clearance should always exist between the sleeve end fitting and the crimped stop. Tighten the outer cable adjustment locknuts on completion.
8 Kickdown cable renewal is a task that must be entrusted to your Citroën dealer.

BX 16 and BX 19 from Sept 1988

9 The operation for these models is similar to that described for pre 1988 models. Note that the crimped stop movement is now 39.0 mm.

3 Selector control - adjustment

Modification: *BX 16 models from January 1985 have a new selector lever gate fitted in which a curtain replaces the brushes used in previous models. This new gate allows an improved view of the selected gear, the selected position being illuminated in red. New and early type gates are interchangeable. When setting the later type, loosen the gate then move the plastic indicator so that the gear selected and indicated are aligned, then retighten the gate (see illustration).*
1 Fit a spanner onto the flats of the selector rod balljoint and twist it to disconnect the balljoint from the selector lever **(see illustration)**.
2 Move the selector lever (from within the vehicle) to N.
3 Move the gearbox selector lever into the N position **(see illustration)**.
4 The selector rod balljoint should align exactly with the coupling ball on the selector lever so that when reconnected, neither the selector lever within the vehicle nor the selector lever on the gearbox move. Adjust the position of the balljoint on the connecting rod if necessary.

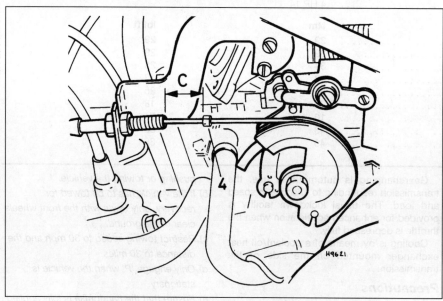

2.6 Crimped stop (4) clearance from sleeve under full acceleration

C = 50 mm (approximately)

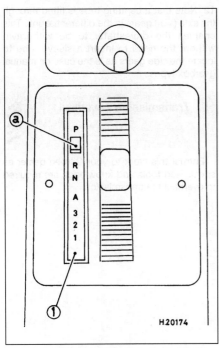

3.0 Later type of automatic transmission selector gate

1 Plastic indicator
a Depress when setting to avoid marking face plate

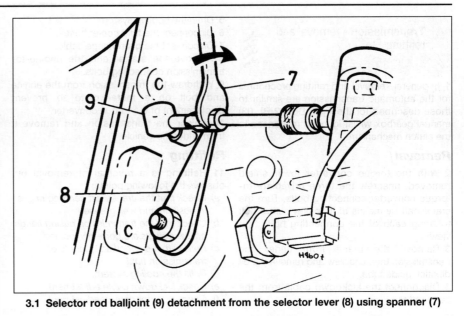

3.1 Selector rod balljoint (9) detachment from the selector lever (8) using spanner (7)

5 If the selector control was adjusted, check the setting by starting the engine and, when it has reached its normal operating temperature, move the selector lever within the vehicle to P. The vehicle should be stationary and the gearbox parking pawl fully engaged.
6 Now move the lever to R with the handbrake off. The vehicle should move rearwards, the pawl having been released.
7 Turn the engine off and then check that the engine will only restart when the lever is moved to P or N. The starter motor must not operate in any other selected position.

7B

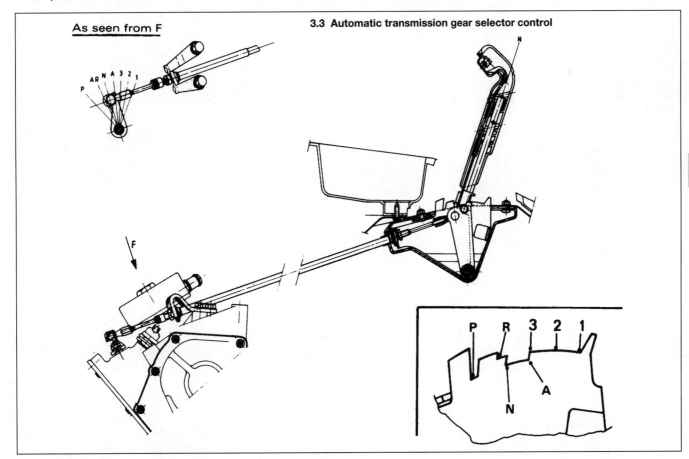

3.3 Automatic transmission gear selector control

As seen from F

4 Transmission - removal and refitting

1 In general, removal and refitting procedures for the automatic transmission are similar to those described for the Type BE1 (2 BL 03) manual gearbox whilst ignoring references to the clutch mechanism.

Removal

2 With the torque converter lower shield removed, unscrew the three driveplate-to-torque converter connecting bolts. Turn the crankshaft by means of its pulley centre bolt to bring each of the connecting bolts into view.

3 Remove the brace from under the transmission then unscrew and remove the oil dipstick guide tube.

4 Disconnect the kickdown cable from the carburettor.

5 Drain the cooling system.

6 Disconnect the fluid cooler hoses.

7 Disconnect the gearchange cable.

8 Remove the starter and the engine-to-transmission connecting bolts.

9 Withdraw the transmission from the engine and bolt on a metal plate to prevent displacement of the torque converter.

10 Lower the transmission and remove it from under the vehicle.

Refitting

11 Refitting is a reversal of removal but observe the following points:

a) *Check that the crankshaft centring ring is in position and well greased.*

b) *Check that the transmission casing flange hollow dowels are correctly located.*

c) *Refill with the specified quantity of transmission fluid.*

d) *Refill the cooling system.*

e) *Check kickdown cable adjustment*

f) *Check selector control adjustment*

12 Note that a centring tube is fitted through the side (sun) gears in the differential unit. This enables the driveshafts to be withdrawn without the need to insert a sleeve tube to locate the side gears as is the case on manual gearbox types.

5 Transmission - overhaul

Entrust this work to your Citroën dealer as specialised tools and knowledge are required to overhaul the transmission.

Chapter 8
Driveshafts

Contents

Degrees of difficulty

| Easy, suitable for novice with little experience | Fairly easy, suitable for beginner with some experience | Fairly difficult, suitable for competent DIY mechanic | Difficult, suitable for experienced DIY mechanic | Very difficult, suitable for expert DIY or professional |

Specifications

For engine to model applications refer to Chapter 2
Driveshafts
Type . . . . Front wheel shafts, each having two tripod constant velocity joints. Inner end splines permit axial movement

Torque wrench settings	Nm	lbf ft
Hub nut (front and rear)	270	195
Driveshaft intermediate bearing nuts (BX and BX 19)	10	7
Lower suspension arm/hub carrier balljoint nut	30	22

1 General information

The driveshafts are conventional with constant velocity joints and splined engagement with the wheel hubs and the differential/final drive unit. They are of two distinct types, these being for the BX and BX 14 models or BX 16 and BX 19 models. The right-hand driveshaft of the BX 16 and BX 19 models differs in that it has an intermediate support bearing.
Constant velocity joints are fitted near each end of each shaft to accommodate the steering and suspension angular movements.

The inner end of each shaft mates with the final drive using sliding splines. This allows changes in overall length of each shaft resulting from suspension and steering movements.
The driveshafts are splined into the front wheel hubs which run on double row ball-races located in the hub carrier at the bottom of each front shock absorber strut.

2 Driveshaft bellows - renewal

1 With the driveshaft removed, loosen the clips on the outer rubber bellows. If plastic straps are fitted, cut them free with snips (see illustration).
2 Prise the bellows larger diameter end from the outer joint housing (see illustration) then tap the centre hub outwards, using a soft metal drift in order to release it from the retaining circlip. Slide the outer joint complete from the driveshaft splines.
3 Extract the circlip from the groove in the driveshaft (see illustration).
4 Prise off the rubber bellows. If necessary, remove the plastic seating from the recess in the driveshaft (see illustration).
5 Loosen the clips on the inner rubber bellows. If plastic straps are fitted, cut them free.
6 Prise the bellows larger diameter end from the inner joint housing and slide the rubber

8

2.1 Plastic ratchet-type clips used to secure driveshaft bellows

2.2 Outer joint with bellows larger diameter end released

2.3 Driveshaft outer joint circlip (arrowed)

2.4 Plastic seating for outer joint bellows

2.6 Removing the inner joint bellows

2.7 Inner joint rollers (arrowed)

2.9 Removing the pressure pad and spring from the inner joint housing

2.11 Injecting grease into the inner joint housing

2.12 Inner joint rubber bellows located on driveshaft

bellows off the outer end of the driveshaft **(see illustration)**.

7 Mark the driveshaft and inner joint housing in relation to each other then separate them, keeping the rollers engaged with their respective spigots **(see illustration)**.

8 Clean away the grease, then retain the rollers using adhesive tape.

9 Remove the pressure pad and spring from inside the inner joint housing **(see illustration)**.

10 Clean away the grease, then commence reassembly by inserting the pressure pad and spring into the inner joint housing, with the housing mounted upright in a soft-jawed vice.

11 Inject one-third of the sachet of grease (supplied in the new bellows repair kit) into the inner joint housing **(see illustration)**.

12 Locate the new inner joint rubber bellows halfway along the driveshaft **(see illustration)**.

13 Remove the adhesive tape and insert the driveshaft into the housing.

14 Inject another third of the grease in the joint.

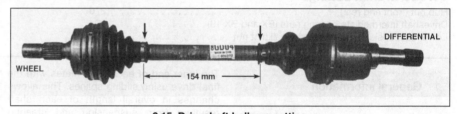

2.15 Driveshaft bellows setting
Dimension shown is for later models only - see text

15 Keeping the driveshaft pressed against the internal spring, refit the rubber bellows. The distance between the inner ends of the bellows is 166.0 mm for vehicles built before June 1987, and 154.0 mm for later models **(see illustration)**.

16 Tighten the clips. Metal-type clips can be retightened using two pairs of pliers, by holding the buckle and pulling the clip through. Cut off the excess and bend the clip back under the buckle **(see illustrations)**.

17 Fit the plastic seating in the driveshaft

recess and refit the new rubber bellows smaller diameter end on it.

18 Refit the circlip in the driveshaft groove.

19 Inject the remaining grease in the outer joint, then insert the driveshaft, engage the splines, and press in until the circlip snaps into the groove.

20 Ease the rubber bellows onto the outer joint and fit the two clips, tightening them as previously described.

3 Driveshafts (BX and BX 14) - removal and refitting

HAYNES HiNT *Before withdrawing a drive-shaft from the differential housing, place a container under the housing to catch any oil which may leak out*

Removal

1 Check that the handbrake is fully applied and remove the roadwheel trim.

2.16a Tightening a bellows clip

2.16b Bellows clip finally secured

3.2 Retaining clip and hub retainer

3.7 Separating driveshaft from front hub - BX 16

3.11 Differential housing oil seal (arrowed)

2 Extract the retaining clip and withdraw the hub nut retainer **(see illustration)**.
3 Loosen the hub nut but do not remove it at this stage.
4 Loosen but do not remove the roadwheel bolts.
5 Place chocks against the rear roadwheels then raise and support the vehicle at the front end so that the front roadwheels are clear of the ground (see "*Jacking and vehicle support*"). Unbolt and remove the roadwheel at the front from the side concerned. Release the handbrake.
6 Loosen the lower arm balljoint nut then detach the joint using a balljoint separator. When the joint is free, remove the separator and the retaining nut. Detach the lower arm.
7 Unscrew and remove the hub nut, then pull the hub carrier outwards and withdraw it from the outboard end of the driveshaft. Pivot the hub carrier as necessary as it is pulled outwards and take care not to strain the hydraulic line connection **(see illustration)**.
8 Before withdrawing the driveshaft from the differential housing, it is advisable to place a clean container under the differential housing to catch any oil leakage once the shaft is removed. Allow for about one litre of oil spillage.
9 Pull the driveshaft from the differential housing, taking care not to damage the housing oil seal. Grip the driveshaft joint cover (not the shaft) when pulling the driveshaft from the transmission, otherwise the CV joint may become dismantled due to displacement of the internal circlip.
10 It is emphasised that if any attempt is made to move the vehicle on its wheels without the driveshafts fitted, there is a danger that the front wheel bearings will collapse.
11 The oil seal in the differential housing can be removed by prising it free using a suitable screwdriver but take care not to damage the housing. Check that the housing is clean before fitting the new seal by driving it carefully into position using a tube of suitable diameter. This seal must not be damaged in any way as oil leakage past it could result in serious damage to both the transmission and the engine **(see illustration)**.

Refitting

12 Refitting the driveshaft is a reversal of the removal procedure but note the following.
13 To ease reassembly and to avoid damaging the oil seal, lubricate the differential hub seal lips and the corresponding hub of the driveshaft with grease prior to refitting.
14 Ensure that the balljoint cone on the hub carrier is clean before refitting the lower arm (do not use a solvent to clean it). Tighten the locknut to the specified torque setting.
15 When refitting the hub nut, lubricate the nut face and threads with grease and tighten the nut to the specified torque before refitting the roadwheel. To prevent the hub from turning, get an assistant to fully apply the brakes. Once the nut is tightened, locate the retainer and refit the retaining clip.
16 With the roadwheel refitted, release the handbrake and check that the hub rotates without excessive binding. A small amount of resistance will probably be present caused by transmission and brake pad drag.
17 On completion, lower the vehicle and tighten the roadwheel bolts to the specified torque settings. Replenish any loss of lubricant from the engine/transmission.

4 Driveshafts (BX 16 and BX 19) - removal and refitting

Manual gearbox

Removal

1 If both driveshafts are to be removed, it is important that the left-hand driveshaft is removed first. This can be removed in the same manner as that described for BX and BX 14 models in the previous Section.
2 With the left-hand driveshaft removed, it is necessary to insert a suitable tube or dowel rod into its aperture in the differential housing **(see illustration)**. The diameter of the tube should be a fraction under the diameter of the driveshaft and its purpose when inserted is to retain the position of the sun gears when the right-hand driveshaft is removed. The tube must remain in position until the right-hand driveshaft is fully refitted.

3 Disconnect the outer end of the right-hand driveshaft as described for BX and BX 14 models in the previous Section.
4 Undo the two intermediate bearing nuts and then turn the screws half a turn. The driveshaft can now be withdrawn from the differential housing and the intermediate bearing carrier then removed **(see illustration)**.
5 Lever out the oil seal in the final drive/differential unit and also the one in the wheel hub. Both seals must be renewed on refitting the driveshaft.

Refitting

6 Lightly grease a new, double-lipped oil seal and carefully tap it into its recess in the final drive/differential unit with the side containing the spring facing into the unit. Make sure that the seal is abutting the internal shoulder in the unit case. Fill the space between the double

4.2 Support differential housing sun gear by inserting tube into left-side driveshaft aperture (manual gearbox)

4.4 Intermediate bearing and retaining nuts

8

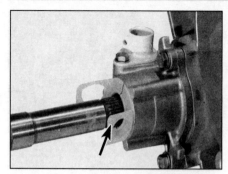

4.8 Oil seal protector bush (arrowed)

lips with general-purpose grease. Similarly, fit a new seal of similar pattern in the wheel hub, making sure that it abuts the bearing retaining ring. Again, fill the space between the lips with grease.

7 Check the driveshaft before fitting to make sure that it is free of obvious defects. Clean the splines at both ends and, at the wheel hub end only, give the splines a thin coat of Molykote 321 R or a suitable alternative anti-friction agent.

8 Protective bushes will have been supplied with new oil seals. The bushes are fitted to the driveshaft aperture in the differential housing to protect the oil seal from damage when refitting the driveshaft(s) **(see illustration)**.

9 Refit the right-hand driveshaft first. Check that the two screws are located in the

intermediate bearing and apply a small amount of lubricant to the bearing outer race prior to engagement of the driveshaft. With the driveshaft in position, tighten the bearing retaining nuts to the specified torque setting.

10 Reconnect the outer end of the right-hand driveshaft, reversing the removal procedures and noting the information given in the previous Section.

11 Withdraw the locating tube from the left-hand driveshaft aperture in the differential housing. The oil seal in the differential housing and the wheel hub can now be removed and renewed on the left-hand side (as described in paragraphs 5 and 6).

12 Clean, check and prepare the left-hand driveshaft for refitting (paragraph 7) and locate the oil seal protector bush to the oil seal in the differential housing on the left-hand side.

13 Refit the left-hand driveshaft, reversing the removal details and noting the information given in the previous Section.

Automatic transmission

14 The differential sun gears fitted to automatic transmission models are different from those fitted to manual gearbox models in that they are supported on a shaft. It is therefore not necessary to insert a tube or dowel through them when removing both driveshafts.

15 The removal and refitting procedures for both driveshafts, and also the renewal of the differential hub and outer wheel hub oil seals,

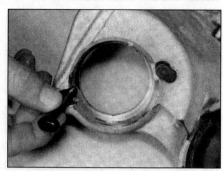

5.2 Driveshaft intermediate bearing carrier (removed) showing special bolts

are otherwise the same as those described for the manual gearbox variants.

5 Driveshaft intermediate bearing (BX 16 and BX 19) - renewal

1 Remove the right-hand driveshaft.
2 Unbolt and remove the engine mounting/ intermediate bearing carrier **(see illustration)**. If the bearing did not come away with the driveshaft, press it and its sealing ring out of the carrier.
3 Fit the new bearing and sealing ring
4 Refit the carrier and the driveshaft. Tighten all fastenings to the specified torque. Use new nuts on the steering and suspension balljoints.

Chapter 9
Hydraulic system

Contents

Degrees of difficulty

| **Easy,** suitable for novice with little experience | **Fairly easy,** suitable for beginner with some experience | **Fairly difficult,** suitable for competent DIY mechanic | **Difficult,** suitable for experienced DIY mechanic | **Very difficult,** suitable for expert DIY or professional |

Specifications

High pressure pump
Type . . . . Five piston volumetric
Operating speed . . . . Half engine speed
Output (per pump cycle) . . . . 4 cc

Pressure regulator
Cut-out pressure . . . . 170 ± 5 bar
Cut-in pressure . . . . 145 ± 5 bar

Accumulator
Capacity . . . . 0.40 litre (0.70 Imp pint)
Calibration pressure . . . . 62 $^{+2}_{-32}$ bar

Security valve
Slide valve return spring calibration pressures:
    Isolation pressure (min) . . . . 80 bar
    Suspension supply pressure (min) . . . . 100 bar

Torque wrench settings

	Nm	lbf ft
Hydraulic pipe unions:		
3.5 and 4.5 mm diameter pipes	8 to 9	6 to 7
6.0 mm diameter pipes	9 to 11	7 to 8

9

1 General information and precautions

General information

The hydropneumatic suspension and the braking system are both pressurised by a common hydraulic system (see illustrations).

Fluid is drawn from a reservoir which is mounted on the right-hand wing valance and delivered under pressure to a pressure regulator which is mounted on the engine crankcase. The system is pressurised by a belt-driven pump, which is mounted on the engine and driven by the crankshaft pulley.

From the pressure regulator, fluid passes to the security valve which has pipe connections running to the compensator control valve and the front and rear suspension height corrector units.

Fluid from the suspension height corrector units (one at the front and one at the rear) flows to the suspension unit cylinders. From the suspension cylinders the low pressure return fluid is returned through pipelines to the hydraulic reservoir.

The height correctors maintain the hydropneumatic suspension at the manually selected height by admitting fluid to, and releasing fluid from, the suspension cylinders according to the movement of the front and rear anti-roll bars to which they are connected.

Four height positions can be selected by the manual height control within the vehicle. They are as follows:

a) *Lever set at second setting position from the front - Normal driving position.*
b) *Lever set at most forward setting position - Minimum height setting for use during repair and overhaul procedures on the vehicle. Should not be used for normal driving.*

c) *Lever set at third setting position from the front - Raises vehicle ride height to intermediate setting. For use when traversing rough road conditions.*
d) *Lever set at fourth setting position (ie. lever moved fully back) - Raises vehicle to maximum height setting. Primary use is to assist when changing roadwheels. Should not be selected when driving except under exceptional conditions such as negotiating undulating surfaces, then only for short distances and at very low speeds.*

Hydraulic pressure for the braking system is supplied from the compensator control valve with separate front and rear circuits. The front circuit is supplied direct from the compensator control valve, whilst the rear brake circuits operate in conjunction with the hydraulic circuits to the rear suspension. This arrangement results in the braking effort being biased in favour of the front brakes and at the same time regulates the braking effort on the

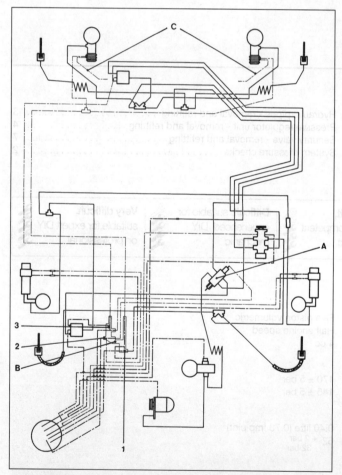

1.1a Hydraulic system circuit diagram - manual steering models

A Security valve
B Return pipes to reservoir (see 1 to 3)
C Rear suspension vent line
1 Overflow return - front and rear suspension cylinders
2 Vent pipe - front suspension cylinders
3 Leakage from front and rear height correctors and security valve

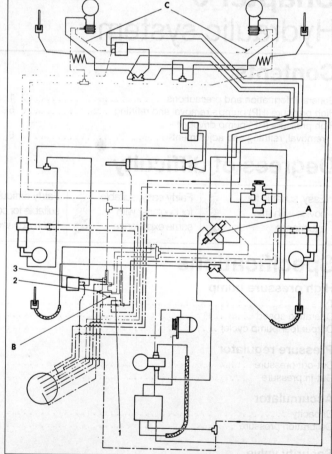

1.1b Hydraulic system circuit diagram - power steering models

A Security valve
B Return pipes to reservoir (see 1 to 3)
C Rear suspension vent line
1 Overflow return - front and rear suspension cylinders
2 Vent pipe - front suspension cylinders
3 Leakage from front and rear height correctors and security valve

rear wheels according to the load on the rear suspension. The heavier the load, the greater the pressure in the rear suspension, thus more braking effort.

Hydraulic pressure is released from the system by slackening the bleed screw on the pressure regulator. This allows the pressure fluid to bleed off to the reservoir.

On power steering models, a flow distributor is fitted between the HP pump and the pressure regulator unit. The purpose of the flow distributor is to control the hydraulic pressure between the steering circuit and the suspension/brake circuits.

Precautions

Cleanliness is of the utmost importance when working on the hydraulic system and its components. Clean all adjacent areas before disconnecting components. After removal, blank off all orifices and ensure that components and pipes do not get contaminated.

Use only LHM mineral hydraulic fluid in the hydraulic system. The use of any other fluid will ruin the rubber rings and seals. LHM fluid is green in colour. Keep the fluid, carefully sealed, in its original container.

Use only genuine spare parts. Components are identified by painting or marking in green. All rubber parts are identified by their white or green colour and are of a special quality for use with LHM fluid.

Before starting work on the hydraulic system, the pressure must be released as follows:
a) Switch the engine off.
b) Place the manual height control lever in the "low" (minimum) height position.
c) Loosen the pressure regulator release screw one and a half turns then wait for the vehicle to reach the low position.
d) Only undo the regulator release screw by the specified amount, do not remove it (see illustration).

Although the maximum height setting is a useful aid when undertaking inspection and repair tasks on the vehicle, it is essential that the vehicle is supported on safety stands when carrying out any service or repairs from underneath.

2 System pressure checks

1 In order to carry out pressure checks on the hydraulic system, a pressure gauge capable of measuring pressure from 0 to 250 bar will be required. A suitable length of high pressure line will also be needed for attachment between the gauge and the operational pipe union on the pressure regulator. A gauge used to check injection pressure on diesel engines may be suitable.
2 Before making any checks, ensure that the hydraulic reservoir filters are clean and also that the fluid level in the reservoir is correct.
3 Release system pressure by loosening the bleed screw on the pressure regulator 1 to 1.5 turns.
4 Disconnect the operational pipe from the pressure regulator by unscrewing the union nut. Move the pipe to one side and plug it to prevent the ingress of dirt.
5 Screw the pressure gauge pipe into the operational pipe port in the pressure regulator. Make the following checks in the order given.

Main accumulator pressure check

6 Tighten the pressure regulator bleed screw.
7 Disconnect the distributor-to-coil leads.
8 Get an assistant to turn the engine over on the starter motor. As the starter motor is operated, check the pressure gauge needle reading. The pressure should gradually rise then stabilise within the calibration pressure readings given in Specifications.
9 If the pressure is not within the specified limits, the main accumulator is faulty.
10 Reconnect the ignition lead on completing this test.

Pressure regulator check

11 Loosen the bleed screw on the pressure regulator by 1 to 1.5 turns.
12 Start the engine and run it at an increased idle speed, then retighten the pressure regulator bleed screw and observe the increase in pressure. When the pressure gauge needle stabilises, the cut-out pressure

is reached and this should be within the pressure range specified.
13 Allow the engine to run at idle speed for a short period to allow the pressure to stabilise. Switch off the engine and note the drop in pressure over a period of three minutes. If this exceeds 10 bar the regulator is faulty.
14 Start the engine again and run it at an increased idle speed. When the cut-in occurs, loosen the pressure regulator bleed screw 1 to 1.5 turns. The pressure reading should gradually fall then rise as the HP pump becomes operational. The minimum pressure reading taken should correspond to the cut-in pressure specified.
15 If the cut-out or cut-in pressure readings taken are incorrect, then the regulator is faulty.
16 On completion, switch off the engine, release the system pressure and detach the pressure gauge. Remove the plug from the operational pipe and reconnect it to the pressure regulator unit.

3 Hydraulic pipes - removal and refitting

Note: Use only LHM mineral hydraulic fluid in the hydraulic system

Removal

1 If at any time it is necessary to disconnect or remove any hydraulic pipeline in the suspension or braking circuits, it is essential that the system pressure is first released. See "Precautions".
2 Before disconnecting the pipe concerned, thoroughly clean the union external surfaces.
3 If a complete pipe section is to be replaced, release the pipe from the retaining clips and/or clamps and bushings. Avoid distorting or damaging the pipe as it is withdrawn (see illustrations).
4 If the pipe is not being replaced immediately, plug the union connections to prevent the ingress of dirt into the system.

Refitting

5 To ensure that a perfect seal exists when

9

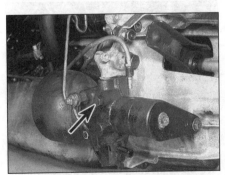
1.13 Pressure regulator unit (BX 16) showing pressure release screw (arrowed)

3.3a Hydraulic pipes and retaining clips which keep them correctly located

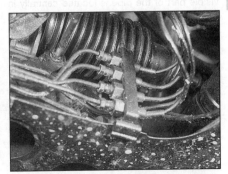
3.3b Hydraulic pipes and union connections - also secured by a clamp for security

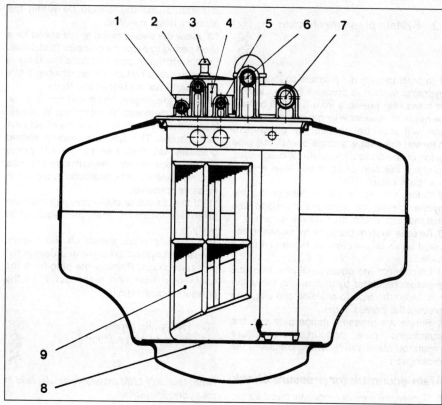

3.3c Hydraulic system reservoir connections

1 Front and rear suspension
   cylinders overflow return
2 Security valve and front/rear
   height correctors
3 Breather
4 Vent pipe - front
   suspension cylinders
5 Operational return/overflow
   return from brake control
   valve
6 Operational return from
   pressure regulator and
   height correctors
7 HP pump suction hose
8 Deflector
9 Filter

hydraulic pipe joints are assembled, the
following procedure must be carried out.
6 Clean the component port, hydraulic pipe,
union nut and sealing rubber and lightly
lubricate them with LHM fluid.
7 Slide the sealing rubber onto the end of the
pipe until the pipe protrudes from it **(see
illustration)**.
8 Insert the pipe into the component so that
the pipe end enters the central hole of the
component port. The sealing rubber must
enter its location hole fully. Check that the
visible part of the pipe is located centrally in
the component port **(see illustration)**.
9 Screw in the union nut by hand whilst
keeping the hydraulic pipe stationary, then
tighten it to the specified torque.
10 The pipe union is designed to provide
increased sealing with increased fluid
pressure. Tightening the nut more than the
specified amount will not improve the seal and
may easily damage the pipe.
11 On completion, check that the hydraulic
system pipes do not touch each other or any
other component which may stress or chafe
the pipes.

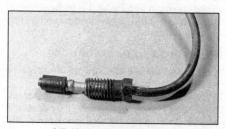

**3.7 Hydraulic pipe union
and sealing rubber**

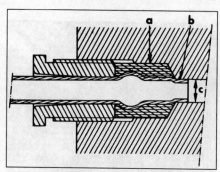

**3.8 Cross-section through
a hydraulic pipe joint**
a Sealing rubber b Pipe c Union bore

4 Pressure regulator unit - removal and refitting

Removal

1 Release the system pressure by loosening
the pressure bleed screw by 1 to 1.5 turns on
the pressure regulator unit **(see illustration)**.
Allow the vehicle to drop to its fully lowered
position.
2 Wipe clean the pressure regulator unit and
the pipe connections in particular.
3 Loosen the retaining clip and detach the
return pipe hose from the regulator. Plug the
hose and position it out of the way.
4 Undo the union nuts and detach the two
rigid pipes from the pressure regulator. Plug
them to prevent the ingress of dirt **(see
illustration)**.
5 Undo the two retaining bolts and the support
bracket nut. Support the regulator unit as the
bolts and nuts are removed and withdraw the
regulator unit. Note the position of the hose
location wire under the lower bolt head.

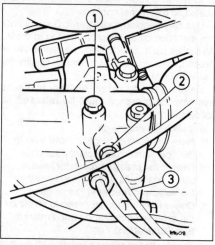

4.1 Pressure regulator

1 Pressure release (bleed) screw
2 Union connector - operational pipe to
   pressure regulator
3 Operational pipe

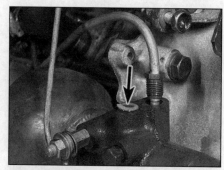

**4.4 Disconnecting the rigid pipes from the
pressure regulator. Note the plug inserted
into the vacated port (arrowed)**

5.3 HP pump showing the supply and output pipe connections

5.4 Detach the output pipe. Pump retaining bolts arrowed

6.2 HP pump drivebelt jockey wheel mounting and adjuster bolts (arrowed) - BX 16

Refitting

6 Refitting is a reversal of the removal procedure. Ensure that the connecting pipe connections are thoroughly clean before connecting them.

7 On completion, top-up the hydraulic fluid level in the reservoir and prime the HP pump.

5 High pressure (HP) pump - removal and refitting

Removal

1 Release the pressure in the hydraulic system as described in "Precautions".

2 Wipe clean the pump and its pipe connections.

3 Disconnect the pump supply pipe from the inlet port and drain the fluid into a suitable container. If a roll type clip is fitted, remove it and obtain a screw type (worm drive) clip **(see illustration)**.

4 Unscrew the high pressure output pipe from the pump **(see illustration)**.

5 Loosen the drivebelt tension and disengage the drivebelt from the pump pulley.

6 Undo the two retaining bolts and withdraw the pump.

Refitting

7 Refitting is a reversal of the removal procedure. Adjust the drivebelt tension.

8 With the pump refitted and the hoses connected, prime the pump.

6 High pressure (HP) pump drivebelt - removal, refitting and adjustment

Removal

1 On BX 16 and BX 19 models, remove the alternator drivebelt.

2 Loosen the HP pump drivebelt jockey wheel mounting and adjuster bolts then pivot the jockey wheel inwards towards the engine to release the drivebelt tension **(see illustration)**.

3 Remove the drivebelt from the HP pump and associate pulleys.

Refitting

4 Refit in the reverse order to removal.

Adjustment

5 With the belt fitted on the pulleys, set the tension by pivoting the jockey pulley outwards as much as possible by hand to take up any play in the belt on its longest run between pulleys. If any form of leverage is employed to achieve this tension great care must be taken not to damage any fittings. Tighten the jockey

pulley mounting/adjuster bolt to set the tension.

6 With the jockey wheel position set, the belt tension must be felt to be taut under a reasonable thumb pressure at the midway point between the pulleys on its longest run. Note however, that the belt tension must not be tightened excessively or the belt life will be shortened and damage to the pulleys and their drive bearings could result. Recheck the tension of a new belt after a nominal mileage has been covered.

7 On BX 16 and BX 19 models, refit the alternator drivebelt and adjust its tension.

7 Security valve - removal and refitting

Removal

1 The security valve is located on the lower left-hand side of the front subframe, behind the steering gear **(see illustration)**.

2 Loosen the pressure regulator bleed screw.

3 Disconnect the rubber overflow return pipe from the end of the valve **(see illustration)**.

7.1 Security valve location

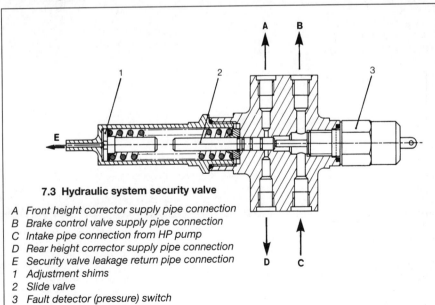

7.3 Hydraulic system security valve

A Front height corrector supply pipe connection
B Brake control valve supply pipe connection
C Intake pipe connection from HP pump
D Rear height corrector supply pipe connection
E Security valve leakage return pipe connection
1 Adjustment shims
2 Slide valve
3 Fault detector (pressure) switch

9

4 Unscrew the union nuts securing the inlet and outlet pipes to the security valve, making a careful note of their location.
5 Disconnect the supply wire from the pressure switch terminal.

6 Unscrew and remove the mounting bolt and withdraw the valve. Where a brake limiter is fitted, this is also detached at the same time.

Refitting

7 Refitting is a reversal of removal. With the pipes and wire connected, tighten the pressure regulator bleed screw.

Chapter 10
Braking system

Contents

Degrees of difficulty

Easy, suitable for novice with little experience 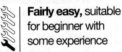	Fairly easy, suitable for beginner with some experience 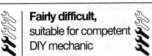	Fairly difficult, suitable for competent DIY mechanic	Difficult, suitable for experienced DIY mechanic	Very difficult, suitable for expert DIY or professional

Specifications

System

Standard type	Discs all round, dual hydraulic circuit supplied by main hydraulic system, automatic rear brake limitation. Front pad wear warning system. Cable operated handbrake to front wheel discs
ABS type	Electro-hydraulic controlled anti-lock brake system, complementary to standard system

Front brakes

Disc diameter	266 mm
Disc thickness:	
Standard:	
New	10 mm
Wear limit	7 mm
ABS:	
Ventilated	20.4 mm
Maximum disc run-out	0.2 mm
Minimum pad lining thickness	Indicated by warning lamp

Rear brakes

Disc diameter	224 mm
Disc thickness:	
New	7 mm
Wear limit	4 mm
Maximum disc run-out	0.2 mm
Minimum pad lining thickness	2 mm - suggested

Pedal

Brake pedal-to-compensator valve clearance:	
1st type	1.0 to 3.0 mm
2nd type	0.1 to 1.0 mm

Wheel sensor - ABS

Air gap (non-adjustable):	
Front	0.30 to 1.0 mm
Rear	0.50 to 1.10 mm

Electronic control unit - ABS

Make	Teves
Reference	ATE 100901 -0014-4

Torque wrench settings

	Nm	lbf ft
Compensator control valve	18	13
Rear brake disc screws	45	32
Rear caliper bolts	45	32
Front caliper bolt	110	80
Wheel sensor (front) - ABS	10	7

1 General information and precautions

General information

Standard system

This dual circuit system, with disc brakes fitted to all wheels, is hydraulically operated from the main hydraulic system. The front brakes are supplied from the hydraulic pressure regulator and the rear brakes are supplied from the rear suspension system. This arrangement favours the front brakes and imposes a braking effort limitation on the rear axle in relation to the load. The braking action is applied through the brake pedal operating a hydraulic control valve which allows pressure to the braking system.

The front brake pads are equipped with internal electric leads which operate a warning lamp on the instrument panel when the linings are due for renewal.

The front brake calipers comprise outer halves which are removable and inner halves which are integral with the steering knuckles.

The rear brake pads and calipers are mounted on the rear suspension arms The pads do not incorporate a warning system.

The handbrake is operated by a floor mounted lever. Cables run to and operate each front caliper to force the friction pads against the discs.

Anti-lock braking system (ABS)

An anti-lock braking system is fitted to the BX 19 GTi from November 1986. The function of the ABS is to prevent the brakes from locking the roadwheels when applied, thereby retaining steering control and giving the shortest-possible stopping distance for emergency braking. The system operates at speeds in excess of 5 mph and when in operation, controls the vehicle deceleration until it is brought to a halt.

The ABS monitors the rotational speed of each roadwheel during braking. If any wheel begins to slow at a faster rate than the others thereby showing that it is on the point of locking, the ABS reduces the hydraulic pressure to that wheel's brake caliper. As the wheel grips again, its rotational speed matches the others and hydraulic pressure to

the caliper is restored. This cycle can be repeated several times per second.

The ABS is operated by the following hydraulic and electronic components, which are complementary to the standard brake system.

a) *Front and rear wheel sensor units - on the driveshaft joints/wheel hubs.*
b) *Hydraulic control block unit - on the left-hand wheel arch in the engine compartment.*
c) *Electronic control unit (ECU) - under the front passenger seat.*

In common with the standard system, the front and rear brake hydraulic circuits are separate but the ABS differs in also separating the right and left-hand front brake circuits. The remaining brake system components and layout are otherwise the same as standard.

The hydraulic control block contains six electro-valves, each of the three brake circuits having its own idle and return valve which work in accordance with the ECU.

The electronic part of the system comprises the ECU and a speed sensor unit for each roadwheel. Each driveshaft outer CV joint and each rear wheel hub has a toothed rotor, the speed of which is recorded by the adjacent sensor unit. This unit in turn relays the signal to the ECU. From the signals received by the ECU from each roadwheel, the average road speed is calculated and any sudden acceleration or deceleration accounted.

An automatic checking device is built into the electronic control unit. Any faults in the ABS will illuminate the yellow warning light on the instrument panel and cancel the ABS (but still allow normal braking). The yellow warning light will also light up when the ignition is initially switched on but will cancel as soon as the engine is started.

If a fault develops or is suspected in the ABS, then the system must be checked by a Citroën dealer at the earliest opportunity.

Precautions

When servicing any part of the system, work carefully and methodically whilst observing scrupulous cleanliness. Always renew components (in axle sets, where applicable) if in doubt about their condition and use only genuine Citroen replacement parts, or at least those of known good quality.

Hydraulic fluid

Hydraulic fluid is poisonous. Wash off immediately and thoroughly in the case of skin contact and seek immediate medical advice if any fluid is swallowed or gets into the eyes.

Certain types of hydraulic fluid are inflammable and may ignite when allowed into contact with hot components. When servicing any hydraulic system, it is safest to assume that the fluid is inflammable and to take precautions against the risk of fire as though it is petrol that is being handled.

Hydraulic fluid is an effective paint stripper and will attack plastics. If any is spilt, it should be washed off immediately using copious quantities of fresh water.

Finally, hydraulic fluid is hygroscopic (it absorbs moisture from the air). Old fluid may be contaminated and unfit for further use. When topping-up or renewing fluid, always use the recommended type and ensure that it comes from a freshly-opened sealed container.

Brake components

When working on brake components, take care not to disperse brake dust into the air or to inhale it, since it may contain asbestos which is injurious to health.

2 Brake pads - renewal

 Warning: When working on brake components, take care not to disperse brake dust into the air or to inhale it, since it may contain asbestos which is injurious to health.

Front

1 The brake pad wear warning lamp will indicate that the front brake pads have worn down to the specified limit. The pads must be renewed as a set.

2 Chock the rear roadwheels, jack up the front of the vehicle and support it on axle stands (see "*Jacking and vehicle support*"). Remove the front roadwheels.

3 Release the handbrake and turn the steering so that the brake caliper is facing outboard.

2.4a Disconnect the pad wear warning leads . . .

2.4b . . . and pull wire from spring clip eyes. Note pad wear indicator studs (arrowed)

2.5a Extract the lock plate pin . . .

2.5b . . . and withdraw the lock plate

2.6 Removing a front brake pad

2.7 Method used to move caliper piston back into cylinder

4 Disconnect the pad wear warning lamp wires from the wiring loom and the outer wire from the spring clip eyes **(see illustrations)**.
5 Using pliers, grip and extract the pin locating the lock plate then withdraw the lock plate **(see illustrations)**. Pressing down on the pad plates at the lower end will ease removal of the locking plate.
6 Each pad, together with its spring clip, can now be withdrawn from the caliper unit **(see illustration)**.
7 The caliper piston must now be moved back into its cylinder to allow room for the new pads. To do this, turn it in a clockwise direction whilst simultaneously applying pressure to it. To rotate the piston, engage a screwdriver with a 7 mm square shaft into the groove in the piston end face. Insert a second

screwdriver or suitable lever between the disc outer face and the caliper frame and lever it outwards, but take care not to apply pressure on the disc friction surface **(see illustration)**.
8 Remove any dust or dirt from the pad recesses in the caliper. Refer to "Precautions".
9 Locate the springs onto each pad.

10 Set the piston position so that the pad engagement slot is aligned correctly **(see illustration)**.
11 Fit the brake pads into position, together with their springs **(see illustrations)**.
12 Slide the lock plate into position and insert the retaining pin.
13 If new brake pads have been fitted, check that a 1 mm clearance exists between the disc and pads. If required, adjust the piston position accordingly **(see illustration)**. Note that this clearance is to allow the handbrake self-adjusting mechanism to operate correctly and is not the normal running clearance between the pads and disc.
14 Pass the outer pad wear indicator wire through the pad spring eyes, through the insulation sleeve (together with the inner pad

2.10 Piston alignment position with identification mark (a) above (or below) piston groove (b)

2.11a Pad peg (c) must engage in piston groove when fitted
Pad springs correctly fitted

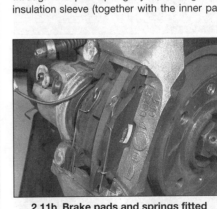

2.11b Brake pads and springs fitted

10

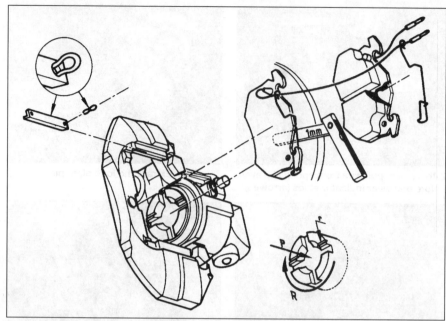

2.13 Front brake pad reassembly - check clearance between disc and pad with feeler blade

2.14 Reconnect pad wear wiring and locate as shown

wire) and reconnect to the wiring loom connector **(see illustration)**.

15 On completion, refit the roadwheel(s) and lower the vehicle to the ground.

16 Avoid harsh braking as far as possible for a few hundred miles to allow the new pads to bed in.

Rear

Modifications: *From October 1988, modified rear brake calipers and pads are fitted. These calipers are modified to provide increased clearance for the disc (now 12.2 mm). The thicknesses of the pad backing plate and friction material are modified accordingly. The pad backing plate is now 5 mm thick (instead of 4 mm previously) and the friction material thickness is now reduced by 1 mm. Vehicles with the early-type calipers can be fitted with the later type pads. It is possible to fit the later-type calipers to early vehicles, in which case the later-type pads must be fitted. Note that the early-type pads must not be fitted to models with the later calipers.*

17 Apply the handbrake, jack-up the rear of the vehicle and support it on axle stands (see *"Jacking and vehicle support"*). Remove the roadwheels.

18 Unscrew and remove the retaining bolt and withdraw the pad cover from the caliper **(see illustration)**.

19 Remove the spring clip and pull out the two pads with a pair of pliers **(see illustrations)**.

20 Brush any accumulated dust and dirt from the pads and caliper recesses. Refer to "Precautions".

21 Examine the pads for wear. If the friction material thickness is less than the specified minimum, the pads must be renewed as a set.

22 When inspecting the pads, it is strongly recommended that they be removed and cleaned even if they appear unworn. Rear pad wear is very slow if the vehicle is driven mostly unladen and it is possible for the pads to seize in place if they are not removed periodically.

23 If new pads are to be fitted, the caliper pistons must be retracted to accommodate the extra friction material. To do this, partially insert the old pads, then lever them apart to depress the pistons.

24 Fit the new pads with the friction surfaces towards the disc.

25 Locate the spring clip with the crossbar at the bottom of the caliper and retain it in position with the through-bolt **(see illustration)**.

26 Refit the pad cover and tighten the bolt.

27 Refit the roadwheels and lower the vehicle to the ground.

2.18 Remove rear brake disc pad cover . . .

2.19a . . . withdraw spring retainer clip . . .

2.19b . . . to extract brake outer pad . . .

2.19c . . . and inner pad

2.25 Locating the through-bolt

3.0a Ventilated type brake disc

3.0b Locating pip (arrowed) on inboard pad

3.2 Front brake disc removal

3 Brake discs - removal and refitting

Front

Note: *Discs fitted to BX 19 GTi 16 valve models are of the ventilated type. Operations detailed in this Section for standard discs apply (see illustrations)*

1 Remove the brake pads.

2 Unscrew and remove the disc-to-hub retaining screws and withdraw the disc **(see illustration)**.

3 Clean and examine the disc for deep scoring or grooving. Light scoring is normal but if it is severe, the disc must be refaced by a competent engineering works or, if worn to the specified wear limit, renewed.

4 Check the disc for run-out to determine whether it is distorted or buckled. To do this accurately, a dial gauge will be necessary. If a gauge is not available, feeler blades can be used against a fixed block as the disc is rotated slowly. Do not confuse wear in the hub bearings with disc run-out. To check run-out, refit the disc to the wheel hub and fully tighten the retaining screws. The mating surfaces of the hub and disc must be perfectly clean or a false reading could be given.

5 Refit in the reverse order to removal. Ensure that no oil or grease come into contact with the disc or pads during assembly.

Rear

Modification: *From October 1988, modified rear brake calipers and pads are fitted. These calipers are modified to provide increased clearance for the disc (now 12.2 mm).*

6 Remove the brake pads.

7 Reinsert the pad/spring retaining bolt and tighten the securing nut to close the half calipers together **(see illustration)**.

8 Unscrew and remove the two caliper retaining bolts.

9 Undo the disc-to-hub retaining screw. Withdraw the disc and simultaneously raise the caliper unit a fraction to allow the disc to be removed **(see illustration)**.

10 If the disc is difficult to separate from the hub, remove the backplate and tap the disc off from behind. Be careful not to fracture or distort the disc if it is to be re-used.

11 Clean and inspect the disc as described for the front.

12 Prior to refitting the disc, check that the mating faces of both the disc and hub are clean. Smear the mating faces and the retaining screw threads with grease. Do not allow any grease to contact the disc friction surfaces.

13 Refit in the reverse order to removal. Tighten the caliper retaining bolts and the disc retaining screw to the specified torque settings.

4 Front brake caliper unit - removal, overhaul and refitting

> ⚠ *Warning: Hydraulic fluid may be under pressure in a pipeline, take care not to allow hydraulic fluid to spray into the face or eyes when loosening a connection*
> *Never refit old seals when reassembling brake system components.*

Removal

1 Loosen the front roadwheel bolts on the side concerned, place chocks against the rear wheels, then raise and support the vehicle at the front so that the roadwheels are clear of the ground (see "*Jacking and vehicle support*").

2 Remove the roadwheel bolts and withdraw the roadwheels.

3 Loosen the pressure release screw on the hydraulic pressure regulator unit by 1 to 1.5 turns. Set the ground clearance height control lever to the "low" position.

4 Unscrew and detach the rigid brake line from the bracket union on the inner wheel arch **(see illustration)**. Plug the exposed pipe and union port to prevent fluid loss and the ingress of dirt.

3.7 Rear brake disc removal showing nut and pad/spring bolt (1 and 5), caliper bolts (4) and disc screw (7)

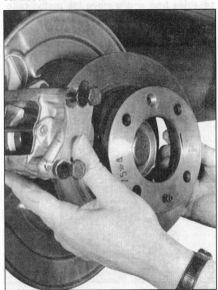

3.9 Rear brake disc removal

4.4 Rigid brake line connection under front wheel arch

10

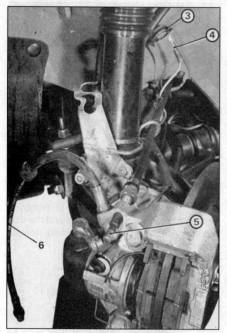

4.5 Front caliper removal

3 *Plate*
4 *Hydraulic supply pipe (rigid)*
5 *Handbrake cable*
6 *Hydraulic supply hose (flexible)*

5 Detach the flexible hose from the locating bracket by pulling the retaining plate free, then disconnect the hose from the support lug forward of the suspension strut **(see illustration)**.
6 Detach the brake pad wear leads from the main harness connector on the top face of the caliper unit.
7 Fully release the handbrake then disconnect the handbrake cable from the operating lever at the caliper.
8 Unbolt and remove the deflector plate **(see illustration)**.
9 Undo the two retaining bolts (on the inner face) and remove the caliper unit, together with the plate.

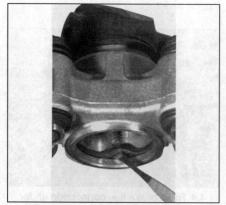

4.15 Prise free the cylinder inner seal

4.8 Front brake caliper deflector (1) and retaining bolt (2)

Overhaul

10 Clean the caliper unit externally. Avoid breathing in any brake dust, see "Precautions".
11 Remove the brake pads.
12 Before dismantling the caliper unit, check that the following repair kits are available, depending on the extent of the overhaul:

a) *Piston seal replacement kit*
b) *Handbrake control repair kit*
c) *Caliper sliding mechanism repair kit*

13 If the control mechanism is to be dismantled it will be necessary to obtain Citroën tool 228-T.
14 Prise free and remove the piston outer seal, then apply low air pressure (eg. from a foot pump) through the fluid inlet pipe aperture to eject the piston. Catch the piston in a cloth to prevent damaging it as it is removed **(see illustration)**.

4.20a Using special tool to compress the dished spring washers

4.14 Piston removal from caliper

15 Prise free the inner seal from the cylinder **(see illustration)**.
16 Inspect the cylinder walls and the piston for signs of damage or excessively deep score marks. If such damage is apparent, renew the caliper unit.
17 To remove the automatic handbrake control mechanism, prise free the rubber cover and withdraw it from the handbrake cable fork arm.
18 Unscrew and remove the brake bleed screw and remove the protective cover.
19 Extract the retaining circlip from the exposed end of the handbrake pivot arm.
20 Locate the compression tool 228-T as shown **(see illustration)** and compress the dished spring washers. Withdraw the handbrake cable pivot arm **(see illustration)**.
21 Remove the compression tool then withdraw the peg, spring, piston locator/adjuster dished spring washers and flat washer.
22 Withdraw the caliper sliding bushes and prise free the rubber gaiters **(see illustration)**.
23 Clean the caliper body thoroughly before reassembling. New repair kits must always be used during reassembly.
24 Relocate the sliding mechanism gaiters (using the new ones from the kit) then

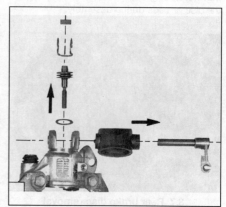

4.20b Remove these handbrake components

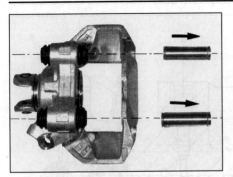

4.22 Remove the caliper sliding bushes and gaiters

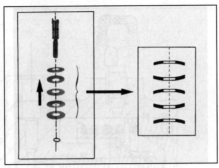

4.25 Caliper washer orientation

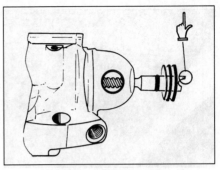

4.26 Correct fitting position of locator/adjuster in caliper

lubricate the bushes with grease from the sachet supplied and push them into position. Check that they are correctly located.

25 Locate the new dished spring washers into position on the piston locator/adjuster, together with the flat washer. The washers must be orientated as shown **(see illustration)**.

26 Lubricate the locator/adjuster with LHM fluid, then fit it into position in the caliper body, passing it through the lower washer. The end slot must be orientated as shown **(see illustration)**. Locate the spring and peg and fit the compression tool (228-T) into position as during dismantling.

27 Locate the new cover onto the handbrake pivot arm and invert it so that it is folded over the cable lever arm to allow fitting.

28 With the dished spring washers held under compression, insert the handbrake pivot arm and position it so that the peg engages with the ratchet as shown **(see illustration)** and the spring end engages as shown **(see illustration)**. Prise the spring down to engage it in the lip of the ratchet.

29 Locate the circlip into the groove in the exposed section of the pivot arm to secure it.

30 Lubricate the pivot arm and adjuster mechanism with grease from the sachet in the repair kit, then fold over the protective rubber cover and engage it in the caliper body groove.

31 Lubricate the cylinder wall and the piston with LHM fluid. Similarly, lubricate and fit the inner piston seal into position in its groove in the cylinder wall. Check that when fitted it is not distorted.

32 Press and screw the piston into position so that, when fitted, the horizontal groove is in line with the bleed screw. To rotate the piston, engage a screwdriver with a 7 mm square shaft into the piston groove in the end face.

33 Lubricate the outer seal with brake grease from the sachet and then fit it in position. When fitted, check that it is fully engaged and not distorted.

34 Refit the bleed screw and protector.

Refitting

35 Refitting is a reversal of the removal procedure but note the following:

a) *Tighten the caliper retaining bolts to the specified torque setting*

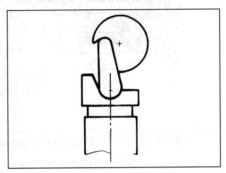

4.28a Engage peg with ratchet

b) *Ensure that the brake hose is correctly located and secured in the location brackets. When reconnecting the rigid supply pipe use a new seal sleeve*

c) *On completion, bleed the brakes then refit the roadwheel and lower the vehicle*

d) *Remove the chocks from the rear roadwheels and check that the handbrake operates correctly*

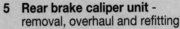

5 Rear brake caliper unit - removal, overhaul and refitting

Removal

1 Loosen the rear roadwheel bolts, check that the handbrake is fully applied, then place chocks against the front roadwheels.

2 Raise the rear of the vehicle and support it with safety stands (see "*Jacking and vehicle support*"). Remove the rear roadwheel(s).

3 Loosen the pressure release screw on the hydraulic pressure regulator unit by 1 to 1.5 turns. Set the ground clearance height control to the "low" position.

4 Clean the hydraulic pipe union to caliper connection then unscrew and detach the pipe at the union. Plug the pipe to prevent the ingress of dirt.

5 Undo the caliper retaining bolts and withdraw the caliper unit.

Overhaul

6 Remove the brake pads and separate the two halves of the caliper unit.

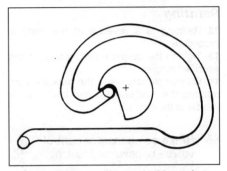

4.28b Engage spring end with ratchet

7 To remove the pistons, apply low air pressure (eg. from a foot pump) through the hydraulic pipe connection port whilst holding a piece of rag over the piston face to catch and cushion the piston in as it is ejected from its bore **(see illustration)**.

8 Clean the caliper and piston components. If, on inspection, the cylinder bore or piston is badly scored, damaged or corroded, then the caliper unit must be renewed.

9 Note the position of the seals and their orientation before removing them. These must always be renewed.

10 Reassemble the caliper in the reverse order to removal. Lubricate each part as it is fitted with LHM fluid and ensure absolute cleanliness.

11 Compress the pistons back into their bores to ease fitting of the brake pads.

10

5.7 Rear brake caliper piston and seals removed

6.3 Brake compensator control valve

Refitting

12 Refitting is a reversal of the removal procedure.

13 Tighten the caliper retaining bolts to the specified torque.

14 On completion, bleed the brakes before refitting the roadwheel(s) and lowering the vehicle to the ground.

6 Brake compensator control valve - removal and refitting

Pre October 1988

1 Raise the vehicle at the front end and support it on safety stands (see "*Jacking and vehicle support*"). Chock the rear wheels.

2 Move the ground clearance control lever to the front ("low" position) then unscrew the hydraulic system pressure regulator bleed screw 1 to 1.5 turns. Operate the brake pedal a few times to release the pressure.

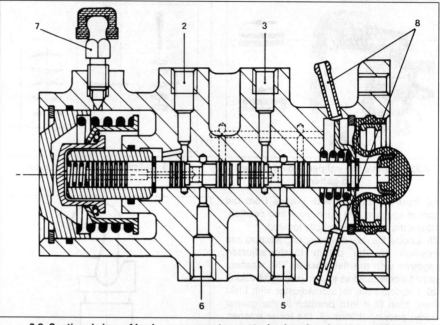

6.8 Sectional view of brake compensator control valve showing connections

2 *Rear suspension pressure line (from 4-way union)*
3 *High pressure connection to front brakes (from security valve)*
5 *Operating pressure to front brakes*
6 *Operating pressure to rear brakes*
7 *Bleed screw*
8 *Reservoir return*

3 Clean the control valve and the hydraulic pipe connections then identify each pipe before detachment to ensure correct reassembly **(see illustration)**.

4 Unscrew the union nuts and pull the pipes clear of the valve.

5 Disconnect the overflow and return pipes from the valve.

6 Working from within the vehicle, unscrew the valve retaining bolts at the bulkhead (directly in front of the brake/pedal assembly) then withdraw and remove the valve.

7 If the internal slide valves are worn, the valve must be renewed. If only the seals are worn, they can be removed separately. Check with a Citroën garage before removing the old seals.

8 Dismantling is straightforward **(see illustration)**. Note that there are several different types of valve, identification being by various paint marks on the valve body. The return outlet is located in different positions on the various types.

9 Refitting is a reversal of removal. Bleed the braking system and make sure that the pressure regulator bleed screw is tightened before using the vehicle on the road.

10 On completion, check that the pedal-to-operating rod clearance is as specified according to type **(see illustrations)**. Adjust as necessary.

From October 1988

11 From October 1988, all models are fitted with a new type of valve, which incorporates three slide valves instead of the previous two.

12 If the new type of valve is being fitted as a replacement for the older assembly, then remove the calibrating plug **(see illustration)** and connect the rear brake pipe to the tapped port.

13 If a new type is being renewed, it will be supplied with a bleed valve screwed into the rear brake pipe connecting port. Remove the bleed screw.

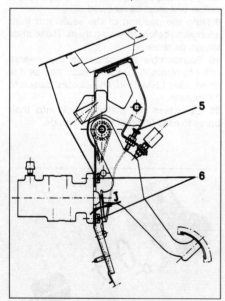

6.10a Footbrake pedal adjustment - type 1

5 *Pedal adjustment stop screw*
6 *Brake compensator retaining bolts*
J = 1.0 to 3.0 mm

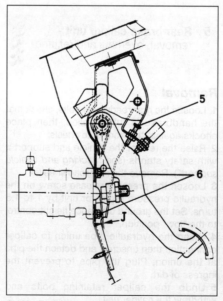

6.10b Footbrake pedal adjustment - type 2

5 *Pedal adjustment stop screw*
6 *Brake compensator retaining bolts*
J = 0.1 to 1.0 mm

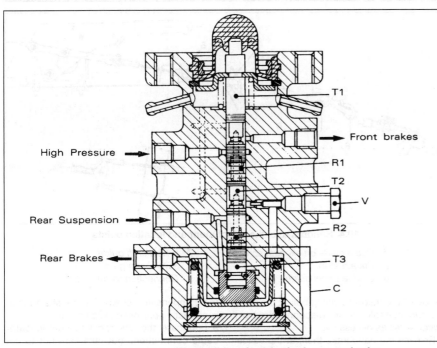

6.12 Sectional view of three slide valve type brake control valve

C	Valve body	R2 Spring	T2 Intermediate slide	T3 Lower slide valve
R1	Spring	T1 Upper slide valve	valve	V Calibrating plug

7.2 ABS electronic control unit

2 Disconnect the sensor wiring plug and free the wiring from any clips or ties **(see illustrations)**.
3 Undo the retaining bolt and remove the sensor.

Refitting

4 Refitting is a reversal of the removal procedure but note the following additional procedure when fitting a new sensor to the front hub swivel.
5 Fit the sensor with the adjuster screw loosened off. Position a feeler blade, of a thickness corresponding to the specified air gap, between the tip of the sensor and the toothed wheel. Tighten the retaining bolt to the specified torque. Make sure that the sensor tip, feeler blade and toothed wheel are in contact, then tighten the adjuster screw until its head shears off. Withdraw the feeler blade.
6 Refit the roadwheel and lower the vehicle.

7 ABS electronic control unit - removal and refitting

Modification: *Later models are fitted with a modified ECU and hydraulic unit. The brake stop-light switch is connected to the ECU by means of pin No. 12, as shown in the relevant wiring diagram*

Removal

1 Unbolt and remove the front passenger seat for access to the electronic control unit (ECU).
2 Unbolt the ECU and its cover plate from the brackets **(see illustration)**.

8.2a ABS wheel sensor - front brake

1	Wiring	4	Toothed wheel
2	Retaining bolt	5	Air gap
3	Adjuster screw (shear type)		

3 Disconnect the multi-plug and remove the ECU.

Refitting

4 Refit by reversing the removal operations.

8 ABS wheel sensor - removal and refitting

Removal

1 Raise and support the vehicle at the front and/or rear as applicable (see *"Jacking and vehicle support"*). Removal of the appropriate roadwheel will provide improved access.

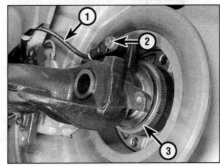

8.2b ABS wheel sensor - rear brake

1	Wiring
2	Retaining bolt and sensor
3	Toothed wheel

9 ABS hydraulic control block - removal and refitting

Removal

1 The hydraulic control block cannot be repaired. If it develops a malfunction then it must be renewed **(see illustration)**.
2 Detach the wiring connectors from the block.
3 Clean and disconnect the hydraulic pipes from the block.

9.1 ABS hydraulic control block

10

10.2 Handbrake console retaining screw positions (2 and 3)

4 Undo its retaining bolts and remove the block.

Refitting

5 Refitting is a reversal of the removal procedure. On completion, the brake hydraulic system will need to be bled.

---

10 Handbrake cable - removal, refitting and adjustment

Removal

1 Position chocks against the rear roadwheels, loosen the front roadwheel bolts, raise the front of the vehicle and support on safety stands (see "*Jacking and vehicle support*"). Remove the front roadwheels.
2 Working inside the vehicle, prise free the rear cubby from the centre console. Reach through the cubby aperture and undo the console retaining bolt at the rear **(see illustration)**.
3 Remove the rubber bung and unscrew and

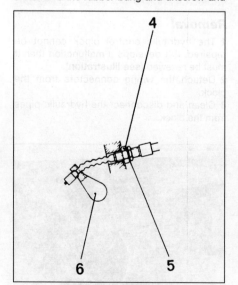

10.14a Handbrake cable adjustment at link rod end
4 Adjuster nut   5 Locknut   6 Lever

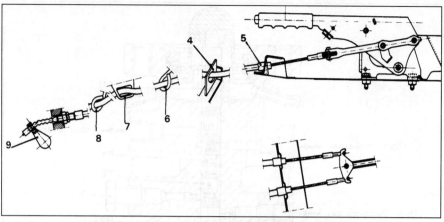

10.4 Handbrake cable attachment and location points

4 Cable guide on exhaust screen
5 Sheath stop
6 Scuttle panel guide
7 Wheel arch guide
8 Swivel arm guide
9 Connection to link rod

remove the console retaining bolt at the front. Lift the console clear, disconnecting any switch wires as necessary.
4 Release the handbrake then, at the caliper end of the cable, unhook the cable from the link rod **(see illustration)**.
5 Back inside the vehicle, pull the cable and disengage it from the compensator.
6 Withdraw the cable, passing it through the various location guides in the body.

Refitting

7 Refit in the reverse order of removal. As the cable is fitted, pass it through the guides in the following order.
a) Cable swivel guide
b) Cable wheel arch guide
c) Cable scuttle panel guide
d) Cable exhaust screen guide
8 When the cable is refitted and hooked onto

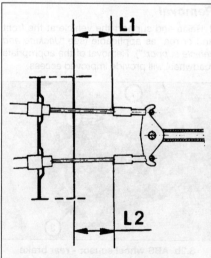

10.14b Check cables at compensator for equal adjustment
Distances at L1 and L2 to be equal (within 1.5 mm)

the compensator, check that the sheath stop is correctly positioned in its housing.
9 Lubricate the link rod and compensator cable connections but take care not to get grease onto the brake disc. Also lubricate the cable/wheel arch guide.
10 Check that the handbrake operates in a satisfactory manner and adjust if necessary.

Adjustment

11 Handbrake adjustment is automatic, being taken up when the handbrake travel reaches 12 to 15 notches.
12 Adjustment is possible after a new cable has been fitted by depressing the brake pedal and bringing the pads into contact with the discs. Release the pedal then move the handbrake lever to the 4th notch position.
13 Adjustment is now made at the link rod end of the cable. Loosen the locknut and turn the adjuster nut in the required direction to bring the lever (on the side being adjusted) into contact with the cam. Tighten the locknut.
14 Repeat the procedure with the cable to the other front wheel brake then check that the cable compensator is equalised **(see illustrations)**.
15 Check that, when the handbrake is released, the pads do not contact the disc irrespective of steering position. Tighten the locknuts then operate the handbrake several times to ensure that the handbrake is satisfactory. Refit the roadwheels and the console inside the vehicle.
16 Lower the vehicle, apply the handbrake and remove the chocks.

---

11 Brake pedal - adjustment

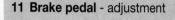

1 The clearances between the footbrake pedal and the rubber damper of the brake compensator control valve must be as specified. If not, loosen the locknut and adjust

the stop screw located over the pedal as necessary. Tighten the locknut when adjustment is complete (see illustrations 6.10a and 6.10b).

2 The pedal must now be checked for correct operation. First move the ground clearance lever fully to the minimum height position.

3 Loosen the pressure regulator bleed screw 1 to 1.5 turns.

4 Depress the brake pedal several times to release the pressure.

5 Fully depress the pedal three or four times, making sure that it returns to its stop freely.

6 Check that the clearance adjusted in paragraph 1 has not altered. The pedal operation is correct if the clearance remains the same.

7 Tighten the pressure regulator bleed screw.

12 Stop-lamp switch - adjustment

1 Before adjusting the stop-lamp switch, the footbrake pedal must be adjusted.

2 The stop-lamp switch is located beneath the footbrake pedal. The internal contacts should switch on the stop-lamps as soon as the pedal touches the brake valve.

3 If adjustment is necessary, loosen the switch locknut and turn the adjuster nut in the required direction. When the adjustment is correct retighten the locknut.

13 Hydraulic system - bleeding

Note: When bleeding the system on models fitted with ABS, the procedure is the same as given below for the standard braking system.

1 The system must be bled after renewing any components. If this procedure is not carried out, air will be trapped in the circuit and the brakes will not function correctly.

2 Before starting work, check all brake lines and connections for possible leakage.

3 If there is any possibility of fluid other than genuine LHM type being in the system, then drain the complete hydraulic system as described in Chapter 9 and fill it with the special rinsing solution obtainable from Citroën. Bleed the system and leave the solution in the circuit for approximately 600 miles (1000 km), then drain it out and fill with LHM fluid. If the rubber seals are damaged by the incorrect fluid, it will also be necessary to renew these items at the same time.

4 The brake bleeding procedure for the front and rear brakes differs, the procedures and requirements being given separately as follows.

Front brakes

5 When bleeding the front brakes, there must be no pressure in the hydraulic system. Undo the release screw by 1 to 1.5 turns on the pressure regulator (engine switched off).

6 You will now need two lengths of bleed tubing long enough to connect over the caliper bleed screws at one end, and to the reservoir at the other. The tubes must be transparent and clean.

7 Get an assistant to sit in the vehicle and depress the brake pedal.

8 Loosen the front brake bleed screws and restart the engine. Run the engine at idle speed and then, with the brake pedal still depressed, tighten the pressure regulator relief screw.

9 When the fluid flowing through each bleed hose to the reservoir shows no signs of air bubbles, retighten the bleed screws and release the brake pedal.

10 Switch off the engine and detach the bleed tubes from the calipers.

Rear brakes

11 The rear brakes draw their hydraulic fluid from the rear suspension system circuit and therefore, when bleeding the rear brakes, the circuit must be under pressure.

12 Check that the handbrake is fully applied and chock the front roadwheels.

13 Loosen the rear roadwheel bolts then raise and support the rear of the vehicle using safety stands (see "Jacking and vehicle support"). Remove the rear roadwheels.

14 Clean each rear brake bleed nipple then attach a length of transparent and clean hose to the nipple on each side. Place the free end of each hose into a clean container.

15 Allow the pressure in the rear suspension to drop, then move the height control lever within the vehicle fully rearwards to the "high" position.

16 Get an assistant to sit in the vehicle and depress the brake pedal. Restart the engine.

17 Loosen the bleed nipples approximately half a turn. The fluid will then flow through the bleed nipples into the jars.

18 When no more air bubbles are visible in the fluid, tighten the bleed nipples immediately then release the brake pedal. The pressure should now build up in the hydraulic system, with the suspension arms assuming the "high" position. If this fails to occur, increase the engine speed to 3000 rpm,

unscrew the pressure regulator bleed screw and leave it open for 30 seconds. Close the bleed screw, allow the engine to idle and recheck the position of the suspension arms.

Front and rear brakes

19 Remove the bleed tubes and locate the rubber caps over the bleed nipples.

20 Check the bleed nipples for leakage by fully depressing the brake pedal.

21 Switch off the engine, refit the roadwheels and lower the vehicle to the ground (where applicable).

22 Check and top-up the hydraulic fluid level in the reservoir.

Compensator control valve

23 Note that on some models fitted with ABS, the bleed nipple for the compensator control valve is located in the hydraulic line connection bracket on the bulkhead (see illustration).

Two slide valve type

24 Have the engine running and the hydraulic circuit pressurised with the brake pedal depressed.

25 Bleed at each of the three bleed screws, as follows:
   a) Control valve.
   b) Front brakes.
   c) Rear brakes.

Three slide valve type

26 Bleed at the two bleed screws.

27 If the compensator is removed and refitted for any reason, it will be necessary to bleed both it and the front and rear brakes. The compensator has a bleed nipple fitted into its top face towards the front.

28 When bleeding, the hydraulic system must be under pressure.

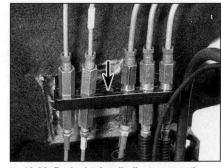

13.23 Brake hydraulic line connection bracket at bulkhead. Compensator valve bleed screw on some ABS models (arrrowed)

10

Notes

Chapter 11
Suspension and steering

Contents

Degrees of difficulty

Easy, suitable for novice with little experience	**Fairly easy,** suitable for beginner with some experience	**Fairly difficult,** suitable for competent DIY mechanic 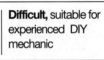	**Difficult,** suitable for experienced DIY mechanic	**Very difficult,** suitable for expert DIY or professional

Specifications

Suspension

Front type	Independent, with upper and lower arms and steering knuckle, hydropneumatic suspension cylinders supplied with fluid from main hydraulic system via front height corrector, anti-roll bar, bump and rebound stops
Rear type	Independent, with trailing arms, hydropneumatic suspension cylinders supplied with fluid from main hydraulic system via rear height corrector, anti-roll bar, bump and rebound stops

Height - normal driving position (engine idling):
Front . . . . 166 $+ \frac{10}{-7}$ mm

Rear . . . . 223 $+ \frac{10}{-7}$ mm

Anti-roll bar diameter:
Front:
  BX 19 GTi, BX 19 GTi 16v and Estate . . . . 23.0 mm
  All other models . . . . 22.5 mm
Rear:
  BX and BX 14 . . . . 16.5 mm
  BX 16 and BX 19 (not Estate) . . . . 17.0 mm
  BX 16 and BX 19 (Estate) . . . . 18.0 mm
  BX 19 GTi and BX 19 GTi 16v (pre March 1989) . . . . 19.0 mm
  BX 19 GTi 16v (from March 1989) . . . . 21.0 mm

Steering

Type . . . . Rack-and-pinion with optional power steering, steering column with universal joint and coupling

Turns (lock to lock):
  Manual steering 3.76
  Power steering 2.83
Shaft length:
  Manual steering . . . . 384.5 mm
  Power steering . . . . 329.5 mm

Wheel alignment

Front:
Toe-out	0 to 3 mm
Camber angle	0° ± 30'
Castor angle	2° ± 35'
Wheel offset	- 7.9 mm

Rear:
Toe-in	1.6 to 5 mm
Camber angle	- 1 ± 20'

Wheel hub bearings

Type	Twin track ball-bearings

Wheels

Type	Pressed steel or alloy

Size

Steel:
BX and BX 14	4.50 B 14 FH 4.30 or 120 TR 365 FH 4.30
BX 14 Estate	4.50 B 14 FH 4.30
BX 16	120 TR 365 FH 4.30
BX 19	5.00 B 14 FH 4.25
BX 16 and BX 19 Estates	5.00 B 14 FH 4.25

Alloy:
BX 14 RE and BX 16	120 TR 365 FH 4.30
BX 16 RE	5.00 B 14 FH 4.25
BX 19	5.00 B 14 CH 4.25
BX 19 GTi	5 1/2 J 14 FH 4.18
BX 19 GTi 16v	6 J 14 CH 4.15

Tyres

Type	Radial ply, tubeless
Pressures	See end of "Weekly checks"

Torque wrench settings

	Nm	lbf ft
Front suspension		
Suspension strut unit upper mounting	20	14
Suspension strut to steering swivel	70	51
Suspension arm to steering swivel balljoint	30	22
Track rod balljoint	38	27
Suspension arm pivot (spindle) nut	160	116
Anti-roll bar connecting link	45	33
Anti-roll bar to subframe	27	20
Subframe bolts:		
BX and BX 14 (front, centre and rear)	57	41
BX 16 and BX 19 (front and centre)	57	41
BX 16 and BX 19 (rear)	95	69
Rear axle		
Suspension arm shaft	130	94
Anti-roll bar bearing flange	65	47
Axle mountings:		
Front	50	36
Rear	28	20
Steering		
Column upper mounting	12	9
Column upper joint clamp	20	14
Column lower flange joint	25	18
Rack mountings	57	41
Track rod inner to outer locknut	38	27
Track rod balljoint nut (outer)	38	27
Track rod balljoint nut (inner)	50	36
Roadwheels		
Bolts:		
Steel wheels	80	58
Alloy wheels	90	65
Hub nut (front and rear)	270	195
Lower suspension arm/hub carrier balljoint nut	30	22

1 General information

The suspension is of independent hydropneumatic type. At the front, it comprises a vertically mounted hydraulic suspension strut unit, a lower suspension arm and an anti-roll bar. The suspension cylinders are supplied with hydraulic fluid from the main hydraulic system via the front height corrector which is actuated by the front anti-roll bar. The anti-roll bar is attached to the suspension arms with two links.

A trailing arm rear suspension system is used. The rear suspension cylinders are supplied with hydraulic fluid from the main system via the rear height corrector. As with the front, the height corrector is actuated by the rear anti-roll bar.

Ground height clearance is adjusted with a lever mounted inside the vehicle, the lever being connected by operating rods to the front and rear height correctors. Automatic damping is incorporated in the suspension cylinders.

Steering is of rack-and-pinion type, mounted on a crossmember attached to the front subframe. The steering column incorporates a universal joint and a coupling.

Power steering is fitted to some models and this system incorporates a self-centring action which varies according to the speed of the vehicle. Power assistance is derived from a power-operated hydraulic ram cylinder mounted on the steering rack. The hydraulic pressure to the ram is supplied by the main suspension and braking system hydraulic circuit, the pressure being controlled by a flow distributor unit and a control valve.

2 Front wheel hub bearings - removal and refitting

Removal

1 Disconnect the relevant driveshaft from the outer hub. Unless necessary, do not withdraw the driveshaft from the differential housing but leave it in position and supported so that the inner joint is not strained.
2 Set the height control to the "low" position.
3 Remove the brake disc.
4 Insert two bolts into the threaded holes in the flange face of the hub and tighten them evenly in a progressive sequence to withdraw the hub from the hub carrier (swivel unit) **(see illustration)**.
5 Remove the bearing inner race from the hub using Citroën tool 2405-T or a similar puller. Take care not to damage the hub.
6 Extract the bearing retaining circlip from the inboard side of the hub carrier.
7 To remove the bearing from the hub carrier, Citroën tool OUT 30 71 04-T should be used **(see illustration)**. Apply grease to the tool friction washer (B). Tighten the centre bolt to push the bearing inwards.
8 If no special tool is available, fabricate a similar tool to that shown, or try removing the bearing by using a suitable tube drift to drive the bearing from the hub. The drift must locate on the outboard end of the bearing outer race and the bearing drifted inwards to remove it. Support the inboard side of the hub carrier during removal.
9 Clean and inspect the hub, hub carrier and bearings for signs of excessive wear or damage and renew as necessary. The inner and outer seals are integral with the bearing and cannot be renewed individually.
10 If the circlip was damaged or distorted during removal then it must be renewed.

Refitting

11 Refitting is a reversal of the removal procedure **(see illustrations)**.

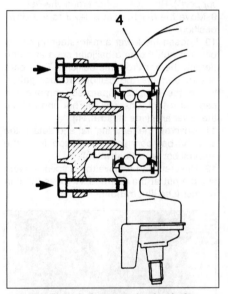

2.4 Front hub removal using bolts (arrowed). Note circlip location (4)

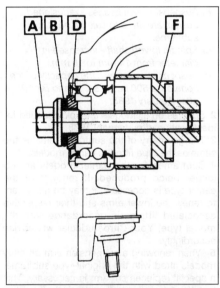

2.7 Citroën tool OUT 30 7104-T (A, B, D and F) assembled for bearing removal from hub carrier. Tighten centre bolt (A)

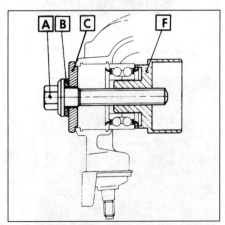

2.11a Reverse the position of tool item F to pull bearing into position in hub carrier. Note support plate C

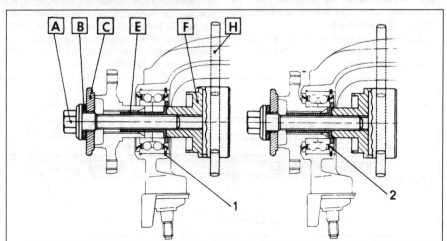

2.11b Hub refitting method using items shown from Citroën tool kit

11

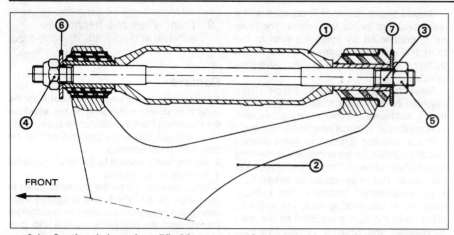

3.1a Sectional view of modified front suspension arm and associated components

1	Subframe	3	Pivot shaft
2	Suspension arm	4	Front nut
5	Rear nut	7	Rear washer
6	Front washer		

12 Take care when fitting the circlip not to damage the inboard seal and ensure that the circlip is fully engaged in its groove in the hub carrier.

13 Lubricate the hub with grease prior to fitting. Also lubricate the seal lips with grease.

14 Refit the driveshaft.

15 Refit the brake disc, taking care not to get grease onto the disc.

16 With the roadwheel refitted, spin it to ensure that the bearings run freely without excessive play or drag.

3 Front suspension arm - removal, overhaul and refitting

Modifications from September 1985

1 From the above date, all models are fitted with a modified front suspension arm which has a revised type of flexible pivot bush fitted **(see illustration)**. In addition to the suspension arm, the following associated items are also modified.

a) Subframe - of modified design and no longer fitted with taper roller bearings **(see illustration)**.

b) Suspension arm bushes - redesigned bushes are fitted to suit the new subframe.

c) Spindle (pivot) shaft - increased in diameter from 14 mm to 16 mm.

d) Suspension spheres - the capacity of the spheres is 500 cc on BX 16 and BX 19 after January 1988.

2 Spheres on all models are colour-coded for identification after January 1988.

3 The geometry of the subframe remains the same as the type fitted to earlier models.

4 Subframes for the earlier models are no longer being produced. If renewal of the earlier type is necessary, it may be necessary to renew the lower arms and their respective associated fittings in accordance with the model type. Your Citroën dealer will advise accordingly.

5 When renewing a suspension arm on early models fitted with the original-type subframe, a special replacement arm is necessary. This has the 14 mm spindle (pivot) shaft rubber bushes and washers **(see illustration)**.

6 When fitting the later-type suspension arms and subframe assemblies to early models, the suspension geometry remains the same and the original suspension spheres can be used.

7 Renewal of the suspension arm bushes on the later types is identical to that described for early types, as follows:

3.1b Later type of front suspension arm and subframe

Removal

8 Position chocks against the rear wheels, loosen the front roadwheel bolts then raise and support the vehicle at the front end on safety stands (see "Jacking and vehicle support"). Remove the front roadwheel(s).

9 Move the height control lever to the "low" position.

10 Loosen the lower arm-to-steering swivel balljoint nut, locate a balljoint separator and detach the arm from the balljoint. Take care not to damage the balljoint rubber gaiter. When the joint is separated, remove the separator tool, unscrew the nut and detach the lower arm **(see illustration)**.

11 Unscrew the retaining nut and detach the anti-roll bar connector track rod from the anti-roll bar **(see illustration)**.

12 Unscrew and remove the suspension arm spindle nut at the rear end. Remove the cup washer **(see illustration)**.

3.10 Separate swivel balljoint from suspension arm

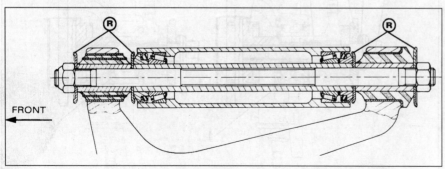

3.5 Special replacement suspension arm with 14 mm diameter pivot shaft
R Washers

3.11 Anti-roll bar and connecting rod. Remove retaining nut (arrowed)

3.12 Remove suspension arm retaining nut at rear (arrowed)

3.13a Remove suspension arm retaining nut at front (arrowed)

3.13b Front suspension arm spindle removal method using Citroën special tools

13 Unscrew and remove the suspension arm spindle nut at the front end **(see illustration)**. Support the suspension arm and withdraw the spindle to the front. It may be necessary to attach a slide hammer to remove the spindle **(see illustration)**. As the spindle is withdrawn from the suspension arm and subframe, make a note of the location of the cup washers and any shims or spacers used.

Overhaul

14 If the pivot bushes in the suspension arm are worn and in need of replacement, then it is also probable that the pivot bearings in the subframe are also in need of renewal.
15 To remove the bushes from the suspension arm, first mount the arm in a soft jaw vice.
16 If possible, use Citroën tool 7104-T to remove the bushes and subsequently refit them. If this tool is not available, you will need to fabricate a similar tool which comprises a length of threaded rod (14 mm diameter), some tube spacers, nuts and washers. The threaded rod should be of suitable length to pass through both suspension arm eyes and protrude enough at each end to enable the spacers and nuts to be fitted so that the bushes can be withdrawn.
17 Remove the rear bush first. Fit the tool through the arm and tighten the nut as indicated (at the front end of the rod) to draw the rear bush from its housing **(see illustration)**.
18 Reverse the procedure to withdraw the front bush **(see illustration)**. Care must be taken during the removal and refitting of the bushes not to distort the suspension arm by applying excessive force.
19 Clean out the bush bores in the suspension arm.
20 Draw the front bush into position by reversing the withdrawal procedure. When fitted, the bush must be positioned as shown **(see illustration)**.
21 Lubricate the rear bush before drawing it into position with a rubber lubricant or liquid soap. Check that the bush is correctly aligned when fitting and locate the index mark on the outer face to the rear **(see illustrations)**.

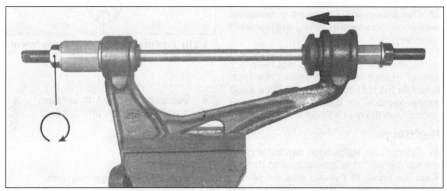

3.17 Suspension arm rear bush removal using Citroën special tool. Note direction of removal (arrowed)

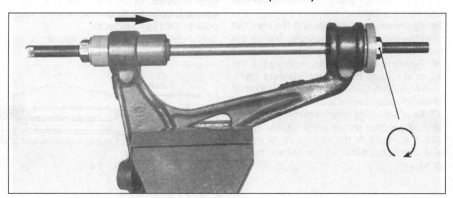

3.18 Suspension arm front bush removal using Citroën special tool. Note direction of removal (arrowed)

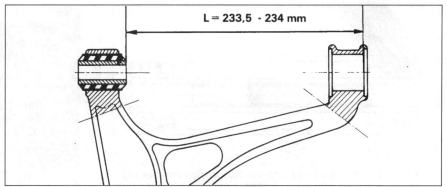

L = 233,5 - 234 mm

3.20 Suspension arm front bush position

11

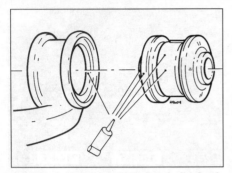

3.21a Lubricate suspension arm rear bush prior to fitting

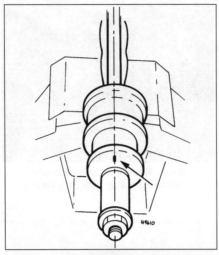

3.21b Position rear bush with alignment mark as shown

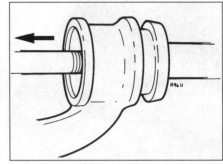

3.21c Draw rear bush into suspension arm eye in direction indicated

22 Check the spindle for signs of excessive wear or damage before refitting and renew it if necessary.

23 Fit a new Nylstop nut onto the front end of the spindle and position it so that there is 7 mm of thread exposed beyond the nut. Lubricate the spindle with grease. Slide a cup washer into position against the inner face of the nut, with the cupped side towards the nut.

Refitting

24 Relocate the suspension arm and engage the spindle. As the spindle is pushed through (from the front), fit the cup washers so that they are facing the subframe **(see illustration)**. If it was removed, ensure that the adjustment shim for the subframe bearings is refitted.

25 Fit the rear cup washer and the plain nut onto the rear end of the spindle. Tighten the nuts hand tight.

26 Reconnect the balljoints, ensuring that the joints are clean but do not lubricate them. New Nylstop nuts must be used and tightened to the specified torque settings.

27 Final tightening of the spindle (pivot) nuts to the specified torque must be carried out with the weight of the vehicle on its wheels and the suspension in the normal driving position.

4 Subframe/front suspension arm bearings - removal and refitting

Removal

1 Remove the front suspension arm.

2 If the subframe unit or spacers are being renewed, then the bearing free play will need to be adjusted. As this necessitates the use of special Citroën tools, bearing renewal should be entrusted to your dealer.

3 Withdraw the spacer tube, washer, spacer

and seal and the bearing inner race from the front end **(see illustration)**. Take note of the fitted position of the seal.

4 To remove the front bearing track, Citroën tool 1671-T will be required. This tool has an expanding end piece fitted which can be passed through the bearing track and expanded beyond the inside diameter of the bearing track. The tool can then be used as a slide hammer to withdraw the bearing track **(see illustration)**.

5 The rear bearing assembly is removed in a similar manner to that described for the front bearing. Note that an adjustment shim is located between the bearing and spacer. When removing the rear outer bearing track, Citroën recommend that the bearing be driven out from the front end rearwards. This will entail fitting Citroën tool 6308-T onto the end of the special tool 1671 -T **(see illustration)**.

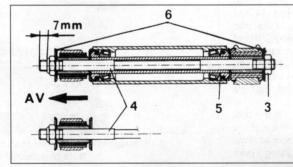

3.24 Cross-section view of suspension arm, spindle and subframe. Arrow indicates front

3 Retaining nut - rear
4 Spindle
5 Adjustment shim
6 Cup washers

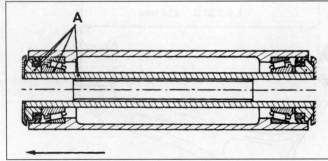

4.3 Cross-sectional view of subframe/suspension arm bearing
Remove items A for access to remove front bearing track
Arrow indicates front

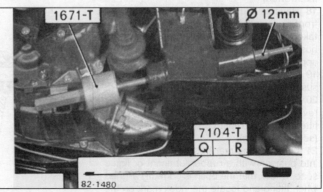

4.4 Citroën special tools in position to remove front bearing track

4.5 Citroën special tools in position to remove rear bearing track

4.7 Bearing, seal and spacer assemblies, rear (top) and front (lower). Note shim location for rear bearing

Refitting

6 Refitting is a reversal of the removal procedures. Drive the new bearing tracks into position and ensure that they are fully fitted and flush against the inner shoulder.

7 Lubricate the new bearing races before fitting. Ensure that the adjustment shim is located between the rear bearing and the spacer (see illustration).

8 Fit new seals onto the spacer washers, ensuring that they face the correct way, as noted during removal.

9 Refit the suspension arm on completion and check that it pivots freely but without excessive play before reconnecting it to the steering swivel hub.

<table>
<tr><td>**5**</td><td>**Front hydraulic suspension unit** - removal and refitting</td></tr>
</table>

Removal

1 Loosen the front roadwheel bolts, chock the rear roadwheels and then raise and support the vehicle at the front end on safety stands (see "Jacking and vehicle support"). Remove the front roadwheel(s).

2 Undo the pressure release screw on the pressure regulator by 1 to 1.5 turns and move

the height control lever to the "low" position.

3 If a suitable spare jack is available, position it under the suspension unit on the side concerned and raise it to disperse as much oil as possible from the suspension unit being removed. This procedure is recommended rather than essential.

4 Unscrew and remove the sphere from the suspension unit at the top end (within the engine compartment). Grip the sphere with a chain or strap wrench to loosen it, then unscrew it by hand. It is important to note at this stage that the sphere support should not be removed (see illustration).

5 Unscrew and detach the rigid feed pipe union from the sphere support. Plug the union and port.

6 Undo the three top mounting nuts and unbolt and detach the rigid feed pipe location clips.

7 Working under the wheel arch, detach the hydraulic overflow and vent pipes (see illustration).

8 Unscrew and remove the swivel hub-to-suspension unit clamp bolt and nut (see illustration). Prise open the clamp using a suitable lever and separate the suspension unit from the hub. The suspension unit can then be withdrawn.

Refitting

9 Refitting is a direct reversal of the removal procedure, but note the following:

a) Tighten the retaining nuts and bolts to the specified torque settings

b) Ensure that the hydraulic pipe and hose connections are unplugged and clean before reconnecting them. When reconnecting the feed pipe union use a new seal

c) Ensure that the overflow return and vent pipe connections are correctly made

d) When refitting the sphere to the support, grease the mating face of the support

10 On completion, tighten the release screw on the pressure regulator unit, top-up the fluid level as required and check that the height control system operates correctly.

<table>
<tr><td>**6**</td><td>**Front anti-roll bar** - removal and refitting</td></tr>
</table>

Modification: From 1987, the front anti-roll bar bearings incorporate a rubber bush instead of the earlier plastic half-shells. This bush may be fitted to earlier bars but both bushes must be renewed. When fitting, make sure both bush and bar are dry. Centre the bar within the subframe and only tighten the bush fixing bolts when the vehicle is at normal driving height, with its roadwheels on the ground.

1 Jack-up the front of the vehicle and support it on axle stands (see "Jacking and vehicle support"). Chock the rear wheels then remove the front wheels.

2 Move the ground clearance lever fully to the minimum height position.

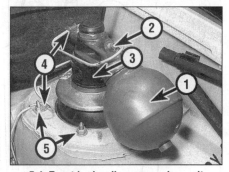

5.4 Front hydraulic suspension unit

1 Sphere
2 Rigid feed pipe union
3 Sphere support
4 Pipe clamps
5 Top mounting nuts (inboard side)

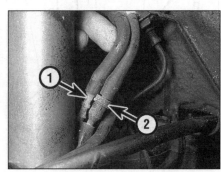

5.7 Hydraulic overflow (1) and vent (2) pipe connections under the wheel arch

5.8 Swivel hub-to-suspension unit clamp bolt (arrowed)

11

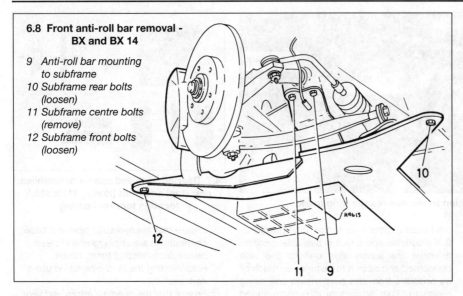

6.8 Front anti-roll bar removal - BX and BX 14

9 Anti-roll bar mounting to subframe
10 Subframe rear bolts (loosen)
11 Subframe centre bolts (remove)
12 Subframe front bolts (loosen)

6.9 Front anti-roll bar removal - BX 16 and BX 19

3 Relay   6 Height control
4 Relay   linkage collar
5 Balljoint

3 Loosen the hydraulic system pressure regulator bleed screw 1 to 1.5 turns.

4 Undo the retaining nut and detach the anti-roll bar link rod on each side.

5 Raise and support the steering swivels as high as possible then move the height control lever to the "normal" height position.

6 Mark the anti-roll bar and height corrector clamp in relation to each other, then unscrew the clamp bolt and remove the clamp.

7 The procedures now differ according to model.

BX and BX 14

8 Loosen the front subframe securing bolts at the front and rear by approximately 10 mm and leave them set at this position. Now unscrew and remove the subframe centre securing bolts (see illustration).

BX 16 and BX 19

9 Disconnect the gear control linkage rods and position the relay (3) to detach the balljoint and locate the relay (4) at the rear of the anti-roll bar (see illustration).

10 Move the protector back out of the way then loosen the collar securing bolts on the left-hand end of the anti-roll bar (see illustration).

11 Follow the procedure described in paragraph 8.

All models

12 Unscrew and remove the anti-roll bar-to-subframe mounting bolt and nut on each side. Remove the anti-roll bar components but leave collar and protector in position on the right-hand side.

13 Slacken the flange from the hydraulic return pipes (see illustration).

14 Detach the hydraulic return pipes from the left-hand suspension cylinder (see illustration).

15 To remove the anti-roll bar, move it towards the right-hand side, underneath the left-hand driveshaft, then back towards the left. Move the right-hand side of the bar towards the inner body. Now locate the left-hand end of the bar between left-hand lower suspension arm and the steering arm and remove it.

16 Before refitting the anti-roll bar, relocate the protector and collar so that they are in a straight position (see illustration).

17 Refitting is mostly a reversal of the removal procedure but note the following.

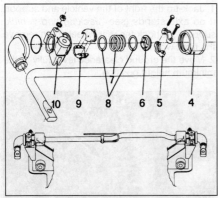

6.10 Anti-roll bar and associated components

4 Protector   8 Washer
5 Collar   9 Balljoint
6 Thrust cap   10 Bearing
7 Spring

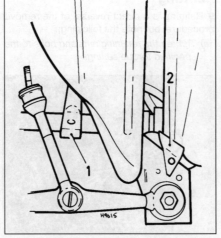

6.13 Anti-roll bar (1) and hydraulic circuit return pipe flange (2)

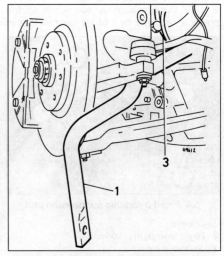

6.14 Anti-roll bar (1) and hydraulic return pipes (3) on left-hand side

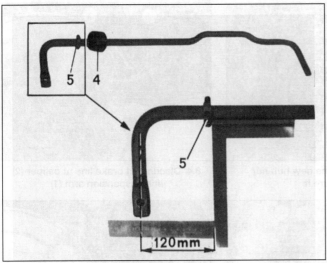
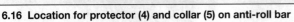

6.16 Location for protector (4) and collar (5) on anti-roll bar

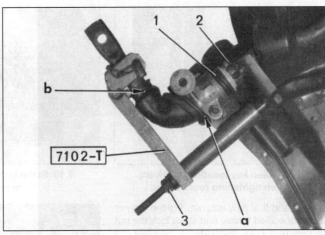

6.20 Front anti-roll bar adjustment using Citroën tool 710 2-T

1	Spring	3	Nut	b	Collar clip
2	Collar	a	Protector clip

18 Lubricate the respective parts with grease prior to assembling them onto the anti-roll bar. Tighten the anti-roll bar bearing to sub-frame to the specified torque setting.

19 Refit the central subframe retaining screw then tighten the front, centre and rear subframe retaining bolts (in that order) to their specified torque settings.

20 The anti-roll bar will now need to be adjusted and to do this Citroën tool 7102-T is necessary. Locate the tool so that it rests behind the collar, and tighten the nut so that the spring coils are touching **(see illustration)**. Loosen the nut 1 full turn and then tighten the collar.

21 Lubricate the anti-roil bar bearings with Total Multis MS grease (about 30 grams), then refit the protectors and their circlips.

22 Reconnect the anti-roll bar to the link rods and tighten the nuts to the specified torque setting.

23 On completion, check the vehicle height settings.

7 Rear wheel hub bearings - removal and refitting

Removal

1 Remove the rear wheel trim, prise free the hub cap, being careful not to distort it, then loosen (but do not remove at this stage) the hub nut and the roadwheel bolts **(see illustrations)**.

2 Raise and support the rear of the vehicle so that the rear roadwheels are clear of the ground (see "Jacking and vehicle support"). Remove the roadwheel from the side concerned.

3 Remove the rear brake pads and the brake caliper unit.

4 Undo the retaining screw and remove the brake disc.

5 Unscrew and remove the hub nut and the washer.

6 Withdraw the hub using a suitable puller or slide hammer **(see illustration)**.

7 Remove the bearing inner race using a suitable puller.

8 Remove the hub seal thrust cup.

9 Clean the components and inspect for excessive wear or damage. Renew as necessary.

Refitting

10 Using a suitable tube drift, tap the thrust cup into position **(see illustration)**.

7.1a Prise free the hub cap . . .

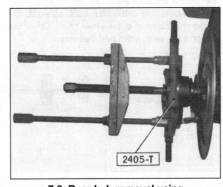

7.6 Rear hub removal using Citroën tool 2405-T

11 Refit the hub inner race by driving it home using the hub nut and a suitable bush. Clean and lubricate the race with grease.

12 Engage the hub onto the stub axle and drive it partially into position so that the thread of the stub axle protrudes a sufficient amount to allow the hub nut to be fitted onto it. Complete the refitting of the hub by tightening the hub nut. Prevent the stub axle from turning by holding it with an Allen key from the rear **(see illustration)**.

13 With the hub fitted, remove the nut. Clean and lubricate the hub/stub axle and bearing outer face with grease then locate the hub

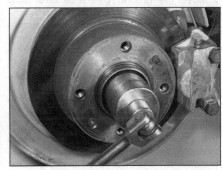

7.1b . . . and loosen the hub nut

7.10 Rear hub thrust cup (5) - fitting method with Citroën tool

11

7.12 Allen key location (arrowed) when tightening rear hub nut

7.13 Stake lock the new hub nut to secure it

8.4 Disconnect brake line at caliper (2) and suspension arm (1)

washer and fit a new hub nut. Tighten the nut to the specified torque and stake lock the nut to secure it **(see illustration)**. Remove the Allen key used to hold the stub axle then check that the hub spins freely.
14 Tap the hub cap into position.
15 Refit the brake disc and brake unit.
16 Refit the roadwheel and lower the vehicle to the ground.

8 Rear suspension arm - removal, overhaul and refitting

Removal

1 Jack-up the rear of the vehicle and support it on axle stands (see "*Jacking and vehicle support*"). Apply the handbrake and remove the rear roadwheel.
2 Move the ground clearance lever fully forward to the minimum height position.
3 Loosen the hydraulic system pressure regulator bleed screw 1 to 1.5 turns.
4 Unscrew the rear brake line union nut from the caliper and disconnect the brake line from the clip on the suspension arm top face **(see illustration)**.
5 Working underneath the vehicle, extract the pin and remove the anti-roll bar clamp on the side concerned **(see illustration)**.
6 Support the suspension arm with a jack then unscrew and remove the pivot shaft nut, withdraw the shaft then allow the suspension arm to drop to the vertical for removal **(see illustration)**.

Overhaul

7 Remove the brake caliper and disc.

8.5 Remove pin (3) and clamp (4) from anti-roll bar

8.6 Remove the suspension arm pivot bolt (6)

8 Remove the wheel hub and bearings from the stub axle.
9 The brake backplate can be removed by undoing the three retaining bolts.
10 To remove the pivot bearings from the suspension arm, first mount the arm in a vice fitted with soft jaws but do not grip the arm by the brake caliper lug.
11 To remove the bearings you will need Citroën tools 1671 -T and 7104-T, also expanding mandrels 12 mm and 35 mm in diameter.
12 Pass tool 1671-T through the pivot bore and locate the 12 mm diameter mandrel onto the tool. If this particular Citroën tool is not available, a proprietary slide hammer and mandrel of suitable dimensions will do the job **(see illustration)**.
13 Withdraw the bearing tube, bearing cone, seal and spacer.
14 Use a suitable tube drift to pass through the suspension arm and butt against the opposing bearing cone inner race. Drive out the spacer, seal, shim and bearing.

15 Insert the 35 mm diameter mandrel into the bearing cone within the suspension arm and attach the mandrel to a slide hammer and draw the bearing out. Repeat the procedure on the opposing bearing cone and, if re-using the bearings, keep them with their respective assemblies.
16 If the suspension arm is being renewed, then the bearing free play will need to be adjusted. As this necessitates the use of specialised tools, this task should be entrusted to your Citroën dealer.
17 Reassembly of the bearings is a reversal of the removal procedure. Ensure that the bearing housings in the suspension arm are cleaned out thoroughly **(see illustration)**.
18 Drive the outer races (cups) into position so that they are flush against the inner shoulder.
19 Lubricate the bearing cones with bearing grease when refitting them.
20 Ensure that the adjustment shim is fitted between the bearing cone and the seal when reassembling the outer (wheel hub side) bearing assembly.

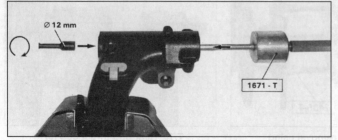

8.12 Rear suspension arm bearing removal tools

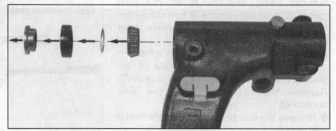

8.17 Outer bearing cone, shim, seal and spacer fitted to rear suspension arm

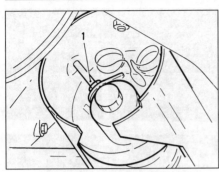

9.5 Disconnect supply pipe (1)
at rear suspension unit
(shown with sphere removed)

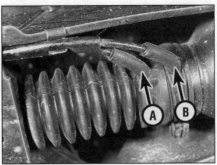

9.6 Rear suspension unit vent pipe (A)
and return pipe (B)

9.7 Rear suspension unit rod clip

21 Refit the brake backplate, caliper unit and wheel hub assemblies to the suspension arm.

Refitting

22 When refitting the suspension arm to the vehicle, grease the pivot shaft along its entire length before inserting it. Ensure that the brake hose is positioned towards the rear of the arm. Use a new Nylstop nut to secure the pivot shaft and tighten it to the specified torque.

23 Check that the suspension arm pivots freely without excessive binding or free play then reconnect the anti-roll bar and tighten the mounting clamp bolts to the specified torque. Relocate the suspension cylinder rod pin.

24 Use a new seal when reconnecting the brake hose to the caliper and engage the brake line in the location clip on the location arm.

25 Bleed the brakes and refit the roadwheel to complete.

9 Rear hydraulic suspension unit - removal and refitting

Removal

1 Loosen the rear roadwheel bolts, check that the handbrake is fully applied and check the front roadwheels. Raise the vehicle at the rear and support on safety stands (see "*Jacking and vehicle support*"). Remove the rear roadwheel(s).

2 Undo the pressure release screw on the pressure regulator by 1 to 1.5 turns and move the height control lever to the "low" position.

3 If a suitable spare jack is available, position it under the suspension arm and raise the rear suspension arm. This will disperse most of the fluid from the suspension cylinder.

4 Unscrew and remove the pneumatic sphere using a chain or strap wrench.

5 Unscrew and detach the rigid supply pipe at the union to the cylinder unit **(see illustration)**.

6 Disconnect the vent pipe and overflow return pipe from the cylinder **(see illustration)**.

7 Withdraw the suspension rod clip **(see illustration)**.

8 Allow the arm to hang free and pass the suspension rod between the subframe rear section and the stop. The suspension cylinder unit can then be withdrawn.

Refitting

9 Refitting is a reversal of the removal procedure. Note the following:

a) *When refitting the cylinder into position, engage the suspension rod and locate the spring end part to the rear of the cylinder union*

b) *Ensure that the supply pipe union is perfectly clean and use a new seal when reconnecting*

c) *When refitting the pneumatic sphere, use a new seal and grease the support face of the cylinder*

10 On completion, tighten the release screw on the pressure regulator unit, top-up the fluid level as required and check that the height control system operates correctly.

10 Rear anti-roll bar - removal and refitting

Modification: *From March 1989, with the increase in bar diameter, the ends of the bar fitted to BX 19 GTi 16v models are located by splines instead of flats. The following procedures are unaffected.*

Removal

1 Check that the handbrake is fully applied and chock the front roadwheels. Loosen the rear roadwheel bolts.

2 Start the engine, allow it to idle and move the ground clearance lever to the fully raised position. Once fully raised, switch off the engine.

3 Jack up the rear of the vehicle so that the rear wheels are clear of the ground and support with safety stands (see "*Jacking and vehicle support*"). Remove the rear roadwheels.

4 Move the ground clearance lever back to the "normal" height setting.

5 Mark the anti-roll bar and height corrector clamp in relation to each other, then unscrew and remove the clamp bolt **(see illustration)**.

6 Unscrew and remove the anti-roll bar mounting flange each side, at the same time noting the location of the bearing flange blocks and thrust plates.

7 Move the anti-roll bar towards the right-hand side then withdraw it from the left-hand side.

Refitting

8 To refit the anti-roll bar, reverse the removal procedure.

9 Locate the thrust plate between the bar and the arm before refitting the bearing flange block each side. Tighten the bearing flange block bolts to the specified torque.

10 Re-engage the height corrector automatic control with the manual control setting still in the "normal" position. Align the clamp-to-anti-roll bar marks made during removal, semi-tighten the clamp bolt and check that the control articulation point free play is between 1.5 to 2.0 mm. Adjust the clearance if necessary and then tighten the clamp bolt.

11 Refit the rear roadwheels and lower the vehicle to the ground.

12 Check and if necessary adjust the vehicle height.

11

10.5 Rear anti-roll bar and height
corrector clamp

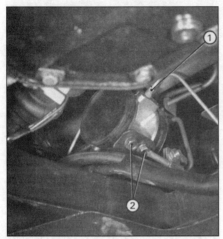

11.5 Front height corrector location, showing feed pipe (1) and retaining bolts (2)

11 Suspension height correctors - removal and refitting

Removal

1 Jack-up the front or rear of the vehicle and support it on axle stands (see "*Jacking and vehicle support*").
2 Move the ground clearance lever to the minimum height position. Unscrew the pressure regulator bleed screw 1 to 1.5 turns.
3 Remove the right-hand side roadwheel.
4 Remove the plastic height corrector cover (where fitted).
5 Identify all the hydraulic pipes for location then disconnect them from the corrector **(see illustration)**.
6 Unscrew the mounting bolts, disconnect the balljoint from the control lever and withdraw the height corrector from the vehicle **(see illustration)**.
7 It is not possible to repair the height correctors. If faulty, they must be renewed.

Refitting

8 Refitting is a reversal of removal. The balljoint should be lubricated with multi-purpose grease. Tighten the hydraulic pipe union screws to the specified torque. Check and adjust the suspension height after tightening the pressure regulator bleed screw.

12 Suspension height - adjustment

1 Check that the tyre pressures are correct. Ideally the vehicle should be parked over an inspection pit as access underneath the vehicle is required with it standing level and at its normal height.

Automatic height control

2 Set the ground clearance lever to the

11.6 Rear height corrector

"normal" position and start the engine. Allow the engine to run at idle speed.
3 Before making the height check, raise the vehicle by lifting it by hand as much as possible then release the weight and allow the vehicle to drop and rise, then stabilise. Before measuring the front height, move the vehicle back and forth slightly to relieve any stress in the suspension.
4 Check that the front and rear suspension heights are as given in *Specifications* **(see illustrations)**. Measure the suspension height at each end twice and take the mean of the two as the height reading.
5 If adjustment is necessary, it is made by rotating the automatic height control collar around the anti-roll bar **(see illustrations)**. When set, a clearance of 1.5 to 2.0 mm must exist between the balljoint and the bottom of its recess.

Manual height control

6 Set the automatic height control.
7 For adjustment at the front, loosen the bracket clamp bolt then move the bracket along the control rod to position the corrector control under the bracket pointer and meet

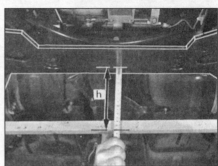

12.4a Front suspension height check
h = ground to axle unit rear crossmember

12.4b Rear suspension height check
h = ground to axle crossmember tube

the dimensions (a and b) shown **(see illustration)**. Tighten the clamp bolt.
8 For adjustment at the rear, set the reversing lever axis of rotation so that the corrector control is central in the reversing lever hole **(L1 and L2 in illustration 12.7)**.
9 With the engine still idling and the ground clearance lever still in the "normal" position, check the front and rear suspension heights as follows. Lift the vehicle by hand as far as possible, then release it and let it stabilise. Note the suspension height. Press the vehicle

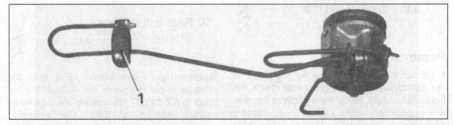

12.5a Front height corrector adjustment - move collar (1) as required around anti-roll bar

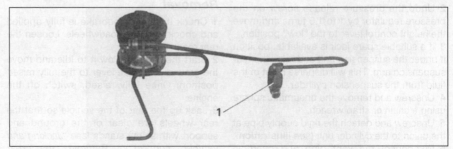

12.5b Rear height corrector adjustment - move collar (1) as required around anti-roll bar

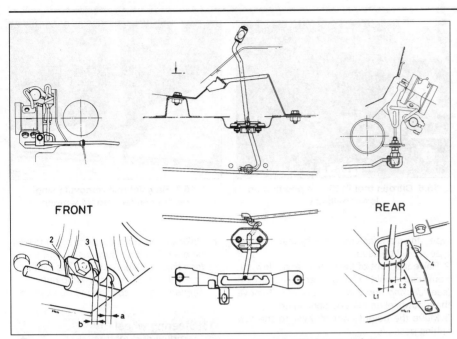

12.7 Automatic height control levers and adjustment points

Front	Rear
2 Bracket	4 Reversing lever
3 Bracket pointer	L1 to equal L2
a = 7 to 7.5 mm	
b = 4 to 4.5 mm	

down as far as possible, then release it and let it stabilise. Note the suspension height again. The average of the two measurements should be within the specified limits.

13 Track rod/balljoint - renewal

1 Set the steering wheel and the front roadwheels in the straight ahead position. Loosen the front roadwheel bolts then raise the vehicle at the front and support it on axle stands (see "*Jacking and vehicle support*"). Remove the roadwheel.
2 Loosen the track rod end balljoint nut then, using a suitable balljoint separator, detach the track rod from the steering arm on the swivel hub **(see illustrations)**.
3 At the inner end of the track rod, measure the amount of exposed thread and make a note of it. This will act as an adjustment guide when refitting the track rod **(see illustration)**.
4 Grip the inboard end of the track rod hexagonal section and unscrew the outer rod from it after loosening the locknut a quarter of a turn.
5 Screw on the new track rod to the same position as the old one and tighten the locknut one quarter of a turn. The section of exposed thread should measure the same as that noted during removal.
6 Ensure that the balljoint taper pin is clean and unlubricated, then insert it into the swivel

arm and tighten the retaining nut to the specified torque.
7 Refit the roadwheel and lower the vehicle to the ground.
8 Check the front wheel alignment.

13.2a Loosen the balljoint nut . . .

13.3 Track rod inner end showing the exposed thread

14 Steering swivel (knuckle) - removal and refitting

Removal

1 Remove the roadwheel trim, extract the split pin from the driveshaft and withdraw the lockplate from the nut.
2 Have an assistant depress the footbrake (with the engine running), then loosen the nut. An extension bar will be necessary as the nut is very tight.
3 Jack-up the front of the vehicle and support it on axle stands (see "*Jacking and vehicle support*"). Chock the rear wheels.
4 Remove the roadwheel and release the handbrake.
5 Move the ground clearance lever fully to the minimum height position.
6 Loosen the hydraulic system pressure regulator bleed screw 1 to 1.5 turns.
7 Undo the brake hose bracket bolts, the deflector retaining bolts and the two caliper securing bolts. Remove the caliper and suspend it from a suitable point so that the hydraulic lines are not distorted or stretched.
8 Disconnect the track rod balljoint.
9 Loosen the suspension arm-to-swivel balljoint and separate the joint using a balljoint separator, then remove the nut and disconnect the joint **(see illustration)**.
10 Unscrew and remove the hub nut, then pull the hub outwards and disengage the driveshaft from it.
11 Unscrew and remove the suspension

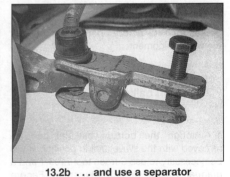

13.2b . . . and use a separator to detach the joint

14.9 Detaching steering swivel/suspension arm balljoint using Citroën separator

11

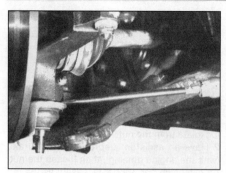

15.5 Prise free the protector plate

15.6 Citroën tool 7103-T in position on lower balljoint
1 Nut

15.7 Balljoint unit removal using recommended impact wrench

strut-to-swivel clamp bolt and nut. Prise apart the clamp and separate the swivel unit from the strut.

Refitting

12 Refitting is a reversal of removal. Note the following:
a) *Lubricate the hub seals with grease prior to refitting the driveshaft*
b) *The bottom balljoint stem must be wiped clean and be assembled dry. Use a new Nylstop nut*
c) *When reconnecting the suspension strut to the swivel, engage the centre tenon with the slot in the swivel. Use a new Nylstop nut to fasten the clamp bolt*
d) *The track rod-to-steering arm balljoint must be assembled dry and a new Nylstop nut used to secure*
e) *Wipe the driveshaft nut and threads with grease then tighten and secure*

13 On completion, check the steering and brakes for satisfactory operation and check the wheel alignment.

15 Steering swivel (knuckle) bottom balljoint - renewal

1 Although the bottom balljoint can be removed with the swivel unit in position, it will be necessary to use Citroën tool 7103-T and a manual impact wrench (Dynapact, Facom

type - the manufacturers specify that no other type should be used).
2 Raise the front of the vehicle and allow the front roadwheels to hang clear of the ground (see "*Jacking and vehicle support*"). Remove the roadwheel on the side concerned.
3 Move the height control lever to the low setting position.
4 Loosen the balljoint locknut, fit a balljoint separator to the joint and separate the lower suspension arm from the taper pin. Remove the separator and nut then detach the suspension arm from the balljoint.
5 Prise the protector plate from the balljoint rubber **(see illustration)**.
6 Locate special tool 7103-T into position on the balljoint and fasten with a nut **(see illustration)**.
7 Unscrew the balljoint unit from the swivel hub unit using the recommended impact wrench **(see illustration)**.
8 Refit in the reverse order to removal noting the following special points.
a) *When refitting the balljoint, use the special tools recommended and take care not to damage the rubber gaiter*
b) *When tightening the balljoint, stop the swivel from rotating. Bolt Citroën tool 6310-T into position on the hub using the wheel bolts as shown* **(see illustration)**. *Tighten the joint to the specified torque setting, then lock in position by peening into the notches at the points shown* **(see illustration)**

c) *Relocate the protector plate over the joint before refitting the suspension arm to it* **(see illustration)**. *Assemble the joint to arm dry and use a new Nylstop nut. Tighten it to the specified torque setting*

16 Steering wheel - removal and refitting

Early models

Removal

1 The steering wheel and upper column shaft are removed together. First disconnect the battery earth leads.
2 Remove the steering column lower shroud and facia by unscrewing the screws indicated **(see illustration)**.
3 Unscrew and remove the column universal joint upper bolt and loosen the lower bolt.
4 The universal joint can now be slid downwards to free the shaft splines.
5 Use a suitable pair of circlip pliers and release the circlip retaining the cup washer and spring, then withdraw the steering wheel and upper shaft.
6 If required, the ball-bearing units at the top and bottom ends of the column housing can

15.8a Type of tool used to prevent swivel hub from turning
1 Wheel bolts

15.8b Lock lower joint by stake punching at points indicated (a)

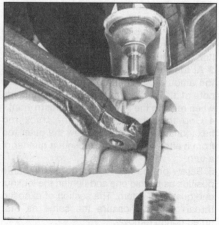

15.8c Carefully drive protector plate into position

16.2 Steering column lower shroud/ finishing panel retaining screw positions - left-hand drive shown

now be withdrawn. Use a suitable puller if necessary.

7 Two distinct upper steering column and wheel/shaft assembly types have been used **(see illustration)**.

Refitting

8 To refit the first type, locate the bearings into the column housing and insert the steering wheel/shaft. The centring cup must face towards the upper bearing. At the lower end, engage the spring, cup washer and circlip over the shaft.

9 To refit the second type, the bearings must be in position in the column. Fit the upper split ring to the steering wheel then insert the upper shaft and steering wheel. Locate the second split ring at the base of the lower bearing then engage the coil springs, cup washer and circlip over the shaft lower end.

10 To engage the circlip in the shaft groove,

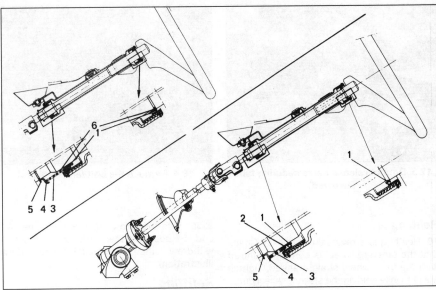

16.7 The first (lower) and second (top) steering column types

1 Ball-bearings
2 Centre cup - first type (chamfer to bearing)
3 Spring
4 Thrust cup
5 Circlip
6 Split rings

you will need to compress the coil spring and cup washer. In the workshop we engaged an open jaw spanner over the shaft and pulled the spanner upwards against the cup washer and spring so that the spanner cleared the spring. An assistant simultaneously moved the circlip into position in its groove and once engaged, the spanner was withdrawn **(see illustrations)**.

11 Align the upper steering shaft and refit it

to the universal joint. With the front roadwheels in the straight-ahead position, the steering wheel spoke should point vertically down and the pinion flange be parallel to the steering rack housing.

12 Refit the upper retaining bolt and tighten it and the lower bolt.

13 Refit the column lower shroud to complete.

Later models

Removal

14 Set the front wheels in the straight-ahead position.

15 Prise out the centre pad, then use a socket to unscrew the retaining nut **(see illustrations)**.

16 Mark the hub in relation to the inner column, then pull off the steering wheel. If it is tight, a rocking action may release it from the splines.

17 If required, the upper column oil seal can be prised free for renewal. Note the seal fitting position and orientation **(see illustration)**.

16.10a Use a spanner to compress the spring and washer . . .

16.10b . . . then locate the circlip in its groove

16.15a Remove the centre pad from the steering wheel . . .

16.15b . . . to expose wheel retaining nut (arrowed)

16.17 Upper steering column oil seal (arrowed)

11

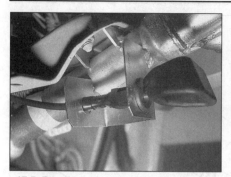

17.5 Bonnet release cable securing tabs (arrowed)

18.4 Remove the bolt (arrowed) . . .

18.5 . . . and press pin to withdraw the lock/switch unit

Refitting

18 Refitting is a reversal of removal. Check that the steering wheel is correctly centred with the front wheel straight-ahead. Tighten the nut while holding the steering wheel rim.

17 Steering column housing (early models) - removal and refitting

Removal

1 Remove the steering wheel and upper shaft.
2 Disconnect the steering lock/ignition switch wiring harness at the connector.
3 Raise and support the bonnet. Remove the air deflector grille in front of the radiator then detach the bonnet release cable from the lock unit. Retain the cable clamp and sheath stop.
4 Unscrew the four column housing mounting nuts and lower the column.
5 To remove the bonnet opening cable, squeeze the two tabs together behind the mounting bracket and withdraw the cable through the bracket (see illustration).

Refitting

6 Refitting is a reversal of the removal procedure. Ensure that the steering lock/ignition switch wiring harness passes over the steering column. Tighten the housing mounting nuts.

18 Steering lock/ignition switch (early models) - removal and refitting

Removal

1 Disconnect the battery earth lead.
2 Undo the retaining screws and remove the steering column lower shroud.
3 Detach the ignition switch wiring from the multi-connector.
4 Unscrew the small bolt with shakeproof washer from the switch unit housing (see illustration).
5 Set the ignition switch so that the key slot

aligns with the arrow mark between the "A" and "S" positions then press in the pin and withdraw the lock/switch unit (see illustration).

Refitting

6 Refitting is a reversal of the removal procedure. Check the operation of the steering lock and ignition switch functions to ensure that they are satisfactory on completion.

19 Steering column and lock (later models) - removal and refitting

Removal

1 Disconnect the battery earth lead, then undo the retaining screws and remove the lower steering column cover. As the cover is removed, detach the wiring connector from the dimmer switch and relay unit.
2 Remove the upper column cover and if required, the steering wheel.
3 Unscrew and remove the column clamp bolt from the intermediate shaft universal joint (see illustration).
4 Undo the upper column retaining bolts/nuts (see illustration) and carefully lower the column from its mountings. To fully withdraw the column, it will be necessary to detach the column switch wiring harness connectors.
5 If necessary, the intermediate shaft can be

removed after prising out the grommet and unscrewing the bottom clamp bolt.
6 To remove the steering lock, unscrew the retaining bolt then, with the ignition key turned to position A (first position), depress the plunger in the housing.

Refitting

7 Refitting is a reversal of removal.

20 Manual steering gear unit - removal and refitting

Removal

1 Chock the rear roadwheels and loosen the front roadwheel bolts. Raise the vehicle at the front and support on safety stands (see "Jacking and vehicle support"). Remove the front roadwheels.
2 Remove the lower steering column shroud, then loosen the column universal joint bolt on the lower left side.
3 Loosen the track rod outer balljoint nut then, using a balljoint separator, detach the joint. Remove the separator and nut then repeat the procedure on the opposing side track rod outer joint. Take care not to damage the balljoint rubber during separation.
4 Unscrew and remove the lower column flexible coupling retaining nuts (see illustration).
5 Detach and remove the heat shield from the

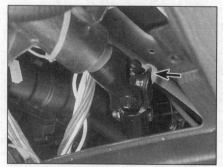

19.3 Steering intermediate shaft universal joint (arrowed)

19.4 Steering column upper retaining nut (arrowed)

20.4 Flexible coupling retaining nuts (arrowed)

20.5a Undo heat shield retaining screw (arrowed) . . .

20.5b . . . and release retaining clip on underside (arrowed)

20.7 Gearchange control pivot bolt and cover - BX 16 and BX 19

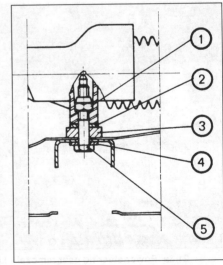

21 Power steering gear unit - removal and refitting

Removal

1 Chock the rear roadwheels and loosen the front roadwheel bolts. Raise the vehicle at the front and support on safety stands (see *"Jacking and vehicle support"*). Remove the front roadwheels.
2 Release the hydraulic system pressure by loosening the pressure regulator release screw 1 to 1.5 turns.
3 Rotate the steering wheel from lock to lock to remove as much hydraulic fluid as possible from the steering ram cylinder.
4 Working inside the vehicle, detach and remove the lower steering column shroud then loosen the upper steering column universal joint bolt and the joint-to-steering wheel shaft clamp bolt **(see illustration)**. Prise free the lower column-to-bulkhead gaiter.

steering gear unit. It is secured by a screw on the topside and a wire clip underneath **(see illustrations)**.
6 On BX and BX 14 models, loosen the bolt retaining the speedometer cable support and rotate the support towards the rack housing to disengage the speedometer cable.
7 On BX 16 and 19 models, undo the bolt and disconnect the gearchange control pivot from its balljoint **(see illustration)**.
8 Unscrew the two steering gear retaining bolts and withdraw them from the underside of the subframe **(see illustration)**. The steering gear can now be withdrawn from the side of the vehicle. As it is withdrawn, collect the thrustwashers and shims from the mounting points and mark them for identification. Keep them separate, as they

must be refitted to their original positions or the steering geometry will be upset.

Refitting

9 Refitting is a reverse of the removal procedure. Note the following;
a) *Locate the mounting thrustwashers and shims in their original positions (see illustrations)*
b) *Where fitted, always use new Nylstop nuts*
c) *Tighten all nuts and bolts to their specified torque settings*
d) *When reconnecting the steering column joints, ensure that alignment is correct*

10 On completion, check the front wheel alignment.

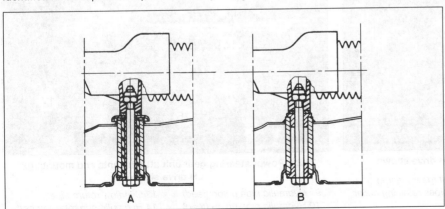

20.9a Steering gear mountings on pre 1984 models
A BX and BX 14   B BX 16 and BX 17

20.9b Steering gear mountings on models from 1984

1 Locknut	4 Flexible washer
2 Adjustment shim	5 Bolt
3 Spacer (11 mm thick)	

11

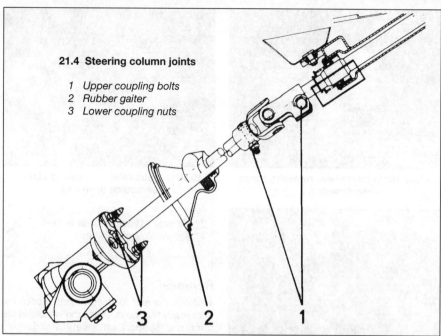

21.4 Steering column joints

1 Upper coupling bolts
2 Rubber gaiter
3 Lower coupling nuts

5 Undo the two lower column-to-flexible flange coupling nuts to disengage the coupling.

6 Loosen the track rod outer balljoint nut then, using a balljoint separator, detach the joint. Remove the separator and the nut and repeat the procedure on the opposite track rod outer balljoint. Take care not to damage the balljoint rubber during separation.

7 Unscrew the bolt and disconnect the gearchange control pivot from its balljoint.

8 Clean the hydraulic supply and return pipe unions at the steering ram connections, also the overflow pipe, then disconnect them from the ram. Plug them to prevent leakage and the ingress of dirt **(see illustrations)**.

9 Detach and remove the heat shield from the steering gear unit.

10 Undo the steering ram retaining bolt at each end and detach the ram from the steering gear unit.

11 Unscrew the two steering gear retaining bolts and withdraw them from the underside of the subframe.

12 The steering gear is now ready to be withdrawn. As it is withdrawn, collect the shims from each mounting, mark them for identification and keep them separate. The shims must be refitted to their original positions or the steering geometry will be upset. As the steering gear is removed, turn it fully on to the right-hand lock, engage the steering to the right and withdraw the steering gear from the underside of the vehicle.

Refitting

13 Refitting is a reversal of the removal procedure. Note the following:
a) Observe the special points outlined in Section 20, paragraphs 9 and 10
b) Use a new seal when reconnecting the high pressure supply pipe. The return pipe and the ram supply pipes do not have seals fitted
c) When reconnecting and securing the steering column universal joint, ensure that the steering is in the straight-ahead position and the steering wheel spoke is pointing downwards

14 Check the front wheel alignment on completion and top-up the hydraulic fluid system. Turn the steering from lock-to-lock with the engine running to ensure satisfactory action. Road test the vehicle.

22 Wheel alignment - checking and adjustment

1 Accurate wheel alignment is essential for good steering and slow tyre wear. Before checking, make sure that the suspension heights are correct and that the tyres are correctly inflated.

2 Place the vehicle on level ground with the wheels in the straight-ahead position.

3 With the ground clearance lever in the

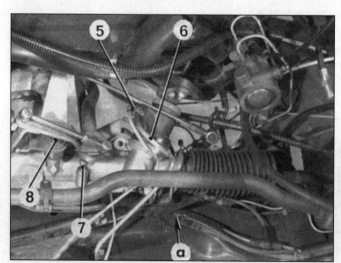

21.8a Power steering gear removal - LH drive shown

5 Supply pipe
6 Return pipe
7 Gearchange balljoint
8 Pivot bolt (gearchange)
a Return pipes retaining collar

21.8b Power steering gear unit attachments and mountings - LH drive shown

9 Hydraulic pipe union (feed)
10 Hydraulic pipe union (feed)
11 Heat shield
12 Hydraulic ram retaining bolt
13 Overflow return pipe
14 Hydraulic ram retaining bolt
15 Steering gear mounting bolts

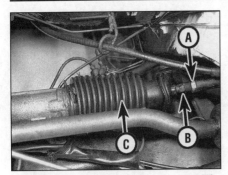

22.5 Track rod locknut (A), inner end (B) and rack gaiter (C)

"normal" position and the engine idling, measure the toe of the front wheels using a wheel alignment gauge. The amount of toe must be as given in *Specifications*.

4 If adjustment is necessary, proceed as follows to adjust the front wheel alignment.

5 Hold the track rod inner end stationary by fitting a spanner onto its hexagonal section and loosen the outer rod locknut **(see illustration)**. Repeat this procedure on the opposing track rod.

6 Adjustment is now made by turning the track rod inner end each side by an equal amount. It may also be necessary to release the steering gaiters to prevent them from distorting as the inner track rods are turned. Turn the track rod inner ends by an equal amount each side until the alignment is correct, then retighten the locknut on each side.

7 A further steering geometry check can be made by checking for any variation of the wheel alignment each side, then set between the normal (intermediate) and high position. The variation per wheel should be between 0.5 mm toe-out and 1.0 mm toe-in.

8 Any adjustment necessary in this instance is made by fitting an alternative shim between the steering gear rack housing and the axle. Shims are available in thicknesses of 0.5, 1.0 and 1.5 mm. A 1.0 mm thick shim gives an equivalent toe-out variation.

9 Castor and camber angles can only be checked with special equipment and this work is best entrusted to a Citroën garage. These angles are set in production and cannot be adjusted. Any deviation from specification must therefore be due to damage or gross wear in the suspension components.

Chapter 12
Bodywork and fittings

Contents

Degrees of difficulty

Easy, suitable for novice with little experience	**Fairly easy,** suitable for beginner with some experience	**Fairly difficult,** suitable for competent DIY mechanic	**Difficult,** suitable for experienced DIY mechanic 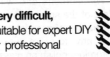	**Very difficult,** suitable for expert DIY or professional

1 General information

The main bodyshell and underframe are of all-steel monocoque construction. Certain components, such as the bonnet, tailgate, rear quarter panels and bumpers, are manufactured in synthetic material. Apart from their rust-free qualities, components manufactured from synthetic material reduce the total weight of the vehicle.

The bumpers are designed to be both light in structure and resistant to low speed impact.

Certain body panels are detachable to reduce the cost of repair and, where necessary, replacement.

The laminated windscreen is bonded in position and provides a considerable increase in the torsional rigidity of the bodyshell.

2 Vehicle exterior and interior - maintenance and inspection

Vehicle exterior

1 The general condition of a vehicle's bodywork is the one thing that significantly affects its value. Maintenance is easy but needs to be regular. Neglect, particularly after minor damage, can lead quickly to further deterioration and costly repair bills. It is important also to keep watch on those parts of the vehicle not immediately visible, for instance the underbody, inside all the wheel arches and the lower part of the engine compartment.

2 The basic maintenance routine for the bodywork is washing - preferably with a lot of water, from a hose. This will remove all the loose solids which may have stuck to the vehicle. It is important to flush these off in such a way as to prevent grit from scratching the finish. The wheel arches and underbody need washing in the same way to remove any accumulated mud which will retain moisture and tend to encourage rust, particularly in winter when it is essential that any salt (from that put down on the roads) is washed off. Oddly enough, the best time to clean the underbody and wheel arches is in wet weather when the mud is thoroughly wet and soft. In very wet weather the underbody is usually cleaned automatically of large accumulations; this is therefore a good time for inspection.

3 If the vehicle is very dirty, especially underneath or in the engine compartment, it is tempting to use one of the pressure washers or steam cleaners available on garage forecourts. Whilst these are quick and effective, especially for the removal of the accumulation of oily grime which sometimes is allowed to become thick in certain areas, their usage does have some disadvantages. If caked-on dirt is simply blasted off the paintwork, its finish soon becomes scratched

and dull and the pressure can allow water to penetrate door and window seals and the lock mechanisms. If the full force of such a jet is directed at the vehicle's underbody, the wax-based protective coating can easily be damaged and water (with whatever cleaning solvent is used) could be forced into crevices or components that it would not normally reach. Similarly, if such equipment is used to clean the engine compartment, water can be forced into the components of the fuel and electrical systems and the protective coating can be removed that is applied to many small components during manufacture; this may therefore actually promote corrosion (especially inside electrical connectors) and initiate engine problems or other electrical faults. Also, if the jet is pointed directly at any of the oil seals, water can be forced past the seal lips and into the engine or transmission. Great care is required, therefore, if such equipment is used and, in general, regular cleaning by such methods should be avoided.

4 A much better solution in the long term is just to flush away as much loose dirt as possible using a hose alone, even if this leaves the engine compartment looking dirty. If an oil leak has developed, or if any other accumulation of oil or grease is to be removed, there are one or two excellent grease solvents available, which can be brush applied. The dirt can then be simply hosed off. Take care to replace the wax-based protective coat, if this was affected by the solvent.

5 Normal washing of the bodywork is best carried out using cold or warm water with a proprietary car shampoo, tar spots can be removed either by using white spirit, followed by soapy water to remove all traces of spirit. Try to keep water out of the bonnet air inlets and check afterwards that the heater air inlet box drain tube is clear so that any water has drained out of the box.

6 After washing the paintwork, wipe off with a chamois leather to give an unspotted clear finish. A coat of clear protective wax polish, will give added protection against chemical pollutants in the air. If the paintwork sheen has dulled or oxidised, use a cleaner/polisher to restore the brilliance of the shine. This requires a little effort, but such dulling is usually caused because regular washing has been neglected. Care needs to be taken with metallic paintwork, as special non-abrasive cleaner/polisher is required to avoid damage to the finish.

7 Brightwork should be treated in the same way as paintwork.

8 Windscreens and windows can be kept clear of the smeary film which often appears, by the use of proprietary glass cleaner. Never use any form of wax or other body or chromium polish on glass.

Vehicle interior

9 Mats and carpets should be brushed or vacuum cleaned regularly to keep them free of grit. If they are badly stained remove them from the vehicle for scrubbing or sponging and make quite sure they are dry before refitting.

10 Where leather upholstery is fitted it should be cleaned only if necessary, using either a mild soap (such as saddle soap) or a proprietary leather cleaner; do not use strong soaps, detergents or chemical cleaners. If the leather is very stained, seek the advice of a Citroen dealer. Fabric-trimmed seats and interior trim panels can be kept clean by wiping with a damp cloth and a proprietary suitable cleaner. If they do become stained (which can be more apparent on light coloured upholstery) use a little liquid detergent and a soft nail brush to scour the grime out of the grain of the material. Do not forget to keep the headlining clean in the same way as the (fabric) upholstery.

11 When using liquid cleaners of any sort inside the vehicle, do not over-wet the surfaces being cleaned. Excessive damp could get into the seams and padded interior causing stains, offensive odours or even rot. If the inside of the vehicle gets wet accidentally it is worthwhile taking some trouble to dry it out properly, particularly where carpets are involved. *Do not leave oil or electric heaters inside the vehicle for this purpose.*

3 Minor body damage - repair

Repair of minor scratches in bodywork

If the scratch is very superficial and does not penetrate to the metal of the bodywork, repair is very simple. Lightly rub the area of the scratch with a paintwork renovator, or a very fine cutting paste to remove loose paint from the scratch and to clear the surrounding bodywork of wax polish. Rinse the area with clean water.

Apply touch-up paint or a paint film, to the scratch using a fine paint brush. Continue to apply fine layers of paint until the surface of the paint in the scratch is level with the surrounding paintwork. Allow the new paint at least two weeks to harden, then blend it into the surrounding paintwork by rubbing the scratch area with a paintwork renovator, or a very fine cutting paste. Finally apply wax polish.

Where the scratch has penetrated right through to the metal of the bodywork, causing the metal to rust, a different repair technique is required. Remove any loose rust from the bottom of the scratch with a penknife, then apply rust inhibiting paint, to prevent the formation of rust in the future. Using a rubber or nylon applicator fill the scratch with bodystopper paste. If required, this paste can be mixed with cellulose thinners, to provide a very thin paste which is ideal for filling narrow scratches. Before the stopper-paste in the scratch hardens, wrap a piece of smooth cotton rag around the top of a finger. Dip the finger in cellulose thinners, and quickly sweep it across the surface of the stopper-paste in the scratch; this will ensure that the surface of the stopper-paste is slightly hollowed. The scratch can now be painted over as described earlier in this Section.

Repair of dents in bodywork

When deep denting of the vehicle's bodywork has taken place, the first task is to pull the dent out, until the affected bodywork almost attains its original shape. There is little point in trying to restore the original shape completely, as the metal in the damaged area will have stretched on impact and cannot be reshaped fully to its original contour. It is better to bring the level of the dent up to a point which is about 3 mm below the level of the surrounding bodywork. In cases where the dent is very shallow anyway, it is not worth trying to pull it out at all. If the underside of the dent is accessible, it can be hammered out gently from behind, using a mallet with a wooden or plastic head. Whilst doing this, hold a suitable block of wood firmly against the outside of the panel to absorb the impact from the hammer blows and thus prevent a large area of the bodywork from being "belled-out".

Should the dent be in a section of the bodywork which has a double skin or some other factor making it inaccessible from behind, a different technique is called for. Drill several small holes through the metal inside the area - particularly in the deeper section. Then screw long self-tapping screws into the holes just sufficiently for them to gain a good purchase in the metal. Now the dent can be pulled out by pulling on the protruding heads of the screws with a pair of pliers.

The next stage of the repair is the removal of the paint from the damaged area and from an inch or so of the surrounding sound bodywork. This is accomplished most easily by using a wire brush or abrasive pad on a power drill, although it can be done just as effectively by hand using sheets of abrasive paper. To complete the preparation for filling, score the surface of the bare metal with a screwdriver or the tang of a file, or alternatively, drill small holes in the affected area. This will provide a really good key for the filler paste. To complete the repair see the Section on filling and respraying.

Repair of rust holes or gashes in bodywork

Remove all paint from the affected area and from an inch or so of the surrounding sound bodywork, using an abrasive pad or a wire brush on a power drill. If these are not available a few sheets of abrasive paper will do the job most effectively. With the paint removed you will be able to judge the severity of the corrosion and therefore decide whether to renew the whole panel (if this is possible) or to repair the affected area. New body panels are not as expensive as most people think and it is often quicker and more satisfactory to fit a new panel than to attempt to repair large areas of corrosion.

Remove all fittings from the affected area except those which will act as a guide to the original shape of the damaged bodywork (eg headlamp shells etc). Then, using tin snips or a hacksaw blade, remove all loose metal and any other metal badly affected by corrosion. Hammer the edges of the hole inwards in order to create a slight depression for the filler paste.

Wire brush the affected area to remove the powdery rust from the surface of the remaining metal. Paint the affected area with rust inhibiting paint, if the back of the rusted area is accessible treat this also.

Before filling can take place it will be necessary to block the hole in some way. This can be achieved by the use of aluminium or plastic mesh, or aluminium tape.

Aluminium or plastic mesh or glass-fibre matting, is probably the best material to use for a large hole. Cut a piece to the approximate size and shape of the hole to be filled, then position it in the hole so that its edges are below the level of the surrounding bodywork. It can be retained in position by several blobs of filler paste around its periphery.

Aluminium tape should be used for small or very narrow holes. Pull a piece off the roll and trim it to the approximate size and shape required, then pull off the backing paper (if used) and stick the tape over the hole; it can be overlapped if the thickness of one piece is insufficient. Burnish down the edges of the tape with the handle of a screwdriver or similar, to ensure that the tape is securely attached to the metal underneath.

Bodywork repairs - filling and respraying

Before using this Section, see the Sections on dent, deep scratch, rust holes and gash repairs.

Many types of bodyfiller are available, but generally speaking those proprietary kits are best for this type of repair which contain a tin of filler paste and a tube of resin hardener, or a 'No-Mix' which can be used directly from the tube. A wide, flexible plastic or nylon applicator will be found invaluable for imparting a smooth and well contoured finish to the surface of the filler.

Mix up a little filler on a clean piece of card or board - measure the hardener carefully (follow the maker's instructions on the pack) otherwise the filler will set too rapidly or too slowly. Alternatively, a 'No-Mix' can be used straight from the tube without mixing, but daylight is required to cure it. Using the applicator apply the filler paste to the prepared area; draw the applicator across the surface of the filler to achieve the correct contour and to level the surface. As soon as a contour that approximates to the correct one is achieved, stop working the paste - if you carry on too long the paste will become sticky and begin to pick-up on the applicator. Continue to add thin layers of filler paste at twenty minute intervals until the level of the filler is just proud of the surrounding bodywork.

Once the filler has hardened, excess can be removed using a metal plane or file. From then on, progressively finer grades of abrasive paper should be used, starting with a 40 grade production paper and finishing with a 400 grade wet-and-dry paper. Always wrap the abrasive paper around a flat rubber, cork, or wooden block - otherwise the surface of the filler will not be completely flat. During the smoothing of the filler surface the wet-and-dry paper should be periodically rinsed in water. This will ensure that a very smooth finish is imparted to the filler at the final stage.

At this stage, the dent should be surrounded by a ring of bare metal, which in turn should be encircled by the finely feathered edge of the good paintwork. Rinse the repair area with clean water, until all of the dust produced by the rubbing-down operation has gone.

Spray the whole area with a light coat of primer- this will show up any imperfections in the surface of the filler. Repair these imperfections with fresh filler paste or bodystopper and once more smooth the surface with abrasive paper. If bodystopper is used, it can be mixed with cellulose thinners to form a really thin paste which is ideal for filling small holes. Repeat this spray and repair procedure until you are satisfied that the surface of the filler and the feathered edge of the paintwork are perfect. Clean the repair area with clean water and allow to dry fully.

The repair area is now ready for final spraying. Paint spraying must be carried out in a warm, dry, windless and dust free atmosphere. This condition can be created artificially if you have access to a large indoor working area, but if you are forced to work in the open, you will have to pick your day very carefully. If you are working indoors, dousing the floor in the work area with water will help to settle the dust which would otherwise be in the atmosphere. If the repair area is confined to one body panel, mask off the surrounding panels; this will help to minimise the effects of a slight mis-match in paint colours. Bodywork fittings (eg chrome strips, door handles etc) will also need to be masked off. Use genuine masking tape and several thicknesses of newspaper for the masking operations.

Before commencing to spray, agitate the aerosol can thoroughly, then spray a test area (an old tin, or similar) until the technique is mastered. Cover the repair area with a thick coat of primer; the thickness should be built up using several thin layers of paint rather than one thick one. Using 400 grade wet-and-dry paper, rub down the surface of the primer until it is really smooth. While doing this, the work area should be thoroughly doused with water and the wet-and-dry paper periodically rinsed in water. Allow to dry before spraying on more paint.

Spray on the top coat, again building up the thickness by using several thin layers of paint. Start spraying in the centre of the repair area and then, with a side-to-side motion, work outwards until the whole repair area and about 50 mm of the surrounding original paintwork is covered. Remove all masking material 10 to 15 minutes after spraying on the final coat of paint.

Allow the new paint at least two weeks to harden, then, using a paintwork renovator, or a very fine cutting paste, blend the edges of the paint into the existing paintwork. Finally, apply wax polish.

Plastic components

With the use of more and more plastic body components by the vehicle manufacturers (eg bumpers, spoilers and in some cases major body panels), rectification of more serious damage to such items has become a matter of either entrusting repair work to a specialist in this field, or renewing complete components. Repair of such damage by the DIY owner is not really feasible owing to the cost of the equipment and materials required for effecting such repairs. The basic technique involves making a groove along the line of the crack in the plastic using a rotary burr in a power drill. The damaged part is then welded back together by using a hot air gun to heat up and fuse a plastic filler rod into the groove. Any excess plastic is then removed and the area rubbed down to a smooth finish. It is important that a filler rod of the correct plastic is used, as body components can be made of a variety of different types (eg polycarbonate, ABS, polypropylene).

Damage of a less serious nature (abrasions, minor cracks etc) can be repaired by the DIY owner using a two-part epoxy filler repair material , or a 'No-Mix' which can be used directly from the tube. Once mixed in equal proportions (or applied direct from the tube in the case of the 'No-Mix)', this is used in similar fashion to the bodywork filler used on metal panels. The filler is usually cured in twenty to thirty minutes, ready for sanding and painting.

If the owner is renewing a complete component himself, or if he has repaired it with epoxy filler, he will be left with the problem of finding a suitable paint for finishing which is compatible with the type of plastic used. At one time the use of a universal paint was not possible owing to the complex range of plastics encountered in body component applications. Standard paints, generally speaking, will not bond satisfactorily to plastic or rubber, but professional spraymatch paints to match any plastic or rubber finish can be obtained from dealers. However, it is now possible to obtain a plastic body parts finishing kit which consists of a pre-primer treatment, a primer and coloured top coat. Full instructions are normally supplied with a kit, but basically the method of use is to first apply the pre-primer to the component concerned and allow it to dry for up to 30 minutes. Then the primer is applied and left to dry for about an hour before finally applying the special coloured top coat. The result is a correctly-coloured component where the paint will flex with the plastic or rubber, a property that standard paint does not normally possess.

4 Major body damage - repair

Where serious damage has occurred, or large areas need renewal due to neglect, it means that complete new panels will need welding in. This is best left to professionals. If the damage is due to impact, it will also be necessary to check completely the alignment of the bodyshell. This can only be carried out accurately by a Citroen dealer using special jigs. If the body is left misaligned, it is primarily dangerous as the vehicle will not handle properly and secondly, uneven stresses will be imposed on the steering, suspension and possibly transmission, causing abnormal wear or complete failure, particularly to items such as the tyres.

12

5 Maintenance - hinges and locks

1 Periodically, oil the hinges of the bonnet, doors and tailgate with a little light oil. A good time is after the car has been washed.
2 Oil the bonnet release catch mechanism and striker pin.
3 Do not over lubricate door latches and strikers. A little oil on the lock spindle is sufficient.

6 Bonnet - removal, refitting and adjustment

Removal

1 Support the bonnet in its open position and place some cardboard or rags beneath the corners by the hinges.
2 The bonnet is not adjustable at the hinges for position so there is no need to mark their relative positions.
3 With the help of an assistant, unscrew the four retaining nuts, noting that an earth strap is located beneath the rear nuts (see illustration). Lift the bonnet from the vehicle.

Refitting

4 Refitting the bonnet is a reversal of removal. When fitted, close the bonnet and check it for correct alignment. An even clearance should exist around the bonnet at the wings, the bulkhead grille and the headlights, and the front bumper at the leading edge.
5 When fully closed, there should be a 10 mm clearance between the bonnet leading edge and the headlamp unit each side, the bonnet top face being flush to the top edge of the wing panels.
6 Check that when fully closed, the bonnet is fully locked, then release the lock and check that the safety catch operates correctly.

Adjustment

7 If necessary, the bonnet lock and safety catch can be adjusted by loosening the retaining bolts or nuts as applicable, repositioning the lock unit or safety catch and

6.3 Bonnet hinge retaining nuts. Note earth strap under lower nut and washer

retightening the bolts/nuts. Recheck the operation of the lock and safety catch on completion.

7 Bonnet lock - removal and refitting

Removal

1 Open the bonnet and support it. If a malfunction of the bonnet lock or cable does not allow the bonnet to open by normal means, it can be released by inserting a suitable length of wire rod hooked over at its end between the headlamp unit and the underside of the bonnet. Hook the end of the rod onto the release lever and pull it towards the left to release the lock.
2 Loosen the cable clamp screw and disconnect the cable from the lock operating lever (see illustration).
3 Mark the location of the lock with a pencil, then loosen the two retaining bolts and withdraw the lock.

Refitting

4 Refit the lock by reversing the removal procedure. Align it with the pencil marks made during removal before tightening the bolts. Adjust the release cable to remove almost all slackness from it. This can be judged by allowing a fraction of free movement at the release knob end.
5 Closure of the bonnet should now be checked and, if necessary, adjusted.

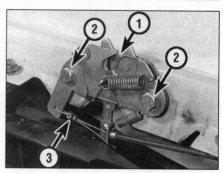

7.2 Bonnet lock (1), retaining bolts (2) and cable clamp (3)

8 Front wing - removal and refitting

Removal

1 Disconnect the battery earth lead.
2 Remove the headlight unit and front indicator unit from the side concerned.
3 Where possible, make pencilled alignment marks of the wing position against corresponding body panels to assist with correct realignment when refitting.
4 Undo and remove the bolts and nuts along the top edge of the wing (five in all).
5 Disconnect the wing at the front leading edge by undoing the two retaining bolts (see illustration).
6 Undo and remove the single retaining bolt and washer (see illustration).
7 Open the front door fully then undo the two rear edge retaining bolts (see illustration).
8 The wing panel can now be lifted away after prising it free from the mastic at the flange joints.

8.7 Front wing rear edge retaining bolt locations (arrowed)

8.5 Remove the retaining bolts and washers (arrowed) from the front wing leading edge

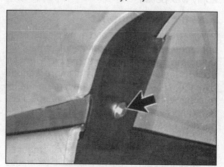

8.6 Remove single retaining bolt and washer (arrowed) from the front wing

8.9 Captive nut locations (arrowed) for attachment of front wing

10.1 Door mirror adjuster knob and gaiter

10.3 Countersunk screw retaining the inner plate (arrowed)

Refitting

9 Before refitting the wing panel, clean away all the old mastic sealant and apply a new bead of sealant. Check the three captive nuts are in the positions shown (see illustration).
10 When refitting the wing, do not fully tighten the retaining bolts until they are all in position and the wing is correctly aligned with the adjacent panels.
11 When the headlight and indicator units are refitted, reconnect the battery and check for satisfactory operation of the lights.
12 Check headlamp alignment.

9 Door rattles - tracing and rectification

1 Check the door is not loose at the hinges and the latch is holding it firmly in position. Check also that the door aligns with the body aperture, if not, then it must be adjusted.
2 If the latch is holding the door in the correct position but the latch still rattles, the lock mechanism is worn out and requires renewal
3 Other rattles from the door could be caused by wear in the window operating mechanism or electric motors, interior lock mechanism, or loose glass channels.

10 Door mirror - removal and refitting

Removal

1 Prise back the rubber gaiter from the trim panel and pull free the adjuster knob and gaiter (see illustration).
2 Undo the inset screw and remove the trim plate.
3 Undo the countersunk screw and remove the inner retaining plate (see illustration).
4 Support the mirror unit and undo the two retaining nuts using a suitable socket or box spanner (see illustration). Remove the mirror unit.

Refitting

5 Refit in the reverse order of removal.

11 Door mirror glass - renewal

1 This can be achieved with the mirror unit in position on the door. To protect the door

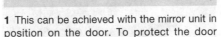

10.4 Door mirror retaining nuts (arrowed)

paintwork, wind down the door window and cover the panel with a suitable cloth.
2 One of two types of mirror will be fitted, being either of Britax or Hohe manufacture (see illustration). The glass replacement for each differs as given below.

Britax mirror

3 With this type, the glass is bonded in position in each corner at the points indicated (see illustration). Break the glass (using care) and remove the remaining fragments.
4 Clean the bonding adhesive from the four points indicated in the mirror unit.
5 Carefully peel off the backing paper from

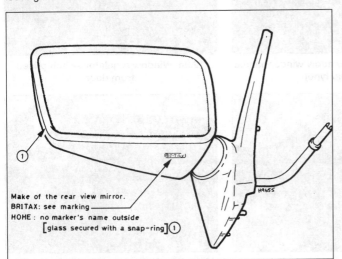

11.2 Door mirror type identification

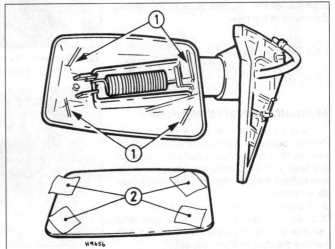

11.3 Britax type mirror showing glass bonding points (1 and 2)

12

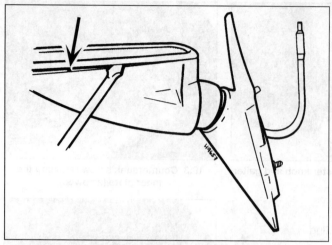

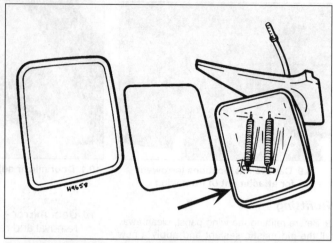

11.6 Prise free the retaining ring (arrowed) to remove the glass - Hohe type mirror

11.8 Apply sealant around perimeter (arrowed) - Hohe type mirror

the adhesive squares on the rear of the new glass then carefully locate and press the glass into position in the mirror unit.

Hohe type mirror

6 Carefully prise free the retaining ring from the perimeter of the glass using a flat-bladed screwdriver and extract the glass **(see illustration)**.

7 A new retaining ring will be supplied with the mirror glass. It will be necessary to cut the ring securing lugs down by half before the mirror and ring can be fitted.

8 Clean the perimeter area of the mirror unit to which the retaining ring is to fit. Apply a thin bead of sealant (epoxy glue Ref ZC 9 865105 U, polyurethane sealant Ref ZC 9 867 433 U or equivalent) around the perimeter area of the mirror unit to which the sealing ring will fit **(see illustration)**.

9 Carefully locate the glass and the retaining ring into position. Secure them in this position using adhesive tape for the period specified by the glue/sealant manufacture to allow full adhesion of the ring and glass to the mirror, then remove the tape.

12 Door trim panel - removal and refitting

Manually operated windows

1 Insert a piece of wire with a small hook at its end, between the window winder handle and the boss on the door inner panel. Engage the hook with the handle securing spring clip and extract the clip. Remove the handle **(see illustration)**.

2 Unscrew and remove the door lock knob.

3 Undo the three retaining screws and remove the door pull/armrest. Unclip and remove the door pull/armrest bezel.

4 Remove the door mirror adjuster knob, gaiter and trim plate.

5 Using a wide-bladed tool inserted between the door inner trim panel and the door, release the panel securing clips.

6 Remove the trim panel and take off the winder handle coil spring.

7 For access to the inner door components, carefully peel back the plastic insulation sheet.

8 Refitting is a reversal of the removal procedure.

Electrically operated windows

9 The switches for electrically operated windows are mounted in the door panels. When removing the door trim panels, it is necessary to prise free the switches from the panel using a thin-bladed screwdriver, then disconnect the wiring from the switches **(see illustrations)**.

10 The window regulator switches are mounted in a secondary panel attached to the main door panel. If required, the panels can be separated by undoing the retaining screws from the rear face **(see illustration)**.

11 If door-mounted radio speakers are fitted, the wires for these will also have to be disconnected to allow the door panels to be removed.

12.1 Removing the window winder handle (manual type)

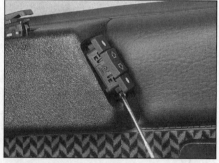

12.9a Window regulator switch prised from door

12.9b Window regulator switches withdrawn to expose wiring

12.10 Extracting a screw from the window regulator mounting panel

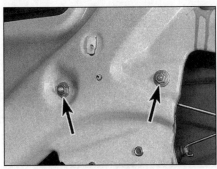

14.2 Door glass runner channel retaining nuts (arrowed)

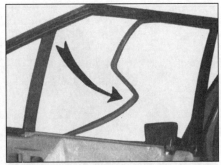

16.2 Fold back the weatherstrip from the rear door window/quarter window

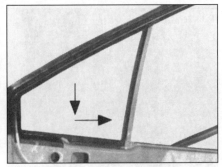

16.4 Direction of rear door quarter window removal

13 Door window lift channels - modification

1 On early models, the window lift channels are glued to the side of the glass. Later models have slotted channels with rubber inserts.
2 If problems are experienced with early-type channels coming unstuck, purchase a modification kit from a Citroën dealer and fit the later-type channels.
3 Mark the position of the old lift channels before removal (saw or prise them off), and fit the new ones in the same position. Measuring horizontally from the front bottom corner of the glass, the front edge of the lift channel should be 207 mm from the corner on the front windows, 124 mm from the corner on the rear windows.

14 Front door window regulator and glass - removal and refitting

Removal

1 Remove the door inner trim panel.
2 Remove the electrically operated window regulator unit. Unbolt the roller runner channel (see illustration).
3 To remove the manually operated window regulator unit, unscrew the regulator retaining nuts and push the regulator into the door cavity.
4 Support the glass and release the rollers from the runner channel.
5 Withdraw the regulator from the door.
6 To remove the door glass, carefully detach and remove the waistline seal by prising it free from the retaining clips. Renew this seal if it is excessively worn or damaged.
7 Tilt the glass upwards at the rear and carefully withdraw it from the door.

Refitting

8 Refitting is a reversal of the removal procedure. Lubricate the regulator guide channels with light grease.

15 Rear door window regulator and glass - removal and refitting

The procedures for removal and refitting are the same as those given for the front doors. However, before removing the door glass it is also necessary to remove the channel weatherstrip from the window aperture at its upper, lower and rear edges.

When refitting the glass, lower it into position and locate it into its guide channels in the lower door section then refit the weatherstrip.

16 Rear door quarter window - removal and refitting

Removal

1 Lower the door window then remove the inner door trim panel. Peel back the insulation sheet from the rear quarter section of the door.
2 Detach the main window weatherstrip from the rear separator and partially along its upper and lower aperture fixings (see illustration).
3 Detach and remove the rear separator and the lower inner strip from the bottom edge of the quarter window.
4 Press the quarter window downwards and

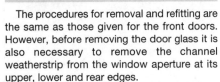

17.2 Door lock retaining screws and nylon grommet

forwards and carefully lever it away inwards at the top corner (see illustration). Remove the quarter window, complete with its weatherstrip.
5 If re-using the weatherstrip, clean it of mastic sealant.

Refitting

6 Refitting is a reversal of the removal procedure. Apply a thin bead of mastic sealant around the outer periphery of the quarter window weatherstrip prior to fitting it into position.

17 Door lock, lock cylinder and handles - removal and refitting

1 Fully raise the door window and remove the inner trim from the door.

Door lock

2 Prise free the nylon grommet from the rear edge of the door (see illustration).
3 Disconnect the control rods from the lock unit, taking care not to damage the nylon fasteners (see illustration). As they are disconnected, note their respective connecting points.
4 Undo the three retaining screws and withdraw the lock unit.
5 Refitting is a reversal of the removal procedure.

17.3 Door lock control rods and nylon fasteners

12

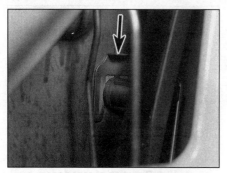

17.6 Door lock cylinder and retaining clip (arrowed)

17.8 Door outer handle retaining nut (arrowed)

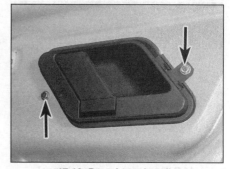

17.10 Door inner handle and retaining bolts (arrowed)

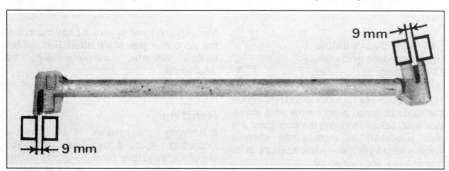

9 mm

9 mm

18.7a Door adjustment tool

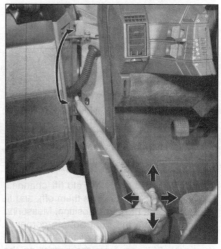

18.7b Adjusting door position by moving a hinge

Lock cylinder

6 Detach the connecting rod, then prise free the retaining clip **(see illustration)**. Withdraw the cylinder.
7 Refit in the reverse order of removal.

Outer handle

8 Detach the connecting rod from the lock unit then undo the two retaining nuts and remove the handle **(see illustration)**.
9 Refit in the reverse order of removal.

Inner handle

10 Detach the connecting rod to the lock unit, undo the two retaining bolts and remove the handle **(see illustration)**.
11 Refit in the reverse order of removal.

18 Doors - removal and refitting

Removal

1 Remove the door trim.
2 Disconnect the wiring from the lock solenoid and the window regulator units, as applicable, and pull the wiring harness from the leading edge of the door.
3 Open the door fully and support it with blocks or a suitable jack. Use a newspaper or rag to protect the paintwork from bring scratched by the support.
4 Use a suitable diameter punch and drive out the roll pins from the door check strap and hinges. Get an assistant to support the door

during this operation. Take care not to distort the hinges when removing the pins. Lift the door from the vehicle.

Refitting

5 Refitting is a reversal of removal. On completion, check the door for alignment, as follows.
6 Close the door gently. If it will not close or if, when it is closed, the door exterior panel is not flush or in correct alignment with the adjacent body panels adjust the door in the following way.
7 Open the door and using a suitably cranked bar, prise the relevant hinge **(see illustrations)**. The hinges are welded to the door and the body pillar, and bending the hinges is the only means of adjustment. Do not overdo this, or it will be virtually impossible to rectify matters and the hinges will have to be renewed using a welding torch.
8 Once the adjustment is correct, release the door striker and adjust its position to engage smoothly in the lock tongue.

19 Tailgate - removal and refitting

Hatchback

1 Disconnect the battery earth lead.
2 Prise free the retaining clips and remove the rear trim panels from the tailgate.
3 Detach the wiring connections to the rear number plate lamps, the rear window demister, the rear wiper motor and the lock

solenoid unit (as applicable). Also disconnect the earth wires whilst noting their connections.
4 Disconnect the hose from the rear washer nozzle.
5 Withdraw the wires and the rear washer hose from the tailgate.
6 Get an assistant to support the tailgate or securely prop it, then disconnect the gas-filled struts by extracting the retaining clip at their top or bottom ends **(see illustrations)**.
7 Carefully prise free the hinge retaining clip each side and remove the tailgate **(see illustration)**. If renewing the hinge pin and clips, note that there are three types used.
8 Refitting is a reversal of removal. On

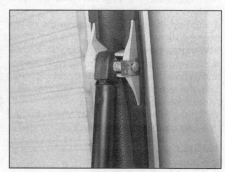

19.6a Support strut and retaining clip to tailgate

19.6b Tailgate support strut and retaining clip to body

19.7 Tailgate hinge retaining clip

19.11 Prising out tailgate strut balljoint clip

19.12 Tailgate hinge pin retaining clip (arrowed)

20.3 Front bumper retaining bolts (arrowed)

completion, check the operation of the tailgate functions prior to refitting the trim panels. Check the tailgate for alignment and satisfactory locking action.

Estate

9 Disconnect the battery.
10 Open the tailgate fully. Disconnect the wiring (heated glass element, rear wiper and central locking) and the washer hose. Extensive dismantling of the interior side trim panels and window surrounds will be required in order to gain access to the wiring plugs.
11 With an assistant supporting the tailgate, prise out the spring clips from the strut balljoints **(see illustration)** and pull the struts off their ball studs.
12 Prise off the retaining clips and tap the hinge pins out. Lift the tailgate from the vehicle **(see illustration)**.
13 Refitting is a reversal of removal.

20 Bumpers - removal and refitting

Front

1 Raise and support the bonnet. Detach and remove the flexible panel between the headlamp units.
2 Unscrew and remove the three bumper retaining bolts from the top face of the bumper (between the headlamp units).
3 From underneath, unscrew and remove the five bolts **(see illustration)**.
4 With the aid of an assistant, simultaneously pull the bumper outwards at each corner and withdraw the bumper forwards from the vehicle.
5 Refit in the reverse order of removal, ensuring that the captive nuts are in position before fitting the bumper into position.

Rear

Hatchback

6 Remove the rear combination light units.
7 Unscrew and remove the three retaining bolts from the top face of the bumper.
8 From underneath, unscrew and remove the three retaining bolts at the rear then remove the bumper in the same manner as that described for the front bumper.
9 Refit in the reverse order of removal, ensuring that the captive nuts are in position before fitting the bumper into position.

Estate

10 The rear bumper comprises a centre section secured to the tailgate by screws, and two end sections held by screws and clips.
11 Remove the screws and withdraw the bumper. The end sections slide rearwards off the clips **(see illustrations)**.
12 Refitting is a reversal of removal.

20.11a Unscrewing a rear bumper lower screw

20.11b Unscrewing a rear bumper upper screw

20.11c Rear bumper end clip viewed from underneath vehicle

12

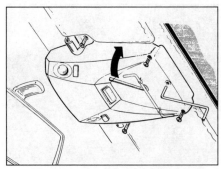

21.3 Crank handle for sunroof manual adjustment is located within roof console

21 Sunroof - manual operation

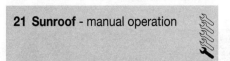

1 In the event of a malfunction of the sunroof electric motor, the roof panel can be closed manually.
2 Check that the sunroof operating switch is in the off position, then undo the four screws retaining the roof console in position and lower the console from the roof.
3 A manual crank handle is contained within the roof console, secured by spring clips. Remove the crank handle and engage it into the manual crank hole in the winder mechanism. Turn the handle to shut the roof panel **(see illustration)**.

22 Sunroof - removal, refitting and adjustments

Removal

1 With the roof panel in the closed position, raise it at its rear edge so that it is in the airflow to the passenger compartment position.
2 If required, undo the three retaining screws and remove them from the mobile frame at the front edge.
3 Unscrew and remove the three retaining screws each side and then lift out the sunroof from its tilt frame.

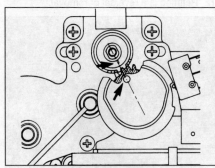

22.6 Sunroof motor reduction gears in alignment

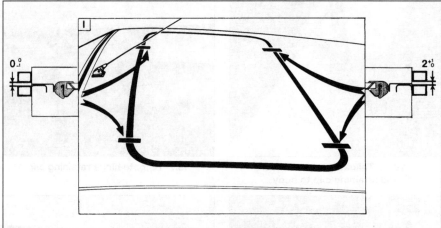

22.5 Sunroof alignment check points
Clearances in mm

Refitting

4 Refitting is a reversal of the removal procedure. Check that the tilt pivots are engaged each side before refitting the panel.
5 On completion, check the roof panel for correct alignment when in the closed position **(see illustration)**. The panel should be parallel at its forward and rear edges with the vehicle roof within the tolerances indicated.
6 If alignment is not within the limits specified, lower the roof console and check to see if the alignment marks of the motor reduction gears correspond **(see illustration)**. If they do not, then proceed as follows.

Adjustment

7 Insert the emergency manual crank handle, check that the roof panel is fully closed and move the reducer lever clockwise to the angle shown **(see illustration)** to disengage the reducer.
8 Undo the two retaining screws and uncouple the motor/reducer unit from the operating cables. Check that roof alignment is now correct.

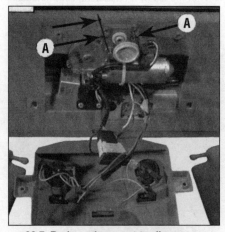

22.7 Reducer lever set to disengage reducer (arrowed)
A - Retaining screws

9 To adjust the reducer gears, turn the small cam anti-clockwise to the point where the large gear cam stops meshing with it. It is particularly important that the microswitch is located on the rear of the large cam and not in the cam recess **(see illustration)**. Holding the cam firmly in this position, turn the small cam clockwise to the point where the gears start to mesh then move the reducer lever back to its original position. Turn the cams to align the gear alignment marks.
10 Reconnect the operating cables, relocate the motor reducer unit and refit the two retaining screws.
11 Refit the roof console and check that the sunroof operates in a satisfactory manner. Recheck the sunroof alignment and free play when closed. If excessive distortion (more than 3 mm) still exists, proceed as follows.
12 Remove the roof console and turn the reducer lever clockwise to the angle shown.
13 Engage the emergency manual handle with the small reduction cam and wind it to fully open the roof panel.
14 Undo the two retaining screws and uncouple the motor reducer unit from the operating cables, then carefully push the two cables with cams towards the front by pressing the frame pivots each side **(see illustration)**.

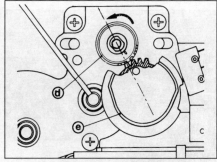

22.9 Reducer gear adjustment
Turn small cam (d) anti-clockwise to disengage from large cam (e)

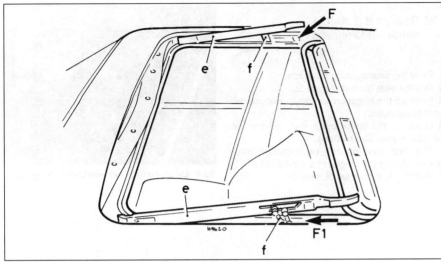

22.14 Sunroof side channels (e) and cams (f) shown with glass panel removed for clarity
F and F1 are the frame pivots

15 Refit the motor/reducer and engage the cables.
16 Manually close the sunroof and recheck the roof alignment and free play. If necessary, adjust the reducer gear alignment marks as described previously. Reset the reducer lever to its original setting before refitting the roof console.

23 Windscreen and tailgate glass - renewal

If you are unfortunate enough to have a windscreen or tailgate glass breakage, the removal and fitting of a replacement is one of the few jobs that the average owner is advised to leave to a Citroën dealer or body repair specialist. Body specialists are familiar with the procedures involved and have the necessary equipment for renewal. Specific sealant products are also required and unless these are used the rigidity of the assembly and its sealing capabilities will be impaired.

24 Dashboard - removal and refitting

Early models

1 Disconnect the battery earth lead.
2 Prise free the glovebox light lens, withdraw the switch/light unit and detach the wiring connections from it.
3 Remove the retaining screws and remove the steering column lower shroud and lower trim panel on the driver's side, and the lower trim panel on the passenger side.
4 Remove the instrument panel.
5 Disconnect the wiring connector at the point indicated **(see illustration)**.
6 Remove the screw from the side of the corner vent trim (open the door for access).
7 Detach the fuse/relay box unit and disconnect from it the wiring loom connections from the steering column switches.
8 Undo the four retaining bolts and lower the steering column from the upper mounting bracket.
9 Remove the upper facia-mounted speaker units from each side.

24.5 Detach the wiring connector (arrowed)

10 Working from the engine compartment, undo the dashboard retaining bolt from each side of the bulkhead **(see illustration)**.
11 The dashboard can now be carefully withdrawn. As it is removed, check that all wiring is disconnected and withdraw the left-hand column switch wiring harness (to the fusebox) through with it whilst noting its route location on the underside of the dashboard.
12 Refitting is a reversal of the removal procedure. Ensure all wiring connections are securely and correctly made and that the loom routing is made as noted during removal.
13 On completion, check the operations of the various switch and instrument functions.

Later models

14 While the dashboard layout differs on later models, the main differences concerning its removal are the associated components attached to it, such as the revised heater controls and the later-type steering column and facia switches. Removal procedures for the dashboard are otherwise similar to those described for early models.

25 Floor-mounted centre console (later models) - removal and refitting

The floor-mounted centre console on later models is secured by two bolts on top and a screw each side at the front. The bolts are recessed in the upper face of the panel and are accessible after removal of the plastic covers. These can be prised free **(see illustration)**.

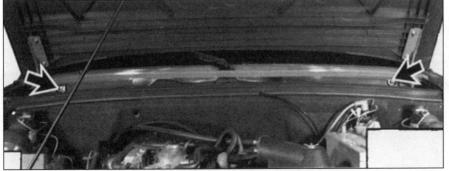

24.10 Undo the two retaining bolts (arrowed)

25.1 Removing plastic cover for access to centre console retaining bolt

12

When removing the console, it may be necessary to detach the wiring connectors from any switches mounted in the console. Some models also have radio headphone jack points mounted in the rear of the console and these will also have to be detached.

26 Rear seat (Estate) - removal and refitting

1 Pivot the seat cushion forwards.
2 Pull the seat back downwards.
3 Prise up the hinge cover flap to expose the seat hinge bolts.
4 Unscrew the hinge bolts and remove the seat back **(see illustration)**.
5 The seat cushion can be removed after disconnecting the hinges in a similar way.
6 Refitting is a reversal of removal.

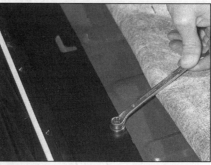

26.4 Unscrewing rear seat back hinge bolt

Chapter 13
Body electrical systems

Contents

Degrees of difficulty

Easy, suitable for novice with little experience	Fairly easy, suitable for beginner with some experience	Fairly difficult, suitable for competent DIY mechanic 	Difficult, suitable for experienced DIY mechanic	Very difficult, suitable for expert DIY or professional

Specifications

System
Type .... 12 volt, negative earth

Fuses

Mark/Ampere rating/Colour | **Protected circuits**

BX and BX 14

F1/10/Red .... Alternator. Reverse lamp. Idle cut-off and cooling fan relay coil
F2/25/White ..... Econoscope. Indicators. Air blower. Engine oil level. Clock.
The following warning lamps:
Engine oil pressure
Fuel minimum level
Hydraulic fluid pressure and level
Coolant temperature
Coolant level
Choke
Battery charge
Emergency STOP
Brake pad wear indicator and handbrake

F3/25/White ..... Windscreen wiper motor and washer pump. Rear window wiper motor and washer pump. Relay coil and indicator lamp for heated rear window. Stop-lamps. Rheostat and dashboard lighting. Ashtray light, cigar lighter and heating control panel lighting. Front/rear window winder relay coil. Horn

F4/25/White ..... Door locking device (unit and motors)
F5/25/White ..... Electric cooling fan
F6/10/Red ..... Hazard warning lamps
F7/25/White ..... Rear door window winder
F8/20/Yellow ..... Side interior lights. Glove compartment and boot lights. Cigar lighter, clock, radio and ashtray lighting

13

Fuses (continued)

Mark/Ampere rating/Colour	Protected circuits
BX and BX 14 (continued)	
F9/25/White	Front door window winder
F10/20/Yellow	Heated rear window
F11/5/Brown	Rear foglamps and warning lamp
F12/5/Brown	Side and tail lamps. Number plate lamps. Side and tail warning lamp. Clock attenuated lighting. Attenuated lighting for heated rear window and hazard warning switches
BX 16 and BX 19	
F1/10/Red	Coolant temperature flasher unit. Alternator. Reverse lamp. Oil gauge unit. Cooling fan relay coil. Idle cut-off
F2/25/White	Indicator. Air blower. Fuel gauge. Tachometer. Clock lighting. The following warning lamps:
	Fuel minimum level
	Engine oil pressure
	Hydraulic fluid level and pressure
	Coolant temperature
	Coolant level
	Emergency STOP
	Door locking device
	Battery charge
	Brake pad wear indicator and handbrake
F3/25/White	Windscreen wiper motor and washer pump. Rear window wiper motor and washer pump. Heated rear window relay coil and indicator lamp. Stop-lamps. Rheostat and lighting for dashboard, ashtray, cigar lighter and heater control. Front and rear window winder relay coil. Horn
F4/25/White	Door locking device (unit and motors)
F5/30/White	Electric cooling fan
F6/10/Red	Hazard warning lamps
F7/30/White	Rear door window winders
F8/20/Yellow	Map reading (swivel) lamp. Side interior lamps. Boot and glove compartment lights. Cigar lighter and lighting. Clock. Radio. Ashtray light
F9/30/White	Front door window winder
F10/20/Yellow	Heated rear window
F11/5/Brown	Rear foglamps. Rear foglamp warning light
F12/5/Brown	Side, tail and number plate lamps. Side and tail warning lamp. Clock attenuated lighting. Attenuated lighting for hazard warning and heated rear window
All later models	
F1/10/Red	Engine cooling fan relay coil, coolant level indicator unit, oil level control unit, tachometer, reversing lights, coolant temperature control unit
F2/25/White	Air blower (and ventilation system), instrument panel
F3/25/White	Heater fan speed control lighting, instrument panel lighting, stop-lights, cigar lighter, on-board computer, heated rear screen relay coil, rear wash/wipe, windscreen wash/wipe (and timer), "door not locked" symbol lighting (and warning lights), electric window relay coil, rear view mirror, sunroof, front seat spotlight, interior light timer unit
F4/30/Green	Engine cooling fan
F5/10/Red	Hazard warning lights
F6/30/Green	Electric rear windows
F7/30/Green	Glovebox lighting, on-board computer (+ direct supply), cigar lighter, supply socket, door locking, roof light and timer unit, boot lighting, radio electrical supply
F8/20/White	Horn, heated rear screen
F9/30/Green	Electric window control unit
F10/5/Brown	Rear foglights and warning light
F11/5/Brown	RH tail light
F12/5/Brown	LH tail light, rear number plate lights
F13/5/Brown	Side and tail warning lights, sidelights, switch lighting, on board computer lighting, front foglight switch (and warning light, relay coil)
F14/10/Red*	Hydraulic unit for ABS

*May be 25 amp White on later models

Bulbs

	Wattage
Headlamps (main/dip)	60/55
Direction indicators	21
Stop-lamps	21
Reverse lamps	21
Rear foglamps	21
Tail lamps	5
Number plate lamps	5
Sidelamps	4
Speedometer lamps	4
Interior lamps	7
Boot lamp	5
Heater control	1.2
Ashtray	1.2
Cigar lighter	1.2
Dashboard warning lamps	1.2
Switch warning lamps	1.2

1 General information and precautions

General information

The electrical system is of the 12 volt negative earth type and comprises a 12 volt battery of which the negative terminal is earthed, an alternator which is driven from the crankshaft pulley, a starter motor and related electrical accessories, components and wiring.

The battery supplies a steady amount of current for the ignition, lighting and other electrical circuits and provides a reserve of electricity when the current consumed by the electrical equipment exceeds that being produced by the alternator.

The alternator is controlled by a regulator. This ensures a high output if the battery is in a low state of charge or the demand from the electrical equipment is high. Alternatively, it ensures a low output if the battery is fully charged and there is little demand for the electrical equipment.

An on-board computer system is fitted to BX 19 models, being located in the floor console forward of the gear lever. This system has fifteen possible functions, the main ones being to log petrol consumption, average speed, journey time elapsed and the estimated time of arrival, plus the range possible on the remaining fuel. The main system components are the computer unit, the distance sensor and the fuel output sensor.

From late 1986, all models are equipped with a dim-dip lighting system to comply with UK regulations. The function of the system is to prevent the vehicle being driven with only the sidelights illuminated. This system uses a relay-controlled resistor circuit. When the sidelights are on (ignition also on), the headlights are automatically illuminated at approximately one-sixth their normal dipped beam power.

Further details of the various systems are given in the relevant Sections of this Chapter. While some repair procedures are given, the usual course of action is to renew the component concerned. The owner whose interest extends beyond mere component renewal should obtain a copy of the `Automobile Electrical & Electronic Systems Manual`, available from the publishers of this manual.

Precautions

It is necessary to take extra care when working on the electrical system to avoid damage to semi-conductor devices (diodes and transistors) and to avoid the risk of personal injury. In addition to the precautions given in the "Safety first!" Section at the beginning of this manual, take note of the following points when working on the system.

a) *Before disconnecting any wiring or removing components, always ensure that the ignition is switched off.*

b) *Disconnect the battery leads before using a mains charger.*

c) *Do not reverse the battery connections. Components such as the alternator or any other having semi-conductor circuitry could be irreparably damaged.*

d) *If the engine is being started using jump leads and a slave battery, connect the batteries positive to positive and negative to negative. This also applies when connecting a battery charger.*

e) *Never disconnect the battery terminals or alternator multi-plug connector when the engine is running.*

f) *The battery leads and alternator multi-plug must be disconnected before carrying out any electric welding on the vehicle.*

g) *Never use an ohmmeter of the type incorporating a hand cranked generator for circuit or continuity testing.*

h) *When carrying out welding operations on the vehicle using electric welding equipment, disconnect the battery and alternator.*

i) *When fitting electrical accessories it is important that they are connected correctly, otherwise serious damage may result to the components concerned.*

Items such as radios, tape recorders, electronic ignition systems, electronic tachometers, automatic dipping etc, should all be checked for correct polarity.

2 Fuses and relays - location and renewal

Note: *Always renew a fuse with one of similar rating and never renew it without finding the source of trouble*

1 The fuse/relay box is located under the lower trim panel on the passenger side.

2 The circuits protected by the fuses, together with their colour and rating, are given in *Specifications*.

3 Access to the fuses is gained by pulling the release handle and swinging the box down **(see illustration)**.

4 Always renew a fuse with one of similar rating and never renew it more than once without finding the source of trouble. If necessary, refer to the wiring diagrams at the end of this Chapter.

5 Relay units rarely give problems but they can easily be renewed by pulling them from their location in the box. The relay units and their functions are also shown in the wiring diagrams at the end of this Chapter. Some relay units are connected in-line and are separate from the main fuse/relay box unit.

2.3 The fuse and relay box

13

2.6 Fuel injection system relays (BX 19 GTi with Bosch LE3 Jetronic fuel injection)

6 On BX 19 GTi models, further relay units are located in the engine compartment, under a plastic cover **(see illustration)**.
7 If suspect, these units should be checked by a Citroën dealer. They are easily renewed by detaching the wiring connector and then unscrewing the retaining bolt.

3 Exterior lights - removal, refitting and bulb renewal

Caution: Avoid touching the glass envelope of a halogen bulb. Failure to do this may result in premature bulb failure.

Headlights
Bulb renewal

1 The bulbs are renewed from the rear of the headlamp unit, access being from the engine compartment.

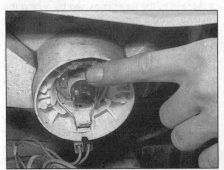

3.4 Align the headlamp bulb

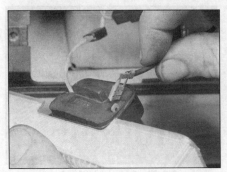

3.10 Disconnecting the foglight wiring

2 Pull free the wiring connector, release the bulb retaining clip and withdraw the bulb **(see illustrations)**.
3 Where halogen bulbs are fitted, do not touch the glass with your fingers or with a fluffy cloth. Allow the bulb to cool before removing it. If the glass is inadvertently touched, clean it with methylated spirit.
4 Refitting is a reversal of removal. When inserting the bulb, it must be correctly aligned with the location notches **(see illustration)**. Check the headlights for satisfactory operation and alignment on completion.

Removal and refitting

5 Raise the bonnet, and pull free the headlamp wiring connector and the sidelight bulbholder.
6 The headlamp unit can then be carefully prised from its ball and socket adjustable mountings **(see illustration)**.
7 Refitting is a reversal of removal. Check lamp operation and alignment on completion.

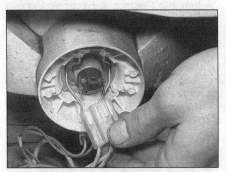

3.2a Disconnect the wiring connector . . .

3.6 Headlamp ball and socket mounting

3.11 Extracting the front foglight bulb

Front foglights
8 Disconnect the battery earth lead.
9 Undo the retaining screws and remove the light unit **(see illustration)**.
10 Detach the wiring and withdraw the cover **(see illustration)**.
11 Release the retaining clip and extract the bulb **(see illustration)**.
12 Refit in the reverse order of removal (avoid touching the new bulb glass with your fingers), then check for satisfactory operation and adjustment. If required, the light beam can be adjusted by turning the adjuster screw.

Front indicators
13 Reach down within the engine compartment and press the front indicator unit retaining tabs to release the unit from the front wing panel **(see illustration)**.
14 Withdraw the bulb holder from the indicator unit and withdraw the bulb **(see illustration)**.

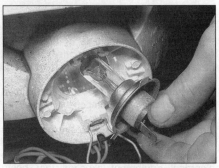

3.2b . . . and remove the headlight bulb

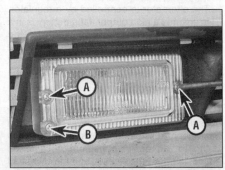

3.9 Front foglight retaining screws (A) and adjuster screw (B)

3.13 Withdraw the front indicator unit . . .

3.14 . . . and extract the bulb holder

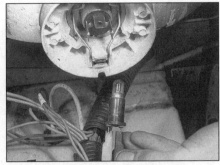

3.16 Sidelight bulb removal

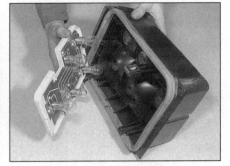

3.19 Removing the bulb holder from the rear lens unit (Hatchback)

3.22 Rear light assembly (Estate)

3.25 Number plate light unit shown with access cover removed from trim panel (Hatchback)

15 Refit in the reverse order of removal. Press the indicator unit fully into position, ensuring that the retaining tabs clip home fully. Check the operation of the indicators.

Sidelights

16 This bulb is located in the rear of the headlight unit, directly underneath the headlight bulb. Pull free the bulbholder, complete with wiring connections, from the headlamp unit then withdraw the bulb from its holder (see illustration).
17 Refit in the reverse order to removal and check the operation of the sidelights.

Side repeater lights

18 To renew the bulb, carefully twist the lens anti-clockwise and withdraw the light unit from the wing. Take care not to allow the wiring to fall back inside the wing. Pull the bulbholder from the back of the light unit for access to the bulb.

Rear combination lights

Hatchback

19 Press the lens forwards with one hand and simultaneously reach within the luggage compartment and release the unit retaining clip by pinching it firmly. The lens, complete with the combination bulbholder unit, can then be withdrawn from the vehicle and separated from access to the bulbs by pressing the retaining catch (see illustration).
20 Withdraw the defective bulb and renew it.
21 Refit in the reverse order of removal. Ensure that the retaining catch and clip are

securely engaged and check the operation of the respective lights in the unit.

Estate

22 Raise the tailgate and remove the lens securing screws. Note the positioning lug at the base of the lens (see illustration). Lower the lens slightly and pull it away from the bulbs.
23 To refit the lens, engage the lower lug at the bottom and secure with the retaining screws.

Number plate light

Hatchback

24 Raise the tailgate and prise free the square cover from the trim panel adjacent to the light unit.
25 Reach through the trim aperture and withdraw the bulb (see illustration).

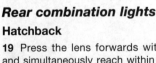

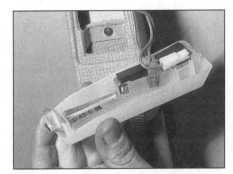

4.2 Interior dome lamp festoon bulb and wiring connections

26 Refit in the reverse order of removal and check the light for satisfactory operation.

Estate

27 Unscrew the fixing screw and pull the assembly from the tailgate.
28 The lens is clipped to the bulbholder and must be removed to renew the bulb.
29 Refitting is a reversal of removal.

---

4 Interior lights - bulb renewal

Interior light

Dome type

1 Prise free the lens unit from its aperture and withdraw the light unit.
2 Ease the festoon bulb free from the terminal springs (see illustration).
3 Refitting is a reversal of removal.

Map lamp type

4 Undo the four retaining screws and remove the roof console. On some types, the light unit is secured by spring clips. In this case prise free the unit (see illustrations).
5 Note that to remove the roof console complete, it will be necessary to detach the sunroof control switch wiring as well as the map reading light wiring (where applicable).
6 Ease the festoon bulb free from the terminal springs (see illustration).
7 Refit in the reverse order of removal.

4.4a Map reading light switch and roof console retaining screw (arrowed)

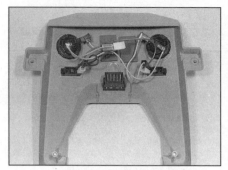
4.4b Map reading light/ sunroof console removed

4.4c Removing the map reading light bulb

4.6 Interior map lamp bulb - festoon type

4.10 Luggage compartment light unit

4.14 Heater control panel bulb (arrowed)

Glovebox

8 Prise free the lens then ease the festoon bulb from the terminal springs.
9 Refit in the reverse order of removal.

Luggage compartment

10 Prise free the light unit then ease the festoon bulb from its terminal springs (see illustration).
11 Refit in the reverse order of removal.

Heater control panel and ashtray

12 Remove the ashtray and pull free the heater control knobs from their levers.
13 Undo the two screws and remove the ashtray support and heater control panel.
14 The bulbs are now accessible and can be withdrawn from their holders as required (see illustration).
15 Refit in the reverse order of removal.

Instrument panel

16 Remove the instrument panel unit. The bulb(s) can then be withdrawn and inspected/renewed as required.

5 Headlamps - alignment

1 Accurate headlamp alignment should be carried out by a Citroën garage. However, in an emergency the following procedure will provide an acceptable light pattern.

2 Position the vehicle on a level surface with tyres correctly inflated. Start the engine and allow it to idle, then check that the ground clearance lever is in the normal running position. The vehicle should be positioned approximately 10 metres in front of a wall or garage door.
3 Mark the headlamp bulb centres on the wall.
4 Switch on the main beam and check that the areas of maximum illumination coincide with the marks on the wall. If not, turn the plastic knobs located on the rear of the headlamps as required (see illustration).
5 Switch off the engine when the adjustment is completed.

6 Horn - maintenance

1 The horn, located near the air inlet grille above the front bumper, should not require any attention or adjustment throughout its life.
2 Provided the circuit fuse and operating switch are in good order, any fault must be in the wiring, the earth bond or the unit itself.
3 A weak or intermittent horn signal may be due to a corroded support bracket connection. Unbolt the horn and scrape the bracket and body contact faces clean.

7 Instrument panel - removal and refitting

Early models

1 Disconnect the battery earth lead.
2 Prise free and lift clear the inspection panel above the instrument panel (see illustration).
3 Unscrew and remove the upper fixing screws (see illustration).
4 Undo the two screws on the underside of the steering column and remove the top cover (see illustration).
5 Unscrew and remove the lower panel fixing bolts from the positions marked by the outer arrows.
6 Disconnect the wiring multi-connectors and the speedometer cable from the instrument panel and carefully withdraw the panel unit.

5.4 Headlamp adjustment screws

7.2 Instrument panel inspection cover removal

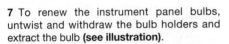
7.3 Remove the instrument panel upper fixing screws (arrowed)

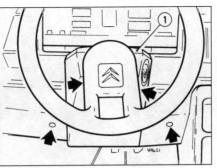

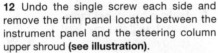
7.4 Remove the fixing screws (arrowed) on the top cover

7.7 Bulb holder removal from the instrument panel

7 To renew the instrument panel bulbs, untwist and withdraw the bulb holders and extract the bulb **(see illustration)**.

8 The instrument panel main body can be detached from the front section by undoing the four retaining screws. Take care not to damage the printed circuits.

9 Further dismantling of the instrument panel is not recommended. If any item in the instrument cluster is malfunctioning, have the unit checked by your Citroën dealer.

10 Refitting is a direct reversal of the removal procedure. If a new vent is being fitted, check that the captive nuts are in position for the lower retaining bolts. Ensure that all wiring connectors are securely made. On completion check the operating of the various instrument panel functions.

Later models

11 Disconnect the battery earth lead.

12 Undo the single screw each side and remove the trim panel located between the instrument panel and the steering column upper shroud **(see illustration)**.

13 Undo the two screws and withdraw the clock/upper facia tray **(see illustration)**. Disconnect the wiring connector and remove the tray.

14 Release the switch panel (located on the right-hand side of the facia) by reaching up behind and depressing the retaining clips each side **(see illustration)**. Withdraw the panel as far as possible to allow access through the aperture.

15 Undo and remove the two instrument panel retaining screws from the front lower edge of the panel **(see illustration)**.

16 Reach through the clock/upper facia tray aperture and, using an 11 mm spanner, undo the upper left-hand instrument panel retaining

nut. The "spire" type nut is threaded onto a plastic stud at the rear of the instrument panel. Later models have wing nuts. Working through the right-hand side switch panel aperture, undo the right-hand side upper retaining nut using the same procedure **(see illustrations)**.

17 Partially withdraw the instrument panel until the wiring connecting plugs can be detached and the speedometer cable disconnected. To do this, pull the sleeve on the connector away from the speedometer head. To reconnect, simply push the sleeve towards the speedometer **(see illustrations)**.

18 The various instrument panel bulbs and their holders are easily accessible in the rear face of the unit. Untwist the holder, and then remove the bulb from it. Take care not to damage the printed circuit on the rear face of the panel.

19 To remove the instrument panel from the

7.12 Unscrewing a trim panel retaining screw

7.13 Unscrewing a clock/upper facia tray securing screw

7.14 Withdrawing the switch panel - retaining clips arrowed

7.15 Instrument panel lower retaining screw

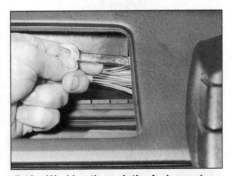
7.16a Working through the facia aperture with a spanner . . .

7.16b . . . to remove an instrument panel retaining nut

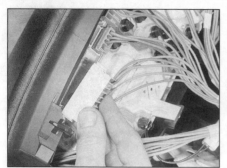

7.17a Instrument panel wiring connectors

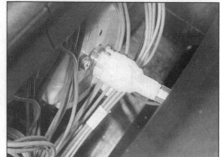

7.17b Speedometer cable connector

8.2 Removing a facia switch

surrounding facia panel, remove the two side screws, and prise free the two clips from the pegs at the lower rear face. Separate the instrument panel from the facia panel.

20 If removing the surrounding facia panel, disconnect the wiring from the four switches, noting the wiring locations given below.

  a) Grey - to the heated rear window switch.
  b) Black - to the hazard warning switch.
  c) Yellow - to the rear window washer/wiper.
  d) Blue - to the rear foglight switch.

21 Refitting of both the instrument panel and its surround is a reversal of the removal procedure. Check the operation of the various switches and controls on completion.

8 Instrument panel facia switches (later models) - removal and refitting

1 Disconnect the battery earth lead.
2 Although it is possible to remove a switch from the facia with it *in situ*, we found it difficult due to the lack of access to the retaining clips on each side of the switch. It may be easier to remove the facia and then push out the switch from the rear whilst compressing the clip each side **(see illustration)**.
3 Detach the wiring connector from the switch and remove it.
4 Refit in the reverse order of removal.

9 Steering column switches - removal and refitting

Early models

1 Disconnect the battery earth lead.
2 Although their functions differ, the switch controls on each side of the steering column are identical. The accompanying illustrations show the removal of the right-hand switch unit but the instructions apply to both the right and left-hand switch units.

Windscreen wiper/washer and horn control

3 Carefully prise free the centre panels and remove them **(see illustration)**.
4 Unscrew the two retaining screws and withdraw the three control switches **(see illustrations)**.

9.3 Removing a central panel

9.4a Remove the two retaining screws (arrowed) . . .

9.4b . . . withdraw the central switch unit . . .

9.4c . . . and selector control unit

9.4d Remove the upper . . .

9.4e . . . and lower switch units

9.5 Withdrawing the multi-connector panel

9.8 Removing the rear window demister switch

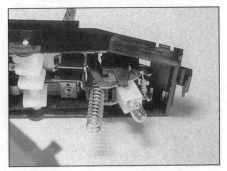

9.9 Switch warning bulb location

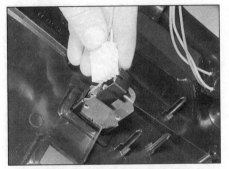

9.12 Detaching the wiring plug from the instrument lighting rheostat

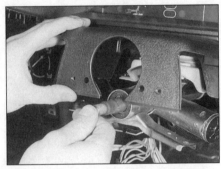

9.13a Removing the steering column upper shroud

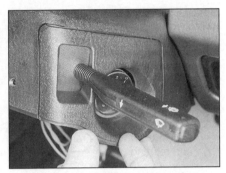

9.13b Removing the steering column upper shroud side panel

9.14a Removing a steering column switch

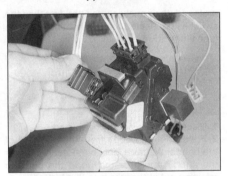

9.14b Steering column switch wiring connectors

5 If required, the switch multi-connector panel can be withdrawn, together with the wires, after detaching the wiring connectors from the main loom **(see illustration)**.

6 Any switch that is defective must be renewed.

7 Refitting is a reversal of the removal procedure. Check the various switch functions on completion for satisfactory operation.

Hazard and rear window demister

8 Use a thin-bladed screwdriver to prise free the switch from its leading edge (the pivot end), then withdraw the switch **(see illustration)**.

9 If the switch warning bulb is to be renewed, carefully prise the outer section away from the inner section and then withdraw the bulb **(see illustration)**.

10 Refitting is a reversal of the removal procedure. Check the switch(es) for satisfactory operation on completion.

Later models

11 Disconnect the battery earth lead.

12 Undo the seven retaining screws and remove the column lower shroud. As it is withdrawn, detach the wires from the instrument lighting rheostat and relay unit **(see illustration)**.

13 Undo and remove the column upper mounting nuts, then loosen the lower mounting bolts to lower the column enough to allow the upper shroud to be removed. The upper shroud has a detachable side panel which is removed sideways by withdrawing it from the windscreen wiper control stalk **(see illustrations)**.

14 To remove either of the column switches, undo the retaining screws and remove them from the brackets. Detach the wiring connectors from the switches **(see illustrations)**.

15 Refitting is a reversal of the removal procedure. Check the switches for satisfactory operation on completion.

10 Door courtesy and boot light switches - removal and refitting

Door courtesy

1 Disconnect the battery earth lead.

2 Open the door then undo the switch retaining screw. Pull the switch from the pillar and detach the wires **(see illustration)**.

3 Refit in the reverse order of removal.

Boot light

4 Disconnect the battery earth lead and open the tailgate.

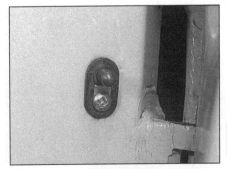

10.2 Door courtesy light switch retaining screw

13

10.5 Boot light switch unit removal

11.2 Electric window operating switch removal

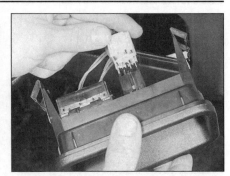

12.3a Disconnecting the wiring from the front foglight switch

5 Reaching up from the underside of the switch, compress the retaining clips and push the switch upwards through its location aperture **(see illustration)**.
6 Detach the wiring connector and remove the switch.
7 Refit in the reverse order of removal.

11 Electrically-operated window switches - removal and refitting

1 Disconnect the battery earth lead.
2 Carefully prise free the switch from the handbrake console. Withdraw the switch and disconnect the wiring **(see illustration)**.
3 Refit in the reverse order to removal.

12 Front foglight and mirror switches (BX 19 models) - removal and refitting

1 Disconnect the battery earth lead.
2 Reach up behind the facia panel, depress the combined switch panel retaining clip each side and push the panel out of its recess in the facia.
3 Disconnect the wiring connector from the rear of the appropriate switch, then push the switch unit(s) out of the panel. The foglight switch has retaining clips which must be depressed to allow its removal **(see illustrations)**.
4 Refit in the reverse order of removal. If

12.3b Front foglight and electric mirror switches and panel

preferred, the panel can be fitted first then the switches connected and pushed into position **(see illustration)**.

13 Handbrake warning switch - removal and refitting

1 Disconnect the battery earth lead.
2 Prise free the cubby from the rear end of the handbrake lever console. Reach through the cubby aperture and undo the console retaining nut at the rear **(see illustration)**.
3 Remove the rubber grommet and undo the console retaining bolt at the front **(see illustration)**. Lift the console clear, disconnecting the wires to any console mounted switches (where applicable) and note their connections.
4 Withdraw the handbrake lever console.

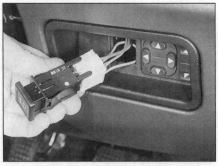

12.4 Refitting the front foglight switch

5 Detach the wiring connector from the handbrake warning light switch, compress the retaining clips and withdraw the switch from its mounting bracket **(see illustration)**.
6 Refitting is a reversal of the removal procedure. Check the operation of the switch on completion.

14 Cigar lighter - removal and refitting

Early models

1 Disconnect the battery earth lead.
2 Remove the radio.
3 The cigar lighter bulb is contained in a shuttle housing on the side of the cigar lighter unit. Withdraw the bulb holder. Extract the bulb if this is to be renewed.

13.2 Handbrake console retaining nut (arrowed)

13.3 Console retaining bolt (arrowed)

13.5 Handbrake warning light switch

14.4 Cigar lighter with bulb and wiring connector detached

14.7 Centre vent grille retaining clip (grille removed for clarity)

14.8 Withdrawing the grille panel

4 Disconnect the wiring connector from the cigar lighter then compress the retaining clips and withdraw the lighter unit **(see illustration)**.
5 Refit in the reverse order of removal.

Later models

6 Disconnect the battery earth lead.
7 Using a suitable screwdriver as a lever, pass it through the centre vent grille on the right-hand side and depress the grille panel retaining clip whilst pulling on the panel **(see illustration)**.
8 With the grille panel withdrawn from the facia **(see illustration)**, detach the wiring from the cigar lighter, compress the retaining clips and withdraw the lighter unit from the panel.
9 Refit in the reverse order of removal.

15 Clock - removal and refitting

1 Disconnect the battery earth lead.
2 Undo the retaining screws and remove the clock/upper facia tray.
3 To remove the clock illumination bulb, twist and remove the holder, then withdraw the bulb from it.
4 To remove the clock unit, detach the wiring connector, then unclip and remove the clock from the tray **(see illustration)**.
5 Refit in the reverse order of removal and reset the clock on completion.

16 Speedometer cable - removal and refitting

1 Disconnect the speedometer drive cable from the rear of the speedometer after sliding back the plastic locking sleeve. The instrument panel will have to be partially withdrawn for access to the connector.
2 Disconnect the cable from the transmission by pulling out the tapered rubber cotter pin. Before withdrawing the cable any further, note how it is routed within the engine compartment as the new cable must be installed in identical fashion to ensure correct operation.

3 Release the bulkhead grommets, and withdraw the cable into the engine compartment.
4 Fitting the new cable is a reversal of the removal operations. Make sure that its routing is as originally taken and avoid bending the cable sharply.

17 Wiper blade - renewal

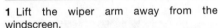

1 Lift the wiper arm away from the windscreen.
2 With a small screwdriver, release the plastic lug and withdraw the wiper blade from the arm **(see illustration)**.
3 Refitting is a reversal of removal.

15.4 Clock unit rear detail - unclip to remove

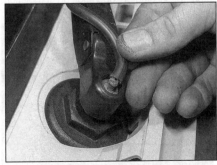

18.2 Detach the washer hose . . .

18 Wiper arm - removal and refitting

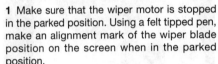

1 Make sure that the wiper motor is stopped in the parked position. Using a felt tipped pen, make an alignment mark of the wiper blade position on the screen when in the parked position.
2 Disconnect the cleaning fluid hose from the nipple on the pivot by pulling it free **(see illustration)**.
3 Lift the cover from the securing nut then unscrew the nut **(see illustration)** and prise the arm from the spindle with a wide-bladed screwdriver. Take care not to damage the paintwork.
4 Refitting is a reversal of removal. Align the

17.2 Wiper blade removal from arm

18.3 . . . and unscrew the wiper arm retaining nut

13

19.3a Peel back the cover seal . . .

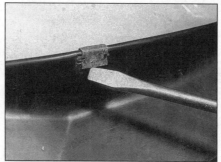

19.3b . . . and prise free the cover clips

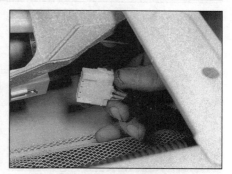

19.4 Detach the wiring connector from the wiper motor

19.5 Wiper arm pivot nut

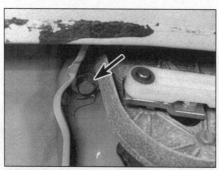

19.6a Wiper motor retaining bolt (arrowed)

19.6b Wiper motor linkage arm spring clip (arrowed)

wiper arm and blade with the temporary alignment marking on the windscreen/rear window. On completion, wipe the alignment mark clean with a dampened cloth and check the operation of the wiper.

19 Windscreen wiper motor - removal and refitting

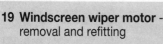

1 Disconnect the battery earth lead.
2 Remove the wiper arm.
3 Raise and support the bonnet. The wiper motor is located in the body cavity above the engine compartment bulkhead (directly in front of the windscreen) under a plastic cover. Remove the plastic cover by peeling back the rubber seal along its leading edge and prising free the retaining clips (see illustrations).
4 Disconnect the wiring connector from the wiper motor (see illustration).
5 Unscrew and remove the wiper arm pivot nut (see illustration).
6 Unscrew the wiper motor mounting bracket retaining bolts and the linkage nut (see illustration). Alternatively, prise free the spring clip and release the linkage arm from the cranked connecting arm pivot but take care not to lose the spring clip (see illustration). Withdraw the wiper motor.
7 Refit in the reverse order to removal. On completion, check the windscreen wiper for satisfactory operation.

20 Rear window wiper motor - removal and refitting

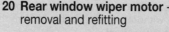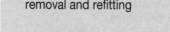

1 Disconnect the battery earth lead.
2 Remove the rear wiper arm and blade.
3 Raise the tailgate and remove the trim panel from it by carefully prising free the plastic retaining clips.
4 Unscrew and remove the wiper motor mounting bracket bolts, noting the earth lead located under the head of one of the bolts (see illustration).
5 Undo the wiper arm pivot nut and lower the motor and bracket away from the tailgate.
6 Disconnect the wiring from the wiper motor and the wiring location clip from the bracket.
7 Unbolt and remove the motor from the mounting bracket.
8 Refitting is a reversal of removal. Check the wiper for satisfactory operation on completion.

20.4 Rear window wiper motor

21 Rear window heater element - maintenance and repair

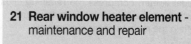

1 The heating elements applied to the glass interior surface should be treated with respect.
2 Clean the glass only with warm water and detergent and wipe in the direction of the element lines. Take care not to scratch the elements with rings on the fingers or by careless stowage of luggage.
3 Do not stick labels over the elements.
4 To repair a break in the element, use one of the conductive paints which are now readily available from motor accessory stores. Follow the manufacturer's instructions carefully.

22 Windscreen and rear window washer units - removal and refitting

Early models

1 These units are located each side at the rear of the engine bay.
2 The pump unit is integral with the filler cap (see illustration).
3 Should the pump fail to operate, check there is sufficient fluid in the reservoir and that the suction and supply hoses are securely connected and clear.
4 Check that the wiring connections are secure. A test light can be used to check the wiring continuity at the pump terminals.

22.2 Washer unit filler cap/pump unit

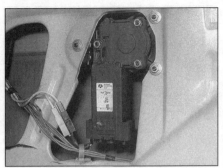

23.3 Electric window regulator unit and wiring connections

24.3 Removing the remote control door locking receiver unit

5 If the pump is defective, renew by detaching the wiring and the suction and supply pipes.
6 The reservoir can be removed by withdrawing the cap/pump unit, releasing the retaining clip and lifting the unit out.
7 Refit in the reverse order of removal and check for satisfactory operation.

Later models

8 Although the location and general details concerning the washer reservoir units remain the same as earlier models, the reservoir pump units are now separate, mounted on the side of the reservoirs rather than being an integral part of the cap as with earlier models.

23 Electrically-operated window regulator units - removal and refitting

1 Disconnect the battery earth lead.
2 Remove the door trim panel.
3 Detach the wiring connectors from the regulator wiring and release the regulator wires from the nylon retaining clip **(see illustration)**.
4 Support the door window, then unscrew the five regulator-to-door retaining nuts and the two nuts securing the lower channel to the door.
5 Slide the regulator rearwards and disengage it from the window channels then remove it through the inner door panel aperture.
6 Refit in the reverse order of removal. Check that the wiring is correctly located and routed so that it will not interfere with the window movement. Check that the window regulator action is satisfactory before refitting the door trim panel.

24 Remote control door locking system - component renewal

Control unit battery

1 The control unit is located next to the handbrake lever. It is accessible after removing the handbrake console.
2 To renew the batteries, depress the battery holder retaining clip each side and withdraw the holder. The batteries can be extracted and

removed but ensure that the correct battery type is used (battery reference V13GA).

Receiver unit

3 The receiver unit is located in the roof console. It is not repairable, and if suspect, must be renewed. Prise free the inspection panel from the roof console, detach the wiring from the receiver unit then unclip and remove the receiver **(see illustration)**.
4 Refitting is a reversal of removal. Check for satisfactory operation on completion.

25 Central locking door solenoid unit - removal and refitting

Side door

1 Disconnect the battery earth lead.
2 Remove the door trim.

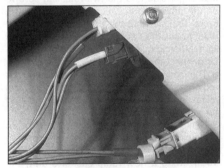

25.3 Wiring connections to door lock solenoid (central locking)

25.9 Lock barrel and retaining clip (central locking)

3 Disconnect the wiring connectors from the end of the solenoid unit **(see illustration)**.
4 Undo the solenoid bolts, detach the solenoid unit from the inner door panel then disengage it from the lock control rod. Withdraw the solenoid unit through the inner door aperture.
5 Refit in the reverse order of removal. Check the operation of the lock on completion.

Tailgate

6 Disconnect the battery earth lead.
7 Raise the tailgate and remove the trim panel from it by carefully prising free the retaining clips.
8 Detach the wiring connector from the solenoid unit **(see illustration)**.
9 Prise the retaining clip free from the lock barrel **(see illustration)**.
10 Undo the retaining bolts and remove the lock solenoid unit **(see illustration)**.
11 Refit in the reverse order to removal.

25.8 Wiring connector to the tailgate solenoid (central locking)

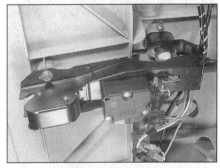

25.10 Tailgate central locking solenoid and lock unit

13

26.3 Removing the door warning panel

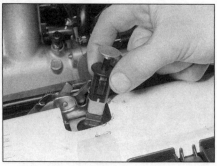

26.4 Removing the bonnet-open warning switch

26 Door-open warning panel - removal and refitting

1 Disconnect the battery earth lead.
2 Tilt, pull and withdraw the coin tray for access to the retaining clip on the left side of the door warning panel.
3 Release the door warning panel retaining clip, then withdraw the panel **(see illustration)**. To renew a warning bulb, twist and remove the holder from the rear face of the panel, then withdraw the bulb. To remove the panel completely, pull free the wiring multi-connector.
4 As well as indicating if any of the doors are open, this warning panel will also indicate if the bonnet and tailgate are not closed properly. If required, the bonnet warning switch can be removed by carefully prising it free from its aperture **(see illustration)** and the wiring disconnected.
5 Refitting is a reversal of the removal procedure. Check for satisfactory operation on completion.

27 Electrically-operated sunroof motor - removal and refitting

1 Disconnect the battery earth lead.
2 Undo the four retaining screws and lower the roof console.
3 Disconnect the wiring from the motor/reducer unit, noting their connections.
4 Undo the retaining screws and partially withdraw the motor/reducer unit so that the operating cables can be detached, then fully remove the motor unit.
5 Refitting is a reversal of the removal procedure. Before refitting the roof console, check the operation of the sunroof and make any adjustments necessary.

28 Radio/cassette - removal and refitting

Early models

1 Disconnect the battery earth lead.
2 Remove the ashtray from its holder and pull free the heater control lever knobs.
3 Undo the two screws from the ashtray holder, remove the holder plate and heater control mounting plate **(see illustration)**.
4 Undo the two diagonally opposed screws securing the centre facia at the heater control **(see illustration)**.
5 Remove the retaining screws and remove the lower trim panel on the passenger side.
6 Remove the retaining screws and remove the steering column lower shroud.
7 Undo the single retaining screw on the passenger side and the two retaining screws on the driver's side which secure the centre facia unit. Withdraw the facia unit and disconnect the wiring to the heater control lights, the cigar lighter and the radio/cassette. Disconnect the radio aerial.
8 The facia unit can now be removed and the radio/cassette retainers (depending on type) released from the rear side to allow the unit to be withdrawn.
9 Refit in the reverse order of removal. Ensure that the wiring and aerial connections are securely made.
10 If fitting a new radio/cassette unit, the aperture in the facia will take any standard-sized equipment.

28.3 Ashtray holder/heater control plate retaining screws (arrowed)

11 The radio must be connected to a power source, the aerial and loudspeaker leads must be plugged in and a good earth bond made between the receiver and a metal part of the vehicle.
12 Once installed, the aerial will have to be trimmed using the small screw provided in the receiver. Tune in to a weak station on the medium wave band and turn the screw until the reception is at its loudest and clearest.

Later models

13 Depending on model, later variants are fitted with a wiring harness and connections for a stereo or a six-speaker radio system, even though the radio and speaker units may not be fitted as standard **(see illustration)**.
14 With the stereo system, there are facilities provided in each front door panel for speaker fitting, the wiring being already provided. The speaker grille can be removed from the door panel by prising it free using a screwdriver as a lever **(see illustration)**.
15 When refitting the grille to the door, locate it at the bottom edge and press it into position at the top.
16 The six-speaker system has a speaker (tweeter) at each end of the dashboard, one speaker in each front door and one each side at the rear, either in the rear quarter panel or above the wheel arches (Estate model). Headphone sockets and an accessories jack may be fitted to the rear face of the centre console, for use by rear passengers. Note that the headphone sockets will only work when the rear speakers are fitted and connected.

29 Speakers (standard) - removal and refitting

Facia mounted - upper

1 Carefully prise free the grille panel from the top of the facia on the side concerned.
2 Undo the two retaining screws and withdraw the speaker unit. Disconnect the leads **(see illustration)**.
3 Refit in the reverse order of removal.

28.4 Remove the panel screws indicated

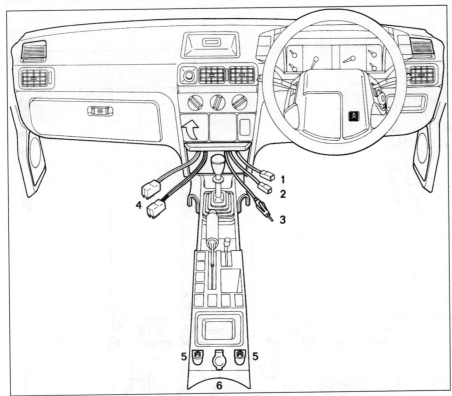

28.13 Later radio and speaker wiring connections

28.14 Using a screwdriver to prise a radio speaker grille from the door

1 Radio supply - grey wire/red connector
2 Radio earth - yellow wire/brown connector
3 Aerial coaxial cable
4 Six-speaker system - four white connectors (two shown):
   Two green wires to left channel
   Two brown wires to right channel
   Black tracer negative/red tracer positive

4 Stereo speaker system - two white connectors:
   One green wire to left channel*
   One brown wire to right channel*
   Black tracer negative/red tracer positive
5 Headphone stereo jacks**
6 Accessories jack (12 volt, 10 amp)
* Speaker wiring to each front door
** Six-speaker system only
   (with rear speakers fitted)

Facia mounted - lower

4 Unscrew the retaining screws from the positions shown (see illustration) and withdraw the lower trim panel and the glove compartment.

5 Undo the retaining screws and lower the speaker unit. Detach the wiring connector.

6 Refit in the reverse order of removal.

29.2 Facia-mounted speaker (upper) shown with grille panel removed

30 Wiring diagrams

The wiring diagrams in this Manual represent typical examples of those available.

To assist in using the diagrams, there

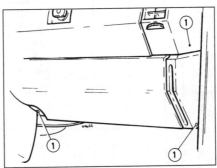

29.4 Remove the lower trim panel screws indicated

follows an explanation of the various letters and their use in conjunction with the wiring diagram keys:

a) Large numbers - identify the various components.

b) Capital letters printed in the middle of a wire - indicate which harness the wire is located in.

c) Small letters located at the connection points - indicate colour, either of the wires (which have an "F" prefix), of the end fitting, of the marking on the wire, or a combination of any two. For example, F.Bl is a blue wire, Mv is a mauve marking, and F.J.Ve is a yellow wire with a green marking.

d) Connecting blocks - the first number and the letters inside the boxes indicate the size and colour of the connecting block. Note that due to lack of space, 0 is used to denote 10. The last number gives the relative location of the relevant wire in that connecting block.

13

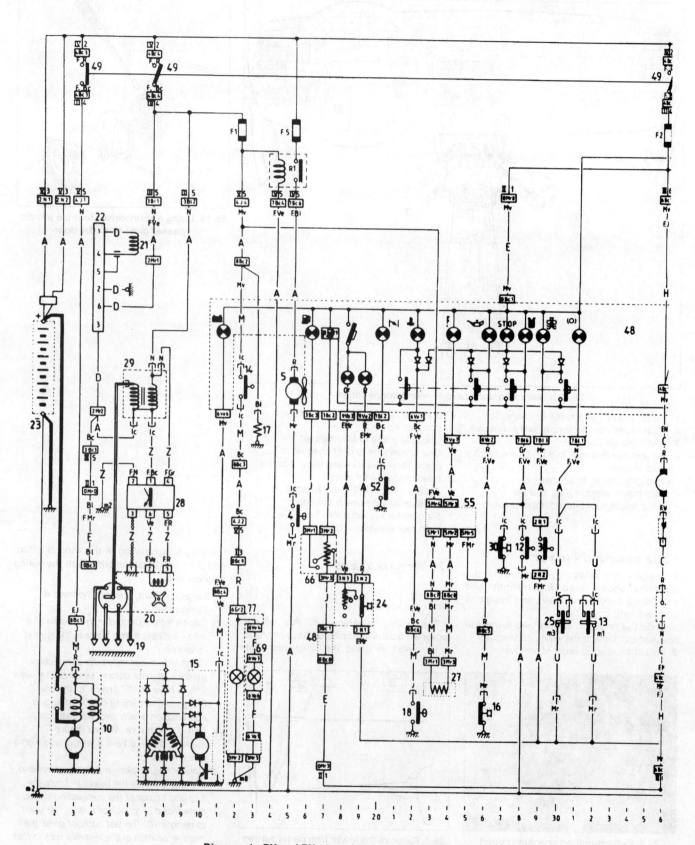

Diagram 1 - BX and BX 14 models from July 1983 (typical)

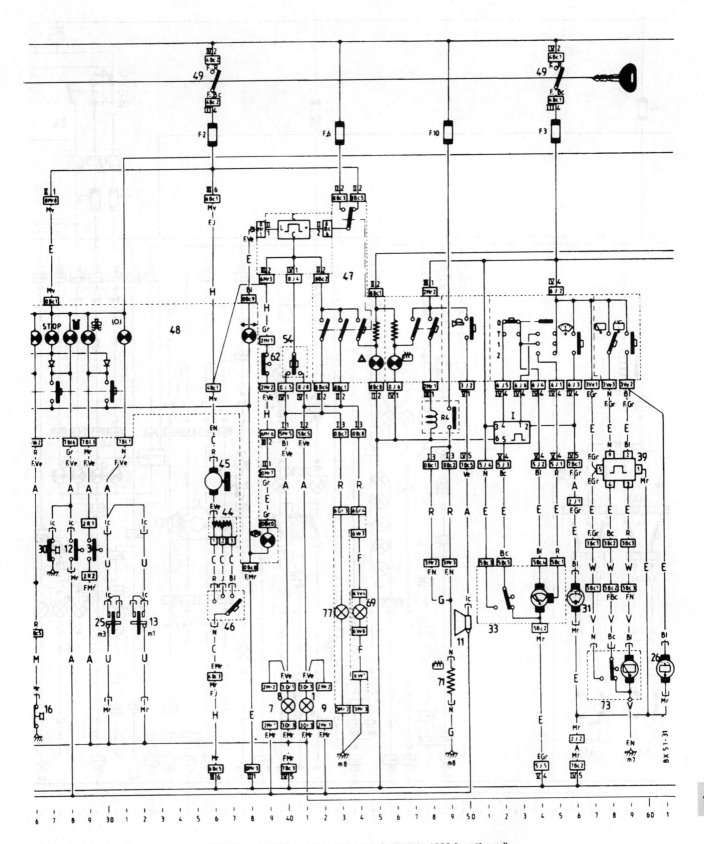

Diagram 1 - BX and BX 14 models from July 1983 (continued)

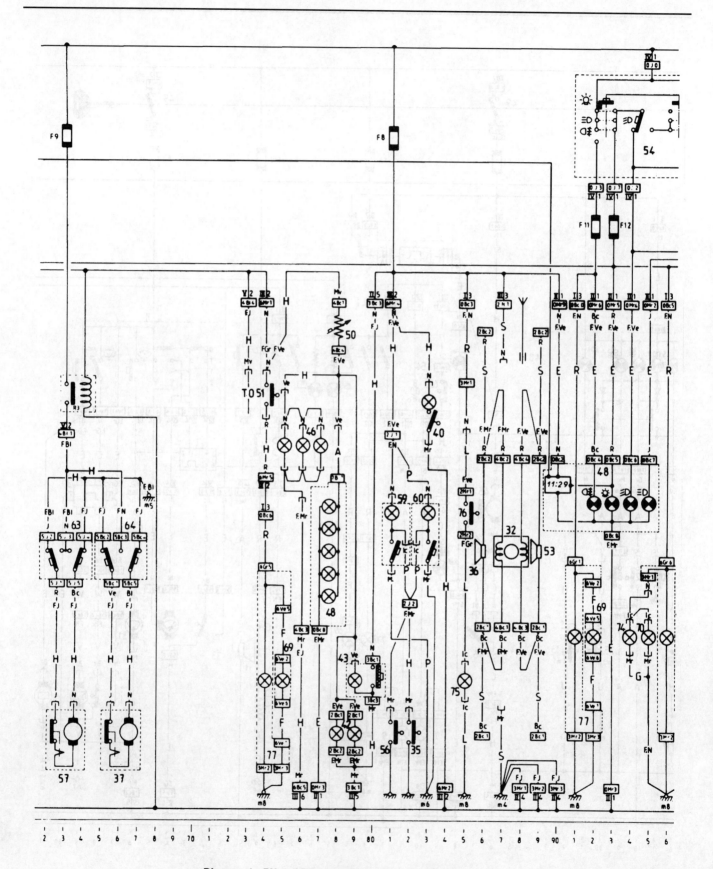

Diagram 1 - BX and BX 14 models from July 1983 (continued)

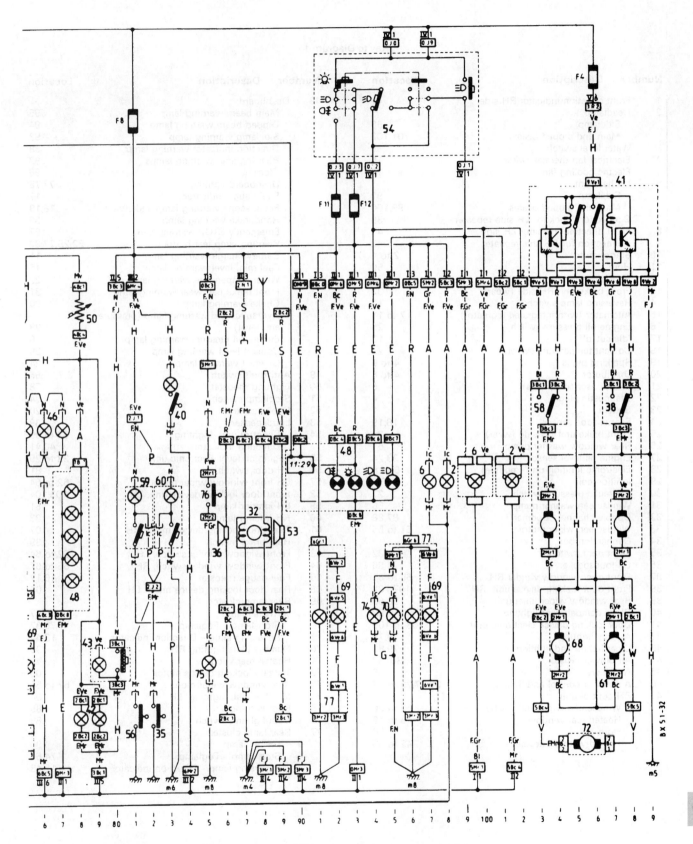

Diagram 1 - BX and BX 14 models from July 1983 (continued)

Key to Diagram 1

Number	Description	Location		Number	Description	Location
1	Front direction indicator RH side	41		48	Dashboard:	
2	Headlamp:				Main beam warning lamp	95
	Sidelamp	98			Dipped beam warning lamp	94
	Main and dipped beams	101,102			Sidelamp warning lamp	93
3	Water level switch	29			Direction indicator warning lamp	38
4	Electrical fan thermal switch	15			Rear foglamp warning lamps	92
5	Electric cooling fan	15			Clock	90
6	LH headlamp:				Dashboard lighting	77,78
	Sidelamp	97			Fuel gauge indicator	17
	Main and dipped beams	99,100			Econoscope warning lamp and switch	18,19
7	Connection block for LH side repeater	39			Handbrake warning lamp	39
8	Front direction indicator LH side	40			Emergency STOP warning lamp	27
9	Connection for RH side repeater	42			Warning lamp test buttom	22,25,27,30
10	Starter motor	2 to 4			Battery charge warning lamp	11
11	Horn	50			Fuel min. level warning lamp	16
12	Hydraulic fluid level switch	28			Water temperature warning lamp	22
13	Front brake unit RH side (wear)	32			Front brake pad wear warning lamp	31
14	Reversing lamp switch	12			Choke warning lamp	20
15	Alternator (with integrated regulator)	7 to 11			Hydraulic fluid warning lamp (pressure and level)	28
16	Engine oil pressure switch	26			Engine oil pressure warning lamp	26
17	Idle cut-off	13			Coolant level warning lamp	29
18	Coolant temperature switch	22			Oil level warning lamp	24
19	Sparking plugs	4 to 6		49	Anti-theft switch	3,7,36,55
20	Distributor	4 to 8		50	Lighting rheostat	78
21	TDC sensor (diagnosis)	6		51	Stoplamp switch	74
22	Diagnostic plug	4		52	Choke control	20
23	Battery	1		53	Loudspeaker	89
24	Econoscope sensor	18,19		54	LH control unit: Lighting	92 to 99
25	Front brake unit LH side (wear)	30			Direction indicators	40,41
26	Rear window washer pump	61		55	Engine oil level electronic unit	23 to 25
27	Engine oil level sensor	23,24		56	LH door switch	81
28	Electronic ignition unit (module)	6 to 8		57	LH front window wiper motor	62 to 64
29	Ignition coil	6,7		58	Front door locking device unit, LH	103,104
30	Hydraulic pressure switch	27		59	LH interior lamp	81
31	Windscreen washer pump	56		60	RH interior lamp	83
32	Double channel "Boomer"	87,88		61	Rear door locking device motor RH	107
33	Windscreen wiper motor	51 to 55		62	Handbrake switch	39
34	Connection box			63	Front window winder switch, LH	62 to 64
35	Front door switch	82		64	Front window winder switch, RH	65 to 67
36	LH loudspeaker	86		66	Fuel gauge rheostat	16,17
37	Front door window winder RH	65 to 67		68	Rear door locking device motor LH	104
38	Front door locking device unit, RH	107,108		69	Rear lamp cluster:	
39	Rear window wiper timer unit	58,59			RH tail lamp	97
40	Glove compartment lighting	83			Stop-lamp – Foglamp	75,92
41	Door locking device electronic unit	103 to 109			Reversing lamp – Direction indicator	13,44
42	Ashtray lighting	78,79		70	Number plate lighting RH	95
43	Cigar lighter and lighting	79,80		71	Heated rear window	49
44	Air blower resistor	36, 37		72	Tailgate locking device motor	105
45	Air blower	36		73	Rear window wiper motor	57 to 59
46	Air blower control and lighting	36,37,75 to 77		74	Number plate lighting, LH	94
47	RH control unit:			75	Boot lighting	85
	Windscreen wiper and washer	52 to 56		76	Boot lighting switch	85
	Heated rear window	46 to 48		77	Rear lamp cluster:	
	Horn	50			LH tail lamp	90
	Hazard warning device	42 to 45			Stop-lamp – Foglamp	74,51
					Reversing lamp – Direction indicator	12,43

Key to Diagram 1 (continued)

Wiring colour code

Bc	White
Bl	Blue
Gr	Grey
Ic	Transparent
J	Yellow
Mr	Brown
Mv	Mauve
N	Black
Or	Orange
R	Red
Ve	Green
Vi	Violet

If the code is preceded by the letter F, it denotes the wire colour. Otherwise it denotes the sleeve colour

Earthing points

m1	Earthing point for RH front brake pad wear	32
m2	Battery earthing point on bodyshell	1,4
m3	Earthing point for LH front brake pad wear	30
m4	Connection box earthing point	87
m5	Earthing point on centre console	67,109
m6	Earthing point on windscreen frame upper part	83
m7	RH rear earthing point (rear window wiper and locking device)	59
m8	LH rear earthing point (rear window, lighting LH and RH rear lamps)	12,43,49,74,85,91,96

Harness code

A	Front
AB	Front foglamp socket
B	Boot locking – intermediate
C	Heater
D	Diagnostic
E	Windscreen wiper and dashboard
F	Ribbon-type – between rear lamps
G	Tailgate – LH
H	Passenger compartment
J	Petrol gauge
L	Boot lighting
M	Engine
P	Interior lamp
R	Ribbon-type – rear
S	Radio
U	Front brakes (pad wear)
V	Tailgate – RH (rear window wiper)
W	Tailgate – RH intermediate
X	Starting safety device
Z	Transistorised ignition

13

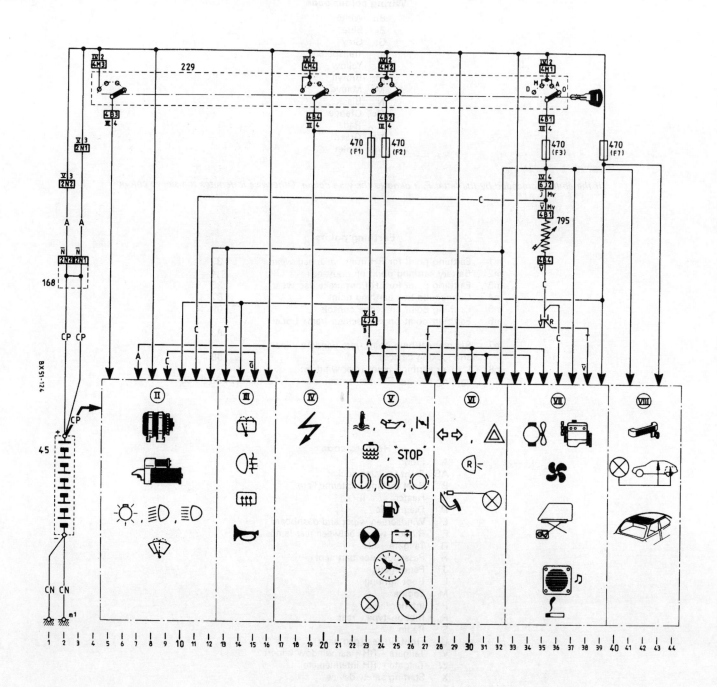

Diagram 2 - BX and BX 14 models from October 1988 - circuit I

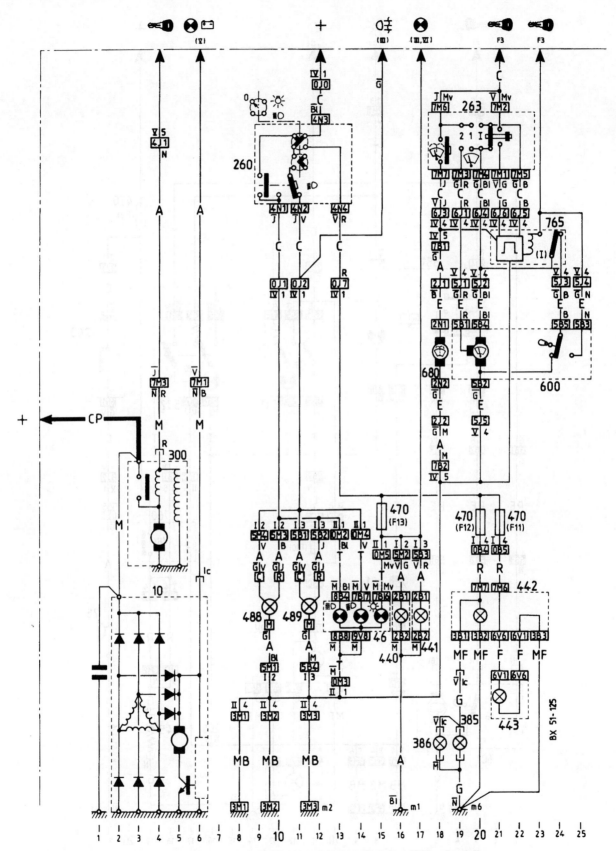

Diagram 2 - BX and BX 14 models from October 1988 - circuit II

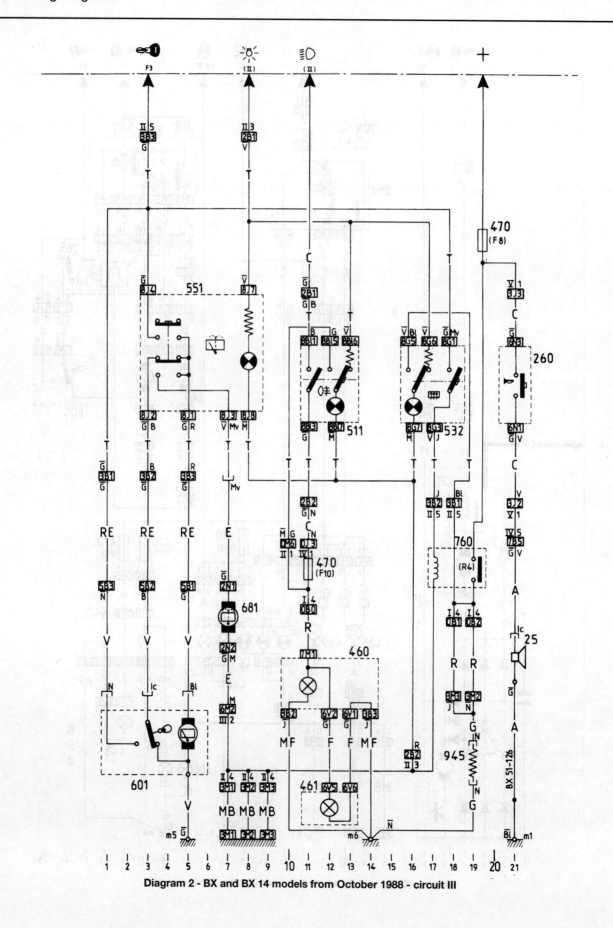

Diagram 2 - BX and BX 14 models from October 1988 - circuit III

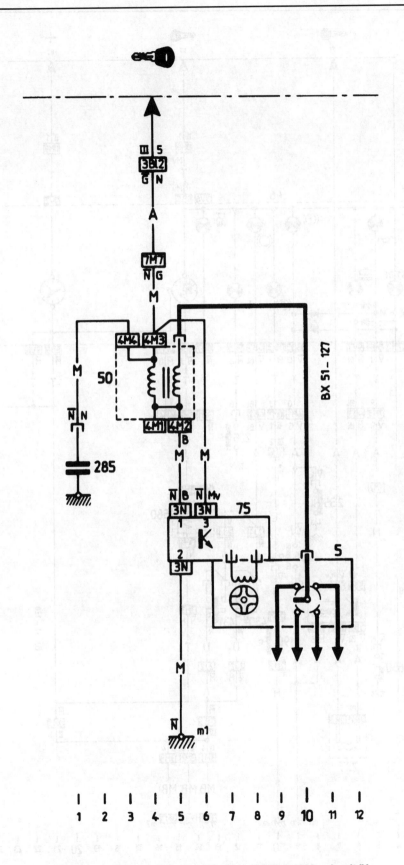

Diagram 2 - BX and BX 14 models from October 1988 - circuit IV

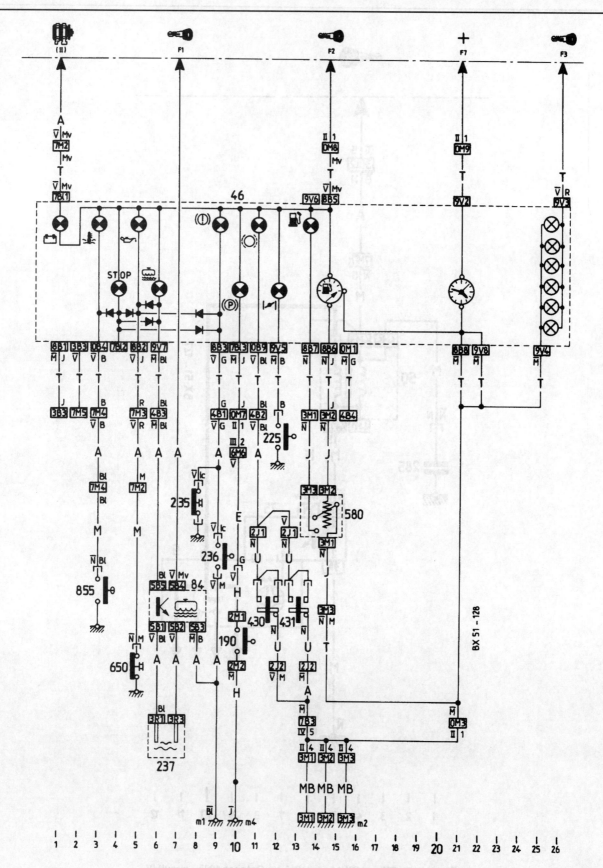

Diagram 2 - BX and BX 14 models from October 1988 - circuit V

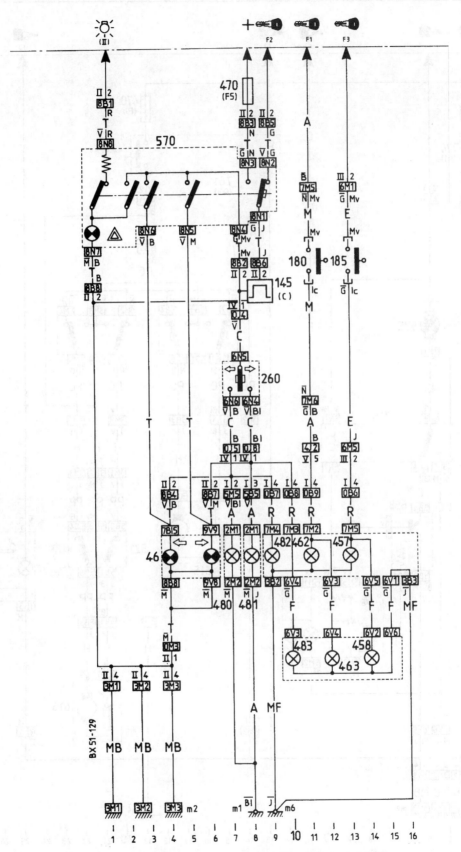

Diagram 2 - BX and BX 14 models from October 1988 - circuit VI

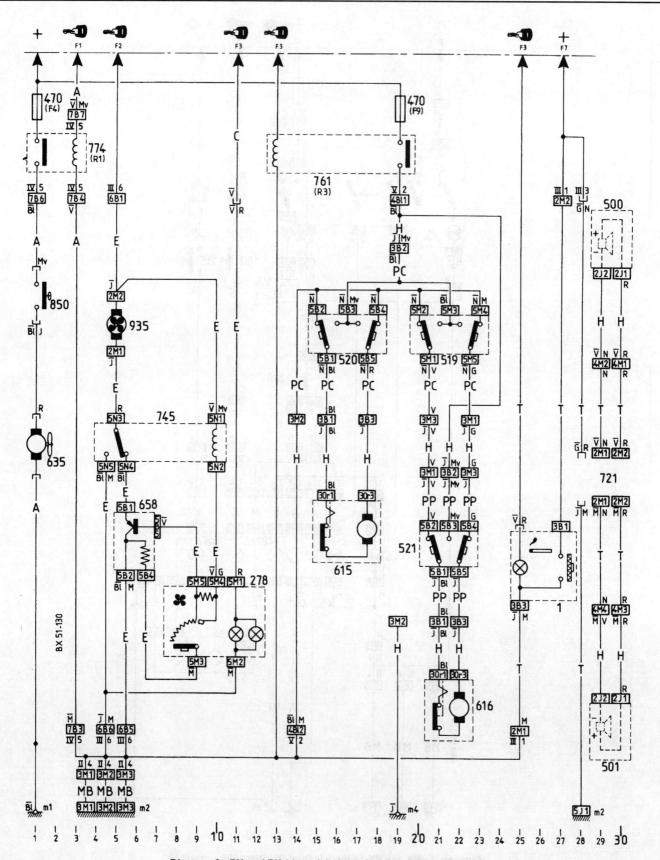

Diagram 2 - BX and BX 14 models from October 1988 - circuit VII

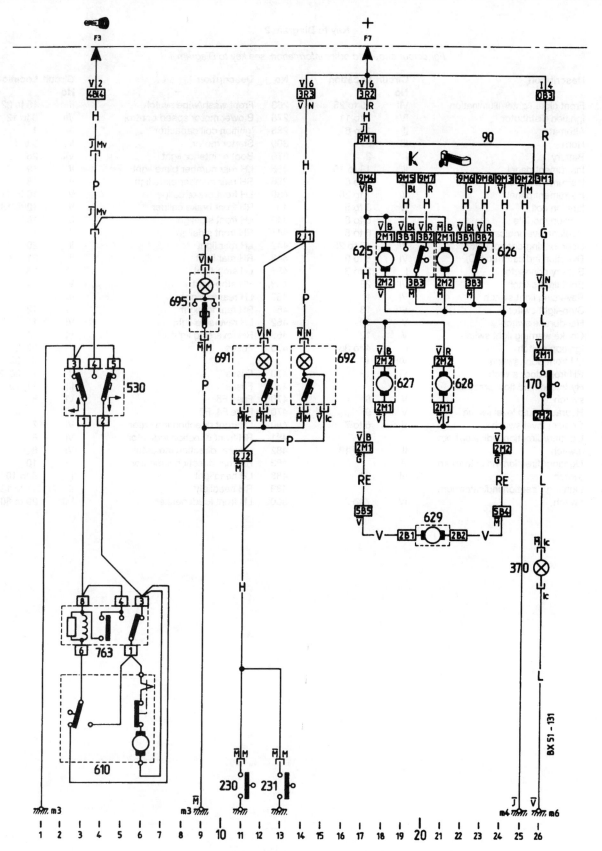

Diagram 2 - BX and BX 14 models from October 1988 - circuit VIII

Key to Diagram 2

For colour code and other information, see key to Diagram 1

No	Description	Circuit No	Location	No	Description	Circuit No	Location
1	Front cigar lighter/illumination	VII	25 to 25	263	Front wash/wipe switch	II	18 to 22
5	Ignition distributor	IV	7 to 11	278	Blower motor speed control	VII	8 to 12
10	Alternator	II	1 to 6	285	Ignition coil capacitor	IV	1
25	Horn	III	21	300	Starter motor	II	3 to 5
45	Battery	I	2	370	Boot or interior light	VIII	26
46	Instrument panel	II	13 to 15	385	LH rear number plate light	II	19
46	Instrument panel	IV	4 to 6	386	RH rear number plate light	II	18
46	Instrument panel	V	1 to 26	430	LH front brake caliper	V	10 to 11
50	Ignition coil	IV	3 to 5	431	RH front brake caliper	V	12 to 13
75	Ignition module	IV	5 to 8	440	LH front sidelight	II	16
84	Coolant level indicator unit	V	6 to 8	441	RH front sidelight	II	17
90	Door locking control unit	VII	17 to 25	442	LH rear light	II	20
145	Direction indicator unit (C)	VI	8 to 9	443	RH rear light	II	21
168	Battery connector	I	2 to 3	457	LH stop-light	VI	13
170	Boot light switch	VIII	26	458	RH stop-light	VI	14
180	Reversing light switch	VI	11	460	LH rear foglight	III	11
185	Stop-light switch	VI	13	461	RH rear foglight	III	12
190	Handbrake switch	V	10	462	LH reversing light	VI	11
225	Choke warning light switch	V	12	463	RH reversing light	VI	12
229	Ignition switch	I	4 to 36	470	Fuses	I	23, 24, 35, 39
230	LH front door switch	VIII	11				
231	RH front door switch	VIII	13	470	Fuses	II	15, 20, 21
235	Hydraulic fluid flow pressure switch	V	8	470	Fuses	III	11, 19
				470	Fuse F5	VI	8
236	Hydraulic fluid level switch	V	9	470	Fuse F4, F9	VII	1, 19
237	Coolant level switch	V	6 to 7	480	LH front direction indicator	VI	7
260	Lighting/direction indicator/horn switch	II	9 to 13	481	RH front direction indicator	VI	8
260	Lighting/direction indicator/horn switch	III	21	482	LH rear direction indicator	VI	8
				483	RH rear direction indicator	VI	10
260	Lighting/direction indicator/horn switch	IV	7 to 8	488	LH headlight	II	9 to 10
				489	RH headlight	II	11 to 12
				500	LH front loudspeaker	VII	29 to 30

Key to Diagram 2 (continued)

For colour code and other information, see key to Diagram 1

No	Description	Circuit No	Location	No	Description	Circuit No	Location
501	RH front loudspeaker	VII	29 to 30	635	LH engine cooling fan motor	VII	1
511	Rear foglight switch	III	11 to 13	650	Engine oil pressure switch	V	5
519	RH window winder switch on driver's door	VII	20 to 23	658	Blower fan control module	VII	6
520	LH window winder switch on driver's door	VII	15 to 18	680	Windscreen washer pump	II	18
521	RH front window winder switch	VII	21 to 22	681	Rear screen washer pump	III	7
530	Sunroof switch	VIII	3 to 4	691	LH interior light	VIII	11 to 12
532	Heated rear window switch	III	16 to 18	692	RH interior light	VIII	14 to 15
551	Rear screen intermittent wiper switch	III	3 to 8	695	Interior spotlights	VIII	9
570	Hazard warning light switch	VI	1 to 9	721	Radio connections (12V and speakers)	VII	28 to 30
580	Fuel gauge	V	14	745	Blower motor high speed relay	II	5 to 10
600	Windscreen wiper motor	II	19 to 25	760	Heated rear screen relay (R4)	III	17 to 19
601	Rear screen wiper motor	III	1 to 5	761	Front window winder motor relay (R3)	VII	13 to 19
610	Sunroof motor	VIII	3 to 6	763	Sunroof motor relay	VII	3 to 6
615	LH front window winder motor	VII	15 to 18	765	Windscreen wiper relay	II	21 to 24
616	RH front window winder motor	VII	21 to 22	774	Engine cooling fan relay (R1)	VII	1 to 3
625	LH front door lock motor	VIII	18 to 20	795	Lighting rheostat	I	35
626	RH front door lock motor	VIII	21 to 23	850	Cooling fan thermal switch	VII	1
627	LH rear door lock motor	VIII	18	855	Water temperature switch	V	3
628	RH rear door lock motor	VIII	27	935	Air conditioning fan	VII	5
629	Boot lid lock motor	VIII	20 to 21	945	Heated rear screen	III	19

Harness code

A	Front		M-B	Junction box earth
C	Switches		M-F	Rear light cluster earth
CN	Battery negative cable		P	Interior lighting
CP	Battery positive cable		PC	Driver's door
E	Window wiper		PP	Passenger's door
F	Rear light cluster connection		R	Rear
G	LH side tailgate		RE	Rear screen wiper
H	Interior		T	Instrument panel
J	Fuel gauge		U	Brake pad wear
L	Boot lighting		V	RH side tailgate
M	Engine		Z	Ignition

13

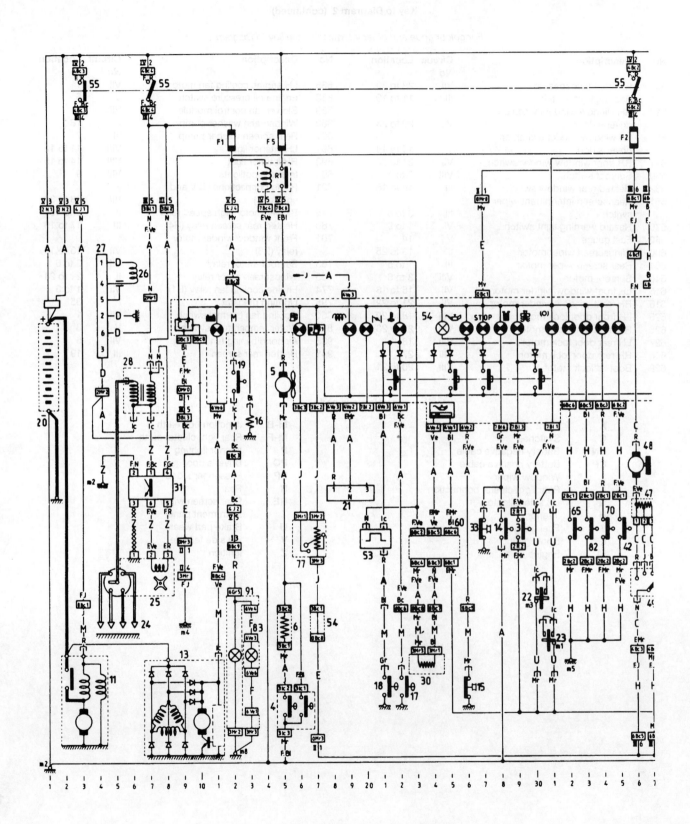

Diagram 3 - BX 16 models from July 1983 (typical)

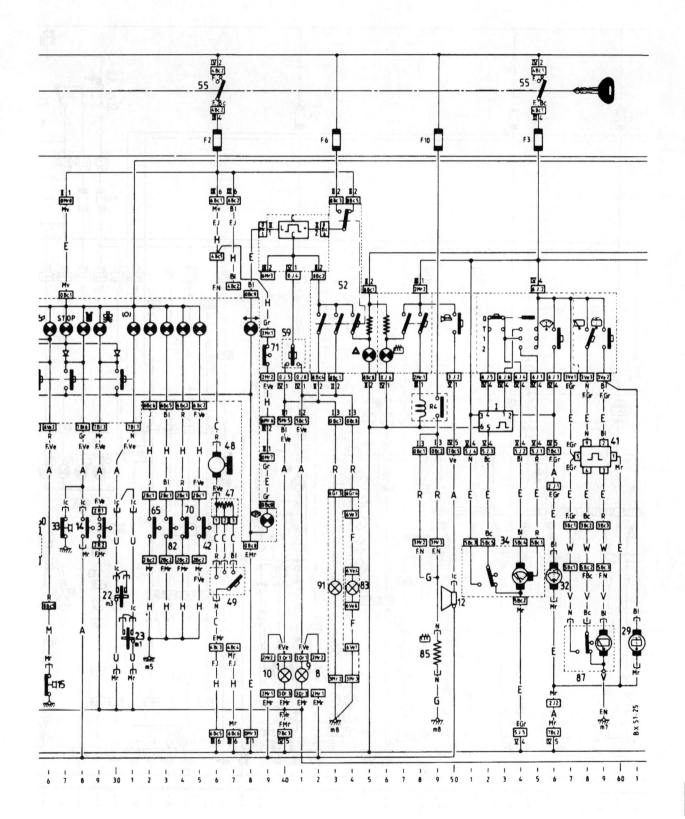

Diagram 3 - BX 16 models from July 1983 (continued)

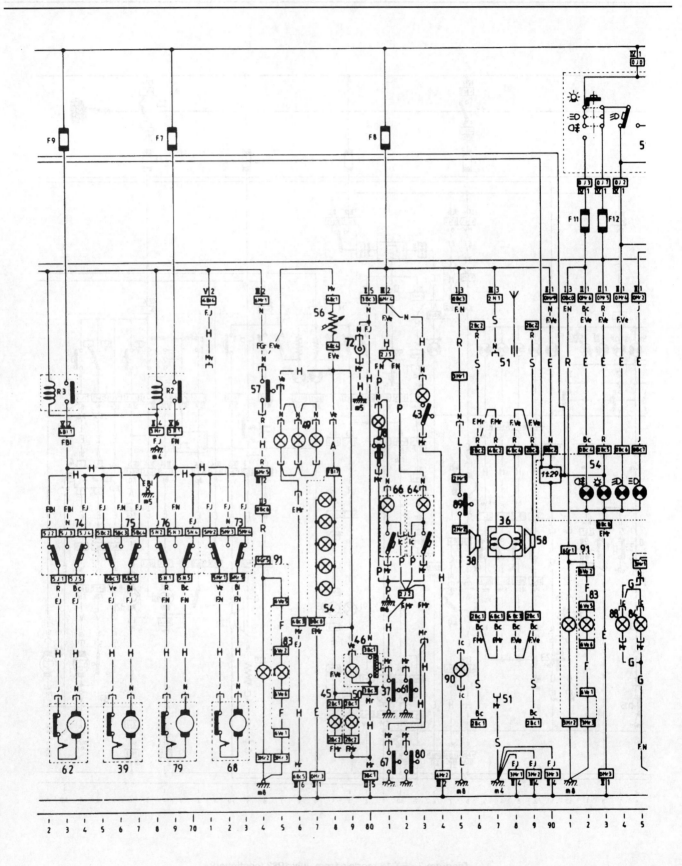

Diagram 3 - BX 16 models from July 1983 (continued)

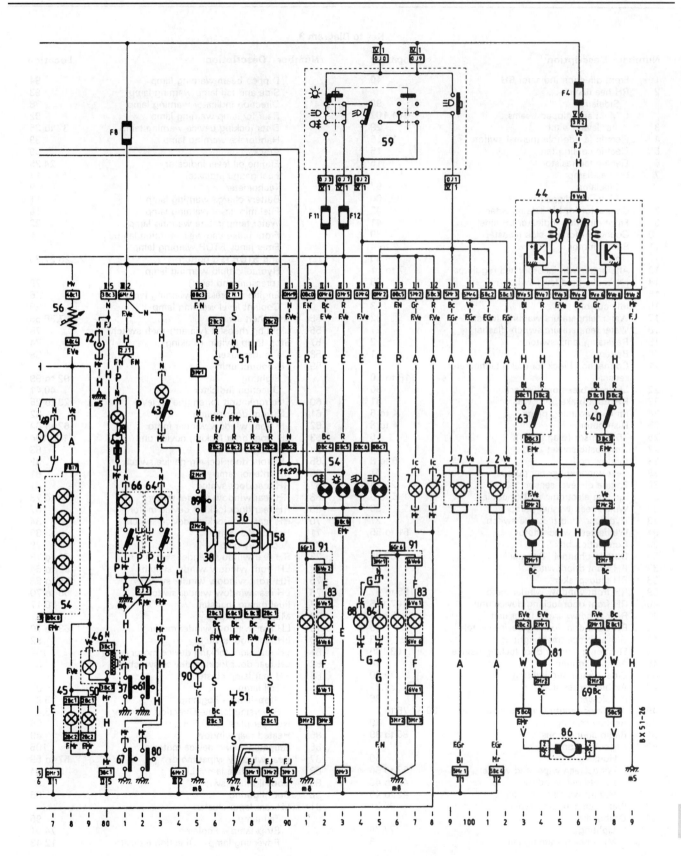

Diagram 3 - BX 16 models from July 1983 (continued)

Key to Diagram 3

Number	Description	Location	Number	Description	Location
1	Front direction indicator RH	40		Dipped beam warning lamp	94
2	RH headlamp:			Side and tail lamp warning lamp	93
	Sidelamp	98		Direction indicator warning lamp	38
	Main and dipped beams	101,102		Rear foglamp warning lamp	92
3	Water level switch	29		Door locking device warning lamp	32 to 35
4	Electric fan double thermal switch	15,16		Handbrake warning lamp	39
5	Electric cooling fan	15		Clock	90
6	Electric fan resistor	15		Engine oil level indicator	24,25
7	LH headlamp:			Fuel gauge indicator	17
	Sidelamp	97		Tachometer	9
	Main and dipped beams	99,100		Battery charge warning lamp	11
8	Connector for LH side repeater	42		Fuel min. level warning lamp	16
9	Front direction indicator LH side	41		Water temperature warning lamp	22
10	Connector for RH side repeater	39		Front brake pad wear warning lamp	31
11	Starter motor	2 to 4		Emergency STOP warning lamp	
12	Horn	50		and STOP test button	22,25,27,30
13	Alternator with incorporated regulator	7 to 11		Hydraulic fluid warning lamp	
14	Hydraulic fluid level switch	28		(pressure and level)	28
15	Engine oil pressure switch	26		Engine oil pressure warning lamp	26
16	Idle cut-off	13		Coolant level warning lamp	29
17	Water temperature warning switch	22	55	Anti-theft switch	3,7,36,55
18	Water temperature switch (flasher)	21	56	Lighting rheostat (via anti-theft switch)	78
19	Reversing lamp switch	12	57	Stop-lamp switch (braking)	74
20	Battery	1	58	LH loudspeaker	89
21	Connection block for diesel tachometer		59	LH control unit:	
	sensor	18 to 20		Lighting	92 to 99
22	LH front brake unit (wear)	30		Direction indicator	40,41
23	RH front brake unit (wear)	31	60	Electronic unit for engine oil level	23 to 25
24	Ignition sparking plugs	4 to 6	61	LH front door switch	82
25	Distributor	4 to 8	62	LH front window winder motor	62 to 64
26	TDC sensor (diagnostic)	6	63	LH front door locking device unit	103,104
27	Diagnostic socket	4	64	LH interior lamp	83
28	Ignition coil	6 to 8	65	LH front door locking device switch	32
29	Rear window washer pump	61	66	RH interior lamp	81
30	Engine oil level sensor	23,24	67	RH rear door switch	81
31	Ignition electronic unit (module)	6 to 8	68	RH rear window winder motor	71 to 73
32	Windscreen washer pump	56	69	RH rear door locking device motor	107
33	Hydraulic fluid pressure switch	27	70	RH rear door locking device switch	34
34	Windscreen wiper motor	51 to 55	71	Handbrake switch	39
35	Connection box		72	Accessory plug	79
36	Double-channel "Boomer"	87,88	73	RH rear window winder switch	71 to 73
37	RH front door switch	81	74	LH front window winder switch	62 to 64
38	RH loudspeaker	86	75	RH front window winder switch	65 to 68
39	RH front window winder motor	65 to 67	76	LH rear window winder switch	68 to 70
40	RH front door locking device unit	107,108	77	Fuel gauge rheostat	16,17
41	Rear window wiper timer unit	58,59	78	Map reading lamp	81
42	RH front door locking device switch	35	79	LH rear window winder motor	68 to 70
43	Glove compartment lighting	83	80	LH rear door switch	82
44	Electronic unit for door locking device	103,109	81	LH rear door locking device motor	104
45	Ashtray lighting	78	82	LH rear door locking device switch	33
46	Cigar lighter and lighting	79,80	83	RH rear lamp cluster:	
47	Air blower resistors	36,37		Tail lamp	97
48	Air blower	36		Stop-lamp – Foglamp	75,92
49	Air blower control and lighting	36,37,75 to 77		Reversing lamp – Direction indicator	13,44
50	Ashtray lighting	79	84	Number plate lamp RH	95
51	Radio connections	86 to 89	85	Heated rear window	49
52	RH control unit:		86	Tailgate locking device motor	105
	Horn	50	87	Rear window wiper motor	57 to 59
	Windscreen wiper and washer	53 to 56	88	Number plate lamp, LH	94
	Heated rear window	46 to 48	89	Boot lighting switch	85
	Hazard warning device	42 to 45	90	Boot lighting	85
53	Water temperature flasher	20,21	91	LH rear lamp cluster:	
54	Dashboard:			Tail lamp	96
	Lighting	77,78		Stop-lamp – Foglamp	74,91
	Main beam warning lamp	95		Reversing lamp – Direction indicator	12,43

Not all items are fitted to all models

Key to Diagram 3 (continued)

Wiring colour code

Bc	White
Bl	Blue
Gr	Grey
Ic	Transparent
J	Yellow
Mr	Brown
Mv	Mauve
N	Black
Or	Orange
R	Red
Ve	Green
Vi	Violet

If the code is preceded by the letter F, it denotes the wire colour. Otherwise it denotes the sleeve colour

Earthing points

m1	Earthing point for RH front brake pad wear	31
m2	Battery earthing point on bodyshell	1,4
m3	Earthing point for LH front brake pad wear	30
m4	Earthing point for connection box and dashboard	9,69,87
m5	Earthing point on console	67,79,109
m6	Earthing point on windscreen frame upper part	81
m7	RH rear earthing point (rear window wiper)	59
m8	LH rear earthing point (heated rear window boot)	49,85
	LH and RH rear lamps	12,43,74,91,96

Harness code

A	Front
AB	Front foglamp socket
B	Boot locking – intermediate
C	Heater
D	Diagnostic
E	Windscreen wiper and dashboard
F	Ribbon-type – between rear lamps
G	Tailgate – LH
H	Passenger compartment
J	Petrol gauge
L	Boot lighting
M	Engine
P	Interior lamp
R	Ribbon-type – rear
S	Radio
U	Front brakes (pad wear)
V	Tailgate – RH (rear window wiper)
W	Tailgate – RH intermediate
X	Starting safety device
Z	Transistorised ignition

13

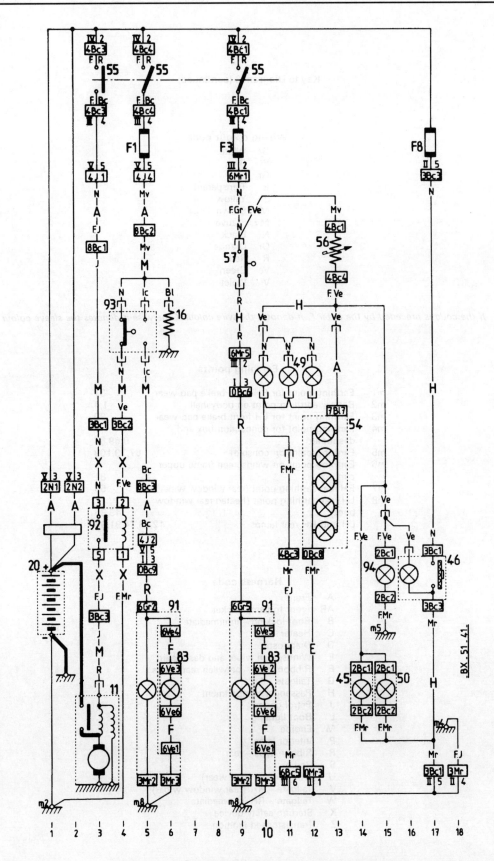

Diagram 4 - BX 16 models with automatic transmission

Key to Diagram 4

Number	Description	Location
11	Starter	2 to 4
16	Float chamber electric ventilation	6
20	Battery	1
45	Ashtray lighting	14
46	Cigar lighter and lighting	16,17
49	Air blower control lighting	10 to 12
50	Ashtray lighting	15
54	Dashboard lighting	12,13
55	Anti-theft switch	3,5,9
56	Lighting rheostat	13
57	Stop-lamp switch	9
83	RH rear lamp cluster	6,10
91	LH rear lamp cluster	5,9
92	Starter motor relay, starter motor	3,4
93	Switch for starter motor, reversing lamps	4,5
94	Gearchange diagram lighting	15

Harness code

A	Front
AB	Front foglamp socket
B	Boot locking – intermediate
C	Heater
D	Diagnostic
E	Windscreen wiper and dashboard
F	Ribbon-type – between rear lamps
G	Tailgate – LH
H	Passenger compartment
J	Petrol gauge
L	Boot lighting
M	Engine
P	Interior lamp
R	Ribbon-type – rear
S	Radio
U	Front brakes (pad wear)
V	Tailgate – RH (rear window wiper)
W	Tailgate – RH intermediate
X	Starting safety device
Z	Transistorised ignition

Wiring colour code

Bc	White
Bl	Blue
Gr	Grey
Ic	Transparent
J	Yellow
Mr	Brown
Mv	Mauve
N	Black
Or	Orange
R	Red
Ve	Green
Vi	Violet

13

If the code is preceded by the letter F, it denotes the wire colour. Otherwise it denotes the sleeve colour

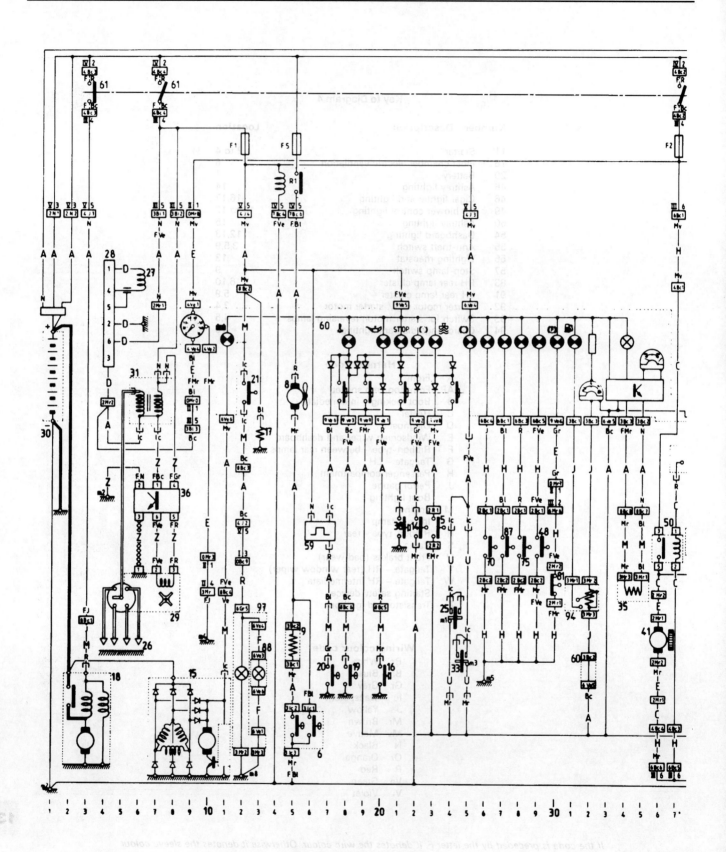

Diagram 5 - BX 19 GT models

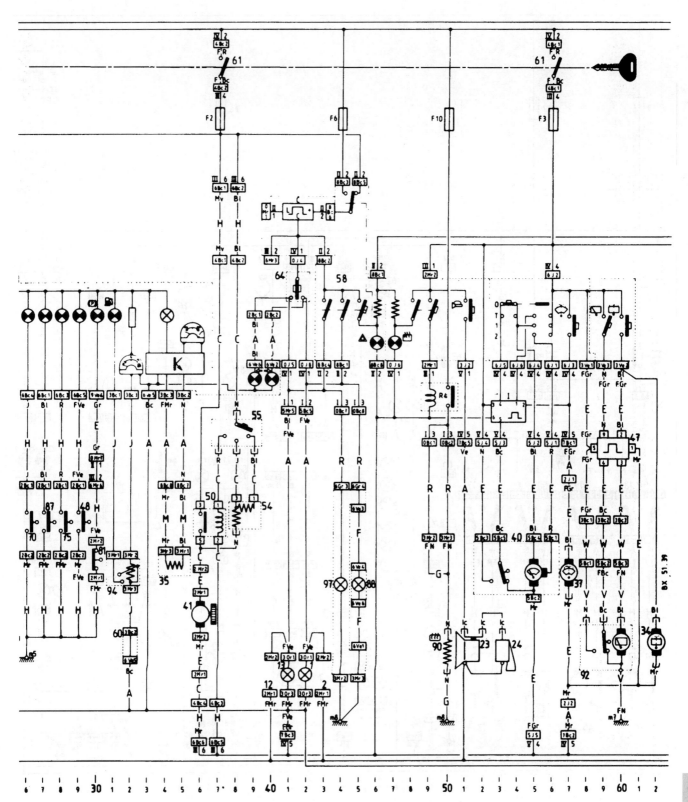

Diagram 5 - BX 19 GT models (continued)

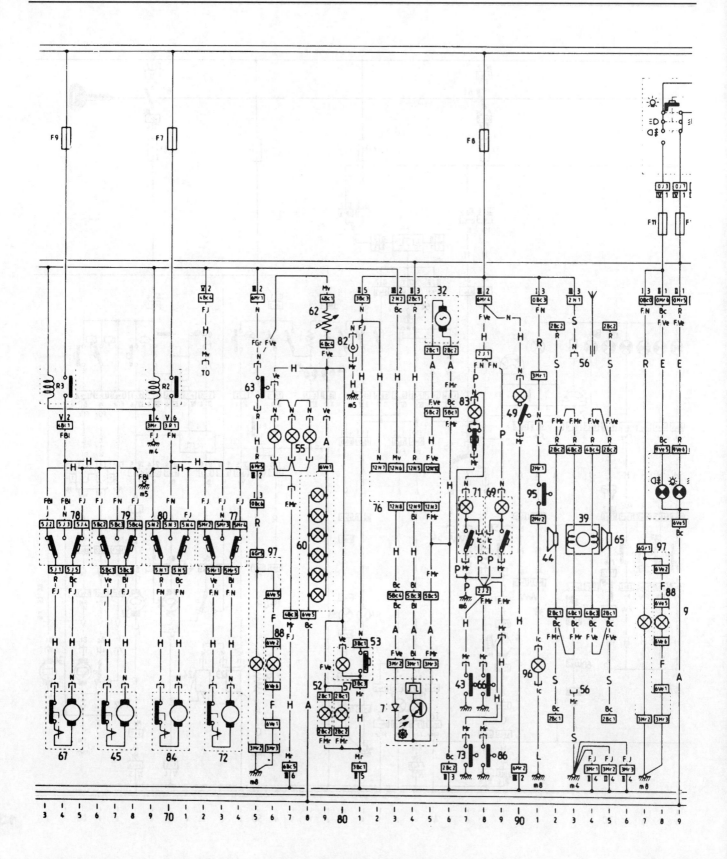

Diagram 5 - BX 19 GT models (continued)

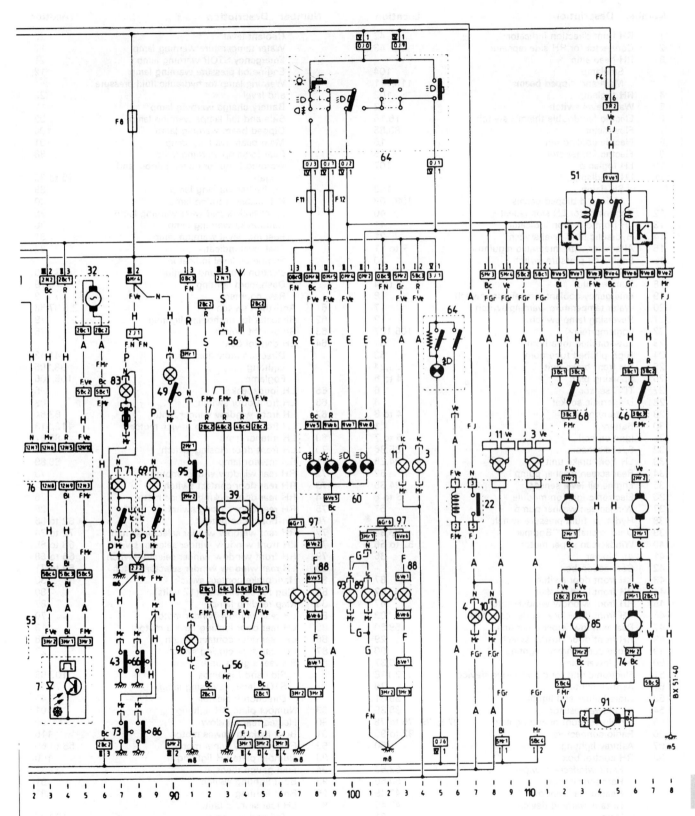

Diagram 5 - BX 19 GT models (continued)

Key to Diagram 5

Number	Description	Location	Number	Description	Location
1	RH front direction indicator	42		Coolant level	23
2	Connector for RH side repeater	43		Water temperature warning lamp	17
3	RH headlamp:			Emergency STOP warning lamp	21
	Sidelamp	104		Engine oil pressure warning lamp	19
	Main and dipped beams	110,111		Warning lamp for hydraulic fluid pressure	
4	RH foglamp	102		and level	22
5	Water level switch	23		Battery charge warning lamp	11
6	Electric fan double thermal switch	15,16		Side and tail lamps warning lamp	99
7	Flowmeter	83,85		Dipped beam warning lamp	100
8	Electric cooling fan	15		Main beam warning lamp	101
9	Electric fan resistor	15		Rear foglamp warning lamp	98
10	LH foglamp	107		Warning lamp for opened doors and	
11	LH headlamp:			tailgate	26 to 30
	Sidelamp	103		LH flasher warning lamp	39
	Main and dipped beams	108,109		RH flasher warning lamp	40
12	Connector for LH side repeater	40		Front brakes pad wear warning lamp	25
13	LH front direction indicator	41		Handbrake warning lamp	30
14	Hydraulic fluid level switch	21		Fuel min level warning lamp	31
15	Alternator with integrated regulator	7 to 11		Fuel level indicator	32
16	Engine oil pressure switch	20		Engine oil level indicator,	
17	Idle cut-off	13		electronic unit and lighting	33,36
18	Starter motor	2 to 4		Dashboard lighting	78,79
19	Emergency coolant temperature switch	18		Rev. counter	9
20	Water temperature warning switch	17	61	Anti-theft switch	2,6,37,56
21	Reversing lamp switch	12	62	Rheostat for dashboard lighting	79
22	Foglamp relay	106,107	63	Stop-light switch	75
23	Low-pitched tone horn	51	64	LH control box:	
24	High-pitched tone horn	53		Direction indicators	41,42
25	RH front brake unit	23,24		Lighting	98,105
26	Sparking plug	4 to 6		Foglamp	105,106
27	TDC sensor	6	65	LH loudspeaker	95
28	Diagnostic socket	4	66	LH front door switch	88
29	Distributor	4 to 8	67	LH front window winder motor	63,64
30	Battery	1	68	LH front door locking device motor	112,113
31	Ignition coil	6 to 7	69	LH interior lamp	86,87
32	Speed sensor	85,86	70	LH front door closing switch	26
33	LH front brake unit	24,25	71	RH interior lamp	88,89
34	Rear screen washer pump	62	72	RH rear window winder motor	73
35	Engine oil level sensor	34,35	73	RH rear door contact switch	87
36	Electronic ignition module	6 to 8	74	RH rear door locking device motor	76
37	Windscreen washer pump	57	75	RH rear door closing switch	28
38	Hydraulic fluid pressure switch	21	76	On-board computer	82 to 85
39	Double channel "Boomer"	93,94	77	RH rear window winder selector switch	72 to 74
40	Windscreen wiper motor	52 to 56	78	LH front window winder selector switch	63 to 65
41	Air blower	36	79	RH front window winder selector switch	66 to 68
42	Connection box	–	80	LH rear window winder selector switch	69 to 71
43	RH front door switch	87	81	Handbrake contact switch	30
44	RH front loudspeaker	92	82	Plug for accessories (12 volts)	80
45	RH front window winder motor	67	83	Map reading lamp	87
46	RH front door locking device motor	103	84	LH rear window winder motor	70
47	Rear window wiper timer unit	59,60	85	LH rear door locking device motor	113
48	RH front door closing switch	29	86	LH rear door contact switch	88
49	Glove compartment lighting	90	87	LH rear door closing switch	27
50	Air blower relay	36,37	88	RH rear signals unit:	
51	Electronic unit for door locking device	112,118		Side and foglamps	103,98
52	Ashtray lighting	79		STOP lamp, reversing lamp	76,13
53	Cigar lighter and lighting	80,81		Direction indicator	45
54	Air blower resistor	38,39	89	Number plate RH lighting	101
55	Air blower control and lighting	37 to 39, 76 to 78	90	Heated rear window	50
56	Radio connectors	92 to 95	91	Boot locking device motor	115
57	Ashtray lighting	80	92	Rear window wiper motor	58 to 60
58	RH control box:		93	Number plate LH lighting	100
	Front windscreen wiper	53,55	94	Fuel gauge rheostat	31,32
	Rear screen wiper	59,60	95	Boot lighting switch	91
	Heated rear window	47,49	96	Boot lighting	91
	Hazard warning device	43,46	97	LH rear signals unit:	
	Horn	51		Tail and foglamp	102,97
59	Water temperature flasher unit	16,17		STOP lamp, reversing lamp	75,12
60	Dashboard:			Direction indicator	44

Key to Diagram 5 (continued)

Wiring colour code

Bc	White
Bl	Blue
Gr	Grey
Ic	Transparent
J	Yellow
Mr	Brown
Mv	Mauve
N	Black
Or	Orange
R	Red
Ve	Green
Vi	Violet

If the code is preceded by the letter F, it denotes the wire colour. Otherwise it denotes the sleeve colour

Harness code

A	Front
AB	Front foglamp socket
B	Boot locking – intermediate
C	Heater
D	Diagnostic
E	Windscreen wiper and dashboard
F	Ribbon-type – between rear lamps
G	Tailgate – LH
H	Passenger compartment
J	Petrol gauge
L	Boot lighting
M	Engine
P	Interior lamp
R	Ribbon-type – rear
S	Radio
U	Front brakes (pad wear)
V	Tailgate – RH (rear window wiper)
W	Tailgate – RH intermediate
X	Starting safety device
Z	Transistorised ignition

13

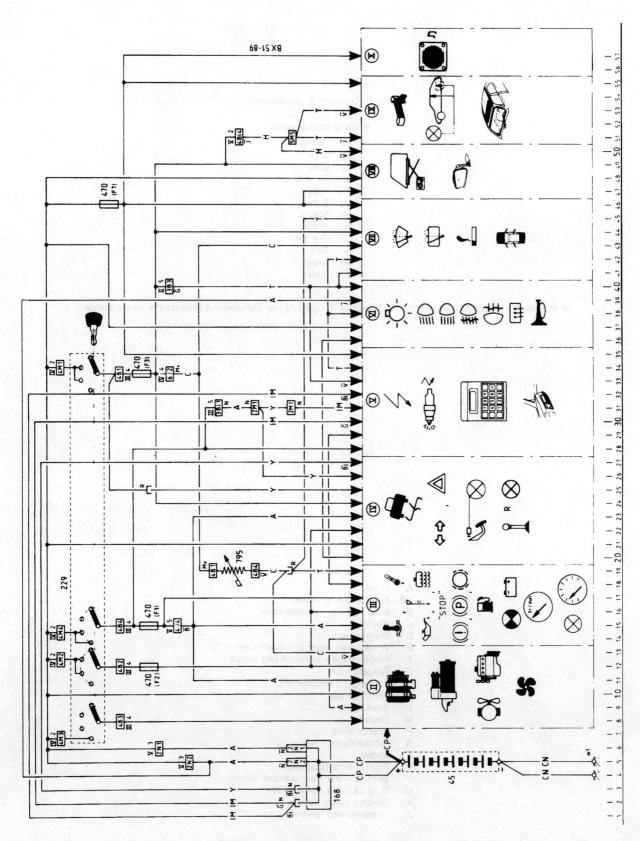

Diagram 6 - All models from 1987 - circuit I

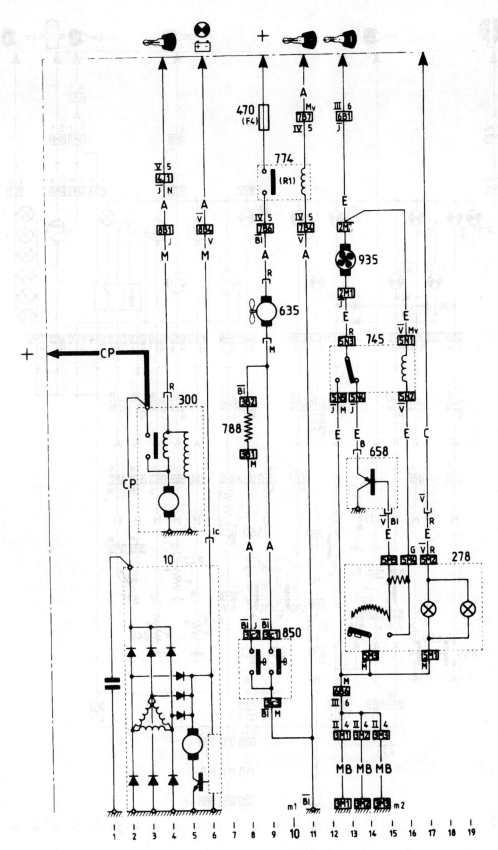

Diagram 6 - All models from 1987 - circuit II

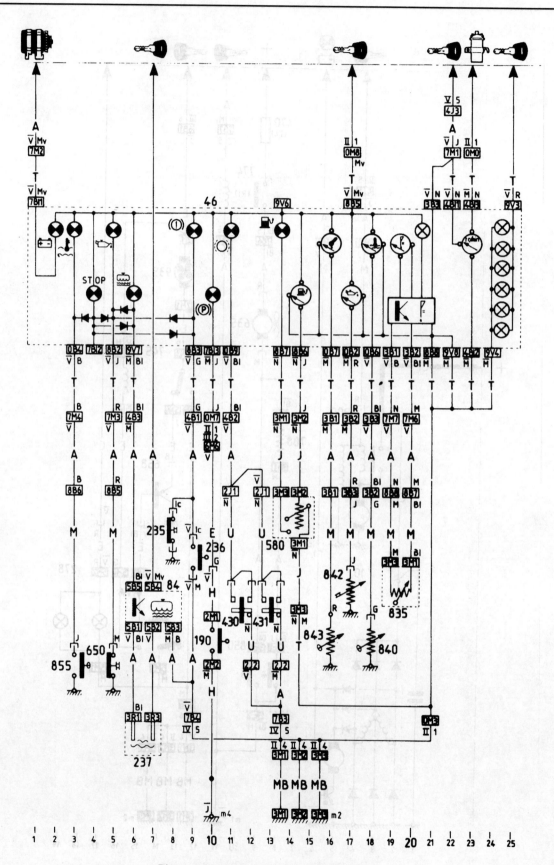

Diagram 6 - All models from 1987 - circuit III

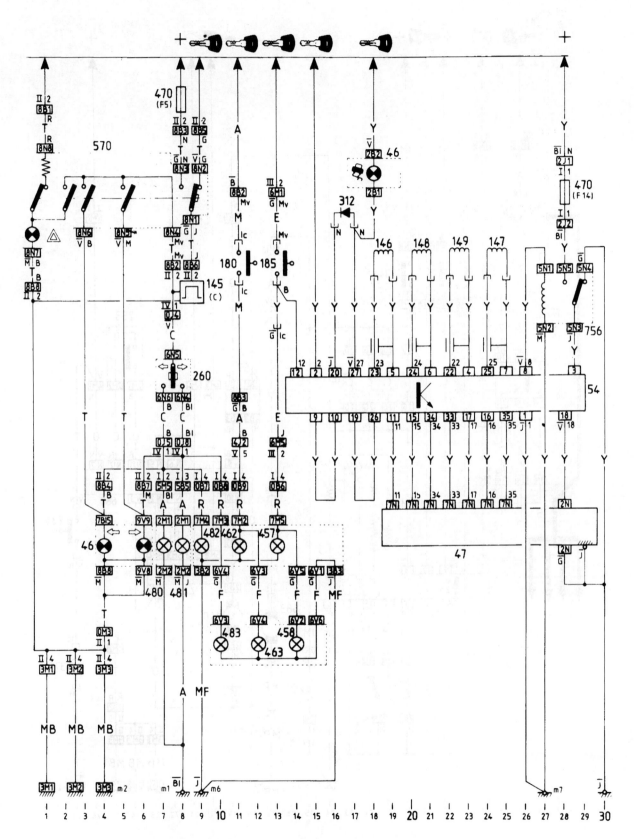

Diagram 6 - All models from 1987 - circuit IV

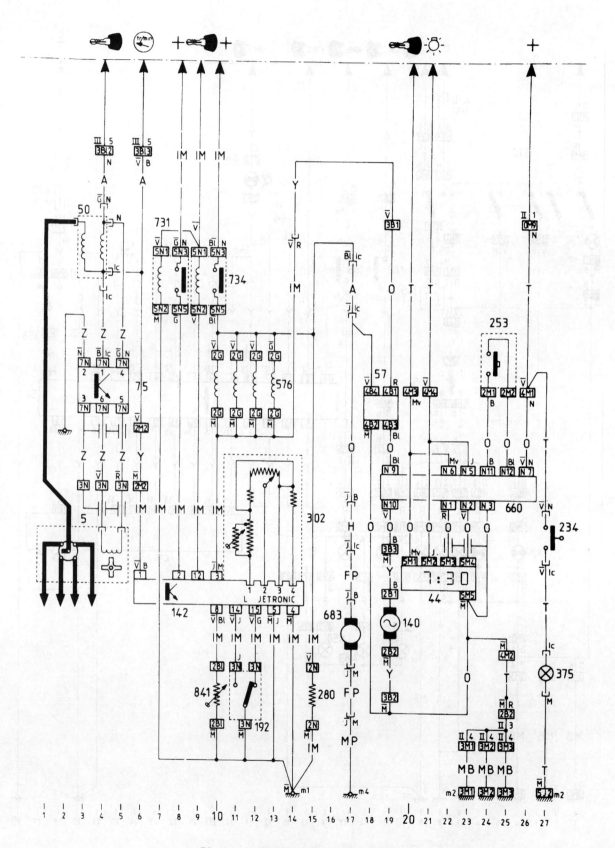

Diagram 6 - All models from 1987 - circuit V

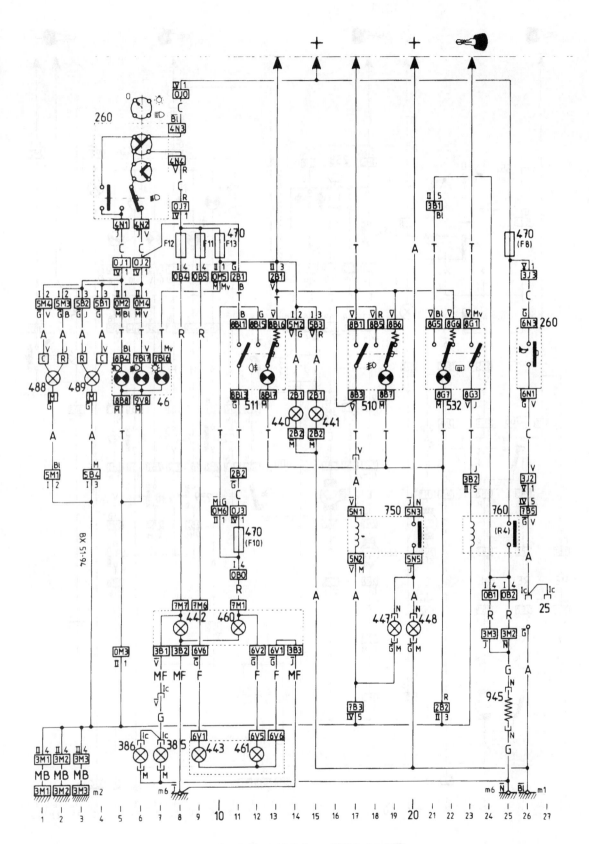

Diagram 6 - All models from 1987 - circuit VI

13

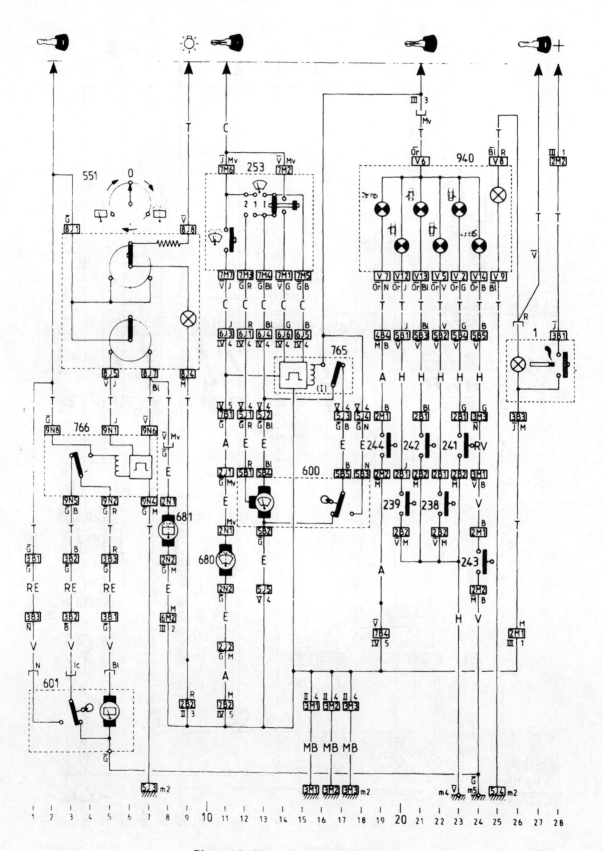

Diagram 6 - All models from 1987 - circuit VII

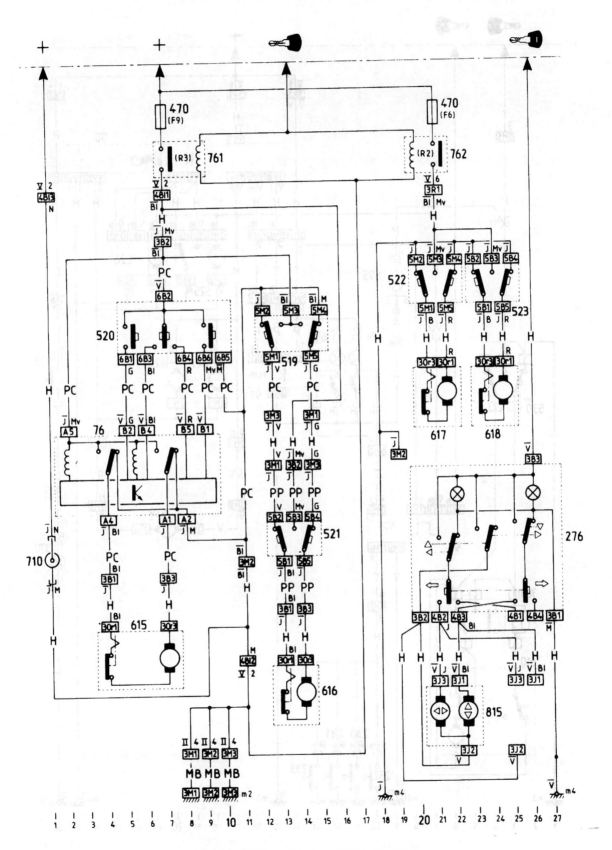

Diagram 6 - All models from 1987 - circuit VIII

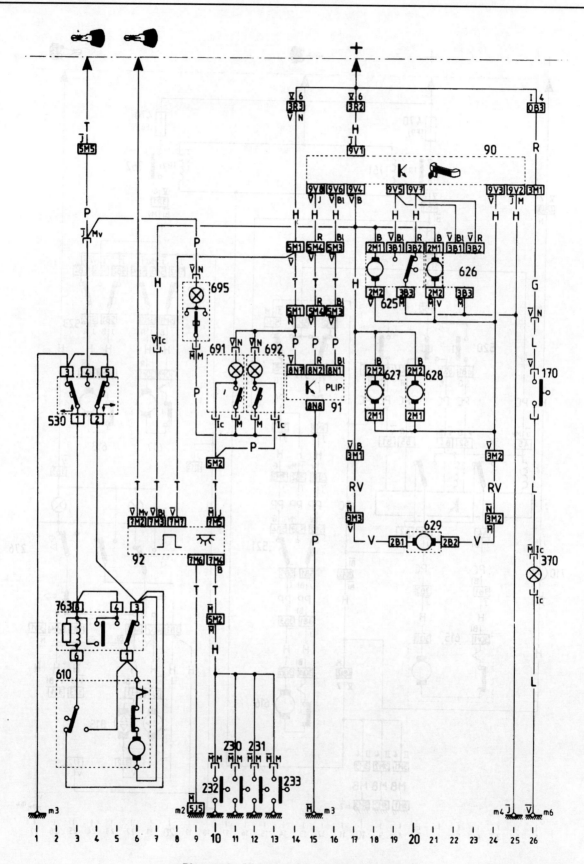

Diagram 6 - All models from 1987 - circuit IX

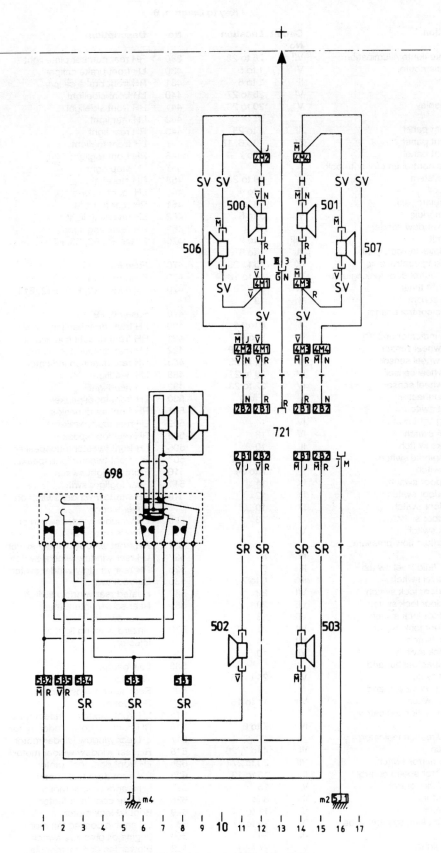

Diagram 6 - All models from 1987 - circuit X

13

Key to Diagram 6

No	Description	Circuit No	Location	No	Description	Circuit No	Location
1	Front cigar lighter/illumination	VII	26 to 28	386	RH rear number plate light	VI	6
5	Ignition distributor	V	1 to 5	430	LH front brake caliper	III	11 to 12
10	Alternator	II	1 to 6	431	RH front brake caliper	III	13 to 14
25	Horn	VI	26 to 27	440	LH front sidelight	VI	14
44	Digital display	V	20 to 23	441	RH front sidelight	VI	15
45	Battery	I	5	442	LH rear light	VI	8
46	Instrument panel	III	1 to 25	443	RH rear light	VI	9
46	Instrument panel	IV	4 to 6, 18	447	LH front foglight	VI	19
46	Instrument panel	VI	5 to 7	448	RH front foglight	VI	20
47	Hydraulic control unit for anti-lock braking system	IV	19 to 29	457	LH stop-light	IV	13
50	Ignition coil	V	3 to 4	458	RH stop-light	IV	14
57	Fuel calculator unit	V	18 to 19	460	LH rear foglight	VI	11
75	Ignition module	V	3 to 5	461	RH rear foglight	VI	12
76	LH front window winder control unit	VIII	2 to 9	462	LH reversing light	IV	11
84	Coolant level indicator unit	III	6 to 8	463	RH reversing light	IV	12
90	Door locking control unit	IX	15 to 25	470	Fuses F1, F2, F3, F7	I	15, 12, 34, 46
91	Remote control door locking unit	IX	14 to 16	470	Fuse F4	II	9
92	Interior light timer	IX	6 to 10	470	Fuse F5, F14	IV	8, 28
140	Distance sensor	V	19	470	Fuse F8, F10, F11, F12, F13	VI	8, 9, 10, 11, 25
142	Electronic control unit for injection	V	6 to 14	470	Fuse F6, F9	VIII	7, 21
145	Direction indicator unit (C)	IV	8 to 9	480	LH front direction indicator	IV	7
146	LH front wheel sensor	IV	18 to 19	481	RH front direction indicator	IV	8
147	RH front wheel sensor	IV	24 to 25	482	LH rear direction indicator	IV	9
148	LH rear wheel sensor	IV	20 to 21	483	RH rear direction indicator	IV	10
149	RH rear wheel sensor	IV	22 to 23	488	LH headlight	VI	1 to 2
168	Battery connector	I	2 to 6	489	RH headlight	VI	3 to 4
170	Boot light switch	IX	26	500	LH front loudspeaker	X	12
180	Reversing light switch	IV	11	501	RH front loudspeaker	X	14
185	Stop-light switch	IV	13	502	LH rear loudspeaker	X	11
190	Handbrake switch	III	10	503	RH rear loudspeaker	X	14
192	Throttle spindle switch	V	11 to 12	506	LH front tweeter loudspeaker	X	10
229	Ignition switch	I	7 to 34	507	RH front tweeter loudspeaker	X	16
230	LH front door switch	IX	11	510	Front foglight switch	VI	17 to 19
231	RH front door switch	IX	12	511	Rear foglight switch	VI	11 to 13
232	LH rear door switch	IX	10	519	RH window winder switch on driver's door	VIII	12 to 15
233	RH rear door switch	IX	13	520	LH window winder switch on driver's door	VIII	5 to 10
234	Glovebox switch	V	27	521	RH front window winder switch	VIII	13 to 14
235	Hydraulic fluid flow pressure switch	III	8	522	LH rear window winder switch	VIII	20 to 22
236	Hydraulic fluid level switch	III	9	523	RH rear window winder switch	VIII	23 to 25
237	Coolant level switch	III	6 to 7	530	Sunroof switch	IX	3 to 4
238	RH front door lock switch	VII	22	532	Heated rear window switch	VI	21 to 23
239	LH front door lock switch	VII	20	551	Rear screen intermittent wiper switch	VII	3 to 9
241	RH rear door lock switch	VII	23	570	Hazard warning light switch	IV	1 to 9
242	LH rear door lock switch	VII	21	576	Injectors	V	10, 11, 12, 13
243	Boot lock switch	VII	24	580	Fuel gauge	III	14 to 15
244	Bonnet lock switch	VII	19	600	Windscreen wiper motor	VII	12 to 18
253	Screen wiper/washer and computer switch	V	24 to 25	601	Rear screen wiper motor	VII	1 to 5
253	Screen wiper/washer and computer switch	VII	11 to 15	610	Sunroof motor	IX	3 to 6
260	Lighting/direction indicator/horn switch	IV	7 to 8	615	LH front window winder motor	VIII	4 to 7
260	Lighting/direction indicator/horn switch	VI	4 to 7, 26	616	RH front window winder motor	VIII	13 to 14
276	Rear view mirror switch	VII	20 to 27	617	LH rear window winder motor	VIII	21
278	Blower motor speed control	II	13 to 19	618	RH rear window winder motor	VIII	24
280	Additional air control	V	15	625	LH front door lock motor	IX	18 to 20
300	Starter motor	II	3 to 5	626	RH front door lock motor	IX	21
302	Airflow meter	V	11 to 14	627	LH rear door lock motor	IX	18
312	Anti-lock braking system diode	IV	16 to 17	628	RH rear door lock motor	IX	20
370	Boot light	IX	26	629	Boot lid lock motor	IX	20 to 21
375	Glovebox light	V	27	635	LH engine cooling fan motor	II	9
385	LH rear number plate light	VI	7	650	Engine oil pressure switch	III	5
				658	Blower fan control module	II	13 to 15
				660	On-board computer	V	19 to 26

Key to Diagram 6 (continued)

No	Description	Circuit No	Location
680	Windscreen washer pump	VII	11
681	Rear screen washer pump	VII	8
683	Fuel pump	V	17
691	LH interior light	IX	10 to 11
692	RH interior light	IX	12 to 13
695	Interior spotlights	IX	9
698	Headphone sockets (2)	X	1 to 9
710	Supply socket	VIII	1
721	Radio connections (12V and speakers)	X	11 to 16
731	Fuel injection relay	V	7 to 8
734	Injector relays	V	9 to 10
745	Blower motor high speed relay	II	13 to 16
750	Foglight relay	VI	17 to 20
756	Anti-lock braking system solenoid relay	IV	27 to 29
760	Heated rear screen relay (R4)	VI	23 to 25
761	Front window winder motor relay (R3)	VIII	7 to 9

No	Description	Circuit No	Location
762	Rear window winder motor relay (R2)	VIII	20 to 21
763	Sunroof motor relay	IX	3 to 6
765	Windscreen wiper relay (1)	VII	14 to 17
766	Rear screen wiper relay	VII	2 to 7
774	Engine cooling fan relay (R1)	II	9 to 11
788	Cooling fan first speed resistor	II	8
795	Lighting rheostat	I	19
815	RH front exterior mirror	VIII	21 to 23
835	Engine oil level gauge	III	19 to 20
840	Coolant temperature sensor	III	18
841	Coolant temperature sensor (injection)	V	10
842	Oil pressure sensor	III	17
843	Oil temperature sensor	III	16
850	Cooling fan thermal switch	II	8 to 9
855	Water temperature switch	III	3
935	Air conditioning fan	II	13
940	Door closed label	VII	19 to 25
945	Heated rear screen	VI	25

Harness code

A	Front	RE	Rear screen wiper
C	Switches	RV	Rear door locking
CN	Battery negative cable	SR	Radio (rear section)
CP	Battery positive cable	SV	Radio (front section)
E	Window wiper	T	Instrument panel
F	Rear light cluster connection	U	Brake pad wear
FP	Fuel pump	V	RH side tailgate
G	LH side tailgate	Y	Anti-lock braking system
H	Interior	Z	Ignition
IM	Injection		
J	Fuel gauge		
L	Boot lighting		
M	Engine		
M-B	Junction box earth		
M-F	Rear light cluster earth		
M-P	Fuel pump earth		
O	On-board computer		
P	Interior lighting		
PC	Driver's door		
PP	Passenger's door		
R	Rear		

Note: Letter/number codes appearing in small boxes on the diagrams convey multi-plug connector information. For example - "3M1": the first number is the number of wires at that connector (three), the letter is a connector colour code (M - Brown, as given below), and the last number is the wire number within the group of wires at the connector (one in a group of three).

Earthing points

m1	Behind battery
m2	Along LH side of the steering column
m3	Roof lighting
m4	Behind console
m5	RH rear lights
m6	LH rear lights
m7	LH front wheelarch

Colour code

B	White
Bl	Blue
G	Grey
Ic	Transparent
J	Yellow
M	Brown
Mv	Mauve
N	Black
Or	Orange
R	Red
V	Green

13

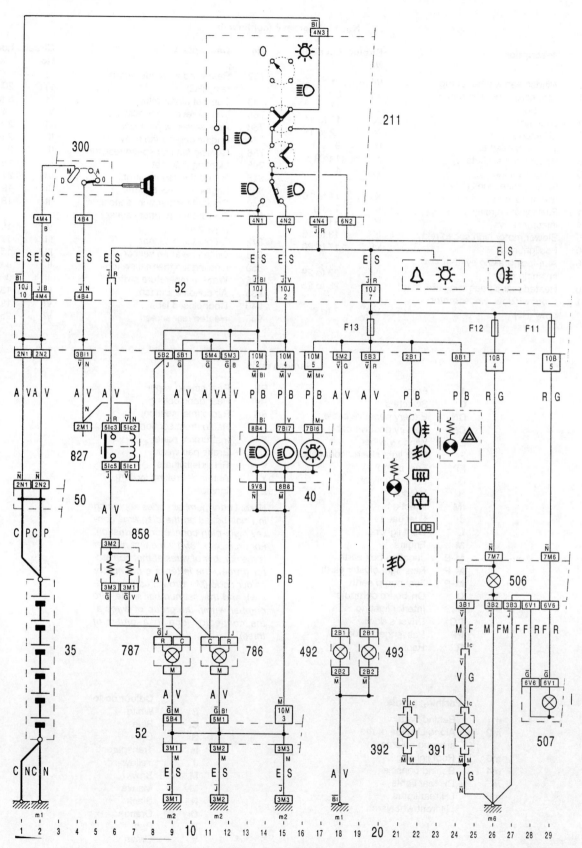

Diagram 7 - All models from July 1986 with Dim-dip lighting

Key to Diagram 7

For colour code and other information, see key to Diagram 6

No	Description	No	Description
35	Battery	787	RH headlight
40	Instrument cluster	827	Dim-dip relay
50	Supply box	858	Dim-dip resistor unit
52	Power supply connector box	**Harness code**	
211	LH combination switch	**AV**	Front
300	Ignition switch	**CN**	Battery negative cable
391	LH number plate light	**CP**	Battery positive cable
392	RH number plate light	**ES**	Windscreen wiper
492	LH sidelight	**FR**	Rear lights
493	RH sidelight	**MF**	Lighting earth
506	LH tail light	**PB**	Dashboard
507	RH tail light	**RG**	Left-hand rear
786	LH headlight	**VG**	Left-hand tailgate

13

Notes

Dimensions and weights

Note: *All figures are approximate, and may vary according to model. Refer to manufacturer's data for exact figures.*

Dimensions

Overall length:
  Hatchback . . . . .4230 mm
  Estate . . . . .4394 mm
Overall height:*
  Hatchback . . . . .1358 mm
  Estate . . . . .1428 mm
Overall width . . . . .1660 mm
Ground clearance* . . . . .160 mm
Engine running - normal setting

Weights

Kerb weight:
  BX . . . . .900 kg
  BX 14 . . . . .900 kg
  BX 16 . . . . .950 kg
  BX 16 Estate . . . . .998 kg
  BX 19 . . . . .1000 kg
  BX 19 Estate . . . . .1037 kg
  BX 19 GTi . . . . .1025 kg
  BX 19 GTi 16v . . . . .1070 kg

Weights (continued)

Maximum towing weight:
  BX . . . . .1000 kg
  BX 14 . . . . .1000 kg
  BX 16 . . . . .1100 kg
  BX 16 Estate . . . . .1100 kg
  BX 19 . . . . .1100 kg
  BX 19 Estate . . . . .1100 kg
  BX 19 GTi . . . . .1100 kg
  BX 19 GTi 16v . . . . .1100 kg
Maximum roof rack load:
  Hatchback . . . . .75 kg
  Estate . . . . .100 kg

Length (distance)

Inches (in)	x 25.4	= Millimetres (mm)	x 0.0394	= Inches (in)
Feet (ft)	x 0.305	= Metres (m)	x 3.281	= Feet (ft)
Miles	x 1.609	= Kilometres (km)	x 0.621	= Miles

Volume (capacity)

Cubic inches (cu in; in³)	x 16.387	= Cubic centimetres (cc; cm³)	x 0.061	= Cubic inches (cu in; in³)
Imperial pints (Imp pt)	x 0.568	= Litres (l)	x 1.76	= Imperial pints (Imp pt)
Imperial quarts (Imp qt)	x 1.137	= Litres (l)	x 0.88	= Imperial quarts (Imp qt)
Imperial quarts (Imp qt)	x 1.201	= US quarts (US qt)	x 0.833	= Imperial quarts (Imp qt)
US quarts (US qt)	x 0.946	= Litres (l)	x 1.057	= US quarts (US qt)
Imperial gallons (Imp gal)	x 4.546	= Litres (l)	x 0.22	= Imperial gallons (Imp gal)
Imperial gallons (Imp gal)	x 1.201	= US gallons (US gal)	x 0.833	= Imperial gallons (Imp gal)
US gallons (US gal)	x 3.785	= Litres (l)	x 0.264	= US gallons (US gal)

Mass (weight)

Ounces (oz)	x 28.35	= Grams (g)	x 0.035	= Ounces (oz)
Pounds (lb)	x 0.454	= Kilograms (kg)	x 2.205	= Pounds (lb)

Force

Ounces-force (ozf; oz)	x 0.278	= Newtons (N)	x 3.6	= Ounces-force (ozf; oz)
Pounds-force (lbf; lb)	x 4.448	= Newtons (N)	x 0.225	= Pounds-force (lbf; lb)
Newtons (N)	x 0.1	= Kilograms-force (kgf; kg)	x 9.81	= Newtons (N)

Pressure

Pounds-force per square inch (psi; lbf/in²; lb/in²)	x 0.070	= Kilograms-force per square centimetre (kgf/cm²; kg/cm²)	x 14.223	= Pounds-force per square inch (psi; lbf/in²; lb/in²)
Pounds-force per square inch (psi; lbf/in²; lb/in²)	x 0.068	= Atmospheres (atm)	x 14.696	= Pounds-force per square inch (psi; lbf/in²; lb/in²)
Pounds-force per square inch (psi; lbf/in²; lb/in²)	x 0.069	= Bars	x 14.5	= Pounds-force per square inch (psi; lbf/in²; lb/in²)
Pounds-force per square inch (psi; lbf/in²; lb/in²)	x 6.895	= Kilopascals (kPa)	x 0.145	= Pounds-force per square inch (psi; lbf/in²; lb/in²)
Kilopascals (kPa)	x 0.01	= Kilograms-force per square centimetre (kgf/cm²; kg/cm²)	x 98.1	= Kilopascals (kPa)
Millibar (mbar)	x 100	= Pascals (Pa)	x 0.01	= Millibar (mbar)
Millibar (mbar)	x 0.0145	= Pounds-force per square inch (psi; lbf/in²; lb/in²)	x 68.947	= Millibar (mbar)
Millibar (mbar)	x 0.75	= Millimetres of mercury (mmHg)	x 1.333	= Millibar (mbar)
Millibar (mbar)	x 0.401	= Inches of water (inH₂O)	x 2.491	= Millibar (mbar)
Millimetres of mercury (mmHg)	x 0.535	= Inches of water (inH₂O)	x 1.868	= Millimetres of mercury (mmHg)
Inches of water (inH₂O)	x 0.036	= Pounds-force per square inch (psi; lbf/in²; lb/in²)	x 27.68	= Inches of water (inH₂O)

Torque (moment of force)

Pounds-force inches (lbf in; lb in)	x 1.152	= Kilograms-force centimetre (kgf cm; kg cm)	x 0.868	= Pounds-force inches (lbf in; lb in)
Pounds-force inches (lbf in; lb in)	x 0.113	= Newton metres (Nm)	x 8.85	= Pounds-force inches (lbf in; lb in)
Pounds-force inches (lbf in; lb in)	x 0.083	= Pounds-force feet (lbf ft; lb ft)	x 12	= Pounds-force inches (lbf in; lb in)
Pounds-force feet (lbf ft; lb ft)	x 0.138	= Kilograms-force metres (kgf m; kg m)	x 7.233	= Pounds-force feet (lbf ft; lb ft)
Pounds-force feet (lbf ft; lb ft)	x 1.356	= Newton metres (Nm)	x 0.738	= Pounds-force feet (lbf ft; lb ft)
Newton metres (Nm)	x 0.102	= Kilograms-force metres (kgf m; kg m)	x 9.804	= Newton metres (Nm)

Power

Horsepower (hp)	x 745.7	= Watts (W)	x 0.0013	= Horsepower (hp)

Velocity (speed)

Miles per hour (miles/hr; mph)	x 1.609	= Kilometres per hour (km/hr; kph)	x 0.621	= Miles per hour (miles/hr; mph)

Fuel consumption*

Miles per gallon (mpg)	x 0.354	= Kilometres per litre (km/l)	x 2.825	= Miles per gallon (mpg)

Temperature

Degrees Fahrenheit = (°C x 1.8) + 32   Degrees Celsius (Degrees Centigrade; °C) = (°F - 32) x 0.56

It is common practice to convert from miles per gallon (mpg) to litres/100 kilometres (l/100km), where mpg x l/100 km = 282

Spare parts are available from many sources, including manufacturer's appointed garages, accessory shops, and motor factors. To be sure of obtaining the correct parts, it will sometimes be necessary to quote the vehicle identification number. If possible, it can also be useful to take the old parts along for positive identification. Items such as starter motors and alternators may be available under a service exchange scheme - any parts returned should always be clean.

Our advice regarding spare part sources is as follows.

Officially-appointed garages

This is the best source of parts which are peculiar to your vehicle, and which are not otherwise generally available (eg badges, interior trim, certain body panels, etc). It is also the only place at which you should buy parts if the vehicle is still under warranty.

Accessory shops

These are very good places to buy materials and components needed for the maintenance of your vehicle (oil, air and fuel filters, spark plugs, light bulbs, drivebelts, oils and greases, brake pads, touch-up paint, etc). Components of this nature sold by a reputable shop are of the same standard as those used by the vehicle manufacturer.

Besides components, these shops also sell tools and general accessories, usually have convenient opening hours, charge lower prices, and can often be found not far from home. Some accessory shops have parts counters where the components needed for almost any repair job can be purchased or ordered.

Motor factors

Good factors will stock all the more important components which wear out comparatively quickly, and can sometimes supply individual components needed for the overhaul of a larger assembly (eg brake seals and hydraulic parts, bearing shells, pistons, valves, alternator brushes). They may also handle work such as cylinder block reboring, crankshaft regrinding and balancing, etc.

Tyre and exhaust specialists

These outlets may be independent, or members of a local or national chain. They frequently offer competitive prices when compared with a main dealer or local garage, but it will pay to obtain several quotes before making a decision. When researching prices, also ask what "extras" may be added - for instance, fitting a new valve and balancing the wheel are both commonly charged on top of the price of a new tyre.

Other sources

Beware of parts or materials obtained from market stalls, car boot sales or similar outlets. Such items are not invariably sub-standard, but there is little chance of compensation if they do prove unsatisfactory. In the case of safety-critical components such as brake pads, there is the risk not only of financial loss but also of an accident causing injury or death.

Second-hand components or assemblies obtained from a car breaker can be a good buy in some circumstances, but this sort of purchase is best made by the experienced DIY mechanic.

Vehicle identification

Modifications are a continuing and unpublicised process in vehicle manufacture, quite apart from major model changes. Spare parts manuals and lists are compiled upon a numerical basis, the individual vehicle identification numbers being essential to correct identification of the component concerned.

When ordering spare parts, always give as much information as possible. Quote the vehicle model, year of manufacture, body and engine numbers as appropriate.

The *vehicle identification plate* is in the engine compartment on the right-hand side wheel arch **(see illustrations)**. It gives the VIN (vehicle identification number).

The *engine number* location depends on engine type. On BX and BX 14 models, it is located on the bottom left-hand side of the engine. On BX 16 and BX 19 models it is located on the top right-hand side of the engine **(see illustration)**.

The *chassis number* is stamped into the manufacturer's plate in the engine compartment on the front panel.

Other identification numbers or codes are stamped on major items such as the gearbox, final drive housing, distributor etc. These numbers are unlikely to be needed by the home mechanic.

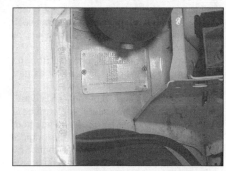

Vehicle identification plate location

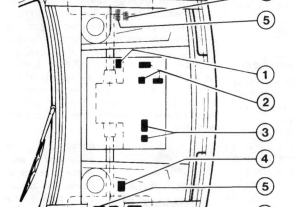

Vehicle identification plate locations

1 Gearbox number
2 Engine number - BX and BX 14
3 Engine number - BX 16 and BX 19
4 Manufacturer's plate
5 Replacement parts organisation number
6 Chassis number
7 Paint reference number
8 Model year

Engine number location - BX 16

Whenever servicing, repair or overhaul work is carried out on the car or its components, it is necessary to observe the following procedures and instructions. This will assist in carrying out the operation efficiently and to a professional standard of workmanship.

Joint mating faces and gaskets

When separating components at their mating faces, never insert screwdrivers or similar implements into the joint between the faces in order to prise them apart. This can cause severe damage which results in oil leaks, coolant leaks, etc upon reassembly. Separation is usually achieved by tapping along the joint with a soft-faced hammer in order to break the seal. However, note that this method may not be suitable where dowels are used for component location.

Where a gasket is used between the mating faces of two components, ensure that it is renewed on reassembly, and fit it dry unless otherwise stated in the repair procedure. Make sure that the mating faces are clean and dry, with all traces of old gasket removed. When cleaning a joint face, use a tool which is not likely to score or damage the face, and remove any burrs or nicks with an oilstone or fine file.

Make sure that tapped holes are cleaned with a pipe cleaner, and keep them free of jointing compound, if this is being used, unless specifically instructed otherwise.

Ensure that all orifices, channels or pipes are clear, and blow through them, preferably using compressed air.

Oil seals

Oil seals can be removed by levering them out with a wide flat-bladed screwdriver or similar tool. Alternatively, a number of self-tapping screws may be screwed into the seal, and these used as a purchase for pliers or similar in order to pull the seal free.

Whenever an oil seal is removed from its working location, either individually or as part of an assembly, it should be renewed.

The very fine sealing lip of the seal is easily damaged, and will not seal if the surface it contacts is not completely clean and free from scratches, nicks or grooves. If the original sealing surface of the component cannot be restored, and the manufacturer has not made provision for slight relocation of the seal relative to the sealing surface, the component should be renewed.

Protect the lips of the seal from any surface which may damage them in the course of fitting. Use tape or a conical sleeve where possible. Lubricate the seal lips with oil before fitting and, on dual-lipped seals, fill the space between the lips with grease.

Unless otherwise stated, oil seals must be fitted with their sealing lips toward the lubricant to be sealed.

Use a tubular drift or block of wood of the appropriate size to install the seal and, if the seal housing is shouldered, drive the seal down to the shoulder. If the seal housing is unshouldered, the seal should be fitted with its face flush with the housing top face (unless otherwise instructed).

Screw threads and fastenings

Seized nuts, bolts and screws are quite a common occurrence where corrosion has set in, and the use of penetrating oil or releasing fluid will often overcome this problem if the offending item is soaked for a while before attempting to release it. The use of an impact driver may also provide a means of releasing such stubborn fastening devices, when used in conjunction with the appropriate screwdriver bit or socket. If none of these methods works, it may be necessary to resort to the careful application of heat, or the use of a hacksaw or nut splitter device.

Studs are usually removed by locking two nuts together on the threaded part, and then using a spanner on the lower nut to unscrew the stud. Studs or bolts which have broken off below the surface of the component in which they are mounted can sometimes be removed using a stud extractor. Always ensure that a blind tapped hole is completely free from oil, grease, water or other fluid before installing the bolt or stud. Failure to do this could cause the housing to crack due to the hydraulic action of the bolt or stud as it is screwed in.

When tightening a castellated nut to accept a split pin, tighten the nut to the specified torque, where applicable, and then tighten further to the next split pin hole. Never slacken the nut to align the split pin hole, unless stated in the repair procedure.

When checking or retightening a nut or bolt to a specified torque setting, slacken the nut or bolt by a quarter of a turn, and then retighten to the specified setting. However, this should not be attempted where angular tightening has been used.

For some screw fastenings, notably cylinder head bolts or nuts, torque wrench settings are no longer specified for the latter stages of tightening, "angle-tightening" being called up instead. Typically, a fairly low torque wrench setting will be applied to the bolts/nuts in the correct sequence, followed by one or more stages of tightening through specified angles.

Locknuts, locktabs and washers

Any fastening which will rotate against a component or housing during tightening should always have a washer between it and the relevant component or housing.

Spring or split washers should always be renewed when they are used to lock a critical component such as a big-end bearing retaining bolt or nut. Locktabs which are folded over to retain a nut or bolt should always be renewed.

Self-locking nuts can be re-used in non-critical areas, providing resistance can be felt when the locking portion passes over the bolt or stud thread. However, it should be noted that self-locking stiffnuts tend to lose their effectiveness after long periods of use, and should be renewed as a matter of course.

Split pins must always be replaced with new ones of the correct size for the hole.

When thread-locking compound is found on the threads of a fastener which is to be re-used, it should be cleaned off with a wire brush and solvent, and fresh compound applied on reassembly.

Special tools

Some repair procedures in this manual entail the use of special tools such as a press, two or three-legged pullers, spring compressors, etc. Wherever possible, suitable readily-available alternatives to the manufacturer's special tools are described, and are shown in use. In some instances, where no alternative is possible, it has been necessary to resort to the use of a manufacturer's tool, and this has been done for reasons of safety as well as the efficient completion of the repair operation. Unless you are highly-skilled and have a thorough understanding of the procedures described, never attempt to bypass the use of any special tool when the procedure described specifies its use. Not only is there a very great risk of personal injury, but expensive damage could be caused to the components involved.

Environmental considerations

When disposing of used engine oil, brake fluid, antifreeze, etc, give due consideration to any detrimental environmental effects. Do not, for instance, pour any of the above liquids down drains into the general sewage system, or onto the ground to soak away. Many local council refuse tips provide a facility for waste oil disposal, as do some garages. If none of these facilities are available, consult your local Environmental Health Department, or the National Rivers Authority, for further advice.

With the universal tightening-up of legislation regarding the emission of environmentally-harmful substances from motor vehicles, most current vehicles have tamperproof devices fitted to the main adjustment points of the fuel system. These devices are primarily designed to prevent unqualified persons from adjusting the fuel/air mixture, with the chance of a consequent increase in toxic emissions. If such devices are encountered during servicing or overhaul, they should, wherever possible, be renewed or refitted in accordance with the vehicle manufacturer's requirements or current legislation.

Note: *It is antisocial and illegal to dump oil down the drain. To find the location of your local oil recycling bank, call this number free.*

The jack supplied with the vehicle should only be used for changing the roadwheels - see *"Wheel changing"* at the front of this Manual. When using the jack, position it on firm ground and locate its head in the relevant vehicle jacking point.

When carrying out any other kind of work, raise the vehicle using a hydraulic (or "trolley") jack and always supplement the jack with axle stands.

When jacking-up the vehicle with a trolley jack, or supporting it on safety stands, locate the jack or stands only at the specified support points **(see illustration)**. Always ensure that they are securely located and the vehicle firmly supported before working underneath.

Jacking and support points

A Support stand - front   B Support stand - rear   C Jacking point

Introduction

A selection of good tools is a fundamental requirement for anyone contemplating the maintenance and repair of a motor vehicle. For the owner who does not possess any, their purchase will prove a considerable expense, offsetting some of the savings made by doing-it-yourself. However, provided that the tools purchased meet the relevant national safety standards and are of good quality, they will last for many years and prove an extremely worthwhile investment.

To help the average owner to decide which tools are needed to carry out the various tasks detailed in this manual, we have compiled three lists of tools under the following headings: *Maintenance and minor repair*, *Repair and overhaul*, and *Special*. Newcomers to practical mechanics should start off with the *Maintenance and minor repair* tool kit, and confine themselves to the simpler jobs around the vehicle. Then, as confidence and experience grow, more difficult tasks can be undertaken, with extra tools being purchased as, and when, they are needed. In this way, a *Maintenance and minor repair* tool kit can be built up into a *Repair and overhaul* tool kit over a considerable period of time, without any major cash outlays. The experienced do-it-yourselfer will have a tool kit good enough for most repair and overhaul procedures, and will add tools from the *Special* category when it is felt that the expense is justified by the amount of use to which these tools will be put.

Maintenance and minor repair tool kit

The tools given in this list should be considered as a minimum requirement if routine maintenance, servicing and minor repair operations are to be undertaken. We recommend the purchase of combination spanners (ring one end, open-ended the other); although more expensive than open-ended ones, they do give the advantages of both types of spanner.

☐ *Combination spanners:*
  Metric - 8 to 19 mm inclusive
☐ *Adjustable spanner - 35 mm jaw (approx.)*
☐ *Spark plug spanner (with rubber insert) - petrol models*
☐ *Spark plug gap adjustment tool - petrol models*
☐ *Set of feeler blades*
☐ *Brake bleed nipple spanner*
☐ *Screwdrivers:*
  Flat blade - 100 mm long x 6 mm dia
  Cross blade - 100 mm long x 6 mm dia
☐ *Combination pliers*
☐ *Hacksaw (junior)*
☐ *Tyre pump*
☐ *Tyre pressure gauge*
☐ *Oil can*
☐ *Oil filter removal tool*
☐ *Fine emery cloth*
☐ *Wire brush (small)*
☐ *Funnel (medium size)*

Repair and overhaul tool kit

These tools are virtually essential for anyone undertaking any major repairs to a motor vehicle, and are additional to those given in the *Maintenance and minor repair* list. Included in this list is a comprehensive set of sockets. Although these are expensive, they will be found invaluable as they are so versatile - particularly if various drives are included in the set. We recommend the half-inch square-drive type, as this can be used with most proprietary torque wrenches.

The tools in this list will sometimes need to be supplemented by tools from the *Special* list:

☐ *Sockets (or box spanners) to cover range in previous list (including Torx sockets)*
☐ *Reversible ratchet drive (for use with sockets)*
☐ *Extension piece, 250 mm (for use with sockets)*
☐ *Universal joint (for use with sockets)*
☐ *Torque wrench (for use with sockets)*
☐ *Self-locking grips*
☐ *Ball pein hammer*
☐ *Soft-faced mallet (plastic/aluminium or rubber)*
☐ *Screwdrivers:*
  Flat blade - long & sturdy, short (chubby), and narrow (electrician's) types
  Cross blade – Long & sturdy, and short (chubby) types
☐ *Pliers:*
  Long-nosed
  Side cutters (electrician's)
  Circlip (internal and external)
☐ *Cold chisel - 25 mm*
☐ *Scriber*
☐ *Scraper*
☐ *Centre-punch*
☐ *Pin punch*
☐ *Hacksaw*
☐ *Brake hose clamp*
☐ *Brake/clutch bleeding kit*
☐ *Selection of twist drills*
☐ *Steel rule/straight-edge*
☐ *Allen keys (inc. splined/Torx type)*
☐ *Selection of files*
☐ *Wire brush*
☐ *Axle stands*
☐ *Jack (strong trolley or hydraulic type)*
☐ *Light with extension lead*

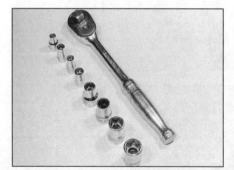
Sockets and reversible ratchet drive

Valve spring compressor

Spline bit set

Piston ring compressor

Clutch plate alignment set

Special tools

The tools in this list are those which are not used regularly, are expensive to buy, or which need to be used in accordance with their manufacturers' instructions. Unless relatively difficult mechanical jobs are undertaken frequently, it will not be economic to buy many of these tools. Where this is the case, you could consider clubbing together with friends (or joining a motorists' club) to make a joint purchase, or borrowing the tools against a deposit from a local garage or tool hire specialist. It is worth noting that many of the larger DIY superstores now carry a large range of special tools for hire at modest rates.

The following list contains only those tools and instruments freely available to the public, and not those special tools produced by the vehicle manufacturer specifically for its dealer network. You will find occasional references to these manufacturers' special tools in the text of this manual. Generally, an alternative method of doing the job without the vehicle manufacturers' special tool is given. However, sometimes there is no alternative to using them. Where this is the case and the relevant tool cannot be bought or borrowed, you will have to entrust the work to a dealer.

☐ Valve spring compressor
☐ Valve grinding tool
☐ Piston ring compressor
☐ Piston ring removal/installation tool
☐ Cylinder bore hone
☐ Balljoint separator
☐ Coil spring compressors (where applicable)
☐ Two/three-legged hub and bearing puller
☐ Impact screwdriver
☐ Micrometer and/or vernier calipers
☐ Dial gauge
☐ Stroboscopic timing light
☐ Dwell angle meter/tachometer
☐ Universal electrical multi-meter
☐ Cylinder compression gauge
☐ Hand-operated vacuum pump and gauge
☐ Clutch plate alignment set
☐ Brake shoe steady spring cup removal tool
☐ Bush and bearing removal/installation set
☐ Stud extractors
☐ Tap and die set
☐ Lifting tackle
☐ Trolley jack

Buying tools

Reputable motor accessory shops and superstores often offer excellent quality tools at discount prices, so it pays to shop around.

Remember, you don't have to buy the most expensive items on the shelf, but it is always advisable to steer clear of the very cheap tools. Beware of 'bargains' offered on market stalls or at car boot sales. There are plenty of good tools around at reasonable prices, but always aim to purchase items which meet the relevant national safety standards. If in doubt, ask the proprietor or manager of the shop for advice before making a purchase.

Care and maintenance of tools

Having purchased a reasonable tool kit, it is necessary to keep the tools in a clean and serviceable condition. After use, always wipe off any dirt, grease and metal particles using a clean, dry cloth, before putting the tools away. Never leave them lying around after they have been used. A simple tool rack on the garage or workshop wall for items such as screwdrivers and pliers is a good idea. Store all normal spanners and sockets in a metal box. Any measuring instruments, gauges, meters, etc, must be carefully stored where they cannot be damaged or become rusty.

Take a little care when tools are used. Hammer heads inevitably become marked, and screwdrivers lose the keen edge on their blades from time to time. A little timely attention with emery cloth or a file will soon restore items like this to a good finish.

Working facilities

Not to be forgotten when discussing tools is the workshop itself. If anything more than routine maintenance is to be carried out, a suitable working area becomes essential.

It is appreciated that many an owner-mechanic is forced by circumstances to remove an engine or similar item without the benefit of a garage or workshop. Having done this, any repairs should always be done under the cover of a roof.

Wherever possible, any dismantling should be done on a clean, flat workbench or table at a suitable working height.

Any workbench needs a vice; one with a jaw opening of 100 mm is suitable for most jobs. As mentioned previously, some clean dry storage space is also required for tools, as well as for any lubricants, cleaning fluids, touch-up paints etc, which become necessary.

Another item which may be required, and which has a much more general usage, is an electric drill with a chuck capacity of at least 8 mm. This, together with a good range of twist drills, is virtually essential for fitting accessories.

Last, but not least, always keep a supply of old newspapers and clean, lint-free rags available, and try to keep any working area as clean as possible.

Micrometer set

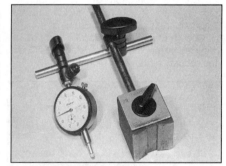

Dial test indicator ("dial gauge")

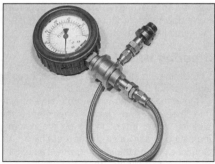

Stroboscopic timing light

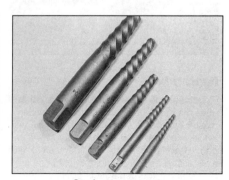

Compression tester

Stud extractor set

This is a guide to getting your vehicle through the MOT test. Obviously it will not be possible to examine the vehicle to the same standard as the professional MOT tester. However, working through the following checks will enable you to identify any problem areas before submitting the vehicle for the test.

Where a testable component is in borderline condition, the tester has discretion in deciding whether to pass or fail it. The basis of such discretion is whether the tester would be happy for a close relative or friend to use the vehicle with the component in that condition. If the vehicle presented is clean and evidently well cared for, the tester may be more inclined to pass a borderline component than if the vehicle is scruffy and apparently neglected.

It has only been possible to summarise the test requirements here, based on the regulations in force at the time of printing. Test standards are becoming increasingly stringent, although there are some exemptions for older vehicles. For full details obtain a copy of the Haynes publication Pass the MOT! (available from stockists of Haynes manuals).

An assistant will be needed to help carry out some of these checks.

The checks have been sub-divided into four categories, as follows:

1 Checks carried out **FROM THE DRIVER'S SEAT**

2 Checks carried out **WITH THE VEHICLE ON THE GROUND**

3 Checks carried out **WITH THE VEHICLE RAISED AND THE WHEELS FREE TO TURN**

4 Checks carried out on **YOUR VEHICLE'S EXHAUST EMISSION SYSTEM**

1 Checks carried out **FROM THE DRIVER'S SEAT**

Handbrake

☐ Test the operation of the handbrake. Excessive travel (too many clicks) indicates incorrect brake or cable adjustment.

☐ Check that the handbrake cannot be released by tapping the lever sideways. Check the security of the lever mountings.

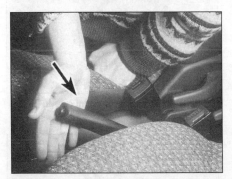

Footbrake

☐ Depress the brake pedal and check that it does not creep down to the floor, indicating a master cylinder fault. Release the pedal, wait a few seconds, then depress it again. If the pedal travels nearly to the floor before firm resistance is felt, brake adjustment or repair is necessary. If the pedal feels spongy, there is air in the hydraulic system which must be removed by bleeding.

☐ Check that the brake pedal is secure and in good condition. Check also for signs of fluid leaks on the pedal, floor or carpets, which would indicate failed seals in the brake master cylinder.

☐ Check the servo unit (when applicable) by operating the brake pedal several times, then keeping the pedal depressed and starting the engine. As the engine starts, the pedal will move down slightly. If not, the vacuum hose or the servo itself may be faulty.

Steering wheel and column

☐ Examine the steering wheel for fractures or looseness of the hub, spokes or rim.

☐ Move the steering wheel from side to side and then up and down. Check that the steering wheel is not loose on the column, indicating wear or a loose retaining nut. Continue moving the steering wheel as before, but also turn it slightly from left to right.

☐ Check that the steering wheel is not loose on the column, and that there is no abnormal

movement of the steering wheel, indicating wear in the column support bearings or couplings.

Windscreen and mirrors

☐ The windscreen must be free of cracks or other significant damage within the driver's field of view. (Small stone chips are acceptable.) Rear view mirrors must be secure, intact, and capable of being adjusted.

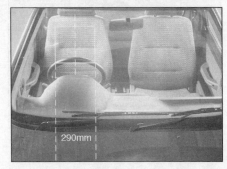

290mm

Seat belts and seats

Note: *The following checks are applicable to all seat belts, front and rear.*

☐ Examine the webbing of all the belts (including rear belts if fitted) for cuts, serious fraying or deterioration. Fasten and unfasten each belt to check the buckles. If applicable, check the retracting mechanism. Check the security of all seat belt mountings accessible from inside the vehicle.

☐ The front seats themselves must be securely attached and the backrests must lock in the upright position.

Doors

☐ Both front doors must be able to be opened and closed from outside and inside, and must latch securely when closed.

2 Checks carried out WITH THE VEHICLE ON THE GROUND

Vehicle identification

☐ Number plates must be in good condition, secure and legible, with letters and numbers correctly spaced – spacing at (A) should be twice that at (B).

☐ The VIN plate and/or homologation plate must be legible.

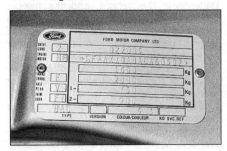

Electrical equipment

☐ Switch on the ignition and check the operation of the horn.

☐ Check the windscreen washers and wipers, examining the wiper blades; renew damaged or perished blades. Also check the operation of the stop-lights.

☐ Check the operation of the sidelights and number plate lights. The lenses and reflectors must be secure, clean and undamaged.

☐ Check the operation and alignment of the headlights. The headlight reflectors must not be tarnished and the lenses must be undamaged.

☐ Switch on the ignition and check the operation of the direction indicators (including the instrument panel tell-tale) and the hazard warning lights. Operation of the sidelights and stop-lights must not affect the indicators - if it does, the cause is usually a bad earth at the rear light cluster.

☐ Check the operation of the rear foglight(s), including the warning light on the instrument panel or in the switch.

Footbrake

☐ Examine the master cylinder, brake pipes and servo unit for leaks, loose mountings, corrosion or other damage.

☐ The fluid reservoir must be secure and the fluid level must be between the upper (**A**) and lower (**B**) markings.

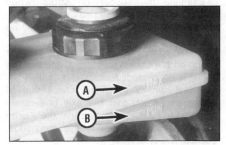

☐ Inspect both front brake flexible hoses for cracks or deterioration of the rubber. Turn the steering from lock to lock, and ensure that the hoses do not contact the wheel, tyre, or any part of the steering or suspension mechanism. With the brake pedal firmly depressed, check the hoses for bulges or leaks under pressure.

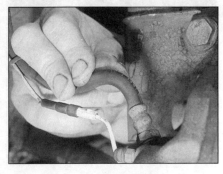

Steering and suspension

☐ Have your assistant turn the steering wheel from side to side slightly, up to the point where the steering gear just begins to transmit this movement to the roadwheels. Check for excessive free play between the steering wheel and the steering gear, indicating wear or insecurity of the steering column joints, the column-to-steering gear coupling, or the steering gear itself.

☐ Have your assistant turn the steering wheel more vigorously in each direction, so that the roadwheels just begin to turn. As this is done, examine all the steering joints, linkages, fittings and attachments. Renew any component that shows signs of wear or damage. On vehicles with power steering, check the security and condition of the steering pump, drivebelt and hoses.

☐ Check that the vehicle is standing level, and at approximately the correct ride height.

Shock absorbers

☐ Depress each corner of the vehicle in turn, then release it. The vehicle should rise and then settle in its normal position. If the vehicle continues to rise and fall, the shock absorber is defective. A shock absorber which has seized will also cause the vehicle to fail.

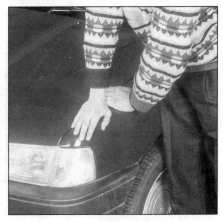

Exhaust system

☐ Start the engine. With your assistant holding a rag over the tailpipe, check the entire system for leaks. Repair or renew leaking sections.

3 Checks carried out
WITH THE VEHICLE RAISED AND THE WHEELS FREE TO TURN

Jack up the front and rear of the vehicle, and securely support it on axle stands. Position the stands clear of the suspension assemblies. Ensure that the wheels are clear of the ground and that the steering can be turned from lock to lock.

Steering mechanism

☐ Have your assistant turn the steering from lock to lock. Check that the steering turns smoothly, and that no part of the steering mechanism, including a wheel or tyre, fouls any brake hose or pipe or any part of the body structure.
☐ Examine the steering rack rubber gaiters for damage or insecurity of the retaining clips. If power steering is fitted, check for signs of damage or leakage of the fluid hoses, pipes or connections. Also check for excessive stiffness or binding of the steering, a missing split pin or locking device, or severe corrosion of the body structure within 30 cm of any steering component attachment point.

Front and rear suspension and wheel bearings

☐ Starting at the front right-hand side, grasp the roadwheel at the 3 o'clock and 9 o'clock positions and shake it vigorously. Check for free play or insecurity at the wheel bearings, suspension balljoints, or suspension mountings, pivots and attachments.
☐ Now grasp the wheel at the 12 o'clock and 6 o'clock positions and repeat the previous inspection. Spin the wheel, and check for roughness or tightness of the front wheel bearing.

☐ If excess free play is suspected at a component pivot point, this can be confirmed by using a large screwdriver or similar tool and levering between the mounting and the component attachment. This will confirm whether the wear is in the pivot bush, its retaining bolt, or in the mounting itself (the bolt holes can often become elongated).

☐ Carry out all the above checks at the other front wheel, and then at both rear wheels.

Springs and shock absorbers

☐ Examine the suspension struts (when applicable) for serious fluid leakage, corrosion, or damage to the casing. Also check the security of the mounting points.
☐ If coil springs are fitted, check that the spring ends locate in their seats, and that the spring is not corroded, cracked or broken.
☐ If leaf springs are fitted, check that all leaves are intact, that the axle is securely attached to each spring, and that there is no deterioration of the spring eye mountings, bushes, and shackles.

☐ The same general checks apply to vehicles fitted with other suspension types, such as torsion bars, hydraulic displacer units, etc. Ensure that all mountings and attachments are secure, that there are no signs of excessive wear, corrosion or damage, and (on hydraulic types) that there are no fluid leaks or damaged pipes.
☐ Inspect the shock absorbers for signs of serious fluid leakage. Check for wear of the mounting bushes or attachments, or damage to the body of the unit.

Driveshafts (fwd vehicles only)

☐ Rotate each front wheel in turn and inspect the constant velocity joint gaiters for splits or damage. Also check that each driveshaft is straight and undamaged.

Braking system

☐ If possible without dismantling, check brake pad wear and disc condition. Ensure that the friction lining material has not worn excessively, (A) and that the discs are not fractured, pitted, scored or badly worn (B).

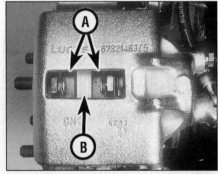

☐ Examine all the rigid brake pipes underneath the vehicle, and the flexible hose(s) at the rear. Look for corrosion, chafing or insecurity of the pipes, and for signs of bulging under pressure, chafing, splits or deterioration of the flexible hoses.
☐ Look for signs of fluid leaks at the brake calipers or on the brake backplates. Repair or renew leaking components.
☐ Slowly spin each wheel, while your assistant depresses and releases the footbrake. Ensure that each brake is operating and does not bind when the pedal is released.

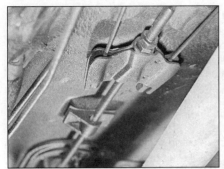

□ Examine the handbrake mechanism, checking for frayed or broken cables, excessive corrosion, or wear or insecurity of the linkage. Check that the mechanism works on each relevant wheel, and releases fully, without binding.

□ It is not possible to test brake efficiency without special equipment, but a road test can be carried out later to check that the vehicle pulls up in a straight line.

Fuel and exhaust systems

□ Inspect the fuel tank (including the filler cap), fuel pipes, hoses and unions. All components must be secure and free from leaks.

□ Examine the exhaust system over its entire length, checking for any damaged, broken or missing mountings, security of the retaining clamps and rust or corrosion.

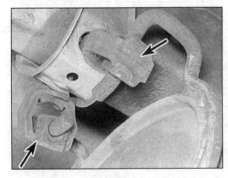

Wheels and tyres

□ Examine the sidewalls and tread area of each tyre in turn. Check for cuts, tears, lumps, bulges, separation of the tread, and exposure of the ply or cord due to wear or damage. Check that the tyre bead is correctly seated on the wheel rim, that the valve is sound and

properly seated, and that the wheel is not distorted or damaged.

□ Check that the tyres are of the correct size for the vehicle, that they are of the same size and type on each axle, and that the pressures are correct.

□ Check the tyre tread depth. The legal minimum at the time of writing is 1.6 mm over at least three-quarters of the tread width. Abnormal tread wear may indicate incorrect front wheel alignment.

Body corrosion

□ Check the condition of the entire vehicle structure for signs of corrosion in load-bearing areas. (These include chassis box sections, side sills, cross-members, pillars, and all suspension, steering, braking system and seat belt mountings and anchorages.) Any corrosion which has seriously reduced the thickness of a load-bearing area is likely to cause the vehicle to fail. In this case professional repairs are likely to be needed.

□ Damage or corrosion which causes sharp or otherwise dangerous edges to be exposed will also cause the vehicle to fail.

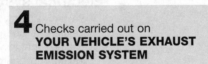

4 Checks carried out on YOUR VEHICLE'S EXHAUST EMISSION SYSTEM

Petrol models

□ Have the engine at normal operating temperature, and make sure that it is in good tune (ignition system in good order, air filter element clean, etc).

□ Before any measurements are carried out, raise the engine speed to around 2500 rpm, and hold it at this speed for 20 seconds. Allow

the engine speed to return to idle, and watch for smoke emissions from the exhaust tailpipe. If the idle speed is obviously much too high, or if dense blue or clearly-visible black smoke comes from the tailpipe for more than 5 seconds, the vehicle will fail. As a rule of thumb, blue smoke signifies oil being burnt (engine wear) while black smoke signifies unburnt fuel (dirty air cleaner element, or other carburettor or fuel system fault).

□ An exhaust gas analyser capable of measuring carbon monoxide (CO) and hydrocarbons (HC) is now needed. If such an instrument cannot be hired or borrowed, a local garage may agree to perform the check for a small fee.

CO emissions (mixture)

□ At the time of writing, the maximum CO level at idle is 3.5% for vehicles first used after August 1986 and 4.5% for older vehicles. From January 1996 a much tighter limit (around 0.5%) applies to catalyst-equipped vehicles first used from August 1992. If the CO level cannot be reduced far enough to pass the test (and the fuel and ignition systems are otherwise in good condition) then the carburettor is badly worn, or there is some problem in the fuel injection system or catalytic converter (as applicable).

HC emissions

□ With the CO emissions within limits, HC emissions must be no more than 1200 ppm (parts per million). If the vehicle fails this test at idle, it can be re-tested at around 2000 rpm; if the HC level is then 1200 ppm or less, this counts as a pass.

□ Excessive HC emissions can be caused by oil being burnt, but they are more likely to be due to unburnt fuel.

Diesel models

□ The only emission test applicable to Diesel engines is the measuring of exhaust smoke density. The test involves accelerating the engine several times to its maximum unloaded speed.

Note: *It is of the utmost importance that the engine timing belt is in good condition before the test is carried out.*

□ Excessive smoke can be caused by a dirty air cleaner element. Otherwise, professional advice may be needed to find the cause.

Introduction

The vehicle owner who does his or her own maintenance according to the recommended service schedules should not have to use this section of the manual very often. Modern component reliability is such that, provided those items subject to wear or deterioration are inspected or renewed at the specified intervals, sudden failure is comparatively rare. Faults do not usually just happen as a result of sudden failure, but develop over a period of time. Major mechanical failures in particular are usually preceded by characteristic symptoms over hundreds or even thousands of miles. Those components which do occasionally fail without warning are often small and easily carried in the vehicle.

With any fault finding, the first step is to decide where to begin investigations. Sometimes this is obvious, but on other occasions a little detective work will be necessary. The owner who makes half a dozen haphazard adjustments or replacements may be successful in curing a fault (or its symptoms), but will be none the wiser if the fault recurs and ultimately may have spent more time and money than was necessary. A calm and logical approach will be found to be more satisfactory in the long run. Always take into account any warning signs or abnormalities that may have been noticed in the period preceding the fault - power loss, high or low gauge readings, unusual smells, etc - and remember that failure of components such as fuses or spark plugs may only be pointers to some underlying fault.

The pages which follow provide an easy reference guide to the more common problems which may occur during the operation of the vehicle. These problems and their possible causes are grouped under headings denoting various components or systems, such as Engine, Cooling system, etc. The Chapter and/or Section which deals with the problem is also shown in brackets. Whatever the fault, certain basic principles apply. These are as follows:

Verify the fault. This is simply a matter of being sure that you know what the symptoms are before starting work. This is particularly important if you are investigating a fault for someone else who may not have described it very accurately.

Don't overlook the obvious. For example, if the vehicle won't start, is there petrol in the tank? (Don't take anyone else's word on this particular point, and don't trust the fuel gauge either!) If an electrical fault is indicated, look for loose or broken wires before digging out the test gear.

Cure the disease, not the symptom. Substituting a flat battery with a fully charged one will get you off the hard shoulder, but if the underlying cause is not attended to, the new battery will go the same way. Similarly, changing oil-fouled spark plugs for a new set will get you moving again, but remember that the reason for the fouling (if it wasn't simply an incorrect grade of plug) will have to be established and corrected.

Don't take anything for granted. Particularly, don't forget that a 'new' component may itself be defective (especially if it's been rattling around in the boot for months), and don't leave components out of a fault diagnosis sequence just because they are new or recently fitted. When you do finally diagnose a difficult fault, you'll probably realise that all the evidence was there from the start.

1 Engine

Engine fails to rotate when attempting to start

☐ Battery terminal connections loose or corroded *(Weekly checks).*
☐ Battery discharged or faulty (Chapter 5).
☐ Broken, loose or disconnected wiring in the starting circuit (Chapter 5).
☐ Defective starter solenoid or switch (Chapter 5).
☐ Defective starter motor (Chapter 5).
☐ Starter pinion or flywheel ring gear teeth loose or broken (Chapters 2 and 5).
☐ Engine earth strap broken or disconnected (Chapter 5).

Engine rotates but will not start

☐ Fuel tank empty.
☐ Battery discharged (engine rotates slowly) (Chapter 5).
☐ Battery terminal connections loose or corroded *(Weekly checks).*
☐ Ignition components damp or damaged (Chapters 1 and 5).
☐ Broken, loose or disconnected wiring in the ignition circuit (Chapters 1 and 5).
☐ Worn, faulty or incorrectly gapped spark plugs (Chapter 1).
☐ Choke mechanism sticking, incorrectly adjusted, or faulty (Chapter 4).
☐ Major mechanical failure (eg camshaft drive) (Chapter 2).

Engine difficult to start when cold

☐ Battery discharged (Chapter 5).
☐ Battery terminal connections loose or corroded *(Weekly checks).*
☐ Worn, faulty or incorrectly gapped spark plugs (Chapter 1).
☐ Choke mechanism sticking, incorrectly adjusted, or faulty (Chapter 4).
☐ Other ignition system fault (Chapters 1 and 5).
☐ Low cylinder compressions (Chapter 2).

Engine difficult to start when hot

☐ Air filter element dirty or clogged (Chapter 1).
☐ Choke mechanism sticking, incorrectly adjusted, or faulty (Chapter 4).
☐ Carburettor float chamber flooding (Chapter 4).
☐ Low cylinder compressions (Chapter 2).

Starter motor noisy or excessively rough in engagement

☐ Starter pinion or flywheel ring gear teeth loose or broken (Chapters 2 and 5).
☐ Starter motor mounting bolts loose or missing (Chapter 5).
☐ Starter motor internal components worn or damaged (Chapter 5).

Engine starts but stops immediately

☐ Insufficient fuel reaching carburettor (Chapter 4).
☐ Loose or faulty electrical connections in the ignition circuit (Chapters 1 and 5).
☐ Vacuum leak at the carburettor or inlet manifold (Chapter 4).
☐ Blocked carburettor jet(s) or internal passages (Chapter 4).

Engine idles erratically

☐ Incorrectly adjusted idle speed and/or mixture settings (Chapters 1 and 4).
☐ Air filter element clogged (Chapter 1).
☐ Vacuum leak at the carburettor, inlet manifold or associated hoses (Chapter 4).
☐ Worn, faulty or incorrectly gapped spark plugs (Chapter 1).
☐ Uneven or low cylinder compressions (Chapter 2).
☐ Camshaft lobes worn (Chapter 2).
☐ Timing belt incorrectly tensioned (Chapter 2).

Engine misfires at idle speed

☐ Worn, faulty or incorrectly gapped spark plugs (Chapter 1).
☐ Faulty spark plug HT leads (Chapters 1 and 5).
☐ Incorrectly adjusted idle mixture settings (Chapter 1).
☐ Incorrect ignition timing (Chapter 5).
☐ Vacuum leak at the carburettor, inlet manifold or associated hoses (Chapter 4).
☐ Distributor cap cracked or tracking internally (Chapter 5).
☐ Uneven or low cylinder compressions (Chapter 2).
☐ Disconnected, leaking or perished crankcase ventilation hoses (Chapters 1 and 4).

Engine misfires throughout the driving speed range

☐ Blocked carburettor jet(s) or internal passages (Chapter 4).
☐ Carburettor worn or incorrectly adjusted (Chapters 1 and 4).
☐ Fuel filter choked (Chapter 1).
☐ Fuel pump faulty or delivery pressure low (Chapter 4).
☐ Fuel tank vent blocked or fuel pipes restricted (Chapter 4).
☐ Vacuum leak at the carburettor, inlet manifold or associated hoses (Chapter 4).
☐ Worn, faulty or incorrectly gapped spark plugs (Chapter 1).
☐ Faulty spark plug HT leads (Chapter 5).
☐ Distributor cap cracked or tracking internally (Chapter 5).
☐ Faulty ignition coil (Chapter 5).
☐ Uneven or low cylinder compressions (Chapter 2).

1 Engine (continued)

Engine hesitates on acceleration

- [ ] Worn, faulty or incorrectly gapped spark plugs (Chapter 1).
- [ ] Carburettor accelerator pump faulty (Chapter 4).
- [ ] Blocked carburettor jets or internal passages (Chapter 4).
- [ ] Vacuum leak at the carburettor, inlet manifold or associated hoses (Chapter 4).
- [ ] Carburettor worn or incorrectly adjusted (Chapters 1 and 4).

Engine stalls

- [ ] Incorrectly adjusted idle speed and/or mixture settings (Chapters 1 and 4).
- [ ] Blocked carburettor jet(s) or internal passages (Chapter 4).
- [ ] Vacuum leak at the carburettor, inlet manifold or associated hoses (Chapter 4).
- [ ] Fuel filter choked (Chapter 1).
- [ ] Fuel pump faulty or delivery pressure low (Chapter 4).
- [ ] Fuel tank vent blocked or fuel pipes restricted (Chapter 4).

Engine lacks power

- [ ] Incorrect ignition timing (Chapter 5).
- [ ] Carburettor worn or incorrectly adjusted (Chapter 1).
- [ ] Timing belt incorrectly fitted or tensioned (Chapter 2).
- [ ] Fuel filter choked (Chapter 1).
- [ ] Fuel pump faulty or delivery pressure low (Chapter 4).
- [ ] Uneven or low cylinder compressions (Chapter 2).
- [ ] Worn, faulty or incorrectly gapped spark plugs (Chapter 1).
- [ ] Vacuum leak at the carburettor, inlet manifold or associated hoses (Chapter 4).
- [ ] Brakes binding (Chapters 1 and 10).
- [ ] Clutch slipping (Chapter 6).

Engine backfires

- [ ] Ignition timing incorrect (Chapter 5).
- [ ] Timing belt incorrectly fitted or tensioned (Chapter 2).
- [ ] Carburettor worn or incorrectly adjusted (Chapters 1 and 4).
- [ ] Vacuum leak at the carburettor, inlet manifold or associated hoses (Chapter 4).

Oil pressure warning light illuminated with engine running

- [ ] Low oil level or incorrect grade (*"Weekly checks"*).
- [ ] Faulty oil pressure switch (Chapter 2).
- [ ] Worn engine bearings and/or oil pump (Chapter 2).

- [ ] High engine operating temperature (Chapter 3).
- [ ] Oil pressure relief valve defective (Chapter 2).
- [ ] Oil pick-up strainer clogged (Chapter 2).

Engine runs-on after switching off

- [ ] Idle speed excessively high (Chapter 1).
- [ ] Faulty anti-run-on solenoid (Chapter 4).
- [ ] Excessive carbon build-up in engine (Chapter 2).
- [ ] High engine operating temperature (Chapter 3).

Engine noises

Pre-ignition (pinking) or knocking during acceleration or under load

- [ ] Ignition timing incorrect (Chapter 5).
- [ ] Incorrect grade of fuel (Chapter 4).
- [ ] Vacuum leak at the carburettor, inlet manifold or associated hoses (Chapter 4).
- [ ] Excessive carbon build-up in engine (Chapter 2).
- [ ] Worn or damaged distributor or other ignition system component (Chapter 5).
- [ ] Carburettor worn or incorrectly adjusted (Chapter 1).

Whistling or wheezing noises

- [ ] Leaking inlet manifold or carburettor gasket (Chapter 4).
- [ ] Leaking exhaust manifold gasket or pipe to manifold joint (Chapter 4).
- [ ] Leaking vacuum hose (Chapter 4).
- [ ] Blowing cylinder head gasket (Chapter 2).

Tapping or rattling noises

- [ ] Wrong valve clearances (Chapter 1).
- [ ] Worn valve gear or camshaft (Chapter 2).
- [ ] Worn timing belt or tensioner (Chapter 2).
- [ ] Ancillary component fault (coolant pump, alternator, etc) (Chapters 3 and 5).

Knocking or thumping noises

- [ ] Worn big-end bearings (regular heavy knocking, perhaps less under load) (Chapter 2).
- [ ] Worn main bearings (rumbling and knocking, perhaps worsening under load) (Chapter 2).
- [ ] Piston slap (most noticeable when cold) (Chapter 2).
- [ ] Ancillary component fault (alternator, coolant pump, etc) (Chapters 3 and 5).

2 Cooling system

Overheating

- [ ] Insufficient coolant in system (Chapter 3).
- [ ] Thermostat faulty (Chapter 3).
- [ ] Radiator core blocked or grille restricted (Chapter 3).
- [ ] Electric cooling fan or thermostatic switch faulty (Chapter 3).
- [ ] Pressure cap faulty (Chapter 3).
- [ ] Timing belt worn, or incorrectly tensioned (Chapter 2).
- [ ] Ignition timing incorrect (Chapter 5).
- [ ] Inaccurate temperature gauge sender unit (Chapter 3).
- [ ] Air lock in cooling system (Chapter 3).

Overcooling

- [ ] Thermostat faulty (Chapter 3).
- [ ] Inaccurate temperature gauge sender unit (Chapter 3).

External coolant leakage

- [ ] Deteriorated or damaged hoses or hose clips (Chapter 1).
- [ ] Radiator core or heater matrix leaking (Chapter 3).
- [ ] Pressure cap faulty (Chapter 3).
- [ ] Coolant pump seal leaking (Chapter 3).
- [ ] Boiling due to overheating (Chapter 3).
- [ ] Core plug leaking (Chapter 2).

Internal coolant leakage

- [ ] Leaking cylinder head gasket (Chapter 2).
- [ ] Cracked cylinder head or cylinder bore (Chapter 2).

Corrosion

- [ ] Infrequent draining and flushing (Chapter 1).
- [ ] Incorrect antifreeze mixture or inappropriate type (*"Weekly checks"*).

3 Fuel and exhaust systems

Excessive fuel consumption

☐ Air filter element dirty or clogged (Chapter 1).
☐ Carburettor worn or incorrectly adjusted (Chapters 1 and 4).
☐ Choke cable incorrectly adjusted or sticking (Chapter 4).
☐ Ignition timing incorrect (Chapter 5).
☐ Tyres under inflated (Weekly checks).

Fuel leakage and/or fuel odour

☐ Damaged or corroded fuel tank, pipes or connections (Chapter 1).
☐ Carburettor float chamber flooding (Chapter 4).

Excessive noise or fumes from exhaust system

☐ Leaking exhaust system or manifold joints (Chapter 1).
☐ Leaking, corroded or damaged silencers or pipe (Chapter 1).
☐ Broken mountings causing body or suspension contact (Chapter 1).

4 Clutch

Pedal travels to floor - no pressure or very little resistance

☐ Broken clutch cable (Chapter 6).
☐ Faulty clutch pedal adjust mechanism (Chapter 6).
☐ Broken clutch release bearing or fork (Chapter 6).
☐ Broken diaphragm spring in clutch pressure plate (Chapter 6).

Clutch fails to disengage (unable to select gears)

☐ Faulty clutch pedal adjust mechanism (Chapter 6).
☐ Clutch friction plate sticking on transmission input shaft splines (Chapter 6).
☐ Clutch friction plate sticking to flywheel or pressure plate (Chapter 6).
☐ Faulty pressure plate assembly (Chapter 6).
☐ Transmission input shaft seized in crankshaft spigot bearing (Chapter 2).
☐ Clutch release mechanism worn or incorrectly assembled (Chapter 6).

Clutch slips (engine speed increases with no increase in vehicle speed)

☐ Faulty clutch pedal adjust mechanism (Chapter 6).

☐ Clutch friction plate friction material excessively worn (Chapter 6).
☐ Clutch friction plate friction material contaminated with oil or grease (Chapter 6).
☐ Faulty pressure plate or weak diaphragm spring (Chapter 6).

Judder as clutch is engaged

☐ Clutch friction plate friction material contaminated with oil or grease (Chapter 6).
☐ Clutch friction plate friction material excessively worn (Chapter 6).
☐ Clutch cable sticking or frayed (Chapter 6).
☐ Faulty or distorted pressure plate or diaphragm spring (Chapter 6).
☐ Worn or loose engine or gearbox mountings (Chapter 2).
☐ Clutch friction plate hub or transmission input shaft splines worn (Chapter 6).

Noise when depressing or releasing clutch pedal

☐ Worn clutch release bearing (Chapter 6).
☐ Worn or dry clutch pedal bushes (Chapter 6).
☐ Faulty pressure plate assembly (Chapter 6).
☐ Pressure plate diaphragm spring broken (Chapter 6).
☐ Broken clutch friction plate cushioning springs (Chapter 6).

5 Manual gearbox

Noisy in neutral with engine running

☐ Input shaft bearings worn (noise apparent with clutch pedal released but not when depressed) (Chapter 7).*
☐ Clutch release bearing worn (noise apparent with clutch pedal depressed, possibly less when released) (Chapter 6).

Noisy in one particular gear

☐ Worn, damaged or chipped gear teeth (Chapter 7).*

Difficulty engaging gears

☐ Clutch fault (Chapter 6).
☐ Worn or damaged gear linkage (Chapter 7).
☐ Incorrectly adjusted gear linkage (Chapter 7).
☐ Worn synchroniser units (Chapter 7).*

Jumps out of gear

☐ Worn or damaged gear linkage (Chapter 7).

☐ Incorrectly adjusted gear linkage (Chapter 7).
☐ Worn synchroniser units (Chapter 7).*
☐ Worn selector forks (Chapter 7).*

Vibration

☐ Lack of oil (Chapter 1).
☐ Worn bearings (Chapter 7).*

Lubricant leaks

☐ Leaking driveshaft oil seal (Chapter 7).
☐ Leaking housing joint (Chapter 7).*
☐ Leaking input shaft oil seal (Chapter 7).*

*Although the corrective action necessary to remedy the symptoms described is beyond the scope of the home mechanic, the above information should be helpful in isolating the cause of the condition so that the owner can communicate clearly with a professional mechanic

6 Automatic transmission

Note: Due to the complexity of the automatic transmission, it is difficult for the home mechanic to properly diagnose and service this unit. For problems other than the following, the vehicle should be taken to a dealer service department or automatic transmission specialist.

Fluid leakage

☐ Automatic transmission fluid is usually deep red in colour. Fluid leaks should not be confused with engine oil, which can easily be blown onto the transmission by air flow.

6 Automatic transmission (continued)

☐ To determine the source of a leak, first remove all built-up dirt and grime from the transmission housing and surrounding areas, using a degreasing agent or by steam-cleaning. Drive the vehicle at low speed, so that air flow will not blow the leak far from its source. Raise and support the vehicle, and determine where the leak is coming from. The following are common areas of leakage:

a) Fluid pan (transmission sump).
b) Dipstick tube (Chapter 7).
c) Transmission-to-fluid cooler fluid pipes/unions (Chapter 7).

Transmission fluid brown, or has burned smell

☐ Transmission fluid level low, or fluid in need of renewal (Chapter 1).

General gear selection problems

☐ The most likely cause of gear selection problems is a faulty or poorly-adjusted gear selector mechanism. The following are common problems associated with a faulty selector mechanism:

a) Engine starting in gears other than Park or Neutral.
b) Indicator on gear selector lever pointing to a gear other than the one actually being used.
c) Vehicle moves when in Park or Neutral.
d) Poor gear shift quality, or erratic gear changes.

☐ Refer any problems to a Citroen dealer, or an automatic transmission specialist.

Transmission will not downshift (kickdown) with accelerator pedal fully depressed

☐ Low transmission fluid level (Chapter 1).
☐ Incorrect selector adjustment (Chapter 7).

Engine will not start in any gear, or starts in gears other than Park or Neutral

☐ Faulty starter inhibitor switch (Chapter 7).
☐ Incorrect selector adjustment (Chapter 7).

Transmission slips, shifts roughly, is noisy, or has no drive in forward or reverse gears

☐ There are many probable causes for the above problems, but the home mechanic should be concerned with only one possibility - fluid level. Before taking the vehicle to a dealer or transmission specialist, check the fluid level and condition of the fluid as described in Chapter 1. Correct the fluid level as necessary, or change the fluid and filter if needed. If the problem persists, professional help will be necessary.

7 Driveshafts

Clicking or knocking noise on turns (at slow speed on full lock)

☐ Lack of constant velocity joint lubricant (Chapter 8).
☐ Worn outer constant velocity joint (Chapter 8).

Vibration when accelerating or decelerating

☐ Worn inner constant velocity joint (Chapter 8).
☐ Bent or distorted driveshaft (Chapter 8).

8 Hydraulic system

Loss of hydraulic pressure

☐ Reservoir filters blocked (Chapter 9).
☐ Pump supply pipe leaking (Chapter 9).
☐ Pressure regulator faulty (Chapter 9).
☐ Pump faulty or drivebelt broken (Chapter 9).
☐ Pressure regulator bleed screw loose (Chapter 9).

Excessive hydraulic pressure

☐ Pressure regulator faulty (Chapter 9).

Loss of suspension pressure

☐ Safety valve faulty (Chapter 9).
☐ Height corrector faulty (Chapter 9).
☐ Suspension cylinders faulty (Chapter 9).
☐ Height adjustment incorrect (see Chapters 9 and 11)

Loss of brake pressure

☐ Brake valve faulty (see Chapters 9 and 10)

9 Braking system

Note: Before assuming that a brake problem exists, make sure that the tyres are in good condition and correctly inflated, the front wheel alignment is correct and the vehicle is not loaded with weight in an unequal manner

Vehicle pulls to one side under braking

☐ Worn, defective, damaged or contaminated front or rear brake pads on one side (Chapter 1).
☐ Seized or partially seized front or rear brake caliper piston (Chapter 10).
☐ A mixture of brake pad materials fitted between sides (Chapter 1).
☐ Brake caliper mounting bolts loose (Chapter 10).
☐ Worn or damaged steering or suspension components (Chapter 11).

Noise (grinding or high-pitched squeal) when brakes applied

☐ Brake pad friction material worn down to metal backing (Chapter 1).
☐ Excessive corrosion of brake disc, especially if the vehicle has been standing for some time (Chapter 1).
☐ Foreign object (stone chipping etc) trapped between brake disc and splash shield (Chapter 1).

Excessive brake pedal travel

☐ Air in hydraulic system (Chapters 9 and 10).

Brake pedal feels spongy when depressed

☐ Air in hydraulic system (Chapters 9 and 10).
☐ Deteriorated flexible rubber brake hoses (Chapters 1 or 10).

9 Braking system (continued)

Excessive brake pedal effort required to stop vehicle

- [ ] Hydraulic circuit failure (Chapters 9 and 10).
- [ ] Seized brake caliper piston(s) (Chapter 10).
- [ ] Brake pads incorrectly fitted (Chapter 1).
- [ ] Incorrect grade of brake pads fitted (Chapter 1).
- [ ] Brake pads contaminated (Chapter 1).

Judder felt through brake pedal or steering wheel when braking

- [ ] Excessive run-out or distortion of discs (Chapter 10).
- [ ] Brake pads worn (Chapter 1).
- [ ] Brake caliper mounting bolts loose (Chapter 10).
- [ ] Wear in suspension, steering components or mountings (Chapter 11).

Brakes binding

- [ ] Seized brake caliper piston(s) (Chapter 10).
- [ ] Incorrectly adjusted handbrake mechanism (Chapter 10).

10 Suspension and steering

Note: *Before diagnosing suspension or steering faults, be sure that the trouble is not due to incorrect tyre pressures, mixtures of tyre types or binding brakes*

Vehicle pulls to one side

- [ ] Defective tyre *(Weekly checks)*.
- [ ] Excessive wear in suspension or steering components (Chapter 11).
- [ ] Incorrect front wheel alignment (Chapter 11).
- [ ] Accident damage to steering or suspension components (Chapter 11).

Wheel wobble and vibration

- [ ] Front roadwheels out of balance (vibration felt mainly through the steering wheel) (Chapter 11).
- [ ] Rear roadwheels out of balance (vibration felt throughout the vehicle) (Chapter 11).
- [ ] Roadwheels damaged or distorted (Chapter 11).
- [ ] Faulty or damaged tyre (*"Weekly checks"*).
- [ ] Worn steering or suspension joints, bushes or components (Chapter 11).
- [ ] Wheel nuts loose (Chapter 1).

Excessive pitching and/or rolling around corners or during braking

- [ ] Defective damping units (Chapter 11).
- [ ] Broken or weak suspension component (Chapter 11).
- [ ] Worn or damaged anti-roll bar or mountings (Chapter 11).

Wandering or general instability

- [ ] Incorrect front wheel alignment (Chapter 11).
- [ ] Worn steering or suspension joints, bushes or components (Chapter 11).
- [ ] Roadwheels out of balance (Chapter 11).
- [ ] Faulty or damaged tyre (*"Weekly checks"*).
- [ ] Wheel nuts loose (Chapter 1).
- [ ] Defective damping units (Chapter 11).

Excessively stiff steering

- [ ] Lack of steering gear lubricant (Chapter 11).
- [ ] Seized track rod balljoint or suspension balljoint (Chapter 11).
- [ ] Incorrect front wheel alignment (Chapter 11).
- [ ] Steering rack or column bent or damaged (Chapter 11).

Excessive play in steering

- [ ] Worn steering column universal joint(s) or intermediate coupling (Chapter 11).
- [ ] Worn steering track rod balljoints (Chapter 11).
- [ ] Worn steering gear (Chapter 11).
- [ ] Worn steering or suspension joints, bushes or components (Chapter 11).

Tyre wear excessive

Tyres worn on inside or outside edges

- [ ] Tyres under inflated (wear on both edges) *(Weekly checks)*.
- [ ] Incorrect camber or castor angles (wear on one edge only) (Chapter 11).
- [ ] Worn steering or suspension joints, bushes or components (Chapter 11).
- [ ] Excessively hard cornering.
- [ ] Accident damage.

Tyre treads exhibit feathered edges

- [ ] Incorrect toe setting (Chapter 11).

Tyres worn in centre of tread

- [ ] Tyres over inflated *(Weekly checks)*.

Tyres worn on inside and outside edges

- [ ] Tyres under inflated *(Weekly checks)*.

Tyres worn unevenly

- [ ] Tyres out of balance *(Weekly checks)*.
- [ ] Excessive wheel or tyre run-out *(Weekly checks)*.
- [ ] Defective damping units (Chapter 11).
- [ ] Faulty tyre *(Weekly checks)*.

11 Electrical system

Note: *For problems associated with the starting system, refer to the faults listed under "Engine" earlier in this Section*

Battery will only hold a charge for a few days

- [ ] Battery defective internally (Chapter 5).
- [ ] Battery electrolyte level low (*"Weekly checks"*).
- [ ] Battery terminal connections loose or corroded (*"Weekly checks"*).
- [ ] Alternator drivebelt worn or incorrectly adjusted (Chapter 1).
- [ ] Alternator not charging at correct output (Chapter 5).
- [ ] Alternator or voltage regulator faulty (Chapter 5).
- [ ] Short-circuit causing continual battery drain (Chapter 5).

Ignition warning light remains illuminated with engine running

- [ ] Alternator drivebelt broken, worn, or incorrectly adjusted (Chapter 1).
- [ ] Alternator brushes worn, sticking, or dirty (Chapter 5).
- [ ] Alternator brush springs weak or broken (Chapter 5).
- [ ] Internal fault in alternator (Chapter 5).
- [ ] Broken, disconnected, or loose wiring in charging circuit (Chapter 5).

11 Electrical system (continued)

Ignition warning light fails to come on

- ☐ Warning light bulb blown (Chapter 13).
- ☐ Broken, disconnected, or loose wiring in warning light circuit (Chapter 13).
- ☐ Alternator faulty (Chapter 5).

Lights inoperative

- ☐ Bulb blown (Chapter 13).
- ☐ Corrosion of bulb or bulbholder contacts (Chapter 13).
- ☐ Blown fuse (Chapter 13).
- ☐ Faulty relay (Chapter 13).
- ☐ Broken, loose, or disconnected wiring (Chapter 13).
- ☐ Faulty switch (Chapter 13).

Instrument readings inaccurate or erratic

Fuel or temperature gauge give no reading

- ☐ Faulty sender unit (Chapters 3 or 4).
- ☐ Wiring open circuit (Chapter 13).
- ☐ Faulty gauge (Chapter 13).

Fuel or temperature gauges give continuous maximum reading

- ☐ Faulty sender unit (Chapters 3 or 4).
- ☐ Wiring short-circuit (Chapter 13).
- ☐ Faulty gauge (Chapter 13).

Horn inoperative or unsatisfactory in operation

Horn operates all the time

- ☐ Horn push either earthed or stuck down (Chapter 13).
- ☐ Horn cable to horn push earthed (Chapter 13).

Horn fails to operate

- ☐ Blown fuse (Chapter 13).
- ☐ Cable or cable connections loose, broken or disconnected (Chapter 13).
- ☐ Faulty horn (Chapter 13).

Horn emits intermittent or unsatisfactory sound

- ☐ Cable connections loose (Chapter 13).
- ☐ Horn mountings loose (Chapter 13).
- ☐ Faulty horn (Chapter 13).

Windscreen/tailgate wipers inoperative or unsatisfactory in operation

Wipers fail to operate or operate very slowly

- ☐ Wiper blades stuck to screen, or linkage seized or binding (Chapter 13).
- ☐ Blown fuse (Chapter 13).
- ☐ Cable or cable connections loose, broken or disconnected (Chapter 13).
- ☐ Faulty relay (Chapter 13).
- ☐ Faulty wiper motor (Chapter 13).

Wiper blades sweep over too large or too small an area of the glass

- ☐ Wiper arms incorrectly positioned on spindles (Chapter 13).
- ☐ Excessive wear of wiper linkage (Chapter 13).
- ☐ Wiper motor or linkage mountings loose or insecure (Chapter 13).

Wiper blades fail to clean the glass effectively

- ☐ Wiper blade rubbers worn or perished *(Weekly checks)*.
- ☐ Wiper arm tension springs broken or arm pivots seized (Chapter 13).
- ☐ Insufficient windscreen washer additive to adequately remove road dirt film *(Weekly checks)*.

Windscreen/tailgate washers inoperative or unsatisfactory in operation

One or more washer jets inoperative

- ☐ Blocked washer jet (Chapter 13).
- ☐ Disconnected, kinked or restricted fluid hose (Chapter 13).
- ☐ Insufficient fluid in washer reservoir *(Weekly checks)*.

Washer pump fails to operate

- ☐ Broken or disconnected wiring or connections (Chapter 13).
- ☐ Blown fuse (Chapter 13).
- ☐ Faulty washer switch (Chapter 13).
- ☐ Faulty washer pump (Chapter 13).

Washer pump runs for some time before fluid is emitted from jets

- ☐ Faulty one-way valve in fluid supply hose (Chapter 13).

Electric windows inoperative or unsatisfactory in operation

Window glass will only move in one direction

- ☐ Faulty switch (Chapter 13).

Window glass slow to move

- ☐ Incorrectly adjusted door glass guide channels (Chapter 12).
- ☐ Regulator seized or damaged, or in need of lubrication (Chapter 12).
- ☐ Door internal components or trim fouling regulator (Chapter 12).
- ☐ Faulty motor (Chapter 13).

Window glass fails to move

- ☐ Incorrectly adjusted door glass guide channels (Chapter 12).
- ☐ Blown fuse (Chapter 13).
- ☐ Faulty relay (Chapter 13).
- ☐ Broken or disconnected wiring or connections (Chapter 13).
- ☐ Faulty motor (Chapter 13).

Central locking system inoperative or unsatisfactory in operation

Complete system failure

- ☐ Blown fuse (Chapter 13).
- ☐ Faulty relay (Chapter 13).
- ☐ Broken or disconnected wiring or connections (Chapter 13).

Latch locks but will not unlock, or unlocks but will not lock

- ☐ Faulty master switch (Chapter 13).
- ☐ Broken or disconnected latch operating rods or levers (Chapter 12).
- ☐ Faulty relay (Chapter 13).

One motor fails to operate

- ☐ Broken or disconnected wiring or connections (Chapter 13).
- ☐ Faulty motor (Chapter 13).
- ☐ Broken, binding or disconnected latch operating rods or levers (Chapter 12).
- ☐ Fault in door latch (Chapter 12).

Glossary of technical terms REF•19

A

ABS (Anti-lock brake system) A system, usually electronically controlled, that senses incipient wheel lockup during braking and relieves hydraulic pressure at wheels that are about to skid.

Air bag An inflatable bag hidden in the steering wheel (driver's side) or the dash or glovebox (passenger side). In a head-on collision, the bags inflate, preventing the driver and front passenger from being thrown forward into the steering wheel or windscreen.

Air cleaner A metal or plastic housing, containing a filter element, which removes dust and dirt from the air being drawn into the engine.

Air filter element The actual filter in an air cleaner system, usually manufactured from pleated paper and requiring renewal at regular intervals.

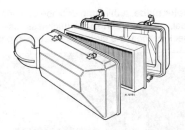

Air filter

Allen key A hexagonal wrench which fits into a recessed hexagonal hole.

Alligator clip A long-nosed spring-loaded metal clip with meshing teeth. Used to make temporary electrical connections.

Alternator A component in the electrical system which converts mechanical energy from a drivebelt into electrical energy to charge the battery and to operate the starting system, ignition system and electrical accessories.

Ampere (amp) A unit of measurement for the flow of electric current. One amp is the amount of current produced by one volt acting through a resistance of one ohm.

Anaerobic sealer A substance used to prevent bolts and screws from loosening. Anaerobic means that it does not require oxygen for activation. The Loctite brand is widely used.

Antifreeze A substance (usually ethylene glycol) mixed with water, and added to a vehicle's cooling system, to prevent freezing of the coolant in winter. Antifreeze also contains chemicals to inhibit corrosion and the formation of rust and other deposits that would tend to clog the radiator and coolant passages and reduce cooling efficiency.

Anti-seize compound A coating that reduces the risk of seizing on fasteners that are subjected to high temperatures, such as exhaust manifold bolts and nuts.

Asbestos A natural fibrous mineral with great heat resistance, commonly used in the composition of brake friction materials.

Asbestos is a health hazard and the dust created by brake systems should never be inhaled or ingested.

Axle A shaft on which a wheel revolves, or which revolves with a wheel. Also, a solid beam that connects the two wheels at one end of the vehicle. An axle which also transmits power to the wheels is known as a live axle.

Axleshaft A single rotating shaft, on either side of the differential, which delivers power from the final drive assembly to the drive wheels. Also called a driveshaft or a halfshaft.

B

Ball bearing An anti-friction bearing consisting of a hardened inner and outer race with hardened steel balls between two races.

Bearing The curved surface on a shaft or in a bore, or the part assembled into either, that permits relative motion between them with minimum wear and friction.

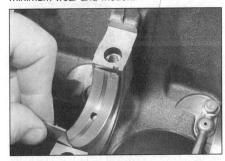

Bearing

Big-end bearing The bearing in the end of the connecting rod that's attached to the crankshaft.

Bleed nipple A valve on a brake wheel cylinder, caliper or other hydraulic component that is opened to purge the hydraulic system of air. Also called a bleed screw.

Brake bleeding Procedure for removing air from lines of a hydraulic brake system.

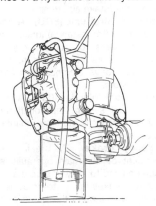

Brake bleeding

Brake disc The component of a disc brake that rotates with the wheels.

Brake drum The component of a drum brake that rotates with the wheels.

Brake linings The friction material which contacts the brake disc or drum to retard the vehicle's speed. The linings are bonded or riveted to the brake pads or shoes.

Brake pads The replaceable friction pads that pinch the brake disc when the brakes are applied. Brake pads consist of a friction material bonded or riveted to a rigid backing plate.

Brake shoe The crescent-shaped carrier to which the brake linings are mounted and which forces the lining against the rotating drum during braking.

Braking systems For more information on braking systems, consult the *Haynes Automotive Brake Manual.*

Breaker bar A long socket wrench handle providing greater leverage.

Bulkhead The insulated partition between the engine and the passenger compartment.

C

Caliper The non-rotating part of a disc-brake assembly that straddles the disc and carries the brake pads. The caliper also contains the hydraulic components that cause the pads to pinch the disc when the brakes are applied. A caliper is also a measuring tool that can be set to measure inside or outside dimensions of an object.

Camshaft A rotating shaft on which a series of cam lobes operate the valve mechanisms. The camshaft may be driven by gears, by sprockets and chain or by sprockets and a belt.

Canister A container in an evaporative emission control system; contains activated charcoal granules to trap vapours from the fuel system.

Canister

Carburettor A device which mixes fuel with air in the proper proportions to provide a desired power output from a spark ignition internal combustion engine.

Castellated Resembling the parapets along the top of a castle wall. For example, a castellated balljoint stud nut.

Castor In wheel alignment, the backward or forward tilt of the steering axis. Castor is positive when the steering axis is inclined rearward at the top.

Catalytic converter A silencer-like device in the exhaust system which converts certain pollutants in the exhaust gases into less harmful substances.

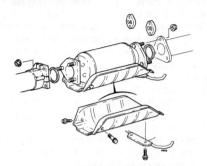

Catalytic converter

Circlip A ring-shaped clip used to prevent endwise movement of cylindrical parts and shafts. An internal circlip is installed in a groove in a housing; an external circlip fits into a groove on the outside of a cylindrical piece such as a shaft.

Clearance The amount of space between two parts. For example, between a piston and a cylinder, between a bearing and a journal, etc.

Coil spring A spiral of elastic steel found in various sizes throughout a vehicle, for example as a springing medium in the suspension and in the valve train.

Compression Reduction in volume, and increase in pressure and temperature, of a gas, caused by squeezing it into a smaller space.

Compression ratio The relationship between cylinder volume when the piston is at top dead centre and cylinder volume when the piston is at bottom dead centre.

Constant velocity (CV) joint A type of universal joint that cancels out vibrations caused by driving power being transmitted through an angle.

Core plug A disc or cup-shaped metal device inserted in a hole in a casting through which core was removed when the casting was formed. Also known as a freeze plug or expansion plug.

Crankcase The lower part of the engine block in which the crankshaft rotates.

Crankshaft The main rotating member, or shaft, running the length of the crankcase, with offset "throws" to which the connecting rods are attached.

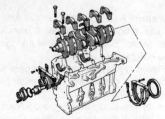

Crankshaft assembly

Crocodile clip See Alligator clip

D

Diagnostic code Code numbers obtained by accessing the diagnostic mode of an engine management computer. This code can be used to determine the area in the system where a malfunction may be located.

Disc brake A brake design incorporating a rotating disc onto which brake pads are squeezed. The resulting friction converts the energy of a moving vehicle into heat.

Double-overhead cam (DOHC) An engine that uses two overhead camshafts, usually one for the intake valves and one for the exhaust valves.

Drivebelt(s) The belt(s) used to drive accessories such as the alternator, water pump, power steering pump, air conditioning compressor, etc. off the crankshaft pulley.

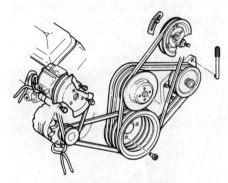

Accessory drivebelts

Driveshaft Any shaft used to transmit motion. Commonly used when referring to the axleshafts on a front wheel drive vehicle.

Drum brake A type of brake using a drum-shaped metal cylinder attached to the inner surface of the wheel. When the brake pedal is pressed, curved brake shoes with friction linings press against the inside of the drum to slow or stop the vehicle.

E

EGR valve A valve used to introduce exhaust gases into the intake air stream.

Electronic control unit (ECU) A computer which controls (for instance) ignition and fuel injection systems, or an anti-lock braking system. For more information refer to the *Haynes Automotive Electrical and Electronic Systems Manual.*

Electronic Fuel Injection (EFI) A computer controlled fuel system that distributes fuel through an injector located in each intake port of the engine.

Emergency brake A braking system, independent of the main hydraulic system, that can be used to slow or stop the vehicle if the primary brakes fail, or to hold the vehicle stationary even though the brake pedal isn't depressed. It usually consists of a hand lever that actuates either front or rear brakes mechanically through a series of cables and linkages. Also known as a handbrake or parking brake.

Endfloat The amount of lengthwise movement between two parts. As applied to a crankshaft, the distance that the crankshaft can move forward and back in the cylinder block.

Engine management system (EMS) A computer controlled system which manages the fuel injection and the ignition systems in an integrated fashion.

Exhaust manifold A part with several passages through which exhaust gases leave the engine combustion chambers and enter the exhaust pipe.

F

Fan clutch A viscous (fluid) drive coupling device which permits variable engine fan speeds in relation to engine speeds.

Feeler blade A thin strip or blade of hardened steel, ground to an exact thickness, used to check or measure clearances between parts.

Feeler blade

Firing order The order in which the engine cylinders fire, or deliver their power strokes, beginning with the number one cylinder.

Flywheel A heavy spinning wheel in which energy is absorbed and stored by means of momentum. On cars, the flywheel is attached to the crankshaft to smooth out firing impulses.

Free play The amount of travel before any action takes place. The "looseness" in a linkage, or an assembly of parts, between the initial application of force and actual movement. For example, the distance the brake pedal moves before the pistons in the master cylinder are actuated.

Fuse An electrical device which protects a circuit against accidental overload. The typical fuse contains a soft piece of metal which is calibrated to melt at a predetermined current flow (expressed as amps) and break the circuit.

Fusible link A circuit protection device consisting of a conductor surrounded by heat-resistant insulation. The conductor is smaller than the wire it protects, so it acts as the weakest link in the circuit. Unlike a blown fuse, a failed fusible link must frequently be cut from the wire for replacement.

G

Gap The distance the spark must travel in jumping from the centre electrode to the side electrode in a spark plug. Also refers to the spacing between the points in a contact breaker assembly in a conventional points-type ignition, or to the distance between the reluctor or rotor and the pickup coil in an electronic ignition.

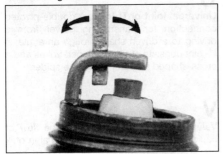

Adjusting spark plug gap

Gasket Any thin, soft material - usually cork, cardboard, asbestos or soft metal - installed between two metal surfaces to ensure a good seal. For instance, the cylinder head gasket seals the joint between the block and the cylinder head.

Gasket

Gauge An instrument panel display used to monitor engine conditions. A gauge with a movable pointer on a dial or a fixed scale is an analogue gauge. A gauge with a numerical readout is called a digital gauge.

H

Halfshaft A rotating shaft that transmits power from the final drive unit to a drive wheel, usually when referring to a live rear axle.
Harmonic balancer A device designed to reduce torsion or twisting vibration in the crankshaft. May be incorporated in the crankshaft pulley. Also known as a vibration damper.
Hone An abrasive tool for correcting small irregularities or differences in diameter in an engine cylinder, brake cylinder, etc.
Hydraulic tappet A tappet that utilises hydraulic pressure from the engine's lubrication system to maintain zero clearance (constant contact with both camshaft and valve stem). Automatically adjusts to variation in valve stem length. Hydraulic tappets also reduce valve noise.

I

Ignition timing The moment at which the spark plug fires, usually expressed in the number of crankshaft degrees before the piston reaches the top of its stroke.
Inlet manifold A tube or housing with passages through which flows the air-fuel mixture (carburettor vehicles and vehicles with throttle body injection) or air only (port fuel-injected vehicles) to the port openings in the cylinder head.

J

Jump start Starting the engine of a vehicle with a discharged or weak battery by attaching jump leads from the weak battery to a charged or helper battery.

L

Load Sensing Proportioning Valve (LSPV) A brake hydraulic system control valve that works like a proportioning valve, but also takes into consideration the amount of weight carried by the rear axle.
Locknut A nut used to lock an adjustment nut, or other threaded component, in place. For example, a locknut is employed to keep the adjusting nut on the rocker arm in position.
Lockwasher A form of washer designed to prevent an attaching nut from working loose.

M

MacPherson strut A type of front suspension system devised by Earle MacPherson at Ford of England. In its original form, a simple lateral link with the anti-roll bar creates the lower control arm. A long strut - an integral coil spring and shock absorber - is mounted between the body and the steering knuckle. Many modern so-called MacPherson strut systems use a conventional lower A-arm and don't rely on the anti-roll bar for location.
Multimeter An electrical test instrument with the capability to measure voltage, current and resistance.

N

NOx Oxides of Nitrogen. A common toxic pollutant emitted by petrol and diesel engines at higher temperatures.

O

Ohm The unit of electrical resistance. One volt applied to a resistance of one ohm will produce a current of one amp.
Ohmmeter An instrument for measuring electrical resistance.
O-ring A type of sealing ring made of a special rubber-like material; in use, the O-ring is compressed into a groove to provide the sealing action.
Overhead cam (ohc) engine An engine with the camshaft(s) located on top of the cylinder head(s).

Overhead valve (ohv) engine An engine with the valves located in the cylinder head, but with the camshaft located in the engine block.
Oxygen sensor A device installed in the engine exhaust manifold, which senses the oxygen content in the exhaust and converts this information into an electric current. Also called a Lambda sensor.

P

Phillips screw A type of screw head having a cross instead of a slot for a corresponding type of screwdriver.
Plastigage A thin strip of plastic thread, available in different sizes, used for measuring clearances. For example, a strip of Plastigage is laid across a bearing journal. The parts are assembled and dismantled; the width of the crushed strip indicates the clearance between journal and bearing.

Plastigage

Propeller shaft The long hollow tube with universal joints at both ends that carries power from the transmission to the differential on front-engined rear wheel drive vehicles.
Proportioning valve A hydraulic control valve which limits the amount of pressure to the rear brakes during panic stops to prevent wheel lock-up.

R

Rack-and-pinion steering A steering system with a pinion gear on the end of the steering shaft that mates with a rack (think of a geared wheel opened up and laid flat). When the steering wheel is turned, the pinion turns, moving the rack to the left or right. This movement is transmitted through the track rods to the steering arms at the wheels.
Radiator A liquid-to-air heat transfer device designed to reduce the temperature of the coolant in an internal combustion engine cooling system.
Refrigerant Any substance used as a heat transfer agent in an air-conditioning system. R-12 has been the principle refrigerant for many years; recently, however, manufacturers have begun using R-134a, a non-CFC substance that is considered less harmful to the ozone in the upper atmosphere.
Rocker arm A lever arm that rocks on a shaft or pivots on a stud. In an overhead valve engine, the rocker arm converts the upward movement of the pushrod into a downward movement to open a valve.

Rotor In a distributor, the rotating device inside the cap that connects the centre electrode and the outer terminals as it turns, distributing the high voltage from the coil secondary winding to the proper spark plug. Also, that part of an alternator which rotates inside the stator. Also, the rotating assembly of a turbocharger, including the compressor wheel, shaft and turbine wheel.

Runout The amount of wobble (in-and-out movement) of a gear or wheel as it's rotated. The amount a shaft rotates "out-of-true." The out-of-round condition of a rotating part.

S

Sealant A liquid or paste used to prevent leakage at a joint. Sometimes used in conjunction with a gasket.

Sealed beam lamp An older headlight design which integrates the reflector, lens and filaments into a hermetically-sealed one-piece unit. When a filament burns out or the lens cracks, the entire unit is simply replaced.

Serpentine drivebelt A single, long, wide accessory drivebelt that's used on some newer vehicles to drive all the accessories, instead of a series of smaller, shorter belts. Serpentine drivebelts are usually tensioned by an automatic tensioner.

Serpentine drivebelt

Shim Thin spacer, commonly used to adjust the clearance or relative positions between two parts. For example, shims inserted into or under bucket tappets control valve clearances. Clearance is adjusted by changing the thickness of the shim.

Slide hammer A special puller that screws into or hooks onto a component such as a shaft or bearing; a heavy sliding handle on the shaft bottoms against the end of the shaft to knock the component free.

Sprocket A tooth or projection on the periphery of a wheel, shaped to engage with a chain or drivebelt. Commonly used to refer to the sprocket wheel itself.

Starter inhibitor switch On vehicles with an automatic transmission, a switch that prevents starting if the vehicle is not in Neutral or Park.

Strut See MacPherson strut.

T

Tappet A cylindrical component which transmits motion from the cam to the valve stem, either directly or via a pushrod and rocker arm. Also called a cam follower.

Thermostat A heat-controlled valve that regulates the flow of coolant between the cylinder block and the radiator, so maintaining optimum engine operating temperature. A thermostat is also used in some air cleaners in which the temperature is regulated.

Thrust bearing The bearing in the clutch assembly that is moved in to the release levers by clutch pedal action to disengage the clutch. Also referred to as a release bearing.

Timing belt A toothed belt which drives the camshaft. Serious engine damage may result if it breaks in service.

Timing chain A chain which drives the camshaft.

Toe-in The amount the front wheels are closer together at the front than at the rear. On rear wheel drive vehicles, a slight amount of toe-in is usually specified to keep the front wheels running parallel on the road by offsetting other forces that tend to spread the wheels apart.

Toe-out The amount the front wheels are closer together at the rear than at the front. On front wheel drive vehicles, a slight amount of toe-out is usually specified.

Tools For full information on choosing and using tools, refer to the *Haynes Automotive Tools Manual*.

Tracer A stripe of a second colour applied to a wire insulator to distinguish that wire from another one with the same colour insulator.

Tune-up A process of accurate and careful adjustments and parts replacement to obtain the best possible engine performance.

Turbocharger A centrifugal device, driven by exhaust gases, that pressurises the intake air. Normally used to increase the power output from a given engine displacement, but can also be used primarily to reduce exhaust emissions (as on VW's "Umwelt" Diesel engine).

U

Universal joint or U-joint A double-pivoted connection for transmitting power from a driving to a driven shaft through an angle. A U-joint consists of two Y-shaped yokes and a cross-shaped member called the spider.

V

Valve A device through which the flow of liquid, gas, vacuum, or loose material in bulk may be started, stopped, or regulated by a movable part that opens, shuts, or partially obstructs one or more ports or passageways. A valve is also the movable part of such a device.

Valve clearance The clearance between the valve tip (the end of the valve stem) and the rocker arm or tappet. The valve clearance is measured when the valve is closed.

Vernier caliper A precision measuring instrument that measures inside and outside dimensions. Not quite as accurate as a micrometer, but more convenient.

Viscosity The thickness of a liquid or its resistance to flow.

Volt A unit for expressing electrical "pressure" in a circuit. One volt that will produce a current of one ampere through a resistance of one ohm.

W

Welding Various processes used to join metal items by heating the areas to be joined to a molten state and fusing them together. For more information refer to the *Haynes Automotive Welding Manual*.

Wiring diagram A drawing portraying the components and wires in a vehicle's electrical system, using standardised symbols. For more information refer to the *Haynes Automotive Electrical and Electronic Systems Manual*.

Note: *References throughout this index are in the form - "Chapter number" • "page number"*

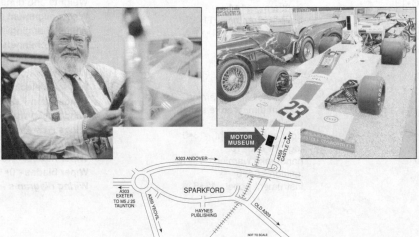